THE BEST PLAYS OF 1937-38

EDITED BY

BURNS MANTLE

Photo by Vandamm Studio, New York.

"OF MICE AND MEN"

She has come lookin' for Curley, Curley's wife informs them. They don't know any more th[an] that Curley had been there and left. George is quite curt in admitting even this much. Len[ny] might have been more interested if George hadn't kept pressing him back in his seat.

(Broderick Crawford, Wallace Ford, Claire Luce)

THE BEST PLAYS
OF 1937-38

AND THE
YEAR BOOK OF THE DRAMA
IN AMERICA

EDITED BY
BURNS MANTLE

With Illustrations

DODD, MEAD AND COMPANY
NEW YORK   -   -   -   1938

INTRODUCTION

FOR a second year the play producers and the independent dramatists of the American theatre, insofar as that theatre is represented by Broadway, New York, have done without financial assistance from the movie barons.

During the season of 1937-38, the cinema masters continued to sulk in their gold-lined bungalows on the Pacific coast, refusing to take any part in the production of plays until the American Dramatists' Guild gave way in the matter of its demand for a more liberal sharing of profits and percentages in the sale of the picture rights of successful plays.

You may if you like trace to this circumstance the cause for a definite upturn in the quality of the better plays produced. Money is seldom intelligently selective. Restricted budgets have to be. No other recent theatre season has been as bright with novelty and alive with experiment as this one has been. True, the sceneryless stage as such represents neither novelty nor experiment, seeing that it was both invented and employed by the Elizabethans. But the sceneryless stage has not been as effectively used in years as it was this season in the production of Thornton Wilder's "Our Town" and the Orson Welles-John Houseman version of Shakespeare's "Julius Caesar" in mufti.

Even the International Ladies' Garment Workers' Union profited from the restricted list of productions. Greatly to their surprise they found their musical revue, "Pins and Needles," accepted in fair competition with other music plays on Broadway. This probably will inspire the lady garment workers to continue the expansion of their talent school, thus making a place for honest workers at a Capitalists' table where only the privileged few have heretofore been served.

The prize-winning plays of the year were nicely contrasted. John Steinbeck's "Of Mice and Men," which received the Drama Critics' Circle award, was forcefully representative of the realistic drama in its most acute expression. Thornton Wilder's "Our Town," which was given the Pulitzer prize, impressively combined a homely and sensitive study of native character with a novelty of form that completely detached it from the ordinary drama of commerce. Both dramas found responsive publics. The realists

v

flocked to the Steinbeck story of two lonely California vagrants who were both pitifully and profanely human, while the dreamers, the idealists and the sentimentalists gave their devoted attention to Mr. Wilder's saga of a small town populated by our earlier kin.

Paul Vincent Carroll's "Shadow and Substance," a moving story of a child's faith in a patron saint that was stronger than a scholar's belief in the accumulated wisdom of the ages, was, properly enough, awarded a Critics' Circle citation as the most distinguished of the imported dramas shown during the year.

Paul Osborn's "On Borrowed Time" found a receptive audience because, in transferring the novel of Lawrence Edward Watkin to the stage, Mr. Osborn was able to retain its tender and enormously appealing story of a very old man and a very young boy and combine it with a theatrically manipulated plot of fine holding quality. Gramps' defiance of Death, while he struggles to protect his orphaned grandson, was one of the most satisfying of the season's emotional exhibits.

Rachel Crothers, having been in picture-land for five years, returned to Broadway and to her accepted task of setting the American home in order. Her "Susan and God" also won a quick response from audiences that take a personal and frequently an intimate interest in those social problems that are common gossip. The flighty Susan's contact was with the religion of a cult. Her experience in being caught up in its all-embracing tentacles was close enough to common experience to give it a hold on play-goers who were not at all troubled by the sometimes obvious theatricalism of the plot development.

The same was true of Maxwell Anderson's "The Star-Wagon." The nostalgic appeal of the story, which dipped back to the eighteen-nineties, was compelling. Combined with the familiar experience of the defrauded inventor who comes through at last to some sort of victory, it was sufficiently strong to overcome the theatricalism exposed in the story's telling. The further use of a time-machine device by which all the comedy's wonders are made possible was accepted with glee.

Professor Conkle's story of the 22-year-old Lincoln in "Prologue to Glory" set a bright new feather in the cap of the WPA Federal Theatre. This is historical drama that reveals sympathetically the homeliness and sincerity of the people and the times in which it is cast. The success the Federals enjoyed with this play, and with their ". . . one-third of a nation . . ." has strengthened the hope that some part of the better work they have done may be salvaged. Possibly through the organization of a circuit of national theatre units that shall continue to carry on if and when the relief rolls are again absorbed by private industry.

"Amphitryon 38," worked over by S. N. Behrman from the original of Jean Giraudoux, perfectly lived up to its promise as an ideal vehicle for Alfred Lunt and Lynn Fontanne. A witty and sophisticated comedy, it utilized, for the thirty-eighth time say the authors, the story of Jupiter's earthly dalliance in search of an unselfish love. "Amphitryon 38" proved the one consistent success of the Theatre Guild list.

Clifford Odets' "Golden Boy" belongs also with the realistic dramas. It tells, in language that is plain and direct, the story of an Italian boy who might have been a great violinist had his lust for money and power not turned him to prizefighting. It, too, reveals that keenness of observation and incisiveness of statement that give force to the Odets dramas, and continue their author as one to be reckoned with in the theatre's future.

"What a Life" is not at all a weighty opus. Clifford Goldsmith, who wrote it, has set down simply his observations of high school life and what it does to certain types of adolescents. As producer and director George Abbott has added a touch here and there and the comedy has the advantage of touching upon and appertaining to situations and characters that have a great universality in appeal. Student problems and faculty problems will endure so long as schools endure, and this gives the editor an excuse for including Mr. Goldsmith's first play in this issue.

"The Best Plays of 1937-38" is the nineteenth volume in this Year Book series begun with the issuance of the first volume in 1919-20. Its various divisions have become more or less standardized and do, it is the editor's hope, cover all the major and many of the minor activities of the theatre year with fair completeness. An addition has been made to the index to include producers, directors and scene designers, which the editor believes will add to the value of "The Best Plays" as a book of reference. The consistent support of a friendly and growing public provides the editor's compensation, and for this he is duly grateful.

B. M.

Forest Hills, L. I., 1938.

CONTENTS

ILLUSTRATIONS

THE BEST PLAYS OF 1937-38

THE BEST PLAYS OF 1937-38

THE SEASON IN NEW YORK

THIS has been frequently referred to as an exciting theatre season. Meaning that it has been punctuated with novelties and that it has exceeded expectations in the matter of the quality of plays produced. Statistically it has fallen somewhat behind the two previous recovery seasons, which is in keeping with the record, there having been a recession noted in the commercial world. Ask any theatre devotee and he will quickly insist that he had much rather have a season boasting an artistic advance than he would one that merely produced more plays than another. However, being of native origin, he is pretty sure also to speak pridefully of box office records.

It has been a season of interesting experiments. An experiment with sceneryless plays. An experiment with Shakespeare in mufti, so to speak. An experiment continuing the successes of one season through the Summer following their production, and also through the Fall and Winter of a second season. The hardiest of the tireless dramas, "Tobacco Road," continued smartly through its fifth year and is moving briskly toward its sixth year and its objective, which is to break the record of 2,532 performances hung up by Anne Nichols' "Abie's Irish Rose." Interesting, but unimportant.

It was the third year of the government's participation in show business. Some twenty new plays and revivals were staged or sponsored by the WPA Federal Theatre, including four successes that were sufficiently outstanding to excite comment—a story of Abraham Lincoln's youth called "Prologue to Glory," written by E. P. Conkle of the University of Iowa; an impressively dramatic arraignment of the housing problem entitled ". . . one-third of a nation . . ." assembled by the WPA's Living Newspaper staff headed by Arthur Arent; William Du Bois' historical drama concerned with the revolt of the Haitian natives under Christophe called "Haiti," and a late spring production of George Bernard Shaw's "On the Rocks."

The future of the WPA Federal Theatre enterprise continues in

3

doubt. Created as a relief project, it has developed certain valuable assets that could well be salvaged in the organization of a national theatre movement of potential importance to the whole country. A movement started by the WPA in the Spring of 1938, looking to the formation of a touring circuit that should inspire the co-operation of interested minor theatre centers, gave promise of important accomplishments.

It was a season that gave encouragement and courage as well to the more soundly established of the progressive groups. Labor Stage, representing the cultural activities of the International Ladies' Garment Workers' Union, broke into Broadway company with the production of a timely revue, "Pins and Needles," and started a tour of the country that may reasonably inspire other labor groups to similar activity. The Mercury Theatre, organized by John Houseman and Orson Welles, achieved so pronounced a success that it was invited to co-operate with the Theatre Guild in a series of 1938-39 productions. The Group Theatre recovered considerable lost ground through reorganization and the production of Clifford Odets' successful "Golden Boy."

In addition to these gains, the American Theatre Council started a search for talent that may in time off-set the raids of Hollywood on the gifted youth of the theatre. Under the direction, and moved largely by the inspiration of Antoinette Perry, the Council set up a plan for the reception of applications from those who wanted to become actors, and later expanded this into the formation of groups of both amateurs and professionals who were given a chance to rehearse plays and act them before audiences of representative producers and producers' executives.

The extent to which this volunteer work developed may be gathered from the figures that were given out by Miss Perry's committee at the end of the season. Nearly 7,000 letters of inquiry were received from all parts of the United States and Canada. Approximately 2,500 asked for auditions. Fourteen hundred of these were interviewed, and arrangements were made for auditions for 1,200. Three hundred and fifty reached final auditions, in which the plays of forty-nine playwrights were used in giving the young folk a chance to prove their quality.

Concrete results will begin to show the coming season, the Perry committee believes. At least a new and workable plan has been evolved bringing the producer into more direct touch with new and available acting talent, and much practical good it is hoped will come of that.

The season proper was delayed. The producers were worried

but still hopeful. There were, for the first time in years, no late August openings. Not until September 2 was there a new play on view, and that one was disappointing. The Rockefellers, as represented by their agents, had been looking for a proper successor for their first stage success at the Center Theatre. They had done well with "The Great Waltz" and pretty well with "White Horse Inn." Now they turned to American writers and suggested that something should be done in the way of an American story. What better, then, than a story of early Colonial days centering in Williamsburg, Va., the restored village on which the Rockefellers already had spent something like $13,000,000? Laurence Stallings was engaged to write the book and Arthur Schwartz provided the musical setting. When things went wrong at rehearsal Owen Davis was called in to help point up the story, but there was still something wrong when the production was finally made. "Virginia," with Anne Booth, an English soprano, and Ronald Graham, an American baritone, playing the leads, finally emerged as the story of the first theatrical troupe to land in America. The plot revolved about the attempt to smuggle a letter to Col. George Washington from the colonists' sympathizers in England. It was an expansive production scenically, though not as huge nor as exciting as were its two predecessors. Several attempts were made to sharpen the story, but the larger public was not interested. "Virginia" was withdrawn after sixty performances and the Center went back to displaying motion pictures.

On the 15th Maurice Evans, who had been vacationing at home in England, resumed his previous season's run with "King Richard II," adding thirty-eight to the hundred and seventeen performances he had given before he took the tragedy on tour. "The Show Is On," which had also done well the previous season with Beatrice Lillie and Bert Lahr, was revived with Rose King and Willie and Eugene Howard as substitute stars. Not so good. Two weeks and they were gone, closing on the road after a poor reception in Chicago.

Two importations were English successes—"George and Margaret," a domestic light comedy written by a young English actor, Gerald Savory, and "French Without Tears," a comedy relating the adventures of several young Englishmen studying French in a French town. This was the work of another youngster named Terence Rattigan. Both were disappointing in that their clever characterization was definitely aimed at English rather than American audiences, but both, helped by occasional cut-rate priming, lingered for approximately eleven weeks.

"The Lady Has a Heart," featuring Elissa Landi and the Vincent Price who the year before had scored as Victoria's Alfred in Helen Hayes' "Victoria Regina," was also helped to a fair run by the cut-rate merchants. The one success of the month was Maxwell Anderson's "The Star-Wagon," a fantastic comedy that he had patched together for Burgess Meredith. There were popular values in this play. Mr. Meredith was agreeably assisted by Lillian Gish, the two playing a middle-aged couple who are whisked back to their youth and given a second chance at marrying for money instead of love, and then whisked back to the present to confess that they had made the right choice the first time. "The Star-Wagon" played through until April.

There was only one success in October, too. That was Rachel Crothers' "Susan and God," with Gertrude Lawrence, the English comedienne, playing Susan. There was also popular appeal in this drama, despite an obvious theatrical quality in the story development. Susan, impressed by a new religious cult in England, whence she has fled to escape an alcoholic husband, returns home prepared to save all her friends. The contrite husband's request to be included in the new salvation, his eagerness to take it on in the hope of reclaiming his wife, his home and his neglected daughter, involves Susan in unexpected complications which she is happily able to adjust. The play, produced in Washington, suffered the loss of its leading man, Osgood Perkins, who died in his hotel a few hours after the first performance. Mr. Perkins' understudy, Paul McGrath, was able to step into the role and, following a succession of trial performances, continued to play it through the New York run. This continued for 288 performances, being discontinued then because of Miss Lawrence's request for a vacation.

The Abbey Theatre Players from Dublin were back for another season of Irish plays. Their company had been weakened by the withdrawal of several of its more popular members, and the repertory had not been strengthened by the addition of any plays of outstanding merit. The Abbey's one success at home the season before had been Paul Vincent Carroll's "Shadow and Substance," which had been sold to another producer and was later brought to New York by Eddie Dowling. As a consequence enthusiasm was muffled. A revival of Lennox Robinson's "The Far-off Hills," however, brought back the old following with something of a rush and the Irish held on till holiday time.

The Theatre Guild began its season with Ben Hecht's "To Quito and Back." This, the story of an idealist seeking peace for his soul in an elopement with his secretary, did not please either the Guild's subscribers or the play's professional critics, and was withdrawn after six weeks of playing.

A hit-and-miss entrant was "Many Mansions," written by Jules Eckert Goodman and his son, Eckert Goodman. It was a serious revealment of a young and liberal clergyman's struggle with the hopelessly conventionalized forces of orthodox Christianity, and won a respectful hearing, but only the cut-rates kept it playing.

Now came a series of inspiriting successes: "Amphitryon 38," with the popular Lunts, on Nov. 1; "I'd Rather Be Right," the year's sensation in the way of political satires, with George M. Cohan cavorting impertinently but amusingly as President Roosevelt, on Nov. 2; Clifford Odets' bid for reinstatement as a Broadway dramatist with his "Golden Boy" Nov. 4, and the Mercury Theatre's stripped "Julius Caesar" on the 11th, after being postponed from the 6th. Four hits and not a miss among them.

The success of "Amphitryon 38" had been discounted because of the reports that had preceded it, as well as by the established popularity of the Lunts. Yet both these factors have been known on occasion to fail. In this instance they did not. The Giraudoux-Behrman version of Jupiter's visit to the earthly Alkmena ran gaily through the Winter, and until the players themselves, seeking a change of role, determined to revive Chekhov's "The Sea Gull" before going to London with "Amphitryon."

"I'd Rather Be Right," having been first-page news from one end of the country to the other following its production in Boston, was welcomed to Broadway by an audience that represented probably more riches and more political power than any other that has ever been gathered in an American theatre. It was an audience that would have either secretly or openly delighted in a chance to boo any attempted defense of New-Deal policies and personages, but so deftly had the authors, George S. Kaufman and Moss Hart, concealed the metallic fist within the velvet glove, and so good-naturedly had the cast been trained in even the broadest of its caricatures, that "I'd Rather Be Right" passed into history as just another musical comedy given an ingratiating touch by Mr. Cohan.

Odets' "Golden Boy" quieted the fears of that playwright's friends that he had gone hopelessly Hollywood, being an incisive character drama written with the feeling for drama and the sympathetic understanding of human types that had characterized both the author's "Awake and Sing" and "Waiting for Lefty." It, too, ran through the season.

The sceneryless "Julius Caesar" established in a single night both the purpose and intent of the Mercury Theatre promoters, John Houseman and Orson Welles. They had come from the WPA Federal Theatre, where they had experimented successfully with the Haitian version of "Macbeth" and the resurrection of Marlowe's "Dr. Faustus." They had left the Federals because they had been stopped by Washington from doing a radical labor play called "The Cradle Will Rock." And they were hell-bent on proving that the new type of theatre they had in mind would find an audience. It did. Those younger playgoers who never had seen an adequately staged production of the Shakespeare tragedy were thrilled to discover that, in modern clothes and on a bare stage, "Caesar" became a thrilling tragedy of a dictator-ruled country. Older playgoers, troubled with memories of the older Shakespearean theatre, were not so keen in enthusiasm, but something more than respectfully interested in the outcome of the experiment, and the unquestioned vitality of the revolutionary treatment. The new "Caesar" ran on for weeks, being transferred to a larger theatre to accommodate its audiences.

Curiously, a real sufferer from this success was Tallulah Bankhead, who preceded the Houseman-Welles "Caesar" the night before with a costly and handsome production of "Antony and Cleopatra" done in the old manner and made possible by the generosity of Rowland Stebbins. This gave the play reviewers a chance to turn odious comparisons to smart account, an opportunity no one of them overlooked. And this, added to the obvious fact that Miss Bankhead had elected to play Cleopatra historically rather than traditionally, as a somewhat common and designing siren rather than as a regal and commanding Shakespearean queen, doomed her efforts to quick defeat. The production was in the storehouse and the actress and her husband, John Emery, who played her Octavius, Conway Tearle being the Antony, were free to seek other jobs a week after they started.

The Theatre Guild tried again with "Madame Bovary," a drama of romance and frustration extracted from the Flaubert novel by Gaston Baty of France and put into English by Benn Levy, principally so his wife, Constance Cummings, could play the name part. Everything was done for the play that the Guild can do—nice setting, good cast, well-directed performance—but there was little sympathetic interest aroused in the fate of the Flaubert heroine and "Madame Bovary" was also through in six weeks.

There were still hits to come, however, in November. "Father

Malachy's Miracle," a heart-warming fantasy taken by Brian Doherty, a Toronto attorney, from a novel by Bruce Marshall, brought Al Shean, erstwhile vaudeville comedian, to the legitimate stage and greatly pleased its first audiences as well as its first critics. The fantastic story of a modern miracle that moved an objectionable dance hall away from a neighborhood otherwise dominated by a church, as the result of a trusting priest's prayers, seemed destined for a long engagement. It probably lacked the full support of Catholics, however, though it was named in the church's white list of plays. Interest began to slip after a hundred performances. The play was withdrawn in March, after having played 125 performances and sent on tour. Chicago failed to react kindly and the tour was canceled.

The Theatre Guild now made a third attempt to recover prestige as America's first producing unit with the production of Sidney Howard's "The Ghost of Yankee Doodle." Again the season's jinx whipped the Theatre Guild. Mr. Howard's thoughtful play, concerned with the last stand of a family of liberal Americans against the mob sentiment that is likely to sweep the country into another great war, provided serious and sane discussion of timely problems, which probably was its weakness so far as popular appeal is concerned. We as a people have been so eternally fed up with discussions of serious problems the last several years it is not easy to find satisfying entertainment in them any longer. "The Ghost of Yankee Doodle," even with Ethel Barrymore returned to the stage as a featured member of the cast, along with the well-liked Dudley Digges, could hold on no longer than the subscription list lasted, which was six weeks.

And then came dramatically the most sensational and most powerful drama of the season's output, which was John Steinbeck's "Of Mice and Men," as staged by George S. Kaufman. A bit startling in the ruddiness of its language and a little ugly in its honest exposure of the true lives of a couple of California farm vagrants, one a half-wit, "Of Mice and Men" naturally met a divided public. The initial impact, however, was definitely in its favor. Its critics were enormously impressed with its significance as a dramatic contribution and it continued for many weeks to capacity audiences. Later interest waned until the play was awarded the New York Drama Critics' plaque as the best drama of American authorship of the season. This doubled the size of the audiences for another two weeks, after which the play was withdrawn for the Summer, a road tour to follow in the Fall.

Just as November was passing out the International Ladies'

Garment Workers' Union, of all people, came in with what turned out to be the surprise musical revue performance of the season. This was a little something the ladies had run together called "Pins and Needles." It was performed by amateurs and semi-professionals taken from the trade, was bright with humorous sketches, lightly satirical in furthering labor's cause, adequately if not brilliantly played and surprisingly good entertainment. Within a fortnight "Pins and Needles" had become a hit with both workers and employers, as well as with many rich loafers. It not only continued through the season, but a second company was organized and installed in the home theatre while the first organization was sent on tour. The international lady garment workers are in show business to stay.

The holiday weeks through December were not particularly interesting. Ed Wynn came off the radio and punned his way happily through a revue called "Hooray for What!" this being the story of an inventive horticulturist who thought up a gas to kill bugs and discovered it would kill humans, too. All the war-eager countries of Europe were after it for their approaching conflicts, and Mr. Wynn had a terrible time keeping his gas and his conscience free. The Wynn addicts were happy, but as usual the crowd that just can't understand how anybody finds the comedian funny was resentful. "Hooray for What!" ran the season out.

Cornelia Otis Skinner played all eight characters she had written into a dramatization of "Edna His Wife," which proved greatly pleasing to her friends. Ruth Gordon came in with a Thornton Wilder editing of Ibsen's "A Doll's House," satisfying a goodly public with her modernized Nora—enough to keep Mr. Ibsen on Broadway for eighteen weeks, which was a record. And there were two musical entertainments, "Three Waltzes," with Kitty Carlisle and Michael Bartlett playing a three-generation romance, and "Between the Devil," which was saved principally by its three principals, Jack Buchanan, Evelyn Laye and Adele Dixon, all British. "Three Waltzes" was the more popular, but "Between the Devil" managed to hang on for twelve weeks, which was only three weeks less than its rival played.

The new year brought a little excitement, but not much added entertainment. The Houseman-Welles Mercury Theatre did an interesting revival of "The Shoemakers' Holiday" with true Elizabethan quaintness in the staging and playing, and "The Cradle Will Rock," which the Mercury had fathered, was moved to another theatre, where it continued for something more than a hundred performances, exciting a labor-conscious following.

An English success, "Time and the Conways," showing what nineteen years did to embitter and practically ruin an English family, was found too leisurely to satisfy American audiences, and a story of the animals in a circus, amusingly told in human terms by Vincent Duffy, called "The Greatest Show on Earth," and quaintly produced by Bonfils and Somnes, just missed success.

A second John Steinbeck play, taken from his popular "Tortilla Flat," by Jack Kirkland, proved a quick failure. A good melo-drama, "Stop-over," written by Mat and Sam Taylor and well played by Arthur Byron and Sidney Blackmer, also missed. Fredric March and Florence Eldredge came bravely from Holly-wood to test their screen popularity on the stage with a comedy of manners called "Yr. Obedient Servant," by Horace Jackson, and met a cool reception. An awful something called "Journey-man," by the Erskine Caldwell who wrote "Tobacco Road," went down by the head in short order.

There was a rewarding experience in the production of "Shadow and Substance," however, that made up for a lot of cheap fail-ures. This eloquently written drama, detailing a contrast of the faith of a scholarly minded and severely ritualistic high priest of Catholicism with that of his house servant, a simple child whose patron saint was the Saint Brigid whose voice she was sure she heard in answer to her prayers for guidance, was impressively cast and acted. Sir Cedric Hardwicke, a first actor of England, and Julie Haydon, an ambitious child of Hollywood, played the contrasting roles and the play ran through until mid-Summer. In the Spring it was awarded a citation by the New York Drama Critics' Circle as the most distinguished play of foreign author-ship to be presented during the season. The author, Paul Vincent Carroll, came from Glasgow, Scotland, where he teaches school, to receive the award in person. He had a grand month in New York and went back to his old job a richer and happier man.

Soon there were two more hits added to the expanding list, and a note of exultation began creeping into the editorials of the season's severer critics. Early in February there appeared a curi-ously happy and satisfying comedy about Death called "On Borrowed Time," extracted by Paul Osborn from a novel by Lawrence Edward Watkin. With Dudley Digges, who had long been a favorite Theatre Guild actor, playing opposite a wonder child named Peter Holden, "On Borrowed Time" tells a fascinat-ing story of an old man who chased Death up a tree and held him there while he tried to find a proper home for his grandson. It was immediately hailed as a popular hit.

The same week saw the production of Thornton Wilder's "Our Town," a story also having to do with Death in its concluding scenes, and this, too, was hailed as a drama that was vastly creditable to its author and to the native drama. In the Spring "Our Town" was awarded the Pulitzer prize as the season's best play of American authorship. The Wilder drama was also produced on a bare stage, with a novel employment of a narrator as stage manager, played by Frank Craven, as is more fully explained in later pages. It ran through to hot weather, and bids fair to be something of a touring sensation when it takes to the road in the Fall.

Two plays by Robert Ardrey, a new writer of definite talent, were produced within a week of each other. One was called "How to Get Tough About It," and was the story of a couple of Illinois mill-town characters who find a solution for their frustrated lives in finding each other. The other told of a famous railroad engineer who fought off the physical impairments of age, beginning with a weakening vision at 50. It was named "Casey Jones" after the fabled hero of the Salt Lake line. Both plays were commended for many virtues by the experts, but neither was quite up to standards demanded of realistic romance. Four weeks and both were in storage. Ina Claire, having failed with Thomas Job's "Barchester Towers," came back with a Frederick Lonsdale conversation piece called "Once Is Enough," which turned out to be the one about the fascinating Lady Bletchley who kept her Duke of Hampshire from making a fool of himself over Liz Pleydell. Miss Claire, taking her ladyship in her stride, kept "Once Is Enough" playing for 105 times.

The Theatre Guild, down but far from out, now tried another Behrman piece, a slightly socialistic drama entitled "Wine of Choice." In this a number of interesting people (including one played by Alexander Woollcott) tried to unravel certain tangled skeins involving this thing called life and seemed only to tie them into harder knots. Katharine Dayton, whose first try resulted in "First Lady," with George Kaufman as her collaborator, offered another on her own, a comedy called "Save Me the Waltz," which had intimate contact with a mythical kingdom plot and failed to survive the experience. The original English company, headed by Robert Speaight, which had played T. S. Eliot's "Murder in the Cathedral" 600 times on the other side, tried to pick up the interest in this poetic tragedy where the WPA Federal Theatre had laid it down the season before. People were not interested in this $3 version, however, having been quite satisfied with what they had seen for a third that admission cost.

And now we began to coast gently toward the season's close, even though by the calendar the end was still three months away. Hardly anything worth the doing came to production in March. Another spoof of Hollywood called "Schoolhouse on the Lot," making sport of the infant phenoms; a good old-fashioned drama from England, "Whiteoaks," which served a good purpose in that it gave Ethel Barrymore a second chance to make her expenses for the year. Miss Barrymore played a matriarch who had lived for a hundred years and was still able to make up her mind that she wanted to leave her money to the weakest and not the strongest member of her clan.

There was an impressively dramatic study of life in a sanitarium for the mentally touched called "All the Living," which Hardie Allbright, actor-playwright, adapted from Dr. Victor Small's "I Knew 3,000 Lunatics." It was splendidly cast and directed by Lee Strasberg, but playgoers were not sufficiently interested. Fifty-two performances was all. The Lunts gave five weeks to Chekhov's "The Sea Gull" to rest their minds, and that revival was pleasing to their following. After closing "The Sea Gull" they took boat for England, and scored again with "Amphitryon 38" with the Britishers, of whom, of course, Mrs. Lunt is one.

Now the season was practically in the doldrums. Happily George Abbott obliged with a comedy called "What a Life," written by a high school lecturer named Clifford Goldsmith. This gave a lift to early April. It tells of the somewhat backward son of a Phi Beta Kappa father who was expected to make Princeton, but could not even make the Junior prom. "What a Life" was received with such favor that it ran well into Summer.

William A. Brady, feeling in his 75th year an urge to do another one of the spectacular revivals that punctuated the years of his greater activity, selected Somerset Maugham's "The Circle," which was a hit seventeen years ago with John Drew and Mrs. Leslie Carter playing the leads. Mr. Brady cast his wife, Grace George, for the Carter role and Tallulah Bankhead for the second feminine lead, co-starring the two of them. The result was most satisfactory, both to the players and to the playgoers. A nine week run followed.

Robert Henderson and Estelle Winwood, who had directed a Western tour of "Tonight at 8.30," elected to spend their profits in a revival of "The Merry Wives of Windsor" in New York. The result was lightly catastrophic. The Messrs. Welles and

Houseman revived George Bernard Shaw's "Heartbreak House,"
Mr. Welles playing the philosophical octogenarian, Capt. Shotover, and scoring as pronounced a personal success in the part
as he had playing Brutus in "Julius Caesar." The Shaw drama,
written out of the resentment awakened by a socially disintegrating England just previous to the Great War, was plentifully sup-
plied with scenery and continued a popular feature of the Mercury repertory for forty-eight performances.

The Theatre Guild, thoroughly downhearted by now, and still
owing its subscribers a production to make up for one missed the
season before, decided to sponsor the production of a satirical
political revue called "Washington Jitters," written by John
Boruff and Walter Hart and produced originally by the Actors'
Repertory Company. For three weeks "Washington Jitters" was
shown to subscribers only. At the end of three weeks it was
thrown open to press and public, which did not appear to make
a great deal of difference. A series of indifferent press reviews for
this indifferent satire followed, and "Washington Jitters" was
gone with the wind in another fortnight.

That was all until mid-May, when Dwight Deere Wiman, who
had been lucky with "On Borrowed Time," and had produced a
musical comedy called "I Married an Angel" on tour, intending
to take it to Chicago for a Summer run, changed his mind and
brought it into New York instead. The piece, with a cast headed
by Dennis King, Vera Zorina, Vivienne Segal and Walter Slezak,
a book by Lorenz Hart and a musical score by Robert Rodgers,
found immediate favor and was quickly headed for a Summer run.

This was followed the last of the month by "The Two Bouquets," a quaint Victorian operetta by Herbert and Eleanor
Farjeon, with music assembled from the compositions of some
twenty different composers. Following a mixed reception, "The
Two Bouquets" continued hopefully for a few weeks and was
then withdrawn.

And so another theatre season came to an end. There were
fewer new productions than there had been the last several years,
about the same number of revivals as usual and as healthy an
interest otherwise as might be expected.

THE SEASON IN CHICAGO

By Charles Collins

Dramatic Critic of the *Chicago Tribune*

CHICAGO'S stage activities of the year 1937-1938 form a shorter story than one should expect from the Second City of the nation. It is, moreover, a tale that began well and ended badly. For six months the playgoing season seemed like a renaissance in its first flush of optimism, but the last quarter of the year was a *débâcle*, sliding down close to the zero point. The evolutionary advance was halted almost as if fate had slammed a door in its face on or about March 1—a date that is here set down for the benefit of economists in their study of time-lags—and afterward symptoms of degeneration were painfully in evidence. All this coincides, of course, with the onrush of the new depression in business and industrial life.

Perhaps one should write about his favorite subject in a reassuring mood, stoutly maintaining that although apparently washed up for the time being it would soon be coming around the corner again with a rainbow on its shoulder and vine-leaves in its hair. When this happy event comes to pass I shall be there, I hope, with a brass-band to welcome it; but in the meantime I must face the fact that the Chicago stage reached the month of June, 1938, with nothing but "Pins and Needles," a sporadic victory of amateurism loaded with labor union propaganda, to offer its customers. The man on the street has begun to talk about this state of affairs and to ask me what is the matter with the theatre and the town. I cannot give him a satisfactory answer; but on the other hand I cannot refuse to admit that such a condition exists. I may, like Nature, abhor a vacuum, but I will not take the witness stand to testify that there ain't no such animal.

As official score-keeper of the stage year in this region, I must report 20 professional theatrical engagements, many of them of high quality. This is a decline from the preceding year by six. I might pad the score by adding strays, casuals and aliens; but I prefer to keep them in separate categories, thus: Federal Theatre Project productions, 9; Yiddish troupes from New York, 2; special dramatic productions of an ambitious and worthy nature by

15

eminent stars, 2 (Helen Hayes and Maurice Evans).

The Chicago stage started the summer period of 1937 with two dramatic companies carrying over from the preceding year. (The activities of the Federal Theatre Project are excluded from this chronological scheme and will be dealt with separately.) They were Maxwell Anderson's "The Wingless Victory," with Katharine Cornell as star, and "You Can't Take It with You," the comic prodigy by George S. Kaufman and Moss Hart. Miss Cornell remained only until June 12 and then began her sabbatical year of the contemplative life. "You Can't" et cetera (I am tired of writing that title in its full length) remained as Chicago's only show of the summer of 1937 and kept on running until Jan. 15, 1938. Its final record here was 49 weeks, which is a new "high" since the 58 weeks of "Abie's Irish Rose" in 1924-1925. Its chief actor, Aldrich Bowker, in the role of the philosophic loafer called Grandpa, was unknown here until this play arrived, but he is now a civic legend ranking with Frank Bacon of "Lightnin'."

The arrival of "Brother Rat" on August 22 gave the fall season an early opening. This company did not contain a heavy representation from the New York cast, but there was no reason to complain of its "second" quality. The play was heartily enjoyed as a comedy of college life with a fresh atmosphere, and Edwin L. Philips, as the first jester among the cadets of Virginia Military Institute, was singularly ingratiating in his behavior. The play ran in the Selwyn Theatre for 17 weeks, and before it departed one of its young women flitted away to Hollywood with a movie contract in her hand-bag. This unimportant fact is mentioned merely to suggest one of the handicaps under which the American stage is staggering.

On September 19 "The Women" came to the Erlanger Theatre to utter its disheartening message about the meanness and viciousness of Park Avenue's hoity-toity dames. Chicago's cynics, largely of the female sex, were there to gloat over this satire written in sulphuric acid; but the cast contained so many second- or third-grade personalities that there was a reaction of antagonism at the première. Lois Wilson, known only as a film actress, had the central role in place of Margalo Gillmore, and was pleasant enough; but most of the others lacked distinction and the air of ultra-sophistication. Max Gordon, the play's impresario, hurried to Chicago to lift the curse, and two or three changes were made, without much improvement. Nevertheless the play remained for ten weeks and the box-office prospered, although rebels against the old theatrical custom of second companies for Chicago could be found in every tavern and woman's club meeting.

"The Show Is On" came to the Grand Opera House on Oct. 5 as a successful revue from Broadway, but without its original principals it was a feeble affair. After two weeks it vanished, not only from Chicago but from "the road" in general. Willie and Eugene Howard, Rose King and Chic Yorke were the co-stars. This was the only disastrous failure of the year. The anti-second-company revolutionaries were getting in their deadly work by word of mouth.

The Theatre Guild began its annual subscription program on Oct. 18, at the Grand Opera House, with the dramatization of "Madame Bovary" which has been greatly admired in Paris. It met with favor here also, and Constance Cummings was a happy girl when she read her notices. But after two weeks of much better than subscription business, it moved to New York to meet its doom through what was, to my mind, hair-splitting reviewing. This, I believe, was a good thing in drama with a literary background, put out of existence by the exacerbations of supercilious criticism.

The next new title on the playbills was "Yes, My Darling Daughter," which came into the Grand Opera House on Nov. 1, sponsored by the Theatre Guild although not of its own coinage. There were two weeks of this light comedy of modern youth and parenthood, adeptly acted by its original cast. The Guild's subscribers, however, said that they hoped to get bigger and better things for signing on the dotted line.

A new Nora Helmer was added to the Ibsen acting tradition when "A Doll's House," textually smoothed by Thornton Wilder, came to the Grand Opera House with Ruth Gordon as its star. Chicago saw and approved this production before Broadway's firstnighters endorsed the verdict. This was the third play on the Theatre Guild program; the engagement was for three weeks, starting Nov. 29.

The next opening was also under the Guild's subscription plan and from its own workshops—"Wine of Choice," a comedy in which S. N. Behrman struck a glittering intellectual attitude toward political and social problems of the times and over-talked his nebulous theme. The result was pretentious boredom, in spite of Miriam Hopkins, Leslie Banks and other able players. Alexander Woollcott's association with this piece began in Chicago; the Guild appealed to him as a rescuer and flattered him, probably, into acting a character that was cut to his pattern. On Christmas Day he was scheduled to join the show as a secret recruit, but rehearsals got into a mess and the matinée performance was omitted without notice to the public. The rest of this play's brief and painful history belongs to New York, whither it and Mr. Woollcott went to do and die. The entire episode is to be scored as an error by the Theatre Guild in strategy, tactics and public relations.

Then came a period that formed the glowing heart of the season—a succession of magnificent successes which caused many playgoers to believe that the brave days of old had returned. "Tovarich," with Eugenie Leontovich, McKay Morris and admirable associates, opened on Dec. 20, at the Selwyn, to remain for nine weeks. "Victoria Regina," with Helen Hayes and all the others (Werner Bateman as the Prince Consort) opened at the Erlanger on Dec. 27 to stay for eight weeks. "Stage Door," with Joan Bennett acting like her father's daughter, reached the Grand Opera House on Jan. 10 to abide for four weeks. "Tonight at 8.30," with a new and surprisingly brilliant company (Bramwell Fletcher, Helen Chandler, Estelle Winwood, Jessie Royce Landis and Roland Bottomley as principals) came into the Harris on Jan. 30 with a two weeks' booking and flourished for five. Feb. 7 started two weeks of the Abbey Theatre Company of Dublin at the Grand. Shakespeare in the true heroic style arrived at the Grand, in the form of Maurice Evans' staging of "Richard II," on Feb. 21, to hold forth for five weeks. The addition of Mr. Evans' magnificent Falstaff, in "King Henry IV, Part 1," made this engagement a repertory affair.

Miss Hayes added glamour to this rich period of playgoing by giving three matinée performances of "The Merchant of Venice." Her classic début in the role of Portia was exceedingly happy. She had a strong and intelligent Shylock in Abraham Sofaer; a first-class Bassanio in Alexander Clark; an impressive Duke of Venice in McKay Morris; and a remarkable Prince of Morocco in Cecil Humphreys. The latter two were borrowed from the "Tovarich" company. Cornelia Otis Skinner's annual monodramatics, this year based upon Margaret Ayer Barnes' novel, "Edna His Wife," was a minor incident in this halcyon period.

"Room Service" reached Chicago at the tail-end of this harvesttime (Feb. 20). This farcical comedy of show-business antics was better humor for Broadway than for the Middle West, and the audience reaction to it was much more temperate than to its forerunner, "Three Men on a Horse." Nevertheless it ran for ten weeks at the Selwyn Theatre.

"Julius Caesar" after the fashion of Orson Welles and the

Mercury Theatre of New York, with a new cast which had Tom Powers in the role of Brutus, opened at the Erlanger Theatre on March 7 under Theatre Guild sponsorship and stayed four weeks. New York's hurrahs over this parable of Fascism did not reverberate strongly along the shores of Lake Michigan; but many customers, mainly of the younger generation, rejoiced over this bizarre business because it was in the fashion. My own reaction was a growing fatigue from the monotony of young men in overcoats, portentously muttering lines from Shakespeare in the gloom. Perhaps the unlettered millions need an Orson Welles to teach them the implications of Roman history when the republic was in its death throes; but I myself feel no need of him on this subject.

"Father Malachy's Miracle," the last item on the Theatre Guild's subscription schedule, appeared at the Harris Theatre on March 14 with its original cast. Here was admirable acting in the relatively neglected field of modern Scottish character. The play itself was an eccentricity of humorous folk-lore against a religious background which did not arouse a strong theatre-going interest. When people heard that it dealt with the miraculous levitation of a cabaret from its city site to a distant island, they said, "Oh, folderol," and went to some movie which probably told an equally preposterous tale. The character of the miracle-making monk was acted by Al Shean, an ancient low comedian of Chicago's musical comedy past, when the LaSalle Theatre was a local institution.

A month without a première followed; then came "The Star Wagon," Maxwell Anderson's dramatic variant of the good old "time machine" plot. Burgess Meredith, Lillian Gish and the others in the fine cast that Guthrie McClintic assembled, kept the customers of the Grand Opera House well contented for three weeks.

The last opening of the season brought the second musical show in nine months—a new frolic called "You Never Know," which Broadway will see next fall. It has a plot of mixed identities and masquerades in Viennese high life, and is an adaptation of an Austrian play called "Candle Light" when Gertrude Lawrence and, later, Eugenie Leontovich acted it five or six years ago. The music and lyrics are Cole Porter's inventions and in his happiest vein. This was an ambitious cast, with Clifton Webb, Lupe Velez and Libby Holman as co-stars, and with Toby Wing and Rex O'Malley as important assistants.

On Memorial Day, when the Chicago stage had prepared itself for the most empty summer in its history, "Pins and Needles," a well-drilled and alert revue with which the International Ladies' Garment Workers' Union had surprised New York, entered the Grand Opera House. It may be accounted for in the theatrical annals of 1938-1939.

The Federal Theatre Project's activities in Chicago during this period, centering in the Blackstone and Great Northern theatres, may be described as work-relief for jobless actors as usual. Stage direction and acting were generally improved. The choice of plays left much to be desired by utopians who believe that something culturally important will eventually come out of this government bureau. Here is a catalogue of the productions:

"The Lonely Man," a drama dealing with Lincoln's reincarnation as a liberal professor in a small college and lawyer for labor unions; it was produced in May, 1937, and ran well into the summer. "An Evening of Short Plays," four in number, containing an early example of Eugene O'Neill's work, and a bit of *pastiche* by Thornton Wilder. "Monesh," a Yiddish folk-drama. "The Straw," a revival of O'Neill's early drama with a tuberculosis sanitarium as its scene. "The Devil's Disciple," costume piece out of Bernard Shaw's repertory. "Holy Night," a Christmas mystery play by Martinez Sierra. "See Naples and Die," by Elmer Rice, produced on Broadway without much cheering about ten years ago. "Ballet Fèdre," a program of modern dancing. "The Tailor Becomes a Shoemaker," a Yiddish comedy. "The Great Barrington," a fantasy of grim humor on the subject of old American families and their villainous forbears. "Big White Fog," a Negro play, all-colored in cast and authorship, which had some merit as a picture of characters in Chicago's black belt. "Spirochete," a series of sketches dealing with syphilis in its historical and clinical aspects, effective as medical propaganda.

These Federal Theatre productions ran up a total of 472 performances during the year, according to my calculations.

THE SEASON IN SAN FRANCISCO

By FRED JOHNSON

Drama Editor of *The Call-Bulletin*

SAN FRANCISCO'S leanest theatrical year in number of touring attractions also brought the longest continuous parade of Broadway successes of the previous season.

The twelve-month period, beginning as Alfred Lunt and Lynn Fontanne concluded their engagement in "Idiot's Delight" and the première run of "Amphitryon 38," was near its fade-out as Helen Hayes came in for a three weeks' stay, playing to capacity business in "Victoria Regina" for receipts totaling $90,000.

Between these lustrous events and along with the hit road shows came the most variegated and experimental series of entertainments the city had ever known. Five of these ventures represented coast producers' testing of pieces they believed might have a chance on Broadway.

It might have been coincidental or a result of the Lunts' and Tallulah Bankhead's ("Reflected Glory") successes, following San Francisco tryouts. Anyway, as the season ended, Miss Bankhead was reported bound for this city for the proving of a new play by Zoe Akins and Lili Hatvany, appropriately titled "I'm Different." A fall opening in New York was projected.

It will be recorded as the year of Arthur J. Beckhard's west coast Waterloo, with a perfect score of three disasters in a row. The product of his Santa Barbara laboratory, the Lobero Theatre, all were bound up with hopes of an eventual Broadway showing.

Rather than saying Walter Huston was a sacrificial offering that led the Beckhard list, it might be explained that Mr. Huston was an entirely willing sacrifice in "The Miles of Heaven," David Hertz's biographical romance of the eighteenth century English astronomer, William Herschel. He was enamored of the role for its possibilities in characterization, of which he made the most. But his followers, who had packed the Curran Theatre to view him as Dodsworth, saw only stodginess in his new creation. Such brightness as Barbara O'Neil contributed as the belated love interest was offset by the dourness of Nan Sunderland as a sisterly possessor of the ardent scientist. Doubtful beforehand of

21

the play's appeal, Huston's dubiousness was confirmed in the two lean weeks that followed.

Following a September to January interlude, Mr. Beckhard again acquired a ranking star in Pauline Frederick and a play for which she shared his enthusiasm. This was an English murder mystery piece by Edward Percy and Reginald Denham ("Rex Judd"), in which Miss Frederick enacted an elderly recluse, under revived accusation for an ancient double homicide. Her well-studied characterization and a sensational climactic scene won considerable word-of-mouth interest, but the star's illness while continuing in the role brought the play to a close, and abrupt shelving, after a fortnight's run at the Curran.

One month later, Beckhard chose a new comedy, "Rhyme Without Reason," by the Hollywood screen writers, Edmund North and James Gow, as his next venture, at the Geary Theatre. In this feather-weight affair, linking Hollywood and Broadway theatrical characters, were John Eldredge, Leona Maricle, Esther Dale (Mrs. Beckhard) and Kay Linaker. Its folding came after one week.

Preceding these experiments in coast production, Arch Selwyn and Edgar MacGregor presented "for New York Productions, Inc.," at the Curran, a new play by William Hurlbut, dealing with the silver bonanza days in Nevada. Marjorie Rambeau made a perennial return to the stage in the starring role of a brothel keeper, supported by Weldon Heyburn, Herbert Corthell, Minnie Dupree (now in film assignments) and Edith Kingdon. The drama's realistic bawdiness was too much for the younger generations of California mining pioneers and its slow death occupied an even fortnight.

As an anti-climax of the season at the Geary, and of ill-starred new play projects as well, the New York firm of Hilbert and Ames presented Alan Dinehart in "Thanks for My Wife," a comedy by Joseph Carole of Hollywood. Marking Dinehart's return to the stage as director as well as star, the piece dealt wittily with the Broadway theatrical scene and showed potentialities as diverting fare for that sector, toward which it was aimed later on. It had fair patronage for two weeks, and for good entertainment reasons, but was then withdrawn for further rewriting in a Hollywood workshop. The supporting cast included James Spottswood, Regis Toomey, Mozell Britton (Mrs. Dinehart), Virginia Howell and Kay Linaker.

George Abbott's "Room Service," with a competent road company that included Michael Dalmatoff, Clinton Sundberg and

Matt Briggs, stayed through most of August with only fair patronage.

"Yes, My Darling Daughter," starring Florence Reed, with Lawrence Grossmith, did much better in its three weeks.

"The Women," with a less brilliant cast, fared equally well for the same period and "You Can't Take It with You," featuring Clarence Oliver as Grandpa Vanderhof, outstripped them all in the seven weeks that set a record in length of runs for the season.

Aside from Dinehart's offering, the same house presented but one other coast-produced attraction, a three weeks' festival of Gilbert and Sullivan by the San Francisco Light Opera Guild, with Frank Moulan as a New York guest star.

Homer Curran maintained his standards in taste and costliness with a single production during the year, at the theatre bearing his name, in early spring. This was his staging of "Golden Boy," starring Francis Lederer, who was regarded as miscast in the title role by some of his previous matinée admirers of the "Autumn Crocus" period. But other followers rallied to make the engagement successful, under the staging of Stella Adler. Louis Calhern and Betty Furness also absented themselves from Hollywood for the roles of Tom Moody and Lorna Moon for the three weeks that has become the expected, or hoped-for, period of a San Francisco play run.

This span was exceeded, however, by the month's duration of the Noel Coward vogue at the same theatre in October. The "Tonight at 8.30" cycle of nine short plays was made brilliant by such principals as Estelle Winwood, Bramwell Fletcher, Helen Chandler and Jessie Royce Landis, with Carole Stone and Mary Astor as guest artists.

Came Billy Rose and his "Show of Shows," equipped with Texan pulchritude and further publicized by the divorce rumors which coincidentally broke around the showman's defenseless head. Strongly avowing that there are no more yokels left anywhere, he found the populace backing him up in his assertion by limiting the fee-ments at his carnival. After three weeks he packed up for further operations under the heading of Casa Mañana.

Morris Gest's production of "Lady Precious Stream," a Merle Armitage attraction, opened the calendar year at the Curran for a fortnight's run. Clarence Derwent, who originally directed the play in America, portrayed the prime minister and Lotus Liu appeared in the title role.

"Tobacco Road" returned for the same period with James Barton's Uncle John in the Jeeter role.

Merle Armitage, in association with Paul Posz, a new San Francisco impresario, and in arrangement with the New York Theatre Guild, then revived "Porgy and Bess" under Rouben Mamoulian's direction. The latter, associated in the original "Porgy's" staging, was the late George Gershwin's choice as pilot of the music drama's presentation. Todd Duncan, Anne Brown and Ruby Elzy came on from New York to re-create the principal roles. And a revival of interest in Gershwin, who had previously conducted the San Francisco Symphony Orchestra in a concert, augmented patronage of the two weeks' engagement.

The Abbey Theatre Players returned to the Curran after a three years' absence, Barry Fitzgerald coming from Hollywood as guest star in "Juno and the Paycock" and "The Plough and the Stars." Cormac O'Daly's comedy, "The Silver Jubilee," was added to the regular repertoire.

Helen Hayes attracted less than her usual capacity houses for the two matinée performances in "The Merchant of Venice," during the run of "Victoria Regina." Abraham Sofaer won critical praise for his Shylock equaling that given her Portia, which she had played some months earlier in Chicago.

John Charles Thomas returned to the light opera stage, after an absence of fifteen years in grand opera and concert, to sing the Franz Schubert role in "Blossom Time." The single week's run, closing the season at the Curran, drew sell-out business, justifying his assertedly record salary at $7,500. Edwin Lester, who brought the Los Angeles Civic Light Opera Association's attraction here, also discussed the project of an annual season of operettas, to be divided between the two cities.

San Francisco's Federal Theatre Project, maintained its pace in achievement, with 22 productions for the year. The most successful of its offerings included Eugene O'Neill's "Beyond the Horizon," Galsworthy's "Justice," Barry Lyndon's "The Amazing Dr. Clitterhouse," Elmer Rice's "Judgment Day" and Professor E. P. Conkle's "Prologue to Glory."

Thespians of the two largest universities showed zeal in their activities, with prodigious results by the University of California Little Theatre on its now famed postage stamp platform. On it were managed Strindberg's "The Dance of Death," Paul Green's "Johnny Johnson," and Clifford Odets' "Awake and Sing," for their first non-professional productions anywhere. Spaciousness of the near-by Greek Theatre gave the student actors a refreshing freedom in their notable production of Maxwell Anderson's "High Tor." In the same amphitheatre was staged "Of Thee I Sing."

At Stanford, in addition to its "Big Game Gaieties," was produced Martin Flavin's "Blue Jeans," a story of the Salinas Valley lettuce strike, which, oddly enough, he completed one month before the strike began. This was the Dramatic Council's first production of a professional playwright's experimental endeavor. Flavin also conducted a Stanford winter class in playwriting.

The Palo Alto Community Players, maintained under a municipal budget, used but one old standby, "The Dover Road," as a major production. Best-acted plays were "Biography" and "Night Must Fall." The seat of Maxwell Anderson's alma mater (Stanford) offered his "Winterset" and "High Tor"; "Pride and Prejudice," "The Old Maid," "Journey's End," "Pygmalion" and "Excursion."

The Wayfarer's Civic Repertory Theatre, in San Francisco, gained in prestige with its Shakespearean repertoire, Gorky's "The Lower Depths," Mary Hay's original "Glass Splinter," a comedy of theatrical life, and "Delightful Dishonor." Other items were Wilde's "Ballad of Reading Gaol" and Molière's "The Miser."

The Berkeley Playmakers, in continuous existence since 1923, made longer strides as the only known group confined to first productions of one-act plays. Its fifteenth annual playwriting contest, like others, has brought entries from many states in competition for the larger prizes offered.

THE SEASON IN SOUTHERN CALIFORNIA

By EDWIN SCHALLERT

Drama Editor of the *Los Angeles Times*

DEMONSTRATION that there are enormous audiences for the right type of stage attraction in Southern California was one of the major developments of the 1937-38 season—a season that was far from uniformly bright, but which had superbrilliant peaks and summits. Severally, these included the engagement of Alfred Lunt and Lynn Fontanne in "Amphitryon 38" at the very outset of the twelve-month period, and Helen Hayes in "Victoria Regina," and a single performance of "The Merchant of Venice," at the very close. To these must be added the remarkable light opera series, which garnered more than $120,000, with $40,000 the revenue for a single week of John Charles Thomas in "Blossom Time."

The 1937-38 was a disappointing season from the standpoint of enthusiasts for Coast-made productions. The number of these in the commercial theatre was reduced to the minimum, with, perhaps, a few more in San Francisco than Los Angeles. The best center for activities, though, was Santa Barbara, where Arthur Beckhard held forth valiantly from time to time with new plays and new presentations. His premières included "The Miles of Heaven," written by David Hertz, with Walter Huston, Barbara O'Neil and Nan Sunderland; "American Primitive" by Ernest Pascal, with Grant Withers, Nydia Westman, Robert Cummings and John Arledge, Helen Craig and William Mansell, and he offered various other productions like the English mystery play "Suspect," with Pauline Frederick, "Spring in Autumn" by Martinez Sierra, "Pilate" by H. Campbell Duncan and R. A. Lennon, and one or two others, none of which was seen in Los Angeles.

Beckhard inaugurated his season impressively with "Tonight at 8.30," Noel Coward series, his casts including Glenn Anders, Genevieve Tobin, Mary Astor, Bramwell Fletcher, Helen Chandler, Barbara O'Neil, Nydia Westman and various others. Subsequently and under other sponsorship these plays were given in Los Angeles without Miss Tobin and Mr. Anders, and with Estelle Winwood prominently featured, as well as Miss Astor, Fletcher and Miss Chandler. This followed shortly after the Lunt-Fontanne appearance in "Amphitryon." Only once did Homer Curran achieve a full-fledged manifestation, when "Golden Boy" was offered late in the season with Francis Lederer, Betty Furness, Louis Calhern and Lee Cobb in prominent parts, all benefiting by the exceptional direction of Stella Adler. This production did better business in Los Angeles than in San Francisco, and was at one time slated for a Chicago booking.

"Golden Boy," "Amphitryon 38" and "Prologue to Glory" (Federal) are the only three plays on the Burns Mantle ten-best list for the season to have been seen in Southern California. In the season of 1938-39 showgoers will have the chance to view early presentations of "On Borrowed Time" with Victor Moore and Guy Bates Post in leading roles (a Coast production), and "Susan and God" with Gertrude Lawrence. Doubtless, too, they will see "Our Town" and "Of Mice and Men."

Most auspicious is the increase in visiting attractions, and the results that attend. Even downright second companies do pretty fair business. Such plays as "The Women" and "You Can't Take It with You," which had a rather lengthy engagement, "Room Service," "Brother Rat" and "Yes, My Darling Daughter" had little or no cause for complaint. "The Women" drew exceptionally well, with Lois Wilson heading its cast. Champion one-week offering was "Tobacco Road," on a return trip, which rivaled Helen Hayes and the Lunts in playing to "standing room only," and not much of that. The Abbey Theatre Players remained consistently popular on their return tour with repertoire.

"Victoria Regina" was the decisive visiting lure. First reservations for seats had been made months in advance of the opening, and the theatre was constantly packed during the three weeks' engagement. Speculators were heavy purchasers of tickets, and they are not a usual phenomenon in such a sensational way in Southern California. A great contrast was this Hayes season and the one that she played in "Coquette" some years ago, when she drew rather scanty audiences. She was nominated a favorite comparable with Katharine Cornell and Alfred Lunt and Lynn Fontanne by the Western theatregoers, and "The Merchant of Venice," in which she played Portia for a lone Sunday evening, had probably the most amazing professional audience since the days of Raquel Meller. This play which was admirably and beautifully presented by the star and her company proved more than a mere curiosity for this curious throng, but a source of satisfaction as well.

The Hayes three weeks derived approximately $100,000, and was matched by the Lunt-Fontanne engagements in "Idiot's Delight" and "Amphitryon." The light operas rose higher financially because of a longer season. In addition to "Blossom Time," there was one week of "Student Prince" and "New Moon"—the best production, and a truly spectacular one; and two weeks of "Roberta" with Bob Hope, Tamara, and one or two others of the original cast. Stanley Morner and Della Lind, European light opera star, both under contract to Metro-Goldwyn-Mayer at that time, were in "Student Prince," while George Houston and Francis White, and the clever and comical Sterling Holloway were successful in "New Moon." Thomas was aided by Miss White, Melville Cooper and others in "Blossom Time," which gave the real fillip to the season. The interest was astonishing, because it had no precedent in other attempts at the same sort of entertainment.

Among other attractions originated in Los Angeles during the season were "Lady Precious Stream," staged with marked charm, but failing of popular appeal, and "Porgy and Bess," as a sort of memorial to George Gershwin, which had good audiences during its stay at Philharmonic Auditorium. Perhaps the "Ice Follies," which visited late in the spring, might be considered a theatrical attraction; anyway this did excellent business.

One misses, of course, the name of Henry Duffy whose efforts for more than a decade were so entirely dependable. He has embarked on a new activity in his school of the theatre, and hopes to crystallize this in occasional festivals of plays, and possibly later professional productions. In this way his path may lead back to the theatre.

In the same field of development of new talent Max Reinhardt is intent on essaying important things, and has already instituted his workshop with a notable faculty of directors and instructors. His aim is to eschew the school idea. His actual production plans include Thornton Wilder's new comedy of the gay nineties, "The Merchant of Yonkers," and Goethe's "Faust" at this writing. Reinhardt hopes permanently to establish the Salzburg festival type of presentation in Southern California. He is especially interested in staging Maeterlinck's "Blue Bird" in the Hollywood Bowl at some future time, though that will hardly be possible of realization during the 1938-39 season. The success of the Reinhardt "Midsummer Night's Dream" in the Bowl during the early fall of 1934 is still something to conjure with in Southern California.

Little theatres and community theatres faced a major battle, with Equity rulings requiring payment of $25 per week to senior members and $15 to juniors, while amateur players were required to pay $5 to Equity for the privilege of appearing with professionals. There was a mass meeting at which opinion even among the professionals was found to be divided on the attitude toward community playhouses. Some professional actors rather favor accepting these engagements under any terms, but the majority rule of their organization decided against this. Tendency therefore of the little theatres is to cut down on use of professionals, even, say, in the instance of so important an institution as the Pasadena Community. Whether the quality of productions can be maintained under the circumstances is one of the topics of debate.

Pasadena as usual led all forces among the community group. Several important premières distinguished the season. "Knights of Song," by Glendon Allvine, woven around the lives of Gilbert and Sullivan, was a stunning achievement, which served to lift up the theatre's record to a level attained in many of its other gallant originations. Highly commendable also, and with an even earlier historical setting was "Sing, Sweet Angels," written by Belford Forrest, concerning the crusading for the theatre of James Burbage. This had genuine quality in the writing.

"Star of Navarre," written by Victor Victor, and detailing romantic phases of the life of Marguerite of Navarre, was another première, and during the Midsummer Drama Festival, dedicated to the Great Southwest, two new plays were given, including "Miracle of the Swallows" by Ramon Romero and "Miner's Gold" by Agnes Peterson.

Strikingly during this series of productions the old "Girl of the Golden West" was a big winner with audiences. Maxwell Anderson's "Night over Taos" and Franz Werfel's "Juarez and Maximilian" were impressive offerings of the group, which also contained "Montezuma" by Gerhardt Hauptmann and "Rose of the Rancho" by Belasco and Tully. It was a rather conglomerate assembling of plays.

This year (1938) for its festival Pasadena Community is presenting "Seven from Shaw," including "Arms and the Man," "Major Barbara," "Heartbreak House," "On the Rocks" and three parts of "Back to Methuselah." The last trio are given their Coastal première.

Other very worthy plays and productions during the 1937-38 Pasadena season included "The Amazing Dr. Clitterhouse," "Idiot's Delight," "Merrily We Roll Along," "First Lady," "Pride and Prejudice," "Accent on Youth," "The Breadwinner" by Somerset Maugham, "Case of the Frightened Lady" by Edgar Wallace, and "Three Men on a Horse."

The theatre rounded out in complete style its Shakespearean repertoire by offering the previously ungiven "Winter's Tale," "Measure for Measure," "All's Well That Ends Well" and "Titus Adronicus." These were to celebrate the twentieth anniversary of the organization, which curiously enough established itself as a theatre for extended engagements some years ago with a performance of the Bard's "Tempest," Gilmor Brown, the director, himself appearing as Prospero. A Shakespearean play marked a turning point in the history, therefore, of the Pasadena Community.

The number of little theatres in Southern California remains approximately the same, with a group of about half a dozen continuously doing their stint in the offering of new shows and new talent. Much necessarily in this field is mediocre, but Hollywood and the films provide an ever-present stimulus and will probably go on doing so for many days to come. Just in passing, these names of offerings might be registered to keep the record straight: "One More Genius," "Madrid Madness," "Miracle for Two," "Man with Portfolio," "The Duchess Receives," "God Out of Heaven," "Little Town of Bethlehem," "Dump Heap," "Show in August," "Shadow that Passes," "Geometric Pattern," "You're the Doctor," "Stray Greeks," "Gudrun," "Savage Beast," "Chaperoned by Three," "High as the Heaven," "One Hollywood Day," "Lagniappe," "The Duggan Family," "Every Saturday Night." These were among the more successful attempts at playwriting and play offering—in a very few cases unusually interesting.

The Federal output of theatrical productions meanwhile exceeded forty and aimed apparently to entertain with a more popular sort of attraction. Especially well performed were "Judgment Day," "Prologue to Glory," "Allison's House," "The Weavers," "Caesar and Cleopatra," "Captain Brassbound's Conversion," "Androcles and the Lion," "Accent on Youth," "Roadside," "Brothers," "Days Without End," "Ready! Aim! Fire!", "Mary's Other Husband," "Boy Meets Girl," "Merry Wives of Windsor," "The Nativity" and "Pursuit of Happiness." Other plays included "Ah, Wilderness," "Night Must Fall," "Will Shakespeare," "The Amazing Dr. Clitterhouse," "The Bishop Misbehaves," "Loyalties," "The World We Live In," "Gods of Lightning" and "American Exodus."

Road improvement is still the leading motif in Southern California discussions of the stage. The hope here is that more companies will visit, the increase having been steady during the past few seasons. Coast production activities, which were at a low ebb during 1937-38 may show some tendency to pick up during 1938-39. Momentous gains in that department are not, however, anticipated, and the summer theatre has yet really to establish itself. But there is one show that goes on forever, and that's "The Drunkard," now in its sixth year.

OF MICE AND MEN
A Drama in Three Acts

By JOHN STEINBECK

THE theatre season was moving sluggishly and a little uninterestingly toward the holidays when John Steinbeck's "Of Mice and Men" was ready for production. Nothing particularly cheering had occurred in the discovery of new plays. Nothing particularly promising was to be found in the published announcements. Therefore the stage was nicely set for a play of character, substance and dramatic power.

"Of Mice and Men" startled its first-night audience into upright sitting positions and such emotional quivers as no other Broadway audience had enjoyed since Jeanne Eagels cussed out a psalm-singing clergyman in "Rain." No other spoken text had been as freely profane as this one since "What Price Glory?" was a success, and no other drama had offered so thrilling a dramatic climax as was discovered in the concluding tragedy of the Steinbeck story.

As a natural result, "Of Mice and Men" was the play sensation of the next several weeks. There were auditors who recoiled from its ruddy boldness, and were free spoken in their resentment. But the greater number accepted and approved the drama for its obvious sincerities and its appealing exposure of the tragedy that is found in human loneliness.

"Of Mice and Men" ran through till spring and was then given the silver plaque awarded annually by the New York Drama Critics' Circle to the play of American authorship considered by the professional reviewers to have been the best of the season. An added fortnight of capacity audiences followed, after which the drama was withdrawn until Fall.

The play opens in Salinas valley in California on a particular Thursday afternoon, when a short wiry man called George and a huge hulk of a man called Lennie are making their way through the willows skirting the sandy bank of the Salinas river. A descending sun is nearing the horizon. Its slowly deepening rays filter through the foliage. The call of quail can be heard, and, in the distance, the bark of a ranch dog.

31

The men, George and Lennie, are carrying blanket rolls slung across their shoulders. "Bindles" is the word for them out Salinas way. Lennie, discovering a pool of water near the edge of the bank and at the foot of a huge sycamore tree, has dropped his bindle to the ground and fallen on his stomach to quench his thirst. The more particular George would stop Lennie if he could. It may be this water is not fresh. No man should drink water unless it is running. But Lennie—well, Lennie, in the frank estimation of George, is a crazy bastard who is likely to do anything any time, and forget what he has done the minute after he has done it.

That George is right is soon made evident. Lennie can't even remember where they are going, or why. Lennie can't remember anything except something about rabbits. George, with a good deal of sarcasm and a slight tinge of self-pity for his own martyr-dom, is obliged to go over the whole story again:

They were settin' in a gutter watchin' a blackboard; they went into Murray and Ready's and got a couple of work cards and bus tickets; (Lennie can't find his work card, but that doesn't matter, because George never gave it to him); they got on the bus and rode to where the guy on the bus told them they should get off and walk a little stretch down the road to the ranch they were looking for; "a little stretch," he said, and George thinks they've walked damned near four miles—

There is a slight interruption while George takes a dead mouse away from Lennie. Lennie, who likes to pet soft things, was hiding the mouse in his pocket and found it when he was looking for his card. He is reluctant to give it up. After all, he didn't steal it, and it is dead anyway. Why can't he keep it? But George is firm. The mouse must be thrown away—

"Well, look," continues George, "we are gonna work on a ranch like the one we come from up North. The ranch we're goin' to is right down there about a quarter mile. We're gonna go in and see the Boss."

"See the Boss," repeats Lennie, as though this were a lesson.

GEORGE—Now, look! I'll give him the work cards, but you ain't gonna say a word. You're just gonna stand there and not say nothing.

LENNIE—Not say nothing!

GEORGE—If he finds out what a crazy bastard you are, we won't get no job. But if he sees you work before he hears you talk, we're set. You got that?

LENNIE—Sure, George . . . sure. I got that.

GEORGE—Okay. Now when we go in to see the Boss, what you gonna do?

LENNIE (*concentrating*)—I—I—I ain't gonna say nothing—jus' gonna stand there.

GEORGE (*greatly relieved*)—Good boy, that's swell! Now you better say that over two or three times so ya sure ya won't forget it.

LENNIE (*drones softly under his breath*)—I ain't gonna say nothing—I ain't gonna say nothing. . . . (*Trails off into a whisper.*) I ain't gonna . . .

GEORGE—And you ain't gonna do no bad things like you done in Weed neither.

LENNIE (*puzzled*)—Like I done in Weed?

GEORGE (*looking up at* LENNIE)—So you forgot that, too, did you?

LENNIE (*triumphantly*)—Oh— They run us out of Weed!

GEORGE (*disgusted*)—Run us out hell! We run! They was lookin' for us, but they didn't catch us!

LENNIE (*happily*)—I didn't forget that, you bet!

GEORGE—God, you're a lot of trouble! If I was alone, (*Rising*) I could live so easy, so nice, if I didn't have you poundin' on my tail. I could live so easy!

LENNIE (*hopefully*)—We gonna work on a ranch, George.

GEORGE—All right, you got that. But we're gonna sleep here tonight, because—I want to. I want to sleep out.

LENNIE—Why ain't you goin' on to the ranch to get some supper? They got supper at the ranch.

GEORGE (*untying bindle*)—No reason at all. I just like it here. Tomorrow we'll be goin' to work. I seen thrashing machines on the way down—that means we'll be buckin' grain bags. Bustin' a gut liftin' up them bags. Tonight I'm gonna lay right here an' look up! Tonight there ain't a grain bag or a boss in the world! Tonight, the drinks is on the—house. Nice house we got here—Lennie. (*A whip-poor-will is heard.*)

LENNIE (*plaintively*)—Ain't we gonna have no supper?

GEORGE (*kneeling at bindle*)—Sure we are. You gather up some dead willow sticks. I got three cans of beans in my bindle. I'll open 'em up while you get a fire ready. We'll eat 'em cold.

LENNIE (*companionably*)—I like beans with ketchup!

GEORGE—Well, we ain't *got* no ketchup. You go get the wood, and don't you fool around none. Be dark before long!

Lennie is gone longer than he should be and George senses why. Lennie has been wading into the river to recover the dead mouse George has thrown away. Now George must take it away from him again and throw it farther into the brush. Still Lennie can't understand. It ain't nobody's mouse, and he ain't hurtin' nobody petting it. Lennie, "blubbering like a baby" now, doesn't know where he can find another mouse; he can remember when a kind lady used to give him all the mice she caught, but she ain't here no more—

"Lady, huh!" snorts George. "Don't even remember who that lady was. That was your own Aunt Clara. She stopped givin' 'em to you. You always killed 'em!"

"They was so little," explains Lennie. "I'd pet 'em and pretty soon they bit my fingers and then I pinched their head a little bit and then they was dead . . . because they was so little. I wish we'd get the rabbits pretty soon, George. They ain't so little."

"The hell with the rabbits. . . . Come on, let's eat."

The fire they have built is sputtering fitfully, the light shining on their faces, as they pry the covers from the beans and dive in, George with a spoon, Lennie with two fingers.

"I like 'em with ketchup," ventures Lennie.

GEORGE—Well, we ain't got any! Whatever we ain't got, that's what you want. God Almighty, if I was alone, I could live so easy. I could get a job of work and no trouble. No mess—and when the end of the month come, I could take my fifty bucks and go into town and get whatever I want. Why, I could stay in a cat-house all night. I could eat any place I want. Order any damn thing.

LENNIE (*plaintively, but softly*)—I didn't want no ketchup.

GEORGE (*continuing*)—I could do that every damn month. Get a gallon of whiskey or set in a pool room and play cards or shoot pool. And what have I got? (*Disgustedly.*) I got *you.* You can't keep a job and you lose me every job I get!

LENNIE (*in terror*)—I don't mean nothing, George.

GEORGE—Just keep shovin' me all over the country all the time. And that ain't the worst. You do bad things—you get in trouble, and I got to get you out. It ain't bad people that raises hell. It's dumb ones! (*Shouts.*) You crazy son-of-a-bitch, you keep me in hot water all the time! (LENNIE *tries to stop* GEORGE'S *flow of words with his hands.*) You just wanta feel that girl's dress. (*Sarcastically.*) Just wanta pet it like it was a mouse. Well, how the hell'd she know you just wanta feel her dress? How'd she know you'd just wanta pet it like it was a mouse?

LENNIE (*in panic*)—I didn't mean to, George!

GEORGE—Sure you didn't mean to. You didn't mean for her to yell bloody hell, neither. You didn't mean for us to hide in that irrigation ditch all day with guys out lookin' for us with guns, alla time it's somethin' you didn't mean. God damn it, I wish I could put you in a cage with a million mice and let them pet *you!* (GEORGE'S *anger leaves him suddenly. For the first time he seems to see the expression of terror on* LENNIE'S *face. He looks down ashamedly at the fire.*)

LENNIE (*after a pause*)—George! (GEORGE *purposely does not answer him.*) GEORGE?

GEORGE—What do you want?

LENNIE—I was only foolin', George. I don't want no ketchup. I wouldn't eat no ketchup if it was right here beside me.

George is overcome with "a sullenness of shame" now. He refuses to look at Lennie as Lennie, pressing his triumph, protests his willingness to go away and leave George, if that is what George wants. He could go off in the hills and find him a cave, Lennie insists. He could get along somehow. He could find food. Perhaps he could find another mouse—and there wouldn't be no one to take it away from him.

George is properly reproved and compassionate. He did not want to be mean. He was just foolin'. Of course he wants Lennie with him—

"Jesus Christ, somebody'd shoot you for a coyote if you was by yourself," explodes George. "Stay with me. Your Aunt Clara wouldn't like you runnin' off by yourself, even if she is dead."

"George," pleads Lennie, craftily, "tell me—like you done before."

GEORGE—Tell you what?

LENNIE—About the rabbits.

GEORGE—You ain't gonna put nothing over on me!

LENNIE (*pleading*)—Come on, George . . . tell me! Please! Like you done before.

George—You get a kick out of that, don't you? All right, I'll tell you. And then we'll lay out our beds and turn in.

Lennie—Go on, George.

George (*rhythmically, as though he had said it many times before*)—Guys like us that work on ranches is the loneliest guys in the world. They ain't got no family. They don't belong no place. They come to a ranch and work up a stake and then they go in to town and blow their stake. And then the first thing you know they're poundin' their tail on some other ranch. They ain't got nothin' to look ahead to.

Lennie (*delightedly*)—That's it, that's it! Now tell how it is with us. (*Takes hat off—places it above him on ground.*)

George (*still almost chanting*)—With us it ain't like that. We got a future. We got somebody to talk to that gives a damn about us. We don't have to sit in no bar-room blowin' in our jack, just because we got no place else to go. If them other guys gets in jail, they can rot for all anybody gives a damn.

Lennie (*who cannot restrain himself any longer. Bursts into speech*)—But not us! And why? Because—because I got you to look after me—and you got me to look after you—and that's why! (*He laughs.*) Go on, George!

George—You know it all by heart. Do it yourself. (*Spreading out blanket.*)

Lennie—No, no. I forget some of the stuff. Tell me how it's gonna be.

George—Some other time.

Lennie—No—please, George—tell how it's gonna be!

George (*holding ends of the blanket*)—Okay. Some day we're gonna get the jack together and we're gonna have a little house, and a couple of acres and a cow and some pigs and . . .

Lennie—And live off the fat of the land! And have rabbits. Go on, George! Tell about what we're gonna have in the garden. And about the rabbits in the cages—and the rain in the winter—and the stove and the cream is so thick you can hardly cut it. Tell about that, George!

George—Why don't you do it yourself—you know all of it!

Lennie—It ain't the same if I tell it. Go on now. How I get to tend the rabbits.

George (*resignedly*)—Well, we'll have a big vegetable patch and a rabbit hutch and chickens. And when it rains in the winter we'll just say to hell with goin' to work. We'll build up a fire in the stove, and set around it and listen to the rain comin' down on the roof— Nuts! (*Resumes spreading blanket on ground.*) I ain't got time for no more.

They have spread their blankets and crawled between them. Darkness is rapidly approaching. There is still time before they sleep for a light rehearsal of what Lennie is going to do when they get to the ranch. He isn't gonna say a word. And also time for a few words of further instruction from George: If Lennie ever gets into trouble on this ranch he is to come right back here where they are and hide in the brush until George can come for him. Lennie thinks he can remember that. But he ain't gonna get in no trouble. He ain't gonna say a word.

They are mumbling drowsily now. "It's gonna be nice sleeping here," sighs George. "Jesus, you feel free when you ain't got a job—if you ain't hungry."

"George, let's have different-colored rabbits," suggests Lennie. "Sure. Red ones, blue ones, green ones," agrees George. The big fellow is protesting sleepily that he can go away and live in a cave, when George shuts him up and the curtain falls.

It is late Friday morning before George and Lennie arrive at the bunk house on the ranch. A quick look around reveals a bare room lined with bunks at both ends. In a back wall there is a large double window, and nailed to the wall either side of the window are old boxes with shelves for toilet articles. On one bunk post a comb dangles from a string and there is a small mirror nailed to the post.

In the center of the room is an old wood-burning "belly stove" and an old kitchen table. Around the table a backless stool and a couple of kitchen chairs. There is a hanging light above the table, a grimy deck of cards on the table and a litter of dirty towels have been hung over the window sill to dry.

Candy, a gray and aging cripple, is in charge of the bunk house and is prepared to assign George and Lennie to their bunks. Candy lost a right hand at the wrist in a grain binder, but has learned to use the stump of his arm with great dexterity. He limps as he shuffles across the floor. Candy gives the impression of a beaten man crouching to protect himself from expected blows.

George and Lennie throw down their bindles and prepare to unpack. George will take the upper bunk to be sure Lennie won't be falling down on him. He is also a little curious about the guy

that's been sleepin' in that bunk before him. There's a suspicious looking can on the box shelf. "Positively kills lice,
roaches and other scourges" reads the label. "What the hell
kinda beds you givin' us, anyway?" demands George. "We don't
want no pants rabbits."

Candy is ready with an explanation. The former bunk holder
was a blacksmith and "as clean a guy as you'd want to meet."
The blacksmith had quit, but not on account of the bunk. The
food was his complaint. . . .

The Boss, "a stocky man dressed in brown Stetson hat, flannel
shirt, black coat, old trousers, belt and high-heeled boots," has
arrived to take over the examination of the new men. He is not
in a particularly good temper, having expected George and Lennie
earlier. They had been given a bum steer by the bus driver,
George explains, with a warning wink at Lennie.

"Well, I had to send the grain teams out short two buckers,"
says the Boss. "It won't do any good to go out now until after
dinner. You'd get lost. (*Takes pocket size time book and pencil
from coat pocket, opens it.*) What's your name?"

GEORGE—George Milton.

BOSS (*writing*)—And what's yours?

GEORGE (*quickly*)—His name's Lennie Small.

BOSS—Lennie Small. (*Writing.*) Le's see, this is the twentieth.
Noon the twentieth— (*Makes positive mark.*) Where you boys
been workin'?

GEORGE—Up around Weed.

BOSS (*to* LENNIE)—You too?

GEORGE (*quickly*)—Yeah. Him too.

BOSS (*to* LENNIE)—Say, you're a big fellow, ain't you?

GEORGE (*quickly*)—Yeah, he can work like hell, too.

BOSS—He ain't much of a talker, though, is he?

GEORGE—No, he ain't. But he's a hell of a good worker.
Strong as a bull.

LENNIE (*smiling*)—I'm strong as a bull. (GEORGE *scowls at
him and* LENNIE *drops his head in shame at having forgotten.*)

BOSS (*sharply*)—You are, huh? What can you do?

GEORGE—He can do anything.

BOSS (*addressing* LENNIE)—What-can-you-do?

GEORGE (*quickly*)—Anything you tell him. He's a good
skinner—can wrestle grain bags, drive a cultivator. He can do
anything you tell him. Just give him a try.

BOSS (*turning to* GEORGE)—Then why don't you let *him* answer? (LENNIE *gives a high nervous chuckle.*) What's he laughing about?

GEORGE—He . . . laughs when he gets excited.

Boss—Yeah?

GEORGE (*loudly*)—But he's a God damn good worker. I ain't saying he's bright, because he ain't. But he can put up a four hundred pound bale.

Boss (*hooking his thumbs in his belt*)—Say, what you sellin'?

GEORGE—Huh?

Boss—I said what stake you got in this guy? You takin' his pay away from him?

GEORGE—No. Of course I ain't!

Boss—Well, I never seen one guy take so much trouble for another guy. I just like to know what your percentage is.

GEORGE—He's my—cousin. He got kicked in the head by a horse when he was a kid. Just ain't bright. But he can do anything you tell him.

Boss (*turning half away—crossing below to L.C.*)—Yeah?— Well, God knows he don't need no brains to buck barley bags. (*He turns back.*) But don't you try to put nothing over, Milton. I got my eye on you. Why'd you quit in Weed?

GEORGE (*promptly*)—Job was *done.*

Boss—What kind of job?

GEORGE—Why—we was diggin' a cesspool.

Boss (*after a pause*)—All right. But don't try to put nothing over 'cause you can't get away with nothing. I seen wise guys before. Go out with the grain teams after dinner.

"He talked like a kinda nice guy toward the last," ventures Lennie, when the Boss has left.

"He's the Boss, ain't he?" snaps the experienced George. "Well, he's the boss first an' a nice guy afterwards. Don't you have nothin' to do with no boss, except do your work and draw your pay. You can't never tell whether you're talkin' to the nice guy or the boss. Just keep your God damn mouth shut. Then you're all right!"

Candy has come back. He is carrying an old dog in his arms, a sheep dog he has raised from a pup. George thinks perhaps Candy has been listening to what they said to the Boss, but he hadn't. "A guy on a ranch don't never listen," says Candy. "Nor he don't ask no questions."

Their next caller is Curley, the Boss' son. Curley is a smallish, active sort, "dressed in black cotton shirt, pink sleeve garters, black trousers and black high-heeled boots. On his left hand he wears a leather glove."

Curley is looking for his father, but has time to cast an inquiring word or two at the newcomers. If they're the guys his father was lookin' for, why didn't they get there? George explains that they got off the bus too soon. Curley wants to know more than that. Especially from Lennie. George is answering for Lennie, as usual, and Curley doesn't like that. Like it or not that's the way it is.

"What yer pickin' on him for?" George wants to know. "He didn't do nothin' to you!"

"Are you drawin' cards this hand?" sneers Curley.

"I might," answers George, meeting the threat.

"Well—I'll see you get a chance to ante," Curley flings back as he goes out the door.

"Say, what the hell's he got on his shoulder?" George wants to know. "Lennie didn't say nothin' to him."

"That's the Boss' son," Candy reminds them. "Curley's pretty handy. He done quite a bit in the ring. Prizefightin'. . . . Curley's like a lot of little guys. He hates big guys. Kinda like he's mad at 'em because he ain't a big guy. You seen little guys like that, ain't you—always scrappy?"

"Sure, I see plenty of tough little guys. But this here Curley better not make no mistakes about Lennie. Lennie ain't handy. See, but this Curley punk's gonna get hurt if he messes around with Lennie."

"You know, it never did seem right to me. S'pose Curley jumps a big guy and licks him. Everybody says what a game guy Curley is. Well, s'pose he jumps 'em and gits licked. Everybody says the big guy oughta pick somebody his own size. Seems like Curley ain't givin' nobody a chance."

"Well, he better watch out for Lennie. Lennie ain't no fighter. But Lennie's strong and quick and Lennie don't know no rules."

Candy has a further explanation. Curley got married a couple of weeks ago and he's been worse'n ever since he got married. His wife is living over in the Boss' house. Purty? Yeah, she's purty, but she's got the eye, too. Candy has seen her givin' a couple of mule skinners the eye.

"I think Curley's married himself a tart," is Candy's conclusion.

"He ain't the first," agrees George. "Yes, sir—there's plenty done that!"

Candy has gone to set out the wash basins for the men coming in from the fields when George decides to have a serious talk with Lennie.

"Look, Lennie, this here ain't no set-up," warns George, stopping a solitaire game he has started. "You gonna have trouble with that Curley guy. I seen that kind before. You know what he's doin'? He's kinda feelin' you out. He figures he's got you scared. And the first chance he gets he's gonna take a sock at you."

LENNIE (*frightened*)—I don't want no trouble. Don't let him sock me, George!

GEORGE—I hate them kind of bastards. I seen plenty of 'em. Like the ole guy says: "Curley don't take no chances. He always figures to win." (*Thinks for a moment.*) If he tangles with you, Lennie, we're goin' to get the can. He's the Boss' kid.

LENNIE (*mourning*)—I don't want no trouble. I never done nothing to him!

GEORGE—Well, that won't do you no good, if Curley wants to set himself up for a fighter. Just don't have nothing to do with him. Will you remember?

LENNIE—Sure, George—I ain't gonna say a word. (*Sounds of teams coming in from the fields, jingling of harness, creak of heavy laden axles.*)

SLIM (*off stage*)—Stable buck! Hey! Stable buck!

GEORGE—Here come the guys. Just don't say nothing.

LENNIE (*timidly*)—You ain't mad, George?

GEORGE—I ain't mad at you. I'm mad at this Curley bastard! I wanted we should get a little stake together. Maybe a hundred dollars. You keep away from Curley.

LENNIE—Sure I will. I won't say a word.

GEORGE—Don't let him pull you in—but—if the son-of-a-bitch socks you—let him have it!

LENNIE—Let him have what, George?

GEORGE (*after looking hopelessly at* LENNIE)—Never mind . . . Look, if you get in any kind of trouble, you remember what I told you?

LENNIE—If I git in any trouble, you ain't gonna let me 'tend the rabbits?

GEORGE—That ain't what I mean. You remember where we slept last night. Down by the river?

LENNIE—Oh, sure I remember. I go there and hide in the brush until you come.

GEORGE—That's it. Hide till I come for you. Don't let nobody see you hide in the brush by the river. Now say that over.

LENNIE—Hide in the brush by the river. Down in the brush by the river.

GEORGE—If you get in trouble.

LENNIE—If I get in trouble.

There is a good deal of racket as the grain teams draw up outside the bunk house, and loud calls from the skinners for the stable boy. George and Lennie are sitting at the table and George is going on with his solitaire game when Curley's wife appears in the door. "She is dressed in a cotton house dress and red mules on the insteps of which are little bouquets of red ostrich feathers. She is heavily rouged, her fingernails are bright red, her hair hangs in little rolled clusters, and her eyes are made up."

She has come lookin' for Curley, Curley's wife informs them. They don't know any more than that Curley had been there and left. George is quite curt in admitting even this much. Lennie might have been more interested if George hadn't kept pressing him back in his seat every time he started up. Curley's wife decides she might as well look somewhere else, but she is in no hurry to start. Sometimes, she confesses, she just likes to talk to someone. Still they are not interested.

"Jesus, what a tramp!" explodes George when she has gone. "So that's what Curley picks for a wife. God Almighty, did you smell that stink she's got on? I can still smell her. Don't have to see her to know *she's* around."

"She's purty!" says Lennie.

GEORGE—Yeah. And she sure ain't hidin' it. Curley's got his work ahead of him.

LENNIE—Gosh! She's purty!

GEORGE (*turning furiously to him*)—Listen to me, you crazy bastard. Don't you even look at that bitch! I don't care what she says or what she does. I seen 'em poison before, but I ain't seen no piece of jail bait worse than her. Don't you even smell near her!

LENNIE—I never smelled, George!

GEORGE—No, you never. But when she was standin' there showin' her legs, you wasn't lookin' the other way neither!

LENNIE—I never meant no bad things, George. Honest I never!

GEORGE—Well, you keep away from her. You let Curley

take the rap. He let himself in for it. I bet he's eatin' raw eggs and writin' to patent medicine houses.

LENNIE—I don't like this place. This ain't no nice place. I don't like this place.

GEORGE—Listen—I don't like it here no better than you do. But we gotta keep it till we get a stake. We're flat. We gotta get a stake. If we can just get a few dollars in the poke we'll shove off up the river and pan gold. Guy can make a coupla dollars a day there.

LENNIE (*eagerly*)—Let's go, George. Let's get out of here. It's mean here.

The men are in from the yard now, dripping with water and looking for their towels. There are meetings and explanations. Slim, a tall, tanned man, is glad George and Lennie are going to work with him. George is pleased, too. He (George) is not so good, but his friend, Lennie, is a hell of a good worker and a nice fella, too.

Carlson, "a big-stomached, powerful man," joins the group and is included in the introductions. Soon the gossip of the workers is in full swing. Slim's bitch has had her pups—nine of them— and Slim had drowned four right off. She couldn't feed nine. They're gonna be some kind of Shepherds, Slim thinks. Carlson's chief interest in the pups is to get Slim to give one to Candy, so's they can get Candy to shoot his old dog.

"You know, Slim—that dog of Candy's so God damn ole he can't hardly walk," protests Carlson. "Stinks like hell. Every time Candy brings him in the bunk house, I can smell him for two or three days. Slim, why don't you get Candy to shoot his ole dog, and give him one of them pups to raise up. Got no teeth, can't eat, and Candy has to carry him around all day so he don't bump into things."

The ring of steel on an iron wagon wheel hoop is the signal for dinner and the skinners are out of the bunk house with a rush. George and Lennie better hurry, Slim advises, if they want to get there while there's anything to eat.

They are about to start when Curley barges in again. He is still looking for his wife. Again they can't help him. She was there a half hour ago. What was she doin'? "She *said* she was lookin' for you," George answers a little insultingly.

"You know, Lennie! I'm scared I'm gonna tangle with that bastard myself," admits George, as Curley rushes from the room. "I hate his guts."

Lennie isn't thinking of Curley. He is remembering what Slim had said about the pups.

"George—will you ask him about a brown and white one?" pleads Lennie, as the curtain falls.

ACT II

It is seven-thirty, Friday evening. The bunk house for the moment is deserted. A lantern hanging to one of the bunk posts adds feebly to the evening light that filters through the window. Outside the men are engaged in pitching horse shoes, their expressed exultations over good pitches and disgust with poor ones can be heard. George's and Lennie's bunks are spread with their blankets and their toilet articles have been placed in the box on the wall.

Presently Slim, carrying an unlighted lantern, comes through the door, followed by George. They are concluding a conversation having to do with Slim's kindness in giving Lennie a pup. George is grateful because of what it means to Lennie. It is going to be pretty hard to keep Lennie in the bunk house from now on, George thinks. He will be wanting to sleep in the stable with the dogs.

Slim would make light of the puppy gift. He would have had to drown most of them anyway. He has been considerably impressed with Lennie as a worker, too. "Funny how you and him string along together," ventures Slim, filling his lantern with kerosene.

"What's so funny about it?" asks George, who has begun rubbing oil into "the best God-damned pair of shoes" he ever owned.

Slim—Oh, I don't know. I hardly never seen two guys travel together. You know how the hands are. They come in and get their bunk, work a month and then they quit and go on alone. Never seem to give a damn about nobody. Jest seems kinda funny. A cuckoo like him and a smart guy like you.

George—I ain't so smart neither or I wouldn't be buckin' barley for my fifty and found. If I was bright, if I was even a little bit smart, I'd have my own place and be bringin' in my own crops 'stead of doin' all the work and not gettin' what comes up out of the ground.

Slim—A guy'd like to do that. Sometimes I'd like to cuss a string of mules that was my own mules.

George—It ain't so funny, him and me goin' 'round together.

Him and me was both born in Auburn. I knowed his aunt. She took him when he was a baby and raised him up. When his aunt died Lennie jus' come along with me, out workin'. Got kinda used to each other after a little while.

SLIM (*leaning on table—facing* GEORGE)—Uh huh.

GEORGE—First I used to have a hell of a lot of fun with him. Used to play jokes on him because he was too dumb to take care of himself. But, hell, he was too dumb even to know when he had a joke played on him. (*Sarcastically.*) Hell, yes—I had fun! Made me seem God damn smart alongside of him.

SLIM—I seen it that way.

GEORGE—I tell you what made me stop playing jokes. One day a bunch of the guys was standin' aroun' up on the Sacramenta River. I was feelin' pretty smart. I turns to Lennie and I says, "Jump in."

SLIM—What happened?

GEORGE—He jumps. Couldn't swim a stroke. He damn near drowned. And he was so nice to me for pullin' him out. He clean forgot I tole him to jump in. Well, I ain't done nothin' like that no more. Makes me kinda sick tellin' about it.

SLIM (*rolling cigarette*)—He's a nice fella. A guy don't need no sense to be a nice fella. Seems to me sometimes it's just the other way round. Take a real smart guy, he ain't hardly ever a nice fella.

GEORGE—I ain't got no people. I seen guys that go around on the ranches alone. That ain't no good. They don't have no fun. After a while they get mean.

SLIM—Yeah, I seen 'em get mean. I seen 'em get so they don't want to talk to nobody. Of course, most times they got to keep their traps shut. You take a bunch of guys all livin' in one room an' by God they got to mind their own business. 'Bout the only private thing a guy's got is where he comes from and where he's goin'.

Of course, George admits, Lennie's a damn nuisance most of the time, but after you get used to him "you can't get rid of bein' used to him." Lennie gets into trouble all the time, too. Like he did in Weed. George has an urge to tell Slim about what happened in Weed. Slim does not encourage him but listens interestedly.

There was a girl in a red dress in Weed. Lennie liked the red dress and, "dumb bastard like he is," George explains, Lennie reached out to feel the dress. The girl, being frightened, let out a squawk, and the louder she squawked the more scared Lennie became and the tighter he held on. George, running in to find out what was happening, finally had to hit Lennie over the head with a fence picket to make him let go.

The girl ran to "the law" and told him she'd been raped. The guys in Weed were getting ready to lynch Lennie when he and George made a run for it. They sat in an irrigation ditch all day with only their heads above water, and finally got away at night. . . .

Lennie has come into the bunk house, walking hunched over in an effort to conceal the puppy dog he is carrying inside his denim coat. He shuffles guiltily toward his bunk and is lying down with the pup when George senses what is happening. George had told Lennie he could not bring the pup in the bunk house and now he sends him back to the barn with it. Lennie will probably be sleepin' in the barn, alongside the dogs, thinks George, but if he does that won't be doin' any harm. . . .

Candy has come in with his dog in his arms. He is followed shortly by Carlson, and now the question of the old dog has been brought up again by Carlson, who is prepared to make an issue of it.

"I don't know nothin' that stinks as bad as ole dogs does," protests Carlson.

"I been round him so much I never notice how he stinks," says Candy.

CARLSON—Well, I can't stand him in here. That stink hangs round even after he's gone. Look at him. All stiff with rheumatism. He ain't no good to you, Candy. Why don't you shoot him?

CANDY (*uncomfortably*)—Well, hell, I had him so long! I herded sheep with him. (*Proudly.*) You wouldn't think it to look at him now. He was the best damn sheep dog I ever seen.

GEORGE—I knowed a guy in Weed that had an Airedale that could herd sheep. Learned it from the other dogs.

CARLSON (*sticking to his point*)—Lookit, Candy. This ole dog jus' suffers itself all the time. If you was to take him out and shoot him—right in the back of the head . . . (*Leans over and points.*) right there, why, he never'd know what hit him.

CANDY (*unhappily*)—No, I couldn't do that. I had him too long.

CARLSON (*insisting*)—He don't have no fun no more and besides he stinks like hell. Tell you what I'll do. I'll shoot him for you. Then it won't be you that done it.

CANDY—I had him from a pup.

WHIT—Aw, let 'um alone, Carl. It ain't a guy's dog that matters. It's the way the guy feels about the dog. Hell, I had a
mutt once I wouldn'ta traded for a field trial pointer.

CARLSON (*being persuasive*)—Well, Candy ain't being nice to
him, keeping him alive. Lookit. Slim's bitch got a litter right
now. I bet you Slim would give ya one of them pups to raise up,
wouldn't ya, Slim?

SLIM—Yeah—you can have a pup if you want to, Candy.

CANDY (*helplessly*)—Mebbe it would hurt. I don't mind
taking care of him.

CARLSON—Aw, he'd be better off dead. The way I'd shoot
him he wouldn't feel nothin'. I'd put the gun right there. (*Points
to the back of dog's head.*)   Right in back of the head.

Candy is holding the old dog a little closer now, and Whit is
moved again to suggest that Carlson let him alone. The situation
assumes an intensity that even Whit's reading from a magazine
cannot dispel.

"You ain't got no gun," ventures Candy, hopefully, as Carlson
stands firm.

"The hell I ain't. Got a Luger—right here—right here in my
bag," quickly answers Carlson, producing the gun. "It won't
hurt him none at all."

Again a long pause. Candy suggests that they wait until tomorrow. Carlson refuses to yield. And now Slim has chipped in
quietly to advise Candy that he had better let the dog go.
Candy holds out a moment or two longer, but finally he gives up.
Carlson takes the dog, pushes the pistol into his belt and is gone.

An oppressive silence overcomes the group. George goes on
perfunctorily with his solitaire game at the table. Candy moves
over to one of the lower bunks and sits with his head bowed in
his hands. Whit has followed Carlson to the door and closed it.
Slim, taking up his lantern, starts for the barn.

"Candy . . . You can have any of those pups you want," says
Slim. But Candy doesn't hear.

Now George and Whit have organized a rummy game. Once
or twice they try for conversation. No good. It seems hours
since Carlson left. And still there is no shot. The silence is becoming unbearable.

"What the hell is takin' him so long?" shrills Whit, his nerves
snapping.

George starts the deal again. Slowly, one by one, he lays down the cards. Neither he nor Whit is paying any attention to the game.

Both are watching the bowed and silent Candy. At last a single shot is heard. Candy goes rigid against the impact. George and Whit go on with their game. . . .

Crooks, the stable buck, "a lean-faced Negro with pained eyes," has come to tell Slim that the tar he wanted for his mule's foot is warm now. Also Crooks would like to report that "that big new guy is messin' 'round Slim's pups." Slim doesn't think that will hurt the pups any. . . .

Whit brings up the subject of Curley's new wife. "Ain't she a lula?" "I ain't seen that much of her," answers George. "Well, stick around and keep your eyes open. You'll see plenty," promises Whit. "I never seen nobody like her. She's just workin' on everybody all the time. Seems like she's even workin' on the stable buck. I don't know what the hell she wants."

"Been any trouble since she been here?" George asks, casually.

WHIT—No, they ain't been no trouble yet. She's only been here a couple of weeks. Curley's got yellow jackets in his drawers, but that's all so far. Every time the guys is around she shows up. She's lookin' for Curley. Or she thought she left somethin' layin' around and she's lookin' for that. Seems like she can't keep away from guys. And Curley's runnin' 'round like a cat lookin' for a dirt road. But they ain't been no trouble.

GEORGE—Ranch with a bunch of guys on it ain't no place for a girl.

WHIT—If she's give you any ideas you ought to come in town with us guys tomorrow night.

GEORGE (gathering cards)—Why, what's doin'?

WHIT—Just the usual thing. We go into Susy's place. Hell of a nice place. Old Susy is a laugh. Always cracking jokes. Like she says when we come in last Saturday night: Susy opens the door and she yells over her shoulder: "Get your coats on, girls, here comes the Sheriff." She never talks dirty neither. Got five girls there.

GEORGE—How much it set you back?

WHIT—Two and a half. You can get a shot of whiskey for fifteen cents. Susy got nice chairs to set in too. If a guy don't want to flop, why, he can just set in them chairs and have two or three shots and just pass the time of day. Susy don't give a damn. She ain't rushin' guys through, or kicking them out if they don't want to flop.

GEORGE—I don't know—I might go in and look the joint over.

WHIT—Sure. Come along. It's a hell of a lot of fun—her crackin' jokes all the time. Like she says one time. She says: "I've knew people that if they got a rag rug on the floor and a kewpie doll lamp on the phonograph they think they're runnin' a parlor house." That's Gladys's house she's talkin' about. And Susy says: "I know what you boys want," she says. "My girls is clean," she says. "And there ain't no water in my whiskey," she says. "If any you guys want to look at a kewpie doll lamp and take your chance of gettin' burned, why, you know where to go." She says: "They's guys round here walkin' bowlegged because they like to look at a kewpie doll lamp."

Carlson has come back. Candy looks up, inquiringly, for the first time. Slowly he moves over to a box by the side of the window. Again his head sinks to his knees. Carlson is cleaning his pistol.

"We don't never go to Gladys's," Whit is saying. "Gladys gits three bucks, and two bits a shot and she don't crack no jokes. But Susy's place is clean and she got nice chairs. A guy can set in there like he lived there. Don't let no Manila Goo-Goos in, neither."

"Aw, I don't know," fidgets George. "Me and Lennie's rollin' up a stake. I might go in and set and have a shot, but I ain't puttin' out no two and a half."

"Well, a guy's got to have some fun sometimes!"

Lennie is back, and without the pup. A moment later Curley has come excitedly through the door. Again he is looking for his wife. Not finding her, he'd like to know where the hell Slim is. They tell him Slim has gone to the barn to look after a mule with a split hoof, and Curley is out of the door like a shot, barely missing a collision with the returning Carlson.

"Curley must be spoilin' or he wouldn't start for Slim," suggests Whit.

"Thinks Slim is with his wife, don't he?"

"Looks like it. 'Course Slim ain't. Least I don't think Slim is."

Carlson has tossed his Luger back into his suitcase and started for the barn. He wouldn't want to miss a fight. Whit has gone, too. George is staying. He doesn't want to get mixed up in anything. "Me and Lennie got to make a stake," repeats George.

Lennie didn't see Curley's wife in the barn, he assures George.

He saw Slim and Slim told him not to pet the pups so much. But he didn't see Curley's girl, or see Slim talkin' to her.

"Okay. I guess them guys ain't gonna see no fight," concludes George. "If there's any fightin', Lennie, you get out of the way and stay out," warns George.

"I don't want no fight, George," agrees Lennie. But he would like to know about how long it is going to be before they are going to get that little place and live off the fat of the land.

George can't tell about that. They've got to get a stake first. He knows a little place they can get cheap, but—Lennie would like to hear about that place again—

"Well," sighs George, organizing a solitaire game; "it's ten acres. Got a little windmill. Got a little shack on it and a chicken run. Got a kitchen orchard. Cherries, apples, peaches, cots and nuts. Got a few berries. There's a place for alfalfa and plenty water to flood it. There's a pig pen. . . ."

LENNIE (*breaking in*)—And rabbits, George?

GEORGE—I could easy build a few hutches. And you could feed alfalfa to them rabbits.

LENNIE—Damn right I could. (*Excitedly.*) You God damn right I could.

GEORGE (*his voice growing warmer*)—Every Sunday we'd kill a chicken or rabbit. Mebbe we'll have a cow or a goat. And the cream is so God damn thick on the pan you got to cut it off with a knife.

LENNIE (*watching him with wide eyes—softly*)—We can live off the fat of the land.

GEORGE—Sure. And we wouldn't sleep in no bunk house. Nobody could can us in the middle of a job.

LENNIE (*begging*)—Tell about the house, George.

GEORGE—Sure. We'd have a little house. And a room to ourselves. And when we put that crop in, why, we'd be there to take that crop up. We'd know what come of our planting.

LENNIE (*eagerly*)—Tell about the rabbits, George, and how I get to tend 'em!

GEORGE—Sure. You'd take a sack, go out in the alfalfa patch and fill up the sack, bring it in and put it in them rabbit cages.

LENNIE—They'd nibble and they'd nibble, the way they do. I seen 'em.

GEORGE—Every six weeks or so them does would throw a litter. So we'd have plenty rabbits to eat or sell. (*Pauses for inspiration.*) And we'd keep a few pigeons to go flying round the wind mill, like they done when I was a kid. (*Seems entranced.* CANDY *begins to show interest.*) And it'd be our own. And nobody could can us. If we don't like a guy we can say: "Get to hell out"—and, by God, he'd have to do it. And if a friend come along, why, we'd have an extra bunk. Know what we'd say? We'd say, why don't you spen' the night? And, by God, he would. We'd have a setter dog and a couple of striped cats. (*Looks sharply at* LENNIE.) But you gotta watch out them cats don't get the little rabbits.

LENNIE (*breathing hard*)—You jus' let 'em try. I'll break their damn necks. I'll smash them cats flat with a stick. I'll smash 'em flat with a stick. That's what I'd do.

Candy has been listening. He can keep silent no longer. He wants to know more about this wonderful place. George at first is of a mind to keep Candy, and everybody else, out of this particular secret, but soon Candy has convinced him of the honesty of his curiosity and interest. How much could George get a place like that for? George thinks he could get it for six hundred bucks. The ole people who own it are broke and need medicine. But what's it to Candy?

Well, look— When Candy lost his hand they gave him two hundred and fifty bucks, and he's got another fifty bucks saved up. That's three hundred, and he gets another forty at the end of the month. Candy would put that three hundred and forty bucks in—and make a will leavin' his share to George and Lennie in case he kicked off— That gives George an idea—

"Say, look!" says George. "If me and Lennie work a month and don't spend nothin' at all, we'll have a hundred bucks. That would be four forty. I bet we could swing her for that. Then you and Lennie could go get her started and I'd get a job and make up the rest. (*They look at each other in amazement. Reverently.*) Jesus Christ, I bet we could swing her. (*His voice is full of wonder.*) I bet we could swing 'er."

"I got hurt four years ago," Candy goes on, nervously scratching the stump of his wrist. "They'll can me pretty soon. Maybe if I give you guys my money, you'll let me hoe in the garden, even when I ain't no good at it. And I'll wash dishes and little chicken stuff like that. But, hell, I'll be on our own place. I'll be let to work on our own place."

"We'll do 'er!" cries George, standing up with a fistful of playing cards. "God damn, we'll fix up that little ole place and we'll go live there. (*Wonderingly.*) S'pose they was a carnival,

or a circus come to town or a ball game or any damn thing.
(CANDY *nods in appreciation.*) We'd just go to her. We
wouldn't ask nobody if we could. Just say we'll go to her, by
God, and we would. Jest milk the cow and sling some grain to
the chickens and go to her."

"And put some grass to the rabbits. I wouldn't forget to feed
them. When we gonna do it, George?"

"In one month. Right squack in one month. Know what I'm
gonna do? I'm goin' to write them old people that owns the place
that we'll take 'er. And Candy'll send a hundred dollars to bind
her."

They are agreed that they won't tell anybody; just go on like
a bunch of punks and then, all of a sudden, bang—

The window at the back has opened. Curley's wife stands
listening as George finishes with his plans. George doesn't see
Curley's wife, but—

"You know seems to me I can almost smell that carnation stuff
that Gad damn tart dumps on herself."

"Who you callin' a tart?" angrily demands Curley's wife. "I
come from a nice home. I was brung up by nice people. Nobody never got to me before I was married. I was straight.
I tell you I was good. (*A little plaintively.*) I was. (*Angrily
again.*) You know Curley. You know he wouldn't stay with
me if he wasn't sure. I tell you Curley is sure. You got no
right to call me a tart."

"If you ain't a tart, what you always hangin' 'round guys for?
You got a house an' you got a man. We don't want no trouble
from you."

"Sure I got a man. He ain't never home. I got nobody to
talk to. I got nobody to be with. Think I can just sit home
and do nothin' but cook for Curley? I want to see somebody.
Just see 'em an' talk to 'em. There ain't no women. I can't
walk to town. And Curley don't take me to no dances now.
I tell you I jus' want to talk to somebody."

The sound of approaching voices is an interruption. Slim and
Curley are coming. Their talk is loud. Slim isn't mad, but he
is getting damned sick of having Curley question him. Let Curley take care of his own wife.

Then Carlson chips in: Why doesn't Curley tell his wife to
keep to hell out of there? And Whit adds a word.

Curley is flaming with anger. Suddenly he sniffs the air like
a hound. His wife's been in that room. George was there, too.
The other guys was outside. Curley turns savagely on George—

"Now, God damn you . . . you talk. . . ."

George is worried. He hesitates, then slowly "makes up his mind to face an inevitable situation."

"Somebody's got to beat hell outa you," he says, calmly. "I guess I'm elected."

George is slowly taking off his coat and putting it on a chair when Lennie gives a high, nervous chuckle. Curley, rasped by the laughter, turns on Lennie and with a "Come on, you big bastard! No big son-of-a-bitch is gonna laugh at me," has lashed out at Lennie with both hands.

Lennie is crouching to defend himself with his arms. Whit is shouting to Curley that Lennie hasn't done anything. George is trying to separate the fighters and appealing to Slim for help. Blood is trickling from Lennie's mouth. Curley is slashing away and Lennie is helpless, trying to cover. Suddenly George can stand no more. He begins to shout—

"Let him have it, Lennie! Let him have it!"

There is a sharp cry of pain from Curley. As the men move away from the fighters "Curley is seen flopping about—his right hand lost in the crushing grip of Lennie's hands."

"That's it, big boy—break his God damn arm!" encourages Carlson.

George, seeing what is happening, has closed in on the fighters and is trying to break Lennie's hold on Curley. He slaps the confused Lennie repeatedly in the face—

"Let go his hand, Lennie!" he calls. "Carlson, come help me while this guy's got a hand left!"

Carlson comes in grumbling. He'd like to see the fight go on. Slim lends his aid. Now George has both hands in Lennie's hair and is pushing him away. Suddenly Lennie lets go and Curley falls back to the floor. There isn't much left of his hand.

Curley will have to go to the doctor. Slim can see that, and orders them to get the wagon ready. George is filled with fear. Will he and Lennie get canned? Will Curley's old man can them now? Slim doesn't know. He turns to the suffering Curley—

"You got your sense enough to listen?" Curly nods. "Well, then you listen. I think you got your hand caught in a machine. If you don't tell nobody what happened, we won't. But you jest tell and try to get this guy canned and we'll tell everybody. And then will you get the laugh!" He helps Curley to his feet. "Come on now. Whit's goin' to take you to a doctor."

"Maybe you'd better go in the wash room and clean up your face," George says to the still confused Lennie. "You look like hell."

"I didn't want no trouble," wails Lennie.

"Come on—I'll go with you."

"George?"

"What you want?"

"Can I still tend the rabbits, George?"

They go through the door together as the lights dim and the curtain falls.

The room of Crooks, the stable buck, is a lean-to off the barn. It is cluttered with an assortment of harness and various farm tools, and with the broken ends of many things. There are several horse collars hung on pegs against the wall; a littered work bench; an iron cot, covered with a patch quilt. An old and exploded upholstered chair stands under an oil lamp with a tin reflector, hung between two windows in a side wall.

Crooks is puttering around the room. It is 10 o'clock Saturday evening and the ranch is practically deserted. Presently Lennie comes hesitantly through the door. Crooks, with a frown, would have him out. Nobody has any right in that room except Crooks. Just as Crooks has no rights in the bunkhouse. That's because he's black.

Lennie didn't mean anything by coming; he just wanted to see his pup and talk to somebody. George had told him to stay there and not get into no trouble and that is what Lennie is trying to do. There isn't anyone else to talk to, except Candy. And Candy just sits in the bunk house sharpenin' pencils and figurin', figurin' all the time. Figurin' about the place they're gonna get, and live on the fat o' the land.

Crooks is contemptuous about the place Lennie's talking about. Crooks thinks Lennie is crazy as a wedge. S'pose George doesn't come back no more? What's goin' to happen to Lennie then?

"Want me to tell you what'll happen?" Crooks proceeds. "They'll take you to the booby-hatch. They'll tie you up with a collar like a dog. Then you'll be just like me. Livin' in a kennel."

Slowly the idea reaches Lennie. Perhaps something has happened to George. "Who hurt George?" Lennie bellows, drawing himself up furiously, and threatening the surprised Crooks.

"I was jus' supposin'," quickly explains Crooks. "George ain't hurt. He's all right. He'll be back all right."

"What you supposin' for? Ain't nobody goin' to s'pose no hurt to George," growls Lennie.

Crooks is quick to make peace. Still he can't take the land talk seriously.

"I seen hundreds of men come by on the road and on the ranches, bindles on their head. Every damn one of 'em is got a little piece of land in his head. And never a God damn one of 'em gets it. Jus' like heaven. Nobody never gets to heaven, and nobody gets no land."

Now Candy is standing in the door. He has come excitedly looking for Lennie to tell him the result of the figurin'. They can make money on the rabbits, Candy figures, if—

That is another laugh for Crooks. They're just kiddin' themselves, these guys. Where's George now? In town in a whore house spendin' their money. George hasn't got the money, Candy explains. The money's in the bank—and they got just a little more to get—

"I've never seen guys really do it," persists Crooks. "I seen guys nearly crazy with loneliness for land, but every time a whore house or a black jack game took it away from 'em."

"Well, they ain't gonna get it this time!"

For a second Crooks is thoughtful. Now he is out of his chair and pacing the floor nervously. "If you guys would want a hand to work for nothin'—just for his keep, why, I'd come and lend a hand," he says timidly. "I ain't so crippled I can't work like a son-of-a-bitch."

Suddenly they are aware of the presence of George. He has been standing in the door listening.

"You couldn't go to bed like I told you, could you, Lennie?" George's voice is gentle but half-satiric. "Hell, no—you got to get out in society an' flap your big mouth!"

LENNIE (*defending himself*)—You was gone. There wasn't nobody in the bunk house. I ain't done no bad things, George.

GEORGE (*still casually*)—Only time I get any peace is when you're asleep. If you ever get walkin' in your sleep I'll chop your head off like a chicken.

CROOKS (*defending* LENNIE)—We was jus' talkin'. Ain't no harm in that.

GEORGE—Yeah. I heard you. (*A weariness has settled on him.*) Got to spend all my time with you, I guess. Got to watch ya! (*To* CROOKS.) It ain't nothin' against you, Crooks. We just wasn't gonna tell nobody.

CANDY (*trying to change subject*)—Didn't you have no fun in town?

GEORGE (*pacing—kicking keg—pacing again, placing hat on shelf*)—Oh—I set in a chair and Susy was crackin' jokes—an' the guys was startin' to raise a little puny hell. Christ Almighty —I never been this way before. I'm jus' gonna set out a dime and a nickel for a shot an' I think what a hell of a lot of carrot seed you can get for fifteen cents.

CANDY—Not in them damn little envelopes—but bulk seed, you sure can!

GEORGE—So purty soon I come back. I can't think of nothin' else. Them guys slingin' money around got me jumpy.

CANDY—Guy got to have some fun. I was to a parlor house in Bakersfield once. God Almighty what a place. Went upstairs on a red carpet. They was big pictures on the wall. We set in big sof' chairs. They was cigarettes on the table—an' they was free. Purty soon a Jap come in with drinks on a tray an' them drinks was free. Take all you want. (*In a reverie.*) Purty soon the girls come in an'—

GEORGE—And they was free?

CANDY—No—but they was jus' as polite an' nice an' quiet an' purty. Didn't seem like hookers. Made ya kinda scared to ask 'em.—That was a long time ago.

GEORGE—Yeah? An' how much them soft chairs set you back?

CANDY—Fifteen bucks.

GEORGE (*scornfully*)—So ya got a cigarette an' a drink an' a look at a purty dress an' it cost ya twelve and a half bucks extra. You shot a week's pay to walk on that red carpet.

CANDY (*still entranced with his memory*)—A week's pay? Sure. But I worked weeks all my life. I can't remember *none* of them weeks. But—that was nearly twenty years ago—And I can remember that! Girl I went with was named Arline. Had on a pink silk dress.

Curley's wife is standing in the door. She has come to ask Crooks something, she quickly explains, when George would savagely send her away. She isn't looking for Curley. This being Saturday night she knows where Curley is, even with his arm in a sling. She wants to ask Crooks what happened to Curley's hand.

George makes a quick sign to Crooks not to answer, seeing which convinces Curley's wife that, as she suspected, Curley had not caught his hand in a gear, as he said he had. So it was George who hurt Curley. She smiles at that. Perhaps now, since he isn't scared of Curley anymore, George will be willin' to talk to her once in a while.

"Look! I didn't sock Curley," protests George, seriously. "If he had trouble, it ain't none of our affair. Ask Curley about it. Now listen. I'm gonna try to tell ya. We tole ya to get the hell out and it don't do no good—so I'm gonna tell ya another way. Us guys got somepin' we're gonna do—an' if you stick around you'll gum up the works. It ain't your fault. (*Trying to explain.*) If a guy steps on a round pebble an' falls down an' breaks his neck—it ain't the pebble's fault, but the guy wouldn't of did it if the pebble wasn't there!"

Curley's Wife (*puzzled*)—What ya talkin' about pebbles? If you didn't sock Curley, who did?

George—Nobody socked him.

Curley's Wife (*looking at others—then stepping quickly to* Lennie)—Where'd you get them bruises on your face?

George (*quickly*)—I tell you he got his hand caught in a machine!

Lennie—He caught his han' in a machine.

George—So now get out of here!

Curley's Wife (*goes close to* Lennie. *Speaking softly, with a note of affection in her voice*)—So—it was you. Well—maybe you're dumb like they say—an' maybe you're the only guy on the ranch with guts. (*Placing her hand on* Lennie's *shoulder.*) You're a nice fella! (Lennie *giggles a little.*)

George (*suddenly leaps at her ferociously, grabs her shoulder and whirls her around facing him*)—Listen!—you! I tried to give you a break. (Lennie *takes a step back.*) We ain't gonna let you mess up what we're gonna do. You let this guy alone an' get the hell out of here!

Curley's Wife (*defiant*)—You ain't tellin' me what to do. I got a right to talk to anybody I want to!

The Boss appears in the doorway. He stands there, looking on. As George raises his hand to strike Curley's wife, he sees the Boss out of the corner of his eye. The Boss walks down closer to them and stands surveying the pose. Curley's wife turns slowly and walks away. George's arm drops to his side. With a shrug of his shoulders he turns to face the Boss as the curtain falls.

ACT III

Sunday afternoon. The boys can be heard pitching horseshoes outside the big barn. Inside the barn the hay is stacked against

the end and slopes up nearly as high as the roof. In front of the
hay loft there are stalls. Into one, a part of a box-stall, the hay
is spilled over and boards at the end form a sort of bench. 'The
sound of horses in adjoining stalls can be heard. There are sacks
of grain against the walls and harness is hung on long pegs on
the wall. "Streaks of afternoon sun come between the boards,
made visible by dust in the air."

Presently Lennie lets himself in through a door at the upper
end of the barn. He is carrying the body of his dead puppy,
stroking it from time to time. "God damn you, why you got
to get killed?" he mutters, angrily. "You ain't so little as mice.
I didn' bounce you hard." He has bent the pup's head up and
is looking in its face. "Now maybe George ain't gonna let me
'tend no rabbits if he finds out you got killed."

Candy has been looking for Lennie. Wants to tell him, with
some excitement, that the Boss isn't going to can him and George.
Slim has spoken for them. They're good buckers and the Boss
has got to move his grain. The Boss had given Curley's wife
hell, too—worse hell than George gave her. Told her never to
go near the men no more.

Candy goes in search of George to repeat the good news.
Lennie lays down on the hay with the pup. Outside, the clink
of the horseshoes is frequently punctuated by the excited comments of men.

Again the back door opens. Curley's wife tiptoes in. She is
carrying a small, cheap black suitcase and has a coat over her
arm. Quietly she crosses to a grain box, puts the suitcase and
her coat inside and is ready to tiptoe her way out when she sees
Lennie.

Curley's wife knows that Lennie has seen her hide her things.
She is eager to get him to promise that he won't tell. Lennie,
suspicious and afraid, would keep her away. "I ain't gonna have
nothin' to do with you," says Lennie, sullenly. "George tole me.
I ain't to talk to you or nothin'."

"George give you all your orders?" she asks, flippantly.

"Not talk nor nothin'," sullenly repeats Lennie, swinging to a
sitting position on the bench.

"You won't tell about that suitcase?" pleads Curley's wife.
"I ain't gonna stay here no more. Tonight I'm gonna get out.
Come here an' get my stuff an' get out. I ain't gonna be pushed
around no more. I'm gonna go in pitchers."

Lennie has got to his feet and is backing away, holding the
dead pup behind him. Curley's wife would reassure him.

Everything's all right. "Them guys ain't gonna leave that tenement. They got money bet," she explains. "You don't need to be scared to talk to me."

Gradually Lennie becomes a little more sociable. He tells her about the dead pup. "He was so little," says Lennie, sadly. "I was jus' playing with him—an' he made like he's gonna bite me —an' I made like I was gonna smack him—an' I done it. An' then he was dead."

Curley's wife would console him. The country's full of mutts. . . . They are sitting on the bench side by side. Tomorrow, she is saying, she will be gone. She ain't meant to be livin' the way she has been livin'. Lennie seems to be listening, but he has tomorrows of his own to be thinking of—tomorrows on the place with George. Lennie doesn't hear Curley's wife and she doesn't hear him, yet both keep talking.

"I come from Salinas," Curley's wife is saying. "Well, a show come through an' I talked to a guy that was in it. He says I could go with the show. My ol' lady wouldn't let me, 'cause I was on'y fifteen. I wouldn't be no place like this if I had went with that show, you bet."

"We gonna have a little house an' raspberry bushes," mumbles Lennie. "Gonna take a sack an' fill it up with alfalfa an'—"

CURLEY'S WIFE—'Nother time I met a guy an' he was in pitchers. Went out to the Riverside Dance Palace with him. He said he was gonna put me in pitchers. Says I was a natural. Soon's he got back to Hollywood he was gonna write me about it. I never got that letter. I think my ol' lady stole it. Well, I wasn't gonna stay no place where they stole your letters. So I married Curley. Met him out to the Riverside Dance Palace too.

LENNIE—I hope George ain't gonna be mad about this pup.

CURLEY'S WIFE—I ain't tol' this to nobody before. Maybe I ought'n to. I don't like this Curley. I might a stayed with him but last night him and his ol' man bot lit into me. I don't have to stay here. (*Moves closer to him confidentially.*) Don't tell nobody 'til I get clear away. I'll go in the night an' thumb a ride to Hollywood.

LENNIE—We're goin' away from here purty soon. This ain't no nice place.

CURLEY'S WIFE—Gonna get in the movies an' have nice clothes —all them nice clothes like they wear. An' I'll set in them big hotels and they'll take pitchers of me. When they have them openings, I'll go an' talk in the radio—an' it won't cost me nothin'—'cause I'm in the pitcher. (*Puts her hand on* LENNIE'S *arm for a moment.*) All them nice clothes like they wear—because this guy says I'm a natural.

LENNIE—We gonna go way—far away from here.

CURLEY'S WIFE—'Course when I run away from Curley, my ol' lady won't never speak to me no more. She'll think I ain't decent. That's what she'll think. (*Defiantly.*) Well, we ain't really decent, no matter how much my ol' lady tries to hide it. My ol' man was a drunk. They put him away.

LENNIE—One time George an' me was to the Sacramento Fair. I fell in the river an' George pulled me out an' saved me, and then we went to the Fair.

CURLEY'S WIFE—My ol' man was a sign painter, when he worked. (LENNIE *looks at her. She sits at his right.*) He used to get drunk an' paint crazy pitchers an' waste paint. One night when I was a little kid, him an' my ol' lady had an awful fight. They was always fightin'. In the middle of the night he come into my room, and he says—"Let's you an' me go away." (*She becomes lost in reverie, and her voice takes on a curious wondering tenderness.*) I guess he was drunk. . . . I remember the night—walkin' down the road, and the trees was all black. I was pretty sleepy. He picked me up, an' he carried me on his back. He says, "We gonna live together. We gonna live together 'cause you're my own little girl. Why, you'll bake little cakes for me, an' I'll paint pretty pitchers all over the wall." (*Sadly.*) But in the morning they caught us—an' they put him away. (*Pause.*) I wish we'd a went.

LENNIE—Maybe if I took this here pup an' throwed him away, George wouldn't never know.

There is the clang of a horseshoe outside, followed by a great shout. Somebody evidently has made a ringer. Curley's wife has quit dreaming. Lennie is still going on about the rabbits. He's nuts, that's what Curley's wife thinks. He ain't nuts, Lennie insists. He just likes to pet nice things, with his fingers. Soft things, like velvet. Once he had a piece of velvet a lady gave him—Lennie wishes he had a piece of velvet right now—

"You're nuts," repeats Curley's wife, with increasing conviction. "But you're a kinda nice fella. Jus' like a big baby. A person can see kinda what you mean. Sometimes when I'm doin' my hair I jus' set there and stroke it because it's so soft." Outside there is still the ring of horseshoes and the laughter of men. "Some people got kinda coarse hair," Curley's wife goes on. "You

take Curley, his hair's jus' like wire. But mine is soft and fine."
She has taken Lennie's hand and put it on her head. "Feel there
and see how soft it is."

Lennie's fingers fall to stroking her hair. "Oh, that's nice,"
he cries, and strokes harder. "Oh, that's nice!"

She is pulling away from him now. "Look out now, you'll
muss it," she warns, as she raises her hands to stop him. "You
stop it now! You'll mess it all up." She would jerk her head
away. "Let go!" she calls, excitedly.

Lennie's fingers close on her hair and he hangs on. He is in
a panic now, and crying with fright as Curley's wife struggles to
be free. "Oh, please don't do that!" he begs. "George'll be
mad. . . . George's gonna say I done a bad thing. . . ."

Curley's wife is screaming now and Lennie, blanched with fear,
has put a hand over her nose and mouth. "I don't want you
to yell," he says. "You gonna get me in trouble, just like George
says you will. Now don't you do that—"

Curley's wife has increased her struggles to get away. Lennie's
grip tightens. He has thrown her down on the bench. "I don't
wanta hurt you," he protests. "Don't you yell! Don't you
yell!!!" He is shaking her violently. Suddenly her neck snaps
sideways and she lies still. Her left hand lies limp near the
floor. Her feet are up on the bench. He looks down at her
and cautiously removes his hands from her mouth and hair. . . .

"I done a bad thing. I done another bad thing," he mutters,
a pitiful whine creeping into his voice. Dazedly he puts a handful
of hay on her body, "in a childish attempt to cover her."

"Oh, I done a real bad thing. I shouldn't a did that. George
is gonna be mad." Slowly he picks up the dead pup. "I'll
throw him away," he says; "it is bad enough like it is. . . ."

Lennie has disappeared through the door. For a moment there
is silence, broken only by the mumbling of the horseshoe pitchers
outside. A few minutes and then Candy shuffles in, calling loudly
for Lennie. A shaft of sunlight breaks through the door he has
opened and falls on the body of Curley's wife. "Oh, I didn't
know you was here," exclaims Candy. "You was tol' not to be
here." He notices the awkward position and goes to her. "Oh,
Jesus Christ!" he exclaims. The next second he is calling excitedly for George.

George kneels beside the body. He feels heart and wrist.
Slowly and stiffly he stands up. "I should of knew," he mutters.
"I guess way back in my head I did."

Candy is hysterical with fear. Dully George takes command

of the situation. The guys will have to be told. He knows that.
And he guesses they will have to catch Lennie and lock him up.
They can't let Lennie get away. "The poor bastard would
starve," says George. "Maybe they'll lock him up and be nice
to him."

"You know better'n that, George," wails Candy. "You know
Curley's gonna want to get him lynched. You know how Curley
is." George knows. . . .

"Now, you listen," George is saying. "The guys might think
I was in on it. I'm gonna go in the bunk house. Then in a
minute you come out and yell like you just seen her. Will you
do that? So the guys won't think I was in on it?"

"Sure, George. Sure. I'll do that."

"Okay. Give me a couple of minutes then. And then you
yell your head off. I'm goin' now."

George has run out the door. Candy stands looking down at
the body of Curley's wife. He speaks in sorrow and in anger.
"You God damn tramp," he says, "you done it, didn't you?
Everybody knowed you'd mess things up. You just wasn't no
good. I could have hoed in the garden and washed dishes for
them guys. . . . If there was a circus or a baseball game—we
would o' went to her . . . just said to hell with work and went
to her. . . ."

With an effort Candy has called the boys. They come, hatless,
curious, inquiring. Slim is first. Then Carlson. Curley is with
them, his arm in a sling. . . . Now they have found Curley's
wife. They are gazing at her, stunned, when George comes running in. He is wearing hat and coat and has thrust Carlson's
Luger in his belt under his coat.

George has pushed his way through the group. "What's the
matter? . . . What's happened?"

Curley turns to him. "I know who done it," he shouts, working himself into a fury. "That big son-of-a-bitch done it. I
know he done it. Why, everybody else was out there playing
horseshoes. I'm gonna get my gun. Why, I'll kill the big son-
of-a-bitch myself. I'll shoot him in the guts. Come on, you
guys."

Curley has run out the door. Carlson will get his gun. The
others hurry after him.

"I guess Lennie done it, all right," says Slim, confirming the
broken neck. "Her neck's busted. Lennie could o' done that.
Maybe like that time in Weed you was tellin' me about. Well,
I guess we gotta get him," he adds, gently. "Where you think

he might o' went?"

George doesn't know. "Couldn't we maybe bring him in and lock him up? He's nuts, Slim. He never done this to be mean."

"If we could only keep Curley here. But Curley wants to shoot him. . . . And s'pose they catch him, George—lock him up, strap him down and put him in a cage, that ain't no good. . . . I think there's only one way to get him out of it."

George is staring at Slim. Slowly his hand goes to the Luger in his belt. "Yeah—I know," he says as he puts the gun back.

Carlson has rushed back to report the loss of his Luger. Curley follows him, a six-shooter in his hand. Crooks has found a shotgun. Carlson should take the shotgun, Curley orders. Whit can get a gun from Curley's old man—

"Don't give him no chance," orders Curley. "Shoot for his guts, that'll double him over." He has turned to George. "You're comin' with us, fella!" he says, menacingly.

"Yeah! I'll come," agrees George. "But listen, Curley, the poor bastard's nuts. Don't shoot him; he didn't know what he was doin'."

"Curley, maybe you'd better stay here with your wife," suggests Slim.

"Naw. . . ." For a second Curley hesitates, then hardens again. "Naw!! I'm gonna shoot the guts outta the big bastard. I'm gonna get him myself. Come on—you guys!"

Curley has rushed out, followed by Carlson and the others. "Look out for him! He's got my Luger!" calls Carlson.

George starts to follow, then turns back to wait for Slim. "All right, Candy—you stay here then," says Slim. He has put a hand on George's shoulder. Gives him a push toward the door. "Poor bastard!" says Slim. The lights dim quickly as the curtain falls.

Again the sandy bank of the Salinas river. Again the shadows are deepening. Through the willows Lennie makes his way, holding the dead pup under his coat and muttering to himself. "I didn't forget, you bet," he is saying. "I come right here. Hide in the brush and wait for George." He looks sadly at the pup. "George gonna give me hell—I bet," he adds. And then, with sudden resolution, "I won't tell him. I'll bury him."

He scoops out a hole at the base of the big elm. He puts the pup in and pats down the sand, still mumbling. "I can go right up in the hills and find a cave."

George comes in hurriedly. He has barely time to push

Lennie ahead of him into the brush before the men have caught up with him. George shouldn't get so far ahead, seeing he ain't got a gun, calls Whit, coming through the brush.

The men have come on now. The Boss is with them, carrying a rifle, and there are a couple of ranch hands with shotguns. This is the way Lennie must have come, they are agreed. This is the way the tracks pointed. George is acting as though he had searched the willows where he stands. Slim thinks they had better split up. They'll never find him stickin' in a bunch that way. They ought to spread out. Curley thinks Lennie might be lyin' in the thick brush, but George gets in front of him when he starts to look—

"Look— Up there's the county road an' open fields an' over there's the highway," says Slim. "Le's spread out and cover the brush. . . . We better drag up to the roads an' then drag back. . . . Me an' George'll go up to the county road. You guys gets the highway an' back."

"If we get separated, we'll meet here," adds the Boss. "Remember this place."

"All I care is getting the bastard," growls Curley, leading off. Slim rolls a cigarette. The men's voices trail off.

"Where is he?" asks Slim, softly.

George looks at Slim for a long moment. Then he nods toward the bushes. "You want—I should—go away?" asks Slim. George nods slowly, staring at the ground.

Making sure the men are out of hearing, George calls softly and Lennie comes lumbering through the tules. He is curious about the other guys. Where they goin'? Huntin'? Why can't he and George go with 'em? Lennie likes huntin'—

"Is it because I done a bad thing?" asks Lennie, puzzled by George's silence. "Is that why we can't go huntin' with them guys?"

"That don't make no difference," says George, huskily. "Sit down, Lennie—"

"George! Ain't you gonna give me hell?" pleads Lennie, sitting on a rock and facing George anxiously.

"Give ya hell?"

LENNIE—Sure . . . like you always done before. Like—"if I didn't have you I could take my fifty bucks . . ."

GEORGE (softly, as if in wonder)—Jesus Christ, Lennie, you can't remember nothing that happens. But you remember every word I say!

LENNIE—Well, ain't you gonna say it? (*Pause—there is no answer.*) Go on, George, say it!

GEORGE (*reciting*)—"If I was alone I—could live—so easy. (*His voice is monotonous.*) I could get a job and not have no mess . . ."

LENNIE (*rising*)—"And when the end of the month come . . ."

GEORGE—"And when the end of the month come, I could take my fifty bucks and go to—a cat house—"

LENNIE (*eagerly*)—Go on, George—(GEORGE *does not go on.*) I can go away. I'll go right off in the hills and find a cave if you don't want me.

GEORGE (*speaks as though his lips were stiff*)—No, I want you to stay here with me.

LENNIE (*craftily*)—Then tell me like you done before.

GEORGE—Tell you what?

LENNIE—'Bout the other guys and about us!

GEORGE (*recites again*)—Guys like us got no families. They get a little stake and then they blow it in. They ain't got nobody in the world that gives a hoot in hell about 'em.

LENNIE (*happily*)—But not *us*. Tell about us now.

GEORGE—But not us.

LENNIE—Because . . . I got you—

GEORGE—Because I got you and . . .

LENNIE—And you got me and we got each other. That's what gives a hoot in hell about us!

GEORGE (*looks at* LENNIE)—Lennie—

LENNIE—Huh?

GEORGE—Take your hat off, Lennie. . . . (GEORGE *takes off his hat.* LENNIE *imitates* GEORGE *and does the same.*) The air feels fine!

LENNIE—Tell how it's gonna be.

GEORGE (*pushing him toward the willows*)—Lennie—go over there and look acrost the river, and I'll tell you like you can almost see it. . . . We gonna have a little place . . .

LENNIE (*stops*)—Go on! How's it gonna be? "We gonna have a little place. . . ."

GEORGE (*thickly*)—"We'll have a cow. And we'll have maybe a pig and chickens—and down in the flat we'll have a . . . little piece of alfalfa. . . ."

LENNIE—For the rabbits!

GEORGE (*still pushing* LENNIE *toward willows*)—"For the rabbits!"

LENNIE—And I get to 'tend the rabbits?

GEORGE—And you get to 'tend the rabbits!

LENNIE—And we can live off the fat of the land!

GEORGE—Yes. Er . . . why don't you sit down, Lennie— right on that rock. (LENNIE *sits*.) That's it. Now turn around and look over there, Lennie. Like you can really see it.

LENNIE—Where?

GEORGE—Right across the river there. (*Slowly taking the Luger out of pocket*.) Can't you almost see it?

LENNIE—Where, George?

GEORGE—Over there. You keep lookin', Lennie. Just keep lookin'.

LENNIE—I'm lookin', George. I'm lookin'.

GEORGE—That's right. It's gonna be nice there. Ain't gonna be no trouble, no fights. Nobody ever gonna hurt nobody, or steal from 'em. It's gonna be—nice. (*Placing gun at back of* LENNIE's *head*.)

LENNIE (*happily*)—I can see it, George. I can see it! Right over there—I can see it!

George fires. As Lennie crumples and falls his heavy body carries a small willow tree crashing down with it. The voices of the men can be heard gathering volume in the distance. George is walking slowly toward Lennie as the voices of the men grow louder.

THE CURTAIN FALLS

OUR TOWN

A Drama in Three Acts

By Thornton Wilder

SUDDENLY, in late January and early February, the Broadway theatre, considerably to its own surprise, turned metaphysical. Soul themes and the concurrent problems of life and death became common—or at least as common as three plays produced in succession could make them seem.

The first was Paul Vincent Carroll's "Shadow and Substance," dealing with the reclaiming of a scholarly and acetic churchman's soul. The second was "On Borrowed Time," telling fantastically of an old man's effort to fight off Death until certain earthly tasks were completed. And the third was Thornton Wilder's "Our Town," dealing with three great adventures of living—sub-captioned as "Life," "Love" and "Death."

Broadway was a bit awed by "Our Town." A majority of the reviews were mildly ecstatic. A few were modestly doubtful of the complete impressiveness of Mr. Wilder's statement. One or two questioned the effectiveness of the sceneryless stage, with the story told in a fantastic combination of pantomime and Greek Chorus recital by a Narrator performing as a Stage Manager.

Audience response was also divided, but generally favorable. In the spring, when "Our Town" was given the Pulitzer award as the best play of the year of American authorship, a new interest developed that carried the play well into the summer.

Attendance upon "Our Town" provides a new experience in playgoing. There have been other plays produced without scenery, and a number have been shown without the curtain that in the tradition of the theatre shuts out the fourth wall of an interior, or the fourth boundary of such landscape as may be revealed.

Entering the theatre for "Our Town" the spectator's first view is of a completely bare stage, exposed in semi-darkness. The side walls of the stage are remote and hazy. The rear wall is likely to be latticed with steam pipes and speckled with an odd assortment of hooks, rings and perhaps a light bracket or two.

"Presently the Stage Manager, hat on and pipe in mouth, en-

67

ters and begins placing a table and several chairs down stage left, and a table and chairs down stage right," reads Mr. Wilder's directions. " 'Left' and 'right' are from the point of view of the actor facing the audience; 'up' is toward the back wall."

When he has completed the setting of the stage the lights in the auditorium start to fade out and those on the stage to brighten. The Stage Manager saunters casually over to the right proscenium pillar, looks a little patronizingly over the audience, watches a few late arrivals slide self-consciously into their seats, takes the pipe out of his mouth and begins to speak.

"This play is called 'Our Town,' " he says, pausing a second to give the audience time to adjust itself to this new way of beginning a play. "It was written by Thornton Wilder, produced and directed by Jed Harris. In it you will see—"

He names the principal actors of the company, dwelling a little pridefully upon those who are best known. Another brief pause and he continues:

"The name of the town is Grover's Corners, New Hampshire—just across the Massachusetts line: longitude 42 degrees 40 minutes; latitude 70 degrees 37 minutes. The First Act shows a day in our town. The day is May 7, 1901. The time is just before dawn. *A rooster crows.* The sky is beginning to show some streaks of light over in the East there, behind our mount'in. The morning star always gets wonderful bright the minute before it has to go. *He stares at it for a moment, then goes up stage.*

"Well, I'd better show you how our town lies. Up here— *That is: parallel with the back wall*—is Main Street. Way back there is the railway station; tracks go that way. Polish Town's across the tracks and some Canuck families. *Toward the left:* Over there is the Congregational Church; across the street's the Presbyterian. . . . Methodist and Unitarian are over there. . . . Baptist is down in the holla' by the river. . . . Catholic Church is over beyond the tracks. . . . Here's the Town Hall and Post Office combined; jail's in the basement. . . . Bryan once made a speech from these steps here.

"Along here's a row of stores. Hitching-posts and horse blocks in front of them. First automobile's going to come along in about five years—belonged to Banker Cartwright, our richest citizen . . . lives in the big white house up on the hill. . . . Here's the grocery store and here's Mr. Morgan's drug store. Most everybody in town manages to look into those two stores once a day. . . . Public School's over yonder. High School's still farther over. Quarter of nine mornings, noontimes, and three o'clock

o by Vandamm Studio, New York.

"OUR TOWN"

age Manager: I've married two hundred couples in my day. Do I believe in it? I don't
w. M . . . marries N . . . millions of them. The cottage, the gocart, the Sunday afternoon
es in the Ford, the first rheumatism, the grandchildren, the second rheumatism, the deathbed,
reading of the will— Once in a thousand times it's interesting . . . Well, let's have Mendels-
's "Wedding March!"

(Martha Scott, Frank Craven, John Craven)

afternoons, the hull town can hear the yelling and screaming from those schoolyards. . . ."

He has returned to the table at the right. As he continues, two of his assistants appear bearing trellises, each with a climbing rose attached. One is set up at the right, the other at the left, close to the proscenium pillars.

"There's some scenery for those who think they have to have scenery," says the Stage Manager, smiling a twisted, quizzical smile. "There's a garden here. Corn . . . peas . . . beans . . . hollyhocks . . . heliotrope . . . and a lot of burdock."

The house on the right, the Stage Manager explains, is Doc Gibbs' house. That on the left is Editor Webb's. The gardens are just alike, except Mrs. Webb has a lot of sunflowers, too.

He is back leaning against the pillar now and continuing his narrative. It's a nice town, even though nobody very remarkable ever came out of it. . . . Earliest tombstones in the cemetery are dated 1670-1680. . . . It's dark now, but there are a few lights to be seen in the house where a Polish mother is having twins; in Joe Crowell's, where Joe, Jr., is getting up so as to deliver the paper; in the depot, where Shorty Hawkins is gettin' ready to flag the 5:45 for Boston. A second later you hear the train whistle. . . .

Now there is more activity. Doc Gibbs is reported as comin' down Main Street . . . Mrs. Gibbs illustrates coming downstairs by stepping off a steep platform and going through the motions of lighting a fire in the stove and starting breakfast; Joe Crowell is seen starting down Main Street and going through the motions of tossing the morning paper into yards. . . . Presently Howie Newsome, a gangling native, appears, delivering milk in pantomime, leaving bottles at both the Gibbses' and the Webbs'.

Howie also passes the time of day with Doc Gibbs. . . . Stops to have a pleasant word with Mrs. Gibbs and report the approach of the Doc. . . . Mrs. Webb has come into her kitchen, and is duplicating the breakfast preparations of Mrs. Gibbs. . . . Now the children have been called. . . . George and Rebecca Gibbs. . . . Emily and Wally Webb. . . . Time to get up if they don't want to be late for school. . . .

"I declare, you got to speak to George," fusses Mrs. Gibbs, irritably. "Seems like something's come over him lately. He's no help to me at all. I can't even get him to cut me some wood."

"Is he sassy to you?"

"No. He just whines! All he thinks about is that baseball. . . ."

There is still more trouble getting both the Gibbs children and the Webb children down to breakfast, Rebecca Gibbs being displeased with the dress her mother has laid out for her, and there being considerable suspicion in Mrs. Webb's mind as to whether Wally and Emily are washing themselves good. . . .

The factory whistle blows. "We've got a factory in our town, too," explains the Stage Manager. "Makes blankets. Cartwrights own it and it brung 'em a fortune."

The breakfasts finished and first bell having rung, the Webb and Gibbs children go out through the trellised gates, merge and turn left into Main Street. . . . Mrs. Gibbs goes into the yard to feed the chickens. . . . Mrs. Webb has seated herself by her trellis and is stringing beans. . . . The gossip of the day has begun. . . . Mrs. Webb's cold is better but she doesn't think she will go to the choir practice. . . . Mrs. Gibbs thinks Mrs. Webb should certainly try to go. . . . Mrs. Gibbs is quite excited because a second-hand furniture man from Boston has offered her three hundred and fifty dollars for Grandmother Wentworth's highboy. . . . Mrs. Webb thinks she ought to take it. . . . Mrs. Gibbs would sell it in a minute if she thought the Doctor would take her on a real trip—like to Paris, France—but she can't depend on the Doc—

"You know how he is," says Mrs. Gibbs. "I haven't heard a serious word out of him, ever since I've known him. No, he said, it might make him discontented with Grover's Corners to go traipsin' about Europe; better let well enough alone, he says. Every two years he makes a trip to the battlefields of the Civil War and that's enough treat for anybody, he says."

"Now we're going to skip a few hours in the day at Grover's Corners," continues the Stage Manager. "But before we go on I want you to know some more things about the town—all kinds of things. So I've asked Prof. Willard of our State University to come down here and sketch in a few details of our past history —kind of scientific account, you might say. Is Prof. Willard here? *Prof. Willard, a rural savant, pince-nez on a wide satin ribbon, enters from the right with some notes in his hand.* May I introduce Prof. Willard of our University. . . . A few brief notes, thank you, Professor—unfortunately our time is limited."

PROF. WILLARD—Grover's Corners . . . let me see . . . Grover's Corners lies on the old Archaeozoic granite of the Appalachian range. I may say it's some of the oldest land in the world. We're very proud of that. A shelf of Devonian basalt crosses it with vestiges of Mesozoic shale, and some sandstone outcrop-

pings; but that's all more recent: two hundred, three hundred
million years old. Some highly interesting fossils have been
found. . . . I may say: unique fossils . . . two miles out of
town, in Silas Peckham's cow pasture. They can be seen at the
museum in our University at any time. Did you wish the
meteorological conditions?

STAGE MANAGER—Thank you. We would.

PROF. WILLARD—The mean precipitation is 40 inches. The
mean annual temperature is 43 degrees, ranging between 102 degrees in the shade, and 38 degrees below zero in winter. The . . .
the . . . uh . . .

STAGE MANAGER—Thank you, Professor.

The Stage Manager would like the audience to have a political
and social report of Grover's Corners from Editor Webb. There
is a moment's delay. Editor Webb has just cut his hand while
he was eatin' an apple, Mrs. Webb reports. Presently, he appears, a kindly, mentally alert little man with his finger bound
in a handkerchief.

"Hm. . . . I don't have to tell you that we're run here by a
Board of Selectmen," begins Editor Webb. "All males vote at
the age of 21. Women vote indirect. We're lower middle-class,
sprinkling of professional men . . . 10% illiterate laborers. Po-
litically, we're 86% Republicans; 6% Democrats; 4% Socialists;
rest, indifferent. . . . Religiously, we're 85% Protestants; 12%
Catholics; rest indifferent. . . . Do you want the poverty and
insanity statistics?"

"Thank you, no."

There are a few queries. A woman in the balcony would like
to know if there is much drinking in Grover's Corners. Editor
Webb answers that that depends on what you'd call much.
"Satiddy nights the farmhands meet down in Ellery Greenough's
stable and holler some. Fourth of July I've been known to taste
a drop myself—and Decoration Day. . . ."

A tall man in the back of the auditorium asks if there is anyone in town "aware of social injustice and industrial inequality."
Editor Webb thinks practically everybody is. "Seems like they
spend most of their time talkin' about who's rich and who's
poor," says he.

A lady in a box would know whether there is any culture or
love of beauty in Grover's Corners. Editor Webb, a little hesitantly, admits a suspicion that there isn't—not in the sense the
lady means. So much culture as High School Commencements

reveal, perhaps, and such love of beauty as is concerned with sunrises and the panorama of the changing seasons. *"Robinson Crusoe* and the Bible; Handel's 'Largo,' we all know that; and Whistler's 'Mother'—those are about as far as we go," smilingly admits Editor Webb.

"We'll go back to the town now," announces the Stage Manager, as Editor Webb retires. "It's middle of the afternoon. All 2,642 have had their dinners and all the dishes have been washed. There's an early afternoon calm in our town: a buzzin' and a hummin' from the school buildings; only a few buggies on Main Street—the horses dozing at the hitching-posts; you all remember what it's like. Doc Gibbs is in his office, tapping people and making them say 'ah.' Mr. Webb's cuttin' his lawn over there; one man in ten thinks it's a privilege to push his own lawn mower. No, sir. It's later than I thought. There are the children coming home from school already."

Emily Webb is coming down Main Street, carrying her schoolbooks, and apparently doing a bit of day dreaming . . . George Gibbs is not far behind her. . . . Soon they have met to saunter the rest of the way together. . . . George would compliment Emily on the speech she had made in class. . . . Emily might have done better if she had talked about the Monroe Doctrine, as she expected to, but her teacher had insisted upon the Louisiana Purchase. . . . George greatly admires the way Emily sticks to her home work; from his room he can just see the top of her head when she is studying in her room. . . . George thinks perhaps they might work out a sort of telegraph from room to room and then once in a while Emily could give him a kinda hint or two about one of those Algebra problems. . . . Emily thinks perhaps she could. . . . Emily is just naturally bright, George guesses, but Emily is convinced it's just the way a person's born.

"Yeah. But, you see, I want to be a farmer," says George; "and my Uncle Luke says whenever I'm ready I can come over and work on his farm and if I'm any good I can just gradually have it."

"You mean the house and everything?" Emily's eyes are wide with surprise. George was prepared to enlarge upon his prospects, but Mrs. Webb appears and drafts Emily as a help with the string beans. . . .

There are some things about which Emily would like her mother's confirmation: For one, is she (Emily) good-looking? . . . She's got good features, Mrs. Webb admits. . . . But is she pretty enough to get anybody—to get people interested in her?

. . . "Emily, you make me tired," Mrs. Webb snaps finally. "Now stop it. You're pretty enough for all normal purposes."

And that is the best answer Emily can get before the Stage Manager returns to send her and her mother away. He has come back to continue his report of the town, but he has decided to go about it in a little different way. "We're going to look back on it from the future," he says. He won't tell what became of the Webbs and the Gibbses. The rest of the play will show that. But he does want to talk about some of the others.

Joe Crowell, Jr., the paper boy, for instance, "graduated with honors and got a scholarship to Boston Tech,—M.I.T., that is. But the war broke out and Joe died in France. All that education for nothing. . . . Howie Newsome's still delivering milk at Grover's Corners. He's an old man now, has a lot of help, but he still delivers it himself. Says he gets the feel of the town that way. Carries all the accounts in his head, never has to write down a word—"

Morgan's drug store has been all citified; Morgan himself retired and went to San Diego to live with his daughter. Died there in 1935. . . . The Cartwrights got richer and richer and are off "eating big dinners in hotels in Virginia Hot Springs and Miami Beach." . . . The Cartwright interests are building a new bank in Grover's Corners, and there is a good deal of talk as to what should be put in the cornerstone—

"Of course they've put in a copy of the New York *Times* and a copy of Mr. Webb's *Sentinel*," the Stage Manager reports. "We're kind of interested in this because some scientific fellas have found a way of painting all that reading matter with a kind of glue—silicate glue—that'll make it keep a thousand—two thousand years. We're putting in a Bible . . . and the Constitution of the United States and a copy of William Shakespeare's plays." . . . I'm going to have a copy of this play put in the cornerstone and the people a thousand years from now'll know a few simple facts about us—more than the Treaty of Versailles and the Lindbergh flight. See what I mean?

"Well—you people a thousand years from now—in the provinces north of New York at the beginning of the Twentieth Century, people et three times a day: soon after sunrise; at noon; and at sunset. . . . Every seventh day, by law and by religion, was a day of rest and all work come to a stop. . . . The religion at that time was Christianity. I guess you have some other records about Christianity. . . . The domestic set-up was marriage: a binding relation between a male and one female that lasted for

life. . . . Christianity strictly forbade killing, but you were allowed to kill animals, and you were allowed to kill human beings
in war and government punishings. . . . I guess we don't have
to tell you about the government and business forms, because
that's the kind of thing people seem to hand down first of all. . . .
Let me see now if there's anything else. Oh, yes—at death
people were buried in the ground just as they are.

"So, friends, this is the way we were in our growing up and in
our marrying and in our doctoring and in our living and in our
dying. Now we'll return to our day in Grover's Corners. A lot
of time has gone by. It's evening. You can hear choir practice
going on in the Congregational Church. All the children are at
home doing their school work. The day is running down like a
tired clock."

From the orchestra pit come the sounds of the choir practicing
on "Blessed be the tie that binds." . . . From the rear of the
stage two tall stepladders are pushed out in the Gibbs and Webb
territory. . . . When Emily Webb and George Gibbs have
mounted them they represent the second stories of their respec-
tive homes. . . . There is considerable "Hsssting!" until George
and Emily attract each other's attention. . . . Emily can't work
because the moon's so *terrible*. . . . George can't work because he
can't get the third problem. . . . Emily helps him with the
problem and then George's father calls him. . . .

It is an intimate talk Dr. Gibbs has with his son. It has to do
with George's future as a farmer and his present as a son—

"You'll be willing, will you, to get up early and milk and
feed the stock?" Dr. Gibbs asks. "And you'll be able to hoe
and hay all day?"

"Sure, I will. What are you . . . what do you mean, Pa?"

"Well, George, while I was in my office today I heard a funny
sound . . . and what do you think it was? It was your mother
chopping wood. There you see your mother—getting up early;
cooking meals all day long; washing and ironing;—and still she
has to go out in the back yard and chop wood. I suppose she
just got tired of asking you. She just gave up and decided it was
easier to do it herself. And you eat her meals, and put on the
clothes she keeps nice for you, and you run off and play baseball,—like she's some hired girl we keep around the house but
that we don't like very much. Well, I knew all I had to do was
call your attention to it. Here's a handkerchief, son. George,
I've decided to raise your spending money twenty-five cents a
week. Not, of course, for chopping wood for your mother, because

that's a present you give her, but because you're getting older—
and I imagine there are lots of things you must find to do with
it."

"Thanks, Pa."

Two or three of the neighbor women, coming from choir practice, have stopped at the corner. . . . There is considerable gossip
about Simon Stimson, the choir leader. . . . Simon drinks. . . .
Simon either drinks worse than he usta or he doesn't. . . . Complete agreement is lacking on that subject. . . .

The Gibbses have gone to bed. . . . Constable Warren has been
trying a few doors on Main Street. . . . Editor Webb is just
getting home after putting his paper to bed. . . . Simon Stimson
rolls unsteadily along Main Street, nor stops to pass a word
with Constable Warren and Editor Webb when they speak to
him—

"I don't know how that's goin' to end, Mr. Webb," allows
Constable Warren.

"Well, he's seen a peck o' trouble, one thing after another,"
recalls Editor Webb.

George Gibbs is still at his window when his sister Rebecca
climbs the stairs and insists on sharing it with him. Rebecca can't
see the moon from her room.

"I never told you about that letter Jane Crofut got from her
minister when she was sick," volunteers Rebecca, being entertaining. "The minister of her church in the town she was in before she came here. He wrote Jane a letter and on the envelope
the address was like this: It said: Jane Crofut; The Crofut Farm;
Grover's Corners; Sutton County; New Hampshire; United States
of America."

"What's funny about that?"

"But listen, it's not finished: the United States of America;
Continent of North America; Western Hemisphere; the Earth;
the Solar System; the Universe; the Mind of God,—that's what
it said on the envelope."

"What do you know!"

"And the postman brought it just the same."

"What do you know!"

"That's the end of the First Act, friends," announces the Stage
Manager, coming again into the picture. "You can go and smoke
now, those that smoke."

The lights fade.

ACT II

Tables and chairs indicating the Webb and Gibbs kitchens are still on the stage. The second story ladders have been removed. Lights on the stage go up slowly. The Stage Manager, again leaning against the proscenium pillar, is watching the audience return to its seats.

"Three years have gone by," announces the Stage Manager when the audience has settled. "Yes, the sun's come up over a thousand times. . . . Summers and winters have cracked the mountains a little bit more and the rains have brought down some of the dirt. . . . Some babies that weren't even born before have begun talking regular sentences already; and a number of people who thought they were right young and spry have noticed that they can't bound up a flight of stairs like they used to, without their heart fluttering a little. . . . Some older sons are sitting at the head of the table, and some people I know are having their meat cut up for them. . . . All that can happen in a thousand days."

The First Act, he explains a moment later, was called the Daily Life. This Act is called Love and Marriage. And he will let anyone guess what the next Act is going to be about.

The day is starting about the same as it did before. It's early morning, but this time it has been raining all night and everything is drenched. . . . Howie Newsome's still delivering the milk. . . . Si Crowell has his brother's place as the paper boy. . . . Mrs. Gibbs and Mrs. Webb are again getting breakfast—

"I don't have to point out to the women in my audience that those ladies they see before them," the Stage Manager is saying; "both those ladies cooked three meals a day,—one of 'em for twenty years, the other for forty,—and no summer vacation. They brought up two children apiece; washed; cleaned the house, —and never a nervous breakdown. Never thought themselves hard-used, either. It's like what one of those Middle West poets said: You've got to love life to have life, and you've got to have life to love life. . . . It's what they call a vicious circle."

Howie Newsome is quite chatty this morning. . . . Talks with Si Crowell about George Gibbs giving up baseball to get married. . . . Talks with Mrs. Gibbs about the weather and the wedding. . . . Talks with Mrs. Webb about the wedding and the prospects of Mrs. Newsome's gittin' there. . . .

Dr. Gibbs has come down to breakfast in his shirt sleeves. . . . The Doc is inclined to make light of the wedding, but Mrs. Gibbs is about ready to cry—

"The groom's up shaving himself," reports Dr. Gibbs. "Whistling and singing, like he's glad to leave us. Every now and then he says 'I do' to the mirror, but it don't sound convincing to me."

"I declare I don't know how he'll get along," sighs Mrs. Gibbs. "I've arranged his clothes and seen to it he's put warm things on,—Frank! they're too young. Emily won't think of such things. He'll catch his death of cold within a week."

George has come rattling down the stairs, cheerful as can be. "Good morning, everybody. Only five more hours to live," he calls, making a gesture of cutting his throat.

Despite his mother's protests George is determined to call on the bride, and does. . . . Despite Mrs. Webb's insistence that the groom should never see his bride on his wedding day until he sees her in the church, George is determined to see Emily. . . . A kind of compromise is effected. . . . George stays to have a cup of coffee with Mr. Webb while Mrs. Webb goes to warn the still sleeping Emily that he is there.

A bride, Editor Webb explains, is likely to be pretty nervous on her wedding day. . . . Still George doesn't believe in those foolish superstitions. . . . George wishes a fellow could get married without all that marching up and down. . . . So does every other man, admits Mr. Webb, but the women won't have it that way—

"George, I was thinking the other night of some advice my father gave me when I got married," Mr. Webb is saying. "Charles, he said, Charles, start out early showing who's boss, he said. Best thing to do is to give an order, even if it don't make sense; just so she'll learn to obey. And he said: if anything about your wife irritates you,—her conversation, or anything—just get up and leave the house. That'll make it clear to her, he said. And, oh, yes! he said never, *never* let your wife know how much money you have, never."

"Well, Mr. Webb. . . . I don't think I could . . ."

"So I took the opposite of my father's advice and I've been happy ever since. And let that be a lesson to you, George, never to ask advice on personal matters."

George has gone home, and now the Stage Manager is ready to carry on—

"Thank you. Thank you, everybody. . . . Now I have to interrupt again here. You see, we want to know how all this began,—this wedding, this plan to spend a lifetime together. I'm awfully interested in how big things like that begin. . . .

You know how it is: you're twenty-one or twenty-two and you make some decisions, then whisssh! you're seventy: you've been a lawyer for fifty years, and that white-haired lady at your side has eaten over fifty thousand meals with you. . . . How do such things begin? . . . George and Emily are going to show you now the conversation they had when they first knew that . . . that . . . as the saying goes . . . they were meant for one another. But before they do it I want you to try and remember what it was like when you were young, when you were fifteen or sixteen. For some reason it is very hard to do: those days when even the little things in life could be almost too exciting to bear. . . . And particularly the days when you were first in love; when you were like a person sleep-walking, and you didn't quite see the street you were in, and didn't quite hear everything that was said to you. . . . You're just a little bit crazy. Will you remember that, please? . . . Now they'll be coming out of High School at three o'clock. George has just been elected President of the Junior Class, and as it's June, that means he'll be President of the Senior Class all next year. And Emily's just been elected Secretary and Treasurer. . . . I don't have to tell you how important that is."

The Stage Manager places a board across the backs of two chairs, and puts two high stools behind it. This is the counter of Mr. Morgan's drug store. . . . Now Emily has started down Main Street with an armful of imaginary books. She has been having an animated conversation with Ernestine about the Algebra, and isn't Caesar terrible? . . . George catches up with her. . . . They are standing at the head of Main Street, hesitating about going on. . . . There has been some feeling between them. . . . George doesn't understand. . . . Why is Emily mad at him? . . . Emily isn't mad . . . just disappointed. . . . Why?

"Well, up to a year ago I used to like you a lot," explains Emily. "And I used to watch you as you did everything . . . because we'd been friends so long . . . and then you began spending all your time at baseball . . . and you never even spoke to anybody any more; not even to your own family you didn't . . . and, George, it's a fact, you've got awful conceited and stuck-up, and all the girls say so. They may not say so to your face, but that's what they say about you behind your back, and it hurts me to hear them say it, but I've got to agree with them a little. I'm sorry if it hurts your feelings . . . but I can't be sorry I said it."

"I . . . I'm glad you said it, Emily. I never thought that such a thing was happening to me. I guess it's hard for a fella not to have faults creep into his character."

Emily admits that she expects George to be perfect. . . .
George doesn't think men are ever perfect; only women can be
perfect. . . . No, insists Emily, no girl can be as perfect as a
man; she's too nervous. . . .

They have got as far as Mr. Morgan's drug store and George
has asked Emily if she wouldn't like an ice-cream soda. . . .
Emily would. . . . The Stage Manager is now Mr. Morgan.
. . . He thinks he detects a trace of tears on Emily's face. . . .
It's only because Emily's just had an awful scare, George is quick
to explain. . . . She nearly got run down by Tom Huckins. . . .
And they'd like two strawberry ice-cream sodas—

"Yes, sir. I tell you, you've got to look both ways before you
cross Main Street these days," admits Mr. Morgan, pretending to
draw the sodas from imaginary taps. "There is a hundred and
twenty-five horses in Grover's Corners this minute I'm talking to
you. . . ."

They have the sodas and Mr. Morgan has gone to wait on Miss
Ellis. . . . George insists that he is glad to buy expensive drinks
for such a celebration. . . . First they're celebrating their election
and then George is celebrating because he's got a friend who tells
him all the things that ought to be told him. . . . Emily wishes
he would forget that, but George wants her to stick to it. . . .
"I'm going to change so quick—you bet I'm going to change,"
promises George. . . . And as a favor, when he goes away to
Agricultural College will she write him a letter once in a while?
. . . She certainly will. . . . Three years certainly seems like a
long time. . . . Perhaps letters from Grover's Corners wouldn't
be very interesting after a while. . . . The day wouldn't come
when George wouldn't be interested, he knows that. . . .

George has asked a lot of people about going to Agricultural
College and he has about made up his mind it isn't necessary.
He's practically ready to take over his Uncle Luke's farm right
now. . . . Emily isn't sure about that, but George is. . . . There
are other things George has been thinking a good deal about
lately, too. . . . Mostly they are about Emily—

"Listen, Emily," he is saying, very earnestly, "I'm going to tell
you why I'm not going to Agricultural School. I think that once
you've found a person that you're very fond of . . . I mean a
person who's fond of you, too—at least enough to be interested
in your character . . . well, I think that's just as important as
college is, and even more so. That's what I think."

"I think it's awfully important, too," agrees Emily.

"Emily, if I improve and make a big change . . . would you be . . . I mean, *could* you be . . ."

"I . . . I am now; I always have been," admits Emily.

There is an impressive pause, and then George continues. "So I guess this is an important talk we've been having. . . . Wait just a minute and I'll take you home."

George and Emily walk out in grave silence, go down the street and disappear through the Webbs' trellis.

"Now before we go on to the wedding," the Stage Manager is saying, "there are still some more things we ought to know about this—about this marriage. I want to know some more about how the parents took it; but what I want to know most of all is: oh, you know what I mean,—what Grover's Corners thought about marriage anyway. You know's well as I do: people are never able to say right out what they think of money, or death, or fame, or marriage. You've got to catch it between the lines; you've got to *over*-hear it."

Doctor and Mrs. Gibbs are called. . . . The drug store counter becomes Mrs. Gibbs' ironing board and there is a Gibbs family scene. . . . The Doctor has had a talk with George and found it pretty embarrassing. . . . George wants to marry Emily as soon as school is out and take her right to the farm. . . . "Julia, he's just a green, half-grown kid. He isn't ready to be a family man," insists the Doctor.

"No, he ain't—you're right," agrees Mrs. Gibbs. "But he's a good boy and I wouldn't like to think of him being alone out there . . . coming into town Satiddy nights, like any old farm hand, tuckered out from work and looking for excitement. He might get into bad ways. It wouldn't be enough fun for him to come and sit by our stove,—and holding hands with Emily, for a year mightn't be enough either. He might lose interest in her."

The decision is difficult. . . . There are remembrances of their own early married life, some sustaining, others worrisome, but in the end the Gibbses are agreed that George should be told it's all right—

As the Stage Manager talks the actors help to clear the stage of chairs and tables, trellises, etc. The new scene is to represent the pews of a church facing a small platform that has been placed in front of the back wall. The Stage Manager will act as Minister.

"There are a lot of things to be said about a wedding," observes the Stage Manager; "there are a lot of thoughts that go on during a wedding. We can't get them all into one wedding,

naturally, and especially not into a wedding at Grover's Corners
where they're awfully plain and short. In this wedding I play
the Minister. That gives me the right to say a few more things
about it. For a while now, the play gets pretty serious. Y'see,
some churches say that marriage is a sacrament. I don't quite
know what that means, but I can guess. Like Mrs. Gibbs said a
few minutes ago: People were made to live two by two. This is
a good wedding, but people are so put together that even at a
good wedding there's a lot of confusion way down deep in
people's minds and we thought that that ought to be in our
play, too."

The organ is playing Handel's "Largo" as the congregation
streams into the church. . . . Mrs. Webb pauses on her way up
the aisle to confide to the audience that she has been crying all
day, and can't understand why. . . . Emily, her mother reports,
has been crying, too. . . . "There's something downright cruel
about sending our girls out into marriage this way," insists Mrs.
Webb. . . .

George has come down the right aisle of the theatre. . . . As
he nears the church some of his friends from the baseball club
start cat-calling and whistling to him. . . . "Eh, George, George!
Hssst-yaow! If things don't go right, call us in. We know what
to do." . . . They would say a lot more but the Stage Manager
drives them away. . . . "There used to be an awful lot of that
kind of thing at weddings in the old days—Rome and later," he
says. "We're more civilized now,—so they say. . . ."

For a moment, in the aisle, George hesitates. . . . Panic
threatens him. . . . He is ready to run. . . . Mrs. Gibbs comes
from her place to set him right. . . . He comes out of the mood
as out of a dream and is eager again for the wedding to go on.

Now Emily has come through the audience, in white and wearing her wedding veil. . . . She, too, has a moment of doubt and
indecision. . . . Emily doesn't want to get married. . . . She
wants to stay with her father, who is trying to comfort and reassure her. . . . Mr. Webb calls George and George brings new
confidence to Emily. . . .

The organist has started the March from "Lohengrin." . . .
George has taken his place beside the minister. . . . The ceremony goes on, punctuated momentarily by Mrs. Soames in the
congregation assuring those assembled that this is a lovely wedding and Emily a lovely bride.

The ceremony is completed in pantomime. . . . "I've married
two hundred couples in my day," the minister confides. "Do I

believe in it? I don't know. M. . . . marries N. . . . millions of them. The cottage, the go-cart, the Sunday afternoon drives in the Ford, the first rheumatism, the deathbed, the reading of the will,— Once in a thousand times it's interesting. Well, let's have Mendelssohn's 'Wedding March'!"

The organist starts the March, the bride and groom come happily down the aisle. . . . Mrs. Soames repeats her conviction that it has been a lovely wedding. . . . A bright light picks out the bride and groom as they run joyfully up the aisle of the theatre—

"That's all the Second Act. Ten minutes' intermission, folks," says the Stage Manager.

The lights are dimmed.

ACT III

The scene has been changed during intermission. There is now a group of ordinary chairs at the right side of the stage, arranged in rows. These are the graves of the Grover's Corners dead, and the dead are sitting upright in them—Mrs. Gibbs, Simon Stimson, Mrs. Soames, Wally Webb and others.

The Stage Manager has taken his usual place. "This time nine years have gone by, friends—summer, 1913," he explains. "Gradual changes in Grover's Corners. Horses are getting rarer. Farmers are coming to town in Fords. Chief difference is in the young people, far as I can see. They want to go to the moving pictures all the time. They want to wear clothes like they see there . . . want to be citified. . . . Everybody locks their house doors now at night. Ain't heen any burglars in town yet, but everybody's heard about 'en_ . . But you'd be surprised though —on the whole, things don't change much at Grover's Corners."

He describes the location of the cemetery on a windy hilltop. And the view that can be seen from it. . . . He tells of the old stones over in a far corner—1670, 1680—and of the Civil War veterans: "New Hampshire boys . . . had a notion that the Union ought to be kept together, though they'd never seen more than fifty miles of it themselves. All they knew was the name, friends—the United States of America. And they went and died about it."

He tells of this new part of the cemetery and of the people who have been brought here and something of their last illnesses—

"This certainly is an important part of Grover's Corners," he continues. "A lot of thoughts come up here, night and day, but

there's no post office. . . . Now I'm going to tell you some things
you know already. You know'm as well as I do; but you don't
take'm out and look at'm very often. . . . I don't care what they
say with their mouths—everybody knows that *something* is
eternal. And it ain't houses and it ain't names, and it ain't earth,
and it ain't even the stars . . . everybody knows in their bones
that *something* is eternal, and that something has to do with
human beings. All the greatest people ever lived have been
telling us that for five thousand years and yet you'd be surprised
how people are always losing hold of it. There's something way
down deep that's eternal about every human being. (*Pause.*)
You know as well as I do that the dead don't stay interested in
us living people for very long. Gradually, gradually, they let
hold of the earth . . . and the ambitions they had . . . and the
pleasures they had . . . and the things they suffered . . . and
the people they loved. They get weaned away from earth—that's
the way I put it,—weaned away. Yes, they stay here while the
earth-part of 'em burns away, burns out, and all that time they
slowly get indifferent to what's goin' on in Grover's Corners.
They're waitin'. They're waitin' for something that they feel is
comin'. Something important and great. Aren't they waitin' for
the eternal part in them to come out clear? Some of the things
they're going to say maybe'll hurt your feelings—but that's the
way it is: mother'n daughter . . . husband'n wife . . . enemy'n
enemy . . . money'n miser . . . all those terribly important
things kind of grow pale around here. And what's left? What's
left when memory's gone, and your identity, Mrs. Smith?"

Joe Stoddard, the undertaker, has been hovering around in the
background. Sam Craig, a Grover's Corner boy back from the
West, strolls in. These two renew an old acquaintance and Sam
hears the recent town news. He has returned for the funeral of
his cousin, he explains, walking over toward the graves. He
stops before Mrs. Gibbs, staring at her knees; but seeing only
her headstone.

"Why, this is my Aunt Julia. . . . I'd forgotten that she'd
. . . of course, of course."

"Yes, Doc Gibbs lost his wife two-three years ago . . . about
this time," confirms the undertaker. "And today's another pretty
bad blow for him, too."

As Craig and Stoddard move on, the dead speak, their voices
colorless and even. . . . "That's my sister Carrie's boy, Sam,"
volunteers Mrs. Gibbs, speaking to Simon Stimson. . . . "I'm
always uncomfortable when *they're* around," answers Simon;

"they and their nonsense and their damned glee at being alive"
. . . "Simon, be patient. . . ."

It has begun to rain. . . . Shortly a funeral procession enters.
. . . "Four men carry a casket invisible to us." . . . As the
crowd gathers around the new grave the umbrellas shut the services from view. . . . Again the dead are speaking—

"Who is it, Julia?" asks Mrs. Soames.

"My daughter-in-law, Emily Webb."

"Well, I declare! The road up here must have been awful
muddy. What did she die of, Julia?"

"In childbirth."

"Childbirth. (*Almost with a laugh.*) I'd forgotten all about
that! My, wasn't life awful—(*With a sigh.*) and wonderful. . . ."

Mrs. Soames grows reminiscent. . . . She can remember
Emily's wedding . . . and how bright Emily was in school. . . .
The group at the grave is singing "Blessed be the tie that binds."
. . . The dead like that.

Now, from among the umbrellas Emily appears. "She is wearing a white dress. Her hair is down her back and tied by a
white ribbon, like a little girl." She walks slowly, wonderingly,
toward the dead. They greet her with cheerful Hellos. She sits
down next to Mrs. Gibbs.

"It seems thousands and thousands of years since I—" Emily
is saying when her attention is attracted by the mourners. "How
stupid they all look. They don't have to look like that!"

"Don't look at them now, dear. They'll be gone soon."

"Oh, I wish I'd been here a long time. I don't like being new
here."

Again she notices the funeral group. To keep her mind away
from them she talks freely to Mrs. Gibbs, telling her the news
of earth—about George and the farm. . . .

The umbrellas are leaving the stage. The funeral is over. Dr.
Gibbs has taken some of the flowers from Emily's grave and is
bringing them to Mrs. Gibbs. Emily notices the grief in his
face—

"Oh, Mother Gibbs, I never realized before how troubled and
how . . . how in the dark live persons are. From morning till
night, that's all they are—troubled. . . ."

The Stage Manager has appeared at his post, calmly smoking.
Emily is still trying to adjust her mind to the new conditions.
As she thinks of the farm she feels that she has been there, with
her baby on her lap, as plain as day—

Yes, Mrs. Gibbs tells her, she can go back if she wants to,

but it wouldn't be wise—

"When you've been here longer you'll see that our life here is our hope that we'll soon forget all that, and think only of what's ahead, and be ready for what's ahead. When you've been here longer you'll understand," explains Mrs. Gibbs.

Still, Emily is persistent. The Stage Manager and the friendly dead advise her against going back, but she will not be swayed. She will go back and live again a happy day. She chooses a birthday—her 12th birthday. And there, with the Stage Manager's help, she finds herself at early morning, with the sun just coming up. The town's the same as it was then. And the people, too. Howie Newsome. And the policeman. Constable Warren and Joe Crowell. Emily can hear them talking and what they're saying. Now Mrs. Webb has come into her kitchen to start breakfast, and is calling: "Chil-*dren!* Wally! Emily! . . . Time to get up."

Mr. Webb comes along Main Street. He is just home from making a speech at his college in New York State. No, he hasn't forgotten that this is Emily's birthday. He's got something for his birthday girl—

"I can't bear it," murmurs Emily, softly, more in wonder than in grief. "They're so young and beautiful. Why did they ever have to get old? Mamma, I'm here. I'm grown up. I love you all, everything.—I can't look at everything hard enough. There's the butternut tree. (*She wanders up Main Street.*) There's Mr. Morgan's drug store. And there's the High School, forever and ever and ever. And there's the Congregational Church where I got married. Oh, dear. Oh, dear. Oh, dear!"

The Stage Manager has called her attention to the house and to her mother. It is an eventful birthday for Emily, but just another day of work and routine for Mrs. Webb. She greets her daughter with a perfunctory kiss, wishes her many happy returns and goes on with the breakfast.

Emily would remind her mother of the fourteen years that have passed, and of all that has happened. . . . Of Wally's death. . . . And of her own death, but there is no taking Mrs. Webb's attention away from her work—

Now Emily has found her presents and thanks her mother profusely for her gift. Mrs. Webb is pleased, but too busy to show it. . . . Mr. Webb is heard approaching, but before he comes Emily has had enough of her return to life. "I can't—I can't go on," she says to the Stage Manager. "It goes so fast! We don't have time to look at one another. I didn't realize. . . . Take me back—up the hill—to my grave. . . . Do any human beings ever realize life while they live it?—every, every minute?"

"No," says the Stage Manager. "The saints and poets, maybe —they do some."

Emily is back with the dead now, satisfied to be quiet for a while. Human beings are just blind people—

"Yes, now you know," agrees Mr. Stimson. "Now you know! That's what it was to be alive. To move about in a cloud of ignorance; to go up and down trampling on the feelings of those . . . of those about you. To spend and waste time as though you had a million years. To be always at the mercy of one self-centered passion, or another. Now you know—that's the happy existence you wanted to go back and see. Did you shout to 'em? Did you call to 'em?"

"Yes, I did."

"Now you know them as they are: in ignorance and blindness."

"Simon Stimson," interjects Mrs. Gibbs, spiritedly, "that ain't the whole truth and you know it."

The dead have begun to stir restlessly. Emily's rebellious spirit is responsible for that, Mrs. Gibbs thinks. And now someone is coming into the cemetery. It is George Gibbs. He has come to Emily and his mother and stood before them for a minute. Now he has flung himself prostrate at Emily's feet. The dead murmur their disapproval. Emily looks down wonderingly at George—

"Mother Gibbs?" she murmurs.

"Yes, Emily?"

"They don't understand much, do they?"

"No, dear, not very much."

The Stage Manager starts across the stage pulling the curtain with him. A clock can be heard softly striking the hour.

"Most everybody's asleep in Grover's Corners," says the Stage Manager. "There are a few lights on: Shorty Hawkins, down at the depot, has just watched the Albany train go by. And at the livery stable somebody's setting up late and talking—Yes, it's clearing up. There are the stars—doing their old, old criss-cross journeys in the sky. Scholars haven't settled the matter yet, but they seem to think there are no living beings up there. They're just chalk . . . or fire. Only this one is straining away, straining away all the time to make something of itself. The strain's so bad that every sixteen hours everybody lies down and gets a rest. (*He winds his watch.*) Hm. . . . Eleven o'clock in Grover's Corners.—You get a good rest, too. Good night."

The lights dim slowly.

SHADOW AND SUBSTANCE

A Drama in Four Acts

By Paul Vincent Carroll

IT was late January before Paul Vincent Carroll's fine play, "Shadow and Substance," arrived. It would have been in the repertory of the Abbey Theatre Players, who first produced it in their home theatre in Dublin, if the active and ambitious Eddie Dowling had not heard of it first. Mr. Dowling, stirred to a new interest in the higher drama by his success as co-producer with Maurice Evans of "King Richard II" a year ago, had heard of the Dublin success of "Shadow and Substance" through a Dublin friend. Confirming the friend's enthusiastic report as best he could, Mr. Dowling determined to buy the American rights to the Carroll play, which he did. The Abbey Players were therefore forced to tour America with revivals from their old repertory, the while their newest and greatest play was produced by and played to the enrichment of strangers.

Playwright Carroll, who left Ireland seventeen years ago to take up teaching in Glasgow, Scotland, did his first playwriting for the Abbey Theatre and insists that, despite such offers as he may receive from either Hollywood's picture magnates or Broadway's play producers, he will remain loyal to that institution. He had previously written several short plays for the Abbey Players, one entitled "Things That Are Caesar's" creating the best impression.

Writing of the inspirations entering into the creation of "Shadow and Substance" Mr. Carroll has said: "For years I had been studying the Augustan period of English literature, and always have been fascinated by its chief character—Dean Swift. . . . I decided one day to resurrect Dean Swift, make him not only a Catholic but a learned interpreter of Catholicism, and throw him into the modern mental turmoil in Ireland, which could be complicated by contact. From him came the character of the Canon. How I came upon Brigid is a secret which I will not sell to any damned publicity hound. The cringing schoolmaster I got from a snug in an Irish country pub. The rebel schoolmaster and the Canon represent the conflicting forces that crush Brigid

87

(the spirit of the nation) between them."

"Shadow and Substance" was an immediate success in New York. On a February visit to America, made possible by that success, Mr. Carroll quite frankly admitted that his income had been increased from $37.50 a week, which is his salary as a schoolmaster, to approximately $1,000 a week, which he has received in royalties from his play.

It is midday late in January when we are let into the living room of the Very Reverend Thomas Cannon Skerritt in Ardmahone, "one of the small towns lying round the feet of Mourne, on the borders of Louth." It is a pleasant room, excellently furnished and giving evidence of the refined character of the Canon. "The one incongruous note in the harmony of the whole design is a large, gaudy oleograph of the Sacred Heart over the door."

At the moment Brigid, a servant, is showing in Dermot Francis O'Flingsley, a schoolmaster. Brigid is about 18, "small, possibly a little stupid looking, with large eyes; neat, but not to any degree Quakerish. She is obviously not mentally outstanding, but capable of deep affection and pleasing in her person." O'Flingsley is a young man, "very alert, alive and intelligent, obviously capable of feeling things acutely, and of passion and pride. He is bright in manner and has a pleasing sense of humor."

The Canon, Brigid reports, is not at home. He might be back for lunch, he said, and he mightn't. It was to Dublin he went, probably, Brigid thinks, to see one of his old Spanish friends. She would have O'Flingsley wait and make himself comfortable, though she is a bit apprehensive lest when the Canon does come the two of them will be quarreling again, as they always do.

"Isn't it funny now that I think there's no one like ayther of yous," ventures Brigid. "Would that not mean that the two of yous are maybe the one? Or am I blatherin'?"

"You certainly are blatherin'," answers O'Flingsley, with some spirit. "If you love him, you hate *me,* and if you love me, you hate *him.*"

"That's maybe the way it would show on paper, but in the mind it's not maybe as true. . . . St. Brigid wouldn't deceive me like that," says Brigid, slowly.

And this brings up a subject—and a secret—that has been an issue between them—this same belief in the frequent appearance of St. Brigid herself to the lesser Brigid of the Canon's household. It is a belief that worries O'Flingsley. He thinks Brigid should speak to the Canon about it, or the curates. But Brigid wouldn't do that.

"Sure, they'd question, and cross-question, and then make me promise never to see her again," protests Brigid. "That would be somethin' too terrible for me to bear—the same as you could bear the burn of a hot poker or of scaldin' water."

O'FLINGSLEY—Then—you *do* see her actually?

BRIGID (*rapt*)—Yes . . . often. I'm used to her now. She is always smilin', smilin' and in great humor, as if she was enjoyin' makin' me happy. It's lovely that she's not sour like a nun, at the convent school or like a priest in the box.

O'FLINGSLEY (*seriously*)—I don't want to hurt you, Brigid, but if you're a wise girl, you'll put this thing absolutely away from you. Some day, maybe she or it, whatever it is, will desert you, and you'll go crazy with despair. Are you listenin' to me?

BRIGID (*softly*)—Yes . . . but she promised . . .

O'FLINGSLEY—Supposing she's an evil thing? It could well be.

BRIGID—If she was evil, I would feel the fear in me. Doesn't God make us like that?

O'FLINGSLEY—Why don't you ask her for a proof, as I told you?

BRIGID—I did. I asked her one night to make the bed-chair move. Wasn't that what you said?

O'FLINGSLEY—And did she?

BRIGID—No . . . She just smiled, and her eyes laughed the way she was amused at me.

O'FLINGSLEY—Maybe it was at me she was amused— O'Flingsley, the idiot.

BRIGID—It was never that. She loves you too. I can see it. She told me you had a secret.

O'FLINGSLEY (*startled*)—What sort of a secret?

BRIGID—She said—a dark secret, and that you were a blunderer, but that God loved blunderers because they were the children of Peter.

O'FLINGSLEY (*concerned*)—Brigid, you dreamed this! You *did!*

BRIGID (*slowly*)—No. . . . Sure I know I didn't. . . . She told me about the Canon too.

O'FLINGSLEY—*Him?* What did she say about him?

BRIGID—She said that there was great holiness in him, but that his pride would need the tears of a hundred just men and the soul of a child, to soften it.

O'FLINGSLEY (*tensely*)—Did she say—what child?

BRIGID—She only smiled and went away.

O'Flingsley—Good God! What creature is this at all? I'm warning you, Brigid. I'm warning you, mind.

Brigid—I love her too much now to be afraid . . . (*Pause.*) *Have* you a secret?

O'Flingsley (*secretively*)—I have written a book and published it. No one knows it's mine.

Brigid—Is it a *good* book?

O'Flingsley—It might be. It's a *bitter* book.

Brigid—She will not be pleased. Why could you not make it full of love?

O'Flingsley (*tensely*)—I don't believe in love.

Brigid—St. Brigid does. She stood near me at the bed last night when the new moon was in it. I said, "There's the new moon, God bless it," and I blessed meself, and she laughed without any noise, and her eyes had the moon in them like a mirror. She stood lookin' out at the big boulders of the hills, and her speakin' low. Then she said when I came close to her that the hills were just like that long, long ago, and that they were God's hint to man to build in the heart forever and ever, instead of with stone and mortar and the pride that puts a stone on another stone without meanin'. And a lot more that the words will not come to me for. I fell asleep listenin' to her—her voice was sinkin' me all the time into sleep.

A shadow of fear crosses the young woman's features as she considers the consequences of her confession. O'Flingsley could put it in a bitter book and publish it! But O'Flingsley has no intention of doing that. He only wants to be sure that Brigid is not lying to him. He is impassioned in repeating that he thinks she should tell the Canon, and worried afresh when Brigid refuses to do so.

"Not yet," she says. "I won't be separated from her. I love her. Some day I shall come to her, she said. . . ."

O'Flingsley has gone now, leaving a sarcastic message for the Canon—asking him when the school is to have coal to heat it, and whole windows, and a roof that doesn't leak and someone beside the schoolmaster to clean it up. It won't matter if Brigid forgets to relay the message, O'Flingsley sourly admits. The Canon wouldn't pay any attention to it anyway. . . .

O'Flingsley is leaving as Thomasina Concannon bounces into the room. Thomasina is "a very 'bunty' girl of about 22, with full animal spirits, round fat face, all dimples, given to giggling laughter and eternally sucking sweetmeats." She is also the

Canon's step-niece, it develops, a schoolteacher who has recently finished her course and has been doing substitute work. She has come to see the Canon about a place, which O'Flingsley realizes with no slight horror is that of his assistant.

Brigid's hurried return to report the Canon home on the train, and stopped in the postoffice to write a postcard, excites Thomasina. She had decided to sleep in the Canon's bed the night before and she suddenly remembers that she had left a copy of *Love's Purple Passions* under his pillow. . . .

The approach of Canon Skerritt is attended by considerable excitement. Brigid is nervously anxious for fear the room will not be just as it should be and the table laid just as the Canon expects it to be laid.

The curates, Father Kirwan and Father Corr, who apparently grow a little slack in the matter of their routines when the Canon is not in residence, are brought up smartly with the announcement of the arrival. Corr "is a young man, small and round-shouldered, with a face easily affected by fervor or sentiment." Kirwan "is athletic, good-humored and well meaning." Kirwan is the less serious of the two, and given to making covert sport of the Canon behind that worthy's back. It is Kirwan who is the more worried of the two at the moment. Not only has he parked a somewhat disreputable motor car at the gate, which he realizes is likely to distress the Canon, but he is also unshaven. For that offense he has been spoken to before. . . .

The curates have left when Canon Thomas Skerritt enters the room. He is a man "finely built, but a little too full in the stomach, fine face, but a little too red. His eyes are vividly living always, and at times his whole being concentrates in them. He has a perfect bow, his voice is cultured, he can be very charming and courteous, can quickly adapt himself to suit people, and has a kingly walk and dignity. He is excellently dressed. He is wearing a tall silk hat, and carries an umbrella." The Canon's greeting of Brigid is austere but friendly. He is pleased to report a pleasant week-end with his friend, Don Miguel Barzan y Perdito, to whom he had mentioned Brigid.

"I said to Don Miguel, 'My truest friend in this fallen land is Brigid,' " the Canon reports. To which Don Miguel had smiled and replied: "Where we have truth we have God."

The Canon is quite distressed at the news of his niece's arrival, and Brigid is moved to warn him, as his irritation mounts, that he should be careful not to make himself ill again.

"You are wise, child. I forget myself. I always forget myself in the face of this recurring decimal of relationship. (*Holding* BRIGID's *arm.*) Consider, Brigid! My name—grave and classical —purloined—that's the word for it—to gain a—nomenclature for a human dumpling who reeks eternally of peppermints."

BRIGID—Sure, you're angerin' yourself, Canon. Sure, maybe if she got married, it would settle her down, and you wouldn't be pestered with her no more.

CANON—There is wisdom there, Brigid. I will consider that. I shall turn that over carefully.

BRIGID—Sure, I try to help ye, Canon.

CANON—As you say, Brigid, you try to help me, and as I say, there is wisdom in you. Let it be written of you, Brigid. You are a good child—an excellent child. Go, Brigid!

BRIGID (*going*)—Yis, Canon.

CANON—Wait, Brigid. Where did she stay last night?

BRIGID (*in fear*)—She—she said the spare room was draughty and there was a mouse in the wardrobe, and she—she—

CANON—She what?

BRIGID—She took *your* room, Canon.

CANON (*fuming*)—Eh? She—she what? Brigid! I am incensed beyond words. You are arraigned! You are in the dock!

BRIGID—But I could do nothin', Canon. Says she to me, "I'm the Canon's niece, and the place for his servant is at me footstool."

CANON—The Canon's niece! That Irish matrimonial luggage label! That ecclesiastical buckle on a female shoe! Go, Brigid! Restore my room to its—austerity.

BRIGID—Yis, Canon. Sure it'll be lovely and grand for you now, if you'll not be vexin' yourself.

CANON (*softening*)—There, child, I do not blame you. We are thwarted. We shall die outwitted by boobs and idiots. Mark it, Brigid, mark it! Go, Brigid!

The Canon's meeting with Thomasina is less than enthusiastic. He manages, by blowing his nose with one hand and holding the other up defensively, to escape her embrace, but he has considerable difficulty thereafter pretending that he is glad to see her. Thomasina has come with the endorsement of her parish priest and the complete confidence of her mother to ask her uncle to appoint her to a vacancy in his school—

"Your mother, my dear, I regret to say, is, and has ever been, a woman bereft—that's the word, bereft—of one iota of sound

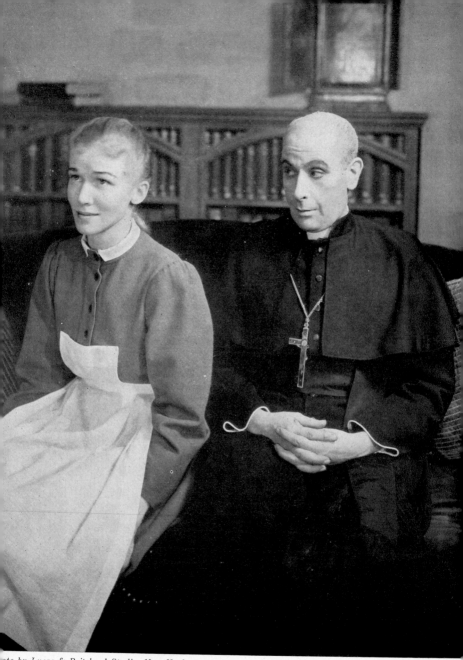

"SHADOW AND SUBSTANCE"

Canon: If it is a matter of your soul, Brigid, I must know it.
Brigid: Please, Canon, not—not now. I'll tell you when I'm able. I—I don't want it taken
ay from—from me yet.

(*Julie Haydon, Sir Cedric Hardwicke*)

sense or dignity. The fact burns me. But it is—irrefutable."

"Sure, maybe you're right, Uncle. The talk and blatherin' of her—you'd think I had no name o' me own—I'm the Canon's niece to everyone we meet."

"I am well aware of it. But it is a national disease, and I am no surgeon. You must leave me now, and I shall let you know in a few days about the school."

Employing a deft persistence the Canon is finally able to get Thomasina started for her bus, but not without her excited assurance that she will be back. They have gone out together when Brigid summons Father Corr and Father Kirwan to lunch. The young men are free in their hope that the food will be to their liking for a change, but Brigid can promise no more than another Spanish dish such as the Canon likes.

"I wish to God I could get a transfer to some old P.P. that loves cabbage and eats peas with his knife, and snores after his dinner," explodes Father Kirwan.

The Canon enters with dignity. The curates rise in their places at the luncheon table. The greetings are formal. They have quietly said grace when the Canon begins, with great suavity, to call certain lapses to the attention of his assistants.

He would know who owns the motor car at the gate and when they admit joint ownership, he would know if they consider the possession of it necessary. When they would justify the car on the ground that it contributes to the comfort of their job he is not particularly pleased, but is willing to admit that there is no law against "owner-driver clerics."

Now the Canon has caught sight of a copy of the Ballyelphinstown *Courier* protruding from the pocket of Father Kirwan's coat and is distressed that the curate should permit the exhibit to detract from the dignity of his person.

"There's a very strong leader in it this week, Canon, on that outrageous book that is just after comin' out," explains Father Kirwan in justification of his carrying the paper. "It's called *I Am Sir Oracle.*"

"I was just goin' to mention that, Canon," puts in Father Corr. "It's a very grave matter altogether, and I think it calls for action. The people's demandin' it."

"They say, Canon, the author is a schoolmaster with a spite agin the local P.P. He calls himself Eugene Gibney."

"Are *you* prepared to take anny action, Canon?"

"There is no such word as 'anny,' except of course the female appellation, and the verb agrees with its subject, always—even in

Ireland," acidly replies the Canon.

Now Brigid would serve the coffee (with both curates preferring tea instead), to the quite evident disgust of their superior, and the Canon has asked that a special bottle marked "Vino de Amontillado" be brought to him from the locked cupboard under the bookshelves.

"Are you having a little wine, Fathers?" the Canon asks, solicitously.

"I'll take a thimbleful, Canon," Father Corr replies modestly.

"And I, too, thanks," adds Father Kirwan, as Brigid brings a small flagon of rich golden wine, expensively wrapped, from the cupboard.

"I'm afraid there are no thimbles reasonably convenient, Father," the Canon is saying. "Better take a wineglassful. You may bring Fathers Corr and Kirwan the bottle of Empire wine that's on the left-hand side," he adds to Brigid.

"Is it the one, Canon, that Martin Reilly sent up last Christmas for a present?"

"Precisely, Brigid. (*Ironically.*) It should be considerably matured by this."

They have returned to a discussion of the outrageous book. The curates report their entire sympathy with those incensed citizens who would like to see it burned in every market square in Ireland.

"And on what grounds are we to have this extensive series of rural bonfires?" demands the Canon.

"Why, the whole book is a dastardly attack on the Catholicism of Ireland, Canon!" protests Father Corr, heatedly.

"Grave news surely out of Bally—Ballyeffelstown," calmly admits the Canon, looking appreciatively at his bubbling wine. "A seamew blunders against a lighthouse and the keeper sends up distress rockets. (*With suave irony.*) Your health, Fathers."

The curates repeat their sympathy with those who would hang the author of *I Am Sir Oracle,* or at least burn his work in public, but the Canon is not impressed. He would, however, call their attention to one or two other things that are on his mind.

"Father Corr, I am given to understand that since your arrival here you have attained quite an inordinate amount of popularity mixed with a particularly abhorrent form of sentimentality, and that this copious bathing—shall we say—springs from your antics with bouncing babies, and such like, the prescribing of cures for old ladies' rheumatics and for carious diseases in horses and cows. I suggest to you, that since Catholicism rests on a classical, almost abstract, love of God, rather than on the frothy swirl of stirred emotionalism that these popular heroics of yours are not, canonically speaking, the duties of a Catholic curate."

FATHER CORR (*blushing and abashed*)—I—I was only tryin' to be kind, Canon.

CANON—*I* call it hunting after popular glory—an Irish clerical disease.

FATHER CORR (*rising with fire*)—I'm a farmer's son, Canon, and I'm not ashamed of it.

CANON—I am not interested in your antecedents. I am interested instead in the behavior of my curate. You may be seated. (FATHER CORR *sits down, crushed.* FATHER KIRWAN *shifts uneasily in his seat, with one eye on the* CANON *who presently regards him with calm brutality.*)

CANON (*with slight cough*)—Father Kirwan, may I ask if it is the custom in *your* part of the country for the curate to don football-regalia, and er—kick ball?

FATHER KIRWAN—Sure it's quite common down in Ballyedminstown, Canon. The curate in me father's place is a very noted center-half.

CANON (*cruelly, leading him on, hand to ear*)—I—I didn't quite catch that word, Father Kirwan. Center—what?

FATHER KIRWAN—Center-half, Canon. The fellow, Canon, that the team most depends on when the enemy makes an onslaught.

CANON (*suavely*)—Incongruous as it may seem, Father Kirwan, it is *not* the custom here for the curate to be the fellow that —er—does what you say he does.

FATHER KIRWAN—But you misunderstand me, Canon. I strip and play with the men to entice them all into the Sacred Heart Confraternity. Sure, Canon, that's a grand motive for a grand end!

CANON—I see . . . And since when has the Sacred Heart of our Redeemer, that kings and emperors and queens like Violanti and Don John of Austria and the great Charles V, and the soldier Ignatius, walked barefooted for the love of—since when has it become a sort of snap door chamber where dolts and boobs come to—to kick ball and find themselves tripped up on an altar step instead of a goal post?

FATHER KIRWAN (*aghast*)—I—I never looked at it that way, Canon. Doesn't it justify itself if it brings people to the Sacred Heart?

CANON—Am I justified then, in staging amateur theatricals on
the high altar to coax boobs along the Latin way of salvation?
(*There are awesome ejaculations from the two curates.*)

FATHER KIRWAN and FATHER CORR—God forbid, Canon!
There is no comparison, surely.

CANON—To my thinking, there is a parallel. As a consequence,
Brigid will be instructed that—er—football regalia is barred from
the parochial clothes line.

FATHER KIRWAN—As you wish, Canon.

CANON—There is just one other matter. Is it the custom also
in Bally—Bally—eskerstown, to sit down to lunch unshaven?

FATHER KIRWAN—I'm afraid it's not, Canon.

CANON—Interesting to compare the topographical similarities.
It is *not* the custom in *this* part of the country either.

The luncheon is finished. The Canon has risen and the curates
have followed his example. Suddenly the Canon's eye alights
upon the gaudy German oleograph of the Sacred Heart. He is
completely astounded. What is this "nightmarish conception of
some uncouth vulgarian?" Where did it come from? And when
he learns that the picture had been presented to his curates by
the Woman's Confraternity he still can see no reason why he
should have to suffer its presence. Brigid is quite worried by the
Canon's irritation. Perhaps he isn't well again.

"I was just followin' the pious custom, Canon, of havin' colored
pictures of religious subjects near us to give a feeling of sanctity,"
explains Father Corr, in an effort to justify the hanging of the
Sacred Heart.

"A feeling of sanctity from that!" explodes the Canon. And
then he adds, with great quietness: "I am a man, Fathers, who
by study, travel and observation, has seen the decline and decay
of the great classic ideals and the steady vulgarization of our life
by that tributaried stream of barbarians who have taken all that
was royal in conception, and given nothing but their vulgar deluge in return. Their achievement is the Nordic civilization, in
which the passport to fame is financial scoundrelism, and the
scholar of taste is ever the avowed 'enemy of the people.' They
have vulgarized our reading, our music, our art, our very privacy.
They have thrust books into the hands of herds who are forever
misreading them; they have reduced us all to the lowest social
class by teaching us how to get from excess the same emotionalism that classicist used to get from music and art; they have
taken away our aesthetic sense and given us in exchange a rather

spurious ethical sense, and as you can see here—(*He points to picture.*)—they deal with a whitewash brush in terms of the divine. Yet you stand aghast when I point it out to you—when I refuse to allow barbarians to impose on me their vulgar conception of Christ and His Saints. If, for a moment, I felt our Redeemer's heart was akin to that monstrosity on the wall, I should go back to Socrates, and be a pagan."

There is some little suggestion of comfort for Canon Skerritt in the presence of Brigid. She, at least, is clean and simple; she is one in a wilderness of "knaves, fools, spirit-grocers and their women, clerical football-kickers, palavering C.C.'s and only one scoundrel." All about them is the very smell of vulgarity. Brigid thinks that perhaps if she were to open the window—

"You are the Canon's friend, Brigid," the Canon is saying.

"Yis, Canon. Thank you, Canon." She is looking at him timidly. "Can—can I speak to you, Canon?"

"You can always speak to me, Brigid. It is your privilege."

But now Brigid cannot say what she was going to say. A great fear assails her and she draws back. The Canon is firm in his command that she shall tell him what is troubling her, and as his insistence mounts her own fear grows.

"If it is a matter of your soul, Brigid, I must know it," firmly insists the Canon.

"Please, Canon, not—not now. I'll tell you when I'm able. I—I don't want it taken away from—from me yet," protests the unhappy Brigid.

CANON (*rising*)—This is a serious matter, Brigid. I insist. The Canon insists.

BRIGID (*hands to face*)—N-no, Canon. I want it. I want it.

CANON—Did I say that I insist, Brigid?

BRIGID (*backing against the wall*)—Not for a while yet, Canon. Not—not now.

CANON (*coming to her*)—I will dismiss you, Brigid, for this disobedience.

BRIGID (*hands to face, back to wall*)—Yis, Canon.

CANON—I will cast you down—down!

BRIGID (*pathetically*)—Yis, Canon.

CANON—You will be the Canon's friend no longer.

BRIGID—Yis, Canon.

CANON—You will tell me then?

BRIGID—N-no, Canon.

CANON—You will suffer all these things?

BRIGID—Yis, Canon.

CANON (*terribly*)—The Canon commands it.

BRIGID—N-no, no, Canon. N-no. I—I couldn't. Not—now . . .

CANON—Put down those hands and look at me. (*She puts down her hands. Head is held up, but tears in her eyes. She is firmly against the wall like one at bay. An incongruous pride sits upon her. The* CANON *observes her strangely, as if deeply moved at a discovery.*)

CANON—You defy me!

BRIGID—N-no, Canon.

CANON—But you—refuse to tell me!

BRIGID (*pathetically but proudly*)—Y-yis, Canon. (*Long pause. He stands watching her as if fascinated.*)

CANON (*as if to himself*)—My God, my God, that—that is what we have come from . . . pride . . . loyalty . . . a classic race . . . a royal conception . . . A thousand years ago, someone with that brow and face held up His head and died like a prince. . . . It was that . . . (*He stares at her, his face working visibly.*) Come here to me, Brigid.

BRIGID (*as she comes slowly and looks humbly up at him*)—Yis, Canon.

CANON—I shall ask you—nothing.

BRIGID—Th-thank you, Canon. (*She looks gratefully at him.*)

CANON (*slowly*)—You are the Canon's friend, Brigid. Let it be written of you. Let it be written of both of us. (*They are looking at each other, the* CANON *with deep emotions stirred, and* BRIGID *with the tears glistening in her eyes, as the curtain falls.*)

ACT II

The following day the Canon is discovered in his living room reading "the castigated novel," *I Am Sir Oracle,* the while he sips occasionally from a glass of wine. The picture of the Sacred Heart has been removed.

Presently Brigid comes to remind the Canon that Miss Jemima Cooney and her nephew, Francis Xavier O'Connor, are still in the waiting room, and have been there, off and on, the better part of the day. The Canon would have them continue waiting—or go away and come again tomorrow, but he gives way finally before the gentle but firm insistence of Brigid, who would also be rid of the visitors for her own peace of mind. The Canon can be rid of them in a minute "with a grand word and a clap on the back," Brigid points out.

"Excellent, Brigid," agrees the Canon. "An answer and a suggestion at once plausible and philosophic. The Canon, Brigid—the Canon shall do exactly as you say."

And so the callers are brought in. "Jemima is a thin, gaunt spinster, secretly vicious but very virtuous before the Canon." Francis "is a sheepish, obsequious youth, his whole being in the grip of an inferiority complex."

Jemima and Francis approach the Canon with elaborate obsequiousness, scraping and bowing and protesting their reluctance to disturb him. The Canon receives them with a dignity that thinly veils his contempt and a certain "scoundrel grace." Francis has brought, and exhibits with a pride that almost equals that of his beaming aunt, the teacher's certificate he has just been given. It is Francis' hope, and that of Miss Cooney, that the Canon will do all he can about placing Francis in the school. The Canon would remind Francis that such a request is quite superfluous. Is it not written in the Penny Catechism that we must all of us come to the aid of each other?

The Canon is very sympathetic. He is pleased with the picture that Aunt Jemima has taken of Francis in Dublin, showing the boy posed in proud possession of his certificate, and with the prayer book given him by the Canon plainly visible in his waistcoat pocket. The Canon is sure that Francis' mother was a very, very good woman. But—about the school—Francis will have to be a little patient.

"We must *all* be a little patient," warns the Canon. "Your Aunt Jemima with her invaluable experience of life, as we live it, and of the—the idiosyncrasies of our checkered existence, will have impressed *that* upon you, I feel sure."

"Sure, Lord, Canon, isn't it all now in the will o' God!" agrees Jemima.

It is, as Miss Cooney so wisely puts it, in the will of God. And now (Brigid having popped in to announce another caller) now the Canon hopes to have news for Francis very shortly. He should keep within easy call and employ his waiting time properly.

"Indeed, Canon, he'll spend his time of waitin' your command in makin' a novena," promises Miss Cooney.

The knowing Brigid has come to raise the window after Francis and his aunt have left, and the Canon is grateful for the child's understanding. She must never think of leaving him. But, it seems, Brigid has been thinking quite seriously of that very thing.

She has been happy with the Canon, but she may be wanting to go away for a little while.

The Canon is quite disturbed by the news. What Brigid needs is a good rest. She has been working much too hard. Let her know, too, that when he dies she is to have every penny that he leaves. Let her consider that.

But Brigid will not need money where she is going. Brigid has quite made up her mind that she wants to be a nun. If he was disturbed before, the Canon is quite flabbergasted at this announcement. "You—you want to be a nun, eh?" he repeats. "My God, am I not sufficiently stocked with boobs that *you*, Brigid, *you* must add the final straw."

"You're vexed with me, Canon."

"Displeased, Brigid. . . . Displeased that you would go and leave me here alone. And you my friend! You the—the Canon's friend."

"It's not just *you*, Canon, but everythin' I'd be leavin'."

"Brigid, you have been doing too much lately, and you are overwrought. Excess in anything is bad, Brigid—in work, in play, in religion—it is not—classical. I am going to send you away for a holiday. And you must have a new hat too—a new hat with—with a feather in it. There now!"

Brigid is pleased at the suggestion of a new hat, but she would politely remind the Canon that they are not wearing feathers any more. Which is news to the Canon. Brigid shall have whatever it is they are wearing, even to "a white dog and a nose veil," if she wants them. And she shall have a "fit-on" to make sure the hat will be the right size.

"There now, you've forgotten already," concludes the Canon, greatly relieved as he notes the smile on Brigid's face. "When you get your holiday you will be again classically simple and quiescent."

The Canon has sent Brigid for the Baptismal Registers. While she is gone he picks up the copy of *I Am Sir Oracle* that he has been reading and turns to a chapter near the end of the book. He reads a passage aloud—

" 'The Canon lay dying. The mists came white and wraith-like from the bogs to tell him so . . .' (*Puts down book.*) Not a bit. On the contrary, the Canon feels well—feels in fact very well. (*As* BRIGID *comes in and hands him Register.*) It may interest you to know, Brigid, that the Canon feels—excellently." (*He smiles sardonically.*)

"Sure, thanks be to God, Canon," adds Brigid.

The Canon runs his eye down the alphabetical lists of registered births. Mallin and Melling, O'Brien and O'Connell, etc., until he comes shortly to O'Flingsley. "June 8, 1908, Dermot Francis O'Flingsley."

"Is that the Master's birthday, Canon?" asks Brigid.

"That's it, Brigid," the Canon replies, gleefully, as he reads on. His father's name was Francis Eugene O'Flingsley. Mark the princely name, Eugene. Ah, and his mother bore the—storied name of Gibney. Could you credit that now? . . . Incomprehensible in fact. . . . Let me introduce you, Brigid, to Mr. Eugene Gibney—er—author, amateur theologian, Catholic reformer, public moralist, student of Northern apologetics, erstwhile schoolmaster, ex-peasant and—gentleman."

"What does that mean, Canon?"

"To you, Brigid, it shall mean—*nothing*. Put that Register back, Brigid, and not a word to anyone."

The Canon requests that Brigid send word to O'Flingsley that he would like to see him in the morning. Brigid, nearly in tears at the thought of her Master's being in trouble, says nothing. . . .

Now Father Corr and Father Kirwan are there to request a word with the Canon. Their mission is also concerned with the scurrilous book. The Confraternity, they report, has passed a resolution and the members of the football club are greatly excited.

"No doubt it's the warm weather," calmly suggests the Canon. "And I note you haven't as yet found time, even between resolutions, to shave."

The Canon has left the curates standing perplexed in the center of the room. They are frankly disgusted. There's little Irish blood in the Canon's veins, Father Kirwan is convinced of that. It's a pity that his Spanish mother had not stayed at home in place of gallivanting about the continent to meet his Irish father finally in Brussels.

They compare notes of their contact with the parishioners. There are some who want to burn it publicly and insist the Canon is the one to do the casting into the flames. Now they have found the opened copy of the vile book and are certain the Canon must have been reading it.

Father Corr throws *I Am Sir Oracle* venomously on the ground. Father Kirwan "dribbles" it across the room, getting it in position for a vigorous kick. Now he sends it crashing against the door just as the Canon comes through.

"I suppose I am to regard this outbreak of hooliganism in my study as a typical spasm of—Catholic action," observes the Canon, as he waits patiently for the reluctant Father Corr to pick up the book and hand it to him. Nor is he further impressed by their reports of the growing intensity of the press attack against the book—including an editorial in the Irish Press and the re-printing of columns of the contents in the Ballyedminstown *Courier.* . . .

He agrees, however, at their continued urging, to talk with a delegation of incensed citizens. He will, largely to please Brigid, give them another clap on the back and a grand word.

The delegation is composed of Jemima Cooney and her nephew, Francis, Martin Mullahone, referee of the football team and keeper of a public house on the Dublin road, and his wife, Rosey Violet. The Canon recalls Rosey Violet as being neither rosey nor a violet, but lets that pass.

He is seated at his desk in solemn majesty when the delegation is shown in by Brigid. Miss Cooney and Francis are as obse-quious as before. Mr. Mullahone "is a large, awkward man, with a large stomach and a red nose." Rosey Violet "is typical in dress and voice of the 'social status' aspirants in rural Ireland."

The Canon, surveying them pitilessly with a sardonic eye, would call attention to Martin Mullahone's shiftless slouch, with his hands in his pockets. He would have them all sit erect and not loll. "Decorum and personal dignity are not by any means the least of the Christian virtues," he reminds them.

He would know then what has suggested their coming to pro-test against this certain book which, Mr. Mullahone assures him, is a "terror and a fright to the world." Rosey Violet has come because she agrees with what Father Kirwan had said when he thumped the table at the meetin' of the Football Club. Her son, she would have the Canon know, is the fullback of the team.

Miss Cooney has been moved to come because Father Corr had told her it was her duty to God and Ireland. Francis would re-peat his aunt's feeling of loyalty in Irish, but more than that will not venture an opinion. It is only the Canon's right to express an opinion, says Francis. Rosey Violet would offer the further endorsement of her brother, Father Jamsie of Dunaree. Which brings on something of a Mullahone altercation, seeing that Mr. Mullahone resents Mrs. Mullahone's continual bargin' in with Father Jamsie, just because he is her brother.

"How many of you have read this book?" suddenly demands the Canon. There are negative murmurs and a general shaking of heads.

"Not a one, Canon."

"And you come here to condemn a book you have not read! What nonsense is this?" The Canon taps his desk. "Preposterous and ridiculous. The deputation is dismissed."

Before Canon Skerritt can rise Father Corr has jumped to his feet, only to be ordered back into his chair. Francis has also indicated a desire to protest, but his aunt hurls him down without ceremony. It is Francis the Canon chooses to hear. Francis would like to admit that, as a certified teacher, he had read the book "judiciously." At least he had read parts of it, and when he came to such sections as threatened to get bad he skipped.

With Francis' admission before her, Jemima is moved to confess that she, too, has read parts of the book and turned down certain pages she thought Francis should know about in his study. Mr. Mullahone admits that, while he cannot read, he had listened to Joey Hardy read bits of it in the bike shop on Friday—

CANON (*rounding on them*)—I am to take it then that four of my parishioners, deliberately—I might even say, wantonly—and without right or lawful authority from me either in person or by proxy, committed themselves to the reading of a book gravely alleged to be pernicious, immoral and—subversive. (*He sizes up the four, severely.*) Of these, one is the sister of a priest, (ROSEY VIOLET *sobs.*) another presumptuously aspires to the position of teacher of the young, (JEMIMA *gives* FRANCIS *a vicious elbow dig in the ribs.*) a third is or should be a father and a husband, (MARTIN *sags visibly.*) and a fourth—(JEMIMA *bows her head and sniffs.*)—I can find no words to castigate the curiosity that tempted the fourth to this grave indiscretion. (*He rings the bell.*) I shall deliver my directions to the two Fathers here who will communicate them to you for your unswerving acceptance. You will leave immediately. I shall contemplate whether it is humanly possible to pardon any or all of you. (CANON *rises, as* BRIGID *appears. The deputation also rises. The* CANON *waves. They go out in confusion following* BRIGID. *The two curates turn nervously to the* CANON. *Curtly.*) Be seated. (*They sit.* CANON *resumes his seat.*) I may take it, I suppose, that you two have also presumed to read this book.

FATHER CORR—I frankly considered it my duty, Canon.

FATHER KIRWAN—So did I, Canon.

CANON—Bad theology, Fathers, bad theology. And equally bad theology of course to have any—er—unofficial conflagrations on the public street without my express approval. (*Pause.*) The

author of this book which I have read, Fathers, is obviously a
very young man. I fear his education cannot be more—adequate
than that of the average young man of the present, either lay
or—er—clerical. (*He coughs.*) The theme I take to mean that
Ireland has dangerously materialized the outlook of the Church,
and that its profound spiritual essence has been stolen by a small
band of learned men whom it does not even recognize. A dangerous theme, Fathers, I grant you.

FATHER CORR (*blazing out*)—A blasphemous lie on Catholic
Ireland!

CANON (*calmly*)—A theme, Fathers, that in the hands of an
abler controversialist with a claim to scholarship or a classic status, might possibly cause alarm amongst us, especially when we
have presently no known Irish Catholic scholar with that delicacy
of touch, subtlety of culture and profundity of classical knowledge
to defend and even rescue the Church intellectually. Coming in
contact with such an immaturity as this the insufficiently schol-
ared mind, fed mostly on sentimentalisms in the form of learning,
is often shocked, and—vulgarly agitated. Violent emotionalism
results, followed by a quite ridiculous hubbub, tawdry heroics,
even bigoted physical violence under holy names, and generally a
quite ludicrous procedure that the classic dignity of the mind of
the Church recoils from. As I have no desire, Fathers, to make
a presumptuous young man bogusly important in an age that is
itself bogusly important, or to condone a procedure too undignified to be Catholic, I therefore decree that no action of any sort
be taken in the case of this book, except such action as I, in my
official capacity, shall think fit to perform. (*Pause.*) That, I
think, Fathers, will be all.

FATHER CORR (*livid*)—Are we then actually to take it that our
efforts to deal with this disgraceful libel are banned?

CANON—You are!

FATHER KIRWAN (*touching* FATHER CORR, *as he is about to
burst out*)—That's enough now. You'll only be sayin' things
you'll be sorry for.

FATHER CORR (*in a temper*)—I'll say what I like.

FATHER KIRWAN—Now can't you see that's wild talk?

FATHER CORR (*cooling*)—I suppose it is. But he's never done
belittlin' and humblin' me. But I'll try not to mind. It's in my
nature to be humble.

CANON—Inoculated would be a better word. Inoculated with
the prevalent deluge of sentimentalism.

FATHER CORR—I'm afraid, Canon, there's nothin' for me to do

but ask the Bishop for a shift and to give my reasons.

CANON—And in spite of your impertinences, Father, I shall be prepared to give his Grace an—adequate report on your work. (FATHER CORR *abruptly leaves the room, left. The* CANON *looks after him quietly and then turns to* FATHER KIRWAN.) And you, Father Kirwan? Are you also going to the Bishop?

FATHER KIRWAN (*confused, and crossing*)—I'm goin' for a— for a shave, Canon.

CANON—Dear me! We—progress!

Dusk is falling. The Canon has settled into an arm chair and is preparing for an evening of reading when suddenly Brigid rushes in with a cry. Brigid is greatly frightened, but the presence of the Canon reassures her. She also is greatly troubled in mind. She would be assured that the Canon does really love St. Brigid, because when she was drying the dishes the Saint had appeared to her and told her to ask the Canon if he loved her (St. Brigid) more than he did the rest.

    "Brigid, you are, I fear, stubborn, disobedient and even defiant, and—I am seriously annoyed and displeased with you," says the Canon, gravely.

"I—I knew you would, Canon."

"If you were a boob, Brigid, or a footling trifler, I should expel you from my presence. But you are my friend, and I try to bear with you."

"Yis, Canon."

"I have borne all day with fools, Brigid, knowing that at the end you would come to me, and ask my wants and find no fault in me. There now. You see how it is with me."

"Yis, Canon," agreed Brigid, sadly. "I'm a wretch and a villain."

"On the contrary, child, you are a good girl, and you have wisdom and grace. God, Brigid, is not *always* pleased with girls who want to be nuns. Sometimes He expects them to remain at their posts as His soldiers."

"If only I could just be a nun instead of a soldier! Soldiers make so much noise."

That Brigid's nerves are shaken the Canon is convinced. She must go away on Friday for a holiday. Right now she must go to bed and get plenty of sleep and rest. "Rest to the body, Brigid, is like prayer to the soul," the Canon reminds her. Soon she will forget her imaginings.

But Brigid cannot forget. Not in bed. It is then that St.

Brigid comes to her—"her face is there in the curtains, and the mark on her cheek where she struck the loveliness out of her face."

There is no historical authority for the St. Brigid legend, the Canon irascibly reminds her. It is probably a myth. And who should know better, he or she? The Canon knows better, Brigid weakly agrees.

"Well, now, I say this thing you foolishly think you see is not— not of God. Dismiss it!" demands the Canon.

"Canon! . . . Oh, Canon! . . . how—how could you be sayin' that?" cries the unhappy Brigid, her head in her hands.

CANON (*sympathetically*)—There, there! God tempts most those whom He loves best. You should be proud. The soul's great battles are not fought by common boobs. The great Ignatius was tempted like this, and so were Theresa and Augustine and Dominic, but they were not deceived. They rose up and conquered the tempter. So must you conquer this, Brigid.

BRIGID (*tearfully*)—So must you conquer this, Brigid.

CANON—Not more beautiful, Brigid, than the demon that twisted himself around the crucifix St. Ignatius prayed before. He had to lie on his face to save himself. You too, Brigid, must turn away from this thing you think you see. You must be wise. Wise, Brigid, and brave. Promise me, Brigid.

BRIGID (*sobbing*)—I want to die, Canon. . . . I want to—to die. . . .

CANON (*softly*)—Come now, Brigid. That is not being brave! That is being merely heroic, like these modern vulgarians. Say, Brigid, "I want to live and conquer." (*She is silent.*) Say it, Brigid. Be proud like a soldier and say it.

BRIGID (*sadly*)—I want to live and—conquer. . . .

CANON (*clapping her on back*)—Ah, Brigid, excellent! Go now, Brigid, to bed and sleep. And none of these dreams, remember, or foolishness. To sleep is safe, to dream is dangerous. I shall go out and send Dave Dooley for Miss Cooney to take your place.

BRIGID (*emotionally*)—Yis, Canon. (*He crosses to window, opens it and passes out, into the garden.*)

CANON'S VOICE (*without*)—Dooley! Are you there! Come here, Dooley! (BRIGID's *emotional stress now visibly shakes her, as she stands undecided and forlorn in the deepening shadows. She sobs pathetically, her head down, like a child. She gives the impression of having lost someone very beloved. She lifts her head suddenly, and stares stealthily over her own shoulders at the slightly swaying curtains, that reach to the ground. Her body shudders, and she covers her face with her hands.*)

BRIGID (*sobbing*)—I'm not to look at you. . . . I—I promised him. . . . I'm not to see your face. . . . No, no. I—I mustn't. . . . I daren't. . . . I must keep my eyes covered from you. . . . I must be—be wise and brave . . . I must sleep but not dream . . . but I—I . . . (*She draws her hands from her eyes, shakingly, stretches out her two arms to the curtains, and with a sob, rushes to them as to a loved one.*) But I—I love you. . . . I love you. . . . I love you . . . (*Her face is buried sobbingly in the great curtains, and her arms are about them pathetically, as the curtain falls slowly.*)

ACT III

A few days later the Canon is finishing breakfast. An early caller is Father Corr, who has come to examine a Register of Births in the book case above the writing desk. Jemima, having taken Brigid's place temporarily, is fussing about with extravagant solicitude for the comfort and the approval of the Canon.

Brigid, Jemima reports, has had a fairly good night. "A wee bit feverish, maybe, and her eyes are shinyish, but the doctor says it is nothing to worry about."

"As a good woman, Miss Cooney, what do you think yourself?" the Canon would know.

"Sure, I'd say, Canon, I'd say nothin' much," answers Jemima, squirming a little under his gaze. "I'd put it down, if you'd allow me, Canon, to what—what she came from. Her mother, Canon, was none too strong—(*Hoarsely.*) in the mind, I mean, Canon. They had to—remove her in the end."

"Remove her? Enlarge on that, Miss Cooney."

"Sure—take her away, Canon: to—to Dublin, I mean. It was before your time, sure."

"Ah! . . . And her father?"

"Sure they say, Canon, he didn't die a Christian death in Scotland. But sure God's good, Canon."

"As you say, Miss Cooney, God is good."

Jemima is dismissed with a reminder that she is to give Brigid very careful attention and the Canon turns to Father Corr. The father had heard Brigid's confession that morning, and had, by instruction, been particularly firm about those matters of which the Canon had spoken. He is, however, a little doubtful in his own mind. Does the Canon know that Brigid was born on Feb. the first, nearly twenty-one years ago? Which is St. Brigid's day. The coincidence, as the Canon calls it, has given Father Corr cause for reflection.

"The danger with you, Father Corr, is that some trivial happening is always liable to hurl you headlong into violent emotionalism," declares the Canon.

FATHER CORR—Sure, I'm doin' nothin' violent, Canon—I'm as calm as any priest could be. I'm only just quietly turnin' over a few things in my mind, such as, for instance, the fact that Brigid was born on St. Brigid's day, and that St. Brigid lived and worked in this very locality here in Fanghart.

CANON—I dislike your attitude. If a leaf turns unaccountably in these credulous days ten thousand ferrety nonentities cock their ears and gibber.

FATHER CORR—Suppose, Canon, that Brigid—*did* see this— well, this vision?

CANON—If Brigid saw ten thousand visions, our attitude to the accumulated wisdom of the Church should be unaltered. I wish you, in particular, and this country in general, could digest just *that* much, and cease chasing emotional red-herrings. (*Pause.* FATHER CORR *shifts uneasily.*)

FATHER CORR—With all respect to you, Canon, I don't think you understand this country.

CANON (*acidly*)—I understand the mind of the universal Church, and that alone concerns me. (*Pause.*) Besides, didn't you hear Miss Cooney just now on the matter of Brigid's antecedents?

FATHER CORR—That might mean nothing.

CANON—It generally means everything. But you *will* strain after miracles, in spite of my previous observations. One can conceivably understand her father dying an unchristian death in a barbarous nation like Scotland, but there is no escaping the significance of the fact that her mother was—removed, as Miss Cooney so Celtically phrased it.

FATHER CORR—That may be, Canon. What worries me, is her insistence that she saw the face and eyes of the Saint. Poor Brigid is not a liar.

CANON—Brigid, as you observe, is not a liar. But the reflections, Father, in an unstable mind are not—shall we say—theologically significant? (*As* JEMIMA *enters.*) Let us dismiss the subject.

Francis O'Connor has come for news, but the Canon has none for him—none that might be considered good. And yet— The Canon finds himself in an awkward position. There is, of course, his niece, Thomasina Concannon, whom Francis has had the honor of meeting on divers occasions. Thomasina has been promised the first vacancy in the school. Naturally that promise must be fulfilled. But— There is another matter. The man O'Flingsley, the Canon admits in great confidence, is to be dismissed—

"A grave step, Francis—a very grave step," the Canon submits, "but necessary. We must never hesitate in our duty. That is the sum and essence of conduct. Note it down, Francis."

"I'll write it in me 'Things to Remember' book this very night," promises Francis.

O'Flingsley's removal will leave the position of principal vacant, the Canon continues, and there is no one to whom he had rather give that position than Francis—

"But, mark my problem, Francis, my dilemma, my moral embarrassment. An attractive young man and a comely young girl in the one building all day. Mark it gravely, Francis!"

"There—there would be scandal, Canon, and . . . and talk. I see it all."

But if Francis, whose "brain is young and nimble," could hit upon a way out!

"If the two of them was married, Canon!"

Francis is a little frightened by his own inspiration. The Canon is apparently greatly perplexed. "If which two were married?" he asks, blandly. Oh—the two in the school! That, of course, would solve everything. That would be "an approximation of the ideal," admits the Canon.

It might be arranged that way, thinks Francis, with growing enthusiasm, if neither his Aunt Jemima, or the Canon, offered any objection—

". . . Francis, what on earth is this? What is that brain of yours propounding?" demands the Canon, play-acting admirably. "I asked you to hit on a way out, and you—you bring the house down about my ears without warning! By my soul, Francis, you're a—a scoundrel; a—a desperado! I insist on your Aunt Jemima taking you in hand this instant!"

Aunt Jemima is duly acquainted with the conspiracy the

scoundrel Francis has had the audacity to propose and, past her
first indignation, when she realizes that they are laughing at her,
she is as greatly enthused as Francis.

"It's God, Canon, that's Who it is!" declares Jemima.

Soon Francis has gone to further the plan. Thomasina is back
and can be found, it may be, in the kitchen. . . .

While he is waiting to see the Canon, who has gone into the
garden, Dermot O'Flingsley is suddenly conscious of Brigid's
presence. She has come, wrapped in a dressing gown and bare-
footed, because she has been dreaming of him. Brigid has seen
the Master going down a long road and waving back, and knows
that he is to "take up his bed."

"And you're to try to love people when they're dirty because
any ass can love them when they're clean," reports Brigid. Her
Saint had told her that. "She said you'd know," adds Brigid.
And O'Flingsley does know.

"If I could just shake this fear off me—this fear of hunger
. . . of money . . . of the cold. . . ."

"It will be terrible, Master, when I see you comin' up the
school road, and you not comin' at all. But I'll still have the
Canon."

"The Canon!   That man!"

"Yis, Master . . . Oh, I know you have the dagger for him
because he can hurt and say killin' words. . . . *You* see him
when he's proud, but I see him when he's prayin' in his little
place and the tears on his cheeks; *you* see him when he dines
but *I* see him when he fasts; *you* see him when his head is up
and fiery like a lion, but *I* see his head when it's down low and
his words won't come . . . It's because of that, that *you* hate
him and *I* love him . . . St. Brigid says that if we could all
see each other all the time in big hangin' mirrors, the whole hate
of the world would turn into dust."

"I'll remember that always, Brigid," says O'Flingsley, visibly
touched. "And I'll remember you, too."

"It wouldn't matter not rememberin' me," says Brigid, "if
you'd remember *it*." They are staring at each other as the
Canon comes into the room. He is greatly perturbed at finding
Brigid out of bed and angered that Jemima should have been so
careless of her charge. But Brigid explains that she wanted to
come—

"I just wanted to—to be sure that I loved the two of yous
and could serve you always," explains Brigid.

Jemima is taking Brigid back to her bed, and would be none

too gentle with her had the Canon not spoken. Brigid has turned back to O'Flingsley.

"Good-by, Master. And—I love you," she says, looking up at him emotionally. He bends to kiss her hair softly. The Canon "stands like a statue, his feelings masked completely."

And now the men are alone. The Canon is frank in saying that he has for some time had "ample grounds for complaint" against both the O'Flingsley person and his work. O'Flingsley replies that he also has a "goodly few" complaints that may cancel out the others. He counts them over rapidly on his fingers—

"No coal, no handle on sweeping-brush, no caretaker for the school, no windows that aren't stuck fast; eighteen crumbling desks, six broken panes of glass, no lighting on dark days, and the public highway of the Saorstat Eireann for a playground. And these complaints render my attitude—unsuitable."

CANON (*unperturbed*)—Your enunciation is very imperfect for a teacher, O'Flingsley. I missed quite half of them. Besides, these alleged deficiencies are not complaints. They are officially termed "Recommendations in writing to the Very Reverend Manager."

O'FLINGSLEY—Or alternately, "Words Scrawled on the Sands by an Innocent."

CANON (*coldly*)—I will not—descend to you, O'Flingsley.

O'FLINGSLEY—You sent for me, Canon, to say something and you haven't said it yet.

CANON—I'll say it now, O'Flingsley. I'll say it now. (*Bending over.*) Your mother's name was Gibney.

O'FLINGSLEY (*with a slight start*)—So it was, Canon.

CANON (*grimly*)—Your father's second name was Eugene.

O'FLINGSLEY (*now reckless*)—It was. And if you're as interested as all that in my genealogy, I had a grandmother that was called Poppet, an uncle that could spit over his own shoulder, and a paralyzed aunt that was christened Delia Diana. But I never had a niece that was called after me, thank God.

CANON (*controlling his anger*)—I'll be—calm, O'Flingsley. I'll be—logical. I—I won't descend to you. (*Holding up press cuttings from desk.*) I note from these cuttings of *your* book *I Am Sir Oracle*, that the Church in Ireland is controlled by a—a red army of turkey-cocks.

O'FLINGSLEY—If you have, Canon, that's always a big step forward.

CANON (*grimly, his eye gleaming*)—And I see that our educational system is the—the sewage of European culture. I'd never have thought it, O'Flingsley. Could you tell me, on what page of your teacher's Penny Catechism I could find it?

O'FLINGSLEY (*with venom*)—On the page, Canon, the Bishops won't add until they're made.

CANON (*striking desk*)—Damnation! I'll not have—*that!* (*He jumps up fiercely.*)

O'FLINGSLEY (*also jumping up*)—And hell and blazes, but you'll have to! (*They face each other on the floor, the masks now off completely. A pause as they regard each other venomously. The* CANON *composes himself with a great effort.*)

CANON (*with composure*)—O'Flingsley, do you know Francis Ignatius O'Connor?

O'FLINGSLEY—Who doesn't? (*Imitating* FRANCIS.) "Sure, Lord now, Canon!"

CANON (*grimly*)—I—I'm expecting him.

O'FLINGSLEY—I rather thought you were. And his—virgin consort, Aunt Jemima too, of course.

CANON (*fuming*)—In my—my forty years as a priest—

O'FLINGSLEY—You played the turkey-cock with your teachers, and made them your slavish handymen.

CANON (*with some composure*)—No. . . . I—I will not stoop! I will not argue. To argue is to assume equality.

O'FLINGSLEY—And equality of course would mean the end of your precious managerial system of education that's the laughing-stock of Europe. That would never do, Canon. By all means, spit on me.

Francis Ignatius O'Connor is back with great news—news that simply will not keep. The fair Thomasina has promised to be his wife and everything is lovely and grand.

"Hurrah for the Catholic ideal!" shouts the rebellious O'Flingsley. "A rebel knocked out; a niece married off; and a school made safe for a stagnant tradition all in the one move! Canon, you deserve a seat in Maynooth."

There is little more for the Canon to add. O'Flingsley is dismissed. Francis will take over O'Flingsley's school at the end of the month.

O'FLINGSLEY (*turning*)—I'll leave tomorrow, Canon, without pay, and give over the school to your handyman, if you'll answer me one question before I go.

CANON—Your question, O'Flingsley, may have an answer from us if it is—suitable.

O'FLINGSLEY—As a scholar who knows what he won't publicly admit, you loathe and detest the whole miserable fabric of things here. You detest that disgraceful apology for a school down there, even more than *I* do. I know that because I'm not a fool whatever else I am. Why then do you deliberately prepare to perpetuate it through that poor spineless imbecile there beside you?

FRANCIS (*outraged*)—Canon! He's insultin' me. I'd make him take that back. (*The* CANON's *eyes meet* O'FLINGSLEY's *eyes challengingly, in a silent tense duel. Pause.*)

CANON (*tensely*)—That will be all, O'Flingsley.

O'FLINGSLEY (*venomously*)—Afraid, Canon? But the heart-break is there all the same. *You* know it, and I know it. However, I'll always owe you something for taking me by the scruff of the neck out of a mouse's hiding place and putting me back on the high road. Good-by, Canon, you will be remembered, if at all, not as a classicist, nor as a priest, but for your love for a poor little miserable child.

CANON (*his voice trembling with passion*)—That will—be all, O'Flingsley. (O'FLINGSLEY *turns and snapping up his hat, walks quickly off. The* CANON, *oblivious of* FRANCIS, *stares after him unseeingly.* FRANCIS *is standing flabbergasted and open-mouthed.*)

FRANCIS—Is he mad or what, Canon?

CANON (*after a pause*)—Conceivably, Francis . . . conceivably. . . .

The curtain falls.

ACT IV

It is the next morning. The Canon is finishing his breakfast. The red curtains that were at the windows formerly have been replaced by long, flowing white ones, and on the table is a great vase of white lilies. Jemima has come to report that Brigid has had a restless night, when suddenly the changed furnishings strike her eye. And who, she wonders, could have changed them? Suddenly she knows. It was Brigid.

"It was the meanderin' talk of her durin' the night, Canon," she explains. "She kept sayin' that someone went always in white a long time ago."

The Canon is angered. The thought that Jemima has been so negligent as to let a sick child go wandering about a cold room, bare-footed and undressed, is distressing to him. The fact that Jemima thought she must attend Mass is no excuse. She should have missed Mass under the circumstances.

Apprehension is added to anger later when Jemima rushes back from Brigid's room to report the bed empty and the child gone. Nor can she be found any place in the house. It is the opinion of Father Kirwan, just now arrived, that Brigid may have crossed the fields to St. Brigid's Shrine, this being the Saint's feast day. A search is about to be started when Brigid appears suddenly in the doorway. "She is dressed all in white, is neat and comely, and is smiling slightly. She leans against the curtains—a white picture in a white frame."

Brigid accepts the Canon's anxiety lightly. She had things to do and she had "riz" to do them. He must not be angry— not this day. Tomorrow, maybe—but not today. She is sorry the Canon is displeased. Where has she been? She has been in the chapel—the Canon had given her communion himself, and didn't recognize her in her white dress. Brigid nearly laughed at that. And now she does not want to be put back to bed. Nor will she eat the breakfast the Canon orders. She would fast till midday. And she is eager to speak with the Canon.

Father Corr and Father Kirwan, called to a meeting of the Football Club, are worried about leaving Brigid. What is it she wants to talk to the Canon about? After Father Kirwan has gone Father Corr would make sure. Canon Skerritt is curious.

"If Mr. O'Flingsley done one thing wrong, he'll surely do twinty things right," Brigid suddenly bursts out. And when they stare at her she adds: "The men's havin' a meetin', Canon. There's goin' to be talk, then stones and sticks."

Father Corr, grown moderately defiant, is willing to admit that there has been some indication of trouble brewing for Dermot O'Flingsley. The men of the Football Club, incensed because they were not told that O'Flingsley was the author of *I Am Sir Oracle*, have warned that hated author to leave the locality at once or suffer whatever may happen to him.

These are new times, Father Corr insists. He and Father Kirwan are perfectly willing to take the Canon's orders in all canonical matters, but not in "all matters affecting the dignity of the Church," as the Canon insists. It is not enough that the Canon has dismissed O'Flingsley from his position of principal—

"As usual, Father Corr, you are intemperate in your language and chaotic in your feelings," declares Canon Skerritt. "I place both you and Father Kirwan under a strict rule of obedience. Any attempt at Dublin's holy hooliganism in *my* parish, will be rigorously met by *me*. Go down and acquaint this meeting of *that*. And in my name, dismiss it."

Sulkily, Father Corr agrees to deliver that message. . . .

Jemima, back to insist again that Brigid shall come to her breakfast, brings the Canon a letter. It is from his friend in Bray, and reports that all is in readiness for Brigid's holiday. With a whole five-pound note in her bag, and the new hat with a veil over her nose, Brigid should be happy to go. But Brigid is not happy. She is quite miserable.

"I—I could cry, Canon," she says softly. "I'll anger you again and vex you. I—I know it."

CANON—No, Brigid. God will help you not to. You will be my friend instead. It is good to have a friend on a dark day. If anything is ever said of me, child, I want it to be that I found your face always full of grace and comely.

BRIGID—Don't say anythin' nice about me face, Canon, or I would want it to be like St. Brigid's face with the niceness torn out of it with pain.

CANON (*chidingly*)—There! There! Your mind must not dwell on these myths and fancies. What is God's nothing can destroy. Go now, child, and have a good breakfast, and then we shall fit on your hat and arrange about your train. (BRIGID *moves towards door, and then comes back pathetically.*)

BRIGID (*shrewdly*)—Canon, if—if you made a great promise to—to Don Miguel or Don Pedro, would you keep it in face of everythin'?

CANON—Keep it? Why, most certainly, Brigid. A gentleman *always* keeps his promises, under penalty of dishonor. (*She looks at him pleadingly.*)

BRIGID (*after a pause*)—That's why I don't want to—to eat till midday, Canon. I—I promised St. Brigid. (*The* CANON *starts visibly, realizing he is caught. He controls his feelings.*)

CANON—Brigid, you are very trying. Will you eat if I, as the Canon, give you a special—a very special dispensation?

BRIGID—But it's for—the love of her, Canon, not as a penance. She asked me to prove I loved her.

CANON—To say she asked you is—inaccurate, Brigid. What you mean is that in praying to St. Brigid, you *told* her you would fast yourself. In that you were harder on yourself than the Church allows. Anything excessive, Brigid, is not classically Catholic.

BRIGID—She *did* ask me, Canon. But you won't believe me.

CANON (*ruffled*)—I thought, Brigid, we finished with this matter long ago!

BRIGID—I tried, Canon. But—she kept pleadin'—as if everythin' else was standin' waitin'. . . . She said I was to offer my Communion this mornin' for *you*, and my fast till midday for *you* too.

CANON (*after a pause*)—Brigid, for offering your Communion for me, I am indeed grateful. It is the act of my friend. But you must not think any *figure told* you to do this. The Church *frowns* at such imaginings, and she is very, very wise.

BRIGID—But there's—somethin' else, Canon. It's—killin' and killin' me. . . .

CANON (*holding himself in*)—I feel you're going to make me angry, Brigid.

BRIGID (*trembling*)—I—I know. . . . I'm tremblin'. . . .

CANON (*touching her*)—There! My poor child, there! You are ill, and I will say no word. You may tell me. I will contain myself, Brigid. I will bear with you. Let it be written of me.

BRIGID—She told me to ask you, Canon, to—come with me, wearin' your surplice and soutane, and I in this white dress, into the chapel yard today at twelve when the Angelus is ringin' and the people are comin' and goin'. (*The* CANON *is staring at her, holding himself desperately in leash.* BRIGID, *with tearful eyes, is looking up pleadingly at him.*) We are to kneel down on the seventh flag from the door and I am to keep sayin' the prayer to St. Brigid. And you are to invoke her three times, and then kiss the stone and say, "Mary of the Gael, show us the way through the dark." And she promises that a stream of water, waitin' there for years, will gush out over the flagstone, and that the fingers of everyone will dip into it forever. (*Pause.*) That— that's all, Canon. (*She stands visibly trembling, looking up at the* CANON *whose face is strained and masklike.*) Please don't— shout and be angry with me, C-Canon. Just—just say, "G-go, B-Brigid!"

It is some moments before the Canon, fighting desperately to control himself, feels sufficiently in command of his emotions to answer Brigid. When he does speak it is softly and with understanding compassion. She is very ill, he tells her, even more ill than he suspected. If she were not ill he would not be able to control his anger, or his disgust.

"I make you my friend," he says, "and in return you ask me to be a—boobish sort of conjurer who draws rabbits out of a hat or water out of a stone for the gratification of oafs and idiots."

"But sure, Canon, St. Brigid wouldn't belittle *you* and deceive *me*. She—she *couldn't*."

"As you rightly say she couldn't, Brigid. As I explained, child, she wasn't—there."

"But I saw her, Canon. And the mark on her face and all."

"I know, Brigid. Our poor sick minds play with terrible pictures. But *you* know nothing of such things. When you return from your holiday, you will say to me, 'Canon, I was a little fool in the wind, and you were a big tree that gave me shelter.'"

Jemima has again come to ask what is to be done with Brigid's breakfast and is quite disturbed when the Canon insists that she put it on the priests' table. Again the Canon has taken Brigid to a seat beside him to reason with her about St. Brigid and the miracle.

"Listen to me, Brigid. When a woman in marriage gives birth to men, she proves herself a mother. Her men are all about her —justifying her. Suppose, Brigid, a fool came along and said, 'Prove yourself a mother again,' what would happen?"

"Sure, they'd laugh, Canon."

"They'd laugh! Excellent, Brigid. You are following me with intelligence. Now, it is just like that with the Church. Her children have justified her eternally. She is venerable with holiness and heavy with the wisdom of ages. And yet, Brigid, you want her to give birth to a new child—to prove herself by a new miracle. St. Brigid would laugh heartily at such a thing. She, Brigid, that redeemed the world, you want her to produce rabbits out of a boob's hat!"

Brigid is in tears, but still she cannot see. Not within her understanding is that "whole world of spiritual rowdies willing to sell themselves to anything that can produce signs and wonders to please their vanity." She only knows that she is completely and utterly miserable. "It's like people that you love pullin' against each other," she cries. "It's hard, Canon, the things that you love goin' crashin' down, as if they were timber fallin'!"

"You must learn to laugh, child, at the big shaky things that our poor sick minds build up, and our healthy minds pull down. There is great safety in the right kind of laughter."

Jemima spreads Brigid's breakfast on the priests' table, and this time Brigid agrees to eat, if the Canon so orders it. St.

Brigid would feel as he does, the Canon is sure, because St. Brigid was a very sensible saint indeed. But when Brigid tries to eat her promise again assails her and she draws away from the food. She has walked now to the curtains and stands as though hoping for a sign from her beloved Saint. And what will St. Brigid be thinking of her, after her promise? And with her white dress on too?

Jemima is back to hurry her, roughly, but Brigid cannot be hurried. She is hoping that the Angelus will ring, and is glad of the interruption of Thomasina and Francis, who have come to ask the Canon to marry them in person. It is Thomasina and Francis who finally eat the breakfast, to Brigid's great relief.

These two have brought bad news, too. They have heard of the plan in the village to give Dermot O'Flingsley a blatherin', and that news distresses Brigid. She would cry out against such an outrage. Even the Canon would not permit that. With sudden resolution she has dashed through the curtains and out toward the village.

"That one will get hurt if the stones start flyin'," observes Francis, his mouth full of cake. . . .

The Canon has come now to hear what it is that Thomasina and Francis would have him do. Marry them? He will not. Permit his name to be written in the marriage notice in the papers? No. Nor in any future birth notices either. And where is Brigid?

Brigid, they tell him, has heard them talkin' of what the town people were sayin' about O'Flingsley and away she had run, like a madhead. The Canon is greatly excited by the news. Brigid is a very sick child. She must be brought back immediately. Let them run, both of them, and tell her the Canon wants her at once.

Thomasina and Francis are no more than out of the house before Father Kirwan is in at the other door. He has come rushing back from town in his motor car to ask that the Canon come and help him and Father Corr. The Football Club has started a march on O'Flingsley's house. The men are threatening to get out of hand. They're booin' and shoutin'. The Sergeant of Police might help them, true, but the Sergeant's wife is having a baby and he is not available.

Now Father Corr has rushed in to report that O'Flingsley is jeerin' at the people instead of getting out, as he has been told. It is true that he and Father Kirwan had led the march to O'Flingsley's house, but it was an orderly mob until O'Flingsley started jeerin'.

"You are a sentimental youth, Father Corr, or you would know that all men in the mass are barbarians," declares the Canon. "Every year scores of decent Christians in America sprinkle Negroes with petrol and burn them because they love God and his justice. Yet, you *will* indulge in this—free Presbyterianism, this Lutheran zeal that the Church has never had any nonsense with in history. And in *my* parish too."

Now Jemima has rushed in to report that the milkman has seen Brigid holding on to O'Flingsley on the road, while the crowd pelts him with sticks and stones. The Canon, seized with fear, calls to Jemima to get his hat and coat. A moment later, with top hat and cane, he is ready to step forth.

"I long enough have suffered boobs gladly without and within," he says, as his curates would protest that what is happening was no fault of theirs. "Now, I, the Canon, will act, and I will have obedience and authority."

Before the Canon can reach the window there is a commotion outside and O'Flingsley appears with Brigid lying in his arms. "His hair is disheveled and his face streaked with blood and mud. Brigid's head is almost covered with a large white cloth, and there are bloodstains upon her white dress."

Above the protests of Father Corr and Father Kirwan that they had intended no wrong, Canon Skerritt manages to start Jemima for a doctor and to ask O'Flingsley to lay Brigid on the couch. He is standing over her now, muttering, "God of mercy, do not take this, my one consolation, away from me." And then to O'Flingsley: "Is—is it serious, O'Flingsley?"

"I'm afraid it is." They are avoiding each other's gaze.

"What happened? Tell me. . . ."

"She got half a brick that one of your hirelings intended for me," replies O'Flingsley, without passion.

"They are not my hirelings, O'Flingsley. We are surely better enemies than that," answers the Canon. "Where is the wound?"

"Side of the head and upper part of the face. I'm afraid of concussion. It was a cruel blow. . . . As I ran with her, a woman poured a bottle of oil over it and tied her apron about her to stop the bleeding."

"And this in the name of the Communion of Saints. . . ."

Their anxiety grows as the doctor does not come. There might be a chance for Brigid if he would hurry. She had only spoken once after she was struck, reports O'Flingsley. That was a whispered something about the Angelus bell and the Canon.

And now the bell is ringing clearly from the church tower outside. Brigid stirs weakly and moves her head. They are regarding her emotionally.

"Brigid—it's the Canon and I," says O'Flingsley, softly.

"The man O'Flingsley . . ." mutters Brigid, weakly. "The . . . the Angelus . . . the Angelus . . . and I'm not—able . . . Canon, make me able. . . ."

CANON—I am here, Brigid. But you must not speak. You are very ill, poor child.

BRIGID (*as in a dream*)—There's blood on the Master's head. . . . I felt it. . . . Then the stone came . . . with the pain in it . . . and I knew my face was like St. Brigid's then . . . torn and hurt. . . . My mouth is burnin' . . . me. . . . (*The* CANON *pours a little of his Spanish wine into a glass and brings it towards her.*)

O'FLINGSLEY—The Canon is right this time, Brigid. You must lie very still and not talk till the doctor comes.

BRIGID—But how can I rest . . . and that bell ringin'. . . . The Canon knows. . . . Canon! . . .

CANON—There, child! I am here with you. . . . You must take a sip of this wine to strengthen you. . . . (*She takes a few sips from the glass.*)

BRIGID—Don Miguel's wine. . . . He said to the Canon, "Where there is truth there is God." . . . I wish I could rise up and be *true* to her . . . and not false. . . . But I'm not able. . . .

CANON (*striving to hold in his emotions*)—Brigid, if you will live for me, live on as the Canon's friend, I will do what you want. I will bend for you. The Canon will bend. He will stoop. He will—believe. . . .

BRIGID (*weakly, struggling*)—C-Canon . . . I—I want to live for that. . . . I must live. . . . I must show you the stone . . . and my white dress on . . . me. . . .

O'FLINGSLEY (*tenderly supporting her*)—Yes, Brigid, but not till the doctor examines you.

BRIGID (*weakly moving*)—But there is no time, Master . . . no time. . . . The Angelus will soon not be ringin'. . . .

O'FLINGSLEY—She's fighting hard as if there was something that mattered a lot.

CANON—So there is. . . . (*Emotionally.*) So there is. . . .

BRIGID (*rising a little, painfully*)—Make me able, Canon. I want to keep faith with her. I want her to see me face like hers. . . . I want to be a white rose in her mouth . . . not a smut of soot brushed away. . . . (*She rises still more—only her eyes and brow and hair visible and glowing above the bandages.*) I want to see your face stooped, Canon, in the way she said . . . and the love of the little things in it. . . . I want to dip me fingers in the new water, and to say what she told me, "Mary of the Gael, show us the way . . . through the dark." . . . (*For a moment her face is poised eloquently. The Angelus bell ceases. She suddenly collapses back and lies still. The* CANON *buries his face in his hands.* O'FLINGSLEY *stifles a sob.*)

CANON (*shakingly*)—Tell me, O'Flingsley. No, no. Don't— don't say it. . . .

O'FLINGSLEY (*simply*)—It's one of the things must be said, Canon. She's dead. . . .

CANON—God . . . God . . . Have I blundered? (O'FLINGS- LEY *takes up a coverlet to draw it over* BRIGID's *face, but the* CANON *pathetically intervenes, childishly.*) No, no. Let—let me, O'Flingsley. . . . Let me.

O'FLINGSLEY (*slowly*)—Let both of us. . . . (*Terribly.*) It will be—worthy of us. . . . (*Together they draw the coverlet over* BRIGID's *face. Their eyes meet fully for the first time, and hold each other over* BRIGID's *body. Then slowly each moves back in different directions.*)

CANON (*huskily, as* O'FLINGSLEY *nears the door*)—No, no. . . . Do not leave me, O'Flingsley. . . . I am alone. . . .

O'FLINGSLEY (*turning, slowly*)—I must. (*Very low.*) We must work this out. . . . Innocent blood. . . .

CANON (*hands to face, shakingly*)—Am I just an embittered old man . . . living here with shades too glorious to forget? (*For a moment,* O'FLINGSLEY *regards him from the doorway, his face a study—in mingled hate, pity and respect. He turns slowly and goes out. A moment passes. The* CANON *sits down heavily. He lifts heavy weary eyes to the couch and the empty room.*)

CANON (*his head down again, slowly*)—I am not well. . . .

THE CURTAIN FALLS

ON BORROWED TIME
A Comedy in Two Acts

By Paul Osborn

(Based on a novel by Lawrence Edward Watkin)

THE theatre season of 1937-38 was half spent by the time Paul Osborn's "On Borrowed Time" was produced. That was in early February, and those who keep close track of such things were just about to settle back and call it a season of few plays worth either talking or writing about. Then, quite suddenly and surprisingly, there was a burst of good plays—Carroll's "Shadow and Substance" having been done the week before, and Wilder's "Our Town" following the week after.

Both the latter won citations from those who award best play prizes at the close of the season. "Our Town" was given the Pulitzer award as the best play of American authorship produced during the winter. "Shadow and Substance" was voted by the Drama Critics' Circle the most distinguished drama of foreign authorship that had been imported.

"On Borrowed Time" proceeded calmly without a prize or a citation to boast about, but it may easily outlast and outdraw either of the other two. Its appeal is, if anything, a wider appeal and is based on a human response to sentiment and humor that is a shade more universal than either Mr. Carroll's contrast of an intellectualized Catholic faith opposed to that of childlike acceptance of the religious mysteries, or Mr. Wilder's simple study of life and death in a small New England town.

"On Borrowed Time" was enthusiastically welcomed by the professional play reviewers, both for its own sake and because it brought one of their favorite actors, Dudley Digges, to stardom after forty years of fine service to the theatre. Mr. Digges had been associated with the New York Theatre Guild since its earlier productions and had given many excellent performances.

The living room into which we are admitted at the opening of "On Borrowed Time" is typical of no particular locality. There may be a touch of New England in it, or it may be rather definitely on the Middle Western side. But in general it is just a living room, comfortably and conventionally furnished, with a

122

regulation number of easy chairs, a table and reading lamp, a cabinet of curios, treasures, etc.

At the moment an old gentleman known as Gramps is busy at the table apparently engaged in engraving. He is an amiable old gentleman, probably well in his eighties, his thin white locks softly ruffled over a scalp that shows pink wherever the thatch leaves it bare.

Sprawled on the floor, practically under Gramps' chair, is a small boy, also of indeterminate age, but probably about six. A serious, inquisitive youngster, still carrying some of his baby fat, but beginning to thin out and shoot upward.

It would appear from the conversation that Gramps is engraving a name on a watch fob. The name might be Pud, which would be the boy's name, or, as Gramps suggests, it might be shikepoke. But seeing that a shikepoke is a bird, and that birds don't have watch fobs, it isn't going to be shikepoke. Neither is it going to be Pud. It is going to be John Gilford Northrup, which is Pud's rightful name, and nothing else.

That matter having been settled with some degree of definiteness, certain other items are taken up. For one there is the question of the collection of treasures that is evidently showing signs of depletion. A frog recently added appears now to be getting pretty old, and will probably have to be discarded. A bone that Gramps picked up near the meatshop is a nice addition and looks pretty human in the main. But human or not, it is, as Pud insists, a very fine specimen.

Then there is the question of Aunt Demetria. Aunt Demetria, Pud breaks into song to suggest, is a pismire. That's what Gramps had told Granny. And, Gramps admits, Aunt Demetria is a pismire, even though she shouldn't be called that. A pismire is one of the meanest of ants, and that's what Aunt Demetria is, but it makes Granny mad to say so. Demetria was the oldest of a large family, Gramps explains, the first child Pud's other grandfather ever had, and he didn't know much about being a father at the time. But the last child he had was Pud's mother, and by that time he had learned a lot, because Pud's mother was pretty near a perfect job.

Now Granny, a pleasant, fussy little old lady in her late seventies, has come looking for Gramps to take the dog, Betty, out for a walk. Gramps doesn't care for Betty, nor for the way Betty smells. He is of the opinion, too, that she should be able to find her own tree by this time, an observation that is quite shocking to Granny in the presence of Pud.

"Go with your Grandpa, Betty," says Granny, quickly, to cover the situation.

"I'll thank you not to claim kin to me with that bitch!" snorts Gramps.

GRANNY (*protestingly*)—Julian!

GRAMPS (*rising*)—Pshaw, that's what she is . . . no more, no less than a bitch.

PUD (*singing, suddenly*)—A dog or a bitch, you never know which.

GRANNY (*as they both look at* PUD)—There you are!

GRAMPS—I never taught him that, Miss Nellie, I swear.

GRANNY—Turning your own grandson into a smutty mouth like yourself.

GRAMPS—Honest, I never taught him that, Miss Nellie.

GRANNY—That I should live to see the day . . . !

GRAMPS—Oh, come along, Petunia.

GRANNY—And her name isn't Petunia.

GRAMPS—All right, come along, Sweet Pea.

PUD—I'll take her, Gramps. It's kinda *hot* for you to be out today.

GRAMPS—I guess you're right, it is. Thank you kindly. Go with your uncle, Betty. (*He gives leash to* PUD.)

PUD—Am I her uncle?

GRAMPS (*looking toward* GRANNY)—Seems so.

GRANNY—Just walk her up toward the Browns', darling.

PUD—I know where her twalet is. (PUD *and dog go off.*)

GRANNY—That boy's gettin' to be the limit. You're not only making a smutty mouth out of him . . . the first thing you know you'll be teaching him to smoke, I suppose. And even drink . . . and goodness knows what all.

GRAMPS—It'll be years yet before he can "What all"!

GRANNY—Julian!

GRAMPS—Oh, Miss Nellie.

GRANNY—He mimics everything you do. He hardly has a chance to see his own father. Jim's always so busy. First thing you know, that boy'll grow up and be just like you. Is that what you want?

GRAMPS—Nope. I want him to go further'n I have.

GRANNY—Then you'd better set him an example. You gotta stop swearin' and smokin' that smelly pipe. You never draw a breath that it ain't full of smokin' and swearin'. You better change your ways, Julian Northrup. If you don't, I'm gonna talk

"ON BORROWED TIME"

Gramps: I got you up that tree and you're gonna stay there until I tell you to come down.
Pud: You got him, Gramps, you got him!

(Frank Conroy, Dudley Digges, Peter Holden)

to Jim and Susan about sending Pud away to school.

GRAMPS—Send him away to school? At his age?

GRANNY—It'd be better for him than being around you so much.

GRAMPS—There ain't no school what'd take him. He's too little.

GRANNY—Yes, there is. Demetria knows a school in . . .

GRAMPS—Demetria! By God, I might have known she was at the bottom of this. Old bird-stuffer!

GRANNY—Demetria's a fine Christian woman and I won't hear a word against her.

GRAMPS—She's a bird-stuffer!

GRANNY—She's no such thing.

GRAMPS—Oh, Miss Nellie—I don't see why you're always sticking up for Demmie. She's a bird-stuffer and you know it.

GRANNY—Demmie may have her faults but she's a God-fearing woman. She's warned Susan time and time again how you're poisoning Pud's mind, and now she's found this nice boarding-school run by a Baptist woman.

GRAMPS—Baptist woman! By God, Pud's not goin' to no school run by a Baptist woman.

GRANNY—Then you better change your ways, Julian Northrup. You are a bad influence on the boy and it's gotta be stopped.

Granny doubtless would have had more to say, but an attack of "gas" on the stomach stops her. Stops her for a moment, but does not quiet her curiosity. She must know what Julian meant by a bird-stuffer. Julian didn't mean anything much—

"Adam saw a dog and it looked like a dog and he called it a dog," he explains. "I saw Demmie, she looked like a bird-stuffer and I called her a bird-stuffer, so she is a bird-stuffer."

Through the window Gramps has caught sight of the Widow Tritt and is noticeably interested. The Widow Tritt is one whom Demetria insists should be run out of town, according to Granny. The Widow Tritt is always making advances to the men. Gramps, of course, never took any notice of such things. Once, in the grocery store, he had patted the Widow Tritt's dog, but— And he didn't even know it was her dog. . . .

Granny has left the room a little haughtily and Gramps is still staring out the window, humming a gay tune, when Mr. Brink appears. Mr. Brink is a stranger, a pleasant enough person, but a little forbiddingly assertive in manner. Gramps has barely caught sight of him when he is stricken with a sudden pain and falls back into a chair.

"Mr. Julian Northrup, I believe?" says Mr. Brink, quietly.

"What's that? I didn't catch it?" demands Gramps, slowly pulling himself together.

BRINK—Most people don't hear me the first time.

GRAMPS—How in blazes could I hear you if I was asleep?

BRINK—Are you sure you were—asleep?

GRAMPS—Guess I musta drowsed off. Felt kind of tired all of a sudden. Who are you? What d'ye want?

BRINK—I request that you come with me.

GRAMPS—Where yuh goin'?

BRINK—Where the woodbine twineth.

GRAMPS—Where the wood . . . ? I just said that. I made it up. It's what yuh say to a child. I ain't no child.

BRINK—Aren't you?

GRAMPS—No, I'm not. Say, look here, who the hell are you?

BRINK—You may call me Mr. Brink.

GRAMPS—Well, look here, Mr. Brink, I don't like you. I wouldn't go with you to a rat fight, so now you know.

BRINK—I'm sorry.

GRAMPS—I don't like the way you snuck up here. I don't like the way you talk. (*He leans over to pick up job and instrument which fell from his hands.*)

BRINK—I'm afraid that will have to be as it may be.

GRAMPS—Oh, you are! Well, you better . . . (*Rises.*) . . . get out of here right awa . . . (*He becomes suddenly weak and sits bewildered.*)

BRINK—You see. It's time for you to come with me.

GRAMPS—No . . . no. . . . It ain't. I ain't goin' nowhere. I'm goin' to stay right here. I'm waitin' for Pud. (*He gets stronger.*) By God, you get the hell out of here! You git off my son's property! You git the hell . . . (GRANNY's *voice off stage stops him.* BRINK *turns swiftly and leaves.*)

GRANNY (*off stage*)—Julian!

GRAMPS—You git the . . . (*He discovers* MR. BRINK *has disappeared and is bewildered.*) Well, I'll be . . .

GRANNY (*comes down on stairs*)—Who you shoutin' at that way?

GRAMPS—Well, I . . . there was a feller here. . . .

GRANNY—Well, where is he?

GRAMPS—He's gone now.

GRANNY—What did he want?

GRAMPS—I don't rightly know, Miss Nellie. I . . .

GRANNY—You better come upstairs out of that hot room, Julian.

GRAMPS—Yes, I guess I better had.

PUD (*coming in from porch with* BETTY)—Gramps, who was that mans?

GRAMPS—You seen him, did you, son?

PUD—Sure. He was coming down the walk. Who was he?

GRAMPS—I don't rightly know who he was.

PUD—What did he want?

GRAMPS—He wanted me to go with him.

PUD—Where?

GRAMPS—Where the woodbine twineth.

PUD—Oh! You mean, Hell.

GRAMPS (*rising*)—By golly, boy, we better both go upstairs out of this hot room.

They go upstairs as the curtain falls.

A week later, in the late afternoon, Granny is sitting by the table in the living room crying softly and dabbing her eyes with a mourning handkerchief. Marcia, a young woman, is solicitous regarding Granny, but there isn't much that she can do.

Gramps is writing at the desk and Pud is lying on his stomach on the floor reading. Suddenly it is Pud who breaks the silence. Why, he asks, do they put dead people in coffings. Granny is again dissolved in tears but Gramps would be helpful. He suggests that Pud do not talk about such things. "Is it comfortable in a coffing?" persists Pud. He had seen them put his father and mother in a coffing and lower them into the ground, and he wants to know.

Granny has controlled her tears to explain to Pud that his father and mother are very comfortable in their coffins and that his father was, indeed, a very brave man—

"He turned his automobile right off the road so he wouldn't hurt a little boy just like me," says Pud.

"That's right, darling," agrees Granny.

"But I must never forget that my dear mamma and papa were taken from me and I will never, never have any others," recites Pud, solemnly. "I'm a—orphan."

GRAMPS—(*quickly*)—Who told you that?

PUD (*turning to* GRAMPS)—Aunt Demetria.

GRAMPS (*roaring*)—There! That damned old—!

GRANNY—Julian!

GRAMPS—Telling things like that to the boy! By God, if that God-damned old hellion—

GRANNY—Julian! If you swear any more like that in front of—

GRAMPS—It's enough to make a preacher swear.

PUD—I'm going to swear when I'm nine.

GRAMPS (*shaking his finger*)—Ah— Ah—

PUD—But you said I could, Gramps. (GRAMPS *motions violently for* PUD *to go back to his book.*)

GRANNY (*angrily*)—There! Did you tell the boy he could . . . Did you tell that boy he could . . . (*She belches sharply.*) Whoops, there it goes again! never know when it's coming. (*She drinks.* GRAMPS *writes.*) Who you writin' to, anyway, Julian?

GRAMPS—Reverend Murdock. Looked pretty shabby when he was preachin' that funeral sermon. I guess preachin' don't pay what it used to.

GRANNY—What are you writin' him for?

GRAMPS—Goin' to send him a check for $50. (*Turning to* GRANNY.) Now, that's a good deed, ain't it, even if I do say so myself.

GRANNY—Good deeds and leadin' a Christian life is two different things.

PUD (*rising to his knees, excited*)—Oh, Gramps, if you do a good deed, you can make a wish and it'll come true.

GRAMPS—What's that?

PUD—If you do a good deed, you can make a wish and it'll come true.

GRAMPS—That so, boy?

PUD—That's what my book says.

GRAMPS—Must be so then.

PUD (*very excited*)—So make a wish, Gramps, make a wish, make a wish.

GRAMPS—All right, boy, soon's I think of a good one. (*Turns to* GRANNY.) Listen, Miss Nellie, how does this sound? "Dear Reverend Murdock: Enclosed is a check for $50, for which please kindly send me one copy of the sermon you preached at the funeral of my son, James Northrup, M.D., and his wife Susan. If you don't have it down on paper, maybe you wouldn't mind writing out the jist of the thing which I thought was very good and proper and appropriate to the occasion. I hope the enclosed check will compensate in some part for the trouble this will make you. Yours truly, Julian Northrup." Now you don't think he'd take offense at that, do you?

GRANNY—I don't think so, Julian.

GRAMPS (*turning back to desk*)—No. Don't want to offend the old bastard.

GRANNY (*rising*)—Julian!

GRAMPS—Sorry, Miss Nellie. Take it back. Forgot. (*Pause.*)

If he can get himself unbuttoned Pud thinks he will go to the twalet. He should not announce that fact to the neighbors, Granny tries to explain to him. And Gramps adds as a lesson in etiquette that he should simply say that he wants to wash his hands, whether they are dirty or not. . . .

And now Granny has come to a decision. She has heard the voice of the Lord telling her that He had taken Pud's father and mother as a warning. Gramps had been ruinin' Pud. They simply cannot raise a little boy all by themselves. They will have to turn Pud over to Aunt Demetria. The suggestion so irritates Gramps that he cannot even help Pud with his buttoning up when he comes back from the twalet.

Gramps is determined now that his correction of Pud will not be longer neglected. With such severity as he can muster he informs Pud that he has got to be nicer to his Granny; that he must not wiggle away when she puts her arms around him, or pull away when she wants to kiss him, even if he has had "too much ladies' arms" around him lately, as Pud protests, or even if Granny does "kiss awful wet."

"And I don't want to ever see you smoke or say dirty things . . . and, above all . . . (*Shaking his finger.*) . . . I don't ever want to hear you swear. . . ."

Out the window Pud has seen somebody stealing apples and calls wildly to Gramps, which adds to the excitement. Gramps is going to get those damned young shikepokes; he'll give them such a tannin', if they'll wait— But they don't wait, and that amuses Pud and Granny.

"I swear I wish that anyone who climbed that tree would have to stay up there until I let them down," storms Gramps.

"Gramps, you made a wish!" shouts Pud. "You wished anyone who climbed that tree would have to stay there until you let him down."

"A lot of good it'll do me."

"Gee, I bet we catch one of those bad boys up there and we can keep him up there for a hundred years," shouts Pud, jumping around excitedly. "Maybe for a million years. Maybe . . ."

The sight of his Aunt Demetria coming up the walk suddenly quiets Pud. Demetria's approach and solicitude for the "poor little lambie" are very unwelcome to Pud and Gramps as well. Pud is wriggling out of her arms when Gramp calls—

"Leave that boy alone, for God's sake!"

"Would you deny the child Christian comfort, his parents hardly cold in their graves . . . ?" demands Demetria.

GRAMPS (*clasping* PUD)—To hell with Christian comfort, you old . . .

DEMETRIA—Come here, Pud.

PUD—I hate you!

GRAMPS—Now you know.

DEMETRIA—Come here to me, Pud.

GRAMPS—Like hell he will!

PUD—Like hell I will!

DEMETRIA (*to* GRANNY)—See! See! (*To* GRAMPS.) You whited sepulcher!

GRAMPS—What! Whited sepulch . . . You—whore of Babylon! You—

PUD—You—pismire!

GRAMPS—That's right, boy. Come along. Let's get out of this company. (*They go out by the porch, leaving* DEMETRIA *and* GRANNY *speechless.*)

DEMETRIA—You heard it, Nellie.

GRANNY—I never thought I'd live to—

DEMETRIA—You heard what he called me! He called me . . .

GRANNY—I know. Revelations 17:5. Don't say it, Demmie.

DEMETRIA—Of course I know I'm a nobody, Nellie. Maybe I'm no better than some folks say I am. But I'm certainly not a whore—

GRANNY—Of course you're not, Demmie. I don't know what Julian was thinking of.

DEMETRIA—And he said it right in front of that sweet little boy. But, then, of course, it's none of my business.

GRANNY—Of course it's your business.

DEMETRIA—No. I guess I better stay home after this. I'm a down-right nuisance.

GRANNY—You're not. You're a dear, sweet, Christian woman and you shouldn't always be runnin' yourself down. You're the only God-fearing woman . . . Well! . . . Maybe that's what the voice of God meant.

DEMETRIA—What?

GRANNY—I wonder if you shouldn't bring Pud up?

DEMETRIA—Me?

GRANNY—Your own sister's child. And you could bring him up the way God wants him to be brought up. Maybe that's what God meant.

DEMETRIA—Well, Nellie, I've thought about it. But I couldn't afford to give Pud all the things he's been used to. That is, unless Jim left a will—or something like that.

GRANNY—Well, he did, Demmie. He left a will.

DEMETRIA—Well, think of that. And how m . . . that is . . . well, is the little lambie well taken care of?

GRANNY—Yes, Demmie. Jim left fifty-five thousand dollars.

DEMETRIA—Fifty-five thou . . . ! Dear little lambie. . . . Well, Nellie, maybe you're right.

GRANNY—About what—?

DEMETRIA—Maybe I should adopt Pud.

GRANNY—Adopt him . . . ?

Granny hadn't meant just that. She did not expect Demetria to adopt Pud. She thought Pud might live with Demetria and come and see Julian in the afternoons. But Demetria is firm. She can't approve of Nellie going on letting Julian bring up Pud like a heathen. And there is that Marcia Giles, who has come to bring Granny a little soda and gone out again. Marcia certainly is no person to be around where Pud is. Not after the way Demetria has seen her carryin' on with Bill Murdock, the minister's son. Kissin'—right in the park, that's what she was doin'.

Kissing may be a sin to Demetria, but it isn't to Gramps, to whom the awful news is later revealed by Granny. Gramps knows Bill Murdock for a fine boy and Marcia Giles for a fine girl, and he hopes they were kissin'. After he has had a talk with Marcia he tells her he hopes she will bring Bill up to the house and kiss him there.

"How the hell's Pud gonna learn about kissin' if he don't never see any of it?" demands Gramps.

"Bill's only got one more year at Law School and then we're gonna be married," reports the relieved Marcia. "He took highest honors in his class last year."

"Well, you just tell that to Miss Nellie and everything'll be all right. And the next time you and Bill meet Demetria in the park you make Bill give you a big smacker right in front of her. Just like this. (*He kisses her.*) . . . You just tell Miss Nellie

that you and Bill are engaged and that Bill got highest honors
in his class."

Pud comes in from the porch as Marcia goes back to the
kitchen. He and Gramps stand looking after her.

"Gee, I wish Granny would knit two bumps on the front of
my sweater the way Marcy's got on hers," sighs Pud.

"What?" yells the dumbfounded Gramps. "Hey, there, you!
None of that from you, young man. Not that there ain't something in what you say." Gramps is dragging Pud off by the ear
as the curtain falls.

In Granny's bedroom Demetria has put Granny to bed and is
straightening the covers. Granny is pretty tired, but not too tired
to pick up her knitting, nor too tired to protest with some vehe-
mence that she is not going to have Julian say she is a fool or say
he's disappointed in her. And about Marcia: Granny can't see
as how there is much harm in kissin'—but if Demetria insists she
supposes she will have to speak to Marcia. Hard to do, though,
because Marcia needs the money so bad.

Granny is weakening a little about Julian too. Julian doesn't
mean all he says; he's just a rough-spoken man. "And he ain't
a blasphemer, either—not exactly," she adds. "He never sneers
at religion. He just don't have no interest in it."

She thinks she would like to see Julian for a minute. When
Demetria goes downstairs she can tell him. No, Granny isn't
goin' to forgive him exactly—she just wants to tell him something.

"Nellie, dear, do you think I should take Pud's things over
with me now?" Demetria asks, softly, as she sees Granny dozing
off. "In the morning I'll go down to Mr. Pilbeam's and have the
papers drawn up for you to sign—about the will and the adoption—and all . . ."

"Now, see here, Demetria," snaps Granny, waking up with a
start. "I didn't say anything about your adoptin' Pud. You're
trying to put words in my mouth. I don't like the way you're
actin', Demmie."

"Nellie Northrup, you said five minutes ago that I should
bring Pud up."

"I just wondered about it, Demmie."

"You said it, Nellie."

"If I did, I was wrong. I can see that now. . . . I don't like
the way you're actin', Demmie."

Granny has fallen back on her pillow. She would like to have
Julian come up, she repeats, weakly. She smiles as she thinks

how Julian always makes a lot of noise bellowin' to give the boys plenty of time to get out of the tree when they're stealin' apples.

Demetria has gone and Marcia has brought tea. Granny is going to sleep in a minute. There was something she wanted to say to Marcia, but she can't remember what it was. Couldn't have been very important.

"Marcia, you just see that Julian always has his pipe. Will you do that?"

"Yes, Mrs. Northrup."

"You're a good girl, Marcy. Now go on back to whatever you're doin'."

Granny tries to go on with her knitting, but is soon dozing again. A moment later Mr. Brink walks out of the closet. Granny thinks he is Julian, and is considerably disturbed when she sees that he isn't.

"See here, what call have you got to come buttin' into a lady's bedroom!" demands Granny.

"I usually come to bedrooms," smiles Mr. Brink. "It's so much more comfortable."

GRANNY—What is?

BRINK—To come with me.

GRANNY—Why should anyone go with you?

BRINK—It's customary.

GRANNY—Oh? Well, you might as well sit down and wait. Because you needn't think I'll stir a step until I've finished this mitten. (*Confidentially.*) I'm narrowin' off at the top now.

BRINK—Yes. I know you are.

GRANNY (*laughing*)—What do you know about knittin'?

BRINK—I don't mean the mitten. I mean you.

GRANNY (*laughing*)—What a fool thing to say. Don't you know a lady from a mitten?

BRINK (*turning away*)—Yes. I know a lady from a mitten.

GRANNY—Now, don't go 'way. You'll just have to wait. I've got to finish this job for my son, Jim. . . . (*Puzzled for a minute, then nods to affirm statement.*) . . . When he drives to Gainesville he says there won't anythin' keep his hands warm but a pair of my mittens. (*Laughs.*) Those boughten things you get at the store—they're no good. A doctor has to be out in all kinds of weather, you know.

BRINK (*smiling*)—He won't need them this year.

GRANNY (*laughing*)—Huh! What do you know about it?

BRINK—Oh, I know many things.

GRANNY—I'll wager I could show you a thing or two about knittin'.

BRINK (*crossing close to bed*)—No doubt. Are you ready now?

GRANNY (*breathlessly*)—Wait . . . just a minute. . . . I'm almost finished. . . . (*Breaks thread.*) . . . There! That's got it! Don't that red stripe look well with the gray?

BRINK—Excellent, my dear. Excellent. Come now.

"He leans over and touches her. She smiles and dies" as the lights fade and the curtain falls.

In Gramps' backyard there is a huge apple tree. There is a hill behind it and beyond the hill the town can be seen hazily. The back porch of the house, with the cellar door and a tool house attached, juts into the yard and there is a picket fence and a gate.

Martin's boy, a young fellow about ten, is up in the tree tugging at his breeches, which apparently have caught on a limb. Demetria, storming out of the house, catches him there and threatens to have the law on him. What if he hasn't stolen any apples—yet, he's trespassin'—

But Gramps follows Demetria out of the house and is quite capable of taking charge of the situation. If trespassers are deserving of a beating he thinks he will start with Demetria. She's trespassin', too.

"Hit her, Gramps, hit her on the rump!" shouts Pud, coming excitedly into the scene.

"Why . . . you little brat!" Demetria would take summary action with the excited Pud, if Gramps hadn't interfered. Now she has been driven off the property with Gramps flourishing a stick behind her.

"All right, Julian Northrup! Maybe you'll find out whose property this is some day," Demetria calls back, angrily.

"You'll find out I can take care of my own," Gramps shouts after her.

Then turning to the Martin boy, Gramps gruffly demands that he come down. The Martin boy would like to, but he can't, on account his breeches are caught.

"Gramps, Gramps! Your wish!" Pud is shouting, jumping up and down. "He can't come down! He can't come down! He can't come down!"

"Sh-h! . . . Now you unloosen your breeches. And come

down from there as fast as you can," repeats Gramps, turning again to Martin.

Once on the ground young Martin is promptly collared and quizzed as to his intentions as a thief. "I'll teach you to steal apples!" threatens Gramps. And he does. He fills the boy's pockets with fruit and makes him promise that the next time he wants apples he will come to the front door and ask for them.

"Them apples I gave him'll be pretty bitter, 'cause he didn't steal them," muses Gramps, as young Martin disappears. Now Pud wants to be boosted into the tree, even if he doesn't have to steal apples. He wants to see about that wish business.

"You know I can't get down until you let me," Pud calls gaily from the crotch of the tree.

"My Lord and Miss Boopydoop, you sure do beat the trolley cars," laughs Gramps, going over to a bench and sitting down.

Pud—You wished *nobody* could come down until you let them. That was your wish.

Gramps—That's right, boy. Guess it was.

Pud—So I can't come down either. I hope you won't keep me up here too long, Gramps.

Gramps—Liable to keep you up there all week. Maybe a hundred years. Depends on how I feel.

Pud—Oh, no, Gramps.

Gramps—Yep. Might leave you there and go down to Milbaur Park and pick up a few new specimens for our collection.

Pud (*starting to climb large branch*)—Then I'm coming down, Gramps.

Gramps—But you can't. You're under my magic spell. Yep, think I'll go along right now . . . good-by. (*Rises.*)

Pud—Wait a minute, I'm coming with you. (Pud *comes part down and hangs.*) Gramps, I can't let loose!

Gramps—'Course you can't. You can't let loose till I tell you.

Pud (*frightened*)—But, honest, I can't, Gramps.

Gramps (*thundering*)—'Course you can't. You can't go breaking my spells like that!

Pud (*more frightened*)—Let me down, Gramps! Let me down! Please! My arms is tired! (Gramps *laughs.*) Gramps! Gramps! Let me go, let me go! Gramps! Gramps!

Gramps—Come on, then. Let go. Let go, honey. (Pud *falls to the ground with a wail.* Gramps *hurries to him.*) What's the matter, boy, what's the matter?

PUD (*wailing*)—I couldn't let go!

GRAMPS (*sitting beside* PUD)—Of course you could.

PUD—No, I couldn't, Gramps. My hands wouldn't move. (*He stops crying.*)

GRAMPS—I thought we were just foolin'.

PUD—I was foolin' at first and then my hands wouldn't move. The tree was holdin' me.

GRAMPS—By golly, you do give a person the creeps sometimes. Doggone if I don't believe you really thought that tree was holdin' you.

PUD—It was, Gramps, it was.

GRAMPS—Oh, that old apple tree couldn't hold anybody!

PUD—Yes, it could, Gramps. You wished it could.

MARCIA (*coming from porch crying*)—Mr. Northrup! Come upstairs! Mrs. Northrup is . . . Mrs. Northrup!

"She buries her face in her hands. Gramps and Pud continue to look at the tree" as the curtain falls.

A week later, when it is nearly dusk, Gramps is sitting mournfully on the bench in the backyard. He wears a mourning band on his arm and his eyes have a far away expression. The coming of Marcia arouses him somewhat. Marcia has come to report that Demetria Riffle has been over again. She's been over every day since the funeral, says Marcia, and is very anxious about Mr. Northrup's health.

"Damned old hellion. Just waitin' for me to die," snorts Gramps.

He will have to take care of himself, warns Marcia. He will have to eat more than he has been eating if he is to keep up his strength. Pud, too. Marcia is worried about Pud. He has been awfully lonely, and he won't eat, either.

"That's what she said," murmurs Gramps. "She said 'he mimics everything you do.' "

The thought of Granny is suddenly strong with Gramps. "If I'd only got there in time, Marcy," he sighs. "We had words and she died before I could take 'em back and say I was sorry."

"She understood."

"She died and she didn't forgive me, she died and she didn't forgive me."

"She did, Mr. Northrup. She would have forgiven you anything," protests Marcia. Suddenly reminded of something, she dashes into the house.

Through the back gate Pud comes running. He stops when he sees Gramps and walks slowly toward the bench. "Gramps," he ventures, hesitantly. "Shall I sit down here, too?"

GRAMPS—Sure thing. What makes you think you shouldn't?
PUD—I think I should.
GRAMPS—Gonna have supper in a minute.
PUD—I'm not hungry.
GRAMPS—Gotta eat, boy. Hungry or not hungry.
PUD—Why?
GRAMPS—Keep up your strength. (*He suddenly clutches* PUD.) There's only me and you left now. Only me and you. I figure we got to stick together.
PUD—You're damn right.
GRAMPS—Shouldn't cuss, boy.
PUD—Why shouldn't I? *You* say that.
GRAMPS—I shouldn't neither. Your Granny didn't like it. Let's you and me turn over a new leaf, Pud.
PUD—What for?
GRAMPS—So your Aunt Demmie won't keep on saying I'm bad for you and won't keep on trying to get you away from me.
PUD—Aw, we'll kill her.
GRAMPS—By the Lord Harry, I almost wish we could.
PUD (*excited*)—We'll kill her; we'll kill her and we'll put her in the ground. We'll lower the coffing and I'll say . . .
GRAMPS (*his head in his hands*)—Hush, boy. Hush!
PUD (*touching him*)—What's the matter, Gramps? Are you sick?
GRAMPS—Growin' pains, I guess.
MARCIA (*coming out of house with* GRAMPS' *pipe*)—Here's your pipe, Mr. Northrup.
GRAMPS—My pipe, Marcy? Oh, I don't believe I can smoke it, thank you kindly. My throat hurts me a little. Fact is, I don't think I'll ever smoke any more. She didn't like it.
MARCIA—But she did, Mr. Northrup. I know she did.
GRAMPS—Nope. Miss Nellie thought it was a dirty habit. And I guess it is. . . .
MARCIA—She told me I was always to keep your pipe filled.
GRAMPS—Miss Nellie what? When?
MARCIA—Just before she died. I took her up a cup of tea and she caught hold of my hand and said . . . wait, I'll remem-

ber her exact words . . . she said: "Marcy . . . Marcy, see that Julian always has his pipe."

GRAMPS—Marcy. . . . You're not just making this up to make me feel good?

MARCIA—No, no, Mr. Northrup. I couldn't do that.

GRAMPS—Give me the pipe.

Gramps has his pipe, but his hand trembles so that Marcia has to help him light it. He guesses that is because he hasn't been keeping up his strength, he tells Pud. And then Mr. Brink appears suddenly. He is friendly and he has come again for Gramps. He thought he would be ready this time. But Gramps isn't ready—

"Now, look here, Mr. Brink. I ain't goin' with you at all. I'm goin' to stay right here with this young fellow. And you're about as welcome as a fly on a currant bun, so now you know."

Mr. Brink will not be turned away. He is plainly disappointed. Mrs. Northrup had been so very charming. How is Miss Nellie? Mr. Brink wouldn't know about that. He only knows that she has changed.

"Miss Nellie changed?" smiles Gramps. "That's what you think!"

"Oh, my dear man, let's not argue the point, and this time you can't fight me away," says Mr. Brink, a trifle testily. "Come now."

But Gramps will not stir. Even though he is suddenly seized with pain he looks hopefully at Pud.

BRINK—You're being difficult again. It's so easy and so pleasant. Now don't worry. Look at me.

GRAMPS (*as* BRINK *advances, hand outstretched*)—Just a minute, please, Mr. Brink. I'd like to have one last apple before I go.

BRINK—Oh, all right.

GRAMPS (*starting to climb tree, fumbles*)—You wouldn't like to get it for me, would you?

BRINK—Curious request. Oh, why not? (BRINK *climbs tree, points to apples.*) This one? Or this one?

GRAMPS (*backs away*)—I don't want none of them! I got you up that tree and you're gonna stay there until I tell you to come down. (*Wind shakes tree, as* BRINK *struggles to get free. Is bewildered.*)

PUD (*putting arms around* GRAMPS)—You got him, Gramps.
You got him!

GRAMPS (*clutching* PUD)—By golly, boy, I believe we have!

The curtain falls.

ACT II

We are still in the backyard. It is two hours later and Gramps
has hired three workmen to start building a fence around the
apple tree. Demetria Riffle, taking advantage of Gramps' absence,
has come over to interview the workmen. The man she talks to
is quite frank. Mr. Northrup had told them he was building the
fence to keep people away from the tree; that if any of them
touched it he would be in danger of his life.

A moment later a Dr. Evans and a Mr. Pilbeam, friends of
Julian Northrup from the village, arrive. They have been sent
for, but not by Northrup, as they suppose. Demetria has sent
for them. Julian, Demetria explains, is just around the corner,
burying his dog, and she wants them to meet a friend of Julian's
—a Mr. Brink—who is at the moment up in the tree.

If they can't see Mr. Brink, it is because he is invisible, Demetria explains further. "You see, a short while after Julian got
Mr. Brink up there, Betty, the old dog, saw him and barked at
him. Mr. Brink didn't like that, so he became invisible. And
right after that Betty touched her nose to the tree and dropped
over dead. Julian and Pud are burying her now."

"Is this supposed to be a joke, Miss Riffle?" Pilbeam wants
to know.

"What would you say if I told you I believed it was the
Gospel truth?"

" 'Fraid I'd say you were crazy."

"I would be crazy, wouldn't I?" continues Demetria. "And
what if I told you that Mr. Brink is a man, just like you, who
goes around taking people away with him when it's time for
them to die. Now, if I believed that you'd surely say I was
crazy, wouldn't you?"

"Come, come, Miss Riffle, what kind of story is this?"

"An hour ago when I happened to be passing, I saw all these
pieces of fence being unloaded from a truck. Naturally, I came
back to find out what was going on. Julian told me he was
building the fence to keep people away from the tree, because

anybody who touched the tree would die."

"Die?"

"And not only that! Touching that tree is the only way any-one can die. There is no more death in the world, Mr. Pilbeam, until Julian lets Mr. Brink come down."

It is Demetria's conclusion that Julian, being an old man who has gone through a great deal, is as crazy as a loon. That is why she has sent for Dr. Evans and Mr. Pilbeam to confirm her belief. Yes, it is true that if Mr. Northrup is insane she would have to take Pud, being next of kin, but she hopes Mr. Pilbeam does not think she is making up this story about Julian to force the courts to let her have Pud.

"I guess a court of law will feel different about it, if they realize a young boy is being brought up by a maniac," snaps Demetria, sensing the Pilbeam opposition. "I'll be frank with you, Mr. Pilbeam, I intend to get that boy away from this insane man's house before something terrible happens. Tonight —if possible!"

Dr. Evans admits that if he is convinced Northrup is crazy he will be impelled to take immediate action.

A moment later Gramps can be heard bellowing in the distance. It is the workmen who have excited him. In spite of his warning they will insist on getting too close to the tree. Don't they know they stand in peril of their lives? Now, let them go and get the rest of the fence unloaded—

Gramps sees Demetria. That is an added irritation. And Evans and Pilbeam— He realizes Demetria has been talking. Yes, they admit, Demetria has told them everything. And what about it?

It is the truth, Gramps admits. Just as true as he's standin' there. There is somebody in that tree, and nobody in the world can die anymore until Gramps says so, unless they touch the tree, or one of the apples, or Mr. Brink himself—

"You're not serious about this, Northrup?" demands Dr. Evans.

"Of course he is, Doctor," breaks in Demetria. "He's perfectly serious, aren't you, Julian?"

GRAMPS (*crossing quickly to* DEMETRIA)—Hey there, what the hell are you up to anyway?

DEMETRIA—Why, nothing, Julian. I'm just interested. . . .

GRAMPS—Well, I don't want you to go telling anybody else about Mr. Brink. I got him up there and now I gotta figure out what the hell I'm gonna do with him.

DEMETRIA—But you don't think you'll be able to keep a thing like this quiet, Julian.

EVANS—Look here, Northrup. Can you talk to Mr. Brink?

GRAMPS—Sure I can talk to him.

EVANS—Have you talked to him since you got him up there?

GRAMPS—Nope. Haven't had time.

EVANS—I wish you'd talk to him now.

GRAMPS—What for? Just so's you can hear him?

EVANS—I just thought, perhaps if you tried to talk to him— well, you'd find out he isn't up there any more.

GRAMPS—Oh, he's up there, all right.

DEMETRIA—Julian, do try to make him talk. I'd love to hear him.

GRAMPS—Oh, you would. (*He turns suddenly and stares at* DEMETRIA.) Well, by golly, Demmie, I believe I'll let you. I'll let you all hear him. (GRAMPS *goes to tree.* MARCIA *enters from porch.*) Mr. Brink, can you hear me if I don't shout?

BRINK—Sir?

GRAMPS—See, he calls me "Sir." . . .

DEMETRIA (*to* EVANS *and* PILBEAM)—There, he thinks someone's answering.

GRAMPS—Well, Mr. Brink, I'm sorry I haven't had more of a chance to talk to you.

BRINK—Perhaps I shouldn't say it but I'm not extremely upset by that.

GRAMPS—You're not mad at me, are you?

BRINK—I think I might justifiably be allowed some slight irritation.

GRAMPS—Well, I wouldn't have put you there without a damn good reason. I got you up there so this old hellion couldn't get Pud and the money his father left him.

BRINK—I appreciate that your motive was probably sincere.

GRAMPS—Now, I got an idea, and it's goin' to settle once and for all this business of her gettin' Pud. (*He pulls* DEMETRIA *toward him.*) Come here, you. Stand out there. (*To* BRINK.) You see this old battle-ax here—her name is Demetria Riffle. Have you got anything on your schedule about when you are supposed to snuff her out?

BRINK—Riffle? There's no such name that has come to my attention yet.

GRAMPS—Well, Mr. Brink, I'm goin' to keep you up there until it's time for you to exterminate her.

BRINK—My dear man, that may be a very long time yet.

There's no telling how long that woman may hang on.

GRAMPS—Well, that's the way it's goin' to be.

BRINK—But for me to stay here any length of time might be considered by my Superior as a considerable dereliction of duty.

GRAMPS—Can't help it. Them's the terms.

BRINK (*with a sigh*)—Ah, well! I was afraid of that. Very well, since you and your tree are so tenacious, I shall have to sit here and wait for Miss Riffle's call.

GRAMPS—Do you think you can hold out that long?

BRINK—My dear man, a human life is like the twinkling of an eye to me.

GRAMPS—Oh, yes, I suppose it is. All right, then, Mr. Brink.

With a satisfied "Well, there you are!" Gramps turns back to the others. They stare at him wonderingly. No one has heard what he has heard! Evans thinks it's probably some sort of dream. Can it be that he is going nuts? Gramps is worried. Didn't anyone hear what Brink said?

"He said a human life was like the twinkling of an eye to him," speaks up Pud. What a relief! At least Pud had heard.

"See what he's doing to the boy?" demands Demetria.

Pilbeam agrees that, as Gramps says, they may all be too dull to hear. But Evans wants further proof. He has decided to try eating an apple. But before he can get to the tree Gramps has excitedly tripped him up and held him to the ground. "Gol-darn fool, tryin' to commit suicide!" shouts Gramps.

"All right, Northrup. I just wanted to make sure you weren't joking," says Evans, getting to his feet. "Are you going to be home a little later this evening, Northrup?"

" 'Course I am."

"I may be over and—er—talk some more about this."

"All right, Evans." . . .

They have all gone. Gramps and Pud have picked up their spades and are about to get back to work.

"Why don't they hear Mr. Brink?" Pud wants to know.

"Don't know, boy. Guess they're all too busy."

Now Mr. Brink is sitting upright in the tree. "Oh, my dear man, that isn't the reason at all," he calls.

GRAMPS (*turning to him*)—Oh, hello, Mr. Brink. Why is it only Pud and me can hear you, then?

BRINK—I won't go into it now if you don't mind.

GRAMPS—Just as you say, Mr. Brink. One thing I would like

to know though.

BRINK—Well?

GRAMPS—You don't think they'll hold it against Pud what I'm doin' to you?

BRINK—I have neither the inclination nor the authorization to dispense information relevant to your inquiry.

PUD (*laughs*)—He still talks funny.

GRAMPS—Well, guess I'll have to take that chance. Come on, boy. Say good-by to Mr. Brink.

PUD—'By, Brink.

GRAMPS—Can't you say "Mr. Brink"?

PUD—Good-by, Mr. Brink—excuse me.

BRINK—That's all right— Good-by, Pud.

GRAMPS—Well, we gotta get that fence finished tonight, boy.

PUD—We gotta work like hell to do it, though, Gramps.

They start for the hill as the curtain falls.

It is ten o'clock the same night. In the living room Gramps has fallen asleep in his chair, with a newspaper over his face. Pud, playing on the floor, is suddenly reminded of something he learned in Sunday school—that the King of Massonia wore his crown upon his seat. He should, he decides, impart that bit of interesting information to Gramps, and does so. Gramps, being aroused, is glad to hear about the King of Massonia, but it occurs to him that Pud probably means the King of Macedonia. Or, maybe, as Pud also suggests, the King of Massachusetts. And the King's reason for misplacing the crown was, again as Pud decides, no doubt due to his desire to sit on it. . . .

The workmen are still at work on the fence in the yard. They should have it finished by dawn. Gramps doesn't know when Dr. Evans will be over, but he does know it is time Pud was going to bed, and sends him away with Marcia. . . .

Dr. Evans and a Mr. Grimes, a large, surly, domineering sort of person, have arrived. Dr. Evans has told Mr. Grimes about Mr. Brink and the apple tree, he explains to Gramps, and Mr. Grimes would like to have Gramps go along with him to explain it to a third fellow. But Gramps is worried—

"Mr. Grimes, I don't want any more people knowin' about this thing until I find out some way of provin' it. This is goin' to be a hard thing to make people believe. 'Tain't everybody that can hear Mr. Brink when he talks. I figger that . . ."

"Oh, what the hell's the use?" breaks in Mr. Grimes, looking

impatiently at Dr. Evans. Turning back to Gramps he blurts:
"Now try to get this straight, will you? I'm taking you to the
state insane asylum!"

Gramps is dazed by both the statement and attitude of Mr.
Grimes. He looks to Evans for an explanation. There is none
forthcoming. It is, he concludes, more of Demetria's doings. And
where is Demetria? She is outside, waiting in the car. She is
going to take Pud, but only while Gramps is in the asylum for
observation. If there ain't anything wrong with Gramps, Mr.
Grimes promises, they'll find that out, so let him come along like
a good fellow or they'll have to put a jacket on him.

Gramps admits it looks as though he'd have to go, but he
would like to go upstairs a minute to say good-by to Pud. Mr.
Grimes will not allow that. He can see Pud at the asylum tomorrow. All right, Gramps agrees to go, but, just as a little favor,
he would like to wear his veteran's badge, just as he does in
parades.

As Gramps is rummaging in the drawer for the badge, Grimes
explains to Dr. Evans that it is all in the way a man's handled;
some have to be humored and some have to be treated tough—

Now Gramps has found what he was looking for and it isn't a
badge. It's a revolver. He turns now and faces Grimes and
Evans. Since they've decided that he is crazy, and since they
are agreed a crazy person has to be humored, they had better
humor him, because if they don't they're likely to drive him quite
wild—

GRAMPS—I ain't goin' to no bug-house and I ain't goin' to let
that old she-cat get Pud. But I see I gotta prove that what I
been sayin' in reference to a certain Mr. Brink ain't no poppycock.

EVANS—Now be reasonable, Northrup.

GRIMES—Yeah, you can prove it to us later.

GRAMPS—Wait a minute. . . . That your medicine kit, Evans?

EVANS—Yes.

GRAMPS—What you got in that kit?

EVANS—Lots of things.   •

GRAMPS—You got anything in it—poison enough to kill a fly?

EVANS—Of course, but . . .

GRIMES (advancing)—You can play with all the flies you want
when—

GRAMPS—Play! Do you consider it playin' when a man is
willin' to risk his freedom on a fly?

EVANS—What's a fly got to do with it?

GRAMPS—I'll make a bargain with you. And you'd best take it, too, because if you don't I'm just liable to go wild as all hell. (*He wiggles gun at them.*)

GRIMES—Well, what's the bargain?

GRAMPS—You take the worst poison you got in that bag and put some of it in a tumbler. Then you catch a fly and put him in the poison. If that fly dies, I'll give myself up to you, to the police, to anyone, go to the insane asylum, do anythin' you say. (GRIMES *and* EVANS *look at each other.*) Well?

EVANS—If the fly dies, you'll come along with us without makin' any trouble?

GRAMPS—Yup. I promise. Hope to die. Cross my heart.

EVANS—Well—

GRAMPS (*pointing gun*)—It's the easiest way, Mr. Grimes.

GRIMES (*with look at* EVANS)—All right.

EVANS—O.K.

GRAMPS—You get the poison. I'll get the glasses and, Mr. Grimes, you catch a fly. (*He goes for tumblers.*)

GRIMES (*to* EVANS)—He's crazy, raving crazy.

EVANS—Looks like it. But don't think he won't use that gun! I know the old boy. . . .

GRIMES—O.K. Let him play with the fly. How do we know he'll keep his word, though?

EVANS—I think he will.

GRIMES—The word of a nut—

EVANS (*sharply*)—Well, what do you want to do? Take the gun away from him?

GRIMES—No, no. Let him do it! No hurry.

GRAMPS (*coming back to table*)—Of course, look here, a bet ain't a bet that don't cut both ways. If the fly lives, you gotta swear I'm sane.

GRIMES—Well, I don't know.

EVANS—Don't worry. I know damn well I can kill a fly.

GRAMPS—No, you can't.

EVANS—If I can't kill a fly, I'll quit medicine. (*To* GRIMES.) You'll agree to this, won't you, Grimes?

GRIMES—Oh, all right.

GRAMPS—You swear?

EVANS—Yes, we swear, Northrup.

GRIMES—Sure, sure, that's all right. You don't have to worry about us.

GRAMPS—All right. Where's the fly?

Grimes manages to catch a fly on the window screen. Evans
gets the poison and a pair of tweezers from his bag, pours the
poison into a tumbler and transfers the fly to the poison—enough
poison, he says, to kill a horse.

For a few seconds they watch the fly intently. Evans is smiling confidently. Grimes looks on with a satisfied chuckle. Gramps
is anxious. Certainly, says Gramps, after practicing for thirty
years Evans should be able to kill a fly. But, then, everybody
has to live and learn.

Now the doctor decides the fly has had time enough to die and
picks it out of the poison with the tweezers, laying it on a newspaper. It certainly acts like a dead fly. Gramps stirs it up a bit
but there is no sign of life. Grimes is getting impatient and
would move on. Then, suddenly, the fly starts to crawl—

"Well, I'll be God-damned!" swears Gramps. "Look, look!
He's drunk as a lord, but we didn't say anythin' about that. He's
movin' right across that God-damned piece of paper!"

Grimes and Evans also profanely admit their surprise, but
Grimes is in no mood to accept defeat. To hell with Mr. Brink.
Grimes is ready to go and he is taking Gramps with him. What's
a promise to a lunatic—

GRAMPS—So you don't believe it yet, eh? Even after I proved
it to you?

GRIMES (softly)—You crazy bastard—

EVANS—Look out, Grimes. Wait a minute!

GRAMPS—And you ain't goin' to keep your word, eh? Well,
by God, there's another way of provin' it and it looks like I got to
use that way right now.

EVANS—For God's sake, Northrup! What—

GRAMPS—I'm goin' to make another experiment and I want
you to witness it.

GRIMES (going toward EVANS)—He's crazy as hell! He's dangerous!

EVANS—What are you going to do, Northrup!

GRAMPS—Evans, at this close range if a man was shot right
through the belly, he'd die, wouldn't he?

EVANS—Good God, man!

GRIMES—Look out there, Northrup!

GRAMPS—Wouldn't he?

EVANS—Yes, of course, but—

GRAMPS—That's all I want to know. (*He fires.* GRIMES *crumples up.* EVANS *rushes to him.*)

GRAMPS—Now, don't worry. He ain't goin' to die.

EVANS (*straightens up and looks at* GRAMPS)—You crazy fool! He'll be dead in an hour.

GRAMPS (*at window*)—Stay up there, Mr. Brink. If you come down now, by God, I'm in a hell of a fix.

The curtain falls.

At dawn next morning Dr. Evans is discovered outside the fence surrounding the tree in Gramps' backyard. He has thrust a fishing pole through the fence and pulls it out now with a small gray object dangling from the end. It is, he tells Marcia, when she comes from the house, a dead mouse.

Presently Evans is joined by Pilbeam. Evans had sent for Pilbeam to report his latest conclusions, among them that Julian Northrup is not crazy.

"Pilbeam, we gotta keep our heads," Evans explains. "Because something's happened that'll turn this world upside-down, unless we can stop it. And you gotta help me."

"Uh?"

"Northrup shot Grimes last night, Pilbeam."

"Good God!"

"Shot him right through the belly. He had internal hemorrhages and it was an hour before I could get him to the hospital."

"What did he shoot him for?"

"He was experimenting."

"He was—experimenting!"

"Wait a minute, Grimes is all right."

"All right?"

"He's practically well. That's the trouble. According to everything I know about medicine, Grimes should have died last night, Pilbeam. But he didn't. (*Wipes face.*) Plenty of things should have died last night, Pilbeam. But they didn't. (*He pauses for a second.*) I've been up all night, trying to kill something. I've experimented on everything I could get my hands on. Insects. Bugs. I've tried to kill every stray cat or dog I could find. I couldn't kill a damn thing. Except that mouse. And do you know how I killed him? I tied him to the end of this fishpole and touched him to that tree."

Evans is as mystified as Pilbeam, but one thing he knows: If there is anything in that tree, by God, it's got to come down!

Gramps has joined them now. He greets them cheerfully; inquires after the health of Mr. Grimes and is glad to hear he came through the accident successfully. Gramps doesn't blame Dr. Evans at all for being doubtful; no doctor could possibly believe a thing like that at first.

Presently Mr. Brink has announced his presence. He has had a very pleasant morning, he admits, except for having a mouse in his face! When Gramps repeats that to Evans and Pilbeam, Pilbeam decides quite suddenly that he has to go; he's got a big day's work—

"This is a sort of a special occasion," Gramps explains. "In fact this is the mornin' Demmie figured I'd be in the nut-house. Yes, sir, I'm feelin' right good this mornin'. Pud's feelin' pretty spry. Mr. Brink sounded pretty pert. Everybody's feelin' fine— 'cept Demmie. God bless her!"

"Northrup, there's a man in my hospital who's been suffering for ten years," says Dr. Evans, abruptly. "He's in constant pain."

GRAMPS—I'm real sorry, Evans.

EVANS—Day before yesterday, I decided to operate on him. The operation wasn't successful. He's in more pain now than he ever was.

GRAMPS—Well, Evans, I'm real sorry to hear that.

EVANS—I expected him to die last night. I hoped he would.

GRAMPS—Yeah.

EVANS—There's a nice old lady up in 2C, Mrs. Trenner, remember her?

GRAMPS—The old lady who used to have all the dogs?

EVANS—Yeah.

GRAMPS—By God, I'd forgot all about her.

EVANS—Everybody has. She's been in there for six years, in bed. She hasn't got much left. Only one idea—to die. And this is what's happening in just one small hospital, you know. In a small town. There are two in Gainesville. There are several million in the world, aren't there—full of people just like that.

GRAMPS—I'm sorry for all those people—sorry for all of 'em— but if you're hintin' for me to let Mr. Brink down, you're off on the wrong track.

EVANS—What do you think is going to happen, Northrup, in the next few days when people find out there's no more death?

PILBEAM—But it isn't true—

EVANS (*crosses to* PILBEAM)—No more death. Think about it for a minute. Nobody died last night. Nobody's going to die tonight. Or tomorrow night. Nobody's going to die . . . (*Looks at* GRAMPS.) until Northrup says they can. What do you think about that?

PILBEAM—It's absurd.

EVANS—That's right. It's absurd. (*Facing* GRAMPS.) Five years from today this world will be so over-crowded that it won't be fit to live in . . . think of the disease . . .

GRAMPS—I don't give a damn! I don't care what happens! I've got Mr. Brink up there and he's gonna stay there!

EVANS—He can't, Northrup. You gotta let him down.

GRAMPS—Why should I? I'm lookin' after Pud and myself.

EVANS—Who the hell are you?

GRAMPS—I'm the feller that got Mr. Brink up that tree and up that tree he's gonna stay until I'm good and ready to let him down.

Again Pilbeam remembers that he must go, and this time he gets away. Gramps is quick to assure Evans that he is not afraid of dying—dying might be interesting—but he wants to stick around in case Pud needs him.

But, counters Dr. Evans, by the time Pud is grown Gramps will be over a hundred years old and of no use to anyone. He might not even be able to call on Mr. Brink then. That thought gives Gramps pause—he had never thought of being a nuisance to Pud—

"You've got to let Mr. Brink come down today," insists Dr. Evans, very solemnly. "I warn you—I'll do everything I can to make you. Better think it over. (*Crosses to tree, picks up bag.*) I'll be back in an hour. (*Starts out, then hesitates.*) Well, thanks for not letting me eat that apple yesterday."

With Evans gone, Gramps takes the matter up with Mr. Brink. "Mr. Brink, do you think Evans is right about me and Pud?" he asks. "Think maybe I might become a nuisance to the boy?"

"My dear man, there's no doubt about it," answers Mr. Brink.

Pud has come trotting out of the house. He is playing steam engine, and gallops solemnly about the yard, clearing the tracks of God and everybody to make way for Casey Jones. Now he has caught sight of Gramps. A moment later he has run into him. Now he has stopped and thrown his arms around Gramps.

"I love you, Gramps," he says. "I love you more'n my engine."
The curtain falls.

Toward the close of that day, Dr. Evans arrives in the backyard with the Sheriff and Demetria. The three stand now facing
Gramps and Pud, who are back of the bench. The Sheriff has
just finished reading an order of adoption and the three are closing in when Gramps stops them.

"Just read the last part of that document again, Sheriff," says
Gramps. "Where Dr. Evans signed—"

"All right, Northrup," agrees the Sheriff and proceeds to read:

" 'Dr. James Evans, having testified that the said Julian Northrup
is incapable of managing himself and his property, it is the order
of this Court that he be committed to the Gainesville Institution
for the Insane, according to the Laws of this State and it is further
ordered that the custody of the child, John Gilford Northrup, be
awarded to his aunt, Demetria Riffle.' "

"Thank you, Sheriff. (*To* EVANS.) You've kinda fixed me up
good and proper, ain't you?"

"I warned you I'd do anything I could," answers Evans.

Gramps admits that he is beaten, but he would like to speak
to Pud before he goes with them. He knows what Evans has
figured on—that since he has lost Pud he will let Mr. Brink down.
Evans admits that that is what he hoped would happen.

They are alone now, Pud and Gramps. It isn't easy for Gramps
to speak, but he finally musters the needed courage. "I'm goin'
away, boy," he says.

"Where, Gramps?"

GRAMPS—Where the woodbine twineth.

PUD—You goin' with Mr. Brink?

GRAMPS—Yep, I'm goin' with Mr. Brink. You see, your
Gramps is gettin' to be a pretty old man. And when you get to
be a pretty old man you begin to get kinda tired.

PUD—Are you tired?

GRAMPS—Right this minute, I'm pretty dog-gone tired.

PUD—Let's lie down and rest.

GRAMPS—That's just what I'm gonna do. But the only way
an old man can really lie down and rest is to go with Mr. Brink.

PUD—I'll go with you, Gramps.

GRAMPS—No, you can't go with me, boy. You've got your
whole life ahead of you.

PUD—Don't want my whole life ahead of me. I want to go

with you. I love you, Gramps. (*Puts arms around* GRAMPS.)

GRAMPS—Shouldn't love me that much, boy. You see, Pud, I been thinkin' things over. Maybe it ain't such a good thing for you to be livin' with me any more. And, you know, maybe your Aunt Demetria ain't as much of a pismire as we thought she was.

PUD (*backing away*)—Gramps!

GRAMPS—No, sir, maybe she ain't. Maybe it'd be better if you was to go over to your Aunt Demetria's house and live with her. (PUD *backs further away*.) What's the matter, boy?

PUD—Don't you love me any more, Gramps?

GRAMPS—Pshaw, boy, I'm just tryin' to make you understand—

PUD (*miserably*)—Gramps, you don't love me any more.

GRAMPS—Of course I do. It's just that I gotta go away.

PUD—But I'll go with you, Gramps.

GRAMPS—But you can't, boy, you can't.

PUD—Please, Gramps, please!

GRAMPS—No!

PUD—Then I don't love you any more either. . . . I don't love you any more either. . . .

Pud has run crying into the house. Gramps might have followed, but Mr. Brink stops him. It is the better way, says Brink. Pud will forget.

The Sheriff, Evans and Demetria have reappeared. They are closing in now. Gramps explains that he is not going with them. He is going with Mr. Brink, but they close in just the same. Now Demetria has given her promise that she will be good to Pud; that she will see that he gets some fun out of life, but that first she is going to start teaching him herself so he will be ready for school and way ahead of any of the others; she will teach him little poems to recite and how to be polite to older people. Finally she will send him to Miss Ramsdell's girls' school, where they are going to let three little boys in next year— That is too much for Gramps—

"You're gonna make Pud into a sissy!" he shouts. "By God, you are still a pismire! I'm gonna change my mind. I ain't goin' with Mr. Brink. I'm gonna stay right here and take care of Pud."

He cannot do that, Dr. Evans points out, because if he stays he will be in the insane asylum. Gramps sees the point. The time has come, he admits to Mr. Brink with a gesture of helplessness. There's no use stretchin' it out. But he would have Mr. Brink understand that he has been acting only in the interest of

Pud, to keep Demetria from getting him. He had always intended letting Mr. Brink down as soon as he was ready to take Demetria, too. If there is any chance of that, even now—

"No, there's been no call for Miss Riffle," answers Mr. Brink, a little petulantly. "There probably won't be for years."

GRAMPS (*suddenly, as a new idea is born*)—What's that? You say you were supposed to take her an hour ago?

BRINK—No, no. I said I probably wouldn't take her for years.

GRAMPS—My God, why didn't you tell me, Mr. Brink? Why, if you're supposed to take Demmie too—

BRINK—But I'm *not* supposed to take her!

EVANS—Northrup, did he really say that?

GRAMPS—Yep. Says he was supposed to take Demmie an hour ago. This changes everything. Come on, Demmie! (*He drags* DEMMIE *to tree.*)

DEMETRIA (*breaking away from him*)—No— No, Julian. This is absurd! This is—! Dr. Evans.

EVANS—I'm sorry, Miss Riffle. But when a person's time comes . . .

DEMETRIA—But—there isn't really anyone up in that tree— This is all so—so silly.

GRAMPS—Thank you, Mr. Brink, for takin' Demmie. I wonder if you'd do one more thing. I wonder if after you've taken Demmie, you'd just slip the Sheriff in for good measure.

SHERIFF—Hey—what the hell—

GRAMPS—The old stiff's tryin' to take me to the nut-house—

EVANS (*crosses to* GRAMPS)—Good God, Northrup! Do you know what you're doing? This is practically murder!

DEMETRIA—M-m-murder! D-d-doctor! M-m-murder!

EVANS—Listen you, all of you, Northrup's as sane as anyone here.

SHERIFF—What's that? Hey, what is this, anyway?

EVANS—Northrup's not insane. You realize what he's going to do? Death is up in that tree. Northrup's talking to him. If he lets him down you're as good as dead, both of you.

DEMETRIA—What! What! I don't believe it—

BRINK—This is—

GRAMPS—Ssh! Ssh!

BRINK—This is the wildest absurdity I ever heard. You know perfectly well I have no authorization to take any of these people. It is utterly out of the question.

GRAMPS—What's that? You say you'll take the Sheriff too? Thank you, Mr. Brink. I appreciate that a great deal.

Demetria is pacing the yard hysterically and denying that there is anybody in the tree, when Marcia suddenly takes a hand. Marcia can also hear Mr. Brink. She can hear him saying that if he can come down he will take anyone Mr. Northrup wants him to. And Demetria would be the first. Mr. Brink is getting nervous, too. He wants to come down right away.

"Yup," chimes in a surprised Gramps. "That's just what he said. So I better get started. Don't want to make him any angrier."

"That would be impossible," shouts Mr. Brink. "You let me down!"

"Well, good-by, everybody," calls Gramps, ignoring Mr. Brink. "But then I'll be seein' you two in a second. Now I'm gonna start the magic words." He has taken Demetria and the Sheriff by the hand. "Come on, Demmie. Sheriff. Line up! Here we go! Off to glory!"

He has started mumbling and walking them around in a circle. Mr. Brink calls to him to stop. Evans calls, excitedly. The Sheriff tears up the adoption papers as a peace offering. Demetria is wildly promising to keep her hands off Pud and to stay the hell away from Gramps, too.

"All right, Mr. Brink, from now on anybody who tries to make me let you down you gotta take them, too."

"I will not! I will not!" shouts Mr. Brink.

GRAMPS—Thank you very much. . . . Now, you get out of here. All of you. I'm gonna stay right here and take care of Pud. I don't care if the whole damn world goes to hell. Git out of here. Git off my property. Go on. Go on! If you ask me, you got off pretty lucky. (*They all go off except* MARCIA.) Marcy, I love yuh. By God, I love yuh. And there ain't nothin' in this world can stop us now. Just you and me and Pud. Nothin' in the world can stop us now.

BRINK (*appearing*)—Which world do you mean?

GRAMPS—What's that, Mr. Brink?

BRINK—Which world do you mean?

GRAMPS—Why, I don't understand, Mr. Brink.

BRINK—Of course you don't. My poor man!

MARCIA—What did he say, Mr. Northrup?

GRAMPS—He said: "My poor man." And I didn't like the way he said it, Marcy. I didn't like the way he said it.

The curtain falls.

It is a few minutes later. Darkness has closed in. From the house Gramps and Marcia appear, calling excitedly for Pud. Gramps has things he wants to explain to Pud and the boy can't be found. The searchers have gone beyond the yard, still calling wildly, when Pud comes up from the cellar. He is sniffling and carrying a few of his belongings tied up in a handkerchief.

Mr. Brink calls to him. Pud answers tearfully. Pud is in trouble because his Gramps doesn't love him any more. He is going to run away, and then his Gramps will be sorry. What has he got in the handkerchief? Just some cookies, and the watch fob and a couple of specimens.

Mr. Brink thinks Pud would be foolish to run away. They would only find him and bring him back. Pud isn't big enough to run away.

Pud is so. Pud is big enough to do anything and he isn't afraid of the biggest giant on earth. Pud isn't afraid of anything. Could he climb that tree? Pud climbed that tree long before Mr. Brink did and came down again, which is more than Mr. Brink can do. Climb the fence? Of course he can climb the fence. And he does, after a trial or two, and after Mr. Brink has shown him the easiest place. Mr. Brink is quite pleased—

"I never thought you could do it," admits Mr. Brink, when Pud is at the crossbeam. "I guess you must be stronger than I thought. Come on now. Just a little more. *Go along the edge there!* Get one leg over. There! That's it! Now you're here. Splendid! I guess you can do anything."

PUD—Golly, I can see far up here.

BRINK—Can you see me now?

PUD—Yes. Gee, why do you make your voice so whispery, Mr. Brink?

BRINK—Don't you like it?

PUD—Yes.

BRINK—Good. Can you see me?

PUD—Yes, I can see you. I'm up as high as you are now.

BRINK—Look at me!

PUD—Gee, you've got funny eyes, Mr. Brink. They make me dizzy. You've got ghost eyes. (*Slowly* PUD *stands up, gripping the post.*)

BRINK—Look at me again. (PUD *does so*.)   That's right.
Keep on looking at me.   Give me your hand.   Lean forward.
(PUD *suddenly loses his balance and falls*.)

PUD (*in terror*)—Gramps! Gramps! Gramps!

The curtain falls.

It is later the same night.   The moon has risen.   Gramps is
standing holding Pud in his arms.   He is calling to Mr. Brink.
Pud, Gramps explains, is in terrible pain.   Dr. Evans has said
the boy will never be able to walk again.

Mr. Brink is sorry about that.   He had no intention of hurting Pud.   Just meant to take him as the only way out.   Nothing
else, says Mr. Brink, would have forced Gramps to let him down.
He would have had to stay in the tree until Miss Riffle died.

Gramps is glad now that Mr. Brink doesn't have to complete
that sentence.   He needs Mr. Brink's help.

"Will you come down, please, and take us both?" pleads
Gramps.

"Gladly."

Now Mr. Brink has come through the gate and Gramps holds
Pud out to him.   But it is Gramps who is to go first.   Gently Mr.
Brink touches Gramps' brow and he suddenly straightens up.

"Well, well," says Gramps, wonderingly.   "He was quite a load
before.   He's light as a feather now."   He holds the suffering Pud
out again.

Mr. Brink leans over and touches Pud.   The next moment the
boy is standing straight and strong before them.   "Hello, Mr.
Brink!" Pud calls, smilingly.

"Hello, Pud."

PUD—Are we deaded, Gramps?

GRAMPS—Must be.   I feel like a two-year-old.   How do you
feel?

PUD—I feel like a two-year-old, too, Gramps.

GRAMPS—Mr. Brink, why didn't you tell me it was goin' to be
like this?

BRINK—My dear man, I've been trying to tell you how pleasant it is to go with me, but you wouldn't listen.

PUD—You talk so funny, Mr. Brink.

BRINK—Well, never mind me—   Come on.   Come along!

PUD (*crossing*, GRAMPS *following*)—But, where we goin',
Gramps?

GRAMPS (*stopping*)—Oh, yes—by golly, that's important.

Where are we goin', Mr. Brink?

BRINK—You'll find out.

PUD (*looking at* BRINK)—How long will we be there?

BRINK—For eternity.

PUD (*looking at* GRAMPS)—How long is eternity, Gramps?

GRAMPS—Right smart piece of time, boy.

PUD—Anyway, we'll be there together, won't we, Gramps?

GRAMPS (*shaking hands with* PUD)—You're damn right we will be! You're damn right!

GRANNY (*off stage*)—Juleyun! Juleyun, do you have to use such language in front of the boy? (*They all look up.*)

GRAMPS—Oh, hell, I thought you said she'd changed! (BRINK *shakes his head disapprovingly.* GRAMPS *throws* GRANNY *a kiss.*)

Gramps and Pud march hand in hand through the gates and up the ramps and

THE CURTAIN FALLS

THE STAR-WAGON

A Comedy in Three Acts

By Maxwell Anderson

THIS popular fantasy, as did the same author's "High Tor" of the previous season, grew out of the Maxwell Anderson-Burgess Meredith friendship, which in turn stems from young Mr. Meredith's success in Mr. Anderson's prize-winning drama of the 1935-36 season, "Winterset."

There were many Anderson-Meredith walks and talks after Meredith moved into the country near the Anderson place at New City, New York. "High Tor," written around an historic mountain facing the Hudson near both the actor's and the dramatist's estates, had barely been produced before the talk turned to its successor. There is no record of these conversations, but knowing actors, I have an idea that it was Meredith who suggested a character of many facets, and a story that should, as the old play criticisms frequently have it, run the gamut of the emotions. Actors who love their profession also love to act, and nothing gives them a greater consciousness of acting than a protean role that demands frequent changes of costume, wigs, facial make-up and general physical and mental deportment.

In "The Star-Wagon" Mr. Meredith, who commands a marked versatility, is able to appear first as a man approaching sixty, then to go back to his early twenties, to come forward again to a wasted old age and close the evening as he was in the beginning. The play is a combination of fantasy and realism, as also was "High Tor," and is therefore of a divided appeal, so far as audiences are concerned. Those of literal minds find the dips into the past a little foolish. Those of keener imagination and a frank liking for the speculative drama revel in the play's novelty.

It is a spring day in the suburbs of a small manufacturing town in eastern Ohio. The dining room of the Minch's cottage is "clean, neat, bare and sunny." The table is set for breakfast with, for the moment, no one in sight to eat the breakfast.

Presently Hanus appears. Hanus is an elderly workman, graying a little and depressed by the encroaching years. He mutters to himself, which is a habit he has, his subject at the moment

157

being largely speculative and pertaining to the weather. It is, Hanus is prepared to admit, a nice, sunny day. But why everybody he meets will feel obliged to comment upon that fact is irritating.

"No use trying to tell 'em you hate a fine sunny day and wish it would rain once in a while," mutters Hanus. " 'Wish it would rain,' you say. 'Huh,' they say. 'There goes Hanus, says he wishes it was going to rain— He's screwy,' they say. Why can't a man like rain? Everybody else likes what he likes."

Martha, an elderly housewife, shuffling and evidently also in a state of irritation, comes from the kitchen. The sight of Hanus does not cheer her. She resents Hanus' absent-mindedness. Why can't he remember to leave his towel in the bathroom? She resents his talking to himself. It will drive them all as crazy as he is if he keeps it up.

Stephen is the next to arrive. Stephen is "a pleasant, gentle, submissive little man of more than fifty," and he also has forgotten to leave his towel where it belongs. Too late now. He thinks to stick it in his pocket and fool Martha.

But Martha is not to be fooled. She has recovered both towels and gone again to the kitchen, which gives Stephen an idea that this is really not one of their best days. "Beautiful morning, birds in the trees, sun out, dandelions looking right back at him, but the wife's under a cloud," observes Stephen. "I wish it would rain," echoes Hanus.

The trouble is deeper than that with Martha, as they shortly learn. She is back in the room now and prepared to state her case, which still has to do with Hanus.

"If we must live in the same house with a complete half-wit," she says, "you might at least try to teach him something instead of picking up his half-wit tricks! You're more like Hanus every day."

STEPHEN—What have I done? What have I done now?

MARTHA—Hanus! Must you dunk your toast in your coffee? (HANUS *drops his toast.*)

STEPHEN—And you're wrong about Hanus! He's smarter than most people. I tell you I couldn't get along without him in the laboratory.

MARTHA—Just the same I can't get along with him here.

STEPHEN—More than that, didn't he save my life?

MARTHA—Yes, tell me all about that again. You'll have just time before the street-car goes. Tell me about the picnic and how you fell in the water and hit your head on a rock and went down for the third time. And how all your life went before your eyes in a flash—only Hanus pulled you out, so you lived. Wasn't that how it was?

HANUS—It wasn't anything. The water was just taking him round the bend, and I reached in and got him by the hair. That's all it was.

MARTHA—Thirty-five years ago?

HANUS—Yes'm. (*He eats.*) On the Fourth of July. The same Fourth of July when you got engaged to Stephen.

MARTHA—It's nice to know gratitude lasts so long. I can't think of any other emotion that hangs on that way.—He saved your life thirty-five years ago, so he still eats off you and cadges off you and has a bed in your house. If you cared half as much for me as for him you'd have told him long since I couldn't stand it and he'd have to board somewhere else.

HANUS—I—I didn't know—

STEPHEN—He wouldn't have anywhere to go, Martha. Besides, you don't know what Hanus does in the laboratory—

MARTHA—Oh, yes, I do.

STEPHEN—No, you don't. We work together, and he earns his share—

MARTHA—Then why doesn't he get paid?

STEPHEN—Because they don't understand about him. When I'm working at something I get stuck sometimes, and just don't know what to try next. And Hanus works right along with me, not saying a word—

MARTHA—Oh, not saying a word?

STEPHEN—Well, just talking to himself, you know, the way he does. Only when I'm really stuck, he'll put his head into whatever I'm supposed to be doing, and then he'll say, "Why don't you try this?" And it'll be some fool thing I never thought of, and probably no good, only it'll make me think of something that is good, so then I'll go ahead—and maybe figure it out.

MARTHA—Oh, that's what Hanus does in the laboratory? Why couldn't you think of it for yourself?

STEPHEN—I don't know. Only I couldn't.

MARTHA—You'd better eat your breakfast. (*She goes toward the kitchen.*)

STEPHEN—I don't want any breakfast.

HANUS—I don't want any, either.

MARTHA—Then you'd better wipe the egg off your chin.

STEPHEN (*mildly*)—Martha. (MARTHA *returns.*)

MARTHA—Look, Stephen—we've been married thirty-five years —and every year of that thirty-five you've told me you had to have Hanus with you to help with inventions. And every year I've hoped and waited, hoped and waited, till my hope's worn thin, and I'm worn thin. Every year you invent something, and every year I think maybe it's going to mean something to you and me. Maybe we'll be able to have an apartment in town, and a servant, and I won't have to cook and wash and make my own garden. And every time an invention comes along what happens? It belongs to the company. And do you get a raise in salary, so we could live a little better, and I could have some clothes and play bridge in the afternoons, or even go to a concert—? No, the company makes the money, and you're still in the laboratory at $27.50 a week, and a barnacle called Hanus star-boarding with us.

STEPHEN—Martha.

MARTHA—Can't you get angry? If you got angry with me just once it might mean there was some hope of your getting mad enough to stand up for your rights at the factory. Twenty-seven fifty a week, a man of your ability, a man with your record! You invented one of the first automobiles, and sold it, and it's made so many millions they don't know what to do with the money! You invented a washing-machine that everybody else in the world can afford except me. You built a piano action but I haven't any piano. The best selling vacuum cleaner in the world is the one you put together to clean Hanus up after the near-beer exploded! I don't know anything you haven't invented except a way to make money! And everybody makes money out of you, and takes the credit away from you, and steals the patents—and nobody's ever seen you angry—nobody's ever heard you complain—or ask for a raise!

STEPHEN—But I'm working for the company, Martha. They pay for my services.

MARTHA—Do they? How many times a millionaire is Mr. Charley Duffy? And what did he ever do?

STEPHEN—I guess I can't explain to you, Martha.

MARTHA—I don't want you to explain it to me. I want something to happen.

STEPHEN—Maybe I'll get a raise.

MARTHA—You know you won't, though, because you'll never have the gumption to ask for it.

STEPHEN—No, I—I guess not.

HANUS—We've got to go, Stephen.

STEPHEN—I'm sorry, Martha.

MARTHA—It doesn't matter. It's too late to do anything about it now.

STEPHEN—Aren't we still in love with each other, Martha?

MARTHA—Are we? Being in love doesn't last forever on $27.50 a week.

STEPHEN—I thought we were.

MARTHA—You haven't thought about it. You haven't thought about me for so many years I can't believe it ever happened. You think about inventions, and Hanus, and the company, and the rights of man, and the war in Spain, but not about me. You should have married someone else.

Martha means that. If Stephen had married Hallie Arlington and Martha had married—well, someone else—they would both be rich now. Her reasoning is a little beyond Stephen. Anyway there's something else he has been wanting to tell Martha. It's something he has been working on sort of on the side—

"Martha, it takes your breath away," says Stephen, his own breath a little fluttery with excitement. "It—it's so incredible I don't dare talk about it. You know how it makes me feel? As if I'd written a poem, a great—sort of poem—all in symbols and lines of light."

"Like Berton Braley," suggests Hanus.

"Only much better," Stephen hurries on; "as if I'd happened on the—the equation they're all looking for—by accident, sort of—because I never would have dared to look for it—only it's there—and I found it—"

"No doubt they'll make a lot of money out of it," ventures Martha.

"And there's another thing I think, Martha," Stephen persists, his eyes alight. "It's that—just working at it, just trying to find it—is better than the money. Sometimes I think they can have the money—because I have the best part.—They can have all the money, if they'll let me work there at things and find them. —That's the best part—it's so good if they knew it they'd take it away from me."

But Stephen's dream means little to Martha. She only knows that she is an old woman and that she has never had anything, nor ever will have anything now. Love? Love isn't enough. Love wears out after a while—and the rest's work. Work may be fun for Stephen. It isn't for Martha. . . .

Stephen and Hanus are hurrying off to work as the curtain falls.

The laboratory in which Stephen and Hanus work at the Arlington-Duffy factory is a small room unfurnished save for a number of stools along a bench and sink that line one wall. There is a small letter file on the sill of the window at back and pushed a bit to one side "stands a peculiar apparatus looking much like a time safe, only taller, narrower, having many dials on its face, a rail or handle on each side, and a silver dome on top. It is set on high casters so that a mechanic may crawl under it to make adjustments."

The fact that it is 9.30 and that Stephen and Hanus are late has been noted by Angela, scrub-woman who is just finishing cleaning up, and by Park and Ripple, two young chemists who have come in search of Stephen. The young men are also interested in the curious-looking safe. It is something Stephen has been working on for a long while, Angela tells them. Of course, Park explains, Stephen is working on company time and using company money, but he doesn't have to report like the rest of them. He has been with the company a long time. He's one of those uneducated guys that works from intuition, and every now and then those guys hit on something. It's a factory belief that Stephen knows more about rubber than any other man in the plant.

Now Apfel, a bustling executive, has barged in. He also is looking for Stephen. The old man wants to see him, Apfel reports, and the old man's about to detonate, he's that mad. This is certainly no morning for anybody to be late. To make it worse the old man came down early just to see Stephen—

And now the old man himself bursts in. He's in an explosive rage. If he can get there at nine, by God, the staff can get there at nine. What's the matter with Steve Minch? "Is this company run for the convenience of a lot of God-damn communistic employees or are we in business by any chance?" Mr. Duffy wants to know. And what is this damn safe thing? Duffy thought Stephen was working on a rubber analysis. Doesn't Apfel know what he's working on? Doesn't he get reports? Who else knows anything about rubber around there? Park?

"Could you handle Steve's work, that's what I want to know?" shouts Duffy. "And, mind you, I want quick results!"

"I think I could. I'm certain I could. I'd like Ripple to help me."

"Then you'll get a chance! By God, you'll get a chance! Tell Minch to report to me when he comes in!"

Duffy has stormed out, slamming the door so hard a pane of glass falls out and is shattered. A moment later Stephen and Hanus come bustling into the room, shedding coats and hats and prepared to get right down to work. They have met Apfel in the hall and they know, before Park relays the message, that Stephen has been summoned by the boss. They are both a little nervous about the summons but soon they have forgotten. The new machine has caught Stephen's eye and his attention. He has a feeling if they just had a little time they could get it working right now. In ten minutes anyway. A second later Stephen is on his back under the machine and calling to Hanus to note certain dials and what they indicate. They indicate, according to Hanus, the year 1600 A.D. And then 1750, in the month of April at 7 P.M. It isn't just right, though. They try again. Now the machine registers December 15, 1878. That's Angela's birthday. Perhaps, Angela thinks, it can tell fortunes. Even if the machine can't she can.

"I can tell your fortune, Mr. Hanus," says Angela.

"What do you mean?"

"You're going to be fired today."

"Don't say that. Don't say it!" protests the distressed Hanus.

"You're going to be fired, and Park and Ripple are going to take over the rubber. They've got it worked out to use the figures in your file there."

This is exciting news. Stephen thinks they had better hurry and see Duffy. Perhaps if they tell him about the machine that will fix everything—

Duffy is back before they can make a move. He is followed by Apfel. Stephen is still on the floor. Hanus is falling all over the place trying to get out of the way. . . . Now Stephen has got to his feet and is dusting himself off as he explains that they were just coming to see Mr. Duffy. They were late, and—

"That explains everything," interrupts Duffy, sneeringly. "You were late this morning. Well, I wasn't late. I came in early to see you. I came in early because that tire you turned out for the spring models will have to be redesigned, and we have only seven days to do it!"

"Was there something wrong with it?" timidly asks Stephen.

"Wrong with it?" Duffy explodes. "We can't wear it out, you dumb cluck! We've worn out two cars on one set of those tires! They've gone a hundred and thirty thousand miles on the

proving track, and we can't wear the tread off on the rear
wheels!"

Patiently Mr. Duffy would explain to Stephen that the profit
in the tire business comes from replacements. If they produce
tires that just won't wear out there are no replacements and they
stand to lose seven million dollars a year.

"I thought you wanted as good a tire as I could make,"
Stephen protests weakly. . . . "It didn't look quite honest to
me not to make it as good as we could make it."

"I thought I told you to work out a whole series, from fifteen
thousand miles to fifty."

STEPHEN—Yes, sir. I haven't got it all yet. Not the low
mileage ones.

DUFFY—Why not? You've had time enough!

STEPHEN—I—I've been doing something else.

DUFFY—What? Something more important, no doubt?

STEPHEN—Yes, sir, much more important.

DUFFY—More important than your job?

HANUS (*muttering*)—What a sweetheart, son-of-a-bitch, what
a sweetheart—

DUFFY—What are you saying—

HANUS—I wasn't saying anything—son-of-a-bitch of a sweetheart—

DUFFY—Who lets that crank in here? Apfel, is he on the
payroll?

APFEL—No, sir.

HANUS—I'll be a son-of-a . . .

DUFFY—They're both fired! Go get his check for him—and
never mind about tomorrow. We'll get along. (APFEL *goes out.*)

STEPHEN—But about this machine, Mr. Duffy—if you knew
what it was—

DUFFY—I don't care what it is!

STEPHEN—You will, though. You will when you hear about
it.

DUFFY—All right—what is it?

STEPHEN—It's something nobody would believe. It's like the
radio was when it first came out—you couldn't believe it. It's
like the airplane was—the papers wouldn't even report it because
they thought it couldn't be true.

DUFFY—I say all right, what is it?

STEPHEN—I can't even tell you the principle of it, because
I don't really know what it is. I just know it acts the way it

"THE STAR-WAGON"

Martha: We're all going to get them (the bloomers)—all the girls in the choir. Don't you
k they're nice, Steve?

eve: Well—they—they—they don't leave much to the imagination, do they?

Martha: You're horrid! You're perfectly horrid!

(Burgess Meredith, Lillian Gish)

does. It's like radio that way—nobody knows why the waves work the way they do; they just know how they work. Marconi didn't know why the wireless worked. He said he didn't. But it worked just the same. This is a machine that picks up waves, too—only it picks them up anywhere—a year ago or two years ago—

DUFFY—You mean it picks up old programs? That's not much good.

STEPHEN—Oh, no, it picks up anything, anywhere. The kind of thing we used to think was a miracle.

DUFFY—Can you give it a name?

STEPHEN—We call it the—Star-Wagon. (DUFFY *steps back a little*.) You don't really ride in it. We just call it that.

DUFFY—That's very interesting—and it picks up—that's very interesting— (*He begins to edge toward the door*.)

STEPHEN—You see, they always thought time was a sort of string with beads on it, as if we were all beads on a string, but it's not that way at all—

DUFFY—No, I can see that—Jesus—beads on a string—

STEPHEN—It's more like a moving platform, but you can get on it anywhere, and off it anywhere—it's hard to explain—you don't have to be in one place or time—you can change it—

DUFFY—Yeah? Write it down—make a report. (*He turns and finds* HANUS *between him and the door, which is closed*.) You hear, Hanus, have him make a report—

STEPHEN—Some people understand it better if you say time is like the banks of a canal, and we're canal boats moving between the banks.—Now the banks are always there—they don't change, but we move on, and if we have a way of making our boats go back and forth in the canal—

HANUS—With this you just press a button, and there you are.

DUFFY—Why, you poor fish—I always knew you were crazy, but I thought you were harmless. What's that door shut for?

HANUS—So they won't listen out there. (*He turns the key in the lock*.)

DUFFY (*he mutters*)—Give me that key! Canal boats! Canal boats! (HANUS *puts the key in his mouth and begins to search his pockets in confusion*.)

STEPHEN—First you set it for place and time, then you press the button and keep hold of the railing on the side. Then you don't move and the machine doesn't move, but everything else moves. Time and place. It all goes past you like a shot and leaves you where you want to be.

DUFFY—Damn it.—Where do you think I want to be?

STEPHEN—I don't know.

DUFFY—I want to be in my own office—

STEPHEN—When?

DUFFY—When? Why, half an hour ago, you lunatic—or last year, if it suits you better!

STEPHEN—I'll make it last year.

Duffy can stand no more. He grabs the key out of Hanus' mouth and starts for the door, stopping only to tell Apfel to see that the nut-machine is scrapped for the materials. Stephen can't understand—

"Don't you see we've happened on the one thing everybody's looking for, Charley—?"

"Don't Charley me—"

STEPHEN (*gulping*)—Mr. Duffy—the one thing they've all said we'd find— Up to now it's all been theory about the fourth dimension.—Everybody said it was there—the mathematicians said it was there—the physicists said it was there, only when they quit writing their books they went right back into Euclid again, and they couldn't find any way out. But Euclid's nothing but an illusion, honest he is—you can walk right through him. There aren't any right angles in space, and there aren't any straight lines—and there's nothing positive about time or space—everything that ever happened is happening all the time—and matter isn't solid—materials aren't any more solid than a wave of light from the sun— I've got it all set down here, but it's in symbols— (*He stops in despair.*)

DUFFY—Treat 'em gently, Apfel. They're raving—! Raving mad!

APFEL—Yes, sir. (DUFFY *disappears.*)

STEPHEN—Mr. Apfel, I don't know how to put things in words—I've never had to use words—but don't take it apart—I'd never have the heart to build another—and I'll pay for it when I can—and it's a thing that's never been in the world before—it's a key to all the great things men are trying to say in all the laboratories there are—it's the alchemist's secret—there's nothing to it but a series of mathematical relations—but when you know them they build up into the mystery of how things happen—clear out into the constellations—of the whole world—like a chord—in music— (*He stops again, looking at* APFEL'S *face.*)

APFEL—Here's your check.

STEPHEN—Yes, sir. (APFEL *ushers them out.*)
HANUS—Sweetheart—
The curtain falls.

It is after midnight. The laboratory is in darkness, save for
the flitting rays of a searchlight being manipulated by someone
outside the window. Presently the window is pried open with a
jimmy. Stephen shoulders his way in, followed by Hanus. They
have come for the safe. Stephen couldn't go home and admit
to Martha not only that they had been fired, but that the company had also smashed his invention. They are going to take
the star-wagon away before anything can happen to it.

A quick inspection assures Stephen that the machine is all
right up to now, and Hanus goes to the door to let in a couple
of hired hands who are to help move it. From their appearance
it is obvious the helpers are also pretty tough and very suspicious.
They want to know what is expected of them. Stephen explains
that they are to get the safe through the window and into the
court below before the night watchman gets around again.
There is a truck gangway in the basement. They can use that.
They can, admits the first thug, if someone will fetch it for them.

"Who is this guy?" the second thug demands, as soon as
Stephen and Hanus have left to get the truck gangway.

"All I know is he came up to me in the skoff-house," explains
the first thug, "and says: 'Want a little job?' and I says, 'Money
in it?' and he says, 'I'll give you twenty bucks. It's all I got.'
'Give it to me now,' I says. 'Oh, no,' he says. 'I'll give it to
you when it's done.' 'Tough,' I says. 'What is this blankety-
blank job?' thinking he was a parson. 'I want to move a safe,' he
says, 'and it'll take anyway two men.' 'I got a friend,' I says,
thinking of you, see?"

"Yeah."

"So I says how far's this safe being moved and he says out a
window. So here we are and there's the safe and there's the
window."

"Yeah."

"But I don't move any safe out any window. I got other
ideas."

Stephen and Hanus are back with the truck gangway. The
thugs do not offer to help them get it through the window.
They are too busy pawing over whatever they find on the shelves,
putting what they take a fancy to in their pockets.

"We wouldn't want you to spoil your hands doing rough work,

of course," mutters Hanus, struggling sweatily with the truck gangway. "A crook has to keep his fingers delicate so he can feel the tumblers dropping in a lock. You might take up something light, like croquet or dominoes."

"I certainly like to watch a couple of good men work," admits the first crook, picking up the card file. "It does me good just to see it. What's this?"

"Oh, those aren't mine," protests Stephen, excitedly.

"What are they?"

"Rubber formulae all worked out for the company. Don't— don't mix them up—they're—"

"What?"

"Well, they're very valuable, and they're all in order."

"Well, now they're mine, see, very valuable and all in order."

The thug has put the cards in his pocket and proceeded to light a cigaret while Stephen and Hanus try to go ahead with the safemoving. They are at the window adjusting the truck gangway when it falls to the courtyard with a crash. The next minute steps are heard and now Misty, the night watchman, has stuck his head in the door. He'd like to know what's going on and is only partially reassured when Stephen tells him everything is all right. Misty doesn't see why Stephen and Hanus can't ever remember to sign their names when they come in at night. How would he know there weren't burglars in there? . . .

The watchman gone, Stephen turns again to the safe and calls for help. The thugs aren't interested. There's only two things to do with a safe, says the first thug. If you're moving it you do it by daylight, and if you're cracking it you do it at night.

"I don't get the philosophy of this, boys," he protests. "We got a safe here with something in it we want. We hoist it out the window and run it into the court. What's the sense of it? You can open it here and save yourself all that exertion."

The crooks are for getting at the safe immediately, but Stephen protests. He has agreed to pay them twenty dollars to help him move the safe, not to tell him what to do with it. They solve that matter by taking the twenty dollars away from him. After that they are prepared to do one of two things: Let Stephen open the safe and share its holdings with them, or they will drill it for soup and blow the top off. If Stephen doesn't stop protesting and get out of the first thug's way he is going to be taken apart himself. Hanus thereupon decides to take a hand and is promptly knocked down for his interference.

"I just want to tell you," pleads Stephen, "I work here, you see—I'm an inventor—and this is something I made—something extra that's my own—only now the company says it belongs to them and I'm fired.—It's not stealing to take it—because they're taking it from me to smash it, and I've worked all these years, and it's the best thing I ever hit on—it's better than anybody knows—better than you know.—If I could only tell you—"

1st Thug (*menacingly*)—The longer you stand there the harder you hit the floor, see?

Stephen—You must have wanted something, back before you —got this way—and it seemed as if you couldn't go on if you didn't get it—

1st Thug—You're certainly asking for something, bo! And you won't go far after you get it.

Stephen—And when I asked you to come here it was because I was desperate, don't you see? I didn't care if they shot me for it, I had to try to save this thing I made—even if I was to die for it—

1st Thug—Are you talking about that safe?

Stephen—Yes—that.—I don't care if you kill me—I'll fight for it—

2nd Thug—Ah, let him have his little machine—

1st Thug—Now what's the matter with you—?

2nd Thug—Come on; we got the twenty dollars—let's get out of here—

1st Thug—Now you're belly-aching. For Christ's sake, what do you think he's putting up the song and dance for if there's nothing in it? I'll play fair with you, professor. I'll give you half. You trust me.

Stephen—You got your twenty dollars, and you didn't do anything for it, and now you get the hell out!

2nd Thug—He's crying, big boy, why don't you let him have his machine?

1st Thug—I'll make hash out of all three of you, you bunch of mushheads! Get out of the way before I fracture your dome!

Angrily the thug pushes Stephen aside and goes to the machine. He has taken a hand drill from his pocket and is looking for the lid. "You'd better do something with it, Steve!" excitedly calls Hanus. "You'd better push the button!"

"It's out of sync, Hanus," answers Stephen. "I never had time to true it up. I don't think it'll work."

"Well, if it don't work you don't lose anything," ventures the thug.

"No, there's nothing to lose now," admits Stephen. "And maybe a lot to gain. I'll try it!"

A second later Hanus has slid under the machine and is adjusting the dials as Stephen calls the date: "One—Nine—Aught—Two! Check! July 4—Nine A.M.! Right!"

"The bicycle shop? It's on the map at the left?" queries Stephen.

"The bicycle shop? On the Fourth of July?" Hanus is peeved. "Look, Stephen, you've got the whole world to pick from and you pick a Fourth of July in a bicycle shop!"

STEPHEN—That's the Fourth where everything happened, Hanus—when you saved my life, and Martha and I fixed it up together.

HANUS—I see.

1ST THUG—What kind of a funny business is this—?

STEPHEN—It's a time-set—see—like I told you.

1ST THUG—It better work.

STEPHEN—Oh, it'll work. Maybe it won't work the way it should, but it'll work.

HANUS—O.K. I got it. The bicycle shop. July Fourth.

1ST THUG—If that's a combination, I'm a Vassar girl.

STEPHEN—It's all right. Just give me a minute. Let me check the platinum a minute. (*He tips the dome, looks inside, and puts it back.*) Grab the other handle now, and help me swing it. (HANUS *climbs out and takes the handle opposite* STEPHEN.) I don't know what's going to happen, so hang on, everybody! (*He looks up at the clock.*) One o'clock. Here goes. (*He pushes the button. The lights dim sharply, there is the noise of an electric motor and the* TWO THUGS *go backward out of the room, through the door that opens of itself. The lights go out entirely. There is a crash outside, and a terrific explosion.*)

HANUS—What's that?

STEPHEN—He must have dropped the nitroglycerin.

The curtain falls.

ACT II

In the corner of such a cluttered bicycle shop as would be remembered by those some part of whose youth was lived in the early nineteen hundreds, Stephen and Hanus are revealed still clinging to the bars of the Star-Wagon. "The place is a large one-room shell, formerly a blacksmith shop, with a window at the rear." There is a repair bench and a rack containing a few bicycles, and practically in the center of the shop is a horseless carriage with an engine under the seat, a whip sticking up bravely from its socket.

Slowly the lights brighten. Stephen and Hanus are still discussing the possibility of the nitroglycerin having been dropped. Gradually their astonished eyes take in the new scene, recognizing one object after another—the car Steve built; the calendar on the wall he had marked; big Minnie's bicycle that Hanus was working on. Stephen was right—the machine was out of sync. This is July 3rd—not the Fourth.

Suddenly they get a good look at each other. They're young again—and funny looking. Hanus understands after one look in the mirror why he never got married. Perhaps, suggests Stephen, it will be different this time—

"What are you going to do—now you're back here, Steve?" Hanus wants to know.

"I'm going to change everything," answers Stephen. "Martha can marry the celluloid collar boy, the way she wanted to. I'm going to marry the other one."

"Do you think you can do it?"

"I'm going to try."

There is a hail from outside. It's Martha—Martha in black bloomers come to ask them to blow up a tire for her. A conscious Martha, more and more fussed the longer and steadier Stephen's gaze. He never thought he'd see Martha in things like that.

"We're all going to get them—all the girls in the choir," chirps Martha, a little defiantly. "Don't you think they're nice, Steve?"

"Well—they—they—they don't leave much to the imagination, do they?"

"You're horrid! You're perfectly horrid!" protests the blushing Martha.

A fellow'd be pretty funny if he didn't look at Martha, whatever she had on, ventures Stephen, which puts him again in her good graces. The talk turns to the choir practice scheduled for that night, and to Stephen's promise to sing a solo. He has a good natural voice, Mrs. Rutledge, the choir leader has said, if he'd only work at it. Steve isn't much for studying, especially voice. If a fellow wants to sing, let him sing. If he doesn't, let him play the piano. Anyway, he's learned his solo by heart and is willing to stay after choir practice and let Martha play it for him.

There is a curious squawk outside, indicating that the Arlingtons' White Steamer has arrived. Hallie Arlington and her father are in it. Martha could have guessed Hallie would be along.

"Maybe you think I don't know what Hallie Arlington's up to," snaps Martha, recovering her bicycle. "She's got her cap all set to marry you."

"Oh, now, say, Martha—what in the world would she want to marry me for?" asks Stephen.

"I don't know, but I'll bet her family's relieved to have her running after you after some of the specimens she's run after."

The girls exchange glances and compliments as they meet and pass in the doorway. Hallie is astonished at Martha's bloomers, and Martha expected she would be. Hallie thinks if there's a law against such things Martha may be arrested. The sheriff might see her, and—

"Probably Hank likes a pair of legs as much as anybody in town," mutters Hanus. "You don't lose your taste for legs by being sheriff."

The real reason for the Arlingtons' visit is soon made apparent. "Tell you what I came in for, Steve," says Mr. Arlington. "No use beating about the bush. That expert that looked over your automobile made a very interesting report. Very interesting. (*They all look at the carriage.*) He says for a young man you've done a most unusual job."

HALLIE—It's much prettier than our car.

STEVE—Oh, no. It's just made out of odds and ends.

ARLINGTON—What I wanted to ask you was, is it patented?

STEVE—Why, no, I just made it for fun—to ride around in. Not much use trying to patent it. Anyway it'd cost a lot.

ARLINGTON—Should be done, though.

STEVE—To tell the truth, it's not really original. I read about the engine in the papers.

ARLINGTON—Well, I don't want to over-praise it, but that expert said it had some remarkable features—the way the valve's set, for example. And the way it started—he said that's unique.

STEVE—That's nothing. That's nothing but a strap around the drive shaft.

ARLINGTON—It saves cranking, doesn't it?

STEVE—Oh, you don't have to crank it. Hardly ever.

ARLINGTON—I wonder if you'd start it for us.

STEVE—Sure thing. Open those doors, will you, Hanus? (*He picks up a pint bottle and looks through it.*) Gasoline's running pretty low. (HANUS *opens the end doors.* STEPHEN *empties the bottle into the fuel tank.*)

HALLIE—I'm so excited! I can't breathe!—Will it go?

STEVE—Once in a while she's balky. (*He climbs in.*) It's going to make a lot of noise, you know. So brace yourselves for it.

ARLINGTON—Burns gasoline?

STEVE—That's right. (*He pulls a strap on the footboard, pulls it again, again and again.*)

HALLIE—I'm going to be so disappointed if it doesn't go.

STEVE—Looks like this was one of its bad days. (*He pulls a strap again, and is rewarded by a terrific concussion. Just one, but it blows* HALLIE *backward.*)

HALLIE—I'm all right! It didn't hit me!

STEVE—It won't hurt you. (*He gets another explosion.*)

HANUS—Has she got power! Land o' Goshen, has she got power!

STEVE—This time. (*Another pull and the engine starts.* STEVE *lets in the clutch and the car moves.*)

HALLIE—Wait! Wait! I want to ride in it! (*She climbs in beside* STEVE, *and they drive out the door.*)

ARLINGTON—I wonder if the thing's safe.

HANUS—With him, it is. He can spin it on a four leaf clover. He can do anything with it.

ARLINGTON—Do you know much about it?

HANUS—I helped him build it.

ARLINGTON—Why did he put the valve on the top?

HANUS—Saves fourteen moving parts, setting it there.

ARLINGTON—How'd you like a little job over in the carriage factory?

HANUS—Me? Maybe I'm better off here.

ARLINGTON—He can't pay you much.

HANUS—I like it here.

ARLINGTON—I see.

With a roar Stephen brings the horseless carriage back after a turn around the yard. Hallie is delighted, but hopes for a longer ride. Her father is greatly impressed. So impressed, in fact, that he straightway offers to buy Steve's car—including all future rights, patents and so on. Offers to pay five hundred dollars for it. Stephen isn't sure it's worth that much and he wouldn't like to cheat Mr. Arlington. Besides he doesn't really want to sell. But—he'd probably be crazy not to take the offer. So he takes it —and the deal is closed.

"And I hope it won't be the last business we do, either," adds Arlington, expansively. "In fact, I'll give you a chance to put that five hundred right back into my carriage factory with me, if you like, and it'll start earning for you from the word go. Only not if you'd rather do something else, mind you. You do just as you please."

"Yes, sir."

ARLINGTON—Hallie there's taken quite a fancy to you, and maybe you two could hit it off, and we could sort of make a little combine. I wouldn't mind it a bit.

STEVE—Yes, sir.

HALLIE—Why, papa, what are you talking about?

ARLINGTON—Just trouble to come, that's all; trouble to come. No harm in looking ahead a little and anticipating your grandchildren. If she doesn't have 'em with one she'll have 'em with another, so it might as well be a good one. As a matter of fact, Steve, I wouldn't advise you to sell that machine unless we can sort of work out a combination.

STEVE—Yes, sir. (*There is a sound of escaping steam outside.*)

ARLINGTON—Well, come on, puss—our boiler's blowing off out here. Tomorrow's the Fourth. See you the fifth—and we'll fix it all up.

STEVE—Yes, sir.

HALLIE—Au revoir.

STEVE—'By, Hallie. (HALLIE *and* ARLINGTON *go out.*)

HANUS—Jeez, I hate to see it go.

STEVE—We can make another one, and make it better. You know what I ought to do?

HANUS—No.

STEVE—I ought to hook up with her, and put the money in his business the way he said.

HANUS—You won't do it.

STEVE—Yes, I will.—I feel a little hollow, though. (*He walks back to the window, looks out, then, turning, touches the Star-Wagon as if by accident. He takes one of the handles.*) Hanus?

HANUS—Yeah.

STEVE—Come here a minute. (HANUS *goes to him.*) Take hold of this thing. This is a hell of an afternoon. I didn't like it the first time and I don't like it any better now. I want to move on a little.

HANUS—Why don't you do something different. You're doing exactly what you did before. You tried to marry Hallie that time, but you didn't.

STEVE—I know. I'll fix it all up tomorrow.

HANUS—Well, if you're going to press that button I wish you'd pick some time before a meal, and not after. I hate to be full of food and not know where I got it.

STEVE—Martha said something about choir practice. I guess I could see Martha just once more. (*He tips the dome, then replaces it.*) Push the button, will you, Hanus? (HANUS *does so. The lights darken—then go out entirely.*)

The curtain falls.

Out of the blackness of the scene change come the strains of Handel's "Largo" being played on an organ. As the scene lightens it reveals the choir loft in a small village church. Martha is at the organ, flanked by the eight members of the choir, including Stephen and Hallie. Mrs. Rutledge, the leader, "elegant in black lace," is standing before them and Hanus can be seen through a small window-door just above Martha's head, holding the pump handle of the organ across his knees.

As the strains of Handel die away Mrs. Rutledge is pleased to compliment Martha on her playing. She would, however, like to suggest one thing. It probably would be better if Martha were to omit certain of the deeper pedal notes "which require a rather unladylike extension of the lower limbs."

"I love the low notes on the pedals," protests Martha.

"I know, dear. But one occasionally sacrifices art to what one might call the decencies. I've hesitated to speak of this, but there are men in every congregation who might be distracted from their devotions by the vision of feminine proportions in more or less athletic attitudes. The playing of the pipe organ requires the use of the feet, but a woman of refinement will instinctively confine herself to the middle register, easily accessible without—without—uh—without—

"She means without spreading the legs apart," the muttering Hanus fills in. For which Hanus is promptly requested to close his door. Now Mrs. Rutledge has rapped for order and called for hymn 172 in the Victory Songs: "Hark 'tis the Shepherd's Voice I Hear—"

The choir renders two verses and the chorus and repeats the chorus pianissimo with good effect. Mrs. Rutledge is quite pleased —but, she must away. The foreign missions are calling. There will be no time to rehearse Mr. Minch's solo—which is very vexing—

"I could stay and play for Mr. Minch," timidly suggests Martha.

"Not without proper chaperoning, of course," protests Mrs. Rutledge. "I fear it is out of the question."

"I'm here," suggests Hanus, sticking his head out of his small door. The suggestion makes no impression on Mrs. Rutledge. If Mr. Duffy and Miss Arlington could stay—

"Yes, of course, Mrs. Rutledge," promptly agrees Hallie.

And so it is arranged. Mrs. Rutledge sweeps out, after a further passage with the impudent Hanus, who is requested to stay away from next day's picnic as punishment of his complete lack of feeling for the proprieties. Now the rest of the choir has gone over to Schmid's for ice cream. Only Hallie and Charley Duffy are left, and Duffy is loudly protesting against their staying. It would be punishment to him to listen to "the bicycle man make noises like 'Jerusalem the Golden.'" Nor would it be any pleasure to Stephen to have Duffy there. If Hallie and Duffy will go on, Martha promises, she and Stephen will come over for ice cream afterward. And that is a promise that pleases Hallie.

Hanus has returned to his pumping job. Martha runs through the prelude of Stephen's solo, and Stephen, clearing his throat nervously, begins to sing "tentatively at first, then with more confidence till at the end he is doing his excellent best."

> "Jerusalem the golden!
>   With milk and honey blest,
> Beneath thy contemplation
>   Sink heart and voice opprest.
> I know not—oh, I know not
>   What joys await me there,
> What radiancy of glory
>   What bliss beyond compare
>
> "They stand, those halls of Zion,
>   All jubilant with song,
> And bright with many a loved one
>   And all the angel throng.
> There lifts the throne of David,
>   And there, from toil released,
> The shout of them that triumph,
>   The song of them that feast."

As Steve finishes Martha puts her head down on the music rest and begins to sob. "It's so beautiful, and you do sing like an angel—" she explains, when Stephen would comfort her. But—he must not touch her now. They must be going.

"Not yet, please," protests Stephen.

"Why?"

STEVE—I can't go just yet.—The music—does something to you—so that you want—I don't know—so that you want—more music—only so much greater—

MARTHA (*taking his hand suddenly*)—Do you feel that, too?

STEVE—I do right now.

MARTHA—Oh, I thought nobody felt that but me. Only I could never say it—so well—

STEVE—I never say anything well.

MARTHA—Wouldn't it be marvelous if we could be great people —and I could play and you could sing—? Somewhere—I could almost imagine it—

STEVE—That would be wonderful.

MARTHA—Only—there's nobody that knows enough to teach us—out here.—We'd have to be where people love music—where a whole nation loves music—not here—

STEVE—Doesn't Mrs. Rutledge know?

MARTHA—No, she really doesn't, Steve.

STEVE—Isn't she kind of a fake, Martha?

MARTHA—Maybe she is. No, it isn't fair to say that. She does as well as she can.

STEVE—I guess an old maid never could be much.

MARTHA—She's not an old maid. She's a widow.

STEVE—Well, she acts like an old maid.

MARTHA—Yes, she does act like one.

STEVE—You're marvelous, Martha.

MARTHA—No, I'm not. I don't like to hear you say that. I'm silly and all I know is just what I could learn in high school, and probably I'll never get any farther—

STEVE—But I do think you're marvelous. Don't you like to hear me say it?

MARTHA—No.

STEVE—Why?

MARTHA—Because I had a glimpse of something—in the music —that was better than just somebody saying you're marvelous— and—wanting to kiss you. (*She takes her hand away.*) I want to love someone—that's much too good for me—and a person like that—never would love me—but that's why I'd love him.

STEVE—Who is it, Martha?

MARTHA—Nobody I ever saw. But you might be like that—some time.

STEVE—I wonder if I could. (HANUS *opens his little door softly, sees them close together, and half closes it again.*)

MARTHA—Does it seem to you as if we said all this once before, once long ago?

STEVE—Yes.

MARTHA—Maybe we did. Away back when the earth wasn't the same—and even the north star wasn't the north star at all.

STEVE—When you were a queen and I was a slave?

MARTHA—No. I wouldn't want you to be a slave. (*He puts out a hand again.*) Don't touch me. It makes me feel as if you're like the others.

STEVE—Maybe I am.

MARTHA—I guess so. I guess we both are. Only I like to think, just tonight—that there's something we can have—that's like the music—nobler than we are—

STEVE—I know.

MARTHA—Do you mind if I play a little more—to see if it will come back?

STEVE—No, Martha. (HANUS *begins to pump, and* MARTHA *touches the keys, playing the "Largo" again.*)

The lights dim and go out as the curtain falls.

Next day we are at the Fourth of July picnic. "The picnic ground is at the edge of a cliff. Above one can see the party gathering with baskets on the grass. Beneath them a shallow cave hollows into the rock, hidden from those on the upper level. A ledge from the side affords an entrance to the cave."

The members of the choir, led by Mrs. Rutledge, are gathering. It is to be noted that Stephen is carrying Hallie's basket and Paul Reiger is carrying Martha's. Hanus, a little hangdoggedly, brings up the rear. After the party is assembled Mrs. Rutledge quiets them long enough to deliver what is evidently an annual request and warning.

"Before anything is unpacked it becomes my duty to say again the few words with which I prefaced our last year's outing," begins our leader. "Your attention, please, Master Hanus. It is, of course, incumbent on all of us to conduct ourselves at all times like ladies and gentlemen. At all times, but even more when an occasion arises which places a certain amount of responsibility upon us. I am here, as you know, in the thankless capacity of chaperon. You will make my duties easier, and my day pleasanter, by conforming to certain rules of decorum, rules of which you are all aware. It is, no doubt, more largely incumbent on the young ladies of our company than on the gentlemen to maintain the standards of society, for women are in general the civilizing and restraining influence. But I shall expect complete co-operation from the young men as well.—Hallie! Miss Arlington! That is exactly the kind of thing I mean! A lady does not put her hand into a gentleman's pocket! For any purpose!"

HALLIE—I was taking a piece of candy, Mrs. Rutledge.

MRS. RUTLEDGE—If Mr. Minch wishes to offer you candy he will do so.

HALLIE—But he wouldn't give me any. He said if I wanted it I could help myself.

MRS. RUTLEDGE—Stephen?

STEVE—Yes, ma'am.

MRS. RUTLEDGE—Is that co-operation?

STEVE—No, ma'am.

HANUS—She wanted to put her hand in his pocket, that's what she wanted.

MRS. RUTLEDGE—Hanus, be quiet.

HANUS—Yes, ma'am.—Only what you think a fellow carries candy for except for bait?

MRS. RUTLEDGE—For what?

HANUS—Nothing.

REIGER—He said for bait.

MRS. RUTLEDGE—Master Hanus was not invited to this outing. He is here on sufferance only. The less attention paid to him the better.

HANUS—Yes, ma'am.

MRS. RUTLEDGE—Now shall we spread our cloth near the rock, as usual? Always remembering that I must keep you all within sight at all times. The girls will understand my reasons for that request, and will obey implicitly, I am sure. I am responsible to your parents.

Mrs. Rutledge, enlisting the help of Martha and several others, has gone to spread the luncheons. Hallie has resumed her search of Steve's pocket for candy corn. Charley Duffy is restlessly walking about. Duffy has heard that Mrs. Rutledge thinks they might play Sacks to the Mill and Farmer in the Dell after lunch. He doesn't care much for that. Likes Hallie's suggestion that they all get down under the ledge, where they can't be seen. It would be more fun. Then, adds Hallie, they could sneak off and go swimming. Swimming's a lot of fun—and she's got a towel. Stephen is not very enthusiastic about the swimming, even when Hallie pleads that she would love to go in with him when she wouldn't think of going in with just everybody. . . .

The crowd has settled to lunch. Martha, Stephen and Paul Reiger are in one group. Hanus is near, tired of the heat and wishing it would rain. Funny about people liking heat better than rain. . . . Now Martha and Steve are alone and Martha is wondering a little if Stephen doesn't wish he had gone swimming with Hallie, seeing he carried her basket. He can go if he wants to—if he wants to see how Hallie looks in the completely now's his chance. Steve allows he can stand it.

"Do you think I'm catty, Steve—I mean just vilely catty?" asks Martha.

"I never noticed."

"I am though. Oh, I can't bear it—and I won't!" Martha has risen. "Why should I care whether you like me or not? Why does a girl have to care whether anybody likes her or not? It's disgusting—to care. It's a curse—and we carry it with us everywhere—just like the curse of Eve! There shouldn't be men and women! There should be just—people."

"Why, Martha. I never heard you talk that way."

"You're a man. You wouldn't understand."

"Where are you going?"

"Anywhere! Nowhere! Only don't come with me unless you want to. I won't play any game for anybody. It's not worth it!"

Stephen has started after Martha, but stops to call Hanus. It is no use trying to go through with their plan, Steve admits.

"I can't do it alone. I'm going right straight ahead and marry Martha again. And she'll hate me for it all over again."

"Well, if that's the way it is—that's the way it is."

"We came back to get another chance, and we can't go all through with it again. Only—I'm falling for her again, Hanus. I'm in love with her all over again—and I just can't quit.—"

"What can I do?"

"You'd better jam the machine, Hanus. Don't spoil it too much. Just fix it so it doesn't work for a couple of minutes."

Stephen has gone in search of Martha. Hanus, starting for the bicycle shop, is stopped by Mrs. Rutledge at the top of the ledge. She is greatly flustered, not being able to find anybody and not getting any replies to her calls.

"I was gone only a moment—one moment, and when I returned there was no one," protests the discouraged chaperone; "not one of them—after all I said about the behavior to be expected of ladies and gentlemen! Is there no such thing as honor among young people? Is the whole world changing—so that there's no principle left, so that girls don't care what's said of them—or—or what they do? Hallie! Martha!"

"They went away by themselves to spoon," explains Hanus. "They don't like anyone to see them when they're spooning."

Mrs. Rutledge is properly horrified at Hanus, but in her rage and disappointment having even him to talk to is some comfort. She wishes he would stay with her. She doesn't really hate Hanus, even if he does say unspeakable things—

But Hanus has something to do, and must see to that. Duffy and Hallie sneak out along the ledge out of sight of Mrs. Rutledge above and are lost in the woods. Stephen and Martha come in from the other direction and stay on the ledge. Mrs. Rutledge continues to call above, but soon goes again in search of her straying charges. Stephen thinks perhaps he should answer the Rutledge call, but Martha insists he should not.

"She seemed pretty excited," suggests Steve.

"I know—but we're not children—and I want you here."

STEVE (*sitting beside her*)—Then I won't answer anything but a fire-alarm.

MARTHA—Are you glad you sold the automobile?

STEVE—Yes.

MARTHA—Why?

STEVE—Because I'll have some money to put into the shop. And when I have a real place—I have some ideas—things I want to make—

MARTHA—Automobiles?

STEVE—Maybe—oh, lots of things.

MARTHA—I thought you might think of going in with Mr. Arlington.

STEVE—I don't know. (MARTHA *leans back and closes her eyes.*) Let me put my coat under your head.

MARTHA—Would you? (*He does so, is tempted to kiss her, then refrains.*)

STEVE—Do you want to talk about music?

MARTHA—If you do.

STEVE—I don't know enough. You're lovely, leaning back

there.

MARTHA—You know, Stephen, a girl that tries to be good is always at a disadvantage.

STEVE—How?

MARTHA—I've never let anybody kiss me, except in games. Some girls let you kiss them, don't they?

STEVE—Only I'd never expect you to. I wouldn't ask it.

MARTHA—Why, Stephen?

STEVE—I wouldn't dare.—It was true, what you said last night, about wanting something better than just being like the others.

MARTHA—Only today—I don't mind at all—

STEVE (*incredulous*)—You mean—if I touch you?

MARTHA (*her eyes still closed*)—Yes.

STEVE (*taking her hand reverently*)—I thought you'd—be angry.

MARTHA—Some days a girl wants—just that—only she doesn't dare—tell you— (*A pause.*)

STEVE (*leaning over to kiss her lips lightly*)—You're sweeter than honeysuckle.

MARTHA—It's sweet—but it's terrible—and tragic, too.

STEVE—Is it?

MARTHA—Because we're alone here—in this world—and so many things could happen—but when I let you kiss me then only one thing can happen—and it's frightening—because if you make a mistake—there's never any way out—

STEVE—It wouldn't be a mistake, Martha.

MARTHA—Men are always so sure. It's like a man to be sure. But a girl. She sees so many things that could happen—and she has just this one life—and when she's tired and lonely and hungry for something—maybe she lets the wrong person kiss her —and then she's a slave—to what he wants to do. All her life long.

STEVE—Do you think I might be the wrong one?

MARTHA—Oh, Stephen—would you always be good to me?

STEVE—Always.

MARTHA—But you don't know. None of us know what we'll be.

STEVE—I know I'd always be good to you.

MARTHA—Men are so sure.

STEVE—Could I kiss you again, Martha?

MARTHA—Yes.—(*He does so.*) There's nothing we can do. There's no use trying to be wise.

STEVE—You mean we just have to fall in love—and—and take

our medicine?

MARTHA—Oh, you poor Stephen—is it as bad as that?

STEVE—It's what I want—that's all I know—the only thing I want.

MARTHA—You say the most blundering, stupid things—and then you say just the right thing—and oh, you darling, you never know which is which—

STEVE (*taking her in his arms*)—Anyway I have the five hundred now, and we can get married.

MARTHA—Oh, but you'll need that—to put in the shop—

STEVE—Only a little of it.

MARTHA—Stephen, Stephen—I don't want to spoil your chances—

STEVE—My chances—! I'm going to be a great man, Martha.

MARTHA—And I won't make it more difficult?

STEVE—You'll make it possible.—I don't care about a lot of money; I just care about the things I want to do. Inventions and mathematics and machines.

MARTHA—But if you don't care about money they'll always take it away from you.

STEVE—Maybe. But they can't take away the things I do. I don't want to put money into Arlington's business. I'd rather you had some furniture—for our house.

MARTHA—You mean we could start out with—real silver, and real linen—

STEVE—Everything real. Especially you and me.

MARTHA—Then we will. (*She sits up.*) And I'll make an end to being afraid of it. You are the one, and you always have been.

STEVE—God knows you're the one, and always will be.

MARTHA—And, Stephen, I have kept myself for you, just for you—and I know people said I was a prude and a blue-stocking—but now—now it's decided—I could even go swimming with you.—I wouldn't care if you saw me. I'd be proud.

STEVE—Let's go. Let's slip away and go.

MARTHA—Stephen—over and over again I have such a strange feeling—didn't we sit here before, and say all these things?

STEVE—Did we, Martha?

MARTHA—Every word, just as we said it now.

There is a "sudden, dramatic darkness, as if a veil had been pulled over the sun." It never has been so dark in the middle of the day before, Stephen is certain of that. It must be Hanus

—he's back at the shop, fixing the machine.

"Now, darling, I know you think a lot of Hanus, but don't get him mixed up with the Creator," Martha protests.

The darkness is deepening. From off in the woods Hallie's voice can be heard. She is calling Stevie! Stevie! Martha is frightened as Stephen takes a step in the direction of Hallie's voice.

"I don't want to go, Martha," Stephen is saying, a little pitifully. "I want to stay and say I love you. But I asked Hanus to fix it so we'd be happier—so you won't be so terribly unhappy—and I won't—"

Hallie's call is louder and more insistent. Stephen starts again to go, nor heeds Martha's cry that she loves him. "You'll know, Martha. You'll know when it happens," he tries weakly to explain. And then, in answer to Hallie's call, "Yes, I'm coming."

The lights have faded entirely. From the darkness comes Martha's last despairing cry: "Stephen, darling—Stephen!"

The curtain falls.

Hanus has been working on Stephen, who lies, face downward on the ledge. Stephen's clothes are wet and there apparently has been an accident, a surmise confirmed when Hallie comes running in, buttoning her dress, her hair down.

The water's out of Steve, Hanus reports, and he will live, no thanks to Hallie, even though "she didn't mean to do it." The least she can do now is to help hold Stephen's head up, which she does by kneeling down and taking it in her lap.

Hanus has found a flask and given Stephen a drink of firewater, and then another drink when he comes to enough to know what is happening.

"I didn't mean to, Stephen," Hallie protests afresh. "You didn't want to go swimming, and I thought if you were all wet you'd have to."

"I certainly got all wet—inside and out," answers Stephen, snuggling his head back. Hallie brushes the hair back from his head and puts her arms around him.

"Now, I'll have to marry you, won't I?" suggests Hallie.

"Yeah, I guess so," mutters Stephen.

With a joyous shout of "Oh, you darling!" Hallie has drawn Stephen into her arms and kissed him. This is Hanus' cue. He is on his way out when Hallie calls to him to bring her back her shoes and stockings.

"Why not? I always have to wait on his women," mutters

Hanus as he leaves them.

Hallie is inclined to pout a little. Why has Stephen run away from her so persistently? Did he have to be hit over the head before he could like her? If he did, Stephen hopes it will be the last time.

"How did I get here?" he wants to know.

"Hanus carried you."

"Good old Hanus. He always rescues me."

"You mean he rescued you before?"

"Yes—all the same. Only it was a different girl that time."

"What are you talking about?"

"I don't know."

"Maybe it will all come out the way papa said, Stevie."

"Maybe it will—this time."

Duffy and Christabel have appeared on the ledge above. Oglethorpe and Della are with them. Noting the affectionate position of Stephen and Hallie, Duffy calls for a song, waving an imaginary baton himself and giving an amusingly exaggerated imitation of Mrs. Rutledge. "I'm dreaming now of Hallie, Sweet Hallie," is what they sing, and a chorus, "Listen to the Mocking Bird," very dulcet, very tender, as an uncalled for encore. Mrs. Rutledge in person breaks in suddenly upon the scene, and is definitely perturbed. Even more so when Hanus walks in, innocently carrying Hallie's shoes and stockings and a discarded chemise. This is the evidence the chaperone has been looking for. Hallie, however, is not the least disturbed. It is true that she has been in swimming with Stephen, if that is what Mrs. Rutledge suspects, and it is quite all right. She and Stephen are going to be married—

Of course that makes everything quite different, Mrs. Rutledge is pleased to admit. She would now embrace them both. But Stephen is quite wet, and about this time Martha runs happily in. She's looking anxiously for Stephen. Someone had told her he was drowned.

"Where did you go?" Martha asks, quickly kneeling beside the unhappy Stephen. "I looked for you everywhere."

"Did you know, Martha? Stephen and Hallie are going to be married?" asks Christabel.

Incredulity, followed by a flash of deep hurt, crosses Martha's face as she turns for confirmation to Stephen. Noting his pained admission, she turns to the others with a hysterical little laugh. "It's—it's marvelous," she cries, gaily. "I must have sounded pretty tragic." She turns to Paul Reiger. "Here we come, dashing to the rescue, and it's—it's a wedding announcement! I hope you'll be—happy."

"You mustn't mind too much, Martha," comforts the triumphant Hallie. "We were so much in love it just had to happen."

"Oh, I can see that! And I don't mind at all. It makes everything so easy."

Martha runs out, followed quickly by Reiger. Mrs. Rutledge has excitedly rallied the others and taken them away so Stephen and Hallie can be assured of a little privacy in which to dress.

"Well, it was all back here, just like we thought it was," mutters Hanus, as he starts after Mrs. Rutledge.

STEVE—Yes, it was all here. Everything that ever happened is right back here, happening all the time.

HANUS—And everything that's going to happen?

STEVE—I don't know what's going to happen.

HANUS—What do we do now?

STEVE—We're not traveling the same direction this time. We went all the way back to the depot, and took another train. Only I guess people don't learn much by experience.

HANUS—Why do you say so?

STEVE—I still want Martha—the worst way.

HANUS—Don't you want to be rich?

STEVE—I'm not thinking about that part of it.

HANUS—Well, I am. What are you thinking about?

STEVE—What we came back here for. Martha was sorry she married me. And now she won't have to.

The curtain falls.

ACT III

The drawing room of Stephen Minch's house, "existing in the false future of his marriage with Hallie, say about 1937," is "a smugly palatial affair." The furnishings include "a grand piano and any amount of Middle Western pictures."

Stephen, an old man now, sits at the piano with a tray full of cocktails near his hand. He downs a couple of them, and has taken up his third when Hanus, also considerably older than he was, appears on the stairway. Hanus is wearing his old clothes, but is struggling with a stiff collar. He resents the power of women over a man and his clothes. "Dress 'em up like so many movie ushers and drive 'em past a grandstand full of butlers—in formation—every woman holding the reins on her own gelding," mutters Hanus. That's what women do to their husbands.

Hanus has left his own home. He couldn't stand his "anthem-croaking old prissie" any longer and he has come back to Stephen. Not, however, with Hallie's approval. Consequently Hanus' future course is a bit doubtful at the moment. Stephen is out of patience with him, too; tired of his constant objection, tired of his "bleeding around like a stuck pig—"

"Do you think I like the place any more than you do—or the clothes I wear, or the company I keep?" demands Stephen, roughly. "I haven't been in the laboratory for ten years! I've done nothing but sit in an office figuring out how to out-smart somebody out of his money! And all you can think of is how to make it tougher for me! I've been trying to make it easier for you! I've been trying to warn you to fit in and play the game, but if you won't learn you won't."

"Maybe I'm too dumb to learn," dolefully admits Hanus.

Now Hallie, "growing old hysterically," comes down the stairs and proceeds to the cocktail tray. She is not in a very good mood, deploring Stephen's impatience—he might at least wait for his guests—and resenting with some vigor the presence of Hanus, who promptly takes himself away to attack the dinner Hallie says is waiting for him.

"This can't go on, you know," warns Hallie, as soon as Hanus is out of the room.

"What?"

"Hanus staying here."

"I never said it could."

HALLIE—But he's here, and he drives me insane, completely insane. His room's a sty, he never changes his clothes, he insults me every time I see him, and he takes it for granted he has as much right in this house as I have.

STEPHEN—When it comes to the value received, maybe he has.

HALLIE—And what does that mean?

STEPHEN—Anything you like.

HALLIE—You've been drinking.

STEPHEN—You'll be drinking yourself, in a couple of minutes.

HALLIE—That's cheap.

STEPHEN—We're all cheap. The whole gang of us, except maybe Hanus.

HALLIE—Well, I warn you, I won't put up with Hanus much longer.

STEPHEN—I guess you won't have to put up with him much

longer.

HALLIE—I'm glad to hear it.—I forgot to tell you—you won't have to bring me home from the Melton dinner. Mr. Duffy's going to be there.

STEPHEN—If you're going to sleep at the club you'd better pack some street clothes. It makes the neighbors talk to see you coming home in a dinner dress around noon.

HALLIE—I have a perfect right to sleep at the club.

STEPHEN—So has my old pal Charley Duffy. And you have a perfect right, under the Constitution, to be a tramp.

HALLIE—I'm not a tramp, but if I can find a little consideration and a little feeling for beauty away from home I shall take it.

STEPHEN—That's what I said. If you can find a little consideration and a little feeling for beauty away from home you have a right to go after it. And when it comes to Charley, he certainly goes around feeling for beauty, right and left.

HALLIE—I don't know why I live with you!

STEPHEN—You don't.—But I can tell you why you don't divorce me.

HALLIE—I've wondered for a long while.

STEPHEN—Because you're afraid the alimony might be less than your present allowance, and Duffy wouldn't marry you any more than I'd do it again myself.

HALLIE—Maybe I know more about that than you do.

Others have come now, Paul and Martha Reiger and Charley Duffy. The Reigers are older, but Duffy is little changed. Now he is acting the clown, playing butler, announcing the Reigers and bidding them "behold our guzzling host with his fair consort." The company is circling the cocktails soon and chattering freely. There is an evident understanding interchange of smiles and greetings between Duffy and Hallie. The men settle to a quick business conference before moving on to dinner. The conference has to do with Hanus. Duffy explains to Hallie:

"We turned over part of that holding company to him—you know, to avoid income tax—and now we've got it all fixed to do a little merry-go-round with the stocks and he won't play ball."

"You mean he won't turn over the stock? But that's dishonest!"

"I'll say it's dishonest!"

"Why do you need him?"

"We haven't got a majority without him."

"It looks as if Master Hanus was in control of the situation."
Duffy, however, has figured a way out of the dilemma. Either
Hanus plays ball, as they explain to him when he is summoned
a moment later, or they declare him to be crazy, have him put
away and let his wife vote his stock. Mrs. Hanus, the former
Mrs. Rutledge, arrives about this time and confirms her understanding of the plan, though she is reluctant to go through with it.

"Look, Charley," protests Hanus, "I don't mind cheating the
government. That's what you put the stock in my name for,
and nobody minds that. But when it comes to wrecking the
holding company to clean out the investors and swipe the whole
kit and kaboodle for yourselves, I can't figure it. It's a dirty
steal of twenty million dollars from people that can't afford it
and I'm not voting."

"Here's something you might consider. You can keep the
stock. Take it as a gift. Only vote our way this once."

"I don't want it. Why are you so hot about reorganizing?
You don't need that twenty million."

"As a matter of fact, we do, Hanus. We pooled our assets
in the new company, and we'll come out plucked if it doesn't go
through."

"Maybe you'd be better off without so much money."

"We'll get it anyway, you know. Only one way'll be unpleas-
ant for you, and the other you'll be on easy street."

Hanus is still obdurate. They can't do anything to him. Stephen won't let them. But even Stephen fails him in the test.
"I wash my hands of you," Stephen shouts, angrily, following
Hanus' final stubborn refusal. "Maybe you think you're a little
tin Jesus being crucified—all right, be a tin Jesus and get yourself
crucified!—What difference does it make? The world's made up
of crooks and thieves, and if you want to do business and eat
regular meals you have to be one of them! We can't afford to
lose all we've got and that officer out there takes orders like a
stenographer! You can vote the stock the way they want it or
else! For all I know you are crazy! I know I am!"

"Stephen—you'd put Hanus away?" exclaims a startled Martha.

"I'm doing it!" snaps Stephen.

Duffy is glancing nervously at his watch. Hanus hasn't much
time. The others want to get on to their dinner with the Tin-
plate King and his collection of Titians. . . .

Martha has found a book from which she would like to read
to Paul a quotation from Dryden. "Listen to this," says Martha:

"All, all of a piece throughout:
Thy chase had a beast in view;
Thy wars brought nothing about;
Thy lovers were all untrue.
'Tis well an old age is out,
And time to begin a new."

"It rhymes," announces Paul.

"Yes, it rhymes," admits Martha. . . .

Now Hanus has given up. Give him the proxy and he will sign. Stephen strikes a few wild chords on the piano as an accompaniment. The others hustle into their wraps and prepare to move on. "You're better than all of them, Hanus," Martha pauses to say. "Anyway, you believe in something."

"Not any more," sighs Hanus.

"You've changed, Stephen. You're like the others, bitter and cruel," continues Martha. "You've never done anything like this before."

STEPHEN—What of it? It had to be done.

MARTHA—I can remember a time when you'd have lost everything, and never given it a thought, before you'd betray Hanus.

STEPHEN—It's Hanus' funeral, not mine.

MARTHA—No, I think it's yours. Your—funeral.

STEPHEN—It all went wrong a long time ago, Martha—when I married Hallie and not you. But it's done with and gone and there's nothing to do now. I know what I am, and I don't like it. I'm not real. And you're not real. We're all a big sham—but there's no changing it. Too much has gone under the bridge.

MARTHA—Why did you marry Hallie then?

STEPHEN—Because you wanted me to.

MARTHA—I never said so.

STEPHEN—Oh, yes, you did. Yes, you did! Don't you remember? Don't you—no, you wouldn't! Go on—go on with the others! They're waiting for you—and it's all too late! Go on! (MARTHA goes out. After a pause STEPHEN makes up his mind and goes to HANUS.)

STEPHEN—Now forget it. (HANUS looks up at him.) Hanus, I'm a—

HANUS (hard)—Yeah, you're everything you can say.

STEPHEN—Because you're my only friend, Hanus—except for Martha. You're the only one I care about, or that cares about me. They'd all cut my throat for a quarter of one per cent of almost anything.

HANUS—Well, you'd do the same to me.

STEPHEN—Maybe I would—but—

HANUS—But what?

STEPHEN—Hanus—where's that machine we used to have?

HANUS—Up in my room.

STEPHEN—What kind of shape's it in?

HANUS—I don't know. It's just sitting there. It wouldn't work a couple of years ago when I tried it.

STEPHEN—You tried it?

HANUS—Yeah. I got desperate. But it wouldn't work.

STEPHEN—We might be stuck here—forever.

HANUS—We are stuck.

STEPHEN—Let's go tinker with it. It's got to work.

HANUS—You think you can fix it?

STEPHEN—Might as well be dead as here.

HANUS—Sure, let's tinker with it.

They clasp hands as the curtain falls.

We are back in the dining room of the Minches' cottage as we first knew it. The table is again set for breakfast. In an upper corner of the room Stephen and Hanus have just let go the handles of the Star-Wagon and are looking about the room wonderingly. They are dressed again as they were when we first met them.

According to Stephen's reckoning, they have been away twenty-four hours. Hanus has long since stopped figuring by hours. They don't mean a thing. But he thinks they might as well sit down to the table. Stephen is hungry, but he must find Martha first.

Stephen is in an inner room when Martha comes through the outside door. She is wearing her hat and coat and, seeing Hanus at table, is immediately concerned for Stephen. Is Stephen all right—

Stephen steps out of the bedroom and Martha is greatly relieved. She would, however, like to know where he has been—all night. "We were trying out a new machine," Stephen explains.

"I wish you'd told me," says Martha, simply, and goes to get their breakfasts.

Suddenly Hanus is struck with an idea. It jumps him right out of his chair. "I'm not married any more!" shouts Hanus, with a trio of "Yipees!" to emphasize his joy. "Give me something to break! Give me my hat! I want to jump on my hat!"

Martha, coming from the kitchen with a pan in her hand, is a little peeved at this exhibition. "If there's any cause for celebration you haven't told me about it! I don't know where you were last night or what you were doing, but whatever it was you left me sitting here all night without a word of explanation! I suppose there were no telephones where you were—and surface transportation broke down all over the city! I suppose you can't remember that yesterday was pay-day and you left me without a cent of money in the house—"

STEPHEN (*softly*)—Martha.

MARTHA—What is it?

STEPHEN—Didn't you sleep last night?

MARTHA—No, I didn't sleep. I sat in the chair by the window.

STEPHEN—Did you want me to come back?

MARTHA—I think you stayed away just to frighten me.

STEPHEN—Martha—did you ever read any of Dryden? (MARTHA *goes slowly to the table and sets the pan down*.)

> Your wars brought nothing about;
> Your lovers were all untrue.
> It's well the old age is out,
> And time to begin a new.

MARTHA—Did you have the same dream?

STEPHEN—Yes.

MARTHA—What does it mean?

STEPHEN—It means I like it better here. And, Martha—when you didn't like it—it was all my fault.

A knock at the door announces Charley Duffy. The plant executive is plainly disturbed, but surprisingly amiable. He even speaks to Hanus. Mr. Duffy is up a little earlier than he likes to be, but Stephen and Hanus are getting him used to that. When they can't think of anything else to do they rob the plant.

Martha is quite appalled but Duffy assures her it is nothing. Just a little matter between friends. Martha isn't satisfied with that. "Tell me what happened, please?" she demands.

DUFFY—Well, the watchman called me up this morning to say there was a window forced in the laboratory last night and somebody'd run a truck gangway out a window and made off with

Steve's contraption there. (*He looks at the Star-Wagon.*) Now I know pretty well who it was, and I didn't give a damn, but pretty soon it turned out there was something else missing.

HANUS—That's all we took.

DUFFY—And now we can prove you took it, because there's the contraption. If you took one you took the other.

STEPHEN—But that's all we took.

DUFFY—Think a minute. Nothing else?

STEPHEN—Not a thing. I didn't have time—that is, I didn't want anything else.

DUFFY—Now, look, Stephen. After you left yesterday I had a little talk with Park and What's-his-name, the fellows who were going to take over the rubber. When I pinned them down it turned out they didn't know much about rubber, but they did know where you kept your analysis. They were all filed away in that little case on your window-sill. And we didn't have brains enough to put those cards away for safekeeping. That filing case was empty this morning. We were slow in the head, Stephen, and you pulled a fast one.

HANUS—The burglar lifted them.

DUFFY—What burglar? I mean which burglar? Because I happen to know who two of them are. (STEPHEN *and* HANUS *exchange glances.*) Now I need those cards. And I could put you boys in jail. Where are they?

STEPHEN—I don't know.

DUFFY—Give 'em back, and we pass the whole thing over, nothing said.

STEPHEN—We don't know where they are.

DUFFY—They're no good to you, Stephen. If you keep 'em it's only to get back at me. But it hurts you worse.

STEPHEN—They got lost—in the shuffle.

DUFFY—Is that your last word?

STEPHEN—I can't do anything about it.

Duffy has clapped his hat on his head and started for the door. At the door, however, he has another idea. He turns back. His mood is again friendly. Stephen is smarter than Duffy thought. It wouldn't do Duffy any good to put Stephen in jail. He's got to have the dope on the tire by the next afternoon and Stephen is the only one who can give it to him. Is Stephen coming back to the laboratory? No. Stephen was fired. But, forgetting that, *will* Stephen come back? No. Stephen has something else to do. Something Duffy would never understand—

"There's a lot of things you wouldn't understand," adds Stephen, with quite unexpected force. "And one of them is that I'll never take orders any more. It's not worth it. I might do you a favor if I liked you, but I won't be threatened and I won't take orders."

DUFFY—What's come over you?

STEPHEN—I know now there's no good or bad fortune. Fortunes are all alike.

DUFFY—I can walk out this door and fetch you more bad fortune than you could shake a stick at.

STEPHEN—No, Charley, you couldn't. And you don't even know what I mean.

DUFFY (*sitting down and taking off his hat*)—I don't know, Steve. Maybe you're bluffing and maybe you're not, but if you're bluffing you ought to play poker. You'd be good.—This is the way I've run the firm, Steve. When a man's too good to lose and you can't keep him any other way I make him a partner. You should have been a partner long ago, only you didn't make any play for it. A partnership carries two hundred shares with an income of about seventeen thousand. What do you say?

STEPHEN—Do I have to do it, Martha?

MARTHA—No. He doesn't want a partnership.

DUFFY—Martha?—What is this, anyway?

MARTHA—I don't want him to have a partnership. I don't want him to be like you or Reiger or any of the others. I want him the way he is. No matter how little we have to live on.

DUFFY—It doesn't hurt a man to be a partner.

MARTHA—I've known it to.—

DUFFY—How about a salary as consulting engineer, no regular hours, just to look in on us when we're in a jam like this one?

STEPHEN—But nobody gives me orders?

DUFFY—Nobody gives you orders.

STEPHEN—Would it be all right, Martha? We could buy a piano then.

MARTHA—I don't need a piano, Stephen.

DUFFY—Say two hundred a week. And Hanus rates fifty.

STEPHEN—All right. (*To* MARTHA.) You're going to have one anyway. (*To* DUFFY.) All right.

DUFFY—God, you had me sweating there for a minute.

Duffy is greatly relieved now, and fairly expansive. He is hoping Stephen doesn't really dislike him. Stephen doesn't.

After all—Duffy did marry Hallie. Yes, Duffy admits with a curious look in his eyes, he did marry Hallie—"Sometime you might do a little more work on that string-of-beads, lines-of-light, time-like-a-canal idea, Stephen," suggests Duffy. "There might be something in that."

"What makes you think so?"

"As a matter of fact—you know, I had a funny—well, never mind. Funny thing about last night—well, never mind. We'll get along better now."

"Yes, we will, Charley," agrees Stephen.

Now Duffy has gone and a pleasant calm has settled upon Martha and Stephen and Hanus. Everything is all right, Martha has assured them, smilingly. Would she rather Hanus lived somewhere else? No. So long as Hanus still believes in Stephen she wants him to live there. Does she want them to tell her about the machine? Yes. Martha would like that. "It's a sort of radio, for picking up—old programs," Stephen explains.

"We call it the Star-Wagon—and it runs along on a thread of time, like a cash basket on a wire," adds Hanus, and would go to the machine to give her a demonstration.

"You don't have to prove it to me," smiles Martha. "I know it's true. I was there."

"Were you, Martha?"

MARTHA—Yes. I don't know how.

STEPHEN—What do you remember?

MARTHA—All of it. I liked the choir practice best.—And now you are a great man—the way you wanted to be.

STEPHEN—No, Martha. If I'm a great man then there aren't any great men. I found out that much.

MARTHA—But suppose you build more of these so people can go anywhere—back and forth—and it changes the whole world?

STEPHEN—That's another thing I found out, Martha. It wouldn't change the world. Nothing changes it. Every new thing we find just makes it more mysterious. And maybe more terrible.

MARTHA—But the people would change.

STEPHEN—Do you think so? I don't. They'd just take it for granted after a while, and they'd be the same. All these new inventions come along, and we think the whole world will be different, but pretty soon they're on the market for a dollar down and two dollars a week, and people go on living as usual. And the inventors aren't any wiser than the others. Look at me,

Martha. I worked for years, and studied, and maybe I had a gift for mathematics and things like that. And finally I put my finger on something—partly by accident—and I saw through the veil—and there was something nobody'd known about.—But I'm not different. I'm just a little man, like the rest, only more stupid about most things.—I looked through the veil and saw a mystery, and pretty soon everybody can look through and see it. But they won't know what it means, and I don't. It's a way of remembering better than we used to, and maybe that'll make us a little wiser, maybe not. But I hope so.

MARTHA—It made me wiser. I don't want to go back any more. And I don't want to change anything.

STEPHEN—We were right all the time, weren't we?

MARTHA—Yes. All the time.—Let's not go anywhere else. It's too sad. But let's have a piano—and sing sometimes.

STEPHEN—I don't know whether I can any more.

MARTHA—It'll all come back when I play for you. I know it will. (*She hums a little and moves her fingers on the table as if pressing the keys.* STEPHEN *sings very softly, then with more assurance as he proceeds.*)

STEPHEN (*singing*)—

> They stand, those walls of Zion,
>   All jubilant with song,
> And bright with many a loved one
>   And all the angel throng.

(*As* STEPHEN *sings,* HANUS *leans to pump the imaginary organ.*)

> There lifts the throne of David,
>   And there, from toil released,
> The shout of them that triumph,
>   The song of them that feast.

I never believed much in a golden city
back there in the choir. I don't believe it now.
But they were right about one thing, the old prophets—
there is a holy city, somewhere. A place
we hunt for, and go toward, all of us trying
and none of us finding it. And it's no wonder
we don't find it yet. Because our lives
are like the bird (you remember) in the old reader
that flew in from a dark night through a room
lighted with candles, in by an open window,
and out on the other side; we come out of dark,
and live for a moment where it's light, and then

go back into dark again. Some time we'll know
what's out there in the black beyond the window
where we came in, and what's out there in the black
on the other side, where it all seems to end.

THE CURTAIN FALLS

SUSAN AND GOD

A Drama in Three Acts

BY RACHEL CROTHERS

TRAGEDY sat in at the birth of one of the outstanding successes of the theatre season of 1937-38. Following the first performance of Rachel Crothers' "Susan and God" in Washington, D. C., the much-loved Osgood Perkins, who was playing the role of Susan's unstable husband, went back to his hotel and was dead of a heart attack before morning.

There was talk of abandoning the week's engagement, but the wisdom of those older showmen who insist that "the show must go on" prevailed. Mr. Perkins' understudy, Paul McGrath, was aroused early and instructed to get up in the part. The assignment set Mr. McGrath shaking in his shoes, and Gertrude Lawrence, the star, spent the day controlling a quite natural attack of hysterics. But the show did go on. The following day Miss Lawrence was confined to her hotel as the result of grief and shaken nerves and a matinée performance was called off.

For two weeks thereafter diligent search was made for a leading man to replace Mr. Perkins, the theory being that an actor of co-star rating would be needed to give the cast a proper balance. During the two weeks Mr. McGrath gave so good an account of his own fitness for the role that he was retained for the New York opening and eventually completed the run of the play.

Miss Crothers has been writing plays for thirty odd years. She has many more successes than failures to her credit. She began as something of a radical feminist as far back as "The Point of View" (1904), "The Three of Us" (1906), and her first notable success, "A Man's World" (1909). Of recent seasons she has been giving a good deal of attention to those common domestic and marital problems growing out of social adjustments in a changing world. She has treated phases of divorce and separation muddles in "Let Us Be Gay," "As Husbands Go" and "When Ladies Meet." Following the success of the last named play she devoted five years to Hollywood and the screen. She returned to the theatre with "Susan and God," which records the reclaim-

ing of a family in a contest with social theories that stand in
danger of vicious expansion.

"Given a current fad for a subject it is reasonable to suppose
that Miss Crothers will make a refreshing play out of it," wrote
Brooks Atkinson. "She is primarily interested in people. She
knows a great deal about women and enough about men to season
the dish agreeably. Although manners change remarkably in a
remarkably short period of time, character remains the constant
factor against which the prevailing fashions can be sardonically
judged."

Irene Burroughs' house in the country, where we first meet
Susan and her friends, has a terrace room enclosed in glass. The
wall at back, through which an arched doorway lets into the
house, is old brick painted white. Ivy, growing in tubs at either
side of the door, has been trained over the wall. The effect is
to give the room a cool, soft, outdoors atmosphere. There is a
medium grand piano in one corner, and the summer furniture is
covered in gay chintz.

Mrs. Burroughs, who is perhaps thirty-seven and whose good
looks "depend largely upon her good grooming," is also "a restless, dissatisfied and hard, but nevertheless an extremely attractive woman." She comes now from a ride on which Michael
O'Hara, a "tall, dark and good-looking young man with a slightly
indolent manner and great charm," has been her companion.
They are tired, but exhilarated and quite ready for a refreshing
drink.

Irene, however, is a little worried. Susan Trexel is coming,
and Irene would have Michael remember to be particularly careful about revealing anything that has happened since Susan went
away. She probably half guesses already. Susan had been willing to wager, before she left, that Irene would not wait for her
divorce and that she and Mike would be living together before
she got back.

"Well, why don't you beat her to it and say—You win—the
minute she arrives?"

"I consider myself much more married to *you*—*now*—than I
ever did to Fred or Tom," answers Irene, throwing herself full
length in a chair. "If Tom had given me my divorce right away
things wouldn't *be*—as they are."

Irene is not regretful. After all her life is her own. She feels
strongly that what she is doing is right—and she will tell Susan
when she gets ready. . . .

There has been a tennis match with Hutchins and Leonora

Stubbs paired against Charlotte Marley and Clyde Rochester. The players are returning to the house. Leonora is "a tall, beautiful woman, about twenty-eight—quite honest and unaffected in manner." Her husband, Hutchins, called "Stubbie," is some years her senior, a nervous, irritable person a good share of the time. At the moment he is furious at having been beaten by Rochester, an actor, about twenty-seven, "fairly good looking in a fresh, healthful way—with a laugh and a cheerfulness very irritating to the uncheerful," and Charlotte, who is herself "a healthy, out-doorsie woman about thirty-five."

Leonora can't see why Stubbie should be sore. Why should he hate the theatre the way he does, when she gave it all up for love of him? Leonora was also supposed to give up theatre people, counters Stubbie, frankly glaring at young Rochester. . . .

They have all been served with drinks when the conversation turns to the expected Susan. She may not come. It is quite like Susan to change her mind again, having already done so three times, according to Irene. But it is Mike's opinion that Susan never changes her mind—only her emotions.

There has been no phone call from Susan, but there has been one from Barrie, who is Susan's husband, asking if she were there. If Barrie should telephone again he is to be told, by Irene's instructions, that Susan isn't coming.

"I will not have them both in my house at the same time," declares Irene, firmly. "I've had enough of that. There'd be the same old scene and row. I adore them—but not when they're together."

Barrie Trexel, it develops, is a considerable problem—both to his wife and her friends. Fearing results, Susan did not let him know she was arriving until after her boat got in.

"If she *had* let him meet her at the boat—he would have arrived with the biggest bunch of flowers in the world—*tight*," says Irene.

"She told him to meet her at Blossom's school—and when he got there Blossom had had another wire from her mother saying she was coming *here* first," explains Charlotte. "Now they don't know *where* she is—I call it *rotten*."

"Foolish, faithful old Barrie," sighs Mike, reaching for another drink. "If he'd only get another gal—Susan would snap back like a shot."

The trouble with the Trexels appears to be of common enough origin, according to Stubbie. Barrie has too much money that he did not have to work for. Susan has too much charm. Life has never disciplined her at all.

"Susan's the most intelligent *fool* I've ever known," insists Irene.

"I've never been sure whether Barrie drinks because Susan's tired of him—or Susan's tired of him because he drinks," chips in Stubbie.

There are many answers to that one, and no two of them are in agreement. In any event the truth appears to be that Barrie does drink like a fish; that he is adorable when sober but terrible when tight, and that there is good reason why Susan should be tired of him.

On the other hand, Susan gets tired of everything. Even her daughter, Blossom. Blossom, to Susan, was the most wonderful of babies until she grew up. Now that Blossom is at the unattractive age of 15 Susan is bored stiff with her. . . .

Now Susan has arrived. They hear her calling from outside, excitedly and with great enthusiasm: "You darlings—you darlings —you darlings!" Then, with both arms spread she is with them. Susan is thirty-five. "A woman with so much charm that it covers most of her faults—most of the time—for most people. She is slender and alert and pretty—with a very individual style and chic. Just now she is delightful in a new Paris creation."

Susan moves from one to the other, kissing, embracing, raving over them. She nearly kisses Leonora Stubbs, though she has never met her, Stubbie having given up bachelorhood while she was away. Now they have all settled down again and Susan has a chance to explain that the reason she looks so wonderful, as they are agreed she does, is due to a perfectly marvelous experience. (SUSAN *has just sipped the highball* MICHAEL *has handed her when she is reminded of the experience and promptly pushes the drink from her. Liquor's out!*)

No, she hasn't exactly gone on the wagon. It's something much more spiritual than that. Something so wonderful that she has given up practically everything to it. She has quite forgotten all about the Riviera and such things.

"I didn't mean to go to England at all," Susan is finally led to explain. "But I met Lady Wiggam on the Riviera and we got awfully keen about each other—and she asked me to go home with her and I thought I might as well sail from— She *is* one of the rarest creatures I have ever known."

IRENE—What's so *rare* about her?

SUSAN (*rushing on excitedly and ceaselessly*)—To begin with she's one of the most *distinguished* women in England and *the* most gorgeously magnificent place in Kent to say nothing of all the others—but *that* isn't it.

CHARLOTTE—That isn't why you're keen about her.

SUSAN—Not at all. It's her *soul* that's developed to such a marvelous— For instance, the first night I was there the house was *filled* with people. I didn't know *anybody*—and I was holding my chin as high as possible and trying to be as insulting to the English as they were to me—when Lady Wiggam *herself* floated in—and we all *loved* each other in a *minute*.

CHARLOTTE—What do you mean? Is she religious—or something?

SUSAN—Oh—it's much more than that. I mean—it's *new*—and fresh and so *practical*—that's why it appeals to me.

IRENE—What appeals to you?

SUSAN—Why, her— It isn't hers—of course. It's anybody's—everybody's. But she began the movement.

CHARLOTTE (*laughing so she can scarcely speak*)—If there's one thing I thought *you'd* never be guilty of—Susan—it's a *movement*.

SUSAN—I know. That's why it's so wonderful. You wait. You'll see. You'll see. I can't even *talk* about it yet—but you can ask me questions.—I want to give, give, *give* all I can—to all of you.

LEONORA—What is it—if it isn't religion?

SUSAN—Well—it *is*—in a way—but you can keep right on being what you *are*—An Episcopalian—or Ethiopian—or Catholic or Jew—or colored—or *anything*. It's just love—love—*love*—for *other* people—not for yourself.

MICHAEL—The good old golden rule, you mean.

SUSAN—What *is* the golden rule—exactly, Mike?

STUBBIE—Didn't you ever go to Sunday School—Susan?

SUSAN—No—I was such a sensitive child they didn't make me. That's why this is so wonderful—there isn't any dogma or anything hard to believe about it. That's why so many intelligent *thinking* people are interested in it. It's *thrilling* and *alive* and *fun*—so people aren't *ashamed to be good*. This was *the* most remarkable collection of people at Lady Wiggam's—all sorts and kinds. I never heard so many titles—all at *once*—in my life—and great thinkers—you never *saw* so much *thinking*—and some were just *people*—and some—well, practically out of the gutter—with the *same light shining in their*— How are the dogs, Charlotte?

Charlotte is a little flustered by the suddenness of Susan's change of thought, but manages to report on her kennels with some interesting details. When Clyde Rochester arrives Charlotte switches from dogs to actors. Being introduced, Susan and Clyde agree to call each other by their first names, just as everybody did at Lady Wiggam's. Even Lord Ramsdale's chauffeur called him Tom—

"The Duchess of Keating said, 'This is a *great* experience—coming into *spiritual* contact with people we never even knew existed,'" reports Susan. "I had the most really thrilling and inspiring talk with one of Lady Wiggam's gardeners. It makes you just open your heart—your *soul* rather—to people—and he told me one morning in one of the marvelous tulip beds that he used to hate his wife so he got all ready to kill her one night—with the gun actually in his hand."

The others make no attempt to control their ribald laughter. "Don't tell me he didn't do it!" protests Michael.

"No—he didn't."

"What stopped him?"

"The gun didn't go off somehow—and he knew afterwards—after Lady Wiggam had brought *him* in *too*—he knew it was the hand of God that stopped him. And now he actually *likes* his wife—very much indeed."

They are off in another burst of laughter, but Susan doesn't mind. They'll see—

It is Stubbie who brings Barrie's name into the conversation. Susan hopes Barrie is all right. She didn't cable him to meet her at the boat for fear he might be— No, Susan isn't planning to open the Trexel house for the summer. After all, why should she? Barrie doesn't care a hang about the place and Blossom adores her camp. Then Susan returns to the news.

Isn't Stubbie terribly flattered that Leonora gave up her stage career to marry him? And what is he going to do when she gives him up to go back to the career? Has Irene got her divorce yet? Not until next month? That will be nice for Mike.

It wouldn't surprise Susan in the least if Lady Wiggam's movement were to wipe divorce right out of the world. "You can't stop it," thrills Susan, back to her proselytizing. "It's marching on like a glorious army."

"I'm *dumb*," admits Charlotte. "What is it? What is Lady Wiggam's movement?"

"Why, she's found God, dear—in a *new way*."

"Really, Susan—I'm not very religious—but I think it's irreverent—talking about sacred things—so *flippantly*."

"It isn't flippant—it's *cheerful*. You're *the* very hardest kind to get at—hard-boiled worldlings. I know—I was one. The first time anybody talked to me about God I was so embarrassed I didn't know where— And the first time they asked me to *confess*—right before everybody—I thought it was too impertinent for words."

"And did you—did you confess your sins before everybody?" Mike wants to know.

"I did."

"What did you tell them?"

"Well, I thought I absolutely *couldn't*. But something guided me—and with everybody looking *straight at me*—I confessed I'd had my hair touched in Paris. (*They shout with laughter.*) And after that—you don't *know* the joy and peace—when I saw people staring at my hair in the sun—I didn't give a *damn.*"

Susan, with Irene, has gone to her room, sending the suggestion back over her shoulder, as it were, that civilization's a failure and that this is a poor, sick, unhappy world. Certainly there is little good in even a marvelous mechanical age if it cannot make people happy.

"Everybody batting around trying to find something to fill up this awful emptiness." Susan has stopped in the doorway for a final word to her listeners. "It is the only thing in the world that will stop war. Oh, Irene—I've brought you the most ravishing panties—"

They are through the door and into the hall. The others are left to wonder whether Susan is kidding herself or kidding them. Or just getting a big kick out of the last thing she has run into. Suddenly there is a startled exclamation from Charlotte. She has caught a glimpse of Barrie through the window. He is getting out of a car. Now, who is going to tell him that Susan isn't there?

Charlotte refuses. Stubbie refuses. Barrie wouldn't believe Mike. So they all run away and leave Clyde Rochester, the only one Barrie doesn't know, to relay the message. A moment later Barrie and his daughter, Blossom, come in from the terrace.

Barrie "is about forty—not striking in any way—but an extremely arresting and lovable personality. Blossom is fifteen— and at her most unpromising stage—tall and awkward. Her teeth are in the process of being straightened. Her vision is being corrected—she is wearing horn-rimmed spectacles. Her hair is straggly—her clothes unbecoming and unattractive. She is one of those well-born products who look unbelievably hopeless in their adolescence."

Clyde gracefully avoids the issue. He introduces himself as

"SUSAN AND GOD"

Susan (to Mike)—Then ask God to help you. He knows what your temptation was. Telling
is only to break down your will—make you humble—bring you closer to Him. No matter
at we are—or what we do—if we're sorry—really—and want His help—we can be made over.
Barrie (who has come quietly through the doorway)—If you believe what you have just said,
san—I believe it, too. . . . Do you mean He can do something about me—if I ask Him? If
u do—I do ask Him.

(Douglas Gilmore, Gertrude Lawrence, Paul McGrath)

a friend; insists he does not know whether or not Mrs. Trexel has arrived; would like to pour Mr. Trexel a drink, which Barrie refuses, "after an eloquent hesitation"; and finally leaves them to see if he cannot dig up some information for them.

Blossom is quite sure her mother must be there. If she isn't, where is she? If she isn't, Barrie insists, it is because she has thought of a better place. Perhaps, thinks Blossom, her mother has gone to the school after all. Maybe they should go back there. Blossom wouldn't mind going back now. She just didn't want to stay there when all the other girls were leaving—

"I didn't want them to think I didn't have any place *to* go," explains Blossom. "I s'pose that sounds silly to you?"

"Not at all. I see your point. We all like to have some place to go. At least we like people to *think* we have. That's almost more important than *going*. Isn't it?"

"Yes, it is. When you didn't come to the last day exercises yesterday—I said you were *sick*—or they'd have thought I didn't have anybody to come."

"Oh. I didn't suppose it really *mattered*—whether I was there or not.—I'm sorry—I meant to get there—but—I got caught in a—jam."

Barrie thinks that if Susan isn't there Mrs. Burroughs will put Blossom up for the night and he will go back to town. Blossom isn't thrilled with that idea. She thinks he wants to go back to town because he is stuck with her. Four hours with her—and he is bored to death. And that's the longest she *ever* has been with him. Blossom's disappointment gives Barrie another idea.

"I'll tell you what we'll do," he says with such enthusiasm that she is a little startled. "You come to town with me for tonight. We'll have dinner at some nice place and see a show.—Wouldn't you like that?—We might even buy a hat—or something." (BLOSSOM *shakes her head—fighting back her tears—then touches the brace on her teeth.*) "Toothache?"

BLOSSOM—No. It's just the darned brace. It slips once in a while.

BARRIE—Is that a feature of the school? Do they all wear one of those?

BLOSSOM—Dad—you fool!—Oh—I should have stayed there.

BARRIE—Why?—After all—why should you?

BLOSSOM—Because there isn't any other place *for* me to stay.

BARRIE (*touched and embarrassed*)—See here! I've got a *real* idea this time. If you don't want to go to New York with me—

how would you like this? Suppose you and I go over to *our* place for tonight. The gardener and his wife are there. *They* might invite us in. They seem like kind people.

BLOSSOM (*with sudden passionate eagerness*)—Oh—*could* we? Could we do that?

BARRIE—Why not?

BLOSSOM—That would be *wonderful!* I'd rather be there than any place in the world. Wouldn't you, Dad?

BARRIE (*meaning a great deal more than he says*)—Just about.

BLOSSOM—If we could all be there together till it's time to go to camp—I wouldn't mind the camp so much.

BARRIE—I thought you liked the camp better than anything.

BLOSSOM—What made you think that?

BARRIE—Well—I've been told it's a nice—healthy place.

BLOSSOM (*with sudden force*)—*If I get any more healthy I'll die!* I *hate* the camp. I *hate* it!—Would you mind asking Mother to let me do that, Dad? It would only be for a little while. *Would* you?

BARRIE (*uncomfortable and unprepared*)—She'd be more likely to do it if *you* asked her.

BLOSSOM—No, she wouldn't. She'd say it's only such a little while till camp, it wouldn't be worth opening the house.

BARRIE—I'm sorry—but you've got the wrong idea. I'm not much good at telling her what *I* want.

BLOSSOM—Why can't we all be together once in a while?—Why can't we be some sort of a family—like other people— Why can't we?— (*She isn't able to hide her emotion this time and shy sobs come.*) *Why—can't—we?*

BARRIE (*amazed and deeply moved*)—I didn't know you felt this way about it. I expect it's all *my* fault.

BLOSSOM (*going to him*)—You're all right, Dad. Why can't you be this way all the time?

BARRIE—Seems simple enough—doesn't it? But somehow what we *mean* to be and what we *are*—are quite different.

BLOSSOM—Maybe if we—

LEEDS (*coming into the entrance at center*)—I beg pardon, sir —Mrs. Burroughs says she is extremely sorry not to see you— but she's in the bath.

BARRIE—Oh—I'm sorry not to see *her*. And Mrs. Trexel?— Is she *also—in the bath?*

LEEDS—Madame says Mrs. Trexel is expected *tomorrow*.

BARRIE—I see.

BLOSSOM—Then she *did* go to school.

BARRIE (*going to couch to get his hat*)—I don't think so.

BLOSSOM—Maybe she's had an accident or something.

BARRIE—If she has—it's a *nice* accident. (*Looking at* LEEDS.) Give my regards to Mrs. Burroughs and say I'll try again to-morrow. (LEEDS *bows and goes.* BARRIE *goes to* BLOSSOM.) Let's go!

BLOSSOM—But, Dad—aren't you sort of worried?

BARRIE—Not a bit. Cheer up. If Susan is lying in the ditch you may be sure she picked it out—and it's a *perfectly good ditch*. (*He takes* BLOSSOM'S *arm.*) Come along!

They go out as the curtain falls.

After dinner that evening the house guests drifted casually back to the terrace room. Now Clyde Rochester is at the piano running over a variety of popular music. The butler brings in a tray of after-dinner coffee.

Irene Burroughs is still a little worried about Barrie Trexel and Blossom. If Barrie should— But Clyde is quite sure Barrie is all right. Clyde, meeting him for the first time, liked Barrie.

Leonora and Mike have come in from the dining-room, and Charlotte, too. They are still a little disturbed by Susan's continued determination to make them acquainted with the glories of conversion. She has told Stubbie that if he isn't "God-conscious" he is nothing but an animal. Which has Stubbie wriggling nervously.

They have all drifted out onto the terrace now. All excepting Clyde and Leonora. This is a moment for an exchange of confidences for them. Leonora is frankly bored. Clyde is as frankly unhappy. Leonora hasn't the nerve to throw Stubbie over and go back to the stage. Clyde hasn't the courage to stay around Leonora when she is the wife of another man.

Then Susan barges in. She is radiant in a very chic dinner gown and seeing Leonora and Clyde, she archly intimates that she knows she is *de trop*. That Clyde and Leonora are in love is quite evident to Susan. That they should confess and exalt their love is also plain. Clyde should go straight to Stubbie and say to him—

"Of course I am in love with your wife—but I'm not hurting *her*—and I'm taking nothing away from *you*—it only puts something fine in *me*."

If Clyde would be that honest— But Clyde isn't. He stands terribly embarrassed now as Stubbie comes through the door. Leonora cannot stand the suspense and starts for the terrace.

Clyde, even though Susan is still urging him to repeat the brave
and beautiful things he has been thinking, seeks a way out by
convincing Stubbie that Susan is only kidding. But Susan isn't
kidding—

"You see, when we run away from things they become dangerous," says Susan. When Stubbie demands an explanation she is
quite ready to give it. "He (Clyde) said so honestly just now—
'Of course I'm in love with Leonora. All the world has always
known it,' " repeats Susan. Stubbie is ready to fight.

"Dear heart—look at me," continues Susan, going quite close
to Stubbie. "Let me say this to you: You've got depths and
fine spiritual forces in your nature which you don't know anything about."

"Neither do you. You let my depths alone," angrily answers
Stubbie, and stalks into the house.

"Everybody behaves that way—at first," smiles Susan. "It
takes time. Stubbie's soul is hardened."

"I ask you one thing, Susan,"—demands Irene—"For heaven's
sake—let our souls alone over the week-end." Irene is getting
anxious.

Susan is not at all dismayed nor yet diverted. She would like
to tell Charlotte what it is she has to fight; to reveal the hidden
something that must be confessed before Charlotte will be able
to change herself and everybody with whom she comes in contact.
She would tell— But now Susan has discovered the heavenly
night—and the stars—"The stars are pulling me up—up to
them!" she exclaims, and drifts a little dramatically out onto the
terrace.

"You have to *think* it's funny or be more furious than you
ever were in your life," declares Leonora, with some spirit.

"What makes me so damned mad is Barrie and Blossom chasing
round trying to find her—while she's reforming *us*," explodes
Charlotte.

But Barrie has quit chasing around. He comes through the
doorway with a huge bunch of peonies in his arms. He obviously
has been drinking, though he manages to keep "perfectly steady
on his feet by moving carefully—and perfectly articulate by
speaking cautiously. There is about him a tremendous sweetness
which is at the moment tragic and pathetic."

Barrie is looking for Susan. The flowers are for Susan, and
he also has something very important that he wants to say to
Susan. They would put him off if they could. Irene would take
him in the house to look for Susan, but Barrie doesn't want to

go inside. He will wait where he is. If one of them will find Susan and send her out without telling her that he is there he will be much pleased.

It is Charlotte's suggestion that Barrie wait until morning before he tries to see Susan, but he will not listen. He's going to see Susan tonight and tell her something she's got to do, or by God—

Now it is Stubbie's turn to try to get Barrie away. Barrie doesn't like Stubbie, and is quite honest in saying so. He doesn't like Stubbie's taking hold of his arm. If none of them can find Susan, he'll find her himself—and he doesn't want any of them to come with him. He has just started out when Leonora arrives with the news that Clyde has said Susan had left him to go to the library. All right, Barrie will go to the library and see if Susan is there. He will go also with Mike, who is a man, and see what can be done about a good stiff drink that, Mike suggests, should help him put over whatever is on his mind.

Barrie and Mike have gone when Susan comes in from the outside, radiant and excited. She has been making Clyde see how he can exalt his love for Leonora. Now she would make Irene see how she might exalt her love life, too. But Irene is only irritated. Irene would shut Susan up, and resents very much her trying to Lady Wiggam her friends. If Susan is so eager for a confession, why doesn't she confess herself?

"Your own life is a mess," declares Irene. "Clean it up before you begin preaching to other people."

"My own life is a great sorrow," protests Susan.

"Sorrow—poppy-cock! If you were decent to Barrie you wouldn't have so much *sorrow on your hands.*"

"What a frightfully nasty thing to say to me, Irene."

"Barrie was here this afternoon."

"What?"

"*Perfectly sober*—and he said he was coming back—tomorrow. I wish I'd let him *see* you. After all he *is* a sweet thing."

"Oh, yes—other people's husbands are always so sweet.—I never know where he is—or what he's doing—or what he'll be like when he does turn up.—It's *ghastly!*—It makes me so nervous I could *scream.* (*Closing her eyes suddenly.*) Now—*peace,* Susan—*peace*— Ask for divine help and it will come. (*She opens her eyes.*) It *does,* Irene—*it does.*—If you and Mike would . . ."

Mike has appeared in the doorway. Susan is not flustered. She repeats to him what she has been saying to Irene. Mike, too, should confess. Before Irene can stop her Susan has gone.

She wants to be alone to pray for Irene. . . .

It is while Susan is praying that her friends agree upon a plan to cure her of this silly religious fad. They are a little fed up now with trying to protect Susan. They would like to do a little exposing. It is agreed, then, that Mike shall pretend that Susan has converted him, and that he wants to confess. They will all play up to Mike and make his confession seem very real. This will be fun. They are in the midst of their plans when Susan comes back. She has come, she says, to give them a demonstration of what love will do. She has come to forgive Irene for all the cruel things Irene has said. She has come to kiss Irene and to forget everything—as though it had never been.

"Susan—I'm awfully impressed with what you've been saying," says Mike, taking advantage of the situation.

"Oh, are you, Mike?" Susan is both amazed and impressed.

MIKE—Something *has* been gnawing at my soul for a long time.

SUSAN (*beginning to be very flattered*)—Darling—how wonderful!

MIKE (*growing convincingly emotional*)—I *want* to confess—but I don't see how I—

CLYDE (*grasping* MIKE's *arm*)—Don't lose your head, Mike! You may regret what you're saying all your life!

SUSAN—*Don't—don't*, Clyde.—Go on, Mike.

STUBBIE (*acting*)—Be very cautious, Mike.

LEONORA (*acting*)—Why should you drag out something from the past—that's *gone?*

MIKE—Because it—I—if I *had* the courage— (LEONORA *pokes* IRENE *to make her do her bit.*)

IRENE (*acting*)—Don't be a *fool*, Mike!

CHARLOTTE—No—no—Mike—I can't bear it! (*Giving a very wooden imitation of* LEONORA.)

MIKE—These people can never forgive me. They won't understand, Susan.

SUSAN (*more and more impressed*)—That doesn't matter. *I* will. *God* will. Go *on*, dear.

MIKE—I—I don't think I can. (*He sinks into a chair—his elbows on his knees—his head in his hands.*)

SUSAN (*going close to* MIKE)—You *must*, Mike—you *must!* Don't stop. Don't kill this impulse. Let it *come!*—You'll be sorry if you don't. (*They are all watching* SUSAN *and* MIKE *so intently—their backs to the hall door—that they don't see* BARRIE come into the doorway. He is dressed as he was when he went out—the flowers still in his arms.)

MIKE—I've done—a *horrible* thing!

SUSAN (*very appealing—carried away by her own dramatic instinct*)—Then ask God to help you. *He* knows what your temptation was. Telling *us* is only to break down your will—make you humble—bring you nearer to *Him*. No matter *what* we are—or *what* we do—if we're *sorry*—really—really and honestly want His help—we can be *made over*. (*She puts a hand on* MIKE's *head*.)

BARRIE (*speaking from the doorway very simply and very honestly*)—If *you* believe what you've just said, Susan—*I* believe it too.

SUSAN (*turning quickly*)—Barrie! (MIKE *rises and moves away. The others turn in awed embarrassment*.)

BARRIE (*coming to* SUSAN)—Do you mean *He* can do something about *me*—if I ask Him?—If you *do*—I *do* ask Him. (BLOSSOM *comes in through the open window*.)

SUSAN (*putting her hands over her face*)—Oh, Barrie!—How could you!

BARRIE (*as he sees* BLOSSOM)—Hello, Blossie!—I forgot all about you out there in the car.

BLOSSOM—I waited such a long time—I thought something must have happened. (CHARLOTTE *puts her arms around* BLOSSOM.)

BARRIE—Something *has* happened.

SUSAN—*Don't*, Barrie—don't—don't—please!

BARRIE—Your mother has just said something that changes the whole stinking rotten world. I never knew you, Susan. You look like a shining angel. You've got *star* dust in your hair. I lay these at your feet. (BARRIE *lets the flowers fall slowly at* SUSAN's *feet. She looks at him in unbelieving wonder as the curtain falls*.)

ACT II

At 7 o'clock the following morning Susan is sleeping peacefully in one of Irene Burroughs' prettiest guest rooms. "The furnishings are luxuriously comfortable in simple good taste." Susan is deep in a wide bed, surrounded by lace and pink silk. Her dressing gown has been thrown over a chair, her slippers are on the floor beside the bed.

There is a light knock at the door. Barrie's voice is heard calling Susan. A second later he comes quietly into the room and stands at the foot of the bed. Susan stirs and demands irritably to know who it is. Opening her eyes wide enough to see that it is Barrie she orders him away. It is an outrageous hour to be waking anybody.

But Barrie has no intention of going away. There is something he must talk to Susan about. He is terribly sorry for any humiliation he may have caused her the night before. That was not what he had planned. He had made up his mind to say to her as soon as she got back that he would give her the divorce she wanted. The kind of life they had been living wasn't living at all—not for either of them. But— Barrie had been thinking. Is there any other man Susan wants to marry? No, there isn't, Susan is quick to assure him. There had been men—plenty of them—but Susan had remained as she is. Barrie can't blame men because their marriage has proved a failure.

"We were frightfully young," Susan reminds him. "We thought we saw things in each other that weren't there *at all*."

"Where are the things you thought were *me*—and the things I thought were you?" demands Barrie. "Where have they gone? *God*—can't we get 'em back?"

Susan doesn't think they can. And she is glad that he has come to think the divorce is right. They will be so much happier once they stop pretending to be married.

Susan has recovered her negligee, slipped into her mules and started brushing her hair when Barrie says, quite calmly:

"I am not going to give you the divorce."

"Now, Barrie—don't wobble back and forth."

BARRIE—Did you mean what you were saying last night when I came in?

SUSAN—Of *course* I meant it.

BARRIE—Are you honest about it?

SUSAN (*brushing her hair*)—Honest?—You see—you *don't* see. —I knew it!—I knew it!

BARRIE—Where did you get it?—Where did it come from?— What's happened to you?

SUSAN—Marvelous things have happened to me. I'm an absolutely changed woman. But I don't expect *you* to believe that.

BARRIE—I believed it last night all right. But in the cold light of morning—it's not so easy.

SUSAN—You didn't even know what I was saying.

BARRIE—You said—no matter *what* we are—or what we've done—we can be made over—if we—ask—God—to help.— That's what made me change my mind about the divorce—that's

what made me think you might want me to try again. Listen,
Susan—this is what I came in to say— Do you think there's
any hope for me?

SUSAN—We can't expect *miracles*, Barrie.

BARRIE—Why not? I want to pull up, Susan—and keep
straight. I'm going to try.

SUSAN—It isn't a question of making promises, Barrie. If you
do mean this—you'd have to *prove* it. You'll have to go off by
yourself and—and prove that you *do* mean it.

BARRIE—Susan—if there *is* anything in what you've got hold
of—why can't it help *me*.

SUSAN—I can't *promise* that it would, Barrie.

BARRIE—Why not?—You were promising everybody else last
night.

SUSAN—Yes—but you may not be one of the ones who *can*
be changed. It means complete *self-abnegation*.

BARRIE—One of the reasons I want to do it is Blossom.

SUSAN—What?

BARRIE (*sitting in the armchair*)—When I saw her in that
school yesterday—with every other kid in the whole damned
place running off to a good time—going *home*—I felt like a
skunk. There she was—nobody wanting her—and no place to go.

SUSAN—Are you blaming *me* for that?

BARRIE—I brought her away with me—and it wasn't anything
like as much of a bore as I thought it would be. She's got a
damned lot of common sense and intelligence. I seemed to be
seeing her for the first time somehow.

Barrie is quite conscious of Blossom's looks—especially with
"that awful bit in her mouth." But he has discovered that Blossom hates camp, and has hated it for a long time. He had never
known that she had been lonely and unhappy—he didn't know
anybody Blossom's age could be lonely and unhappy.

"*You've* neglected her—I *haven't!*" snaps Susan. "*You've*
made her fatherless—I *haven't!* And now you're blaming me for
not having her with me all the time. You were with her *one
day* and got *tight* right before her eyes. Poor, poor dear child!
What can I do?"

"I'll tell you what you can do— You can open the house and
keep her with us this summer."

SUSAN—*Both* of you—under the same roof—*all summer?*—
I couldn't get *through* it. You've no right to ask it.

BARRIE—*She* has a right to ask it. She has a right to expect something of us.

SUSAN—You can't expect me to turn my life upside down just because you're ashamed of yourself for a few minutes.—I've had to learn to get along *without* you. I've had to fill my life with other things.—This summer I'm going to do the most important thing I've ever done in my whole life.

BARRIE—*What?*—*What* are you going to do?

SUSAN—I've promised Lady Wiggam to advance this new movement over here.

BARRIE—What movement?

SUSAN—This new approach to God.

BARRIE—That's the *bunk*, Susan. (*They face each other across the bed—their voices rising.*)

SUSAN—I *knew* you wouldn't know what I'm talking about.

BARRIE—I know every word you said is hot air unless you can forget yourself long enough to do this. I never asked you to do anything you didn't want to do—before. Will you give me a chance—to see what I can do?

SUSAN—And how long would you last, Barrie?—You'd start off so grandly—as if the very birds in the trees were singing a new song—and then—*smash!* (*She sits before her dressing table.*) Don't you suppose I'd like to believe you?—Don't you suppose I'm lonely?—Don't you suppose I'm tired trying to put things into my life to make up for the things that aren't there?

BARRIE—Yes—I s'pose you are.

SUSAN (*rushing on—half honest—half dramatizing herself*)— I came back thinking I wouldn't ask for the divorce. Something high and exalted came to me—right on the boat—right there by the railing—and I felt lifted up—I wanted to *stay* there—*live* there. And when I saw that shore line with all those marvelous things sticking up I said—"After all, this is *home*—Barrie's there —and maybe he *has* bucked up"—and then you walked in last night and I knew how utterly hopeless it all is.—Nothing else will do, Barrie—it's got to be a divorce. (*She rises and goes to the window.*)

BARRIE—Then you won't do what I ask?

SUSAN—You're not fair, Barrie—you ask too much.

BARRIE (*going to* SUSAN)—Susan—I'll make you a proposition. If you'll open the house for the summer—and have Blossom and me *in* it—the first time I slip—*if I do*—I'll give you the divorce.—What do you say?

SUSAN (*hesitating*)—But how can I be sure that you will?

BARRIE—I'll put it in writing. You'll have me sewed up. Here's your chance, Susan. There's my hand on it.

They have shaken hands and are standing, looking deeply at each other, when the door is opened carefully and Blossom appears. She thought she heard them talking, she tells them, timidly. And can she come in? They can think of no reason why not.

Blossom is something of a sight in a suit of Irene's pajamas, over which she is wearing "a trailing affair of brilliant green chiffon and black lace." The effect is a bit startling. "You're gigantic!" explodes Susan. "You look like a girl scout—gone wrong!"

Now they have taken Blossom into their confidence. They had been talking about plans for a happy summer for her, Susan explains. She had expected to go to Blossom's school to arrange something attractive for her, but her father could not wait. "He is so anxious for you to be happy, darling," Susan is saying, the irony of her tone escaping Blossom entirely, but being quite plain to Barrie. "So—since we're all gathered together in this delightfully unexpected huddle—we may as well settle it now. . . . We —thought perhaps we might open the house—and stay there— this summer. That is—of course—if that is what you would like best."

"Your mother suggested that," Barrie puts in, quickly.

"Oh!" exclaims Blossom, in breathless wonder.

SUSAN—Do you think you *would* like that?

BLOSSOM—*All* of us?

SUSAN—Well, what there *is* of us—such as we are.

BLOSSOM—You and Dad—and *me?* (*Her voice breaks slightly.*)

SUSAN—That's quite enough—isn't it?

BLOSSOM—All summer?

SUSAN—All summer—was your *father's* suggestion.

BLOSSOM—Would *you* like that, Mother?

SUSAN—I can't think of anything more thrilling.

BLOSSOM (*throwing her arms about* SUSAN'S *neck*)—Oh, Mother!

SUSAN (*struggling*)—Blossom!—You're *choking* me!

BLOSSOM—I think it's *wonderful*—don't you, Dad?

BARRIE—Sounds all right to me.

BLOSSOM—Do you think I could ask some of the girls to come for a week-end, Mother—sometime—maybe?—I mean, of course —if it would be perfectly convenient—when you aren't having *your* friends.

SUSAN—Oh—*never mind my* friends! Why not have the whole school? Your father would like that. You love playing with the young—don't you, Barrie? Ping pong—basket ball— picnics—and long tramps in the woods?

BLOSSOM—Oh, Mummie—you *are* sweet! Don't you think it's just too wonderful, Dad? (*She slides across the bed to the other side.*)

BARRIE—I do.

SUSAN—Well—since the idea seems to please you both—so much—we may as well begin. We can't stay collected under Irene's roof like this.

The caretakers are still at the house, Blossom and her father report. The furniture is all covered up but Blossom has seen her room and loved it. She had found the bed just too divine, too, and is bouncing happily up and down on her mother's bed to explain what she means. "You can't make the beds at school do this," Blossom assures Susan, and Susan wonders if it is quite necessary that a bed should do that.

It is decided that they shall go over to the house at once. They can't—not the whole army of them—stay there, Susan insists. Barrie thinks he will go first and see if there is any food in the house. Blossom is sure there are more ham and eggs and nothing could be better than the ham and eggs they had for dinner the night before.

Barrie has left them. The experiment is on. For a moment Blossom's excitement cools and she would talk seriously with her mother. Blossom knows. She was awfully sorry about last night—

"I was with him all day yesterday and he couldn't have been nicer," says Barrie's daughter. "Everything was perfectly all right till after dinner. Then I could see him getting restless and then—it *happened*. I expect it was partly *my* fault—because I wasn't very entertaining. But I know he *tried not* to do it. Really—*really* I do—Mother."

SUSAN (*looking down at* BLOSSOM)—I've tried to keep this away from you, Blossom.

BLOSSOM—Isn't there *anything* that can be done?

SUSAN (*moving away to the window*)—Don't you suppose I've done everything on earth I could? It's broken my heart too —but I don't want it to break yours. (*She closes the window with a little bang.*) Now you must stop thinking about it—and *be happy.* (*She goes back to the dressing table.*) You have to *make* yourself happy, my dear.—You can't expect anybody else to do it.—You'll have to learn not to expect anything of anybody but just what they *are.* (*Turning to look at* BLOSSOM.) Do you understand what I'm saying to you?

BLOSSOM—Of course.

SUSAN—Now skip along and get dressed—and we won't talk about it any— *Must* you wear those glasses *all* the time? (*Going to the bed and looking closely at* BLOSSOM.)

BLOSSOM—Not quite *all* the time.

SUSAN—Then the time you don't wear them will be when you're with *me.* Let me see how you look without them. (BLOSSOM *takes off her glasses and gives them to* SUSAN.) Why, your eyes are *good.* You must learn to make the best of what you've got. And you surely don't have to have that thing on your teeth *all* the time.

BLOSSOM—Oh, yes—I do— Dr. Ray says—

SUSAN—Well, I shall tell Dr. Ray I don't believe in it for the daytime. All night is enough for anything on earth. (SUSAN *throws the glasses on the dressing table. Then she lifts* BLOSSOM'S *hair, tucking it up and experimenting with it in different ways.*) If you're not going to be pretty—at least we must make you interesting. It gets a woman further in the long run.—If I had some scissors I'd try something.

BLOSSOM—Mother—Dad said you said something that changes the *whole world* for him. What was it?—What did you say?

SUSAN—Oh—something you wouldn't understand. (*Moving away and sitting on the foot of the bed.*)

BLOSSOM—There's one thing I *do* know. I'm sure—sure— *sure* of it.

SUSAN—What? (*Looking at* BLOSSOM—*arrested by the passionate emotion in her voice.*)

BLOSSOM—When you think somebody doesn't love you—and then you find out they *do*—it does something *wonderful* to you. If that could only happen to *Dad!*—Oh, *Mother!* (*She throws herself across* SUSAN'S *lap.*) It's so wonderful to be with you! (SUSAN *slowly draws* BLOSSOM'S *head to her—holding her a*

little uncertainly—a new and rather puzzled wonder in her eyes.)
The curtain falls.

Sunday morning, back in the terrace room, the week-end guests
are slowly assembling. The room is littered with Sunday papers.
Clyde Rochester and Michael O'Hara are the first ones down.
Then Irene joins them. The talk is mostly of Barrie and what
he has done, and whether he will remember it, and what will
Susan do. Clyde is the only one who has the faintest notion
that anything that Susan has been spouting could possibly help
Barrie. Clyde thinks it might—

"Why not?" he demands, as they are inclined to sneer. "Different things for different people. I don't think it makes much
difference what it is, so long as it is something to believe in and
hang on to."

"Don't tell me Susan's caught a disciple," smiles Mike, as
Clyde goes out onto the terrace.

Irene does not answer. She is troubled in her own mind and
about her own affairs this morning. She would talk with Mike
again about their situation. Does Mike think they are doing
right? Or wrong? Does he think it has been worth it—or
should they have waited until she had her divorce?

Mike is perfectly content. If he has any regrets they are because he is sorry Irene has had to do all the dodging and lying.
And, suggests Mike, if Irene is unhappy about it, why doesn't she
take a long trip to Europe and not come back until just before
they are to be married? "That," says he, "would stop talk and
put the whole thing on a different basis."

"Nobody needs to do any *going away*," snaps Irene. "We'll
call it all off—*now*. I wouldn't marry you for anything on
earth."

"You're acting like a—" But before Mike can finish Charlotte
is in, looking very gay in a brightly colored sweater shirt and
tweed skirt. She, too, is concerned about Barrie's disappearance
and consumed with curiosity as to where he has gone.

And now Stubbie has appeared, and he also is interested in
Barrie. And Leonora. They are all buzzing about the Trexels
when Susan appears suddenly in the doorway and the conversation stops—

" 'Morning, everybody," calls Susan gaily. "And *what* a morning! Did you *ever* hear the birds carry on so?—Oh—(*A pause.*)
You're talking about me. You think what Barrie did last night
was unforgivable.—But—it *wasn't*. Divine help comes in the

most roundabout ways. (*She goes to* MIKE.) Mike, darling—if you hadn't been *trying* to confess—I wouldn't have been saying what I *was* saying to you. The most marvelous thing has happened—the greatest demonstration I have ever— Barrie is *reborn—saved.*—Wait till you see him."

CHARLOTTE (*amazed and skeptical*)—Where is he—now—Susan?

SUSAN—He's gone over to the house to tell them *I'm* coming.

MIKE—What house?

SUSAN (*sitting on the couch*)—*Our* house! We're going to be *in it* this summer. I simply couldn't *wait* to begin. I had to *seize* this electrical thing—and keep it alive. I'm plunging right at it—to keep them close to me—both of them—Barrie and Blossom. I'm so happy I can't *bear* it. Isn't it marvelous, Irene?

IRENE (*standing in the center*)—So marvelous I don't believe a word of it.

SUSAN—*What* have I said that you can't believe?

IRENE—You don't think I believe for a *second* you're going to live in that huge old barracks of a place that's been shut up for years. It will be *filthy.*

SUSAN—Of *course* it will. I said to Barrie—"Never mind the dirt. We'll throw open the windows and let the sun pour in."

STUBBIE—How about getting food in the house? It's Sunday.

SUSAN—What difference does *food* make in a spiritual crisis?

CHARLOTTE—And servants?

SUSAN (*rising and going towards the hall*)—I'm going to get Molly Matthews on the phone now and tell her to send me a cook tomorrow and staff the whole house at once. Those are such little unimportant things compared to the great— (*She goes to the door and turns.*) Let me know when Barrie gets back. (*She goes out. The others immediately begin to talk again—when* SUSAN *re-appears at the door. They stop quickly.*) Oh—you think he isn't coming back. You think he's tight *now.* I'm so sorry for you. Stubbie—you look so silly and so unbelieving. (*CLYDE comes in from the terrace.* SUSAN *points to him.*) Can't you see in Clyde's *eyes* he has *sublimated* his love? Good morning, Clyde. (*She goes out again singing with rather defiant gaiety.*)

It is Irene's opinion, after Susan has left them, that Susan is bluffing; that she and Barrie have had the fight of their lives. Stubbie is inclined to agree. Charlotte and Mike are so curious they decide to hop in a car and go see if anything is really happening at the Trexel place.

Only Clyde and Leonora think there may be a chance that both Barrie and Susan have found a new and promising way, but they, too, have trouble of their own. Clyde has had word from town that a picture job may await him and he is going back to see. Stubbie is relieved but suspicious. Leonora is convinced that Clyde is making a sacrifice for her. After she has kissed him good-by she is suddenly thrilled with the feeling that she, too, should go back to her work, where she belongs. . . .

Now Blossom has come. She has been walking down the road, hoping to meet her father. Now she would like to borrow a car, if her Aunt Irene will agree, and go in search of Barrie. She is sure she should have gone with him in the first place. Irene will not let her have a car. A moment later Mike and Charlotte are back with a report that Barrie had been at his place, and had had breakfast there. Then he had started for the Burroughs place. Blossom is worried. She hopes they will not tell her mother. She will go down to the gate—

Susan has come from the hall in time to see Blossom going out. She is carrying her hat, gloves and bag and she, too, is anxious about Barrie. It is time—

"It's eleven o'clock. I know what you're thinking," says Susan, facing them. "And I don't want you to let him *know* you've been thinking it—when he comes. He needs *faith*—all around him. He needs to know we believe *he can do it.*"

"If you believe in him like that, Susan—it will help him more than anything in the world," encourages Charlotte.

And now Blossom is back to report that her father is coming up the drive. Susan, quite firmly and honestly, asks that she be permitted to see Barrie first alone.

Barrie is smiling as he comes in. He is sober and carries a bunch of violets which he hands to Susan. As he catches the expression of doubt and anxiety in her eyes his smile fades—

"Oh, you thought I'd fallen down before I even started," he says. "Couldn't you trust me for a few hours?"

Susan—I've been lying my head off all morning. They all think you're *drunk* again—and *I* said I *knew* you *weren't*.

Barrie—But you thought I was.

Susan (*shouting at him—her nerves snapping*)—Where on earth have you *been?*—Why didn't you come back when you *said* you would?—*What have you been doing?*

BARRIE (*shouting back at her*)—Digging up Mr. Higgenbottom in the village—to get some food in the house. (*Lowering his voice.*) Are you disappointed?—Were you hoping I *would* come back drunk—so you wouldn't even have to *start off* on our contract? Tell me the truth, Susan—is that it?

SUSAN (*sinking onto the stool in the center of the room*)—No —it isn't. But I've been thinking—a lot—Barrie—since our talk.

BARRIE—Have you?

SUSAN—If you *did* stop drinking—it would be *wonderful—marvelous*—and I *want* you to—with all my heart—but—

BARRIE—But it wouldn't make you want to live with me again.

SUSAN—Not necessarily. But this is what we forgot.—*You may not want to live with me.*

BARRIE—That's not humanly possible.

SUSAN—Oh, but it *is*. Quite—quite possible. You don't know me very well any more, Barrie.

BARRIE—Don't I?

SUSAN—I've changed a *very* great deal.

BARRIE—Have you?

SUSAN—Let's enter into this perfectly honestly—and whatever happens—we'll meet it—and be big about it. Whether *I* want to give *you* up—or *you* want to give *me* up. And while we're going through this, Barrie—we're *friends—good—good—friends.* —Nothing more.

BARRIE (*quietly*)—I won't ask anything more.—Well—at least we know where we *are*—even if we don't know where we're going. —Let's collect Blossom and clear out.

SUSAN (*goes to the hall door and calls*)—Irene.—Irene—we're going now—come and say good-by. (*She comes back to* BARRIE.) And, Barrie—don't contradict anything I say.—Don't make an idiot of me again. (IRENE *comes in from the hall.*) Barrie brought these to you, Irene. (*Giving the violets to* IRENE.) That's one of the things that took him so long—picking them. (BLOSSOM *comes back from the hall.*)

BARRIE (*to* IRENE)—With my very humble—you know.

IRENE—Oh, Barrie—how sweet of you to bother! (CHARLOTTE *and* MIKE *come in from the terrace.*)

CHARLOTTE—Good morning, Barrie.

MIKE—Hello, Barrie.

BARRIE—Good morning. I'm not trying to say anything— except that Susan's being a magnificent sport.

SUSAN—Don't be silly.—Come along. (*She gathers up her hat and bag.*)

IRENE—Why do you go before luncheon?

SUSAN—Oh—we're going to have a marvelous lunch, I adore eating out of a can. Come over for cocktails this afternoon— all of you. We'll give you crackers and rat cheese—and you can help take the sheets off the furniture and make up the beds with them. (CHARLOTTE *and* MIKE *go out onto the terrace.*)

BARRIE—By-by, Irene. Thanks for taking us in.

BLOSSOM—Thank you, Aunt Irene.

SUSAN (*giving* BLOSSOM *a spank with her bag*)—Well—here we are.—The happy little brood—coming home to roost. (BLOSSOM *starts*—SUSAN *following.* BARRIE *steps in front of* BLOSSOM *and the three of them go toward the window—all in step.*)

IRENE (*calling to* SUSAN *as she reaches the window*)—Susan! (SUSAN *turns and comes back to* IRENE—BARRIE *and* BLOSSOM *go on out.*) I take back everything I said. What you're doing is magnificent. And you're going to be awfully happy because you *are* doing it.

SUSAN—Oh, slush, Irene!—That's easy enough for *you* to say. You've got a man you're in love with.

IRENE—You've got them both. They adore you.

SUSAN—And they're going to hang around my neck all summer and choke me to death.—I'm not made for this, Irene. I don't know *why I'm doing it.*—I don't want to do it—at all—at all— At all.—I wish I'd never *heard* of God. (*She goes out through the windows as—the curtain falls.*)

ACT III

The scene changes to the sitting room in Susan's house in the country. "The walls are paneled in very old wood, painted a dull green. The curtains are old silk—soft in colors. The furniture is old French—graceful and charming. . . . The room radiates Susan's gaiety and style—and the ease with which she makes it livable and magnetic."

Irene Burroughs is there now. She has been away all summer and this is the first glimpse Susan has had of her since she returned. Irene had had a terrible fight with her Mike and left him. Now she has come back to marry him. "He's the only thing I want," Irene confesses with a wry little smile. "Mike's the answer to *everything for me.*"

"Because you *did* give him up. And now you love him in a *finer* way," chirrups Susan. "Didn't I tell you?—It's *beautiful!* —I'm proud of you, Irene."

Susan and Barrie have also done pretty well, reports Susan. Barrie isn't drinking—hasn't touched a drop. "It's been a miracle. Deep and beautiful and profound." Has Susan's belief made her do this for Barrie? Irene would know. I couldn't have done it without my belief," declares Susan. "It's *sustained* me. Don't think it hasn't been a hard job, too."

"Of course it has."

"Both of them—Barrie *and* Blossom!—At first I thought I simply could *not* stand it, Irene."

"I know. I know."

"One night I marched upstairs to *leave!*—And then—I didn't. There was a dress of Blossom's lying on the floor. I picked it up to *pitch it out of the*— But it was just like having Blossom in my hands.—You know there's something awfully queer about it. The more I do for them—the better I like them.—Blossom's the sweetest thing you ever— But it's been *awful!* (*Going to the fire.*) I haven't been off the place. Do you think *I've* had any parties? The house is filled with youngsters. They swarm and crawl all over the place. Every time I look up from my soup I see one I never saw before. They wear my clothes—they use my best writing paper.—I found a six-foot boy in my bed the other night."

Blossom has come bouncing in. She is a very pretty girl now, without either glasses or a brace on her teeth. She is wearing tennis shorts and looks radiantly happy. Blossom has come to report that there are no more sandwiches, and nothing to make any of, unless they use the caviar that Susan likes. She gets the caviar and is gone—with an affectionate but lusty spank from her mother.

"I'm so glad you and Barrie are together again," says Irene.

"We're together again—but— It's an entirely spiritual relationship."

"All summer in the same house?—You can't make me think you've got as spiritual as all that."

"That was our agreement—and Barrie hasn't broken his word once."

A dangerous experiment, thinks Irene. Barrie might go looking for another girl. Susan wishes he would, and that it would be Charlotte. Charlotte has long been in love with Barrie, and this summer they have been playing a lot of golf together—

"I've *saved* Barrie—and now I want to make him happy," explains Susan. "He's a darling—a perfect darling— But I've outgrown him. Charlotte never will, of course."

No, Susan is not in love with any other man. It is something
beyond all that. "I can't go back to being an ordinary woman
again," she says, going over to her desk. "Lady Wiggam says
I have a *very rare power*. This summer has been wonderful for
me. It's prepared me for bigger—wider— The meeting at Newport is going to be marvelous. *Brilliant*. Heaps of important
Americans—and as for English titles—Lady Wiggam herself is
coming over."

Susan has been helping to organize the Newport meeting.
And to think that it all started with Mike's confession!—That was
what convinced Susan that she did have the power. Look at
everything that has happened—Irene gave up Mike. Leonora
gave up Stubbie and has gone back to work—looking for a job
—and—

Before Irene can tell Susan the real story of Mike's confession,
Barrie and Charlotte have come in from their golf game. They
are both wearing golf clothes and looking particularly fit. They
greet Irene affectionately. . . . And now, when Susan goes out
with Irene, Barrie and Charlotte have a moment alone as they
make their plans for the next day. They are to play in a match
and Barrie is hopeful that they will win, if Charlotte is as good
as she was today—

"But, I won't be. I always fall down when I ought to make
the shot of my life," says Charlotte.

"That's what you don't do," answers Barrie, with enthusiasm.
"You're the best stander-up I know. Don't think I don't appreciate the time you've put in at this—this summer, Charl—and
don't think I don't know why you've done it. And don't think
I don't know there are a lot of things—a lot more fun for *you*—
than playing golf with me."

"And don't worry about any fun *I've* missed.—It's been a
swell summer. (*She suddenly becomes self-conscious.*) It's been
good for my game—you know—playing with you."

Susan finds them talking interestedly when she comes back.
She would have Charlotte stay for dinner and play backgammon
with Barrie in the evening. She needs Charlotte's help, too, in
finding enough boys for Blossom's birthday party. She had
thought a boy apiece would be enough, but she finds that she
is expected to invite at least six boys for each girl. Otherwise
the party will be a flop. . . .

Charlotte has gone. She is, thinks Susan, developing real charm
of late—real sexy charm. Doesn't Barrie think so? Barrie
thinks Charlotte has something more than that. Charlotte has

character. He can't understand why some man hasn't married her.

"Charlotte's the kind men fall in love with when they grow older— After they get all over that (*She sways alluringly.*) and grow more intelligent."

"Unfortunately intelligence has nothing to do with love at *any* age," says Barrie.

"Meaning that's why you fell in love with me?"

"That's one of the reasons."

Blossom is in to ask if Bobby can stay to dinner, which reminds Barrie not only that Bobby has been staying to dinner pretty often lately, but that Blossom is getting to be a very attractive girl. Isn't it a little dangerous—

"Forty is the dangerous age, lamb," Susan laughs, teasingly. "She's got several safe years yet.—Oh—you're so cunning—being a parent. But if you're going to think up any more things for parents to do—*you* do them.—I can't take on anything more.

BARRIE (*his back to* SUSAN)—You've done a swell job this summer, Susan. I bet there've been times when you wanted to walk out on us—and you've never let us know it.

SUSAN (*sitting up with sudden interest*)—The summer's almost over, Barrie. Blossom goes back to school in three weeks. Let's not put off till the last minute—the things we have to say to each other.

BARRIE (*cautiously—with fear and premonition—keeping his back to* SUSAN)—Well—what *have* we got to say to each other?

SUSAN—You must have something very important to say to me.

BARRIE (*fingering a paper knife*)—Not a thing—but *thank* you. I've managed to pull through—so far.

SUSAN—It's marvelous what you've done, darling. Coming home so fit and *sure*—every— You *are*—*perfectly* sure of yourself now—aren't you?

BARRIE—I guess so.—Thanks to you.

SUSAN—And *Charlotte.*—She's helped—hasn't she?

BARRIE—You bet. She stands up there and swats that ball and pretends she'd rather play golf with me than anything going.

SUSAN—It's too sweet for *me* to have to tell you.

BARRIE—Tell me what?

SUSAN (*rising and going to* BARRIE)—Charlotte's in love with you, dear—and I think you're in love with her and are afraid to tell me.

BARRIE (*throwing down the paper knife*)—Leave Charlotte out of this.—You mean the jig is up—for you and me.

SUSAN—I wouldn't put it that way.

BARRIE (*in quiet level tones*)—How would you put it?

SUSAN—Well—we've done what we *said* we would—and—

BARRIE—And drunk or sober—you're *through* with *me*.

SUSAN—That sounds *horrid*. I love you in a new way—*spiritually*—and I want you to be happy.

BARRIE—Thanks!—Thanks a lot. (*He starts out through the hall.*)

SUSAN (*calling*)—Barrie!—Can't we be *adult* about this? Can't we tell each other the truth *honestly*—as we said we would?

BARRIE (*coming back to face* SUSAN)—Sure we can.—Have you any more truth to tell me?

SUSAN—No, dear. But I wanted you to know that you're free to do what you want to do—and I'm free to do what will fill up *my* life.

BARRIE—And what *will* fill up your life, Susan?

SUSAN—My *work!* Oh, Barrie—this summer has been good for me.—I've reached a great understanding. I'll go to Newport *enriched* because of it.

Susan expects to be in Newport a week, and that is "an awful slice out of Blossom's three," thinks Barrie. Blossom, as Barrie sees it, is the biggest thing in Susan's life, bigger than any message she may think she has to give to waiting thousands anywhere.

"But I shall be back for her party—that's Monday—the twenty-sixth," protests Susan.

"*Saturday* is the twenty-sixth."

The calendar proves Barrie right, even if Susan will not believe it. She just can't be back Saturday—that's the day she is going to lead at Newport! That's the night Susan is going to tell, in her own humble way, how she found God. And what Barrie has gone through. And how gloriously it has all turned out.

"All sorts of people will be there—who know us—know all about us—and if I tell them what's happened to you—they'll have to believe it!"

Barrie will have none of that. What's happened to him isn't anybody's business.

SUSAN—But it *is*. We have no right to hide a thing that's helped us. (*Their voices rise with their emotion.*)

BARRIE—You can't do that, Susan—I *forbid* it!

SUSAN—You can't!

BARRIE—I *do!*

SUSAN (*at full tide*)—You're trying to stop *my work—God's work.*

BARRIE (*at last telling* SUSAN *the truth—his shyness gone—his intelligence on fire*)—I don't think you know anything about God, Susan. It's colossal nerve for you to stand up and talk to people *who do.*

SUSAN—*Stop, Barrie!*

BARRIE—I've tried with everything in me to believe this meant the real thing to you—but I can't. It's the show you like—the emotional excitement.

SUSAN—How can you say that—after what God has done for *you?*

BARRIE—Well—what *has* He done for me?

SUSAN—Barrie!

BARRIE—I've bucked up and hung on this summer—because I was fool enough to think it would *get you back.*—Well—*that's a flop!*—We've cracked up!—*What the hell—what's it all about anyway?* (BARRIE *goes out quickly through the window.* SUSAN *stands amazed—staring after him—as—the curtain falls.*)

Two days later in the same room Blossom is at the telephone. She hesitates a little while Leontine, the maid, finishes straightening up the room. Leontine would know whether or not Blossom's father is expected home this evening and Blossom cannot tell her —not for sure. They are hoping—

When Leontine has left Blossom gets "The House in the Woods" on the phone and inquires anxiously for her father. He is not there.

"If he does come—will you ask him to call up his daughter— *at once*—please?—And—yes— (*Lowering her voice.*) If—if everything isn't quite all right—I mean if he should be a little bit—*sick*—or something—will you please call me—yourself?— Right away?—And don't speak to anyone else, *please.* Thank you—"

She has just put up the receiver when Susan comes in. Susan is not pleased that Blossom should be telephoning the way she has been. Blossom might have known Barrie would not be at The House in the Woods. He is probably with Charlotte, even if Charlotte's maid does insist Charlotte left the house with nothing but her golf shoes the day she and Barrie were to have played the match. The maid was crying. She thought her mistress and Mr. Trexel might have been killed.

Susan doesn't think that. She wishes she did. But Barrie is too fine a driver— Drinking? He has *not* been drinking. Susan is sure of that, too. She will not lose faith in Barrie. If he had only waited— If he had waited Susan would have told him she was giving up the Newport meeting— "I'm making the supreme sacrifice of my life— But he was so strong," she wails. "He told me I could not do it." "Was he right?" "No—he wasn't right—he was strong. I never saw anything so strong. That's why I know he couldn't be drinking." It is Charlotte who is the cause of the trouble. Susan knows now. Charlotte began it. Now Susan will be forced to divorce Barrie. A little cry escapes Blossom at that announcement—

SUSAN—You'll have to accept it, Blossom.—After all—you've had the same father and mother longer than *most* people have.

BLOSSOM (*quietly—after a pause*)—Yes—I have. Nearly every girl in school has only got one of them—*at a time*. Not both together at once. And when you like both of them it mixes things up so. (*Suddenly—looking at* SUSAN.) I'll stay with you —*some*—won't I, Mum?

SUSAN (*startled*)—You'll be with me *all of the time*.—What do you mean?

BLOSSOM—But I'll have to be with Dad *most*.

SUSAN (*with a fierce new jealousy*)—Blossom! Do you love your father *more* than you do *me?* (*Sitting beside* BLOSSOM *again.*)

BLOSSOM—No, Mother—not *more*—but *somebody* will have to be with him.

SUSAN—He'll have Charlotte.

BLOSSOM—I mean someone who belongs to him—who always *has* belonged—from the beginning.—Why couldn't it keep on the way it *was?*—It's been so wonderful with *both* of you. I was going to be so proud when I went back to school and said we'd all been together the *whole* summer.—Oh, Mother. (*Her voice breaks as she puts her head in* SUSAN's *lap.*) I thought everything was *all right.*

SUSAN (*putting her arms about* BLOSSOM, *slowly*)—I've liked this summer too, dear.—It's been sweet—*sweet*—having you.

BLOSSOM—Wasn't *Dad* sweet, too?

SUSAN—Yes— Oh—but I've *grown* so—and your father isn't very *intellectual.*

BLOSSOM (*raising her head*)—Neither are you, Mum.

SUSAN (*giving her a little slap and drawing away from her*)— *What?*

BLOSSOM—You don't *need* to be. You get everything you want anyway.

SUSAN—Don't be silly! I give *up—up—up—all the time.* I try to make things right for other people—and they *change* things. Look at *this.*—I didn't plan this at all.

BLOSSOM—Then how did it happen?—I thought *God* was helping you this summer.

SUSAN—He sometimes does *very* peculiar things.

Someone has come into the house. They start, thinking it may be Barrie, but it is only Irene, and she is greatly excited. She sends Blossom away while she tells Susan that whatever has happened—whether Barrie is drunk or has eloped with Charlotte —that she (Susan) is getting just what she deserved; she is getting a dose of her own medicine. As a result of Susan's interference Irene has lost Mike. Mike is marrying somebody else.

"He was *lonely* this summer—without me—and on the loose. That's why it happened.—I was a fool—fool—*fool* to let anything you said affect me.—It was *right*—for me. It was *right!*—*You* don't know what's right for other people. . . . If you had only let us alone—we would have worked it out our own way. If you—"

Charlotte Marley is standing in the door. Irene starts to go, but Charlotte would have her stay to hear what she has to say. It is Susan, however, who starts the attack. She knows what has happened. She knows Charlotte is responsible for it.

"I know you've pretended to be helping him all summer. That was your method. Your *wholesome—healthy* method. . . . A vulgar—blatant—"

Susan's voice has become shrill. Irene would stop her before the whole house is aroused.

"Do you deny that you're in love with Barrie? Do you?" demands the now slightly hysterical Susan.

"No—I don't deny it. I always have been and I always shall be," Charlotte answers, very quietly.

"Do you deny that you began it?—That you meant from the beginning to get him?—*Do you?*"

"Yes!—I deny that! That isn't true. But I'll tell you this, Susan. If you give him up—*now*—I'll go after him—and I'll get him—if I can."

Charlotte has gone. Irene follows, but not until she has stopped for one final dig. "Now you know how I feel," says Irene.

SUSAN (*after a long pause*)—It isn't the same thing at all. You don't know anything about it.

IRENE—*Oh, don't I?*—I know I've lost Mike.

SUSAN—That's very different. You weren't married to Mike. —You haven't got Blossom. You haven't had them both all summer. (*She moves slowly about the room—taking it in.*) You haven't been here in this room—*alone*—with them, both—*adoring you*—*depending* on you. You haven't felt strange—new—funny little minutes of *peace*—that you never knew anything about before. That only comes after—a *long time*—of *seeing it through.*

IRENE—You didn't know that till you lost him. Till another woman got him away from you.

SUSAN (*speaking through her deep tears—with naked simplicity*)—No—I didn't. I didn't know *anything.*—Everything I've been gabbling about is true. It is! It is!—I know that now. Life has come straight back at me. All the things I've been running away from—are the only ones I want now. (*She sits on the stool before the fire—broken and honest.*)

IRENE (*deeply touched as she listens to* SUSAN)—Life's come back at *me* all right. I wasn't fair just now—Susan. It wasn't anything *you* said that made me lose Mike. It's *myself.*—The way I've lived. (*After a moment* BARRIE *comes in from the hall.*)

BARRIE—Are you going to drive Charlotte home—Irene?

IRENE—Yes—I am.

SUSAN (*getting up quickly from the stool and trying to control her emotion*)—Why do you?—Why don't you let Barrie take her?

IRENE—Good night, Susan. (SUSAN *doesn't answer.*) Good night, Barrie. (*She touches* BARRIE's *arm as she goes out.*)

BARRIE (*after a pause—coming further into the room*)—How much did Charlotte tell you?

SUSAN (*keeping her back to* BARRIE)—She didn't need to tell me anything. She admits she's in love with you—always *has* been and always *will* be.

BARRIE—Did she say that?

SUSAN—She did—and that she'll get you if she *can*. (*She turns to look at him.*) Well—if she hasn't got you now, darling— what *more* can she do?

BARRIE—Nothing. She was great.

SUSAN (*as casually as possible*)—Did *she* do it?—Did *she* sug-

gest going off?

BARRIE (*keeping his eyes away from* SUSAN)—She evidently didn't tell you *this*. I was drunk when I stopped for her in the morning. I began the night before—after we had our fight. (SUSAN *looks at* BARRIE. *He goes on in dead level tones without stopping.* SUSAN *listens—watching him intently—so intently she scarcely breathes.*) But she didn't hesitate to get in the car and go off with me. She did the driving and we *kept going*—till I'd lapped up all I had with me. We landed at some little Inn and she put us up as Mr. and Mrs. Somebody—and she *stayed with me*—till I slept it off—and today she drove three hundred miles to bring me back—and *there it is*.

SUSAN (*after a pause*)—Oh! (*She goes to the couch and sits —a little limp.*) Charlotte was *big*—wasn't she?

BARRIE—She was.

SUSAN—She stood by you—and saw you through.—You slipped because I failed you.

BARRIE—Don't, please! I have nobody to blame but myself.

SUSAN—This had to happen—and it will happen again—but *what of it?*—You've done the *hard* part—*three whole months*— coming home so fit—and *strong*— You're not going to let this once make you think you can't win out—are you?

BARRIE—Oh—don't be *sorry* for me. We'll get down to cases tomorrow. Everything will be all right for *you*, Susan—and exactly as you want it. Good night. (*He goes towards the hall.*)

SUSAN (*calling to him*)—Barrie!—Wait—I have something to tell you. (*He stops in the doorway and turns back.*) Turn out those lights—please. (SUSAN *puts a hand over her eyes.* BARRIE *turns out the brackets—leaving the room lighted from the lamp on the desk. He comes slowly toward her and waits.*) You don't know how rotten I've been. At first—I hoped you *would* come home drunk.

BARRIE (*quietly*)—I know. I *know* you did.

SUSAN—And then—when you didn't—and didn't—I began to be awfully pleased with myself and think *I* was doing it.

BARRIE—Don't try to buck me up.

SUSAN—I know my own stupidity has done all this to me. I know you're tired of my selfishness. Barrie, tell me the absolute truth. Are you in love with Charlotte?

BARRIE—I'm very fond of Charlotte. If she wants to try to pull along with me—why not?—I'm very grateful to Charlotte.

SUSAN—Oh—then you're not in love with her.

BARRIE—I *like* her—which is a damned sight more important.

SUSAN—Oh—I want to be so much more to you than I've ever been before.—Please let me try again.

BARRIE—I'm not worth hanging on to. You know that.

SUSAN—Oh, dearest—I don't think God is something out there —to pray to—I think He's *here*—*in* us. And I don't believe He helps one bit—till we dig and dig and *dig*—to get the rottenness out of us. (*She rises and goes close to him.*) Barrie—hold me. (*She sinks against* BARRIE—*he puts his arms about her—holding her close.*) Oh, *dear God*—don't let me fall down again.

THE CURTAIN FALLS

PROLOGUE TO GLORY

A Drama in Two Acts

BY E. P. CONKLE

WHEN the history of the WPA Federal Theatre is written it will be picked out in high lights of adventure. Some of these came through with surprising, and frequently with rather startling, results. The Federal's early production of Poet T. S. Eliot's "Murder in the Cathedral" was one exhibit in point. Its development of a new technique in the staging of news-drama that became the Living Newspaper series was another.

Its second year brought the people's theatre two outstanding successes in the popular sense that likewise boasted an artistic merit that quite amazed both the project's defenders and its generally lukewarm supporters. These were the newest of the Living Newspaper issues, taking its title from a part of a phrase contained in a Presidential fireside chat, ". . . one-third of a nation . . ." (the one-third that was ill-housed) and the historical drama concerned with the formative years of Abraham Lincoln, entitled "Prologue to Glory," written by Prof. Conkle of the University of Iowa.

There have been several Lincoln plays, notably that bearing the name of the martyred one, written by John Drinkwater, the English poet. Mostly they have been concerned with the later years of the President, and with the more tempestuous political crises of his life. "Prologue to Glory" reveals, with a consistency that is amazingly simple, the young Lincoln, the lad of 22 who had left his father's farm and taken his first job, a clerkship in a country store in New Salem, Ill. Here he drifted a little aimlessly, while those conquering urges for learning and public service were being born within him. His first romance found him here and from its tragedy he extracted a courage and a determination that were character-shaping in force, and a definite influence in setting him on the road that led him both to glory and to death.

The story of "Prologue to Glory" starts in a blackberry thicket near Tom Lincoln's farm. It is a sunny summer day. Abe Lincoln, 22 years old, has come to the field to grub stumps, but at the moment he is seated with his back against a tree reading

233

aloud to Denny, a boy of 13, who had much rather listen to Abe than pick blackberries.

"O admirable man! O great preceptor of his country!" reads Abe, with crude eloquence and considerable depth of feeling; "no wonder everybody loved him, who by his unwearied attention to the public good, manifested the tenderest love for everybody. No wonder his country delighted to honor him. Since the day God created man on earth, none ever displayed the power of industry more signally than did—(*To* DENNY)—George Washington."

Denny can't quite understand how Abe can set such store by reading, seeing that most that he reads is just fibs. But reading is what Abe likes to do most. He can learn by reading. "Readin' l'arns you things you'd never know otherways, Denny," explains Abe. "I never seed Washington nor heard tell of him till I got this book. You can set right yur an' l'arn things—'thout movin' your little finger."

Down the road a piece they can see Tom Lincoln approaching and from the other direction a "furriner" on a sorrel horse. The furriner looks mighty like a town-feller, considering his genuine leather boots. Abe is interested in him. He might know something about how Indianny has come in in the election.

The stranger turns out to be Denton Offut and he can tell them that "Indianny's come in free."

"Mr. Offut—just how do you ca'culate President Adams is goin' t' fare ag'n Mr. Jackson the Demycrats air runnin' from Tennessee?" asks Abe, a little to the disgust of Tom Lincoln, who doesn't greatly approve of his son's quest for knowledge.

"Well, I ca'culate Mr. Jackson is goin' t' beat th' horn-rimmed spectacles off-a Adams. I been all about and I know the country is got its belly full-a that tarnal old hot-headed Yankee. But I come over to see—"

"Reckon maybe the country wants to git its belly full-a hot-headed Andy Jackson, now. Just like people to jump out-a one bonfire into another'n just like it!" That's Abe's conclusion.

Tom Lincoln's all for moving farther West and gettin' rid of this business of politics. "When a feller cain hear his neighbor's shotgun, it's time t' be movin' on," says Tom.

But Abe is interested in news from the outside. Mr. Offut, it appears, is thinking of starting a merchandisin' business in New Salem and expanding from there.

"I ca'culate in two years this-here spot is goin' t' be th' regular buzzum-a God!" declares Mr. Offut. "I ain't goin' East; I ain't goin' West; I'm staying right here! Why, within twelve months this whole Mississippi Valley is goin' to ring with the name of Denton Offut—th' merchant prince of the Middle West—if not of the entire United States."

A chain of stores through Indianny and Illinoy represents the Offut ambition, and he's looking for help. He's heard tell of a smart feller who got a stranded boat over the dam at New Salem by boring a hole in the bottom, letting the water out, then plugging her up and floating her over. That feller was his son, Abe, Tom Lincoln is proud to relate, and Offut decides that Abe is the feller he wants to work for him.

Abe's a good worker, a kind of jack-of-all-trades, with carpenterin' a kind of specialty. "Pa teached me t' work—but he never teached me t' enjoy it!" smiles Abe. To Denny, Abe's "the most powerfullest feller in this yur township." He kin read books, too.

"Well, I reckon mebby you'd do, Abe," decides Offut. "What you say t' comin' down to New Salem and gittin' into my big enterprises? You kin keep m' books, count up m' figgers, an' he'p me build up m' Empire."

"*Me*, Mr. Offut?"

"Shore! Th' fust thing'd be t' raise th' store."

"Ain't the store even riz yet?"

"Big oaks from leetle akerns grows!"

Mr. Offut's further observation is halted by the arrival of Sarah Lincoln, "a large woman carrying a water pail and dipper." Sarah is Abe Lincoln's stepmother, and she is on the side of Abe's taking the job with Offut, against Tom Lincoln's plea that Abe should stay and help him and in a year or two move West.

"Abe, it's time you was goin' on—for your own good," says Sarah, after Tom and Denny have left them together. "Goin' where there's more things for a young feller to do—where there's newspapers and books—where you could get some real l'arnin' and eddycation."

"This-yur Offut feller only thinks he's big punkins, Ma," protests Abe.

SARAH—Th' feller may be a tarnal big talker, but he sees things t' do. He ain't no do-nothin' squatter. You cud see the world and meet other kinds of people you never met b'fore—down there at New Salem.

ABE—Yeh?

SARAH—Git up and git a mite-a gumption about you, Abe.

You cain't set here in the shade of a fence-row all yer life. Offut mayn't be much, but his improvidence'll show ye what not t' be, Abe.

ABE—Person ort t' do a leetle thinkin' 'bout a thing like this, Ma. Better eat beans and bacon in comfort an' peace than cakes and ale in fear an' tremblin'.

SARAH—I don't know nothin' about beans an' ale, Abe. I know your own Ma would want you t' make a man-a yourself.

ABE (*thoughtfully*)—Ma did say that onct.

SARAH—Well—(*Both look at each other—smile.*)—mebby you better had git t' workin' on them stumps right now. It worries your Pa t' see you not workin'.

ABE (*picks up bucket; hands it to* SARAH)—Poor feller worries a sight over how much other folks don't do. (SARAH *crosses to end of fence.*) Sometimes *I* set a-worryin' over th' same thing.

SARAH (*turning to* ABE)—Your Pa's a good feller in th' sight-a th' Lord, Abe, but—

ABE—You don't want it sayed I set all my life on a stump like him, do you? (SARAH *nods; leaves.*) I was worryin' a leetle about *that*, too!

Abe crosses left, takes his ax and swings into the stump as the curtain falls.

Some weeks later we are in New Salem, at a junction of the street where the Rutledge Inn stands. Mentor Graham, Joe Baldwin and several other of the New Salem electorate have gathered to sit on the fence, on the steps of the Inn and other such resting places as they can find. Signs on the Inn indicate that this is election day, and Graham has the pollbook in front of him on a puncheon table.

The gossip of the citizens is mostly political. Every now and then a voter arrives, states his preferences and has Graham record them in a book. Now Doc Allen, a dignified country doctor, comes in, carrying his saddlebags. And Ann Rutledge, a pretty girl who is just back from studying grammar in Mary Cameron's grove—

"And, Doctor, Mary says Offut's to begin his store," reports Ann; "an' he's gettin' a huge fellow, almost as strong as an ox, to clerk for him. Kind of an ogre, she said. You think he can really be an ogre?"

"Undoubtedly!"

"Well, I'm not sure we need any more in New Salem. What

A Federal Theatre Photo, New York.

"PROLOGUE TO GLORY"

rmstrong: Offut's been tellin' us you kin out-wrastle and throw-down any man within fifty
s-a here.
be: I ain't never said such a thing. I ain't got no cause t' wrastle nobody.

(Roderick Maybee, Stephen Courtleigh)

with another store over there, and Henry Onstott's new cabin, and Father talking of putting up a new mill—sakes, what a doings we'll have here."

The Doctor and Ann have disappeared in the Inn. The Merchant Offut has come in, a little high with liquor and with a tale to tell—

"I got a feller Lincoln comin'," Offut tells Squire Green. "Goin' t' clerk for me. He knows more than any other man in the United States, an' he cain out-fight—(*Stepping closer to men.*)—out-wrestle an' throw down any man in Sangamon County!"

The men are moved to loud laughter at such a suggestion. They are used to the Offut blow-hard.

"You better hadn't let Jack Armstrong hear you say that. Be too bad for yer clerk."

"Say, you tell that big tager-eatin' brother-in-law a yourn to skin out-a Sangamon territory before my man blows in. He can lick any man this side-a th' Wabash."

The men are laughing wildly as Offut goes off to make his claims to Jack Armstrong himself. It is while he is gone that Abe and Denny wander in. Abe is carrying a carpet-bag, and looking about confusedly. Denny is footsore and ready to stop. The men of New Salem would make fun of Abe and Denny, but the travelers take their banter in good part.

"What's yer perfession, feller?" Emory Potter wants to know of Abe.

"I s'pect you'd call it carpenterin'. That was my Pa's."

"Looks like a plane tooken t' *you* wouldn't hurt none."

"Abe, they air a-laughin' at you!" warns Denny.

"I don't keer—if they enjoy it," says Abe.

Now Denny, fearing for his hero's prestige, would have Abe tell them a story—the story about the noise and the fellow that got lost in a storm. Being urged, Abe finally agrees—

"Well—this feller was blunderin' and thunderin' about in darkness—except when the lightnin' showed the trees fallin' all about him," relates Abe, sitting on the table. "At last a turrible thunderclap scairt him nigh t' death. He lunged here and he lunged there tryin' t' find his way. He wasn't a prayin'—(DENNY *squats.*)—man; but right then he let up a genuine prayer. He says, says he—'Oh, Lord—if it's all the same t' you, please give us a little less noise, an' a little more light.' (*He looks at* BERT, BERT *laughs; then* GRAHAM *laughs; then rest of men laugh.* ABE, *looking at* JOE.) Mebbe what a feller needs ain't s'much *noise* but more *light*."

"You never heard a feller like Abe t' tell a story," Denny announces proudly, when the men have quit laughing. They admit that they never had, and are inclined to think that New Salem would be a good place for a good story teller to settle down. The call for another—for one with a leetle p'int to it—is insistent, but before Abe can get any farther than: "They was onct a preacher that—" Denton Offut has come back and is all excitement over the discovery of his new clerk. So this is Offut's "wrastlin', throwin', plague-gonned" somebody, is it?

"Fellers, this air him!" proclaims Offut, proudly.

"I kin start hackin' timber, Mr. Offut," says Abe.

"This-here's a star-spangled holiday. I got another job for you, Abe. (*To men.*) Fellers, I'm a-bettin' Linkern here kin throw Jack Armstrong twict out-a three times easy as y' know yer gran'ma—"

From down the street comes the sound of a crowd of men singing "Old Dan Tucker" with more enthusiasm than harmony. Despite Abe's protests that he "ain't got no p'tentions as a wrastler," that he didn't come down there for that; that he doesn't keer to wrastle only when he feels like it, and he doesn't feel like it now, Offut goes to the gate and calls wildly to the singers. "Hi, Jack! My man's yur!"

"Any feller c'nected with me has got to show his gall, by gad," warns Offut. "Two t' one on Linkern."

Now the Clary Grove Boys have crowded in the Inn yard, led by the huge and tough Jack Armstrong. There is a good deal of laughing, singing and back-slapping among the Clary Grove Boys.

"Bring on yer lousy big bum!" yells one. "Well, I'm a son-of-a-gun if it hain't a walkin' bean-pole. Twine up 'er, Jack. Twine up 'er!" shouts another.

Amid the jeers and the shouting Offut manages to introduce Abe to the crowd. They invite him down to Clary's for a swaller-a red eye. Abe doesn't drink. Maybe he wouldn't even drink water, suggests one named Mattling. "Roll the blaggardly dog in a barrel," proposes another named Hoheimer.

"Offut's been tellin' us you can out-wrastle and throw-down any man within fifty miles-a here," says Armstrong, quieting his friends with a wave of his hand.

"I ain't never said such a thing," protests Abe, quietly. "I ain't got no cause t' wrastle nobody."

"You aim t' settle yur in New Salem, don't you?"

"I'm clerkin' for Mr. Offut."

"Well, us fellers jist got a leetle program-a naturalization, then. If you kin stand it, you kin go right on a-clerkin'. If you cain't, you'll jist find yourself draggin' about a mile out-a town and us fellers has had a leetle 'lection day celebration."

A great shout of laughter follows Armstrong's sally. Abe had better wrastle, the crowd warns him. Life won't be worth livin' in New Salem if he don't. Denny, getting into the excitement, is yelling to Abe to "tear inter him."

Abe looks at the men, and then at Armstrong. "Well—I reckon I'm about like th' coon that was up a tree. He says: 'Don't shoot, feller, I'll come down.' "

"You goin' t'?" exclaims the excited Offut.

"I kin do anything fer fun—or necessity," answers Abe. "All right, I'll wrastle."

The men are crowding around the table, yelling their bets. Mentor Graham keeps track of them. Everything from a bottle of liquor to a broken down mare is put up. Abe is slowly taking off his coat. Armstrong has stripped to his shirt. There is a good deal of noise, but Denny can still be heard doing a bit of coaching. "Git yer Indian holt on 'im, Abe."

Offut tosses a dollar for holds. "I'll take what Armstrong don't want," smiles Abe. "Heads got it! You git your holts, Jack," announces Offut. Turning to Abe he adds: "Tear 'im up, Linkern! Lace 'im! You all ready? Give 'em room! Let 'er go!"

The crowd has given the wrestlers a little space and is milling excitedly around them. Squire Green, Colonel Rutledge, Mrs. Rutledge and Dr. Allen have come out on the porch of the Inn. The wrestlers are rolling about on the ground. Suddenly Armstrong lifts Abe up and carries him to the rear; they go down in a heap. Ann Rutledge, coming from the Inn, runs over to the fence. More of the townspeople have joined the crowd. The yelling is excited and confused:

"Wrist-lock!   Give 'im the wrist-lock!" . . . "Look out! He'll flop ye!" . . . "Flop over his legs!" . . . "Yippee!" . . . "Come on there, Linkern—take the arm-lock!" . . . "His legs is over there!"

Armstrong has thrown Abe down and has a hold on him. "Spit in his face! Pull out his hair!" advises Denny.

Abe slides out of Armstrong's hold and gets to his feet. "Look here, feller," he puffs, as Armstrong advances for another hold. "We're evenly matched. Let's quit!"

"Puttin' out th' white feather, air ye?" shrills Clary.

"Licked, air ye? Givin' up?" sneers Armstrong.

"No, I ain't licked."

"Whoever says you ain't's a—a *liar*," growls Armstrong, crossing to the crowd.

"What-say?" demands Abe, sharply. "Looky here, feller. Them's fightin' words, where I come from."

"O-o-oh! Abe's mad!" announces Denny, exultantly.

Now Abe has rushed in, lifted Armstrong up, thrown him down and pinned him to the ground. The crowd closes in. "Dog-fall! Dog-fall!" shouts a loser. "Fair fall! Fair fall!" claims Offut.

"I guess you want another throw, Armstrong," suggests Abe.

"Don't bother y'self, Mister," answers Armstrong, sitting up on the ground, dazed and out of breath. "You air hereby officially natcherlized." He is up now and shaking hands with Abe. "Boys, Linkern is *in!*" he calls to the crowd.

The crowd has gathered around the table. Debts are being paid and collected. Offut has offered to set up the drinks. Abe is dusting himself off and Denny has gone to find a creek for them to wash in.

Squire Green and Doc Allen have lingered to congratulate Abe and welcome him as a citizen of New Salem. The Squire goes further. He would have Abe and Denny come out to his house for the night. "Any feller can lick my brother-in-law is plenty welcome!" confesses the Squire. . . .

There is a good deal of girlish laughter the other side of the road and presently Ann Rutledge, Mary and Lou Cameron come rushing toward the Inn.

"Last one there's an old maid!" shouts Ann, and runs headlong into Abe, throwing her arms around his neck. A second later she has backed away with a curtsey and an apology.

"You go tell your Ma you just been restin' on Abraham's bosom," grins Abe.

"You—you're Mr. Offut's new clerk, aren't you?" asks Ann.

"Yes, ma'am."

"I'm Ann Rutledge. This is Mary Cameron—and Lou Cameron. . . . Well, we'll probably see a lot of you at the New Salem store, Mr.—Mr.—"

"Lincoln!"

The girls have called to Ann to come to supper and she, a little reluctantly, decides that she must go. She curtseys and joins her friends. There is a burst of giggling as they go into the Inn.

Denny has come back from his explorations. "Abe, we can—we—ah—anything wrong, Abe?"

Abe is grinning broadly and still looking after Ann. "I didn't see nothin', Denny," he says as the curtain falls.

The interior of Offut's store shows a counter at the back, the shelves carrying dry-goods and groceries as well. There is a barrel of crackers, a stove with stools and boxes around it, scales, etc.

Abe Lincoln is wrapping up a package of tea for a Mrs. Hankins, but it is not her purchases that most concern Mrs. Hankins. She has come to ask Abe to write a letter home for her. Mrs. Hankins' daughter Carrie is "goin' t' larnin' school," but she cain't tech hand t' paper yit."

Abe is perfectly willing to take on the writing assignment, and a little proud of the reports of his writing ability that are being spread abroad. . . .

Four of the town's most successful "setters" have arrived, and each of them helps himself to a cracker as he passes the barrel and prepares to let Abe start the evenin' session.

"Say, I've done made a new rule for this-here store," announces Abe, with some spirit. "You fellers stay out-a that cracker barrel. It's three-quarters gone a-ready and I ain't sold but one pound. . . . What with Offut drinkin' up the profits and you fellers eatin' us out-a house 'n' home, this-here store's comin' to a perty pass."

Abe has taken up a barrel stave with which to smite the next man who dips into the cracker barrel when Denton Offut appears. He is a little drunk and inclined to extend his celebration. "C'mon back and try m' new keg-a Hammond and Smith," he invites the crowd, throwing an arm around Abe's shoulders. "Hey —I've tooken Abe in 'n' made him m' pardner. Tooken him in on th' wave-a prosperity! C'mon fellers. Abe, did you order them goods?"

"They sent a letter back sayin' they want—money."

"Money? Them sons-a-Satan kin take our credit. They ain't no money out here but wildcat money. You know that."

"I ain't seen none," says Abe, ruefully.

"I give you credit. You give me credit. Potter and Slinkers give us credit. That's th' way business is kerried on. Come on —let's celebrate! Abe takes keer-a th' details, 'n' I go out and boom up th' cater-wallopin' Offut Concerns!"

The men have gone into the back room when Ann Rutledge comes into the store with Aunt Polly and Squire Green. Aunt

Polly has come for sugar. The Squire would like to talk a little law with Abe, seeing they are in agreement on a certain Ohio ferry case, but Ann has come with a serious mission in mind.

"Well, Ann. What cain I do fer you this fine evenin'?" asks Abe, when the others have left. "I got a bran new layout of crocks and hoss-shoe chawin' tobacco!"

ANN—Abe—Henry Onstott asked me to see if you would debate at the Forum meeting tomorrow night. It would be a grand chance for you. Mary's going and so am I. All we girls.

ABE—What's the debate on?

ANN—Which is more valuable, the bee or the ant? Henry Onstott has lots of books to look into, so you'd have to be on your mettle!

ABE—Henry'd be what you'd call havin' a right smart headstart.

ANN—He'll need it to stand against you. You'll do it, won't you?

ABE (*going to counter*)—Aw, I reckon not. I ain't *smart* anough.

ANN—Smart enough? (ANN *comes around to front of counter.*) You sure you're not just too lazy, Abe?

ABE—I ain't got no right t' go about tellin' people which's th' most valuable, th' bee or th' ant. I ain't done enough thinkin' on that subject—nor any other—t' git up b'fore people and—*talk!*

ANN (*coming closer to* ABE)—If it was telling a story to your cronies, I guess you could do it!

ABE—They're kind-a my own people, Ann.

ANN (*turning to him*)—Of course, it's no business of mine, but—(ABE *follows.*)—you could talk as well as David or Henry. An ambitious young man has got to make his mark in oratory now-a-days. (*She sits on box by stove.*)

ABE—Well, maybe.

ANN—Do you mean to tell me you intend to stay in this store all your live-long life?

ABE—I never much thunk-a anythin' else, Ann. If a feller can git along 'thout fightin'—

ANN (*provoked*)—Well, you'd never hear a Rutledge man say that, Abe Lincoln. He'd get out and try to get some independence and respect. He'd try to get some refinement about him, Abe. He'd—

ABE—I've had some etiket lessons, Ann.

ANN (*smiling*)—Oh, it isn't that, Abe.

ABE—I know I'm rough. But there's so many things I want to learn. I know there's places a lot better than around here— I've read of 'em. But all my life I never seed a nicer store than this'n, an' bein' clerk here is two notches higher'n any sityation my Pa ever had. Ever'body here thinks I'm doin' fust-rate. I b'gun t' think so m'self till you come along and set a charge-a gunpowder under me.

ANN (*taken back a little*)—I wasn't aiming to.

ABE—Ann—?

ANN—Yes, Abe?

ABE (*grinning*)—Set some more under me!

Now Ann is thoroughly provoked. What does Abe expect to be? Does he ever expect to get married? If so, how could he ever expect to support a girl in his state of poverty? What kind of a future would that mean for a girl? Because the men praise him to the skies and he wrestled Jack Armstrong he is content to sit around and tell stories—

"You—don't want me to be like my own people—Ann?" Abe asks in an awed voice.

"No, Abe."

"You make things sound plagued serious. I always kind of took it for granted th' Lord would take care of his goats as well as his sheep."

"Don't depend too much on th' Lord, Abe," advises Ann, with a wry smile.

"If you'll just tell me what I ort to do and be—"

"Oh, you're all right, Abe. It's just—you could be so much more. Sitting here with no ambition—satisfied. Sakes-a-mercy, why am I talking like this to you?"

"I was wondering that same thing, Ann," admits Abe, slyly.

Now Ann has found her grammar-book and that has brought them back to the subject of the debate—

"You're not angry with me for what I've said tonight, Abe?"

"I reckon not. 'Twas the God's truth."

"And you'll talk tomorrow night at the meeting?"

"You—you want that I should?"

"I think you ought to. They need someone in there to get them talking *sense*, Abe—talking about bees and ants!"

"Yes. There is so much else to talk about. The land a-growin' around us. People's minds openin' up. Not knowin' what to think—what laws to make. All the politicians talkin' of 'National Problems' and 'Internal Improvements.' Buildin' things. Why—we could dredge that plague-gonned—(*Pointing past the door.*)—Sangamon River—and—"

"That's good, Abe. You go tell them that."

A blustery fellow named Jack Kelso has come in, reciting Shakespeare as he hurries over to the fire. It occurs to Abe that Jack is the fellow to walk out to Mrs. Hankins's with him. The old lady has forgotten her change and Abe thinks she ought to have it. It's an eight mile walk, and the weather's cold and biting—but Jack will have a chance to try his "King Lear" on Abe as they walk along. Abe will be needing a lot of space to think in tonight, he confides to Ann.

Ann sees them to the door. "Blow, winds, and crack your cheeks! Rage! Blow! You cataracts and hurricanes—" Jack is giving full force to his voice as they disappear and the curtain falls.

The Forum Club has a cabin. Inside are rows of puncheon benches, a table for the speaker, a harmonium and bracket lamps on the walls. The crowd is gathering for the debate. Abe is there, talking with Ann up near the table. He feels, he says, a little like "a row of punkins—perty close to earth—"

"You never hear tell of th' feller lit a fuse to the kaig of powder he was settin' on t' see what'd happen?" That's the way Abe feels.

The room is pretty well filled now, and David Rutledge, the Chairman of the meeting, makes the preliminary announcement—

"Ladies and gentlemen, the New Salem Forum Society is happy to welcome you as guests. In this open meeting we will try not only to entertain you, but also to enlighten you. The first thing on the program tonight will be a hymn by the audience. Aunt Polly will lead us in the singing of 'How Tasteless and Tedious the Hours.'"

The hymn is no more than started than the Clary Grove Boys come barging in. They had heard Abe was talkin' and wanted to have a part in the meeting. They do not do so well with—

> "How tasteless and tedious the hours
> When Jesus no longer I see;
> Sweet prospects, sweet birds and sweet flowers,
> Have lost all their sweetness to me."

The hymn finished, young Mr. Rutledge announces the subject of the debate: "Resolved that bees are more valuable than ants.

We are fortunate in having Henry Onstott, who has debated before us many times, to open the question. Mr. Onstott—"

Henry Onstott is a neatly groomed, good-looking young man, entirely sure of both himself and his subject. "I shall not go into a definition of terms," announces Henry, "as I believe it is sufficiently understood that the bee, in general, is a member of the super family Apoides—(*Looking at* ABE.)—and the ant is only a hymenopterous member of the family formicoidea. (*Low murmurs from the crowd.*) I am happy to have for my task the defense of the bee. Not that it is the more easy to defend, but it is my heartfelt conviction that the bee is the more useful animal."

There is a tendency on the part of some of the boys to applaud and encourage Henry. When quiet is restored he proceeds with his argument, basing it upon three main points: (1) "Nature has given the bee one primal function—to pollinate the flower. . . . What would the world be without flowers; hence without bees; hence, without a second generation; hence, barrenness—barrenness everywhere."

Henry has moved back to the table so that he may get another squint at his book, which amuses the Clary Grove Boys. (2) "The bee is the sole maker of honey. What would this vile world be without honey? . . . Can—may I ask—can the ant produce anything of similar value? Can my opponent measure his ant up to my bee in these, or in any other respects?"

There is a generous round of applause and Henry moves on confidently to his next point. (3) "The lessons which the bee teaches us are inestimable. Hour on hour he labors to store away for the winter. The blizzard is on him, but his honey is in the comb. . . . Ladies and gentlemen, no matter who you be, or whom; or where you be, or of what intelligence—it must appear to you that the bee is much more valuable than the ant. First, he fertilizes. Second, he gives honey. Third, he shows how we should live. Can there be any doubt in your minds?"

The ladies answer with a lusty "No!" The Clary Grove Boys would start an argument. The Chairman again takes charge. "Now I am happy to introduce a young man who needs no introduction—Abe Lincoln—who will uphold the negative."

There is considerable applause, mostly from the Clary Grove Boys, and a lusty "Hooray!" from Denny. Abe proceeds slowly, awkwardly from his seat to the table.

"Thankee, David. Ladies and gentlemen, I've done most of my public speakin' on stumps for the benefit of God's green forests and Tom Lincoln's 'tater rows," Abe begins. "So I probably won't show up very bright ag'in an eloquent, polished speaker like th' honorable *positive*. (*To* HENRY.) I should like to add my praises to theirs, though, Henry, for the able manner in which you handled them bees—without gettin' stung! (*Laughter*.) Now—one of the subjects that appears to be botherin' this Forum Club is whether bees are more valuable than ants. It wouldn't take me long to point out a few important functions of the ant if I was a mind to. It is well known that he has moderate intelligence and lives in just as ordered society as the bee. His commerce and trade abound. I've not got any books to prove it, but I maintain an ant can lift many times its own weight, and could, if he was a mind to, outrun, out-wrastle, and out-argue Henry and me both!"

" 'Ray for the ants," shouts the excited Denny. "Give me the bees!" counters Matty Sparrow. The Chairman succeeds in restoring quiet.

"But more important than all these—ants are known to have better sense, and more of it, than to stand arg'yin' on such snivelin' subjects as we are," continues Abe. "Ants ain't ag'in bees. Both of them are valuable and have their God-given purposes, folks. Mr. Speaker, it don't worry me a continental which is more valuable s'long as each keeps into its proper place. Now, if Henry's bees was to git into your bonnets, or my ants was to git into your britches—that would be a subject for discussion— an' immediate action! (*Loud laughter*.) I'm sorry, but I can't imbibe of the same high seriousness for this subject as my opponent. It seems to me that the subjects for debate b'fore this Forum ought to be alive—subjects for action, useful for living. The things we hear, the decisions we arrive at, ought to be helpful to us. The Lord knows there are plenty of problems here with us folks—in Illinoy."

There is loud applause. Henry is on his feet demanding that the Chairman keep the speaker to the subject. The Onstott partisans would start trouble. The Clary Grove Boys wish they would. Abe waits for quiet and then proceeds—

"You fellers hold your 'taters, now. I'll fetch the subject back to ants or bust a hame-string. Folks, I've had some long talks with several ants along th' Sangamon River. (BERT *laughs*. *Boys laugh*.) Do you know what they told me? Well—they said if they was us, they would do something about those bends in the River that keep the *Talisman* from comin' up from St. Louis— that keep New Salem from sending its goods to a market in St. Louis and New Orleans. We've got the land, the pastures, the crops—all we need is a market to sell in, an outlet. We could raise our crops and the broad river would carry them to market and fetch us back sugar and iron, and furniture—(*Low murmurs.*) —things we cain't raise nor otherwise get. Ladies and gentlemen, what I propose to you tonight is—that—"

Now there is more trouble. Objections from the Onstott side. A demand from Abe's supporters that he continue and further objection to the Clary Grove Boys by the incensed Matty Sparrow. Finally Abe is permitted to go on.

"Ladies and gentlemen," he says, holding out his hands for silence and getting it, "I'll set down as soon as you let me say what I came here to say. And th' upshot of my whole speech here t'night is—that, by my own initiative, and through the offices of my kind friends, I want to take this opportunity, hereby and forthwith, to announce myself as candidate for Sangamon County, to the Legislature of the State of Illinois! (ANN *slowly stands. Gasps of surprise from crowd.*) I do wish to announce my platform as one of local reform and 'Internal Developments,' as the politicians say. I am especially interested in the development of waterways and the natural resources of Sangamon County, and its marketing. I am—ladies and gentlemen, further—*done,* I reckon!"

Ann, the Squire, Colonel and Mrs. Rutledge, Doc Allen and the rest of Abe's friends swarm up with congratulations. There is a good deal of loud talk among the rest of the crowd as it slowly filters out. "Did you know Abe was goin' t' do that?" . . . "There goes your ole bees an' ants!" . . . "Runnin' ag'in the Demycrats! Got his nerve!" . . . "I'll vote for him!" . . . "Them long legs is for more than settin'."

"What platform you standin' on, Abe?" Col. Rutledge wants to know.

"The Whig, I reckon," answers Abe.

"Good Gawd! Not a ghost of a chance, sir! Not a ghost!"

"It was perfect, Abe!" says Ann, when all but David had gone on.

"Aw, now, Ann."

ANN—You sure have started something. Whew!
ABE—You're not disappointed at my goin' Whig, Ann?
ANN—Sakes-a-mercy, *yes!*
ABE—Doc Allen, the Squire—all the people but your folks— it's what they stand for, Ann.
ANN—I know, Abe.

DAVID—You coming home, Ann?

ANN—Yes.

ABE (*following*)—I reckon I'm like the feller got on the Texas steer. I don't know where I'm goin', but I'm on my way!

ANN—It takes my breath away. You sure you're feeling all right, Abe?

ABE (*laughing*)—Aw, I reckon I am. Now, I've got to get out and make speeches, shake hands with people—tell 'em where I stand—get out some hand-bills. I got to find what principles Cartwright's standing on.

ANN—He'll fight to the last ditch—he's a Methodist!

ABE—It just don't seem like a Lincoln t' start a thing like this. Ever'thing inside me was saying—"Lord sakes, Abe, set down. Why'd you ever stir up *this* mess?" Tom Lincoln could see me now, he'd not know his boy! It—was right interestin' standin' up there, watchin' people think this-way-and-that. I—feel powerful better—doin' this—thanks t' *you*, Ann!

ANN—Now, Abe.

DAVID (*at the door*)—Coming, Ann?

ABE—I wonder, Ann—

ANN—Yes?

ABE—Could I fetch you home, Ann?

ANN (*smiling*)—It wouldn't seem like a Lincoln to start such a thing as *that*, either, would it?

ABE—Well, I suppose not—but—

ANN (*laughing*)—You can fetch me, Abe.

ABE—Thanks, Ann—! (*He picks up coat and hat; follows.*) My Pa could see me *now!*

The curtain falls.

ACT II

In the early fall Abe Lincoln walks across the lawn back of the Rutledge Inn. He is all dressed up and carries a carpet-bag and a green umbrella. Granny Rutledge is there, but Ann is not, and it is Ann that Abe's looking for.

Granny would like to know the news. Is it true that Denton Offut has left New Salem for good? It is, so far as Abe knows. Offut's gone and left Abe with all the store-debts, but Abe isn't complainin'.

There is one thing that "Abry" can do better than anyone, in Granny's estimation, and that is read from the Bible. "Ann, an' the plagued 'lectioneerin' cain jist wait till you read to Granny

Rutledge," the old lady insists. And Abe, with a twinkle in his eye, agrees to read a mite from "Job."

He starts with Job, but before Granny can make out quite what is happening he has gone into Aesop's Fables, and from Aesop's Fables into a high-powered adventure with a Sultan who awoke suddenly to find himself surrounded with female slaves. But by the time he gets to "Whereat he cried, 'By Allah—either I'm dreaming or this is Paradise!'" Granny has discovered the cheat and is lunging at him with her cane, and laughing delightedly. "I've heard the Bible read many-a time, but I knowed I'd never heard them things in it afore," shrills Granny. "Sakesalive, Ann kin have you. Sakes-a—(*She is shaking with laughter now.*)—Abry—you shore had me goin' plumb galley-west! . . ."

Ann has come into the yard. She is in a teasing mood, but happy in finding Abe there. She is sitting on the wall now, and Abe has parked his hat and umbrella.

"So-o—you're off to the wars, Abe?"

"Yeah, I'm talkin' over toward Antioch t'night. Then around over East—"

"Did you get a horse?"

"No. I'm ridin' with Dave Vance a piece. Then I'll traipse on alone."

"How does it feel to be about elected to something, Abe? The Honorable Abe Lincoln—" (ANN *curtseys.*)

"Aw, Ann—set down and be still. I'll probably not really get it."

"With that brand new white cambric shirt on, Abe—(*Fixes his collar.*)—you can't help it! Isn't it a grand day? Let's run some place, Abe."

"Run?"

"Fly then. Down to Memphis. I've always wanted to see the cotton fields—the long white fields—and songs—"

"Sometimes that ain't such a happy sight. The darkies don't always sing."

"But they are today. And there'll be dancing on the street, Abe—for you—when you're elected!"

"Aw, now, Ann."

"Come on, Abe, let's dance on the greensward."

She has taken hold of her skirts and pointed her toe and is soon dancing to the tune of "Skip to My Lou," backward and forward, toward him, forcing him to take a part against his protests. He's awkward and embarrassed, but Ann is having a fine time.

"You're a very handsome feller, Squire Lincoln," she says, when she has finally given up; "and you may get a seat in the councils of the wise,—but you haven't any way with the gals. I'm going to have to take you in hand. Why, Mary Cameron says you stare at her, and she's afraid you'll step on her toes when she comes in to buy muslin."

ABE—Air *you* a-feared of me, Ann?

ANN (*mock seriously*)—Oh, yes! Terribly!

ABE—Plague take it all, Ann! I've—Ann, will you—you—*marry* me?

ANN (*not too much surprised*)—Marry you, Abe?

ABE—I—(*Almost speechless.*)—reckon so, Ann. I mean—will you—? Aw, Ann—I reckon I love you past any mortal love!

ANN—Do you, Abe?

ABE—Yeh! (ANN *turns to him.*) I've got no right to—no right to hope nor expect anything. But—I do! I can't help it! I've tried and—I just can't!

ANN—Yes, Abe?

ABE—I know I've got no work now. The store's gone. Offut's gone. Debts. It's all I cain do now-days t' keep body and soul together. I ain't much to look at, I know.

ANN—You're not speakin' very well for yourself, are you, Abe?

ABE—I reckon I'd be a good walkin' delegate for a long spell-a bad weather, Ann. A-course I might win. I've thought everything out clear as I could. Folks seem to like to hear me talk. You cain't tell nary a thing how they'll vote, though. I wish I knew. I—I've thought of going into blacksmithing if I don't get it. I never've known a blacksmith that died of starvation. Did you, Ann?

ANN—No-o.

ABE—There you are. And they're always good story-tellers, too.

ANN—That's a lot, Abe!

ABE—I've thought of surveying. And then there's law. Every now and then I get money for writing contracts and deeds. Bowlin wants me t' take up the law. I guess I could make a little pin-money working at harvest,—whip-sawing out coffins,—and such-like, Ann! So's you could have a fol-de-rol now and then.

ANN—A fol-de-rol, Abe?

ABE—Yes. Like for your hair. Or a breast-pin for your dress. Or a poke of sweets.

Ann—I never use fol-de-rols, though, Abe.

Abe—You could have some when we were—married! (*Taking poem from pocket.*) Ann—

Ann—Yes, Abe?

Abe—I've undertooken to write you a snatch of—poetry. I just want you to know before I light out, I—think muchly of you! (*Hands her poem.*)

Ann (*pushing it toward him*)—You read it, Abe.

Abe—I don't know whe'er I can. I—well—

> "Time, what an empty vapor 'tis,
> And days how swift they are;
> Swift as an Indian arrow—
> Fly on like a shooting star.
> The present moment just is here,
> Then slides away in haste,
> That we can never say they're ours
> But only say they're past."

Ann—That's lovely, Abe!

Abe—It's for you, Ann—

Ann—It doesn't say much about love—but it's lovely. I'll put it in my scrapbook. A remembrance of a lovely day.

Abe—Thanks—Ann!

Ann—You know, Abe—once I thought I shouldn't marry you.

Abe—You knew I—was goin' to ask you?

Ann (*smiling*)—Well—every other young fellow here has, Abe.

Abe—Oh.

Ann—No—once I thought I'd not marry you. I thought I'd let Mary Cameron have you. You know—I was engaged once.

Abe—I knew that, Ann.

Ann—He went East—he didn't write.

Abe—Aye, aye, Ann.

Ann—I wanted you to know. Because I—I like you, Abe—muchly! I've never thought of the poverty—the debts—

Abe—You've *not?*

Ann—No. But I never thought you'd speak so soon, Abe—when the prospects were apparently so unfavorable!

Abe—Seems like I always do that, Ann! I just couldn't help it!

Ann—I know that anyone that can write a pretty poem like this, might some day be, oh—the governor!

Abe—Ann—will you marry me? (*He drops to his knees be-*

side her.)   I cain't go on without you.

ANN—I like you, you ganglin' fellow!

ABE—Will you?

ANN—If it'd make you happy—(*Turns from him; she cries softly*.)

ABE—Oh, Ann!

ANN—Yes, Abe.   I think perhaps I will.

She has turned and kissed him and he, beside himself with joy, is jumping about like a wild man. "Dog-gone, Ann! I'm bustin'! I'm plumb bustin'! Whee! Hooray! Hell'n Mariar!"

"For goodness' sake, Abe," protests Ann, running to him and putting her hand over his mouth. "You'll have the whole town over here."

"Let 'em come! I'll tell 'em we're goin' t' be married! (*Embraces her—releases her*.) I'm goin' out to win this 'lection fer you, Ann! I'm goin' to make a big out of it. I'm goin' to put steamboats on the wide breast-a this River! I'm goin' t' work hard, and gain honor and respect, and get myself elected again! I'm goin' to—Ann—did I tell you what that damn fool Offut said in the letter he left me?"

"No, Abe. What?"

"He says, 'You get out of this store-business, keep out of rascally politics and law, and do something honest like tamin' hosses.' (*Laughs*.) Oh, Ann! Lawdy massy!"

He has lifted her high above his head when Dave Vance is heard calling and she makes him put her down. Abe has recovered his hat and umbrella now and is starting off, laughingly admitting that he probably has lost his mind. "I'm goin' to—to sit on th' Seat of the Almighty and consort with the Lord, Ann!"

"Good-by, Abe, dear; I hope you win!" she calls after him.

"Good-by, Ann!"

He has held her in his arms a moment and then, cocking his hat, he has started off singing—

> "Come, thou fount of every blessing,
> Tune my heart to sing thy grace—"

He has disappeared, but still the song floats back to Ann—

> "Streams of mercy, never ceasing,
> Call for songs of loudest praise—"

She is standing by the tree, waving to him. Still his booming voice carries to her—

> "Teach me some melodious sonnet
> Sung by flaming tongues above
> Praise the mount—"

The voice fades. The curtain falls.

At Petersburg a number of men have gathered around Silas' blacksmith shop. Some are leaning against the fence, smoking. One is sharpening a scythe. Several are whittling and none is very busy. The talk is mostly of the campaign and the chances of the candidate Peter Cartwright. There has been some gossip to the effect that the feller Linkern is pretty strong down New Salem way, but it is the general conviction that any man runnin' ag'in Old Hick'ry and the Demycrats ain't got no chance.

George Vorhees, who is the head of the Democratic Party in the Petersburg district, has come bustling in with important news. Judge Higgins has Lincoln in tow down at Vorhees' place, showing him Vorhees' new lightning rod. Lincoln has heard that there was goin' to be a sale there and he has come up to speak. It is up to the Democrats to take care of this fellow.

"Say, George—how much did that high-falutin' lightnin' rod set ye back?" asks a man named Riggins.

"Shet up! I'm gettin' tired talkin' about that rod. It don't make no difference how much it cost. But I can tell you this— if Cartwright ain't elected, it's goin' to cost you fellers a-plenty! Th' plan is—th' Party's goin' to make offices for fifteen or twenty men around here, when it gets in. Old Pete don't know that, but I do, and you fellers do now. Now when th' election's over—"

Riggins has caught sight of Judge Higgins and Abe coming up the road. A second later they have walked into view. Abe is carrying his carpet-bag, umbrella and boat model. "Old Hickory's a good feller, Judge," Abe is saying. "But I cain't make up m' mind t' see no one at Washington that's been mixed up in brawls an' duels, and killed, slashed, and clawed various American citizens."

Such a statement, overheard by the men, stamps Abe as a Whig all right, and there are many sly digs of criticism.

"But I ain't so much interested in that," Abe is saying. "Our Party's got t' git under local improvements. There's where our success lays."

"I reckon mebby so," agrees the Judge. And then, turning to the men, he adds: "Gentlemen, this is Abe Lincoln from down New Salem way—"

The greeting is friendly, and a moment later, when Silas is trying to satisfy his curiosity about the boat model Abe is carrying, the other men are gathering around equally curious. It is, explains Abe, a model for a boat with a couple of bellows hooked below the water line. When the boat comes to the shoals, the bellows are filled with air and she floats over.

"Do tell! Sure that'll work, Lincoln?"

"I'm not sure—but she sounds good, don't she?"

Riggins thinks he might be able to help Lincoln get a patent on his boat. Invites him over to supper to talk it over. But George Vorhees would put a stop to this growing interest. "I'm head-a th' Democratic Party around here!" he announces, defiantly.

"I thought I used t' hear of your bein' a *Whig* once, Mr. Vorhees," says Abe, quietly, and the men laugh.

"That don't make no difference, now!" snaps Vorhees. "I've got better sense since then! I—"

"I was inspectin' your new lightnin' rod as I—come past." The men think this is also cause for laughter. A moment later Abe has asked permission to say a few words to them—

VORHEES—You're out after Pete Cartwright's votes! We got no use—!

ABE (*looking around at* MEN)—No-o. I'm only after a few of my own. I'm one of you men. I know what you have to put up with here. I guess I could do a lot of good, besides helpin' you, in the Legislature down there. (*Steps onto knoll.*)

VORHEES (*facing* ABE)—You're a Whig, by gad! You're a Henry Clay Whig! What's your stand on this secession question, feller? What's your stand on slavery? What about logrolling?

ABE—Now, fellow citizens—

VORHEES—You're a young demagogue and you're goin' to be taken down, by God! I'm running the politics of this precinct and I don't need no upstart bargin' in here tellin' me my business! Look here, Lincoln—

ABE—Mr. Vorhees has said that I'm a young man that should be taken down. (*He starts down from knoll.*)

VORHEES—This territory here is mine!

ABE—It is for you, not for him, to say whether I am up or down. (*He looks at* MEN. *They motion him to continue. He goes up again.*)

VORHEES—You stop this, Lincoln! I warn you!

ABE—I desire to live; and I desire place and distinction; but I would rather die now than, like th'—(*Points finger at* VORHEES.) —gentleman, live to see the day that I would change my politics for an office worth three thousand dollars a year, and then feel compelled to erect a lightnin' rod t' protect a guilty conscience from the wrath of an offended God!

VORHEES (*stepping closer; shaking fists*)—By God, you—! (RIGGINS *stops him.*)

CONOVER—Hey, now, none of that! (*The* MEN *laugh, push* VORHEES *away.*)

RIGGINS—Take 'er easy, George! Don't need no fist fightin' here!

SEESTRUM—Have to do better than *that* to beat this feller, George. (*The* MEN *laugh.* VORHEES *sputters; shakes fist at* ABE.)

MEN (*shoving* VORHEES *farther out*)—Get on home, George! We'll tell you what he said tomorrow. (VORHEES *retires.*) Go on, Lincoln! Speech! Speech!

ABE—There are three ideas I want to stand before you on: internal improvements, a lower rate of usury, and a better system of education. On the former—(*Taking handbills from pocket. Gives some to* SILAS *and the rest to* RIGGINS *who passes them along.*)—I believe these handbills will give you my ideas how the poorest counties can be benefited by the opening of good roads and the clearing of navigable streams like our Sangamon. On the next I may say that the practice of loaning money at exorbitant rates of interest is a baneful practice and as harmful to the interests of the community as a tax of several thousand dollars for the benefit of a few people. I propose to introduce a law fixing the limits of usury. On the subject of education, I should like to say that I view it as one of th' most important subjects in which we can engage. That every individual may receive at least a moderate education, and thereby be enabled to read th' histories of his own and other countries, that they may duly appreciate the value of our free institutions, is of vital importance, to say nothing of the blessings to be derived from all bein' able to read the Scriptures, and other works of religious, educational or moral nature.

MEN—That's right! He's right!

ABE (*comes down to* MEN; *places self among them*)—As—modesty should always attend youth, it is probable that I have already been more forward than becomes me.

MEN—Go on. What else? (RIGGINS *pats him on the back.*)

ABE—But every man is said to have his own ambition. I've got no other so great as that of bein' truly esteemed by my fellow-men, by rendering myself worthy of that esteem. (*Turning to* MEN *on his right.*) I was born twenty-two years ago last February.

SILAS—Yeah?

ABE—And these years have been spent in th' most humble walks of life. (*Turns to* MEN *on left.*) As I have no wealthy or popular relations to recommend me, I throw my case entirely upon th' independent voters. If elected, I shall be unremitting in my labors to serve you; but if your wisdom dictates to keep me in th' background, I am too familiar with disappointments to be very much chagrined. Thank—you.

The men have been impressed and several are eager with their congratulations. Abe is preparing to move on when Dave Vance pushes his way through the crowd. He is looking for Abe.

"Milk-sick! It's struck New Salem, Abe," Dave explains. "It's perty bad there, Abe! People comin' down every night! When I left a couple of days ago, three was tooken dead. Abe—th' leetle gal—"

"Ann?"

"I was comin' to that—I—"

"She's not—bad?"

"Yeh. She's tooken perty bad, Abe. She—was callin' for you to come home."

"I—I've got to go—then! Now!"

"I guess so. The Colonel sent me for you. My buggy's over here, Abe—all ready!"

They have hurried away. The Judge is looking after them, fear in his eyes.

"It ain't struck us—*yet!*" he says, as the curtain falls.

In a room in the Rutledge Inn there is a low fire burning in the fireplace. Granny Rutledge is reading her Bible. Colonel Rutledge is sitting with his head in his hand and Abe is standing by the window.

Mrs. Rutledge can bring no more cheering news from the sick room than that Ann is sleeping.

A stranger, guest at the Inn, would express his sympathy. They call the milk-sick "trembles" where he comes from. "S'pose you've tried barks, and jalap, and boneset tea?" he asks.

"We've tried everything—everything," answers Colonel Rutledge.

The stranger turns to Abe. Abe must have plenty of gumption to run against old Pete Cartwright, he thinks.

"How d'you stand on th' slavery question, Linkern?" he persists.

"I ain't been thinkin' much about slavery lately, Stranger."

"Well, no. But you air a politician, ain't you? These yur Abolitionists says the slaves ort to be set free. Then the—"

"I reckon no one's got more sympathy for the sore-oppressed than me. But we can't afford to make up our minds till we know the facts. Southerners would stand to lose millions if they were freed. Seems to me whether slavery is or is not wrong depends on whether the slave is or is not a *man*. I think—I—don't rightly keer to talk of it now, Stranger."

The stranger decides to go to bed. The Doctor has not come. There is some doubt as to whether he will be able to get any calomel, even in Decatur.

"Do you 'spect the calomel will help her?" Abe asks anxiously of Granny.

"Maybe. Maybe only the dear Jesus can do that now, Abe."

"But she seemed better this afternoon, Granny! She even wanted me to tell her a story and—it can't be that—it—why, she was even sitting up in bed, Granny! And I told her the story about little Bud and she laughed and . . . They cain't carry her off now—in her young years—when she's just beginnin' to live. . . . We'd only begun to know our love—to plan things out in the years—to realize! And now—this! All—going! Going! . . . Waiting! Helpless and waiting! If a man could only rise up and do something! . . . I went through something like this once before! Someone you love—standing helpless—waiting. I set day by day reading Ma parts of the Bible she liked best. On the sixth day she called me to her bed—talked of many strange things—principalities and powers—and things present—and things to come—urged me and Sairy always to walk in paths of goodness and truth—told us many things would come t' him that served God—an' th' best way t'—serve Him was to serve His people. (*Pause.*) She was amongst the lowliest of mankind. She walked the earth with her poor feet in the dust—her head in the stars— (*Pause.*) Pa took me down into the woods t' make her a coffin. Pa was sawin' and I was hammerin' the pegs in. The hammer dropped at my feet; it was like someone was drivin' 'em into my heart. It's—just goin' through all that again—now! . . . How much does the Lord require of a man?"

The Doctor has come. He has the calomel. He hurries into Ann's room. A moment later he comes slowly out again. Ann has been calling for Abe. It is only a matter of minutes—

Abe has disappeared in her room. Through the open door the sound of weeping is heard.

"I guess we've got to bear these things like men, Abe," says Colonel Rutledge, as Abe comes through the door.

"I've—I've got to *feel* it like a man, first," cries Abe, in anguish. He rushes out the door into the night. The curtain falls.

Aunt Polly and Squire Green, sitting on the porch of their log cabin, talking with Dave Vance, are worried about Abe's determination to give up everything and go back to Coles County with his kith and kin.

"Dad-blast me, Dave, that youngster wa'n't never meant to be a farmer," storms the Squire. "I ain't got nothin' ag'in farmin'— I'm a farmer myself—but—"

"Meant t' be a lawyer, mebbe, Bowlin?"

"Abe's a born lawyer—a politician—that's what he is. Shore he lost the 'lection, but he gave Old Uncle Pete the biggest scare a preacher ever got this side th' Jordan, by granny! They're holdin' bar examinations over to Springfield next month. I been tryin' to ease Abe into goin' there and takin' 'em. That's th' only thing for him to do! Doc's talked to him—we have. But he's set on goin' back home. Says it's where he belongs."

They have tried everything to dissuade Abe. The Squire has walked all the way to Athens to borrow a Blackstone thinkin' that might get his mind off things. But it hasn't.

"Won't talk! Won't read. That night they laid her on th' hill—didn't know who he was—talked of her day and night. . . . It's almost like we laid his heart on the hill—that evening." Aunt Polly cannot hold back her tears.

When Abe comes in from the fields, carrying his ax, they make their final pleas. They would have him think again that he should go in for something like the law. He'd done well in the election. The Squire could help him about his studying; he could go down to Springfield, take his examinations, and hang out his shingle. "People all say Springfield is bound to be the capital," Aunt Polly reminds him.

But Abe's mind is set. He is grateful for all Aunt Polly and the Squire have done, but—

"There's nothin' I want to do now," he says, sadly. "Nothin' ahead. You cain't have a light like her come, and lose it, without everything goin' black before your eyes! I've made a failure at everything I've laid hand to!"

AUNT POLLY—Tut-te-tut, Abe! You're just-a startin'!

ABE—Startin'? She showed me my power and strength, and she's gone, and I've got nary wish to go on. I'm just tired of all this—law, and everything.

AUNT POLLY—I don't want to torment you, Abe. I just want you to come to peace of mind before you set out! Cain't you come to look at it like the Rutledges? How they've borne their heads up in sorrow and adversity? They lost her. They've lost their mill. Lost everything. Yet—they ain't goin' back. They're goin' on—out to Ioway—to start over ag'in, Abe!

ABE—I know. You want me to forget—to go on—to be brave. (*Pause.*) What is bravery?

SQUIRE (*sitting in chair*)—Well, why—ah—now Blackstone says—

AUNT POLLY—It's mostly to hold up your head amongst men 'spite of adversity, Abe.

ABE—All I cain think is—she'd ort to be livin' now! It can't be right for a good God to do a thing like this—to take one so promisin'!

AUNT POLLY—Maybe her good work was done, Abe.

ABE—Done? How could her work be done? She was only beginning to live! Why she— (*Silence.*) Never to see her smile no more!

AUNT POLLY—Don't you think there's ary a Hereafter, Abe?

ABE—I'm afeered I cain't! It's awful to think that when we die that's the end of us! That's what hurts! That's why I want to get away from it all!

AUNT POLLY—I won't trouble you no more, Abe. This's all suthin' a person must feel. (*She gets up; goes up steps.*) We've all got to carry out our earthly destiny as best we can.

ABE—*Destiny!*

AUNT POLLY—I've got unbounden faith that, spite of creeds, and churches and sermons, some day you'll come t' b'lieve better than any-a us.

SQUIRE—Now, I look at it this-a-way, Abe. Death air caused by laws that was laid out in the Beginnin's. It ain't a pussonal matter. It ain't unjust to any-a us. Seems t' me a bit preposterous to think the Creator of th' Universe would single out you, or me, or her, or any certain person to chasten.

ABE—I reckon so.

SQUIRE—God-a-mighty, boy! I didn't mean t' open up my mouth—but since Polly's got me started—a young feller of your age and with your book-l'arnin' ought to be out a-usin' it. You got a practical slant on things—you got a good passel of humor— you got strength to do things—

AUNT POLLY (*bending over* ABE. *Puts hand on his shoulder*) —You mustn't forgit, Abe—*Ann* wouldn't be very proud-a you mopin' about and cursin' the Lord. She'd be the first one to want you to take up suthin'.

ABE (*serious; nodding*)—Yes-s. I reckon she'd not be very proud.

This is a new thought. For long moments Abe is lost in contemplation. The Squire motions Aunt Polly into the house. Deftly he brings the conversation back to the law. Mentions Jim Breckenridge, "about the powerfullest talker I ever heard on two legs" by Abe's admission.

"A man o' character and power!" adds the Squire; "servin' his people in the courts and halls-a law! We need upstandin' fellers defendin' the oppressed—handin' out justice over th' country! You know as well as me, Abe, if your kin-folks had knowed the beginnings of law, they could have saved their land in Kentucky! They was bamboozled out-a it."

"Ye-eh. Pa always said he had his belly full-a slavery and bad land-titles down there," admits Abe.

"By Lordy, that's right, Abe! And s'long as every man has to contend with thieves and liars, and since man's a natural-born litigious animal—we've got to have laws and lawyers and judges! God-a-mighty, boy! Go down t' Springfield! Tell Major Stuart a few common-sense things about a law-case! Go out and stand for the Legislature again! Pass your own laws! Why— (ABE *looks at the* SQUIRE. *The* SQUIRE *holds the book out.* ABE *takes it.*) I ain't tryin' to shove you into nothin', Abe. I'm tryin' t' help you!"

Abe has opened the Blackstone, his interest reawakened. He has begun to read aloud. "Now, as municipal law—(SQUIRE *turns and looks at* ABE.)—is a rule of civil conduct, commanding what is right and prohibiting what is wrong—(SQUIRE *goes into house.*)—it follows that the primary and principal object of the law are *Rights and Wrongs.*"

Denny has come charging in, all excitement. Their coach and

four has "just driv in." It is time they were starting.

But Abe has changed his mind. He isn't going. Not back home. He's going down to Springfield to take up the law. It has only been a year since he and Denny were layin' by the fence and Denton Offut drove up on a sorrel horse—

"A person cain live his whole life inside-a year almost sometimes, I guess," muses Abe.

He doesn't want to go away and leave Denny this way. Perhaps, if Denny was to have Abe's pocket-watch to keep, it would soften the parting. It does.

Aunt Polly has come from the house. She has put up a sizable lunch for Abe and Denny—

"Abe ain't goin'—not with me. He's—"

ABE (*firm; happy*)—I'm—goin' to Springfield—Aunt Polly.

AUNT POLLY (*glowing; overjoyed*)—Now—that's just fine, Abe! That is—you're goin' right away, Abe?

ABE—The sooner the better, I guess.

AUNT POLLY—Did you get them pants I had here?

ABE—I've done put 'em in, Aunt Polly. (*Grinning.*) I reckoned I might need 'em if I done as much settin-down labor there as I've done here!

AUNT POLLY—Here's the lunch, Abe. (*Gives basket to* ABE.) You take all of it. I'll put up another bigger one for Denny— if he'll wait for it.

DENNY—Dag-gone, Aunt Polly—I'll wait till the cows comes home!

ABE—I'm leavin' you my ax, Bowlin.

SQUIRE—You swappin' the ax for th' Blackstone, Abe?

ABE—I guess you'd call it just that!

AUNT POLLY—Take keer yourself down there, Abe.

ABE (*shakes hands with* POLLY *and* SQUIRE; *steps closer to* DENNY; *shaking his hand*)—Tell Pa and Ma I'm gettin' along first-rate now, Denny. Tell Pa I won't be back t' stump that land unless—Springfield don't agree with me! (*He smiles.*)

DENNY (*giving* ABE *his bag, with tears*)—I—ah—I will, Abe. I—ah—so long, Abe! (ABE *pats his head; turns slowly and goes toward rise of ground.* DENNY *sits on steps, looking at watch admiringly.*) Just six-thirty-one—(*Then, brightly.*)—and a half!

Abe goes up the slope in the evening—walks on and away— toward Springfield.

THE CURTAIN FALLS.

AMPHITRYON 38

A Comedy in Three Acts

BY JEAN GIRAUDOUX

(Adapted from the French by S. N. Behrman)

THE New York Theatre Guild did not enjoy a particularly happy season, measured in the terms of success at the box office. Its growing list of subscribers, now numbering approximately 30,000, naturally kept the big bad wolves at bay, but there was little joy in the directors' meetings.

Such joy as there was followed the production of the Jean Giraudoux comedy, "Amphitryon 38," gracefully transferred to the English language and lightly adapted to the American mood by S. N. Behrman. Alfred Lunt and Lynn Fontanne, the Guild's No. 1 acting couple, had tried it originally in San Francisco while they were on tour with Robert Sherwood's "Idiot's Delight" a year ago. In the West they found it greatly to the liking of the sophisticated trade.

This reception did not, however, greatly surprise them. "Amphitryon" always has been a comedy of decided popular appeal. As George Jean Nathan assured his readers, "The legend on which the exhibit is based is as old as the Greco-Roman hills, and when its author indicates his belief that there have been only thirty-eight dramatic paraphrases of it he displays himself in the dazzling light of a rather dubious mathematician."

The Behrman version follows that of the Giraudoux original by eleven years and comes several centuries after the first versions were credited to the Greeks, and yet there is no sign that the theme has dated or the adventure staled. The New York production was made November 1, 1937, and ran through until spring. The Guild's opening play, Ben Hecht's "To Quito and Back," was still occupying the home theatre and the Lunts took "Amphitryon" to the Shubert, where they had the previous season enjoyed such a remarkable success with "Idiot's Delight."

The reviews may be generally spoken of as having sounded a note of restrained rapture. "Amphitryon 38," plus the attraction of the leading players, did offer an unusual and delightful evening in the theatre. However—a bedroom farce is a bedroom farce, however classic, they said, and the stretching of a single anecdote to cover three acts of playing time was obviously a stretch.

The first view we have of the characters in Mr. Behrman's adaptation is that of Jupiter and Mercury. They are lying, face downward, upon a particularly buoyant cloud. Their heroic bodies, outlined in exaggerated hills and hollows of celestial flesh, stretch backward and upward. Their chins are pillowed on their mighty arms, "their phosphorescent eyes focused for the moment on the domesticities of a terrestrial couple."

The terrestrial two, it is revealed, are represented by Amphitryon, the warrior, and Alkmena, his lovely wife. For some time Jupiter has been fascinated by the beautiful Alkmena, acquiring some degrees of godly fever even at the sight of her shadow moving about her chamber. Yet, to Mercury's complete mystification, Jupiter has refused to take advantage of those facilities he enjoys as a god to invade that chamber—

"You would have me caress her body with invisible hands, enfold her in a closeness she could not feel?" Jupiter demands of his impatient son.

"But the wind makes love like that, Jupiter," answers Mercury, "and the wind is as much as you are, one of the prime elements of fecundity."

"True, but with her, Mercury, I am tempted to transcend my former conquests. I have a nostalgia for mortality. I would like to experience the same difficulties human beings do—and the same delights. As a god, I feel I should be closer to my subjects!"

That, intimates Mercury, is a foolish conclusion, seeing that love-making among humans is such a boring routine. At least Mercury has found it boring. With nothing particular gained in the end.

"Why then do you bother to go to Earth at all?" demands Jupiter.

"Out of boredom," admits Mercury. "And I confess that for a brief sojourn the Earth has certain advantages. What with its moist atmosphere and its green lawns it is perhaps the pleasantest planet on which to alight—but only for a brief stay—because it has distinct drawbacks. Due to its heavy mineral and oil deposits, it gives off a heady odor. It is, in fact, the only star which smells exactly like a wild animal."

Now the shadows of Amphitryon and Alkmena are moving across the screen of Jupiter's vision and his temperature again is rising. Mercury can understand why Jupiter is willing to forego his celestial eyesight. "To observe merely a shadow husband embracing a shadow wife is less painful than to observe the living substance," concludes Mercury.

The shadows have disappeared but the gods' imagination is still at work. Soon Mercury has caught the vision again and is reporting details that include fairly minute descriptions of Amphitryon and Alkmena in their active persons. He has described the warrior as huge and handsome, and Alkmena as gay, docile and faithful when Jupiter interrupts—

"Faithful to herself or faithful to her husband—that is the question. You know, Mercury, most faithful wives are unfaithful to their husbands with everything except men; with jewels—with perfumes—with reading—with religion and with the contemplation of spring, with everything in fact, except a man. Don't you think these faithful wives deserve some compensation?"

"But Alkmena is faithful only to her husband! Jupiter, by what subterfuge can you make her yours?"

"The difficulty with these virtuous wives is not to seduce them —but to persuade them that they may be seduced confidentially! And the contemplation of this creature paralyzes my invention."

There are, suggests Mercury, two courses for Jupiter to pursue. He can, if he choose, functioning as a god, lift Alkmena to his own plane. Which, Jupiter points out, would rob him of the exquisite sensation of Alkmena's moment of consent. Or, functioning as a human, Jupiter can, for the necessary time, become Alkmena's husband—

"But he's never out of sight," protests Jupiter. "The most persistent stay-at-homes in the world are heroes out of work! They're more domestic than tigers!"

MERCURY—Then employ him. Fortunately there is an infallible recipe for getting heroes out of the house.

JUPITER—War?

MERCURY—Have Thebes declare a war.

JUPITER—But Thebes is at peace with her enemies.

MERCURY—Then have her declare a war against a friend. What are friendly powers for if they can't have a little squabble now and then?

JUPITER—Isn't it singular, Mercury, you and I are gods and yet to achieve human simplicity becomes for us the most devious exercise in style. While we are on Earth fate demands far more of us than she does of mortals. To obtain from Alkmena this exquisite consent—which the most grotesque of human beings can gain by making a few faces—we have to contrive innumerable stratagems, perform wonders, pile up miracles—

MERCURY—Well, contrive them! Pile them up!

JUPITER—How? How?

MERCURY—Have a warrior overcome by an uncontrollable impulse to exercise his profession. Instantly Amphitryon will fly off to head his army.

JUPITER—Of course!

MERCURY—The minute he is gone—assume his appearance—assign to me the exterior of his servant Sosie. I will appear—whisper discreetly in Alkmena's ear that Amphitryon has only made a pretense of departing—that actually he means to return—to spend the night with her.

JUPITER (*with admiration*)—Oh, Mercury, you are your father's son!

MERCURY—Let us go—let us descend. Order a special cloud, Jupiter, to conceal us.

JUPITER—That's hardly necessary, Mercury. For there, on Earth, they have an institution which renders them invisible to creditors, to the jealous—which gives them surcease from their little nervous cares—a great and democratic institution—the only one—I may add—which is even moderately successful—

MERCURY—What is that, Jupiter?

JUPITER—The night! (*The curtains close in and the lights fade as the music swells.*)

MERCURY—The night?

JUPITER—The night . . .

MERCURY—The night.

The curtain falls.

ACT I

Amphitryon's palace in Thebes is built upon an eminence overlooking the city. A flight of steps leads first to an iron grille gate, and then from the gate to the portico of the palace. It is night. A fairly corpulent Trumpeter is sitting on the steps with his trumpet when Sosie, official announcer and scribe, servant to Amphitryon, arrives with a scroll.

Sosie, discovering the Trumpeter, and learning that he is indeed the Trumpeter of the Day, would have him trumpet. But the Trumpeter, being a composer as well, must first know what it is he is to trumpet for—

"If I have attained any celebrity among the one-note trumpeters it is because, before blowing, I compose in my mind a whole musical composition of which the last note is invariably the one I blow. That note is the climax. That is why, when I come to blow it, it has such surprise, such brilliance, such finality. The climax may be always the same but the approach—ah!—the approach . . . !"

"I wish for once you would begin with the climax! The whole town's falling asleep!" protests Sosie.

But the Trumpeter is not to be hurried. First he must know what he is blowing for; then he must compose a silent air; and how can he do that without knowing that he blows for war or peace, lost or found, for marriage, or birth, or death?

It is for peace, Sosie confesses—or at least what passes for peace—"the breathing spell between wars."

For peace the Trumpeter would compose something martial. A martial air, he has found, is irresistible, no matter what the cause. With his instrument to his lips the Trumpeter composes a stirring, military air with his free hand and finally blows a single note.

Sosie carries on, declaiming from the height to the sleeping town below that General Amphitryon has bade him address its citizens on the subject of peace. Instead of rousing them from their beds he would lull them to deeper sleep—

"Is it not good to sleep in a fatherland unscarred by the trenches of war, among friendly birds and dogs and cats, among rats whose appetites have never been whetted by the taste of human flesh?" proclaims Sosie. "Is it not good to wear your national countenance, not as a mask to frighten those who haven't the same blood-count you have but as a oval mirror to reflect smiling and laughter? Thebans, sleep!"

The Trumpeter is quite impressed by Sosie's eloquence and is himself lulled to sleep by the cadence of Sosie's voice. But a professional warrior who has just climbed the hill is not so well pleased. War is the business of warriors and he has come to arouse Amphitryon and bid him get into his accouterments at once—

"The Athenians have mobilized their troops and crossed the frontier," the messenger reports. "Wake up Amphitryon. Do you hear?" Let the Trumpeter now trumpet for war.

"But which aspect of war?" demands the Trumpeter. "Do you wish me to emphasize its sublime side or its pathetic side?"

WARRIOR—Neither. I want you to emphasize its appeal to Youth. (*The* TRUMPETER *composes and blows. The* WARRIOR

leans over the balustrade and shouts.) Thebans awake! All of
you who are vital, whose bodies are strong and unblemished, seg-
regate yourselves from the sweating mass spawning there in the
darkness. Get up! To arms!

TRUMPETER—Some of those lazy people would rather spawn!
They're very weak.

WARRIOR (*continues his harangue*)—You who are poor, all of
you whom fortune has treated badly, war will restore your rights.
And you rich come and experience the final ecstasy—the ecstasy
of the gambler who risks his position, his pleasures, his mistresses,
on one turn of the wheel. You zealots, you prayerful ones, make
Nationalism your religion. And you Atheists and sensualists, war
is your paradise for it legalizes all your excesses—you may whet
your swords on the statues of the gods themselves. You who hate
work—to the trenches—war is the heaven of the lazy. And for
you who are industrious—we have the Commissariat!

TRUMPETER—There's something in what he says—jobs for
everybody!

WARRIOR—Get up! Fall into rank! For who prefers to the
glory of dying valiantly for one's country the inglorious destiny of
staying at home overfed, lethargic and slothful?

TRUMPETER—I do.

WARRIOR—Besides, Citizens, there is nothing really to be afraid
of. I may tell you this in confidence: in this war, on our side at
least, there will be no fatalities whatever, and moreover, whatever
wounds there are will be in the left hand—except among the left-
handed. No more petty squabbles—war unites us! And how
humane it is, for it abolishes the barbaric duel! Here she is—
your war, ready for you, eager to welcome you. War! Welcome!
I salute you! War! It's begun already. See the lights down
there. Citizens—to arms! (*He comes down the steps hurriedly
shouting as he goes.*) You may pick your laws, your pleasures,
your women—Liberty, Equality, Fraternity, War— (*He rushes
across the stage shouting slogans.*) Freedom—license—cruelty—
joy—war— (*His voice trails off as he disappears.*)

The Trumpeter and Sosie have gone. Amphitryon, tall, handsome, of military bearing and in full war regalia, comes from the
palace. He is followed a second later by Alkmena, lovely in her
flowing robes, surmounted by a cerise girdle.

Alkmena has come to remind Amphitryon that she loves him,
and he is back by her side in an instant. She would wish him
well with the war, and chide him a little on the perfection of his

preparation—the fact that he is newly shaved, and wearing his daintiest tunic. How can the enemy be really frightened at him even with his armor and helmet set?

"You know, darling, when you breathe your armor loosens at the fastenings, and your tunic gives your skin a tint of dawn. Breathe, Amphitryon, breathe—deeply—and let me savor, in the darkness of this night, the glow of your body. Stay a little longer. (*Presses close to him.*) Do you love me?"

AMPHITRYON—Yes. I have to wait for my horses anyway. Darling, don't press too closely to me—you'll hurt yourself. You know I'm a husband made of iron.

ALKMENA—Can you feel me—through all that armor?

AMPHITRYON—Through every chink where an arrow might reach me, you reach me. And you—do you feel me?

ALKMENA—Yes—but your own body is a kind of armor. Often I have lain in your arms and felt you remoter and colder than I do now.

AMPHITRYON—Alkmena, often I have held you close to me, and felt you sadder and more desolate than I feel you today. And yet, on those occasions I was departing not for the war but for the hunt. (ALKMENA *smiles.*) Now, why do you smile? Do you find consolation in this sudden declaration of war?

ALKMENA—Did you hear a child crying beneath our window a little while ago? Didn't that seem to you to be a premonition of evil?

AMPHITRYON—No, no, no. Omens are always announced with a thunder-clap in a clear sky, accompanied by a triple flash of lightning.

ALKMENA—The sky was clear and yet the child was crying. That seemed to me to be even a worse augury.

AMPHITRYON—Don't be superstitious, Alkmena.

ALKMENA—Something was hovering over our happiness. Praise be to the gods it was only war.

AMPHITRYON—Why do you say that—only war?

ALKMENA—I was afraid it was our love that might be threatened—it's there I feel the danger. I almost find consolation in war. At least, it's a tangible and visible antagonist. I like enemies whose weapons I can see—my great fear has always been that I would one day find you in the arms of other women.

AMPHITRYON—Other women!

ALKMENA—One or a thousand—what difference does it make? You'd be lost.

"AMPHITRYON 38"

iter: Alkmena is to bear you a son. Will you name him to please me? Will you name him
les?
phitryon: Hercules?
mena: Hercules!
iter: And I shall be his . . . godfather.

(*Alfred Lunt, Lynn Fontanne, Barry Thomson*)

AMPHITRYON—You are the most beautiful woman in all Thebes.
ALKMENA—It's the goddesses I'm afraid of—and those foreigners.
AMPHITRYON—You're not serious.
ALKMENA—Above all—I fear the goddesses. When they emerge from the heavens—rosy without rouge—pearly without powder—their breasts whiter than snow and their arms stronger than crowbars, it must be very difficult to resist them. Don't you think so?
AMPHITRYON—For anyone but me it might be—yes.

It is the goddesses and the foreigners of whom Alkmena is most jealous. They are always in love with married men. . . . Now the horses have arrived and Amphitryon must go. Hasn't Alkmena anything more to say?

"Haven't I said about everything?" the wife demands. "What do other wives say?"

"Well—they make jokes. They hand you your shield and they say things like 'Return on it or beneath it!' They cry out after you, 'Fear nothing,' 'Do or die!' Can it be that my wife has no gift for epigrams like that?"

"I'm afraid not. I couldn't utter a phrase that belonged more to posterity than it did to you. The only words that I can find to utter are those which perish softly even as they touch you. I love you, Amphitryon! Come back soon, Amphitryon! Besides, your name is so long, once you've said it there's hardly breath left to follow it up with an immortal sentence."

"Then say my name at the end. (*Takes spear and shield and lifts his right arm in salute.*) Good-by, Alkmena!"

"Amphitryon!"

Alkmena stands staring after the departing warrior for a moment. As the sound of his horses' hoof-beats diminish in the distance she turns sadly back to the palace. She is on the verge of sobbing. Mercury, disguised as Sosie, has come in quietly and is standing below the gate. Alkmena, startled, knowing that Sosie had just gone off, laughs nervously as Mercury gives her the keys to the gate. She closes the gate but does not lock it and starts up the steps.

Sosie calls. He has a message from his master—a message no one must hear. It is that Amphitryon, only pretending to leave with the army, will, as soon as he has given his orders, be back to spend the night with Alkmena. Alkmena does not understand, but when the Servant would be more explicit she quiets him—

"How dull you are, Sosie! Don't you understand the first principle of keeping a secret—which is to pretend the moment you've heard it—the moment you've grasped it—not to know a thing about it?"

"Very good, my lady. . . ."

"As a matter of fact I haven't understood one word you've been saying."

"You must sit up and watch for my master, my lady. . . ."

"Yes, yes, Sosie. Stop chattering."

Alkmena has gone into the palace when Mercury, turning to the sky, whispers hoarsely to Jupiter, motioning with his thumb to indicate that Alkmena is in the palace. There is a terrific crash, followed by the appearance of Jupiter. He is dressed exactly like Amphitryon, even to the shield and spear. There should have been no crash, Jupiter explains, but he had temporarily forgotten the law of gravity.

Jupiter would hurry on into the palace, but Mercury stops him. He is looking much too spruce to make a proper impression as a husband. He isn't even scratched from contact with the brambles. His clothes haven't so much as a single crease in them. And his back—

"Men think that women never notice their backs," says Mercury. "They are unaware that although they pretend to be overcome by their magnificent padded chests, they are actually maliciously scrutinizing the back view. It's from the back that women estimate a man."

Jupiter's eyes are also far too brilliant—"all iris and no tear duct"—and it is possible that he may have to cry. And his skin—his skin is like a baby's. He must have "a weather-beaten skin—a skin on which the wind has blown for thirty years. In short, a well-seasoned skin—a skin that may be tasted." And finally let Jupiter "contract the sheath of mortality" in which he has encased himself. It is much too big for him as it is. Jupiter obediently flexes his muscles until he feels himself "becoming a filter—an hour-glass of blood."

"The birth of all humanity strains inside me—beating me black and blue! I hope that all my poor human beings don't suffer like this!"

"Twice they do—once when they're born and once when they die."

"How very disagreeable to experience both simultaneously," observes Jupiter, as he straightens up.

Now a gentle aging process has been applied, until Jupiter's heart-beats are not too rapid—like those of a dog or cat. Nor too slow, like those of a fish. It is "by this little ambling inner rhythm" that Alkmena will recognize the heart-beats of her husband.

But now Jupiter has suddenly decided that he wants to be loved for himself alone. "I shall make Alkmena accept a lover," he says with a suggestion of gleeful determination.

"Alkmena, I'm very much afraid, will deny you that pleasure," warns Mercury. "You better stick to being her husband."

JUPITER—Her husband—and her lover. No woman could resist that. We'll begin that way and later on—we shall see—we shall see— (*Starts to go but* MERCURY *raises hand and stops him.*) Any last-minute instructions?

MERCURY—Yes. About your intellect.

JUPITER—What's wrong with my intellect?

MERCURY—We must replace all your god-like conceptions with human ones. What are your beliefs? Recite to me your *man's* idea of the nature of this universe.

JUPITER—My *man's* idea of the nature of this universe? I believe that this flat earth is flat; (MERCURY *picks up helmet, gives it to* JUPITER, *who puts it on.*) I believe that water is water and nothing else; (MERCURY *picks up shield and hands it to* JUPITER.) I believe that air is simple and indivisible; I believe that nature is nature—(MERCURY *picks up spear and hands it to* JUPITER.) and the spirit—well, the spirit—in fact, I believe that there is nothing beyond which I can see, and beyond what I can understand. Is that all?

MERCURY—Not quite. Are you consumed by a desire to part your hair in the middle and keep it set that way unalterably with sticky hair lotion?

JUPITER—I feel that temptation—passionately!

MERCURY—Good! Do you conceive that one day you may die?

JUPITER—That I may die? No, never! That my poor friends may die, alas, yes, my poor friends—but not I!

MERCURY—Splendid! Have you forgotten all the women you've already loved?

JUPITER—I've never loved anyone but Alkmena.

MERCURY—And this sky over us—what do you think of this sky?

JUPITER—I believe that the sky is my own personal property. I believe that I possess it far more than I ever did before.

MERCURY—Oh, Jupiter!

JUPITER—And as for the whole solar system, it seems to me very small!

MERCURY—And the whole vast Earth?

JUPITER—Very small! . . . And, Mercury . . . I feel . . . handsomer than Apollo! Braver than Mars . . . more capable of amorous exploits than—myself. And for the first time, Mercury, I really feel myself, I really see myself, I really believe myself, to be master of the gods!

MERCURY—Well, you're a man all right. Get on with it.

The light in the palace has gone out, but that does not discourage Jupiter. With a slight wave of his hand he causes a sound of knocking at the gate. There is no response. Jupiter knocks again. He knows Alkmena is there, he tells Mercury, because as he was coming down she had leaned out her window and wished on him. Alkmena thought Jupiter was a falling star. At a third knock Alkmena is heard inside the palace. At the sound of her voice Mercury discreetly disappears.

Alkmena would know who it is that disturbs her rest. A general? What is a general doing wandering about at that time of night? Is he a deserter? Or has he been defeated? He has been defeated by love, Jupiter would assure her, and he comes to her as a lover. But, Alkmena insists, she has no lover. True, she did lean from her window to look at the night, but the night was all she was looking at. And if she did exclaim, as she gazed upon a falling star, "Oh, if only while he were at war, I might forego all memory!" it was only because she might have wished to forget that her husband loves his horses and his battles more than he loves her. And what does that prove?

"That you have a lover, and that he is here," answers Jupiter.

ALKMENA—I have a husband and he is evidently not here. And I receive no one in my bedroom who is not my husband. And not even him will I admit if he does not acknowledge his name. You're not very good at passionate disguises—it's not your metier.

JUPITER—Oh, at this hour, when everything between here and heaven is in disguise, may not your husband also disguise himself as a lover?

ALKMENA—Your insight, my friend, is not very keen if you think the night is only the day-time masked, the moon no more than a sun disguised, and that the love of a wife for her husband can be confused with an amour.

JUPITER—Wifely love is a duty. Duty is compulsion. And compulsion kills desire.

ALKMENA—Desire! Desire is a half-god. We here worship only the major ones. The lesser gods we leave to adolescent girls, to the casually married, to the fugitive romantics, the half-wives.

JUPITER—It is blasphemy to speak so even of a lesser god!

ALKMENA—In my secret heart I am more blasphemous even than that for I worship a god that doesn't exist at all. Shall I tell you who it is? It's the god of conjugal love, one that it never occurred to the gods to invent—they are so casual. If you come in behalf of Desire you ask me to betray a greater god for a lesser. If then you are a lover I am sorry but I must ask you to go on. . . . You are handsome and you have a good figure. Your voice is winning. Did it sound in behalf of Fidelity I might love this voice. I might wish to be enclosed in those arms. Your mouth, too, I should say, is dewy and ardent. But I shan't allow it to persuade me. I shall not open my door to a lover. Who are you?

JUPITER—Why can't your husband be your lover?

ALKMENA—Because a lover is closer always to love than he is to the object of his love. Because it is ill-bred to deceive your husband even with himself. Because I like my windows open and my linen fresh.

With this statement Alkmena goes back into the palace. Mercury finds Jupiter pondering the situation and ready to admit that Alkmena is impossible. "She's not a woman, she's a fortress," the god insists, and Mercury agrees. "A fortress that may be taken only by her husband," says Mercury. "Do as I advised you in the first place—be her husband!"

Jupiter agrees to humble himself to this extent. And now the knocking at the gate is resumed and Mercury has again retired. From inside the palace Alkmena would know who this newest visitor is. Being told that it is indeed Amphitryon, her husband, she comes again to the balcony.

"Let me in," pleads Jupiter.

"Are you he by whose side I wake every morning and for whom I cut from the margin of my own day an extra ten minutes of sleep?"

JUPITER—I am he.

ALKMENA—Are you the one whose least footfall is so familiar to me that I can tell whether he is shaving or dressing?

JUPITER—I am the one.

ALKMENA—Are you the being with whom I dine and breakfast and sup? And whom I allow to go to sleep ten minutes every
night before I do?

JUPITER—I am that being.

ALKMENA—Then swear in the presence of the night those marriage vows which hitherto we have spoken only in the presence of
the day.

JUPITER—A wedding ceremony, in the void of the night, with
neither priest nor altar? What for?

ALKMENA—That the invisible beings which surround us may
not be deceived seeing Alkmena receive you like this—like a lover.
That the clear light in which we live by day may transfigure even
the night. Oh, Amphitryon, I have often dreamed of an occasion
like this! Why should the night be the hand-maiden for the
clandestine—the furtive—the illicit? Let her for once be brides-
maid to married love. Do you think I wish this lovely night—
this constellation of stars and little winds—this company of night
moths and shadows—to imagine that I, Alkmena, am receiving
a lover? No! At this hour, when there are consummated so
many false marriages, let us seal our nocturnal, true one! Shall
we begin?

JUPITER—If you only knew, Alkmena, how pitiful to the gods
human beings seem, prating their vows, launching their thunder-
less thunderbolts.

Alkmena will not let him off until they both have taken their
oath—

"I, Amphitryon," swears Jupiter; "son and grandson of former
generals, father and grandfather of future generals . . . indis-
pensable clasp in the twin girdle of war and glory—"

"I, Alkmena, whose parents are no longer and whose children
are yet unborn—poor isolated link in the chain of humanity—"

"I swear so to contrive it that the fragrance of the name of
Alkmena shall survive so long as the hurly-burly of my own."

"And I swear to be faithful to Amphitryon, my husband, or to
die!"

"To what?"

"To die!"

"Don't say that, Alkmena."

"Why not? I mean it. And now, dear husband, the ceremony
is over and I authorize you to come in. You know you've really
been very simple. The gate was open all the time—you had only

to push it—ever so little. . . ."

Jupiter has pushed open the gate and bounded up the first stairs. Now he stands below Alkmena "as if rooted to the spot."

"Why do you hesitate?"

"You really mean it? You really *want me* to come in?"

"My dearest love . . . I command it!"

Jupiter covers the remaining steps at a bound. Reaching to Alkmena's shoulder he strips the sashes from the gown. He has enfolded her in his mantle as the curtain falls.

ACT II

In the darkness Mercury is lying semi-recumbent just outside Alkmena's bedroom. He has been there for some time "soaking in the sweet silence, the gentle resistance, the easy struggle from indoors," but now he is becoming a little bored. "This job that Jupiter has wished on me of prolonging the night till he gets ready to get up is beginning to weigh on me a bit," Mercury mutters. "After all it's midsummer and early in the morning. The great inundation of day canopies out over all the world, thousands and thousands of leagues to the very margin of the sea. Solitary, amid the rose-drenched cubes, this palace is left a cone of black. I really ought to wake my master; he loathes a hurried exit and he will surely wish by way of dressing-gown chatter to reveal to Alkmena that he is Jupiter. He will not willingly forego this sop to his vanity."

An added need of hurry is that Amphitryon, having decided, at Mercury's prompting, to surprise his wife at break of dawn, already has taken secretly to the road and is galloping furiously toward the palace. He will arrive within the hour. Therefore Mercury bids the Sun display his rays that he, Mercury, may choose the one best fitted to kindle the shadows: No, not green! Green is the sinister ray. Nor purple! Nor violet! These are colors that inflame the senses. Amber? That's it!

"Nothing so well as saffron to bring out the insipid quality of the human skin," declares Mercury. "Get on with it, Sun!"

The scene is flooded in sunlight as Mercury scurries off into the darkness.

Now we are in a room in the palace. There is a long couch in the center, with tabourets on either side. Alkmena, lovely in her morning draperies, comes from an inner room and lays her cloak and hat on the couch.

Following her from the inner room is the voice of Jupiter, still a bit heavy with sleep. Jupiter would know where he is. Alkmena assures him that he is "in the last place where husbands think they are when they wake up," which would be in his own home and his own bed and with his own wife. Jupiter pretends to be still mystified. What is his wife's name? Is she still the marvelously dark Alkmena? And won't she please come back to his arms?

Alkmena is in no mood to humor her mate. "The early morning is no time for improvisation," she insists. Let him come along. Breakfast is ready.

Two maids, Nenetza and Kleantha, have brought breakfast trays and presently Jupiter, freshly robed, appears to sit opposite Alkmena on the couch. He smiles with satisfaction when Alkmena gives him an affectionate pat as he passes her and settles to his breakfast, the tray on his lap. It has been, sighs Jupiter, a divine night.

Alkmena considers the adjective feeble. A perfect night, perhaps. Or a charming night. Best of all, a pleasant night. *"What a pleasant night!"* That would suggest many agreeable sensations.

It was, asserts Jupiter confidently, the pleasantest night of all their experience. Again Alkmena disagrees.

"Have you forgotten, my own husband, the night we were married?" she asks. "The miraculous discovery our two hearts made of each other, in the midst of those shadows which for the first time held us in their embrace? That was our most beautiful night!"

Or the night the great fire broke out in Thebes, when Amphitryon had come at dawn "all gilt from the fire and warm as new-baked bread"? Or the night, just two days before, when he had rescued a little boy from drowning in the sea, and had tossed all night, flinging his arms about her to rescue her from imaginary drowning!

"No, my dear, if you wish to sum up this night in an appropriate adjective, I should say that this night, of all nights, was the most connubial," protests Alkmena, sweetly. "There was a sense of security about it which gladdened me. Never have I felt so certain of waking up in the morning to find you beside me; there was mercifully absent that fear which obsesses me constantly—of finding you suddenly dead in my arms."

Jupiter has no liking for that descriptive adjective—connubial! He would cover his irritation by a walk about the room and with varied but irrelevant comments upon the beauty of the landscape.

This creation of the gods—of the Master of the Gods, in fact—
brings Jupiter himself into the conversation. Alkmena admires
Jupiter, Master of the Gods, but with no more enthusiasm than
she admires Neptune. Or Apollo. Anyway, it is her fancy to
think of the gods in pairs rather than singly—of Venus and Mars!
Of Jupiter and Juno! She sees them "wandering about eternally
—hand in hand—on the crests of the clouds—it must be marvelous!"

"Great fun," agrees Jupiter, a little nervously. "You think that
Jupiter has done a good job then, with these rocks and cliffs—
he's done pretty well on this landscape?"

ALKMENA—Yes, it's very nice, but do you think he did it on
purpose?

JUPITER (*shocked*)—Alkmena!

ALKMENA—Well, everything you do, you do on purpose,
whether you are grafting cherry trees on plums or contriving a
double-edged sword. But do you think that Jupiter, on the day
that he created all this, knew what he was doing?

JUPITER (*hurt*)—It is generally assumed that he did!

ALKMENA—We know he created the Earth. But the beauty of
the Earth re-creates itself momentarily. Jupiter seems too settled to have dallied so with the ephemeral!

JUPITER—I'm afraid you haven't a very precise idea of the purpose of creation.

ALKMENA—No, I suppose I haven't. How does it all seem to
you, darling? Doesn't it seem cloudy?

Jupiter—No, no! I see everything perfectly clearly. (*Sits beside her again.*) In the beginning everything was Chaos. It was
then Jupiter's felicitous idea to separate everything into four elements.

ALKMENA—We have only four elements?

JUPITER—Four. And the first is water, and water, I may tell
you, was not so easy to create. Superficially, water looks like
quite ordinary stuff. But imagine, if you had never seen water—
if there were no water in existence, what it would mean to create
it—even to get the idea of creating it.

ALKMENA—What did the goddesses cry—in the pre-water era?
Bronze tears? That stumps you!

JUPITER—Don't interrupt me, Alkmena, I'm trying to give you
some idea of what Jupiter must be—I'm trying to convey to you
something of his scope. He may materialize before you at any
moment, you know, without warning. Wouldn't you like to have

him explain everything to you personally in all his magnificence?
(*He gets up.*)

ALKMENA—No, darling, I'd rather have you explain it to me.

JUPITER (*nonplused, sits again*)—Where was I?

ALKMENA—We've just disposed of original Chaos.

JUPITER—Oh, yes. Once water was in existence it occurred to
him to bank it in with broken coasts, in order to stop the impact
of the storms, and to strew the surface of the waters with Conti-
nents, in order to spare the eyes of the gods the perpetual irritation of a glittering horizon— And so came the Earth and all its
marvels!

Now Alkmena has discovered a hole in Jupiter's stocking and
she must be about mending that. It would never do to let him
go back to war with a hole in his stocking. What would the
enemy think of his wife! It is while she is darning the sock that
Alkmena continues her belittling of the gods. What, for instance,
had Jupiter done?

"He didn't do a thing!" insists Alkmena firmly. "He didn't do
a thing except plunge us into an awful conglomeration of illusions
and stupors from which we have to extricate ourselves—I and my
dear husband."

"Alkmena, are you aware that the gods may be eavesdropping?"

"Oh, they know that my heart is straightforward and honest.
Besides, what does Jupiter expect of me? That I should expire
with gratitude to him for having invented four elements when we
could very well use twenty? I don't think four elements is much,
considering he hasn't had anything else to do for all eternity. I
am far more grateful to you, my dear husband, and my heart
bursts with gratitude to you for having invented a system of
window-pulleys which has lightened my life and for all those
wonderful, new graftings you did for the orchard. (*She puts the
mended sock on his foot.*) You, Amphitryon, have changed for
me the taste of a cherry—(*Puts his sandal on.*) and you have
done more than that—you have enlarged the capacity of my
pantry shelves! Now, for me, it is you who are the creator—
(JUPITER *is staring at her with divine admiration.*) Why do you
look at me like that? Compliments embarrass you, is that it?
I suppose you find me too earthbound?"

"Wouldn't you like to be less so?"

"Less so?"

"You never aspired to be a goddess?"

"A goddess? What on earth for?"

"To be honored and revered by everyone."

"Certainly not!"

Not even a hope of immortality intrigues Alkmena; nor the thought of becoming a star that would shine in the night until the end of time. Such a long evening as that would have no appeal for Alkmena. Nor does any thought of death depress her—

"Oh, sweet, I'm not afraid of death," she says. "It's the stake you give for life. I prefer to identify myself with my own companions, who must also die. I feel so strongly that my very fibers will perpetuate themselves in other men—and animals— plants even—that I should feel cheated if I were not allowed to follow this mysterious destiny. Don't talk to me of not dying, so long as there is a vegetable alive which is not immortal. For a human being to be immortal—is a kind of betrayal of one's own. Besides, when I think of the wonderful surcease death brings; to be irritated for sixty years over meals that don't turn out well—holes in stockings—aches and pains—and then to be offered death—the felicity of death—really, it's a reward we don't deserve!"

That she would like to bear an immortal son Alkmena is ready to admit. But not a son who would become "the greatest of heroes," as Jupiter suggests. Nor can she fully understand him when he would talk to her seriously of her obligations and of the gods—

"Have you lost your senses, Amphitryon? You choose this moment of all moments to talk theology to me. At this time of day, when everybody—drunk with sunlight—just can't wait to go farming or fishing!"

"What's more, isn't the army waiting for you? You have only a few minutes left if you want to kill anybody at all—and you'll have to do that on an empty stomach. No, darling, no. . . . I have my house to attend to—I have my rounds to make—I have the gardener to see—do you think this house runs itself?"

"Alkmena! Dearest Alkmena! Let me apprise you that the gods may appear precisely at the moment when you expect them least."

"Amphitryon, dear Amphitryon, in a moment I shall deliver you an harangue, not about the gods, but about my servant problems. . . . Till tonight, darling, good-by—"

Alkmena has gone and Mercury has reappeared. Mercury has been waiting to see Jupiter emerge from Alkmena's presence in all his glory, as is his usual custom. What has happened?

Jupiter's answers are in a way evasive. He is troubled. He

has even acquired a vertical wrinkle between his eyes. For the
first time he has known what it means to limit the compass of his
mind to that of a husband. As a husband, Alkmena had been
completely victorious over him—

"Do you know, that a few moments ago I had occasion to explain Creation to her and I found myself talking as dry as dust.
The easy eloquence of which I am master when I talk to you—
just—just—dried up—"

Jupiter has made many discoveries concerning humans in general and Alkmena in particular. Humans are not what the gods
think them. Alkmena, for example, has the character of a rock.
"She is the true Prometheus," insists Jupiter. Also she lacks
imagination. She is not ambitious, either to shock or to dazzle.
"It's exactly this single-minded quality in her, this quality of
constancy and devotion, against which our power is futile." Yet
to Jupiter Alkmena is completely adorable. Nor can he overcome her advantages.

"We miss something, Mercury—undoubtedly we miss something," sighs the Master of the Gods; "the poignance of the
transient—the intimation of mortality—that sweet sadness of
grasping at something you cannot hold—"

"It's very simple—make Alkmena immortal!" suggests Mercury.

"And deprive her of her death? She'd never forgive me. . . .
No, I'm too fond of her—and I may tell you now that her son,
of all my sons, will be my most favorite."

"That the Universe knows already."

"The Universe? No one knows anything about this affair."

"Oh, yes, they do. I announced everything this morning!"

The statement angers Jupiter. He raises his arm, with the
index finger crooked, and there is a rumble of thunder as Mercury,
humbled, drops to one knee before him.

"Did you announce that I had visited Alkmena disguised as
Amphitryon?"

"Certainly not! There's something undignified about that
trick. I was afraid it might make a bad impression and since
your desire to spend another evening with Alkmena was so obvious that I could sense it through the very walls, I made the
formal announcement that Alkmena would receive a visit from
Jupiter tonight!"

This announcement, Mercury explains, was made in the order
prescribed by destiny. First to the winds, then to the waters.
Even now the undulations of the Universe, both wet and dry,

are gossiping of nothing else.

Then, protests Jupiter, they are lost indeed. Never will Alkmena agree. She would kill herself first, and Hercules, son of Jupiter, would die. Let Mercury halt all celebrations at whatever cost. But, protests Mercury, what does Jupiter want—

"What do I want?" thunders the god. "What every man wants! A thousand contradictory desires! That Alkmena should remain faithful to her husband and also give herself to me. That she should remain chaste under my caresses and yet that desire should flame up in her under my very sight. That she should know nothing of this intrigue and yet that she should connive at it with all her might!"

Mercury has dropped to one knee before Jupiter to receive his final request. It is that Alkmena shall that night receive, and willingly, a visit from Jupiter—not in the degrading mortal livery, but as a god. Alkmena shall be persuaded in an instant, promises Mercury. . . .

Alkmena has reappeared from the garden. Kleantha is with her, bearing a garden basket filled with vegetables. And now Kleantha has been dismissed and Mercury has revealed himself.

It is easy for Alkmena to recognize Mercury. He has long been one of her favorite gods, and she loves them all. Of course, if she were forced to state a preference it would be for Jupiter. Partly because of his beauty, mostly because of his dignity. And she can understand much that she has heard of Jupiter's passionate impulses that cause him to hurl himself into the arms of mortal women.

This is welcome news to Mercury. Now his way would seem to be clear. But Alkmena only laughs at his report that Jupiter loves her; that, in fact, he has had his eye upon her for a number of days—and nights.

"I know I should blush," blushes Alkmena, "but it kills me to think that Jupiter's been looking at me all this time and I probably wasn't at my best. Why didn't you warn me?"

"And what answer shall I give him now?"

ALKMENA (*rising*)—Tell him—of course—that I shall do my best to earn his gracious favor. I already have a silver altar to him in the Palace. When Amphitryon returns, we'll build a gold one.

MERCURY—It isn't an altar he's interested in.

ALKMENA—Everything here belongs to him. Even my most precious possessions. He has only to choose.

MERCURY—He's already chosen it and tonight he's coming to claim it.

ALKMENA—What is it?

MERCURY—Your bed. I have just given my orders to the night. The day is hardly long enough for the night to get together the brilliant effects and the appropriate sounds for a celestial wedding. It will be less a night than a sample of your immortal future. It gives me pleasure to season your more perishable moments with these pinches of immortality—my engagement present! (ALKMENA *smiles*.) Why do you smile?

ALKMENA—I've smiled at less.

MERCURY—But why?

ALKMENA—Quite simply because this is obviously a case of mistaken identity. I am Alkmena, and Amphitryon is my husband.

MERCURY—But the cosmic forces do not consider husbands.

ALKMENA—But think, Mercury, of all women in Thebes, to have chosen me! I'm a very commonplace woman. I wasn't very good at school and what I did learn I've forgotten. I am not, in fact, considered over bright.

MERCURY—That opinion I do not share.

ALKMENA—At the moment it's not you I'm thinking of, but Jupiter. When it comes to a momentous matter—like receiving Jupiter—I'm simply not up to it.

MERCURY—We've seen you from on high and your body lights up the night of Greece.

ALKMENA—Yes, I have my devices for artificial lighting—I have my powders and lotions—I manage with tweezers and files to put up some kind of an appearance, but I cannot write and I cannot even think.

MERCURY—But you talk very well. Even if you didn't, it wouldn't matter because tonight all the poets of posterity will be carrying on the conversation for you.

ALKMENA—I wish they'd carry the rest as well.

Mercury will not permit Alkmena either to belittle the judgment of the gods or her own surpassing qualities of nobility and beauty. Let her realize the magnificence of her opportunity. He again calls attention to the superlative quality of her figure, the eloquence of her movements. Presently Alkmena is in tears, and this is quite beyond Mercury's understanding.

"What's this, Alkmena? Do I see tears?" demands the messenger. "At this moment you weep; at this moment when a flood of joy is about to inundate humanity in your honor? Tonight a year of joy begins for Thebes. No more epidemics. No more pestilence. No more war. No more famines."

"It's not fair!"

"In your city are eight little children who, this very week, were destined to die. Four little boys and four little girls—among the latter your favorite Charissa. You can save them!"

"Charissa! . . . If anyone else did this it would be called blackmail!"

"Health and happiness are the exclusive blackmail of the gods. Do you hear, Alkmena? The poor and the sick are beside themselves with joy for they will owe to you their happiness and their life. Now, Alkmena, you are apprised of what is to be. Farewell!"

Mercury would be off to tell Jupiter of Alkmena's acceptance, but she still denies the agreement and persists in her denial. She will defend herself with every weapon at her command before she will yield. She might even kill herself—

"Jupiter will reincarnate you, for this son must be born," persists Mercury.

"A child born of adultery, never! Divine son though he be— he shall die!"

"Alkmena, the patience of the gods has its limits. You abuse their courtesy. After all, we don't need your consent. . . . I can't believe, Alkmena, that you really want to see your city infected by pestilence, razed to the ground by fire. Do you want to see your husband defeated? I shall tell Jupiter that you're expecting him."

"You'll be telling him a lie!"

"With women I find the morning lie becomes the evening truth! Till tonight, Alkmena."

The arrival of Queen Leda, who once had known Jupiter as a swan, has given Alkmena an idea. She summons Leda as soon as Mercury has gone. Leda, statuesque and handsomely fair, has heard the news of Alkmena's engagement and wishes to talk with her. First she would acquaint herself with the historic surroundings. Then she would know something of Alkmena's method. Did she pray endlessly? Or cry aloud her misery and her desire? Has she seen him? No? Well, neither has Leda.

"Then it's true what legend tells us, that Jupiter came to you in the guise of a swan?" asks Alkmena.

"Well—up to a certain point he was, a sort of cloudburst— a gust of swan," confesses Leda.

"Was it real down?"

"Certainly. I touched the wingroots with my fingers—a harp of feathers. Alkmena, to be perfectly frank—I would rather, if you don't mind, that with you he wouldn't be a swan again. I'm not of a jealous disposition at all, but if you could leave me this little distinction, it would be so nice of you. After all, there are so many other birds, much rarer ones, even."

The more Leda reveals, the more is Alkmena convinced that she is not happy. Jupiter has acted far too casually about the whole affair, thinks Alkmena. He might at least have shown Leda some little courtesy afterward. Some trifling gift, perhaps, or flowers, or even a little colored egg. Alkmena can understand that Leda, as she says, would not have cared for a prolonged liaison, even with a god, but she does think Jupiter might have paid Leda the compliment of a second visit.

"Leda, you're not happy," declares Alkmena, with conviction. "I can tell. Jupiter hasn't made you happy. . . . It was a shabby trick. Jupiter loved you and abandoned you. . . . If I were you, Leda, I'd revenge myself. He didn't even make an honest legend of you."

"How can I revenge myself on a white swan?"

"I'll tell you how. With a black one. Substitute for me."

"What?"

"That door leads to my room. You go in there—put on my veils, spray my scent about—I can make it very dark. Jupiter will be deceived and to his advantage."

Leda is still deeply puzzled. She cannot understand quite how Alkmena can be so generous, or why she is willing to forego the great honor that is to be conferred upon her. Alkmena's answer that she is in love with her husband seems a little snobbish to Leda. And yet the more she hears from Alkmena the more she is persuaded that the celestial contact might be fatal to her special charm.

At last Leda agrees to help. She will substitute for Alkmena, but only on condition that she can "specify an incarnation that won't be repulsive to me." When Jupiter comes Leda knows that he will naturally assume some shape that haunts Alkmena's dreams. What will that be? Alkmena insists that she is not a haunted woman and she has but one weakness—her husband.

Leda is not impressed with the suggestion until she has been shown a picture of Amphitryon. Then her enthusiasm bubbles.

"Your husband, of course," cries Leda. "Why didn't we think of that before? Your swan will be an Amphitryon. The first time your husband leaves home, Jupiter will enter your bedroom and you'll never know the difference."

The suggestion terrifies Alkmena. Amphitryon is away. There is no telling when he might return.

"Before tonight I promise you that Jupiter will enter that door, so like Amphitryon that you will succumb to him," promises Leda.

"I couldn't possibly be deceived—I should know him."

"For once a human will be a divine imitation, and you will be misled."

"Exactly. He'll be more perfect than Amphitryon, more noble than Amphitryon, and I shall hate him at first sight."

"And I tell you that with me he was a simply enormous swan and I couldn't distinguish him from the swan I see every day on my own river," insists Leda.

There is excitement outside. A second later Sosie has burst into the room to confirm Alkmena's intuition that Amphitryon has arrived. Sosie has seen the general in the distance taking the moats at a single leap. That should be enough to convince Alkmena, Leda thinks. "It's Jupiter, the sham Amphitryon."

"Very well, then he shall find here the sham Alkmena."

Hastily Leda is sent to Alkmena's room. And now Amphitryon, very grand in his war fittings, is through the door and eager to take Alkmena in his arms. But Alkmena draws away. She would conduct a kind of preliminary inspection first. Everything appears to be the same, except a scratch that was in evidence the day before.

"Nothing like fresh air for cuts," explains Amphitryon, sitting on the couch to take off his greaves.

"Marvelously healthy, isn't it, that outdoor exercise on a battlefield?" comments Alkmena, nervously. "What's going on behind that forehead—that forehead that is so much larger than usual?"

AMPHITRYON—What always goes on—adoration for Alkmena.

ALKMENA—And what is that face thinking of—that face that gets bigger and bigger the more I look at it?

AMPHITRYON (*rising and going to her*)—Of kissing your lips!

ALKMENA (*escaping from him*)—Why my lips?

AMPHITRYON (*following more impetuously*)—Of biting the nape of your neck.

ALKMENA—Amphitryon, what's come over you? I've never heard you talk like this before.

AMPHITRYON—Alkmena, what's the matter?

ALKMENA—Where did you sleep last night?

AMPHITRYON—In the brambles—with a bundle of vine-shoots for a pillow. Oh, darling, I have to leave within the hour, for we're giving battle this morning. (*Close to her at last.*) What is this sudden reserve between us? (*He seizes her and kisses her passionately.*) You behave more like a fiancée than a wife.

ALKMENA (*horrified*)—What are you doing?

AMPHITRYON (*kissing her again*)—And now you are coming with me. (*Starts to take her to bedroom.*)

ALKMENA (*breaking away from him*)—Yes—one moment—I'll call you—my sweet—my lover—my husband. (*She exits, leaving* AMPHITRYON *alone. After a short pause* ALKMENA *calls to him from off stage.*) Amphitryon!

AMPHITRYON (*eagerly*)—Yes, darling, here I am— (*He rushes after her. The stage is empty for a moment. Then* ALKMENA *re-enters. She comes down to below the couch.*)

ALKMENA (*with great satisfaction*)—He is there—in her arms! Let me hear no more of the wickedness of life. Let me hear no more about fate—neither the wiles of men nor the caprices of the gods are proof against the clear love of a faithful wife. Echo, what have I to fear from men or gods if I am faithful and loyal? Tell me, Echo, you who have never contradicted me. Nothing—isn't that so, Echo, nothing, nothing? (*Her arms are uplifted to the heavens.*)

ECHO (*from off stage*)—Everything! Everything!

ALKMENA (*terrified*)—What? What is that you say?

ECHO (*relenting*)—Nothing! Nothing! (*Reassured,* ALKMENA *breathes a sigh of relief. Her arms are uplifted in gratitude, her face transfigured.*)

The curtain falls.

ACT III

A stone parapet runs around the roof of Amphitryon's palace. There is a stone bench in the form of an "H" in the center. "There are statues of heroes, gods and goddesses on the cornices of the roof. Their superb backs face the audience." It is late the same day. Nenetza and Kleantha are looking down over the parapet and laughing at something that is going on below. This, it transpires, is the departure of Queen Leda.

Now Leda has departed with a "very self-satisfied look," to the accompaniment of a great stir among the lime trees that appear to be bowing to her as she passes.

"They're not bowing to her—they're bowing to the wind," corrects Sosie. "Anybody'd think this was her day instead of our mistress'."

Sosie has sent the maids about their household tasks when the Trumpeter arrives, quite out of breath as usual, to report that all is festivity and excitement below. Banners blowing in the breeze and a great shouting—a shouting muffled by the low-flying clouds. It is the greatest day that has ever come to Thebes, declares the Trumpeter. The army is victorious, and without a casualty. Everything has been arranged for Jupiter's arrival just as for an eclipse, even the children preparing bits of smoked glass so they may be able to watch without hurting their eyes.

Sosie has mobilized all the invalids of the town, including the paralytics, thinking that Jupiter's touch may make them whole, but the Trumpeter doubts the wisdom of including the paralytics—

"Jupiter thinks that man is perfect because he is created in his own image," says Trumpeter. "If you reveal him now, in his imperfection, you may irritate him. You know how one detests a bad mirror."

It is the Trumpeter's suggestion that the paralytics be replaced by a group of beautiful dancers. Then Jupiter will not blush at having created a world so ridden with ugliness.

Alkmena is reported walking on the terrace wearing an expectant expression which seems quite reasonable. There are rumors that she will refuse to receive Jupiter, that she even may refuse to conceive. But the Trumpeter knows Jupiter. However stubborn Alkmena may be, Jupiter is even more so. "That's what distinguishes gods from men," explains Trumpeter. "If men could push obstinacy to the ultimate point they would be gods, too, like Jupiter."

Alkmena has come from the terrace. She, too, is interested in the excitement of the people and the preparations for the celebration. She would have Sosie order a procession.

And now Amphitryon is there, and in a very bad humor. Alkmena is at a loss to understand why he should look as he does and remain so distant—

"I've just ordered a processional in your honor," Alkmena reports gaily. "All the beauty in Thebes, my darling. Not many wives would do that. All Thebes is awaiting the arrival of the already departed god. I share a secret with Jupiter. Aren't you jealous that I share a secret with Jupiter?"

"It's no secret that Jupiter is coming to you tonight. That's no secret. And you seem radiant at the prospect!"

"I'm radiant at your return and I'm radiant over your victory."

"The victory was won in my absence. For this hour with you—"

"This hour with me—?"

"—cost me this victory. Had we been defeated in my absence, that I might have borne. But a victory without me—it's insupportable!"

"But haven't you just come from the battlefield?"

"What's the matter with you, Alkmena? Have you lost your senses? Have you forgotten already that I have just come from your arms?"

"When did you return?"

"You know perfectly well. You questioned me sufficiently about it. Are you so intoxicated by this honor that you don't remember these last few hours? I can't endure it."

Alkmena's face lengthens, the startled expression of her eyes is intensified. "What have I done? What have I done?" she mutters, largely to herself. Now Amphitryon, noting her expression, would comfort her. He shall, he assures her, put up a fight with Jupiter. Not a physical fight, but one that will be persuasive. Alkmena is fearful of the result of any conference between these two. Jupiter might do anything, might even make them hate each other.

"Dearest, don't cry," Amphitryon is saying. "If we submit to Jupiter—if we consent to this—he will leave us in peace—we shall be left with each other—we'd still have our love."

ALKMENA—No. How could we live with that between us? Imagine us with an unutterable third name always on our lips, withering our kisses, tarnished by immortality. How will you look at me when he who defiled us scrawls his signature across the sky in lightning? (*There is a clap of thunder.*)

AMPHITRYON—We've been so happy. I can't believe it's over!

ALKMENA—I should have loved us to have grown old together. To test the truth of the notion that people grow to look like each other, to experience the tranquil joys of nodding by the hearth, of dying finally. Oh, that wonderful old age of which Jupiter is about to rob us! Long, long years of marriage. Can you imagine us as two very old people? Tell me, my old husband, have you loved me?

AMPHITRYON—My whole life.

ALKMENA—Without exception?

AMPHITRYON—Without exception!

ALKMENA—Can I believe that?

AMPHITRYON—It's true.

ALKMENA—If it's true for you, then that shall be my truth also. Tell me, though, didn't you—just as we were about to celebrate our silver wedding—find a sixteen-year-old virgin, one of those girls at once bold and shy, who was ravished by your distinguished gray hair and your exploits in the past, a creature light as air and as enchanting as moonlight—a perfect monster, in fact?

AMPHITRYON—No, for me you have always been younger than youth itself and I wanted us, when we reached old age, to have no reason for reproach between us.

ALKMENA—Nor have we—(*Kisses him.*) not really. (*Another clap of thunder.*) Now, at last, death may come; not surprising us, but catching up with us. Death may come!

There is a terrific crash of thunder, followed by the sound of trumpets. Out of the clouds Jupiter and Mercury appear. They are in their godly raiment and are godly persons now, Jupiter's imposing head and beard impressively curled. They pause briefly to get the lay of the situation. Jupiter is curious about Amphitryon's presence and not particularly pleased when the general would take issue with him on the inevitability of this night. Certainly Amphitryon would be very foolish to enter the lists with a god! Amphitryon is quite aware of the hopelessness of his attitude, and yet he would persist, even at the expense of death.

"You must understand my forbearance," cautions Jupiter. "I'm fond of you both. As a couple, I'm rather proud of you. I am pleased with the idea of your two superbly sculptured bodies, like prows on galleons, cleaving great furrows in time. I want to sponsor you. It is as a good friend that I wish to be established with you both."

"You are already so established and revered. I refuse!"

"You deny to Alkmena the privileges accident has thrown in your way, when you yourself are not so blameless."

Before Mercury, as Jupiter's suggestion, can blazon to the world the truth of Alkmena's trick with Leda Alkmena intervenes. She has dropped to one knee before the god and begged that they be left alone. With a wave of the hand Jupiter sees to that. Amphitryon and Mercury disappear.

"Alone at last!" sighs Jupiter.

ALKMENA—If one is to believe the legends—it is a kind of solitude which you experience often. Oh, Jupiter, with so many, why do you choose me for an historic role to which I am so little suited?

JUPITER—Because you endow the historic with an air of impromptu which absolutely delights me!

ALKMENA—Why destroy a perfect marriage—leave it in ruins —for one moment's pleasure?

JUPITER—Isn't that the essence of all love?

ALKMENA—Suppose I offer you more than love—better than love—

JUPITER—Am I so repulsive to you?

ALKMENA—If you only were.

JUPITER—You would resist me then because you love me?

ALKMENA—Love! Love you may experience with anyone. But between us I would like to create a bond that is sweeter and more powerful; I, alone among women, can offer you this—I do offer it—and it's friendship!

JUPITER—Friendship? I hear it for the first time. Explain it. What does it mean? Is it a word current on Earth?

ALKMENA—The expression is current.

JUPITER—What is its object?

ALKMENA—To bring together the most totally dissimilar people and make them equal. Have you never seen the most ill-assorted creatures isolate themselves for no reason at all? A cabinet minister and a gardener—a lion sharing his cage with a poodle? And these misfits have a perfect community of interests—they seem drawn together by some strange, chemical substance in their bodies.

JUPITER—I vaguely remember a cabinet minister and a gardener, yes, they were diverting to watch.

ALKMENA—They'd stroll down the hundred paces of the garden path and then—stroll back again.

JUPITER—The cabinet minister would converse learnedly about pruning and weeds—

ALKMENA—The gardener of filibusters and excise taxes—

JUPITER—Then after each had had his say, they'd finally stop at the end of the path—

ALKMENA—look affectionately into each other's eyes—

JUPITER—stroke their beards—

ALKMENA—and wink.

JUPITER—Friendship?

ALKMENA—Friendship!

JUPITER—It sounds an amusing novelty. But if I became your friend—what would we do?

ALKMENA—First of all, instead of believing in you as a god, I should think of you as a friend. My thoughts of you would be from the heart, whereas my prayers to you would no longer be repeated by rote but addressed to you—personally. Instead of ritual gestures of obeisance I should—beckon you with my hands.

And what would Jupiter be doing? Well, Alkmena explains, Jupiter would be visiting Alkmena occasionally, sitting at the foot of the divan, telling her of many interesting things, including creation. And sometimes she would ask great favors of him—as a friend. To find a lost husband, for example. Or to cure a sick child. And then, as a final test—

"In a marriage ideally happy, a husband has been unfaithful through no fault of his own—what can you do for him?" asks Alkmena.

"Cause him never to know it."

ALKMENA—Ah, Jupiter, you are a friend—a true friend!

JUPITER—It seems to me, I'd have more to do than you would.

ALKMENA—Naturally, since you have more power. To do more than one's share is one of the privileges of friendship. Have you never tasted the strange joy of submitting to the will of another?

JUPITER—I've never had the opportunity.

ALKMENA—You have it now. Shall you miss it?

JUPITER—I see through you, Alkmena, I read your thoughts.

ALKMENA—You see, you know my secrets. Therefore you are so much more suited to be my friend than my lover.

JUPITER—I see that no matter what I do, I cannot cross the immutable line that separates us. Therefore, I free you.

ALKMENA—Oh! (*Overjoyed, drops to her knees before him.*)

JUPITER—You've touched me, somehow. You are stubborn, you are obstinate. But you also are forlorn in your devotion. You make fidelity affecting. If you can console the Thebans for depriving them so brutally of this national honor—I give you my word . . . (*Rises.*) I shall not impose my presence on you to-night.

ALKMENA (*rising*)—But why need the Thebans know? Let me appear before them—before the whole world as your mistress. True, it will drive them wild with jealousy, and you know how trying envy can be; but, on the other hand, it'll give Amphitryon and me great pleasure to suffer this inconvenience for you. That's friendship!

JUPITER—You dazzle me, Alkmena. How you fleck your little tricks with gleams of loyalty. How you flavor your little lies with a tincture of sincerity! Nevertheless, I free you!

ALKMENA—Without reservations?

JUPITER—Without reservations.

The ease with which Jupiter accepts the situation rouses Alkmena's suspicions, but these are allayed. She has made friendship sound so attractive, it satisfies him, Jupiter insists. Is he quite sure that he never has been her lover, Alkmena would know. Is he sure he has never taken the shape of Amphitryon? Yes, Jupiter is sure. He has leaned forward now, and is smoothing a lock of Alkmena's hair—

"It seems to me—I have a conviction—it's not the first time you've twisted that lock of hair or leaned over me like this. Was it at night or was it at dawn you came?"

"Neither! Neither!"

"You have obscured everything for me. My whole body rejoices at having met you. I am thrilled in my being at this hour—and yet I'm conscious also of trouble, of uncertainty—of something . . . Can you not rid my mind of this uncertainty?"

"Since you will not believe me, I can grant you forgetfulness."

So it is agreed that forgetfulness shall be Alkmena's gift. She does not care to know before the blessing is bestowed what her future is to be, even though Jupiter assures her it will be happy. She has no curiosity regarding the life of the gods, so declines his offer to share it momentarily before she sinks into oblivion. Nor any wish to see "in one flash of clarity the whole world—past, present and future—and to comprehend its meaning—"

"Do you not wish to see humanity at its labors, from its birth to its final dissolution?" demands Jupiter. "Do you not wish to see the eleven great beings who will constitute the finest ornament in all history? One with his lovely Jewish face; another with her little nose from Lorraine?"

No—Alkmena will be satisfied with forgetfulness. Let him, in his divinity, abandon her to her humanity. And so, with a farewell kiss just this side of oblivion, which is to be her last memory, the compact is sealed.

Now Jupiter lifts his arm. There is music. Amphitryon and Mercury reappear. Jupiter and Alkmena are standing side by side—

"She has won me over, Amphitryon, and I rejoice in my defeat," admits Jupiter. "Is she always like this?"

"She generally manages to be right."

MERCURY—The whole of Thebes is at the foot of the Palace clamoring for you to appear with Alkmena in your arms.

JUPITER—My son and his ceremonials!

MERCURY—Just show yourselves—that will satisfy them completely.

JUPITER (*to* AMPHITRYON)—Do you mind?

AMPHITRYON—It is an honor.

JUPITER—Thank you, General. (*He offers his arm to* ALK-MENA; *they walk to parapet to display themselves to the populace.*) Bear up, Alkmena, for this one instant only.

ALKMENA—These wretches that insult my integrity!

JUPITER—Even they demand their legend.

MERCURY—Just say a few words to them; you can be brief, you know—they'll elaborate it themselves. (*Prompting.*) At last I meet you—

JUPITER and MERCURY—At last I meet you, dearest Alkmena. . . .

MERCURY—Yes, dear Jupiter. . . .

ALKMENA and MERCURY—Yes, dear Jupiter, and so we have to part.

MERCURY (*prompting*)—And so begins this night—

MERCURY and JUPITER—So begins this night—so fertile for all the world.

MERCURY and ALKMENA—So ends this day—this day that I was beginning to love.

MERCURY—Kiss! (JUPITER *kisses* ALKMENA *on the forehead.*)

JUPITER (*leading her back to* AMPHITRYON)—And now that the legend has been duly established, befitting the dignity of the gods—

MERCURY—Amphitryon, your marriage—blessed already—is to be blessed even further—

JUPITER—Alkmena is to bear you a son. Will you name him to please me? Will you name him Hercules?

AMPHITRYON—Hercules?

ALKMENA—Hercules!

JUPITER—And I shall be his . . . godfather. . . .

JUPITER and MERCURY (*together*)—. . . and so will destiny be fulfilled! (AMPHITRYON *and* ALKMENA *are in each other's arms.* JUPITER, followed by MERCURY, *goes to back toward the low-hanging clouds.*)

JUPITER—We must intrude no longer on these two—I have withheld their night too long already— (*The lights slowly dim.* JUPITER *commands the firmament.*) Curtain of the night descend —but for an instant let them be encircled in a glade of light! (*Light from above falls on* AMPHITRYON *and* ALKMENA.) A little island of fidelity! My arm embraces them to bring them closer to their joy—this untarnished couple—forever to remain untarnished! (JUPITER *and* MERCURY *are now on their way to the Empyrean.*)

MERCURY—But I warn you—posterity will gossip!

JUPITER—Alkmena won't mind. By that time she will have forgotten even my farewell. (*He disappears aloft, followed by* MERCURY, *trailing celestial rays.*)

ALKMENA (*transfigured for the moment by the divine, flings up her arms and calls after the departed god*)—Farewell, Jupiter, farewell!

THE CURTAIN FALLS

GOLDEN BOY

A Drama in Three Acts

By Clifford Odets

THERE was, during the season of 1935-36, a fear that the living theatre had lost dramatist Clifford Odets. He had, following the failure of his second long play, "Paradise Lost," gone, a little poutily in all probability, to Hollywood and taken up scenario writing with what appeared to be enthusiasm. Back came reports that Odets had said this, and that, and the other thing, indicating that he was quite through with Broadway and glad of it. George Kaufman and Edna Ferber were not above making capital of the situation by slyly inserting a radical playwright in "Stage Door" who gave up his art in a fit of pique and went Hollywood in a big way, returning East later in white tie and tails, brandishing scads of money and flaunting a deep disgust of the idealists who formerly were his pals.

It was, of course, a personality sketch exaggerated for its satiric value and in truth did not represent the real Odets save in the superficial sense that he frankly had turned to pictures to provide him with the capital necessary if he were to continue his Broadway experiment. Early 1937 found a new Odets play ready for rehearsal by the Group Theatre, with which he had begun his career as a dramatist with "Awake and Sing" and "Waiting for Lefty." This was "Golden Boy." It was produced November 4, and was rapturously received by the Group Theatre subscribers. The professional reviewers' reception was touched with what might be termed a lightly restrained enthusiasm, mixed with unanimous expressions of joy that Mr. Odets was again devoting his talents to a theatre that needed them. "Golden Boy," pungent in dialogue, holding in its salty realism, thereafter builded slowly into a popular success and ran through the season.

The conflict of "Golden Boy" is in reality an inner conflict confined to the breast of an unhappy lad who had some little hope of becoming a great musician, a violinist, but whose inordinate ambition and accidentally discovered talent as a fighter led him to the prize ring.

"In 'Golden Boy' Mr. Odets has trenchantly illustrated the

perniciousness of choices that are false to a man's private character," wrote Brooks Atkinson. "Among other things he has illustrated the false choices that our economic system frequently imposes upon original people."

The Broadway office of Tom Moody, a fight manager, in which the play opens, is scantily furnished, but contains all the necessary appurtenances—a desk, chairs, telephone and couch. Mr. Moody at the moment of discovery is in the midst of a conference—or fight—with his girl, Lorna Moon. Miss Moon, the author would point out, is different. "There is a certain quiet glitter about this girl, and if she is sometimes hard it is more from necessity than choice; her eyes often hold a soft sad glance."

Moody, also, is not all that surface appearances would seem to indicate. "Moody's explosiveness covers a soft, boyish quality, and at the same time he possesses a certain vulnerable quality which women find very attractive."

Mr. Moody is inviting Miss Moon to pack up her things and get the hell out of his life, if she feels the way she says she feels. Miss Moon, on the other hand, has no intention of leaving Mr. Moody thus abruptly, although she is getting pretty tired of his wife—"your sweet goddam Monica," as she calls her. The current Mrs. Moody, it appears, is asking five thousand dollars as the price of a divorce for Mr. Moody.

"Look, Tom," Lorna is saying; "this means as much to me as it does to you. If she's out of the way, we can get married. Otherwise I'm a tramp from Newark. I don't like the feeling."

"Lorna, for Pete's sake, use your noodle! When I get rid of Monica, we'll marry. Now, do I have to bang you on the nose to make you understand?"

"Go to hell. . . . But come back tonight."

Moody has walked over to take Lorna in his arms and kiss her. He would like to buy her something—an ostrich feather, perhaps. And if his boy, Kaplan, wins his fight he will take her dancing.

Lorna is not impressed. Kaplan has no chance of staying ten rounds with the Baltimore Chocolate Drop, and Moody knows it.

"It's the Twentieth Century, Tom—no more miracles," says Lorna, and as Moody turns away, a worried look creeping into his eyes, she smiles: "You know what I like about you—you take everything so serious."

"Who will if I don't?" demands Moody, hotly. "I've been off the gold standard for eight years. This used to be a gorgeous town. New York was hot with money. Kaplan gets four hundred bucks tonight. In the old days, that was nothing. Those were the days when I had Marty Welch, the heavyweight contender—Cy Webster who got himself killed in a big red Stutz. In '27 and 8 you couldn't get to sleep—the town was crawling with attractions. . . ."

"My mother died in '28."

"I haven't had a break in years. 'Carry me back to old Virginny'—that's how I feel. There isn't much of a future."

The Moody depression continues stubbornly. Yet, with a little luck, with a new boy, a good black boy, for example, the vaults of the mint would be accessible. Good boys hard to find? There just aren't any. Hasn't Moody taken trips to Philadelphia? To Boston? To Chicago? And found nothing. Not even a bantamweight. And he is prepared to give his right eye for a good black boy.

Again Lorna is sympathetic and affectionate. She'll stick until hell freezes over. There is gratitude and a lot of love in the embrace she collects for her promise. . . .

Suddenly a boy has appeared in the doorway. He is breathing heavily, is a little flushed of face and is twisting his cap in his hands nervously. He has just come over from the gym he announces, simply, when Moody, angered by the interruption, would know who he is and what he is there for. He has just come from the gym where Kaplan trains. Kaplan has just broken his hand—Tokio, the trainer, is looking after Kaplan—

The news is a shock to Moody. He is, he announces, ready for the bughouse right now. That Kaplan! That phonus bolonus! Now he (Moody) must call up Roxy Gottlieb and cancel the match—and Gottlieb in the red already—

"I don't think it's necessary to cancel, Tom," quietly interrupts the boy.

"Oh, you don't!" Moody has whirled to face him. For the first time he is really aware of his visitor. "Who the hell are you? And who the hell are you to call me Tom? Are we acquainted?" he demands.

Boy—I wrote you a couple of letters. I can do that stretch.
Moody—What stretch?
Boy—Why don't you let me take Kaplan's place tonight?
Moody (*sarcastically*)—Go slow and tell me again . . . what?
Boy (*coolly*)—I can take Kaplan's place. . . .
Moody—You mean you want to fight the Baltimore Chocolate

Drop? *You?* (*The* Boy *remains silent.* Moody *comes out from behind his desk and stands face to face with the* Boy. *With sudden discovery.*) You're cockeyed too.

Boy (*quietly*)—Can't you fix it up with Roxy Gottlieb?

Moody (*suddenly*)—Looka, kid, go home, kid, before I blame Kaplan's glass mitts on *you*. Then you won't like it, and I won't like it, and Miss Moon here, she won't like it.

Boy (*turning to* Lorna)—How do you do, Miss Moon. (Lorna *smiles at the* Boy's *quiet confidence.*) I need a good manager, Mr. Moody. You used to be tops around town—everyone says so. I think you can develop me. I can fight. You don't know it, but I can fight. Kaplan's been through for years. He may be the best fighter in your stable, but he's a stumble-bum for the younger boys growing up. Why don't you give me this chance, Tom?

Moody—I don't want you calling me Tom! (*He glares at the* Boy *and then returns to the desk and telephone.*)

Boy—I'm waiting for your answer. (Moody's *answer is an exasperated glance as he begins to dial the phone. The* Boy *half approaches the desk.*) There are forty-three thousand minutes in a month—can't you give me five?

Moody—I'll give you this phone in the head in a minute! Who are you? What the hell do you want? Where do you fight?

Boy (*with cool persistence*)—We ought to get together, Tom.

Moody—I don't want you calling me Tom. You're brash, you're fresh, you're callow—and you're cockeyed! In fact you're an insult to my whole nature! Now get out! (Moody *turns back to the phone and begins dialing again. The* Boy *stands there, poised on his toes, not sure of his next move. He turns and looks at* Lorna. *She nods her head and gives him a faint smile of encouragement. On phone.*) This is Tom Moody. . . . Is Tokio there? . . . (*He bangs up the phone and holds the instrument thoughtfully.*) Tokio's on his way over.

Boy—The Baltimore Chocolate Drop is not as good as you think he is. (Moody *suddenly whirls around and holds the telephone high over his head in a threatening gesture. The* Boy *steps back lightly and continues.*) I've studied his style for months; I've perfected the exact punch to quench his thirst. Did you ever watch closely? (*Acting it out.*) He likes to pull your lead—he hesitates for a second—he pulls your lead—he slips his face away and then he's in. Suppose you catch that second when he hesitates—he's open for the punch!

Moody (*sarcastically*)—And what do you do with his left hook?
Boy (*simply*)—Avoid it.

Moody decides not to strike the boy with the phone. He has lowered it now and is demanding sarcastically to know if the boy ever heard of Kid Peters, whom the Chocolate Drop had "marked lousy in twelve rounds"; or Eddie Newton, who went down in two; or Frisco Samuels or Mike Mason; or—
"Did you ever hear of me?" quietly demands the boy. "My name's Bonaparte—"
Moody and Lorna are laughing. The boy doesn't think it's funny. They can call him Joe. Still they laugh—until Joe takes Moody by the coat lapels and advises him to quit. Moody has shaken himself loose when Tokio, the trainer, barges into the room. With Joe there Tokio knows Moody has heard about Kaplan. He doesn't wonder the manager is "off the top" with the whole thing. But he is surprised to see Joe there. Joe ought to be ashamed to show his face. He's the boy who did it to Kaplan—
"I went down for an apple," explains Tokio, "and I come back and Kaplan's sparring with this kid—picked him up in the gym. The next thing I know, Kaplan's down on the floor with a busted mitt."
"I took it on the elbow," modestly explains Joe.
Now Lorna takes a hand. She would know more of Joe. Where does he come from? New York. How old is he? Twenty-one. Has he ever fought much? Enough. Syracuse, Albany—
Gottlieb is on the phone. Moody answers. Yes, the worst is true. Kaplan has bust his mitt again. "I can't help it if you've got fifty judgments on your club," shouts Moody into the phone. "The same to you. . . . Your mother, too. . . ."
Then comes the big idea. "If you tie up your big flabby mouth for a minute," Moody is saying, "I'll give you some news. I'm in a position to do you a big favor. I got a replacement —*better* than Kaplan. . . . Bonaparte. . . . No, Bon-a-parte. (*Holds hand over mouthpiece and asks* Boy.) Is that crap?

Joe—No, that's my name.
Moody (*back at the phone*)—That's right, like in Napoleon. . . . (*Looks the* Boy *over appraisingly.*) One hundred and thirty . . .
Joe—Three.

MOODY—Hundred and thirty-three. Your customers'll eat him up. I'll bring him right over . . . you can take my word—the kid's a cock-eyed wonder . . . *your* mother too! (*He hangs up and turns around.* JOE *is the focus of all eyes.*) It's revenge on somebody—maybe God.

JOE (*quietly*)—I think you'll be surprised.

MOODY (*sadly*)—Do your worst, kid. I've been surprised by experts.

JOE—Don't worry, Tom.

MOODY—Call me Tom again and I'll break your neck!!

The scene fades.

We move on to the combination dining and front room of the Bonaparte home. The dining room table, lighted from above, is littered with papers. Two older men are seated at either side, Mr. Bonaparte, Joe's father, a gentle-mannered Italian who speaks with a slight accent, and his friend, Mr. Carp, the Jewish keeper of a candy and stationery store. Presently these two are joined by a young man known as Siggie, an alert but not too prepossessing young man who is Mr. Bonaparte's son-in-law. Siggie brings his own beer from the kitchen. He is in a state of semi-undress, having evidently interrupted his retiring routine to refresh himself with the beer and have another try at Mr. Bonaparte about a certain business matter.

Siggie is eager to be set up in the taxicab business. If his father-in-law will only advance the money to buy a cab Siggie could pay back the loan by the week. He— But Mr. Bonaparte is not interested in the taxicab business.

"I am married to your daughter, and when you do this thing you do it for me and her together," persists Siggie. "A cab in two shifts is a big source of profit. Joe takes the night shift. I'm a married man so you don't expect me to take the night shift."

Siggie's wife, Anna, has appeared in the doorway in her nightgown. She is not interested in the taxicab business either. She would have Siggie stop talking and come to bed—

"Don't you wanna help your own family, Foolish?" Siggie demands, paying no attention to Anna. "After all, Joe's your own son—he's a man, no kid no more—"

"Tomorrow's twenty-one," announces Mr. Bonaparte, with a touch of pride.

"If he don't work he'll turn into a real bum. Look how late he's staying out at night."

"GOLDEN BOY"

Mr. Bonaparte: Joe, I buy you this some time ago. Don't give cause I don't know whatta gonna do. Take him with you now. Play for yourself. It gonna remember you your old s of musical life.

(Luther Adler, Morris Carnovsky, Frances Farmer)

"I don't expects for Joe to drive taxi."

"He's got to do something. He can drive like a fire engine. Why not?"

"He gonna do something."

"What? Play his violinsky in the backyards?"

Again Anna has appeared to urge Siggie to come to bed. This time she is drawn into the argument. She, too, wonders why her father won't buy Siggie a cab, even if it's a used cab. He has the cash. Still Poppa is not interested. Having heard all this many times he is a little bored. He smiles at Siggie's final plea. All he asks is a chance to get Anna out of the kitchen and himself away from driving a company cab. And he warns them all that if things go from worse to worse they needn't expect him to support the family.

"We have-a receive the warning. We are in a conspiracy against you—go to bed," answers Mr. Bonaparte, kindly.

Now Siggie has turned on Anna for having butted in with that second-hand cab idea. He has rolled up a newspaper and is giving his wife a friendly beating over the head with it, promising that the next time he'll break her neck, he's that super-disgusted.

Mr. Bonaparte is moved to soft laughter after Anna and Siggie have gone. He is happy this night, although a little worried about what is keeping his boy, Joe. It's one o'clock, and no Joe—

"You think you got worries?" demands Carp with a friendly challenge. "Wait, you're a young man yet. You got a son, Joe. He practiced on his fiddle for ten years? He won a gold medal, the best in the city? They gave him a scholarship in the Erickson Institute? Tomorrow he's twenty-one, yeah?"

"Yeah."

CARP (*leaning forward and dramatically making his point*)— Suppose a war comes? Before you know it, he's in the army!

MR. BONAPARTE—Naw, naw! Whata you say! Naw!

CARP (*wagging his head in imitation*)—Look in the papers! On every side the clouds of war—

MR. BONAPARTE—My Joe gotta biga talent. Yesterday I buy-a him present! (*With a dramatic flourish he brings a violin case out of the bottom part of the sideboard.*)

CARP (*as the case is opened*)—It looks like a coffin for a baby.

MR. BONAPARTE (*looking down at the violin in its case*)—His teacher help me to picka him.

CARP (*the connoisseur*)—Fine, fine—beautiful, fine! A cultural thing!

Mr. Bonaparte (*touching it fondly*)—The mosta golden present for his birthday which I give him tonight.

Carp—How much, if I'm not getting too personal, did such a violin cost you?

Mr. Bonaparte—Twelve hundred dollars.

Carp (*shocked*)—What?

Mr. Bonaparte—You're surprised of me? Well, I waita for this moment many years.

Carp (*sitting*)—Ask yourself a pertinent remark: could a boy make a living playing this instrument in our competitive civilization today?

Mr. Bonaparte—Why? Don't expect for Joe to be a millionaire. He don't need it, to be a millionaire. A good life'sa possible—

Carp—For men like us, yes. But nowadays is it possible for a young man to give himself to the Muses? Could the Muses put bread and butter on the table?

Mr. Bonaparte—No millionaire is necessary. Joe love music. Music is the great cheer-up in the language of all countries. I learn that from Joe. (Carp *sighs as* Mr. Bonaparte *replaces the violin in the buffet.*)

Carp—But in the end, as Schopenhauer says, what's the use to try something? For every wish we get, ten remains unsatisfied. Death is playing with us as a cat and her mouse!

Mr. Bonaparte—You makea me laugh, Mr. Carp. You say life'sa bad. No, life'sa good. Siggie and Anna fight—good! They love—good! You say life'sa bad . . . well, is pleasure for you to say so. No? The streets, winter a' summer—trees, cats —I lovea them all. The gooda boys and girls, they who sing and whistle—(*Bursts into a moment of gay whistling.*)—very good! The eating and sleeping, drinking wine—very good! I gone around on my wagon and talk to many people—nice!

Frank Bonaparte, oldest son of the family, is home. Frank is "simple, intelligent, observant." Pretty tired, too. He is going South in the morning. More trouble in the South—in textiles. He is taking a hurried look at the papers he has brought in when his eye catches an account of Joe's fight. So that's where he has been.

"Poppa, you better brace yourself in your chair," Frank warns, excitedly. "Looka this, Joe's had a fight. 'Flash: Chocolate Drop fails to K.O. new cock-eyed wonder.'" There it is, picture and all. Mr. Bonaparte refuses to believe it. It must be some other boy—

They have turned to the door. Joe is standing there, in the entrance. As he moves into the light his face is seen to be bruised and there is a piece of adhesive tape stuck over one eye. He has had a fight—with a boy in the park, Joe explains. He's too tired to talk about it. When his brother would pester the truth out of him Joe jumps to his feet in a flash of anger—

"You're a dumb kid," smiles Frank, as the attack subsides.

"Hey, waita onea minute," protests Mr. Bonaparte. "What'sa for this excite-a-ment?"

JOE (*hotly*)—I don't want to be criticized! Nobody takes me serious here! I want to do what I want. I proved it tonight I'm good—I went out to earn some money and I earned! I had a professional fight tonight—maybe I'll have some more.

CARP—You honest to God had a fight?

JOE (*glaring at* CARP)—Why not?

FRANK (*to* JOE)—No one's criticizin'.

MR. BONAPARTE—That's right.

JOE (*half sheepishly*)—I don't know why I got so sore. . . .

FRANK—You're expecting opposition all the time—

MR. BONAPARTE—Sit down, Joe—resta you'self.

JOE—Don't want to sit. Every birthday I ever had I sat around. Now'sa time for standing. Poppa, I have to tell you— I don't like myself, past, present and future. Do you know there are men who have wonderful things from life? Do you think they're better than me? Do you think I like this feeling of no possessions? Of learning about the world from Carp's encyclopaedia? Frank don't know what it means—he travels around, sees the world! (*Turning to* FRANK.) You don't know what it means to sit around here and watch the months go ticking by! Do you think that's a life for a boy my age? Tomorrow's my birthday! I change my life!

MR. BONAPARTE—Justa like that?

JOE—Just like that!

FRANK—And what do you do with music?

JOE—Who says I'm married to music? I take a vacation—the notes won't run away!

FRANK—You're a mysterious kid. Where did you learn the fighting game?

JOE—These past two years, all over the city—in the gyms—

MR. BONAPARTE—Hey, Joe, you sounda like crazy! You no

gotta nature for fight. You're musician. Whata you say, heh?
Whata you do?

JOE—Let's call it a day.

MR. BONAPARTE—Isa no true whata I say?—

JOE—That's all for tonight. (*His lips tightened, he abruptly exits.*)

MR. BONAPARTE (*calling after him*)—Take a gooda sleep, Joe.

FRANK (*smiling*)—It looks like the gold bug has visited our house.

CARP (*sadly*)—Fortunes! I used to hear it in my youth—the streets of America is paved with gold. Say, you forgot to give him the present.

MR. BONAPARTE (*slowly, puzzled*)—I don'ta know . . . he say he gonna fight. . . .

The lights fade out.

Two months later, in Tom Moody's office, Roxy Gottlieb, promoter; Tokio, Joe Bonaparte's trainer, and Moody are in conference. Lorna Moon, listening in, is stretched out on the couch, blowing smoke rings in the air.

The subject of the conference is fighter Joe, and why won't he fight? Joe, it appears, has scored five victories in two months, and still the sports writers and large sections of the fight-going public do not like him. He is too scientific and apparently lacks the killer instinct. For some mysterious reason Joe pulls his punches, and his backers are worried. Tokio tries to argue that they should give Joe his head and let him fight his own way.

"What do you want the boy to do?" asks Lorna, breaking gently into the conversation. "You surely know by now he's not a slugger. His main asset is his science—he's a student."

"Excuse me, Miss Moon," loftily answers Roxy Gottlieb; "in the prizefight ring the cash customer don't look for stoodents. Einstein lives in a college—a wonderful man in *his* line! Also, while I think of it, a woman's place is in the hay, not in the office!"

They are still searching for a password that will inspire Joe to go in and slug when there is a knock on the door. The caller proves to be Joe Bonaparte's father. He has come to see how Joe is getting on. They soon have him worried by their report that Joe is a grand fighter who won't fight. But Mr. Bonaparte reminds them, Joe has fought. He has and he hasn't, they tell him. He "nurses his self," as Tokio puts it. "Is Joe afraid of his hands?" the trainer asks Mr. Bonaparte.

"I don't know. You tella me what'sa what," answers the

puzzled father. "I don't know price fight. His hand coulda get hurt?"

Moody—Every fighter hurts his hands. Sometimes they break—

Tokio—They heal up in no time.

Roxy (*flaring out*)—What's so special about hands? I suppose your kid plays piano!

Mr. Bonaparte—Coulda get hurt? Coulda break!

Roxy—So what?

Mr. Bonaparte (*up on his feet*)—Hey, you! I don't likea you! You no interest in my boy! (*Proudly.*) My boy'sa besta violin' in New York!

Moody (*suddenly sickened*)—What . . . ?

Mr. Bonaparte—Yes, play the violin!

Moody—That's it! . . .

Roxy (*anguished by this stupidity*)—If I had hair I'd tear it out! Five hundred fiddlers stand on Broadway and 48th Street, on the corner, every day, rain or shine, hot or cold. And your boy dares—! (*Turning to* Moody.) How do you like it? (*He waves his hands in despair and retires to the desk, where he sits in fuming disgusted silence.*)

Moody (*repressing a feeling of triumph*)—Your boy's afraid of his hands because he fiddles?

Mr. Bonaparte—Yes, musta be!

Tokio—Why did you come and tell us this?

Mr. Bonaparte—Because I likea to help my boy. I likea for him to try himself out. Maybe thisa better business for him. Maybe not. He mus' try to find out, to see whata he want. . . . I don't know. Don't help Joe to tell him I come here. Don't say it. (*He slowly walks to the door.*)

Moody—That means you won't stand in his way?

Mr. Bonaparte—My boy coulda break his hand? Gentleman, I'ma not so happy as you . . . no! (*He slowly exits.*)

Moody (*joyously*)—I'm beginning to see the light! Joe's mind ain't made up that the fist is mightier than the fiddle.

Roxy (*bouncing up and down*)—I'll make up his mind. For the money that's involved I'd make Niagara Falls turn around and go back to Canada.

Now Moody knows what has to be done. They have got to work on Joe delicately. They will send him on a Midwest tour to start the build-up, with Tokio in charge. The password, as Roxy sees it, is going to be honey.

Presently Joe appears. His friends are soon working on him. Moody tells him of the plans for a tour covering fifteen out of town bouts, and good tough ones, too. Joe, they are all agreed, has a great future. Tokio has even gone so far as to say he thinks Joe can become as good as Benny Simon. He ought to come back from his tour the Number One contender for the lightweight crown. But there will have to be a lot of co-operation. There can't be any side issues. There can't be any holding back—

"You're in the fighting game," the smooth-toned Moody explains to Joe. "It's like being a priest—your work comes first. What had you rather do than fight?"

"I don't know what you mean."

"Some boys, for instance, like to save their looks. They'd practically throw the fight to keep their nose intact."

"My looks don't interest me," protests Joe.

"Then what's holding you back, Joe. You can tell me, Joe. We've set up housekeeping together, Joe, and I want you to tell me if you can't cook a steak—it don't matter. We're married anyway."

"Who's being put to bed?"

"What do you mean?"

"I don't like this seduction scene." (JOE turns to TOKIO.) "What are they after?"

"They think you're afraid of your hands," frankly answers the trainer.

Joe ponders the thought. It may be true. As Moody insists, a fellow can't go in and do his best if he is scared of his mitts. But the expression on Joe's face becomes curiously set as the tactless Roxy remarks that 48th Street is crowded with musicians, like bums in the park, without a dime in a car-load.

"I might give up fighting as a bad job," Joe says, a moment later. "I'm not over-convinced it's what I want. I can do other things. . . ."

Joe has left. He may be at the gym tomorrow and maybe not. Tokio has followed him out. Moody resumes his pacing of the floor and his defeatist mood. A telephone call from his wife asking for another fifty bucks, and suggesting that she might send him back to jail, doesn't help. Lorna would do what she can to compose the situation.

"What was that scene with Bonaparte," she asks.

MOODY—Sweetheart, the jig is up! Believe it or not, Bonaparte's a violinist. Maybe he was on the radio. I don't know what the hell he was. His old man came here and told us. His mitts are on his mind. You can't do a thing with a nut like that.

LORNA—Won't he give up the violin?

MOODY—You heard him stalling. This is the end, Lorna. It's our last chance for a decent life, for getting married—we have to make that kid fight! He's *more* than a meal ticket—he's everything we want and need from life! (LORNA *goes over and slaps him on the back.*)

LORNA—Pick up your chin, little man.

MOODY—Don't Brisbane me, Lorna. I'm licked. I'm tired. Find me a mouse hole to crawl in. . . .

LORNA—Why don't you ask me when you want something? You got the brains of a flea. Do you want Bonaparte to fight?

MOODY—Do I wanna see tomorrow?

LORNA—I'll make him fight.

MOODY—How?

LORNA—How? . . . I'm "a tramp from Newark," Tom. . . . I know a dozen ways. . . .

The scene fades out.

A few nights later Joe and Lorna are sitting on a bench in the park. From the distance the music of a carousel can be heard, and the swish, swish of many passing motor cars is nearer. Deeper in the park a traffic light flashes, first red, then green, then red. . . .

The talk has been of fame and life, riches and ambitions, girls and fighters, Moody and Lorna and Joe. This is Lorna's night out, in a way. Moody always goes to see his kid Tuesday nights. His wife has put the kid with her parents.

"Tokio says you're going far in the fighting game," remarks Lorna.

"Music means more to me," answers Joe, quickly. "May I tell you something?"

"Of course."

JOE—If you laugh I'll never speak to you again.

LORNA—I'm not the laughing type.

JOE—With music I'm never alone when I'm alone—Playing music . . . that's like saying, "I am man. I belong here. How do you do, World—good evening!" When I play music nothing is closed to me. I'm not afraid of people and what they say. There's no war in music. It's not like the streets. Does this sound funny?

LORNA—No.

JOE—But when you leave your room . . . down in the street
. . . it's war! Music can't help me there. Understand?

LORNA—Yes.

JOE—People have hurt my feelings for years. I never forget.
You can't get even with people by playing the fiddle. If music
shot bullets I'd like it better—artists and people like that are
freaks today. The world moves fast and they sit around like forgotten dopes.

LORNA—You're loaded with fireworks. Why don't you fight?

JOE—You have to be what you are—!

LORNA—Fight! See what happens.

JOE—Or end up in the bughouse!

LORNA—God's teeth! Who says you have to be one thing?

JOE—My nature isn't fighting!

LORNA—Don't Tokio know what he's talking about? Don't
Tom? Joe, listen: be a fighter! Show the world! If you made
your fame and fortune—and you can—you'd be anything you
want. Do it! Bang your way to the lightweight crown. Get a
bank account. Hire a great doctor with a beard—get your eyes
fixed—

JOE—What's the matter with my eyes?

LORNA—Excuse me, I stand corrected. (*After a pause.*) You
get mad all the time.

JOE—That's from thinking about myself.

LORNA—How old are you, Joe?

JOE—Twenty-one and a half, and the months are going fast.

LORNA—You're very smart for twenty-one and a half "and the
months are going fast."

JOE—Why not? I read every page of the Encyclopaedia Britannica. My father's friend, Mr. Carp, has it. A shrimp with
glasses has to do something.

The talk turns to Lorna, but she would have that over quickly.
"I'm a girl from over the river," she says. "My father is still
alive—shucking oysters and bumming drinks somewhere in the
wilds of Jersey." And now she would return to the anatomy of
Joe Bonaparte. He is, she finds, much too sufficient to himself.
He should have a look at himself. He doesn't know what's right
or wrong. He doesn't know what to pick, and he won't admit it.

"You're a miserable creature," says Lorna. "You want your
arm in gelt up to the elbow. You'll take fame so people won't

laugh or scorn your face. You'd give your soul for those things. But every time you turn your back your little soul kicks you in the teeth. It don't give in so easy."

Joe knows that Moody has sent Lorna after him as a decoy. He knows more than that, too. He knows Lorna doesn't love Moody. "This is the anatomy of Lorna Moon," he says; "she's a lost baby. She doesn't know what's right or wrong. She's a miserable creature who never knew what to pick. But she'd never admit it."

There has been a long silence. Again Joe's mood has changed. He is going to buy a car, he announces suddenly. He is going to buy a car like Gary Cooper's—and that cost fourteen thousand dollars.

"Tell your Mr. Moody I'll dazzle the eyes out of his head," Joe cries in a burst of enthusiasm.

"You mean it?"

JOE (*looking out ahead*)—Those cars are poison in my blood. When you sit in a car and speed you're looking down at the world. Speed, speed, everything is speed—nobody gets me!

LORNA—You mean in the ring?

JOE—In or out, nobody gets me! Gee, I like to stroke that gas!

LORNA—You sound like Jack the Ripper.

JOE (*standing up suddenly*)—I'll walk you back to your house —your hotel, I mean. (LORNA *stands*. JOE *continues*.) Do you have the same room?

LORNA (*with sneaking admiration*)—You're a fresh kid!

JOE—When you're lying in his arms tonight, tell him, for me, that the next World's Champ is feeding in his stable.

LORNA—Did you really read those Britannica books?

JOE—From A to Z.

LORNA—And you're only twenty-one?

JOE—And a half.

LORNA—Something's wrong somewhere.

JOE—I know. . . . (*They slowly walk out as the curtain falls.*)

The next week, back in the Bonaparte dining room, Joe is packing for his trip. Lorna Moon is there waiting for him. Siggie and Anna are helping by standing around drinking some of the Bonaparte homemade wine. At one side of the room Mr. Bonaparte sits "silently, thoughtfully, watchfully—pretending to read the newspaper."

From time to time Siggie says something funny. At least it

is funny to Anna, who really has never stopped laughing at
Siggie, she admits, since she first met Siggie when he was a
clerk in a United Cigar Store. And that was seven years ago. . . .

Lorna has turned to Mr. Bonaparte. She would like to know
if Mr. Bonaparte likes her. If he does, as he says, why does he
look at her the way he does? "I don't look special," protests
Mr. Bonaparte, and adds: "You gonna travel on the train with
my son?"

"God's teeth, no! I'm a friend of his manager's, that's all.
And a friend of Joe's, too."

"You are in favor for my son to prizefight?"

Joe, noting the drift of the conversation, has quit his packing
and left the room.

"Certainly; aren't you?" answers Lorna.

"Joe has a dream many years to be superior violin'," explains
Mr. Bonaparte. "Was it boyhood thing? Was it real? Or is
this real now? Those area my question, Miss Moon. Maybe
you are friend to my son. Then I asks you, look out for him.
Study him. Help him find what'sa right. Tell me, Miss Moon,
when you find out. Help Joe find truthful success. Will you
do it for me?"

"I'll be glad to keep my eye on him," answers Lorna.

Joe is ready to go now. But he is not ready to have Siggie
drive him to the station. Siggie, insists Anna, is "drunk as a
horsefly," and is quite content to follow Anna to bed.

Now Mr. Bonaparte has brought out a violin case from its
hiding place in the buffet. He hands it to Joe with some little
hesitancy shading his pride.

"Joe, I buy you this some time ago," explains Mr. Bonaparte.
"Don't give cause I don't know whatta you gonna do. Take him
with you now. Play for yourself. It gonna remember you your
old days of musical life."

Joe has put down his suitcase and taken up the violin. "He
plucks the strings; he tightens one of them. In spite of the ten-
sion his face turns soft and tender."

"We better not miss the train," warns Lorna. "Tokio's waiting."

"Take him with you, Joe," suggests Mr. Bonaparte. "Practice
on the road—"

Abruptly Joe turns and leaves the room with the violin. Presently the strains of rich violin music comes from the next room.
A few melodious strains, a familiar chord or two. Then Joe is
back. He lays the violin down before his father. "Return it,

poppa," he says, in a low voice. And then, as father and son look at each other, Joe adds: "I have to do this, poppa." "Be careful fora your hands," says Mr. Bonaparte.

JOE—Poppa, give me the word—

MR. BONAPARTE—What word?

JOE—Give me the word to go ahead. You're looking at yesterday—I see tomorrow. Maybe you think I ought to spend my whole life here—you and Carp blowing off steam.

MR. BONAPARTE (*holding himself back*)—Oh, Joe, shut your mouth!

JOE—Give me the word to go ahead!

MR. BONAPARTE—Be careful fora your hands!

JOE—I want you to give me the word!

MR. BONAPARTE (*crying out*)—No! No word! You gonna fight? All right! Okay! But I don't gonna give no word! No!

JOE—That's how you feel?

MR. BONAPARTE—That'sa how I feel! (MR. BONAPARTE'S *voice breaks and there is nothing for father and son to do but to clutch each other in a hasty embrace. Finally* MR. BONAPARTE *disentangles himself and turns away.* JOE *abruptly grabs up his suitcase and exits.* LORNA *follows, stopping at the door to look back at* MR. BONAPARTE. *In the ensuing silence* ANNA *looks at her father and shakes her head.* SIGGIE *suddenly lumbers to his feet and sounds off like a chime.*)

SIGGIE—Gong gong gong gong!

ANNA—Gee, poppa. . . .

SIGGIE—Come to bed, Anna. . . . Anna-banana. . . . (SIGGIE *exits.*)

ANNA—Gee, poppa. . . . (*She touches her father sympathetically.*)

MR. BONAPARTE (*without turning*)—Gone to bed, Anna. . . . (ANNA *slowly exits.* MR. BONAPARTE *now slowly comes back to the table and looks down at the violin.*)

CARP (*seating himself slowly*)—Come, my friend . . . we will have a nice talk on a cultural topic. (*Looking at the violin.*) You'll work around a number of years before you make it up, the price of that fiddle. . . . (MR. BONAPARTE *stands looking down at the violin.*)

CARP (*sadly*)—Yes, my friend, what is man? As Schopenhauer says, and in the last analysis . . .

The lights slowly fade as the curtain falls.

ACT II

Six months have passed. Joe, back from a successful Western tour, is taking his workout in a gymnasium. Roxy, Moody, Lorna and Tokio stand in a corner of the room looking off at the ring as Joe boxes with a sparring partner. They are an admiring quartet. Wonders have happened. Joe is now a real contender. Only once on the tour was he tagged—an unexpected knockout in Philadelphia. But that, Tokio explains, was an accident. As he and Joe were leaving the hotel in Philly they passed a long-haired man with a violin case under his arm. "He's after me," says Joe, "as if it's cops and robbers." And that night in the ring, Tokio explains, he "kept his hands in his pockets."

Eddie Fuseli, "a renowned gambler and gunman" has joined the onlookers. Eddie also likes the Bonaparte boy's exhibition. Eddie would like to buy a piece of Joe, but Moody says no. Eddie is not discouraged.

"I remember this Eddie Fuseli when he came back from the war with a gun," mutters Roxy, when Fuseli has left. "He's still got the gun and he still gives me goose pimples."

Tokio has a bit of news. Joe has bought his Duesenberg. Cost him five grand, second hand. Moody is excited. Why wasn't he told? He is also perturbed. Joe drives like a maniac. He shouldn't do that.

"Our boy can be champ in three easy lessons—Lombardo, Fulton, the Chocolate Drop," predicts Moody. "But we gotta be careful."

Joe comes from his boxing. He is in fine spirits; glad they have been pleased with him. Sure, he bought a Duesenberg. Why not? He might have some fun— He might, agrees Moody, but they gotta be careful—

"If you're vitally interested in my future, prove it!" says Joe. "Get me some fights—fights with contenders, not with dumb-bunny club fighters. Get me some main bouts in the metropolitan area!—"

"For a kid who got kayoed five weeks ago, your mouth is pretty big!"

"That won't happen again. And how about some mention in the press? Twenty-six bouts—no one knows I'm alive. This isn't a vacation for me—it's a profession! I'm staying more than a week. Match me up against real talent. You can't go too fast for me. Don't worry about autos!"

"We can go too fast! You're not so good!"

"Look at the records," grins Joe, as he goes on into his dressing room.

Eddie Fuseli is back, still persistent in his determination to buy in on Joe. Both Moody and Roxy try to dissuade him, but he insists they put his proposition up to Joe himself. Which, a moment later, they do. Joe listens to the Fuseli proposition—

"I'm Eyetalian too—Eyetalian born, but an American citizen," says Fuseli. "I like to buy a piece of you. I don't care for no profit. I could turn it back to—*you* could take my share. But I like a good fighter; I like a good boy who could win the crown. It's the in-ter-rest of my life. It would be a proud thing for me when Bonaparte could win the crown like I think he can."

Fuseli is also sure he can get Joe good matches and good press notices. He knows the way.

"As long as Mr. Fuseli doesn't mix in my private life . . . cut it up anyway you like," says Joe, and goes to keep a date with his "Miss Duesenberg." . . .

Moody is worried. He feels that again he needs Lorna's help. Joe's getting hard to manage, and now's the time everything has to be right. If Moody and Lorna are ever going to realize the story book way of being "happy ever after" Lorna must help. How?

"Go after the boy. Keep him away from his folks. Get him away from the buggies—" suggests Moody.

"How?"

"You know how."

"You expect me to sleep with that boy?"

"I could tear your ears off for a remark like that," storms Moody. "I'm not a bad guy, Lorna," he continues, seductively. "I don't mean anything bad. . . . All right I'm crude—sometimes I'm worried and I'm crude. . . . But, what the hell, my heart's in the right place." Now he has come up behind her and put his arms about her. "Lorna, don't we both want that sun to come up and shine on us? Don't we? Before you know it the summer'll be here. Then it's the winter again, and it's another year again . . . and we're not married yet. See? . . . See what I mean? . . ."

"Yes. . . ."

"That sounds like the girl I used to know." He is beaming but uncertain.

"I see what you mean. . . ."

"You're not still mad?"

"I'm not mad."

Lorna abruptly leaves the room. For a second Moody stands looking after her. Then, with a shake of his head, he mutters: "Boy, I still don't know anything about women. . . ." The lights fade as the curtain falls.

A few nights later Lorna and Joe are sitting on the same bench in the park. It is a serious time for Joe. He is telling Lorna of his love and his need of the love she represents. Lorna has become real to Joe—as his music used to be real. Neither his car nor his career can overshadow his love. What has he gained by developing the ability to knock down anybody his weight? He's not sure he likes it. And he is sure he doesn't like Moody—

"He's a manager! He treats me like a possession!" says Joe. "I'm just a little silver mine for him—he bangs me around with a shovel!"

"He's helped you—"

"No. Tokio's helped me. Why don't you give him up? It's terrible to have just a Tuesday-night girl. Why don't you belong to me every night in the week? Why don't you teach me love? . . . Or am I being a fool?"

"You're not a fool, Joe."

"I want you to be my family, my life— Why don't you do it, Lorna, why?"

"He loves me."

"I love you!"

"Well. . . . Anyway, the early bird got the worm. Anyway I can't give him anguish. I . . . I know what it's like. You shouldn't kick Moody around. He's poor compared to you. You're alive, you've got yourself—I can't feel sorry for you!"

Joe is not satisfied. His pleading grows earnest. Why is Lorna afraid to give Moody up? Why should they start anything they can't finish? Lorna counters. Moody needs her and Joe doesn't. Moody is a kid at forty-two, Joe's a man at twenty-two—

"What did he ever do for you?" Joe demands.

"Would you like to know?" she answers, with some emphasis. "He loved me in a world of enemies, of stags and bulls! . . . and I loved him for that. He picked me up in Friskin's hotel on 39th Street. I was nine weeks behind in rent. I hadn't hit the gutter yet, but I was near. He washed my face and combed my hair. He stiffened the space between my shoulder blades. Misery reached out to misery—"

"And now you're dead."

"I don't know what the hell you're talking about!" she says, savagely.

"Yes, you do. . . ."

Lorna has withdrawn into a silence she tries to make impassive. Joe starts to whistle. She picks up the last note of his tune and goes on. When she stops he takes up where she left off. For a minute it is a sort of whistling duel. Then Lorna speaks.

LORNA (*beginning in a low voice*)—You make me feel too human, Joe. All I want is peace and quiet, not love. I'm a tired old lady, Joe, and I don't mind being what you call "half dead." In fact it's what I like. (*Her voice mounting higher.*) The twice I was in love I took an awful beating and I don't want it again! (*Now half crying.*) I want you to stop it! Don't devil me, Joe. I beg you, don't devil me . . . let me alone. . . . (*She cries softly,* JOE *reaches out and takes her hand; he gives her a handkerchief which she uses.*)

LORNA (*finally*)—That's the third time I cried in my life. . . .

JOE—Now I know you love me.

LORNA (*bitterly*)—Well . . .

JOE—I'll tell Moody.

LORNA—Not yet. Maybe he'd kill you if he knew.

JOE—Maybe.

LORNA—Then Fuseli'd kill him. . . . I guess I'd be left to kill myself. I'll tell him. . . .

JOE—When?

LORNA—Not tonight.

JOE—Swiftly, do it swiftly—

LORNA—Not tonight.

JOE—Everything's easy if you do it swiftly.

LORNA—He went up there tonight with six hundred bucks to bribe her into divorce.

JOE—Oh. . . .

LORNA (*sadly*)—He's a good guy, neat all over—sweet. I'll tell him tomorrow. I'd like a drink.

JOE—Let's drive over the Washington Bridge.

LORNA (*standing*)—No, I'd like a drink.

JOE (*standing and facing her*)—Lorna, when I talk to you . . . something moves in my heart. Gee, it's the beginning of a wonderful life! A man and his girl! A warm living girl who shares your room . . .

LORNA—Take me home with you.

JOE—Yes.

LORNA—But how do I know you love me?

JOE—Lorna . . .

LORNA—How do I know it's true? You'll get to be the champ.
They'll all want you, all the girls! But I don't care! I've been
undersea a long time! When they'd put their hands on me I
used to say, "This isn't it! This isn't what I mean!" It's been
a mysterious world for me! But, Joe, I think you're it! I don't
know why, I think you're it! Take me home with you.

JOE—Lorna!

LORNA—Poor Tom. . . .

JOE—Poor Lorna! (*The rest is embrace and kiss and clutching
each other.*)

The lights fade as the curtain falls.

Next day Lorna is in Moody's office. She is nervous from a
hangover and restless. Moody is inclined to ride her as to her
drinking habits, and to suggest that she should quit her walks
in the park if this is what they do to her. But Lorna is in no
mood for jests. Nor for love making, either.

Moody, on the other hand, would be lighthearted and gay,
given half a chance. He is there to report that his wife has at
last seen the light. The current Mrs. Moody is running around
with a retired brewer and she now wants a divorce. She goes to
Reno in a few months. After which it won't be long before they
—Moody and Lorna—can be married.

Lorna is no more than lightly stirred by the news. She still
feels like a tramp. But it is nice of Moody to want to marry
her after all this time. He's sweet—

Moody has other good news. He has signed Lombardo. In
six weeks Joe will be meeting Lombardo, and then—

"I'm still not sure what he'll show with Lombardo," the manager confesses, a shade of anxiety creeping into his voice. "But
my present worry is this: help me get that kid straight. Did you
speak to him about the driving last night?"

"I didn't see him. . . ."

"It's very important. A Lombardo win clinches everything. In
the fall we ride up to the Chocolate's door and dump him in the
gutter! After that . . . I don't like to exaggerate—but the kid's
primed! And you and I—Lorna baby, we're set. (*Happily.*)
What do you think of that?"

"You draw beautiful pictures," admits Lorna, evasively.

There is a knock at the door. Siggie has come with a message
from Joe's father. Mr. Bonaparte sends back the $200 Joe has
sent him. He wants no part of it.

"I got a father-in-law nothing's nice to him but feeding his horse and giving a laugh and slicing philosophical salami across the table! He's sore because Joe don't come home half the time. As a matter of fact, ain't he suppose to come to sleep no more? The old man's worried."

"That's not my concern," answers Moody.

"I can't see what it's such a worry," agrees Siggie. "A boy gets in the higher brackets—what's the worry? He's got enough clothes now to leave three suits home in the closet. (*Turning to* LORNA.) It won't hurt if he sends me a few passes—tell him I said so."

"Tell Mr. Bonaparte I saw Joe last night. He's fine," says Lorna.

"I'll see you get some passes," adds Moody.

Siggie has gone, leaving Lorna to speculate on what it is about marriage that will make a pair like Siggie and Anna crazy about each other. It's something special, Lorna decides, and perhaps you have to deserve it.

"I thought you didn't see Joe last night," Moody frowns.

"I didn't, but why worry his father," lies Lorna.

Moody is not entirely satisfied. He is not any too well satisfied the way he has seen Joe looking at Lorna lately. "Looking as if he saw the whole island of Manhattan in your face," says Moody. "I don't like it."

Lorna is not interested. It's pretty late to be giving her warnings. She doesn't need warnings. Anyway, love doesn't last—

"Everything I said about Joe—the opposite goes for you," answers Moody, becoming suddenly serious. "Love lasts . . . if you want it to. . . . I want it to last. I need it to last. What the hell's all this struggle to make a living for if not for a woman and a home? I don't kid myself. I know what I need. I need you, Lorna."

"It has to end. . . ."

"What has to end?"

"Everything."

"What're you talking about?"

"I oughta burn. I'm leaving you. . . ."

"That's what you think," says Moody, with a sick smile.

"I mean it," insists Lorna, not too positively.

"I mean it, too," says Moody.

She looks at him steadily and then her mood changes. "You can't take a joke?" she smiles.

"It all depends. . . . I don't like a joke that pushes the blood down in my feet."

She is sympathetic now. She has come to him and put her arms around his neck. And now, his confidence restored, he has embraced her impulsively and kissed her fully and she has accepted the embrace as Joe Bonaparte and Eddie Fuseli walk into the room.

"The first time I walked in here that was going on. It's one long duet around here," says Joe, as Lorna tries to avoid his eyes. Then he changes the subject quickly to that of the Lombardo fight.

Soon they are quarreling, Moody and Joe. Moody doesn't like the way Joe is driving that Duesenberg around. If he's crazy about speed now he'll be crazy about booze and women next. Fuseli doesn't agree. Speeding is Joe's fun—

"Why did you kiss him?" Joe has turned suddenly to Lorna.

"It's about time you shut your mouth and minded your own goddam business," shouts Moody, moving toward them. "Also that you took some orders."

JOE (*suddenly savage*)—Who are you, God?

MOODY—Yes! I'm your maker, you cock-eyed gutter rat! Outa sawdust and spit I made you! I own you—without me you're a blank! Your insolence is gorgeous, but this is the end! I'm a son of a gun! What're you so superior about?

EDDIE—Don't talk so quick, Tom. You don't know. . . .

MOODY—I wouldn't take the crap of this last six eight months from the President himself! Cut me up in little pieces, baby— but not me!

EDDIE (*quietly*)—You could get cut up in little pieces.

MOODY (*retiring in disgust*)—Sisst!

EDDIE—You hear me?

MOODY (*from his desk*)—You wanna manage this boy? Help yourself—do it! I'll sell my piece for half of what it's worth. You wanna buy?

EDDIE—You are a funny man.

MOODY—Gimme twenty thousand and lemme out. Ten, I'll take ten. I got my girl. I don't need crowns or jewels. I take my girl and we go sit by the river and it's everything.

JOE—What girl?

MOODY—I'm not on speaking terms with you! (*To* EDDIE.) Well?

EDDIE—It would be funny if your arms got broke.

JOE—Wait a minute! Lorna loves me and I love her.

MOODY (*after looking from* JOE *to* LORNA *and back*)—Crazy as a bat! (*He laughs.*)

JOE (*frigidly*)—Is it so impossible?

MOODY—About as possible as hell freezes over. (*He and* JOE *simultaneously turn to* LORNA.)

JOE—Tell him. . . .

LORNA (*looking* JOE *in the face*)—I love Tom. Tell him what? (JOE *looks at her intently. Silence.* JOE *turns and quietly exits from the office.* MOODY *shakes his head with a grin.*)

MOODY—Eddie, I take everything back. I was a fool to get sore—that boy's a real nutsy-Fagan! (*He offers his hand.* EDDIE *looks at it and then viciously slaps it down.*)

EDDIE (*repressing a trembling voice*)—I don't like no one to laugh at that boy. You call a boy like that a rat? An educated boy? What is your idea to call him cock-eyed? When you do it in front of me, I say, "Tom don't like himself" . . . for Bonaparte is a good friend to me . . . you're a clever manager for him. That's the only reason I take your slop. Do your business, Tom. (*To* LORNA.) And that goes for you, too! No tricks, Miss Moon!

Fuseli has walked slowly from the room, leaving Moody staring thoughtfully after him. Lorna moves slowly to the couch. She feels, she admits, like she had been shot from a cannon. She's sorry for Joe.

"You like that boy, don't you?" asks Moody.

"I love him, Tom," Lorna answers quietly.

The lights fade out.

Six weeks later Mr. Bonaparte and Siggie are sitting on a bench in a dressing room of the arena just before the Lombardo fight. The room is furnished with a couple of rubbing tables and a short row of lockers. On one of the tables, Pepper White, a fighter, his hands already bandaged, is being rubbed down by his trainer-manager. From the near distance the roar of the crowd can be heard. There are nine thousand in that crowd, according to Pepper White. . . .

Eddie Fuseli is in, looking for Joe and a little peeved to hear that Moody has Joe upstairs talking to the sports writers. A hell of a thing to be doing, according to Fuseli, just before a fight. Eddie doesn't want Joe to have anything on his mind but the fight. The sight of Siggie and Joe's father waiting adds to his irritation. If they are still there when he gets back Eddie intimates that he will be even more irritated. Siggie decides to go.

Mr. Bonaparte, however, has come to see Joe. He will wait, Fuseli or no Fuseli. When Lorna arrives a moment later, Mr. Bonaparte explains that he has come to see Joe fight. He knows now there is no stopping Joe.

"He gotta a wild wolf inside—eat him up," admits Mr. Bonaparte.

"You could build a city with his ambition to be somebody," smiles Lorna.

"No . . . burn down!" the old gentleman answers cryptically.

There is a distant clang of a bell. A few seconds later Joe comes through the door, followed by Moody. He stops short at sight of "the last two persons in the world he wants to see now." His hands are bandaged and a bathrobe hangs from his shoulders.

Joe's greeting of his father is friendly, but he has no word for Lorna. Girls should be thrown out. This isn't a hotel bedroom, he says. When Moody protests Joe repeats that he doesn't want any girls there. To save the situation Lorna quietly walks out.

Joe is nervous and touchy. He doesn't want any more newspaper interviews before a fight, either. When Pepper White, passing the group, pauses to suggest that he be given a chance at Napoleon, and intimates that up to now Moody has been picking setups for his boy, Joe is at him like a shot. Tokio barely has time to get between them before they reach each other. "Save it for the ring," cautions Tokio.

"You think he'll be the champ?" sneers Pepper. "Where'd you ever read about a cockeyed champ?"

Before they can stop him Joe has dashed across the room and the next second Pepper White is sprawling on the floor. Now Pepper's trainer has started for Joe and Tokio for the trainer. Pepper gets to his feet and finds himself facing Moody. It might have been a good general fight if Eddie Fuseli hadn't come in at the moment. At sight of Eddie everybody is magically calmed down.

"I'm lookin' for you," says Eddie, turning on Moody. "You're a manager and a half! You and your fat friend! (*Meaning* Roxy.) You think this boy is a toy?"

"Eddie's the only one here who understands me," declares Joe.

"Who the hell wantsa understand you?" shouts the enraged Moody. "I got one wish—for Lombardo to give you the business! The quicker he taps you off tonight, the better! You gotta be took down a dozen pegs! I'm versus you! Completely versus!"

"Moody, your brains is in your feet," interjects Fuseli. "This is how you handle a coming champ, to give him the jitters before a bout? Go out and take some air! . . ."

Noting the steady look in Fuseli's eyes Moody and Roxy sullenly sneak out of the room. A few more words of advice to Joe and Fuseli has also left. The silence is intensified by the distant clang of the bell. Suddenly Joe is conscious of his father, sitting quietly on the bench.

"How is Anna, poppa?" he asks.

"Fine."

JOE—Siggie watching the fights?

MR. BONAPARTE—Yes. . . .

JOE—You look fine. . . .

MR. BONAPARTE—Yes, feela good. . . .

JOE—Why did you send that money back? (*There is no answer.*) Why did you come here? . . . You sit there like my conscience. . . .

MR. BONAPARTE—Why you say so?

JOE—Poppa, I have to fight, no matter what you say or think! This is my profession! I'm out for fame and fortune, not to be different or artistic! I don't intend to be ashamed of my life!

MR. BONAPARTE (*standing up*)—Yeah, I understanda you. . . .

JOE—Go out and watch the fights.

MR. BONAPARTE (*somberly*)—Yeah . . . you fight. Now I know . . . isa too late for music. The men musta be free an' happy for music . . . not likea you. Now I see whatta you are . . . I givea you every word to fight . . . I sorry for you. . . . (*Silence. The distant roar of the crowd climbs up and falls down; the bell clangs again.*)

TOKIO (*gently*)—I'll have to ask you to leave, Mr. Bonaparte. . . .

MR. BONAPARTE (*holding back his tears*)—Joe . . . I hopea you win every fight.

The roar of the crowd swells for a second as Mr. Bonaparte opens the door and closes it after him. Tokio turns to the final preparations for the fight. There are still five minutes left for a last tuning up. Joe stretches out on the table and Tokio's busy hands start up the back of his legs.

"I never worried less about a boy . . . in my life," chirps Tokio. "You're a real sweetheart. . . ."

Suddenly Joe begins to cry. His body is shaken, Tokio notices, but goes on with his work. "You're getting good, honey," continues Tokio as the massaging goes on. "Maybe I never told you that before. It seems to happen sudden—a fighter gets good. He gets easy and graceful. He learns how to save himself—no energy wasted . . . he slips and slides—he travels with the punch. . . . Oh, sure, I like the way you're shaping up."

"He needs a straight punch," says Joe. Sitting up, his legs dangling from the side of the table, he goes on, as though speaking partly to himself. "Now I'm alone. They're all against me —Moody, the girl . . . you're my family now, Tokio—you and Eddie! I'll show them all—nobody stands in my way! My father's had his hand on me for years. No more. No more for her either—she had her chance! When a bullet sings through the air it has no past—only a future—like me! Nobody, nothing stands in my way!"

Joe has jumped down from the table and is shadow boxing around the room. "I'm a new boy tonight. I could take two Lombardos." He raises one bandaged hand exultantly above his head. "Hallelujah! We're on the Millionaire Express tonight! Nobody gets me!"

The call has come for Bonaparte. Pepper White and Mickey, his trainer, come in as Joe and Tokio are going out.

"Tell me when you want it," sneers White; "you can have it the way I just give it to Pulaski."

Joe looks Pepper steadily in the eye, flexes his hands and bursts out laughing. The astonished Pepper is still wondering why the laughter as Joe and Tokio leave him. Then his thoughts turn to other things. He wants to grab a cab for Flushing, and to Flushing he will go despite Mickey's warnings that he had better "keep away from her."

"Her husband is an excitable Armenian from the Orient," Mickey reminds Pepper. "There will be hell to pay! Keep away from her!" But there is no dissuading Pepper.

The fighter is on his way to his locker when Mr. Bonaparte comes in. Joe's father has been watching the fighting and doesn't like it. It is, he thinks, terrible, that the boys should be fighting for money. If they fought for a cause, or even a woman, it wouldn't be so bad. But for money—

The roar of the crowd "mounts up to a devilish shriek." It means, laughs Pepper, that Joie Bonaparte is getting a schlocking. It means, counters Mr. Bonaparte, confidently, that Joe is winning. But what difference does it make who wins? It's terrible anyway!

Now Mr. Bonaparte is fascinated by Pepper White's hands.

What happens to a fighter's hands? Do they ever break? Pepper offers an exhibit. His hands aren't broke—they're flat. All the knuckles pushed down. Hurt! A fighter gets used to it. Mr. Bonaparte touches the hands—

"So strong, so hard," he mutters. And again: "So strong . . . So useless. . . ."

He is trembling as the roar of the crowd comes through from the arena. It is the call for a kill. Mr. Bonaparte shudders. He wanders nervously about the room. There is a repeated clanging of the bell. The roar of the crowd "is heated, demanding and hateful." In sudden wrath Mr. Bonaparte jumps to his feet and shakes an angry fist in the direction of the ring—

A Pepper White second has come to get Pepper's clothes. Mr. Bonaparte stops him. How goes the fight, he asks.

"Knockout!" the second answers, laconically. "Lombardo's stiff!"

Now the outside door has been flung open and in troop Joe, Tokio, Moody and Roxy. All save Joe are in a great state of excitement. Joe's face is hard and flushed. Roxy is all but dancing.

"My boy! My dear, darling boy!" Roxy is yelling. "How do you like it, Tom? He knocks him out in two rounds!"

Moody (*stiffly, to* Joe)—It's good business to call the sports writers in—

Roxy—That's right, give a statement! (Moody *gives* Joe *a rapid glance and hurriedly exits.*)

Roxy—I'm collecting a bet on you. All my faith and patience is rewarded. (*As he opens the door he almost knocks over* Eddie Fuseli.) Haha! How do you like it, Eddie? Haha! (*He exits.* Eddie Fuseli *closes the door and stands with his back to it.* Tokio *moves up to* Joe *and begins to remove a glove.*)

Tokio (*gently*)—You're a real sweetheart . . . (Tokio *removes the sweaty glove and begins to fumble with the lace of the other one.* Joe *carefully moves this glove out of* Tokio's *reach, resting it on his opposite arm.*)

Joe (*almost proudly*)—Better cut it off. . . . (Mr. Bonaparte *is watching tensely.* Eddie *watches from the door.*)

Tokio—. . . Broke? . . .

Joe (*holding the hand out proudly*)—Yes, it's broke . . . (Tokio *slowly reaches for a knife. He begins carefully to cut the glove.*)

Joe—Hallelujah!! It's the beginning of the world! (Mr.

BONAPARTE, *lips compressed, slowly turns his head away.* EDDIE *watches with inner excitement and pleasure;* JOE *has become a fighter.* TOKIO *continues with his work.* JOE *begins to laugh loudly, victoriously, exultantly—with a deep thrill of satisfaction.*)

The lights slowly fade out.

ACT III

Again six months have elapsed. Gathered in Moody's office are Joe, Moody, Roxy, Tokio and two sports writers, Drake and Lewis. Joe is sitting on Moody's desk, eating a sandwich. "His success has added a certain bellicosity to his attitude; it has changed his clothing to silk shirts and custom-made suits."

The talk is of the next night's fight, when Joe is to take on the Baltimore Chocolate Drop. Of the two newspaper men Lewis is the friendlier. Drake is plainly irritated by Joe's conceit, and says so.

"Listen, Drake," says Joe, getting down from the desk and facing his critic; "I'm not the boy I used to be—the honeymoon's over. I don't blush and stammer these days. Bonaparte goes in and slugs with the best. In the bargain his brain is *better* than the best. That's the truth; why deny it?"

"The last time you met Chocolate you never even touched him!"

"It's almost two years since I 'never even touched him.' Now I know how!"

"What Joe means to say—" Moody would put in a word.

"He's the genuine and only modest cock-eyed wonder!"

"What good is modesty?" demands Joe. "I'm a fighter! The whole essence of prizefighting is immodesty! 'I'm better than you are—I'll prove it by breaking your face in!' What do you expect? A conscience and a meek smile? I don't believe that bull the meek'll inherit the earth!"

Moody would take Drake and Lewis across the street to buy them drinks, but he does not get them out before Lewis has spilled a small dish of beans by asking Moody when he is going to marry his "big blonde." Joe hadn't known about the wedding. He is a little startled when Moody confirms the date as Sunday. A moment later Joe has pinned Tokio down for the facts. Moody has had his divorce for several weeks. He and Lorna are to be married Sunday.

"Why don't you forget Lorna?" Tokio wants to know. Joe

does not answer. "I'll say it again. . . . Why don't you forget Lorna?" Still no answer. "Joe, you're loaded with love," Tokio goes on. "Find something to give it to. Your heart ain't in fighting . . . your *hate* is. But a man with hate and nothing else . . . he's half a man . . . and half a man . . . is no man. Find something to love, or someone. Am I stepping on your toes?"

"I won't be unhappy if you mind your business," Joe answers, shortly.

Tokio, going out, passes Lorna coming in. She has a pack of newspapers under her arm. The situation is a little strained. Joe and Lorna do not know what to say to each other. She puts the papers down and searches through the desk for a pair of scissors. She is, she says, clipping items on Bonaparte for the press book.

Now Joe has turned suddenly, grabbed the papers from her and stands facing her.

"When I speak to you, look at me!" he shouts.

"What would you like to say?"

JOE—Marry anyone you like!

LORNA—Thanks for permission!

JOE—Queen Lorna, the tramp of Newark!

LORNA—You haven't spoken to me for months. Why break your silence?

JOE—You're a historical character for me—dead and buried!

LORNA—Then everything's simple; go about your business.

JOE—Moody's right for you—perfect—the mating of zero and zero!

LORNA—I'm not sorry to marry Tom—

JOE (*scornfully*)—That's from the etiquette book—page twelve: "When you marry a man say you like it!"

LORNA—I know I could do worse when I look at you. When did you look in the mirror last? Getting to be a killer! You're getting to be like Fuseli! You're not the boy I cared about, not you. You murdered that boy with the generous face— God knows where you hid the body! I don't know you.

JOE—I suppose I never kissed your mouth—

LORNA—What do you want from me? Revenge? Sorry—we're all out of revenge today!

JOE—I wouldn't look at you twice if they hung you naked from a Christmas tree!

Eddie Fuseli comes through the door. He carries two boxes. One is Joe's new headgear. The other a box of shirts, a gift for

Joe, who is far from cordial. He isn't interested in Eddie. Or his shirts. Or his bets. Eddie is giving four to five on Joe and has got eighteen grand spread with the brokers.

"Suppose Bonaparte loses?" suggests Joe.

"I look at the proposition from all sides—I know he'll win," says Eddie.

JOE—What the hell do you think I am? A machine? Maybe I'm lonely, maybe—

EDDIE—You wanna walk in a parade? Everybody's lonely. Get the money and you're not so lonely.

JOE—I want some personal life.

EDDIE—I give Bonaparte a good personal life. I got loyalty to his cause. . . .

JOE—You use me like a gun! Your loyalty's to keep me oiled and polished!

EDDIE—A year ago Bonaparte was a rookie with a two-pants suit. Now he wears the best, eats the best, sleeps the best. He walks down the street respected—the golden boy! They howl their heads off when Bonaparte steps in the ring . . . and I done it for him!

JOE—There are other things. . . .

EDDIE—There's no other things! Don't think so much—it could make you very sick! You're in this up to your neck. You owe me a lot—I don't like you to forget. You better be on your toes when you step in that ring tomorrow night. (EDDIE *turns and begins to dial the telephone.*)

JOE—Your loyalty makes me shiver. (JOE *starts for the door.*)

EDDIE—Take the shirts.

JOE—What do I want them for? I can only wear one at a time. . . . (EDDIE *speaks into the phone.*)

EDDIE—Meyer? . . . Fuseli is speaking. . . . I'm giving four to five on Bonaparte tomorrow. . . . Two? . . . Yeah. . . . (*About to exit,* JOE *stands at the door and watches* EDDIE *as he calmly begins to dial the phone again. The lights fade.*)

It is the next night. We are back in the dressing room at the arena. There is the same clang of the bell at intervals, the same roar of the crowd. There is no one there until Lorna Moon comes quickly through the door. Lorna is nervous. She lights a cigarette. She rouges her lips. She is nervously puffing her cigarette when Eddie Fuseli comes through the door. Eddie is pale and tense. The sight of Lorna stops him short. For a second they stare at each other. Then Eddie speaks, jerkily, tensely.

He would have Lorna leave town. Either leave town or go to Joe. It isn't a suggestion, it is a command. If it hadn't been for Joe they would have found her in a barrel long before this, Eddie tells her; in the river or a bush—

"I'm not afraid of you . . ." says Lorna. There is the clang of the bell.

"That's the beginning of the eighth," reports Eddie. "Bonaparte's unsettled—fighting like a drunken sailor. He can't win no more, unless he knocks the Chocolate out. . . ."

"Don't look at me . . . what'd you . . . I . . ."

"Get outa town!" The roar of the crowd has mounted to a demand for a kill. "He's like a bum tonight . . . and a bum done it!" The roar grows fuller. "I can't watch him get slaughtered. . . ."

"I couldn't watch it myself . . ." echoes Lorna.

The bell clangs loudly. "The roar of the crowd hangs high in the air." Fuseli, accepting it as the end, has turned savagely on Lorna.

"Get outa my sight!" he yells. "You turned down the sweetest boy who ever walked in shoes! You turned him down, the golden boy, that king among the juven-niles! He gave you his hand—you spit in his face! You led him on like Gertie's whore! You sold him down the river! And now you got the nerve to stand here, to wait and see him bleeding from the mouth!—"

Fuseli is still shrieking his wrath. He has half pulled his gun from its holster under his left arm, when Joe appears in the doorway. Moody, Roxy and one of Joe's seconds are back of him. Again Roxy is the bearer of glad tidings. He lifts Joe's arm in the sign of victory. "The monarch of the masses!" proclaims Roxy.

Joe is very tired. "There is a high puff under one eye; the other is completely closed. His body is stained with angry splotches." Roxy has taken up his excited recital for Eddie's benefit—

"The beginning of the eighth: First the bell! Next the Chocolate Drop comes out like a waltz clog, confident. Oh, he was so confident! Haha! The next thing I know the Chocolate's on the floor, the referee lifts our arm, we got on our bathrobe and we're here in the dressing room! How do you like it?"

"I like it," says Eddie.

Joe is sitting on a table. He recalls the fight. It was a straight right that did the work—"with no trimmings or apologies. . . . I gave him the fury of a lifetime in that final punch!"

He, too, is excited now. He can see what the papers will say about the cock-eyed wonder— "He comes from behind in the eighth stanza to slaughter the Chocolate Drop and clinch a bout with the champ!" He is ready now to go outside his weight and beat up the whole damned world!

A bustling little Irishman named Driscoll has pushed his way into the room. He wants to see the happy boy's gloves. He examines them carefully. It looks, he reports, as though the Pride of Baltimore was out for good. And Driscoll means *out*. Joe had better change his clothes.

Slowly, as the facts become known, the situation grows tense. Joe sinks weakly to a bench. Tokio would comfort him. Joe's a clean fighter. He didn't foul the Chocolate Drop. Anything that's happened is an accident—

Barker, the Chocolate Drop's manager, breaks through the crowd. He is "bereft of his senses," hysterical with grief and excitement.

"You murdered my boy! He's dead! You killed him!" shouts Barker, grabbing Moody by the coat lapel. He starts for Joe but Tokio stops him. Tokio and Eddie. Eddie would slug the unhappy Barker out of the room, but Joe stops him. And now Barker is weeping and stammering that he knows that accidents can happen. Suddenly he dashes, weeping, from the room.

"It's in the hands of God, a thing like that," solemnly concludes Roxy.

Eddie Fuseli has cleared the room of everybody except Lorna and Joe. He would send Lorna out, too, but she refuses to go. Lorna would stay and comfort Joe, and Eddie lets her stay.

"It wasn't your fault. You didn't mean it!" says Lorna.

"That's right—I didn't mean it!" Joe finds some comfort in the thought. "I wouldn't want to do that, would I? Everybody knows I wouldn't want to kill a man. Lorna, you know it!"

JOE—But I *did* it! That's the thing—I *did* it! What will my father say when he hears I murdered a man? Lorna, I see what I did. I murdered myself, too. I've been running around in circles. Now I'm smashed! That's the truth. Yes, I was a real sparrow, and I wanted to be a fake eagle! But now I'm hung up by my finger tips—I'm no good—my feet are off the earth!

LORNA (*in a sudden burst, going to* JOE)—Joe, I love you! We love each other. Need each other!

JOE—Lorna, darling, I see what's happened!

LORNA—You wanted to conquer the world—

JOE—Yes—

LORNA—But it's not the kings and dictators who do it—it's that kid in the park—

JOE—Yes, that boy who might have said, "I have myself; I am what I want to be!"

LORNA—And now, tonight, here, this minute—finding yourself again—that's what makes you a champ. Don't you see that?

JOE—Yes, Lorna—yes!

LORNA—It isn't too late to tell the world good evening again!

JOE—With what? These fists?

LORNA—Give up the fighting business!

JOE—Tonight!

LORNA—Yes, and go back to your music—

JOE—But my hands are ruined. I'll never play again! What's left, Lorna? Half a man, nothing, useless. . . .

LORNA—No, *we're* left! Two together! We have each other! Somewhere there must be happy boys and girls who can teach us the way of life! We'll find some city where poverty's no shame—where music is no crime!—where there's no war in the streets—where a man is glad to be himself, to live and make his woman herself!

JOE—No more fighting, but where do we go?

LORNA—Tonight? Joe, we ride in your car. We speed through the night, across the park, over the Triboro Bridge—

JOE (*taking* LORNA'S *arms in his trembling hands*)—Ride! That's it, we ride—clear my head. We'll drive through the night. When you mow down the night with headlights, nobody gets you! You're on top of the world then—nobody laughs! That's it—speed! We're off the earth—unconnected! We don't have to think!! That's what speed's for, an easy way to live! Lorna, darling, we'll burn up the night! (*He turns and as he begins to throw his street clothes out of his locker the lights fade.*)

That night, after the fight, Eddie Fuseli, Moody, Roxy and Siggie are drinking homemade wine in Mr. Bonaparte's dining room. Mr. Bonaparte is a somewhat detached host, standing at one side of the room looking out of the window. His older son, Frank, with a bandage on his head, a strike souvenir, sits near him.

The wine party is a little bit drunk and very anxious. Moody is at the telephone impatiently trying to locate Lorna. He understood that Joe was to come there—but Mr. Bonaparte reminds him that he had only said Joe *might* come.

It is, insists Siggie, a time for drinking and for celebration. Joe's in the lofty brackets and the Bonaparte family will soon be on the move to better quarters. Siggie's one regret is that there isn't a mortgage to be paid off.

There is no celebrating in the heart of Mr. Bonaparte. His son has killed a man. What's that to celebrate?

"Nobody's fault," protests Moody, huskily. "Everybody's sorry—we give the mother a few bucks. But we got the next champ! Bottoms up!"

"You see how a boy can make a success nowadays?" chirrups Roxy to Mr. Bonaparte.

"Yeah. . . . I see."

"Don't worry, Mr. Bonaparte," adds Moody. "Looka me— take a lesson from me—I'm not worried. I'm getting married tomorrow—*this afternoon!*—I don't know where my girl is, but I'm not worried! What for? We're all in clover up to our necks!"

Eddie Fuseli has been looking at Frank. From his size Frank also ought to make a fighter. But Frank isn't interested. The bandage on his head may be a souvenir of strike activity, but he is content.

"I'm not fooled by a lotta things Joe's fooled by," says Frank. "I don't get autos and custom-made suits. But I get what Joe don't."

"What don't he get?"

"The pleasure of acting as you think! The satisfaction of staying where you belong, being what you are . . . at harmony with millions of others!"

"Harmony? That's music! The family's starting up music again!" laughs Roxy.

"That's right—that's music—" agrees Frank.

Now Moody has grown desperately impatient. He is tired of waiting. And it's no use. Lorna's got a helluva nerve riding around Long Island with Joe—without even asking—

Which gives Eddie an idea. Perhaps Moody would like to sell his part of Joe. Eddie figures to be handling Joe alone after tonight. Joe can hold on to his own 30 per cent, but Eddie will take over the rest. Moody wrathfully declares he'll cling to his contract.

As for that, Mr. Bonaparte thinks probably Joe won't be fighting any more after tonight—

"My boy usta could be great for all men," says Mr. Bonaparte. "Whatta he got now, heh? Pardon me for notta feel so confident in Joe's future. Pardon me fora to be anxious—"

The telephone is ringing. Moody jumps up hopefully. That's Lorna—he's sure. . . . The call is for Mr. Bonaparte. Mr. Bonaparte can't take it. He stands in his place, staring helplessly at the phone. Frank has to answer. The others return to their wine and their arguments.

"Yes?" Frank is saying. "No, this is his son. . . . Yes. . . . Yes. . . . Say it again. . . . Yes. . . ."

"You're a killer! A man tries to do his best—but you're a killer!" Moody is shouting at Fuseli.

"You're all killers!" says Frank, lowering the phone.

MR. BONAPARTE—Frank . . . is it . . . ?

FRANK—I don't know how to tell you, poppa. . . .

MR. BONAPARTE (*hopefully*)—Yes. . . .

FRANK—We'll have to go there—

EDDIE—Go where?

FRANK—Both of them . . . they were killed in a crash—

EDDIE—Who?! What?!

FRANK—They're waiting for identification—Long Island, Babylon.

EDDIE (*moving to* FRANK)—What are you handing me?! (EDDIE, *suddenly knowing the truth, stops in his tracks. The telephone operator signals for the telephone to be replaced. The mechanical clicks call* FRANK *to attention; he slowly replaces the instrument.*)

MOODY—I don't believe that! Do you hear me? I don't believe it—

FRANK—What waste! . . .

MOODY—It's a goddam lie!!

MR. BONAPARTE—What havea you expect? . . .

MOODY (*suddenly weeping*)—Lorna! . . .

MR. BONAPARTE (*standing, his head high*)—Joe. . . . Come, we bringa him home . . . where he belong. . . .

THE CURTAIN FALLS

WHAT A LIFE

A Comedy in Three Acts

By Clifford Goldsmith

GEORGE ABBOTT is one producer of plays who does not consider too seriously the time of season at which a new play should be presented. If the play is good, any time is a good time to him, and many of his greatest successes as a producer have been scored in the late spring. "Room Service," which ran through its first summer, following a late start, and continued also through most of the succeeding year, is a notable example.

"What a Life" also arrived late, being produced at the Biltmore on April 13, 1938. It continued also through the hot weather. Not to take any credit from its author, Clifford Goldsmith, this is a typical Abbott comedy, because it is written and played in the Abbott tradition and with a cast of that uncanny fitness that so frequently distinguishes the Abbott productions.

It is a story of High School life that is basically human and sufficiently plausible to re-create for a majority in every audience a picture of their own schooltime adventures. Its character and scene development are both frankly and effectively theatrical and it provides, in sum total, one of the more satisfying light comedy entertainments of the period. It is Mr. Goldsmith's first play but surely not his last.

The Principal's office in the Central High School is a large, heavy, oak-paneled room. On this bright spring morning sunlight is streaming through the window. There are filing cabinets lining the walls. Doors let into waiting rooms and a faculty room. Through double doors at back glimpses of a corridor may be had, masked by a high, oak screen.

"Over the main door, on a narrow shelf, rests a bust of Washington that is yellow with age and draped with dusty and lifeless American flags. Above this entire ensemble, so to speak, painted on the infirm plaster in letters that are scarcely legible, is the motto: "Enter to Learn—Go Forth to Serve."

Miss Shea, an attractive young woman in her late twenties and inclined to be brusque, is at the phone. She is Secretary to the Principal, Mr. Bradley. Mr. Nelson, a personable young man,

332

"WHAT A LIFE"

Henry: Leave me alone, damn you!
Mr. Patterson: Did you say "damn" to me? Did you?
Mr. Nelson: Leave that boy alone. I said leave him alone!

(*Arthur Pierson, William Mendrek, Ezra Stone, Ruth Matteson, Vaughan Glaser*)

about thirty, is seated at his desk. He is the Assistant Principal.

There is more or less routine activity. Teachers come and go. Most of them are interested in learning how much time they are going to have at Easter. One, Miss Pike, a slightly stringy person, is ready to report the janitor because the building is cold. An excited boy in an autographed sweat shirt has rushed in between classes and without permission in search of the Principal. His name, proclaimed by the shirt, is "Bill," and he has come to see the Principal about something that concerns the reputation of all Central High School.

Bill does not get far. "March right back up and get permission from your home-room teacher," instructs Miss Shea with some severity. "There's a good example of Mr. Bradley's open door policy," she adds, as Bill disappears.

As the room clears it becomes apparent that Mr. Nelson is eager to have a few serious words with Miss Shea. Mr. Nelson is "getting tired of being treated like a lamp post." . . . "You won't let me see you outside; so you're going to talk here. I'm not down to writing letters yet. I want to know what I did, or what I said, or what you think I did—"

"I'd like those reports, if you don't mind," answers Miss Shea, in her best office manner, having caught a glimpse of a Mr. Vecchitto, a ruddy-faced Italian, standing in the door, holding a soiled letter.

Mr. Vecchitto is a parent. He has come to see Mr. Bradley about his girl, Mary, and he is considerably surprised to discover that there is more than one Mary in the school. "Sure, you got two Marys?" queries Mr. Vecchitto from the seat to which Miss Shea has assigned him. "We have two Marys? We have thousands of Marys. We have thousands of everybody here," answers Miss Shea, sharply.

Now Henry Aldrich has appeared in the center doors, looking a bit apprehensive. "He is a boy of 16, his hair neither is nor is not combed. Although his features are not fully defined, he might easily develop into a rather attractive young man."

Henry is carrying a book and is also looking for Mr. Bradley. His study-room teacher has sent him there. What for? "Because of a misunderstanding," explains Henry. "She thought I was causing a disturbance."

"But you weren't, of course?"

"No, ma'am. I was scanning Shakespeare."

"Your name is Henry Aldrich?"

"Yes, ma'am."

"Yes—we're getting to know you," says Miss Shea, glancing through a sheaf of reports. "Mr. Patterson was just speaking about you."

"Mr. Patterson was speaking about me?"

"Take that chair there until Mr. Bradley comes in."

"But I've got a study-class."

"Sit down! (HENRY *wilts*.) And if you think you can do it without any additional disturbance, you may go on with your scanning."

Miss Shea has gone about her duties. Mr. Nelson is quietly watching Henry squirming from one side to the other of his chair. Catching Mr. Nelson's eye Henry becomes suddenly interested in his book. After a moment or two Mr. Nelson strolls over and takes Henry's book. "It's *Hamlet*," volunteers Henry.

"How far are you?"

"I'm up to Scene 1, Act 1," answers Henry, truthfully. "That's where he met his father's ghost. That's where he met him—and that's where I left him."

Henry hasn't any clear idea of why he was asked to read *Hamlet*, unless it is because he wants to get into Princeton.

"What seems to be the trouble, Henry?" inquires Mr. Nelson, kindly.

"I don't know . . . I guess it's just the way I'm built or something," answers Henry. "You know what I mean? You can ask any of my teachers and they'll all tell you the same thing. You know what I mean? I guess some people are just built like that."

"Built like what?"

"Like I. . . . And then there are people who can read a book like that. There's a guy in our class by the name of George Bigelow that can make sense out of anything—just so long as it isn't interesting. Or look at Shakespeare. He was even able to write this."

Barbara Pearson appears in the door. "She is a slender girl, lovely eyes, lovely hair, lovely smile." She has been told upstairs that Mr. Bradley would like to see her during her first free period. Miss Shea, back on the job, asks Barbara to come in and sit down. Has she anything to read? No, she hasn't. "You can have this if you want it?" volunteers Henry, extending his *Hamlet*. But Henry is smartly squelched by Miss Shea.

Barbara selects a book from Mr. Bradley's desk and Henry returns to his scanning. A moment later Mr. Nelson, crossing to file reports, stops behind Henry and taps him on the shoulder.

"I am sorry to interrupt—but—how did you happen to choose Princeton?"

"I don't know," answers Henry. "My folks have been saving up for me to go there ever since I was a kid. They call it my sinking fund."

"Your father went to Princeton?"

"Yes, sir. He was a Phi Beta Kappa, and you know what that means."

"What does it mean?"

"It's an honor you never forget. And if you're the son of one, you don't ever forget it either."

A student named Gertie is in trying to sell Henry a couple of tickets for the spring dance. The room that sells the most tickets gets a five-pound box of chocolates and Gertie is an eager salesman. But Henry hasn't got sixty cents. He doesn't even know whether he can go or not. If he can go he'll buy the tickets from Gertie. That's a promise.

When Miss Shea and Mr. Nelson are out of the room Henry thinks Barbara might help him with his scanning. She could if she knew what "parle" means—"So frowned he once when in an angry parle, he smote the sledded Pollaks on the ice," quotes Henry.

"That certainly explains everything," admits Henry. "It must be something you keep on ice. Maybe it's some kind of a drink. Sure. And 'parle' means parlor. They were sitting around in the parlor drinking these pollaks, and they got tight. Or maybe I better just call it a colloquial expression. Any time you aren't sure about something, just call it a colloquial expression. What can they say?"

"Isn't there a footnote?" asks Barbara, thoroughly enjoying herself.

"There are three footnotes. The darned thing is crawling with footnotes. 'Quarto 1, Quarto 2, Folio 1.' Those quartos probably refer to the number of quarts they had drunk. Just a colloquial expression."

Barbara is now practically in stitches. Henry can't see that he has said anything funny, but her laughter indicates friendliness and he asks her if she wouldn't like to go to the spring dance with him Friday night.

Barbara would love to go with Henry, but someone else has already asked her.

"You couldn't tell whoever it is that you're sorry, but you forgot somebody else had already asked you, could you?"

"Would you like it, if I should do a thing like that to you?"

"But I'm not asking you to do it to me. I'm asking you to do it to whosit. Besides, I *might* have already asked you, mightn't I?"

"I wouldn't enjoy a single dance all evening if I did a thing like that," says Barbara.

"But you aren't going to have such a hot time anyway. Gee whiz, why don't you look at it this way? You've got a perfect right to lead your own life, haven't you? Supposing whosit should get the idea he can always tell you who you can go with and who you can't go with?"

"But I'm not going to marry him, am I?"

"No, but a thing like that has led to marriage. Gee whiz!"

Mr. Bradley has arrived. "He is ~~a large man~~, fairly well-dressed, sallow complexion, small, unimaginative eyes. Every word he speaks has the ring of finality."

Mr. Bradley disposes of Mr. Vecchitto first. He will look up Mary Vecchitto's record, if Mr. Vecchitto will wait in the adjoining room. Henry is next. Henry repeats his teacher's suspicion that he was causing a disturbance—

"Who was causing it?" demands Mr. Bradley.

"That's what gets me, Mr. Bradley," says Henry. "All I know is it wasn't I that was doing it. I mean it wasn't me."

"I hope you are more certain of your conduct than you are of your grammar. You were correct the first time."

"But it wasn't me. I was scanning *Hamlet.*"

It might have been anyone, persists Henry. Even the boy in back of him. But when he is pinned down to this he can't remember the boy's name and the more he thinks of it he doesn't see how it could be. Mr. Bradley will ask Miss Eggleston, Henry's teacher, and Henry can wait in the next room.

Barbara is also asked to wait until Miss Shea can get her record, which leaves Mr. Bradley free to see Miss Wheeler, a teacher with "frowsy hair, ruffles, and all that goes with them. She wears glasses that seem always to be out of focus. She carries a baton." Miss Wheeler is in a state of some excitement. Mr. Bradley is afraid she has more orchestra trouble—

"The last time we raised money for your band, through the combined efforts of three thousand students and the entire faculty, we succeeded in putting on an operetta with a resultant net loss of $300," recalls Mr. Bradley.

But it is the instruments, not the orchestra, that are worrying Miss Wheeler. They have been stolen. At least a dozen of the best brasses. Someone had broken into the storeroom the day before, after school.

"You are quite sure that the instruments were not by any chance misplaced?"

"Mr. Bradley, are you accusing me of having lost the best part of a band?" demands Miss Wheeler, who ruffles easily.

"No—but offhand you wouldn't think you could have the best part of a band stolen and not know who did it."

"It's my theory that those instruments were taken by someone who knew the layout," ventures Miss Wheeler.

"Layout?"

"It's a technical term."

"Well—we lost $300 acquiring the instruments, we lost an entire semester losing the $300, and now we've lost the instruments," says Mr. Bradley. "I want a description of everything that was taken."

It disturbs Miss Wheeler to have Mr. Bradley call police headquarters, but he is firm. "We are going to locate that band, and we are going to locate some of the other things that have been disappearing around here lately. Please get the information as quickly as you can. . . ."

Miss Shea has brought the records Mr. Bradley had asked for. He calls Barbara first. It had been decided at a faculty meeting, he tells her, that the daily assembly exercises should be conducted by the President of the Junior Class rather than by one of the teachers, and Barbara is elected. Barbara is terrified at the thought, especially as she will have Miss Wheeler as a guide and counselor, but she can only protest silently.

George Bigelow has arrived. George is the boy who was sitting back of Henry at the time of the alleged disturbance in Miss Eggleston's room.

"George is broad-shouldered, heavy, dark; obviously the school sheik; perpetual smirk on his face." He salutes Barbara with a familiar "Hi!" and is very confident before Mr. Bradley. Henry has been called and both deny that they were talking at the time alleged.

MR. BRADLEY (*looks at* HENRY)—In other words, I take it you were both deeply engrossed in your *Hamlet*. What Miss Eggleston heard was the ghost of Hamlet's father over in your part of the room.

HENRY—I don't think it could have been that, Mr. Bradley.

MR. BRADLEY—I'm glad you feel as I do.

GEORGE—Maybe I laughed once.

MR. BRADLEY—You laughed once. At something Hamlet said, I suppose. (*Hands* HENRY'S *"Hamlet" to* GEORGE.) Will you read me the passage, please.

GEORGE—That isn't what I was laughing at. I was just laughing at what he was doing. He was drawing a picture.

HENRY—I was drawing a picture?

MR. BRADLEY—Where is the picture, Henry?

HENRY—I don't think I remember where I put it, Mr. Bradley. I guess I must have torn it up or something.

GEORGE—It's right there in your book.

HENRY—In what book?

GEORGE—In this book. What book do you think? (*Takes book from desk, ruffles through pages.*) Here! (*He draws out a folded sheet.*)

HENRY—You gimme that! (*Makes a grab.*)

MR. BRADLEY—Hand it to me! (GEORGE *hands it over,* MR. BRADLEY *opens the paper*—GEORGE *crosses to right center.*) Who drew this?

HENRY—Gee whiz—I guess I must have, sir. . . . I didn't know that it was going to turn out to be Mr. Patterson when I started it, Mr. Bradley. . . . I was just drawing around absent-minded and the first thing I knew it came out as Mr. Patterson . . . And I couldn't find an eraser to change it with.

MR. BRADLEY—What is your home address? (*Writing.*)

HENRY—Are you going to write to my parents, Mr. Bradley?

MR. BRADLEY—This is at least the third time you have had to be sent in here, isn't it?

HENRY—Yes, sir, but not for drawing pictures of Mr. Patterson. I give you my word, Mr. Bradley, I won't cause you any more trouble—if I can help it.

MR. BRADLEY—I am pleased to hear that. (*His pen continues to scratch. He finishes, blots what he has written.*)

MISS SHEA (*entering*)—Mr. Ferguson is on the phone, Mr. Bradley.

MR. BRADLEY—Ask him to hold the wire. (*Folds letter, places it in envelope.*) I wonder whether your mother won't be a trifle upset when you hand her this? (*He licks the envelope with a relish.*)

HENRY—My father will be even more upset.

MR. BRADLEY—Could you do anything else if you were in my position?

HENRY—I think I'd give myself another chance, Mr. Bradley.

You don't understand my parents. Sometimes, even I don't understand them.

MR. BRADLEY—Please retire to that room, until Miss Eggleston comes down.

HENRY—Yes, sir.

Mr. Bradley pauses long enough to take the matter of George Bigelow up with George Bigelow, but there does not appear to be much that he can do about it. George stands on his record, which is good; he has both his basketball and football letters and his marks are good. Mr. Bradley is of the opinion that George's laughing at a boy who could find nothing better to do than draw pictures of his instructors "revealed a rather pronounced weakness somewhere."

When Mr. Bradley has left, Barbara takes up Henry's defense. George Bigelow certainly ought to be ashamed of himself. But George is not ashamed. "I let him off easy," says he. "I didn't even show Pussyfoot the best one he's got in there." With which announcement he has taken up Henry's *Hamlet* and found another paper in it.

"Leave that alone!" commands Barbara, grabbing the paper from him. "Henry Aldrich has enough troubles! Don't you know his father's a graduate of Princeton? He's even a member of Phi Beta Kappa club!"

George can't see that that has anything to do with it. Now he has grabbed the paper back from Barbara, and when she protests he puts his arms about her and starts dancing around to the tune of "Bei Mir Bist Du Schone."

"Let me alone, George Bigelow!" cries Barbara, forcing him away from her and putting a chair between them. "Don't you dare hold me! I hate you! The very idea. . . . Anybody'd think . . . Anybody'd think . . . My goodness! I'd give anything in the world if I hadn't told you I'd go with you."

"Go with me where?"

"To the dance Friday night. . . . I suppose you've forgotten you asked me."

"Oh, that's right. I did ask you to go with me, didn't I?"

"Now I won't go with you!" exclaims the infuriated Barbara. "I suppose you want to go with that Henry Aldrich, I suppose."

"Have I even said who I wanted to go with?"

"Boy, if he wouldn't be the original blind date. Phi Beta Kappa! Some time ask Henry Aldrich what it means to have your father asked to join Kiwanis."

"Yeah?" interjects Henry, appearing suddenly at the door. "It means he wasn't good enough to get into Rotary!"

"Nuts to you, wise guy!"

With this parting shot George disappears waving the purloined picture at Henry.

Henry is pretty excited about the loss of the picture. That one is of Bradley, and it would be just like Bigelow— "What's that guy got against me, anyway?"

"Henry, don't get so upset," cautions Barbara, going to him and putting her hand gently on his arm. "Would you still like to have me go to the dance with you?"

Henry is afraid Barbara's kidding him, but she isn't. She can arrange it, if he would like it. She can break her date, if she wants to. Henry is in a perfect dream by this time—

"Geeze—out of all the guys in the school—" he is muttering, as Miss Shea comes back to warn Barbara that Miss Wheeler is waiting for her. . . .

Miss Eggleston has answered Mr. Bradley's summons. It is, Henry submits, probably in regard to his case.

"Do you have this much difficulty with all your teachers?" Miss Eggleston wants to know.

"That's what gets me," admits Henry. "I don't seem to be able to keep my mind on anything these days. The minute I begin to study something important, I get sleepy."

"What time do you go to bed at night?"

"That's another thing. The only time I'm sleepy is in the day time."

Mr. Bradley is back and ready to dispose of the Henry Aldrich matter. He has, he tells Miss Eggleston, written a letter to Henry's parents. Does Miss Eggleston want Henry to take it home, or doesn't she?

"I'll take it home, Mr. Bradley," promises Henry, quickly. "I'll take it home, even if my mother isn't very well."

"What is the matter with your mother?"

"Nobody knows. She just doesn't seem to be able to eat. In the last two weeks she's lost nearly eleven pounds."

"Is your mother confined to her bed?"

"Well, she isn't exactly confined to it."

"I see. Apparently she is just on the edge of it," suggests Miss Eggleston. . . . "Supposing we take your word that your mother isn't well. Do you think enough of her to assume some of the responsibility a young man of your age should assume?"

"Yes, Miss Eggleston. I'll try not to ever do anything again that could possibly upset her."

"How does it sound to you?" Mr. Bradley asks Miss Eggleston.

"Like the vision of Sir Launfal," admits Miss Eggleston. "I'm sure I don't know what to do. . . ."

Mr. Bradley decides that for the present he will keep the note in the drawer of his desk.

"Mr. Bradley, there is a Mrs. Aldrich out here who would like to see you," announces Miss Shea, coming from the hall.

Now Henry is worried. He doesn't think it can be his mother. And he would like to get away. He has a history exam next day and he hasn't even started to get ready for it. But Mr. Bradley insists he should wait in the next room.

Mrs. Aldrich, a plump woman, enters briskly. She is pleased to know Mr. Bradley and surprised to learn that in so large a school he knows her son. But it is just like Henry not to say anything about that. She is also surprised to learn that Henry has been concerned about her health. She is and has been quite well. It is about Henry that Mrs. Aldrich has come to talk with Mr. Bradley.

"You see, since his father was made President of the Parent-Teachers Association here last week, naturally—"

MR. BRADLEY—Henry's father is the same Mr. Aldrich that was —of course— I wonder why I didn't associate the two.

MRS. ALDRICH—Well, you can understand, with Mr. Aldrich President of the P.T.A. here—well, frankly, Mr. Bradley, we can't have any more reports like this. I don't like it. (*She has taken a report card from her bag and now places it on the desk.*)

MR. BRADLEY—You don't like it. I quite understand. Frankly, I don't like it either. Would you say it was quite normal for a boy who has reached his junior year to want to do nothing in class but draw pictures?

MRS. ALDRICH—If we'd let him he'd waste his time in exactly the same way at home. Mr. Aldrich simply won't permit such nonsense.

MR. BRADLEY (*rises*)—Nor do we have any intention of permitting it. (*Goes to door and throws it open.*) Henry, your mother is here. . . . (HENRY *appears in door.* MRS. ALDRICH *rises.*) She has a few questions she would like to ask you.

HENRY (*enters, looking like two cents*)—Hello, Mother.

MRS. ALDRICH—How often have you been sent in here like this, Henry?

HENRY—Not ever what you could call exactly often, Mother.

Mrs. Aldrich—Are you always going through life blindly, never sensing any of your real responsibilities?

Henry—I like to do some kinds of work.

Mr. Bradley—And right there, I believe, is your son's entire philosophy. Supposing I had never schooled myself to do any real work. Where do you think I would be?

Henry—I don't know, Mr. Bradley.

Mr. Bradley—I wonder whether you appreciate what it means for a student of this school to be placed on probation?

Henry—Yes, Mr. Bradley.

Mrs. Aldrich—Probation?

Mr. Bradley—I am ignoring the fact that you lied to me about your mother's illness. But the next time you show the slightest disregard for the rules of this school, you are through until we say you may return. In case I have not made myself clear, you are now going to this school only with that understanding. When your mother is through with you, you will return to your classes. Good day, Madam. (*Exits.*)

Henry (*after an awkward pause, feels that he must say something*)—Are you going to tell Father?

Mrs. Aldrich—Is that the only thing that worries you?

Henry—It's one of the things.

Mrs. Aldrich—I'm sure I don't know how to punish you, Henry. When I think of all the sacrifices Daddy and I have made for you. It is for you that we do everything—so that you can have everything.

Which reminds Henry that he is going to need money for the Friday night dance. He admits that this is no time to ask for it, but he will need it desperately. "Listen, Mother, couldn't I just have two dollars? A dollar and twenty cents for the tickets, 30 cents for carfare. And 50 cents for incidentals. . . . Anybody's liable to have incidentals."

Henry explains also that Barbara Pearson is going with him, and Barbara is not only the President of the Junior Class, but the girl who wrote the cheer that goes: "Central! Be Gentle! Be Brutal! Be Central!"

Mrs. Aldrich cannot understand Henry's enthusiasm for the author of the cheer, but she will agree to his taking Barbara on one condition: If he will pass his ~~Roman~~ history examination with the highest mark in his class he can have the two dollars. But not otherwise.

Henry is completely crushed by the idea. There isn't any chance of his being highest.

MRS. ALDRICH—Your father was always the highest in all of his history examinations.

HENRY—Maybe he was, but he never had to take the history exam I've got to take. And besides, Joe Cameron and Ruth Goldberg and George Bigelow are always the highest. It's a sort of unwritten law.

MRS. ALDRICH—I'm sorry, Henry, but that is exactly the way things stand. (*She stares at him.*) Where's your necktie?

HENRY (*drags a wrinkled tie from his pocket, knotted in a noose*)—It chokes me!

MRS. ALDRICH—Put it on! (*He slips the whole business over his head and slides the knot up. His mother starts to help him, he pulls away.*)

HENRY—I can fix it! (MRS. ALDRICH *crosses to desk to get her things.*) But don't you see, Mother? I've asked her!

MRS. ALDRICH (*taking her bag and gloves*)—Apparently you don't care enough to make the effort.

HENRY—I'll try to be highest. I'll cram all night. I won't even eat dinner. I'll learn every date that Rome ever had. . . . But if I shouldn't—

MRS. ALDRICH—Then you won't go. If you were to plead with me from now until the dance begins, whether or not you go will depend entirely on you.

HENRY—I'll be the highest. I don't know how I will, but I will.

MRS. ALDRICH—Now you are talking like an Aldrich! (*She leans over to kiss him on the cheek.*)

HENRY (*pulling away from her*)—Aw, Mother! (*He wipes his mouth at just the thought of a kiss.* MRS. ALDRICH *goes out the door.* HENRY *follows to door and then spies the stack of old books on top of file. He inspects the titles as* MISS SHEA *enters.*) You haven't had a Roman history book turned in, have you? Mine disappeared about three weeks ago.

MISS SHEA—Three weeks?

HENRY—I didn't lose it. Somebody stole it. The dirty crook.

MISS SHEA—Why didn't you report it then?

HENRY—I didn't need it then.

Henry starts out, scratching his head, as the curtain falls.

ACT II

It is 10:45 the following morning. In Principal Bradley's room Miss Wheeler has been going over with Barbara the routine of conducting assembly. Barbara is pretty miserable about it and Miss Wheeler quite discouraged.

During this rehearsal a Mr. Ferguson appears. "He is a wiry, deliberate fellow, always chewing gum. He wears a top coat and a soft hat."

Mr. Ferguson is looking for a phone and, finding the phone, is eager to get Police Headquarters. He has no success.

"Miss Shea, I understood Mr. Bradley to say we could have some privacy here," protests the ruffled Miss Wheeler.

"Some day you'll learn that this office is the gateway to the West," replies Miss Shea, continuing into the corridor. Miss Wheeler gives up. She and Barbara will have to work in the auditorium, even if the debating team is there.

Henry appears with a sad tennis racquet. The boy Bill has come back, still looking for Mr. Bradley. Henry would like two things from Bill. First, when did Hannibal cross the Alps? Bill doesn't even know who Hannibal was. Second, would Bill like to buy a tennis racquet for $2. Bill does not.

Miss Shea reappears in disciplinarian mood. What does Henry want? Henry has come to report that Miss Pike's ventilating system doesn't work. And Bill? Bill is still looking for Mr. Bradley. Well, Mr. Bradley is in an important meeting of the faculty.

"I expected it," sighs Bill, starting for the door. "I never will get to see old Pussyfoot."

Miss Shea is quick to stop him. "You may go up to your room and write 'I, William Green, have but one purpose and that is to be a gentleman,' seventy-five times," she orders.

"Seventy-five times?" protests Bill.

"And you may write it in Latin!"

"In Latin? I've got to be a gentleman seventy-five times? In Latin?" Bill is disgusted. . . .

Barbara has noticed Henry's worried look. "Henry, don't you feel well?" she asks, solicitously.

HENRY—I feel terrible. . . . I took an exam this morning. . . . I sat up until nearly two o'clock this morning getting ready for it. . . . I chewed nearly a quarter of a pound of coffee.

BARBARA—You chewed it?

HENRY—I promised my father I wouldn't drink any until I'm twenty-one. He's afraid it will stunt my growth. (*Makes a stroke with racquet, then back hand.*) If I don't drink any he's going to give me two hundred dollars. The only trouble is, I'm not going to live until I'm twenty-one.

BARBARA (*giggles*)—I told my father about you last night, Henry. He says that anybody that has the sense of humor you have must have everybody in stitches all the time. He wants to meet you when you call for me tomorrow night. What's the matter, Henry?

HENRY—It's Hannibal. Hannibal—and my mother.

BARBARA—What's she got to do with it?

HENRY—Well—when she went to school she never had Roman history, so she wants me to make up for what she didn't have.

BARBARA—Do you know, Henry, I think that's one of the sweetest things I've ever heard.

GEORGE (*off stage*)—Well the coach said so. (*Enters, followed by two boys, all carrying stacks of books.*) Look out, half-wit! (*Starts out between* BARBARA *and* HENRY. *The boys continue through.*) Let a gentleman pass.

HENRY—Says who?

GEORGE—Do you know what my father says about anybody that belongs to Phi Beta Kappa? He says they can take their logarithms, but watch them try to take their liquor.

HENRY—Yeah? And says who?

GEORGE—I'd show you if I didn't have my arms full.

HENRY—Go ahead. Put them down. I'll wait for you.

GEORGE—So you want to make something out of it, do you? (*Starts to put the books down.*) Look at him. And he couldn't even make the scrub football team.

BARBARA—Stop it!

HENRY—He's not going to insinuate that my father can't take his liquor. I'd like to see your father sit down with my father some time and see who can take it.

GEORGE—Oh, your old man can't take it standing up, eh? He's got to sit down before he can take it.

BARBARA—Stop it!

GEORGE (*to* BARBARA)—What's he wearing to the dance tomorrow night?

HENRY—What do you mean, what am I wearing?

GEORGE—Didn't you ever hear of a gentleman wearing evening clothes when he takes a girl to a dance?

HENRY—And what are you going to wear, pajamas? (*Boys enter and exit.*)

GEORGE—Pardon me while I go into convulsions. Do you know what I bought yesterday?

HENRY—No, but whatever it was you can be pretty sure it was something pretty wonderful.

GEORGE—I'll tell you what I bought. I bought a tuxedo.

HENRY—What are you going to do, wait on table?

BARBARA—You mean you're going to wear a tuxedo tomorrow night, George?

GEORGE—I'm even having it made to order. If you don't believe it, you can come down with me this afternoon when I have my fitting.

HENRY—What's the matter? Couldn't you find a ready-made one that came with short pants?

GEORGE—Short pants? Short pants? And he doesn't even shave yet!

HENRY—Who doesn't shave?

GEORGE—You don't. (*Starts toward door.*)

HENRY—He thinks he's carrying a stack of plates already!

George's armful of books spills to the floor as he rushes at Henry to make him take back that last crack. Henry has fortified himself by grabbing Mr. Bradley's inkwell and is ready to hurl it when Miss Eggleston appears and the fracas is temporarily ended. Miss Eggleston sets George picking up the scattered books. Henry she will report.

Henry is back to worrying about his history exam. He goes over the questions on the examination paper with Barbara and tries his best to remember some of his answers. "When did Hannibal cross the Alps?" "Who was Marius?" "State the cause of the Mithridatic War," etc. Henry is still pretty vague about the whole business. It is Mr. Nelson's advice that he get out of there and let him (Nelson) tell Mr. Bradley about Miss Pike's broken system. . . .

Mr. Ferguson is still trying to get police headquarters. Also he would like a list of the missing band instruments. As near as Miss Wheeler can recall there were four slide trombones, one tuba, one French horn, two silver cornets, slightly dented—

That's enough for Mr. Ferguson. He has been comparing Miss Wheeler's list with a bit of pasteboard he holds. This, it turns out, is a pawn ticket. Mr. Ferguson had picked it up in the boys' washroom. "Looks like one of your kinds here has a date with the state reformatory," says Ferguson. Miss Wheeler is fluttery with excitement.

Mr. Bradley, followed by an excited Mr. Patterson, comes back to the office. Mr. Patterson is trying to tell Mr. Bradley, with force and gestures, that there are some things for which he will not stand. The history examination was over at 10. At 10:15 Mrs. Aldrich had 'phoned to find out if Henry was highest. "I tell you I refuse to be intimidated by any parent, no matter what he is president of," shouts Mr. Patterson.

Mr. Bradley is obliged to stop Mr. Patterson. When he learns that Mr. Patterson had hung up on Mrs. Aldrich, Mr. Bradley is firm—"You will write her a note of apology—today," he orders. "And you will correct Henry Aldrich's paper with exactly the same care with which you correct all the other papers. You know the rules as well as I do."

"The rules! Do the rules say anything about my posing for a series of portraits? Oh, yes—I've heard about that," continues Mr. Patterson as Mr. Bradley looks at him sharply. "I've got one for you, too. It's a drawing of a whale with glasses. 'Moby Bradley.' You should see it!" Mr. Patterson has turned to Nelson.

"I saw it yesterday," admits Mr. Nelson. "I thought he caught the angle of the glasses rather well."

Mr. Bradley is not pleased. "That will be all, thank you!" he says, as he crumples the drawing and throws it into the waste basket.

"Am I to assume that you're going to let the boy get away with this just because his father—"

"He has already been punished. I've put him on probation. There is nothing more to be said. If he is as hopeless as you make him out, sooner or later he'll hang himself. Until then I don't want to hear his name mentioned in this office."

"All right, Mr. Bradley, I'll correct his paper right now, and I think it will be a pleasure," announces Mr. Patterson, storming out.

Mr. Nelson, left alone with Miss Shea, would take up the matter of her regard for him, but Miss Shea is evasive. She does not quite understand why Mr. Nelson, admitting that he doesn't want to teach, and that he is interested in oil geology, has just turned down a job with Standard Oil in South America. Mr. Nelson has no other explanation than that he wants to wait a little longer. "Sure!　Maybe we'll strike oil in the basement!" suggests Miss Shea, cattily, and Mr. Nelson storms out.

Now it is Barbara Pearson who is in trouble.　Things have piled up on Barbara.　She isn't getting along at all happily trying to read the Bible in assembly, and she is worried about going to the dance Friday night, because it is the first one she actually has ever been to.

"You are worried because you think you won't look your prettiest—and for fear no one will ask you to dance," ventures Miss Shea.

"How did you know?"

"I went to a first dance once.　Not so long ago."

"Was it the unhappiest moment of your life?"

"Oh, much.　I sat out a thousand dances—before I went.　In spite of the fact that I had two invitations."

"Did you have two.　So did I."

"Then I shouldn't worry," says Miss Shea, reassuringly. . . .

Mr. Patterson has come triumphantly back to report on Henry's examination paper.　Now he has that young man about where he wants him.　Henry's paper and that of George Bigelow are practically identical.　To Mr. Patterson that can mean but one thing.　Henry has been cheating.

A moment later Mr. Bradley has taken the matter up with Henry, who is back to repeat that Miss Pike's system still doesn't work.

"I understand you took a history examination this morning," begins Mr. Bradley.

"Yes, sir.　In Roman history," Henry answers promptly.

MR. BRADLEY—Who sat next to you when you took that examination?

HENRY—Well—Harry Wood sat right in front of me.　And Joe Cameron sat on my right side.　And I think it was Marni Davis that sat in back of me.

MR. BRADLEY—And who, may I ask, sat on your left?

HENRY—On my left side?

MR. BRADLEY—You have a left side, haven't you?

HENRY—Yes, sir.　That was—oh—I remember—that was George Bigelow.

MR. BRADLEY—George Bigelow.

HENRY—Yes, sir, George Bigelow.　(*He clears his throat and has quite a time of it.*)

MR. BRADLEY—You didn't by any chance receive any help

from him in this, did you?

HENRY—No, sir. Gee whiz, no.

MR. BRADLEY (*holding a sheet of paper*)—Would you mind if I should ask you a few questions from this examination?

HENRY—No, sir.

MR. BRADLEY—Who was Marius?

HENRY—Marius? . . . Marius? . . . He . . . How do you spell that name, Mr. Bradley?

MR. BRADLEY—I am not asking you how to spell it. I am asking you who he was.

HENRY (*trying to laugh*)—Yes, sir. . . . Ah . . . He wasn't a Roman senator, I know that. . . . He . . . I know—he was an officer and liked to proceed into battle and he liked to fight . . . in wars . . . you know what I mean?

MR. BRADLEY—You are sure he was not a senator?

HENRY—Yes, sir. . . . At least, the Marius I'm thinking of wasn't a senator.

MR. BRADLEY—What was the cause of the first Punic War?

HENRY—Greed and jealousy and the desire for expansion.

MR. BRADLEY—When did Rome fall?

HENRY—Rome fell—Rome fell in 300 A.D.

MR. BRADLEY—I always supposed that it fell in 410 A.D.

HENRY—Oh, sure, that's right, 410 A.D. But she really started to go all to pieces about 300 A.D.—at least that's the way it seems to me.

MR. BRADLEY—Then why did you put 410 on your paper?

HENRY—Did I put 410 on my paper? Well—I guess that's right, then.

MR. BRADLEY—What territory did Rome rule at the height of her power?

HENRY—Does that mean—?

MR. BRADLEY—It means exactly what it says.

HENRY—Well, there was the city of Rome, of course,—and there was— Don't tell me, Mr. Bradley.

MR. BRADLEY (*throwing down the paper*)—I have no intention of telling you!

HENRY—But, gee whiz! I'm all mixed up! I'm not even sure of my own name.

MR. BRADLEY—And you still insist that you received no help?

HENRY—I didn't get any help! I didn't cheat, I tell you. I'm just *mixed up!*

MR. BRADLEY—Will you wait in that room, please?

HENRY—Yes, sir. (*He starts for the door.*) I never was any

good at anything oral, Mr. Bradley, even under favorable circumstances.

Presently George Bigelow arrives and is questioned. And George knows the answers—or most of them. George is sent back to his classes and Henry is called again. With the doors shut he is given a last chance to admit that he had cheated. Henry sticks to his story. Confronted with the fact that certain parts of his paper and George Bigelow's are identical Henry thinks it must have been a coincidence.

"Henry—this is your last chance," says Mr. Bradley, solemnly. "Are you going to admit that you cheated?"

"But I didn't."

"Very well. We'll say no more." Mr. Bradley has gone back to his desk and buzzed for Miss Shea. He takes up Henry's paper and a large red pencil. "We'll give you zero on that one. Zero on that one. Zero. Zero. Zero. Zero on that one. Zero. And a large, round zero for the entire paper."

"I can't take that home. I can't do it! It isn't fair!" protests Henry, hysterically.

Mr. Bradley turns calmly to Miss Shea and begins to dictate a letter to Henry's father and mother: "This is formally to advise you that due to the fact that your son apparently finds it impossible to adjust himself to our routine and to co-operate with his teachers, we are finding it necessary to suspend him from Central High School. He is hereby forbidden to attend any further classes for a period of sixty days."

In the corridor crowds of students are talking and laughing. "Oh, my gosh!" wails the unhappy Henry.

"You will get your hat and coat and leave this building at once," concludes Mr. Bradley, and leaves the room.

Now only Henry and Mr. Nelson are left. The assistant principal is friendly. "You *did* cheat in that examination," he says. Henry shakes his head. "I just wanted you to know—in case you did cheat—that you probably aren't the first fellow who ever did. My suspicion is that quite a few have tried it in their time. In fact—just between ourselves—something tells me that everyone who has ever been to school has tried it at least once. . . . At any rate, all the bright ones have."

HENRY—Did you ever?

MR. NELSON—Of course . . . (*Turns to* HENRY.) Did you think I was one of the stupid ones? . . . I tried it on several occasions. And I got away with it very nicely, thank you. Much more cleverly than someone did in this case.

HENRY—You cheated in an examination?

MR. NELSON—Of course. After all, if you have any salt in your blood you have to try everything once, don't you? The disgrace is in failing to see that what you gain by it isn't that—compared with what you lose.

HENRY—I know cheating's bad.

MR. NELSON—That's just the half of it. Denying it when you're caught is just as bad.

HENRY—Sure.

MR. NELSON—It's stupid.

HENRY—Yeah . . . Well—I cheated.

MR. NELSON— . . . Did you? . . . To be quite honest, I thought you did.

HENRY—I didn't mean to, though . . . I didn't mean to tell you, either.

MR. NELSON—What was the idea?

HENRY—I had to. I couldn't help it.

MR. NELSON—I see. . . . In other words, you saw Bigelow's paper there beside you and the temptation was too great.

HENRY—That's not it . . . I'm an Aldrich.

MR. NELSON—What is it, some sort of a secret order?

HENRY—It isn't really anything. All the other Aldriches have just always led in their classes and I had to be the highest or I couldn't go to the dance tomorrow night. And I'd already asked somebody.

MR. NELSON—Well—when Caesar took Rome, didn't he start something?

HENRY—He certainly ruined my life. . . . (*Pauses and looks at* NELSON.) Have I got to tell Mr. Bradley?

MR. NELSON—What do you think? *I don't know*

HENRY—What would you do?

MR. NELSON—I'll be damned if I know. (*Crosses to door.*)

HENRY (*following* NELSON)—Do you think he might give me another chance?

MR. NELSON—Well, of course that isn't the main consideration —but if I were you, I'd give it some serious thought— Naturally, though, it's up to you.

Gertie and Barbara pass Mr. Nelson as he is going out. Gertie has come to bring Henry his tickets for the dance. But Henry won't be going to the dance and doesn't want the tickets. He says so with something more than necessary emphasis.

"You're a fine one!" snaps Gertie, snatching the tickets out of Henry's hand. "Of all the dirty tricks. I hope some day somebody goes back on you some day, and see how you like it!"

Gertie has flounced out of the room, and as Henry turns to watch her he looks at Barbara.

BARBARA—What's the matter, Henry?

HENRY (*turns and sits*)—It's about my uncle.

BARBARA—Your uncle, Henry?

HENRY—I won't be going to the dance.

BARBARA— . . . Oh!

HENRY—It isn't that I can't go. It isn't anything like that. It's just because I just got word my uncle's dying.

BARBARA—He's dying? . . . What's the matter with your uncle?

HENRY—He's got tuberculosis.

BARBARA—Oh!—It won't be any fun without you at the dance. . . . How did he get sick?

HENRY—That's what nobody seems to know. It just came out of a clear sky. (MISS SHEA *starts in, stops as she sees them, stands in doorway unnoticed.*)

BARBARA—I guess that's the way everything happens when you get right down to it. . . . Only yesterday I went downtown with my mother and bought a brand-new dress for the dance. . . . (*Touches him.*) That's all right, though, Henry. It certainly isn't anything you can help. . . . Where is your uncle?

HENRY—He's out in Denver. . . . The doctor says he may die any minute—and then again—he may live for sixty days. I may have to go out there until he dies.

BARBARA—For sixty days, Henry?

HENRY—. . . But of course, we aren't sure yet.

BARBARA—That's eight weeks . . . I'll be thinking of you tomorrow night, Henry. And I hope your uncle gets better. Good-by.

Henry is too miserable to answer. When Mr. Bradley comes back to his office, Henry goes directly to his desk. "Mr. Bradley, I did get help on my examination," he says. "But I had to. Here's what happened. I wanted to go to the dance tomorrow night."

"You wanted to go to the dance! Well, after thirty years that's a new one. I thought I told you to leave this building."

With a meek "Yes, sir," Henry has turned to go when Mr. Patterson, trembling with anger, comes from the corridor and grabs him. "Leave me alone, damn you!" shouts Henry, pulling away.

"Did you say 'damn' to me? Did you?" Mr. Patterson has slapped Henry's face and is shaking him violently.

"Leave that boy alone!" calls Mr. Nelson, leaping across the room and grabbing Patterson, jerking him around. "I said leave him alone!"

"Take your hands off me! Take 'em off—"

"I ought to put them right through you—you overgrown—"

Mr. Bradley's command that they stop is finally heard. Henry has run through the door, "frightened as he never was before."

There is a crash and a feminine scream outside the door. A second later Mr. Ferguson and Miss Wheeler have come into the room loaded down with band instruments. In an effort to retrieve a dropped cornet Miss Wheeler lets an armful of trombones and a tuba fall to the floor.

"Will you stop throwing those things?" demands Mr. Ferguson.

"Have you found out who stole them?" asks Mr. Bradley.

"Yeah," answers Ferguson, casually. "I want to talk to a kid named Henry Aldrich."

"Oh, my God!" wails Mr. Nelson.

The curtain falls.

ACT III

The recovered band instruments are scattered over Mr. Bradley's office, covering a table, chair and the top of one file. Miss Shea is at her desk, okaying the permits of several girl students. Bill, the persistent, is in again, pleading for a chance to talk with Mr. Bradley, and protesting that, after searching all noon hour, he has been unable to find a Latin word for gentleman. "All they had in those days were soldiers and statesmen," insists Bill.

Now Mr. Ferguson has arrived, both arms filled with an assortment of articles. The only thing recognizable is the racket Henry Aldrich tried to sell. Mr. Ferguson has been through Henry's locker. "Somewhere we're going to find some of the other things that have been disappearing around here," explains the detective. "I always said if you wanted to get some practical knowledge in a school, the place to learn it was down in the washroom. And let me tell you another thing. This younger generation's not half as smart as it gets credit for being. There isn't a poem down there that is as good as the ones we used to write. . . . This younger generation can't even think for itself."

He enlists Miss Shea's help in making a list of his findings. There is a book, three shoes, all for the left foot, the tennis racket, a jar of peanut butter, another book on "How to Shag—in Four Lessons," a raincoat, a rubber, three gloves, a doorbell and an umbrella. Also a picture of a girl named Barbara Pearson torn out of a school paper—

"Now then, make two copies. One for us and one to send to Ripley," instructs Mr. Ferguson. "What I want to know," he adds, "is where the hell did he get all this stuff, and why? This kid goes in for anything, just so long's there's only one of it. I'd say he's got the finest collection of shoes for the left foot to be found."

Barbara Pearson, come to learn if anyone has heard how Henry's uncle is, is followed shortly by Henry himself. Henry is much surprised to find a heap of his stuff in Mr. Bradley's room. It was pretty nice of them to clean out his locker. "I guess they thought I'd be needing some of these things," Henry concludes. "I've got some pretty valuable things here."

"Mr. Bradley sent for my mother and me," Henry explains to Barbara. "We just barely got home and there was a message for us to come right back again. I guess he knows I may be out for sixty days—a long time on account of my—and I suppose he wanted me to get all my assignments. . . ."

The matter of the Vecchitto girl is cleared up. Mr. Vecchitto's daughter Mary is on her way downstairs. "You're the man who makes his daughter work on a junk wagon instead of coming to school, aren't you?" accuses Miss Shea.

"Sure—but joosta Thursday . . . Monday, Dominick; Tuesday, Teresa; Wednesday, Giuseppe; Thursday, Mary—"

"How many children have you?"

"Six—I no work on Sunday." The Vecchitto explanation is quite simple. . . .

Mrs. Aldrich has arrived. Soon a conference is organized that also includes Mr. Bradley, Mr. Nelson, Mr. Ferguson and Henry.

Mr. Bradley introduces Mr. Ferguson to Mrs. Aldrich, who thinks he must be some sort of psychiatrist until she learns that he is from police headquarters. She is visibly shocked to learn of the charge against Henry.

As for Henry, he is vigorous in his denials. He never saw the instruments before except when they were being played. He doesn't know anything about the Fourth Avenue pawnshop. And he has no idea how the instruments could have been registered in the pawnshop under his name.

Mr. Ferguson adds to Henry's confusion by producing a cap left in the pawnshop. That cap also has Henry's name in it. Then Henry signs his name for Mr. Ferguson. The detective studies it carefully, puts it in his pocket without change of expression.

"Are you sure you didn't take them?" Mrs. Aldrich asks again.

"I cross my heart. I never even touched them in my life! How many times have I got to tell you?"

"I think I've heard you say things like that before," Mr. Bradley observes, solemnly.

"I can't believe it! My own boy!" Mrs. Aldrich is in tears. "After all we've done for you. I don't think there's a thing on this earth we wouldn't have done if it could have saved you from this."

Miss Wheeler has burst into the room and made for Mr. Ferguson. She has been looking all over the building for him. Finding him she drags him to the door. After a whispered conversation Ferguson announces that he has something more to do and tells Henry to wait for him. Henry, sobbing bitterly, is sent into the next room.

"The next step?" inquires Mr. Nelson, significantly, when Henry has disappeared.

"What would you do, let the boy remain here and exert his influence on the entire student body?" demands Mr. Bradley.

"Supposing he starts exerting it at reform school. Think of the problems they already have. You know he has one definite talent. Have you seen his latest?" Mr. Nelson produces a paper from his pocket. "A final pot-shot at the whole faculty. We're in an aquarium . . . This is you . . . This is Patterson floating on the surface, upside down. (*Turns paper over.*) And this, of course, is a ship being struck by lightning. He seems to have a mania for lightning."

"He evidently thinks he is the Almighty Himself."

"I hate to see this boy go. Isn't there something we can do to help him?"

"We have no time to help any boy who's a thief, Mr. Nelson," and Mr. Bradley has left the room.

George Bigelow has come for an okay on his absence for half of his honor day. He wants to get his tuxedo fitted. Mr. Nelson okays the slip and leaves. Henry, coming in from the next room, catches George's eye. George has been looking for Henry. Mr. Patterson had advised him to knock Henry's block off, and he is ready to do it.

With threats and counter threats the boys circle the room and are soon in a clinch flailing away at each other. Henry swings with everything he has, including his foot, but George is too strong for him. He is punching Henry in the stomach, demanding a promise that there will be no more cribbing, when Barbara and Mr. Nelson appear. Barbara calls excitedly to the boys to quit. Mr. Nelson separates them by grabbing George by the collar and spinning him around.

"Now tell her you didn't crib," dares George, going out.

"I didn't even feel it . . ." boasts Henry, still doubled up.

"Henry—you didn't really—you didn't really crib—did you . . . ?"

Henry doesn't answer.

"She's asking you whether you cheated, Henry," says Mr. Nelson, quietly.

Henry looks up at Nelson and down again, quickly.

'. . . You did . . . didn't you?" exclaims Barbara and unashamedly begins to cry without even covering her face. She is sobbing freely as she goes out.

Henry is miserable. He has decided now that he will run away. He would have Mr. Nelson tell his mother and father that he is sorry and that they should use his sinking fund to get themselves something they need. Mr. Nelson does not try to hold him. Henry has reached the door. There he turns. "Do you really think I did do it?" he asks.

"I don't know," answers Nelson. "But in any case what's done is done. . . . Whoever told you that you had to go through life apologizing for every move you make?"

HENRY—Apologizing?

MR. NELSON—Listen. There never was a human being who didn't make a few mistakes—perhaps not quite as many as you, but we all make some. And if you get ten percent in an examination that everyone else gets one hundred in, don't deny it! Admit it! You can still be just as good no matter how many dates you don't remember. . . . The trouble with you is, you're ashamed of yourself! I know more history than you ever thought of knowing. But do you know what you can do that I can't do?

HENRY—What?

MR. NELSON—Draw a picture of Mr. Patterson that looks like Mr. Patterson.

HENRY—Is that something to be proud of?

MR. NELSON—You can't believe anything good about yourself, can you? (*Rises.*) I'll bet that if I showed one of your drawings to your girl, you'd deny that you ever did it. . . . You'd tell her that your uncle out in Denver did it. . . . And by the way, how is your uncle?

HENRY—Who told you about him?

MR. NELSON—I know the doctor that's taking care of him. . . . And the joke is still on you.

HENRY—Why?

MR. NELSON—Because I talked with your art teacher yesterday. She says you might just possibly have some talent.

HENRY—For what?

MR. NELSON—See that? It's a damned habit! Now listen—if you could do anything on the face of the earth, what would you like to do as a life job?

HENRY—. . . I don't know.

MR. NELSON—Well, what do you think you'd like to do?

HENRY—I never really thought about it. . . . I guess go to Princeton.

MR. NELSON—Good Lord, you don't consider four years at Princeton a life's work, do you?

HENRY—Not an ideal life's work.

MR. NELSON—If I could fix it with the judge down at the court so that you could spend the next sixty days over at the South Side Trade School, where they have a special course in art, just to see how you like it—what would you think?

HENRY—But my mother—

MR. NELSON—Is it your mother who draws or is it you?

HENRY—There isn't anything I'd rather try. But—

MR. NELSON—Go up and bring your mother down here.

HENRY—You don't know her.

MR. NELSON—Do you want to make a bet that she won't let you go?

HENRY—How much will you bet?

MR. NELSON—Anything you want.

HENRY—I'll bet you two dollars.

MR. NELSON—All right! (*Grabs* HENRY *by arm and heads toward door.*) But get this, if you start apologizing in front of her for being able to draw, I'll finish what George Bigelow started! (*Gives* HENRY *a friendly kick.*)

HENRY—Yes, sir.

The Nelson-Shea interlude is adjusted. Mr. Nelson has his telegram from Standard Oil. He is leaving in June. "The poor school teacher is going to be even poorer," he says. "Three years in Venezuela at $1,200 a year."

"You seem happy about it," observes Miss Shea.

"Well, I'm not happy about leaving you—but you've convinced me it's the best thing to do."

"I might grow to like South America. Or wouldn't you let me go even if I wanted to?"

Before Mr. Nelson has a chance to put his answer into action the pestiferous Bill has burst into the room. This time he refuses to be put off. He's just got to see Mr. Bradley because—

"I know who stole the band!" says Bill.

Now there is excitement. Under Mr. Nelson's questioning Bill explains that he saw the fellows who took the band; that he had been trying for two days to tell Mr. Bradley, but, thanks to Miss Shea, all he got was a chance to write Latin; that he can't describe the thieves accurately, because he was going past them too fast on his bicycle.

Mrs. Aldrich and Henry are back. Mrs. Aldrich is now convinced that Henry's trouble can be traced right back to his tonsils. It is Mr. Nelson's idea that Henry belongs in the South Side Trade School, where he can get an art course—

"Or do you consider the reform school a more satisfactory life's work?" adds Mr. Nelson as Mrs. Aldrich is framing a protest. "There is no other choice. Princeton is out! It was out the day Henry was born!"

At the center door Mr. Ferguson has appeared. He is holding George Bigelow by the arm and they are in the midst of a lively argument.

"You can't handle me like that," George is saying. "I know the law." He is wearing his street pants and a basted tuxedo.

"Not half as well as you're going to know it," Ferguson answers, slapping George and turning him swiftly around. "Thought you could get away with stealing a whole band!"

"You can't prove I did it."

"No? I can't prove your brother has a Packard, either, can I?" He turns to Mr. Nelson. "They took the band down there in it. That guy down at the pawnshop wouldn't give them all cash. They had to take out part of it in merchandise. And what do you think this one takes? A second-hand tuxedo."

"A tuxedo?"

"I found him at the tailor's two doors away."

"*We* found him, Mr. Ferguson. It was my idea, you know," interjects Miss Wheeler.

"Yes, my assistant's. That signature this kid gave me. It wasn't the same as the one down there."

Mr. Ferguson takes George away. Mr. Bradley shakes his head in amazement at the proceedings. Mrs. Aldrich is greatly relieved. Something had told her that Henry didn't do it—

"Sure, I'm the one that told you," Henry reminds her.

Everything will be all right now, Mrs. Aldrich feels. Henry won't have to go to South Side Trade School. He can come right back to Central High after his sixty days are up. But Henry doesn't want to come back. Henry has got to have a try at art.

"Are you deliberately disobeying me, Henry?" demands Mrs. Aldrich.

"I can't always go through life doing what you tell me to," protests Henry. "If you can pick Princeton for me, you can pick my children."

"Henry, what are you talking about?"

"My children. I might have children sometime. And if I ever do, I'm going to let them lead their own lives. Why do I have to be like every other Aldrich? What did they ever do, anyhow? They just remembered a lot of dates. Dad was beaten for City Councilman even on the Republican ticket. Can you name anyone in the family beside me that's ever done anything creative?"

There is a heavy pause as Mrs. Aldrich tries to think of an answer. "We're going to have a very difficult time with your father . . ." She sighs.

"No more than we've always had," cries the overjoyed Henry. "Gosh! I can go!"

Henry is piling his stuff together on top of the raincoat. Mr. Nelson, with a nod from Miss Shea, pretends to be helping him when he finds a couple of tickets to the dance.

"Look here! Did you drop these?"

Henry takes the tickets, looks at them "with amazement and longing," and then makes a momentous decision. "No, sir!"

MR. NELSON—Why, you must have! They were under your things there.

HENRY (*bewildered*)—I dropped them?

Mr. Nelson (*starting away*)—You want to be more careful, Henry . . .

Henry (*still bewildered*)—Yeah . . . thanks very much . . . (Mr. Nelson *is at the door.*) Say,—Mr. Nelson . . .

Mr. Nelson—Yes . . . ?

Henry—Would you mind if I take you out sometime and buy you a milkshake or something?

Mr. Nelson—Not at all, Henry.

Henry (*to* Barbara, *who has come in*)—. . . Hello. . . .

Barbara (*coldly*)—I suppose your uncle's much worse.

Henry (*firmly*)—He died.

Barbara—Oh!

Henry—Of tuberculosis—seven years ago. (*His head is high; he seems to stand a bit taller than we have ever seen him stand before.*) And in case you don't know it, it was because I wanted to take you to the dance. That's why I cheated.

Barbara (*still on her dignity*)—Well, I'm sure I didn't ask you to.

Henry—I didn't say you did . . . it's just . . . I mean . . . well . . . (*Stalled, he digs into his pocket and brings out the two tickets.*) If you'd still care to go . . . I've got the tickets.

Barbara—Where did you get them?

Henry—From a friend.

Barbara—Henry . . .

Henry—It's all set. I've got the tickets; we don't have to worry about incidentals; and the carfare is only thirty cents. (*Pause.*) Can you lend me thirty cents?

THE CURTAIN FALLS

THE PLAYS AND THEIR AUTHORS

"Of Mice and Men," a drama in three acts by John Steinbeck. Copyright, 1937, by the author. Copyright and published, 1938, by Covici-Friede, New York.

John Ernest Steinbeck (who doesn't often use the Ernest) was born 36 years ago in the same Salinas Valley, California, that is the scene of his play. "Of Mice and Men" was first written as a novel, but the author confesses that he was a little tricky in that when he wrote the novel he tried to hold it to the form of a skeletonized play, in the hope that eventually it would reach the stage, and that the transfer could be accomplished with comparative ease. That is what happened. George S. Kaufman, who made the transfer, insists that he merely lifted the book's story, filled in the descriptions with scenery, and found the play complete. Through with public schools young Steinbeck took to Stanford University, but not too seriously. He wanted to learn certain things, but he had no intention of cramming for a degree, and never tried for one. He did try free lance writing in New York, but was pretty disgusted with the attitude of editors and went back to California. His first three novels were "Cup of Gold," "Pictures of Heaven" and "To a God Unknown." His fourth, "Tortilla Flat," was his first big success. "Of Mice and Men" followed and clinched that success. Mr. Steinbeck is married, and has a home in Los Gatos, California.

"Our Town," a drama in three acts by Thornton Wilder. Copyright, 1937, by the author. Copyright and published, 1938, by Coward-McCann, Inc., New York.

Thornton Niven Wilder might have been a New Englander by birth as well as inclination if his father, Amos Porter Wilder, had not taken over the editorship of a newspaper in Madison, Wis., about the time of Thornton's arrival. As a result of that move Mr. Wilder belongs to the Middle West, having been born in Madison, Wis., in April, 1897. Shortly after that the paternal Wilder was sent to China as an American Consul General, and it was in China that young Wilder spent his youth. Sent back to America for his schooling he attended high school in Berkeley, Calif., and was afterward a student at the Thacher School in Ojai, Calif. From there to Oberlin, and from Oberlin to Yale, where he won his A.B. He studied for two years at the American Academy in Rome and took his A.M. at Princeton after his return in 1925. His interest has always been centered in writing for the stage. His first play was called "The Trumpet Shall Sound," but after seeing it produced at the Laboratory Theatre in New York in 1926 Prof. Wilder decided to write novels instead. His *Bridge of San Luis Rey* won the Pulitzer award for American novels in 1927. He followed with *The Woman of Andros* and *Heaven Is My Destination* and then turned again to the theatre. Katharine Cornell produced his adaptation of Obey's "Lucrece" in 1932. "Our Town" is his first full-length original drama to reach the stage. It proved one of the outstanding successes of the New York season and was awarded the Pulitzer prize in the spring of 1938 as being the best play by an American author to have been produced the previous season.

"Shadow and Substance," drama by Paul Vincent Carroll. Copyright, 1937, by the author. Copyright and published, 1937, by Random House, Inc., New York.

Paul Vincent Carroll, who was awarded a scroll by the New York Drama Critics' Circle as the author of the most distinguished drama to be imported to America last season, is a modest teacher of 10-year-old boys in a Glasgow, Scotland, school. He was born, however, on the outskirts of Dundalk, County Louth, Ireland, in 1900, and lived there until he was 14. His father, a country schoolteacher, saw personally to his son's early education. At 14 young Carroll departed for Dublin to enter training as a teacher. In Dublin he found the Abbey Theatre and has been a little stage struck ever since. In 1920 he was back in Dundalk, but not very happy. He had been eye witness to the fighting and the tragedies out of which the Irish Republic was born. His father had advised him to go to Great Britain so, boylike, he decided on Scotland. In Glasgow in 1921 he got a job teaching school and has been there ever since. "Soon after landing in Scotland I saw Ireland in a new perspective," Mr. Carroll has written. "I began writing plays for the Abbey directors, who sent them back and pelted me with invectives. And, believe me, I needed it." He had his first play, "The Watched Pot," tried out in 1931. In 1932 he and Teresa Deevey shared an Abbey prize with "Things That Are Caesar's," and in 1934 he wrote "Shadow and Substance." It was produced at the Abbey; reports of its excellence were buzzed over the cables; Richard Madden, play agent, sold the American rights to Eddie Dowling, and, after some weeks of preparation, the little Glasgow schoolteacher found himself in receipt of two incomes—$1,000 a week royalty for his play in New York, $37.50 a week for teaching his 10-year-olds in Glasgow. Mr. Carroll came to America during the winter to see his play. He spent a glamorous month in research and sightseeing and then returned to Glasgow and his old job.

"On Borrowed Time," a comedy in three acts by Paul Osborn, taken from a novel by Lawrence Edward Watkin. Copyright, 1937, by the authors. Copyright and published, 1938, by Alfred A. Knopf, New York.

Paul Osborn really began his career as a playwright as far back as the season of 1928-29, when Brock Pemberton produced a comedy of his called "Hotbed." This had to do with morals and a co-ed institution of learning. It was accepted professionally as a promising first play and was withdrawn after nineteen performances. Mr. Osborn, being persistent, came forward with two other plays, "A Ledge," and "Oliver Oliver," and these also failed. But in 1930 he struck box office oil with "The Vinegar Tree," helped considerably by Mary Boland, who was immensely amusing in the chief role, that of a flighty matron who laid great store by a largely imagined past. "On Borrowed Time" has set Mr. Osborn definitely in the way of further honors. His training has been thorough. He has both an A.B. and an M.A. from the University of Michigan, studied playwriting with George Pierce Baker at Harvard and taught English at his Alma Mater. He has made his home the last ten years in Brattleboro, Vt. He was born in Evansville, Ind., in 1901.

"The Star-Wagon," a comedy in three acts by Maxwell Anderson. Copyright, 1937, by the author. Copyright and published, 1938, by Anderson House, Washington, D. C. Distributed by Dodd, Mead & Co., New York.

Maxwell Anderson continues to be a consistent contributor to the "Best Plays" series, this being his seventh appearance in the twelve years he has been writing plays. He made his début with

Laurence Stallings with "What Price Glory?" in the 1924-25 volume. Other of his plays to be included have been "Elizabeth the Queen," "Mary of Scotland," "Both Your Houses," which won a Pulitzer prize in 1933; "Winterset," which won the Critics' award in 1935, and "High Tor," which duplicated that honor in 1936. Mr. Anderson was born in Atlantic, Pa., fifty years ago, the son of a Baptist minister. Out of college he took to teaching for several years, later to newspaper work and finally to playwriting.

"Susan and God," a comedy in three acts by Rachel Crothers. Copyright, 1937, by the author. Copyright and published, 1938, by Random House, New York.

Rachel Crothers succumbed to the tempters six years ago and went to Hollywood. She made her own rules at the time, dictated the terms of her contract and was happy in anticipation of the fun she was going to have writing screen scripts. It did not, however, work out quite as she had thought it would, so, after five years, with only a few things she considered worth-while accomplished, she came back to Broadway and the living theatre and sold John Golden a social comedy called "Susan and God." With Gertrude Lawrence playing Susan the play was so complete a success Miss Crothers will probably stay East for some time. She frequently has appeared in these volumes—her last appearance being in 1932 with "When Ladies Meet." Previous to that there were "Let Us Be Gay," "As Husbands Go" and others. She was born in Bloomington, Ill. She took naturally to the stage as soon as she was out of school and has devoted a lifetime to it.

"Prologue to Glory," a drama in three acts by E. P. Conkle. Copyright, 1936, 1938, by the author. Copyright and published, 1938, by Samuel French, Inc., New York.

E. P. Conkle's regular job is that of assistant professor of the Department of Speech in the University of Iowa. He is also director of the University Theatre, which is one of the most progressive of the little theatres of the Middle West. He took his B.A. and his M.A. at the University of Nebraska and has a Ph.D. from the University of Iowa. He studied drama with Professor Baker at Yale and had a year in Europe on a Guggenheim Fellowship. He has taught at both the University of North Dakota and the University of Delaware. He has given a good deal of time to playwriting but has never been able, he admits, to make a living at it. He first attracted attention in 1932 when a farce of his called "Forty-nine Dogs in a Meat House" was peddled on Broadway. Also, it found a purchaser, even though it was never produced. His first play to attract attention was a 1936 production, a drama called "200 Were Chosen," telling the story of the Government's experiment trying to re-settle dust bowl farmers in the Mantanuska Valley in Alaska. The play was given thirty-five performances on Broadway and was later taken up by the WPA Federal Theatre for several performances. "Prologue to Glory" was held for a time by commercial managers, but was finally produced by the Federal Theatre and proved an outstanding success of the 1937-38 season. Professor Conkle was born in Peru, Nebraska, in 1899.

"Amphitryon 38," comedy by Jean Giraudoux, adapted by S. N.
    Behrman. Copyright, 1938, by the author. Copyright and
    published, 1938, by Random House, Inc., New York.

S. N. Behrman is another friend of the family, so to speak. Of recent seasons he has been popping up quite regularly with a superior play that almost automatically has found its way to these yearbooks. "End of Summer" (1935-36), "Biography" (1932-33), and "Brief Moment" (1931-32) are Behrman plays that have been favorites of the seasons they decorated. He failed this year with one called "Wine of Choice," but more than made up for it in the matter of returns with the enormously popular "Amphitryon 38." Mr. Behrman is a native of Worcester, Mass., a college man with degrees from three universities, a scenarist of consequence in Hollywood and a playwright Broadway would miss greatly were he ever to decide to retire or devote his whole time to pictures—which isn't at all likely.

Jean Giraudoux, who wrote the original "Amphitryon 38," is celebrated and popular in France as both dramatist and novelist. He was born in 1882 at Bellac (Haut Vienne), and educated at the École Normale, in Paris. In 1918 he spent some time in America as an officer-instructor and afterward wrote a book of American experiences called *Amica America*. A play of his called "Siegfried" was tried briefly by Eva Le Gallienne at the Civic Repertory Theatre in 1930.

"Golden Boy," a drama in three acts by Clifford Odets. Copyright, 1937, by the author. Copyright and published, 1938, by Random House, Inc., New York.

There was a moaning at the bar when Clifford Odets went Hollywood, following the failure of his "Paradise Lost" in 1935. That, declared the young radicals who had pinned all their faith to his studio blouse, would be the last of him. For a time it looked as though they might be right. Mr. Odets did enter with enthusiasm into the work of preparing ideas born in story conferences for the screen. But after a year of this he was reasonably chastened and sent the manuscript of "Golden Boy" back to his old pals of the Group Theatre. "Golden Boy," happily, proved a big success and Mr. Odets was practically reclaimed. This is the second appearance of this playwright in Best Play society. His "Awake and Sing" was included in the 1934-35 volume. He is a Philadelphian by birth, having been born there in 1907. He has lived most of his life in New York, however, and was an actor for some years before he took to writing. "Waiting for Lefty," a labor play, won him recognition; "Till the Day I Die," "Awake and Sing" and "Paradise Lost" followed.

"What a Life," a comedy in three acts by Clifford Goldsmith. Copyright, 1938, by the author.

Playwrights who bloom in the spring occasionally last through the summer, and go on to qualify as candidates for the hardy annuals the following winter. Many playgoers were hoping in the spring of 1938 that Clifford Goldsmith would be one of the lucky few, Mr. Goldsmith having scored a splendid start with "What a Life," the comedy that brought him into these pages. This is practically a first comedy, although Mr. Goldsmith did help Elliott Nugent write one called "Charlie" some years ago. "Charlie," by the record, never amounted to much. The Goldsmith career has otherwise been quite uneventful. He was born in East Aurora, N. Y., in 1900, and lived neighbor to the late Fra Elburtus for many years. He is, by profession, a lecturer on health topics to high school children, and it was while he was pursuing this calling that he gathered stories and incidents that he later put into "What a Life." He has a farm at Paoli, Pa.

PLAYS PRODUCED IN NEW YORK

June 15, 1937—June 18, 1938

(Plays marked with asterisk were still playing June 18, 1938)

VIRGINIA

(60 performances)

A musical play in two acts by Laurence Stallings and Owen Davis; music by Arthur Schwartz; lyrics by Albert Stillman. Produced by the Center Theatre under the direction of John Kenneth Hyatt at the Center Theatre, New York, September 2, 1937.

Cast of characters—

Lady Agatha	Mona Barrie
Captain Somerset	Gordon Richards
Captain Boyd	Lansing Hatfield
Sir Guy Carleton	Dennis Hoey
Fortesque	Gene Lockhart
Minnie Fortesque	Bertha Belmore
Sylvia Laurence	Anne Booth
Miranda	Avis Andrews
Daphne	Helen Carroll
Phyllis	Esta Elman
Major-Domo	Tom Tempest
His Excellency, Governor of the Colony	Nigel Bruce
Scipio	John W. Bubbles
Hannibal	Ford L. Buck
Colonel Richard Fairfax	Ronald Graham
Stage Doorman	Tom Tempest
Prima Ballerina of Drury Lane	Patricia Bowman
Premier Dancer of Drury Lane	Valia Valentinoff
Town Crier	Herbert Garstin
A Patriot	John Ravold

Players of the Fair:

Puppet Master	George Prentice
Fire-Eater	Ajax
Jugglers	James Evans & Co.

Act I.—Virginia, 1775. Scene 1—Wharf at Yorktown. 2—Street in Williamsburg. 3—Outside the Raleigh Tavern. 4—Gates of the Governor's Palace. 5—Slave Quarters. 6—Ballroom in the Palace. 7—Palace Garden. Act II.—Scene 1—A Country Fair. 2—Stage Door. 3—Sylvia's Dressing Room. 4—Fortesque's Dressing Room. 5—Green Room in the Theatre. 6—At the Play. 7—Slave Quarters. 8—Daphne's Room. Raleigh Tavern. Finale.

Staged by Leon Leonidoff; book directed by Edward Clark Lilley; dances by Florence Rogge; music supervised by Don Voorhees; settings by Lee Simonson; costumes by Irene Sharaff.

Fortesque of Drury Lane brings the first company of professional English actors to America. The time is 1775 and the American revolution is in process of fomentation. Fortesque has been entrusted with a letter from British sympathizers to General George Washington in Philadelphia. The Tories have wind of the letter and institute a search for it. Fortesque turns it over to his leading lady, Sylvia Laurence, who in turn gives it to Col. Richard Fairfax of the Virginia militia. Fairfax is taken by the British, but the letter gets through and the revolution is given a big boost.

KING RICHARD II

(Return engagement 38 performances)

A tragedy by William Shakespeare with incidental music by Herbert Menges. Revived by Eddie Dowling and Robinson Smith at the St. James Theatre, New York, September 15, 1937.

Cast of characters—

King Richard, the Second	Maurice Evans
John of Gaunt, Duke of Lancaster	Lee Baker
Edmund of Langley, Duke of York	Lionel Hogarth
Henry, Surnamed Bolingbroke, Duke of Hereford, Son to John of Gaunt: Afterwards King Henry IV	Frederic Worlock
Duke of Aumerle	Winston O'Keefe
Thomas Mawbray, Duke of Norfolk	Donald Randolph
Bushy	John Kennedy
Bagot	Everett Ripley
Green	Sydney G. Smith
Earl of Northumberland	Charles Dalton
Henry Percy, Surnamed Hotspur	Emmett Rogers
Lord Ross	Richard Rauber
Lord Willoughby	Arthur L. Sachs
Lord Marshall	Reynolds Evans
Mawbray's Herald	Arthur L. Sachs
Bolingbroke's Herald	Neal Berry
Earl of Salisbury	Wesley Addy
Captain of a Band of Welshmen	Rhys Williams
Bishop of Carlisle	Reynolds Evans
Sir Stephen Scroop	Donald Randolph
Gardener	A. G. Andrews
Second Gardener	Philip Truex
Duke of Surrey	Neal Berry
Sir Pierce of Exton	Sydney G. Smith
Servant to Exton	Vernon Crane
A Groom	Rhys Williams
A Keeper	Wesley Addy
Queen to Richard	Eleanor Phelps
Duchess of Gloucester	Irene Tedrow
Ladies Attending on Queen	Betty Jenckes, Jessie Dimond, Julia Lathrop

England and Wales Between April, 1398—March, 1400.
Act I.—Scene 1—King Richard's Palace. 2—Duke of Lancaster's Palace. 3—The Lists at Coventry. 4—The Court. 5—Ely House. Act II.—Scene 1—Windsor Castle. 2—Wilds of Gloucestershire. 3—Camp in Wales. 4—Bristol before the Castle. 5—Coast of Wales. 6—Wales before Flint Castle. Act III.—Scene 1—Duke of York's Garden. 2 and 6—Westminster Hall. 3—London. Street leading to The Tower. 4—Windsor Castle. 5—Pomfret Castle.
Staged by Margaret Webster; settings by David Ffolkes.

"King Richard II" was first revived by Maurice Evans at the St. James Theatre, New York, February 5, 1937. It continued for a total of 133 performances. The resumed engagement, with the above cast, preceded a coast-to-coast tour.

THE SHOW IS ON

(Return engagement 17 performances)

A revue assembled by Vincente Minnelli; sketches by Moss Hart and David Freedman; music and lyrics by Vernon Duke and Ted Fetter, George and Ira Gershwin, Rodgers and Hart and others. Returned by the Messrs. Shubert to the Winter Garden, New York, September 18, 1937.

Principals engaged—

Willie Howard	Rose King
Eugene Howard	Chic York
Terry Lawlor	Roy Cropper
Demetrios Vilan	Jack Good
Charles Bowers	John McCauley
Mildred Webb	Lyda Sue Leeds
John Englert	Ruth Sheim
Marcella Swanson	Dave Mallen

Staged by Vincente Minnelli assisted by Frederick de Cordova; sketches directed by Edward Clark Lilley; dances by Robert Alton; settings by Minnelli.

"The Show Is On" was first produced at the Winter Garden, New York, December 25, 1936, and continued there until July 17, 1937, 236 performances. The above is the cast organized for the road tour which followed.

GEORGE AND MARGARET

(86 performances)

A comedy in three acts by Gerald Savory. Produced by John C. Wilson at the Morosco Theatre, New York, September 22, 1937.

Cast of characters—

Gladys	Moya Nugent
Malcolm	Morland Graham
Alice	Irene Browne
Dudley	Arthur Macrae
Frankie	Rosalyn Boulter
Claude	Richard Warner
Roger	Alan Webb
Beer	Gladys Henson

Act I.—Dining Room, Garth-Bander's House, Hampstead, London. Acts II and III.—Drawing Room.
Settings by Geoffrey Nares.

Malcolm and Alice Garth-Bander and their three children are living a little madly and excitingly in a London suburb. They are expecting George and Margaret to arrive as week-end guests and hating the thought of the experience, George and Margaret being such bloody bores. While they wait Frankie, the romantic daughter, falls desperately in love with her brother Dudley's best friend, Roger, and Claude, the elder son, decides that he wants to marry the housemaid, Gladys. Alice, their mother, smilingly approves of Frankie's choice, but is slightly hysterical over the housemaid suggestion. She is forced to make the comic best of things. Then George and Margaret are announced.

BLOW YE WINDS

(36 performances)

A comedy in three acts by Valentine Davies. Produced by Arthur Hopkins at the 46th Street Theatre, New York, September 23, 1937.

Cast of characters—

Tom King	James Doody
Hayden Chase	Henry Fonda
Capt. Terry	Harry Hermsen
George Cosden	Albert Hayes
Amy Baker	Linda Lee Hill
Joseph Allison	Blaine Cordner
Christine Lawrence	Doris Dalton
Benjamin Lessing	Blair Davies
Otto Hardt	Edgar Barrier
Mary Doran	Helen Murdoch
Ruth Lessing	Mary Rockwell
John McKnight	Edgar Stehli
An Elevator Man	James Clairton

Act I.—The *Borealis*. Act II.—Christine Lawrence's Apartment. Act III.—Scene 1—Christine's Apartment. 2—The *Borealis*.
Staged by Arthur Hopkins; settings by Cirker & Robbins.

Hayden Chase, out of college, has no love of either physical labor or mental concentration. He much prefers to loaf and sail his boat, the *Borealis*. When he rents the boat to a society party he meets and is attracted to Christine Lawrence, a brilliant young scientist devoting her life to a career. Later he takes Christine for a sail alone, runs the *Borealis* on a sandbar and anchors there for the night. Next morning Christine would return to her career. Hayden is forced to follow to be near her. Becoming conscious of their clandestine love affair they marry. Christine still refuses to give up her career. Hayden resents being forced to work in an office. He is back on the *Borealis* when Christine comes to arrange about the divorce. They decide suddenly to go sailing again.

THE LADY HAS A HEART

(91 performances)

A comedy in three acts by Ladislaus Bus-Fekete; adapted by Edward Roberts. Produced by Rufus Phillips and Watson Barratt at the Longacre Theatre, New York, September 25, 1937.

Cast of characters—

```
Klari.............................................Judith  Alden
Jean.............................................Vincent  Price
The Countess Mariassy.............................Hilda Spong
The Countess Katinka.............................Elissa  Landi
His Excellency, Count Albert Mariassy..............Lumsden Hare
Count Gyorgy......................................Royal Beal
Radio Announcer..................................Derek Fairman
Ilonka.........................................Katherine Standing
Ferencz...........................................Tom  Bate
Electrician.....................................Richard  Bowler
```
    Acts I and III.—Terrace at the Count's Castle. Act II.—Scene 1—
The Terrace. 2—Town House of Countess Katinka.
    Staged by Rufus Phillips; settings by Watson Barratt.

Jean is the fourth of his line to serve the family of the Count Mariassy, the Prime Minister. Jean is a perfect gentleman's gentleman until the day he is elected a Socialist deputy to represent the Labor party in his master's Conservative government. Jean then tries to serve two masters, political and domestic, which is an embarrassing business. His task is further complicated by his discovered love for the Countess Katinka, daughter of the Prime Minister, and her love for him. The complication is finally composed by the departure of Jean for a neighboring state and the Countess' promise to follow after.

ON LOCATION

(8 performances)

A comedy in three acts by Kent Wiley (Samuel Ruskin Golding). Produced by East Coast Studios, Inc., at the Ritz Theatre, New York, September 27, 1937.

Cast of characters—

```
Annie............................................Nellie Burt
Father Kennedy..................................Jack Norworth
Gene Cabot.....................................Leslie Denison
Windy O'Rourke.................................Leonard Doyle
Doc Howe........................................John F. Kirk
Benny Kaplan....................................Mark Linder
Mackenzie.....................................Ben  H.  Roberts
Dad Kinnear....................................Charles Keane
Will Curran.....................................Lamar  King
Sheriff Bob McLeash..............................Scott Moore
Stella Wallace..................................Mary Drayton
```

Tomlin...John A. Bennett
Amy Rand..Kathleen Hart
Fay Foster.......................................Marjorie Norton
    Acts I, II and III.—Living Room of the Rand Cabin.
    Staged by Samuel Golding.

Amy Rand owns a gold mine which she is trying to operate
with WPA help. Gene Cabot is a motion picture director looking
for new subjects. Gene agrees to put Amy in the movies and
let her write her own story of her adventures, but backs out
when he discovers that Amy's miners are not miners, but WPA
workers. After which Gene falls in love with Amy and agrees
to make the picture anyway. That is how movies are born.

FRENCH WITHOUT TEARS

(111 performances)

A comedy in three acts by Terence Rattigan. Produced by
Gilbert Miller in association with Howard Wyndham and Bronson
Albery at the Henry Miller Theatre, New York, September 28,
1937.

Cast of characters—

Kenneth Lake..Philip Friend
Brian Curtis..Guy Middleton
Hon. Alan Howard................................Frank Lawton
Marianne...Simone Petitjean
Monsieur Maingot.................................Marcel Vallee
Lt.-Commander Rogers...........................Cyril Raymond
Diana Lake.............................Penelope Dudley Ward
Kit Neilan...Hubert Gregg
Jacqueline Maingot..............................Jacqueline Porel
Lord Heybrook.....................................Edward Ryan
    Acts I, II and III.—Living Room of "Miramar," Monsieur Main-
got's Villa in Small Seaside Town in the South of France.
    Staged by Harold French; setting by Raymond Sovey, after original
sketch by G. K. Benda.

The Hon. Alan Howard and a couple of other fellows are
studying French at the villa of Monsieur Maingot in the South
of France, with some thought of entering the diplomatic service.
A fellow student is Diana Lake, sexy and flirtatious. Diana
lures them in turn and, having enjoyed the satisfaction of conquest, practically tosses them over and turns to Lieutenant Com-
mander Rogers, a newcomer. Rogers is taken and, in turn, also
disillusioned. Whereupon all her victims conspire to teach Diana
a lesson by individually and severally ditching her. Diana is
hurt, but immediately begins laying plans for the subjugation
of Lord Heybrook, who is on his way. When his lordship arrives
he is discovered to be a sturdy young lad of 11 years.

THE STAR-WAGON

(223 performances)

A dramatic fantasy in three acts by Maxwell Anderson. Produced by Guthrie McClintic at the Empire Theatre, New York, September 29, 1937.

Cast of characters—

Hanus Wicks	Russell Collins
Martha Minch	Lillian Gish
Stephen Minch	Burgess Meredith
Park	Whitner Bissell
Ripple	Alan Anderson
Angela	Muriel Starr
Apfel	Howard Freeman
Duffy	Kent Smith
1st Thug	Barry Kelley
2nd Thug	Charles Forrester
Misty	John Philliber
Hallie Arlington	Jane Buchanan
Mr. Arlington	J. Arthur Young
Mrs. Rutledge	Mildred Natwick
Paul Reiger	Edmund O'Brien
Christabel	Evelyn Abbott
Della	Edith Smith
Ogelthorpe	William Garner
The Herb Woman	Muriel Starr

Act I.—Scene 1—Dining Room of Cottage Somewhere in Suburbs of Eastern Ohio Manufacturing Town. 2 and 3—Room in Laboratory Wing of Arlington-Duffy Factories. Act II.—Scene 1—Interior of Bicycle Shop, 1902. 2—Choir Loft in Small Church. 3—The Picnic Ground. Act III.—Scene 1—Drawing Room of Stephen Minch's House. In the Nineteen-Thirties. 2—Dining Room of the Cottage. Staged by Guthrie McClintic; settings by Jo Mielziner.

See page 157.

HOW COME, LAWD?

(2 performances)

A Negro folk-drama in three acts by Donald Heywood. Produced by Negro Theatre Guild at the 49th Street Theatre, New York, September 30, 1937.

Cast of characters—

Mom	Mercedes Gilbert
Pa	Homer Tutt
Big Boy	Rex Ingram
Clorinda	Hilda Rogers
Slacks	Alec Lovejoy
Aloes	Leigh Whipper
Sammy	Harry D. Ingram
Boots	Dan Michaels
Rasmus	Edgar Martin
Yamacraw	George L. Ingram
Babes	Dorothy Cadoza

Wallstreet....................................Columbus Jackson
Jackknife..James Fuller
The Deep River Boys.
    Acts I, II and III.—Farmer's Cabin in South.
    Staged by Charles J. Adler; setting by Stagecraft Studios.

Big Boy, an Alabama cotton picker, is emotionally stirred by
an organizer named Aloes who comes from Atlanta with plans
to put the laborers of Alabama in one big union and thus improve
their working and living conditions.   Big Boy confuses the
organizer's work with that of the Lord and is pathetically mystified when the white neighbors gang up on the colored boys and
shoot several of them down.   In his disappointment he takes to
lust and liquor.   His best loved Clorinda is stabbed serving as
his shield.   He is left praying for guidance.

THE ABBEY THEATRE PLAYERS

(85 performances)

A repertory of Irish plays presented by The Abbey Theatre,
Dublin, in association with the Messrs. Shubert at the Ambassador Theatre, New York, beginning October 2, 1937.

KATIE ROCHE

A Play in Three Acts by Teresa Deevy

(5 performances)

Cast of characters—

Stanislaus Gregg................................F. J. McCormick
Katie Roche...Eileen Crowe
Reuben..M. J. Dolan
Michael McGuire..................................Arthur Shields
Amelia Gregg..Ria Mooney
Jo Mahony..Denis O'Dea
Margaret Drybone..............................Maureen Delany
Frank Lawlor.....................................Austin Meldon
    Acts I, II and III.—Sitting Room of the Greggs' Cottage in Lower
Ballycar.

Katie Roche, an illegitimate child adopted into the home of
Stanislaus Gregg and his sister, Amelia, is convinced that she
springs from grand people and awaits a confirmation of her faith.
She gives up the boys of the town to marry her benefactor, the
older Stanislaus, and thinks to become an influence in his life.
When he treats her as a child Katie renews her interest in the
village boys.   Her husband takes her away to Dublin for dis-
ciplining.   She accepts the obligation as a sacrifice that proves
her quality.

THE PLOUGH AND THE STARS

A Tragedy in Four Acts by Sean O'Casey

(October 7)

(4 performances)

Cast of characters—

Commandant Jack Clitheroe......................F. J. McCormick
Nora Clitheroe....................................Eileen Crowe
Peter Flynn...M. J. Dolan
The Young Covey..................................Denis O'Dea
Fluther Good......................................P. J. Carolan
Bessie Burgess..................................Maureen Delany
Mrs. Gogan..May Craig
Mollser...Aideen O'Connor
Captain Brennan, of the I. C. A..................Joseph Linnane
Lieut. Langon, of the Irish Volunteers.................U. Wright
Rosie Redmond....................................Ria Mooney
A Barman..Austin Meldon
The Voice...
Corporal Stoddard, of the Wiltshires.................Austin Meldon
Sergeant Tinely, of the Wiltshires..................Arthur Shields
     Act I.—Scene—The Living Room of the Clitheroes' Three-Room
Flat in a Tenement House in Dublin. Act II.—Scene—A Corner
Public-House in a Street Where a Meeting Is Being Held. Act III.—
Scene—The Outside of the Tenement House in Which the Clitheroes
Live. Act IV.—Scene—Bessie Burgess' Room in the Same Tenement.

"The Plough and the Stars" was first produced in New York
at the Hudson Theatre, November 28, 1927, and played for
thirty-two performances with Arthur Sinclair and Sara Allgood
in the leads. It was revived during the Abbey Players' tour
in 1934.

THE FAR-OFF HILLS

A Comedy in Three Acts by Lennox Robinson

(October 11)

(December 16)

(47 performances)

Cast of characters—

Patrick Clancy....................................P. J. Carolan
Marian...Eileen Crowe
Dorothea, "Ducky"..............................Aideen O'Connor
Anna, "Pet".....................................Frolie Mulhern
Oliver O'Shaughnessy..........................Michael J. Dolan
Dick Delaney......................................Austin Meldon
Harold Mahony...................................F. J. McCormick
Susie Tynan.....................................Maureen Delany
Pierce Hegarty..................................Arthur Shields
Ellen Nolan...May Craig
     The First and Third Acts Take Place in the Clancys' Dining Room,
the Second Act in the Girls'—Ducky's and Pet's—Bedroom.

"The Far-off Hills," played originally by the Abbey Players during their 1932 tour of America and revived for a single performance in 1934, proved the first comedy success of their 1937 engagement and was continued for a run of forty-seven performances. It is Lennox Robinson's story of Marian Clancy, a dominating person, who tried to manage her father's house and her younger sisters, greatly to their distress. To the relief of her family Marian was finally won for a wife by Pierce Hegarty on the promise that with him to help she could run the town.

THE PLAYBOY OF THE WESTERN WORLD

A Comedy in Three Acts by J. M. Synge

(November 20)

(9 performances)

Cast of characters—

Margaret Flaherty	Ria Mooney
Shawn Keogh	Michael J. Dolan
Michael James Flaherty	P. J. Carolan
Philly Cullen	Denis O'Dea
Jimmy Farrell	U. Wright
Christopher Mahon	Arthur Shields
Widow Quinn	Maureen Delany
Sara Tansey	May Craig
Susan Brady	Frolie Mulhern
Honor Blake	Aideen O'Connor
Old Mahon	F. J. McCormick

Acts I, II and III.—Flaherty's Public House, Wild Coast of Mayo.

"The Playboy" was first produced in New York the season of 1911-12, and caused a minor riot in the gallery of the Maxine Elliott Theatre the first night of its showing. It was last revived in November, 1934.

Followed by—

IN A TRAIN

A play in one act dramatized by Hugh Hunt from a short story by Frank O'Connor.

Cast of characters—

Sergeant	P. J. Carolan
His Wife	Ria Mooney
Drunken Traveler	F. J. McCormick
Magner	Austin Meldon
Foley	Arthur Shields
Delancey	Denis O'Dea

Kendillon..Michael J. Dolan
Moll More..Maureen Delany
Two Countrywomen....................May Craig, Frolie Mulhern
The Woman...Eileen Crowe
The Action Takes Places in the Compartment of a Railway Train.

THE NEW GOSSOON

A Comedy in Three Acts by George Shiels

(November 29)

(8 performances)

Cast of characters—

Mag Keogh..May Craig
Rabit Hamil......................................F. J. McCormick
Ellen Carey......................................Maureen Delany
Ned Shay...P. J. Carolan
Luke Carey...Denis O'Dea
Sally Hamil.......................................Eileen Crowe
Peter Carey..M. J. Dolan
John Henly..Arthur Shields
Biddy Henly......................................Aideen O'Connor
The Action Takes Place in Carey's Kitchen.

"The New Gossoon" was first played in New York in November, 1934, by the Abbey Theatre Players.

JUNO AND THE PAYCOCK

A Tragedy in Three Acts by Sean O'Casey

(December 6)

(8 performances)

Cast of characters—

"Captain" Jack Boyle..............................P. J. Carolan
"Juno" Boyle......................................Eileen Crowe
Johnny Boyle......................................Arthur Shields
Mary Boyle.......................................Aideen O'Connor
"Joxer" Daly.....................................F. J. McCormick
Maisie Madigan...................................Maureen Delany
"Needle" Nugents...................................M. J. Dolan
Mrs. Tancred.......................................May Craig
Jerry Devine.......................................Denis O'Dea
Charles Bentham..................................Joseph Linnane
An Irregular......................................Austin Meldon
A Sewing Machine Woman.........................Frolie Mulhern
A Vendor...U. Wright
Neighbors, Furniture Removal Men, Second Irregular
Acts I, II and III.—Living Apartment of a Two-Room Tenancy of the Boyle Family in a Tenement House in Dublin.

"Juno and the Paycock" was first played in New York in March, 1926, with Augustin Duncan the "Capt." Jack Boyle and

Louise Randolph the patient Juno. It was last revived in November, 1934, by the Abbey Theatre Players.

DRAMA AT INISH

A Comedy in Three Acts by Lennox Robinson

(December 13)

(4 performances)

Cast of characters—

John Twohig	Austin Meldon
Annie Twohig	Maureen Delany
Lizzie Twohig	Eileen Crowe
Eddie Twohig	Joseph Linnane
Peter Hurley, T. D.	M. J. Dolan
Helena	Aideen O'Connor
Michael	Arthur Shields
Christine Lambert	Frolie Mulhern
Hector de la Mare	F. J. McCormick
Constance Constantia	Ria Mooney
John Hegarty	Denis O'Dea
Tom Mooney	P. J. Carolan
William Slattery	U. Wright

Acts I, II and III.—Private Sitting Room in Sea-View Hotel.

TO QUITO AND BACK

(46 performances)

A comedy in two acts by Ben Hecht. Produced by The Theatre Guild at the Guild Theatre, New York, October 6, 1937.

Cast of characters—

Railway Official	Joseph Monnert de Villard
Howard Evans	Francis Compton
Lola Hobbs	Sylvia Sidney
Alexander Sterns	Leslie Banks
Zamiano	Joseph Buloff
Officer	Walter Armin
Francisca	Virginia Holden
Tomasa	Eugenia Rawls
Florinda	Isobel Donald
Maria	Virginia Gregori
Alfredo	George J. Lewis
Captain Stewart	Horace Sinclair
Fifi Stewart	Lena Peters
Harold Frazer	Walter N. Greaza
Countess Rivadavia	Evelyn Varden
Dr. Duquesne	Jack Soanes
Manuella	Natalie Danesi
A Soldier	Manuel De Moya
Colonel Pizarro	Manart Kippen
Diaz	Charles H. Pinkham
An Officer	Augustin Gonzales Villaverde
Fortune Teller	Sidonie Espero
Dr. Morodin	Henry Levin
Sanchey	Alfonso Chavez
Comrade Santoya	Jan Ullrich

Comrade Patayo.................................Harry Bellaver
Comrade Rienza.................................Samuel Brown
Comrade Gonzales...................................Fred Clegg
Muggsie..Himself
Natives, Soldiers, etc.: Mildred Levin, Michael Lackman, Louis Hal-
    prin, Albert Allen, Don Kelly, Lone Mountain, Fredericka For-
    tello, Juan De Aguenta, Manuel Risto, Sheila Richart, Tommi
    Bissell, Aristes Corona, Edilberto G. Burgos, Tuan Garcia.
Act I.—Scene 1—Waiting Room of Railway Station on West Slope
of Andes on Ecuadorian Coast. 2 and 3—Living Room in Villa of
Countess Rivadavia, Twenty Miles Outside of Quito, Ecuador. Act
II.—Countess Rivadavia's Living Room.
    Staged by Philip Moeller, Lawrence Langner and Theresa Helburn
assisting in general supervision; settings by Aline Bernstein.

Alexander Sterns is an American novelist seeking escape from
a variety of psychological disturbances. He runs away to
Ecuador with Lola Hobbs. In Ecuador the runaways become
involved in a revolution being conducted by Zamiano, Communist
and defender of the people's cause. Sterns, finding that despite
all his distractions he is still influenced by a lingering sense of
obligation toward, if not of love for, the wife he left at home,
confesses his change of heart and infirmness of character to Lola
and walks out with Zamiano to face the Fascist advance, determined to die a martyr to the cause and leave a song singing in
the hearts of the defeated Zamianistas.

SUSAN AND GOD

(288 performances)

A comedy in three acts by Rachel Crothers. Produced by
John Golden at the Plymouth Theatre, New York, October 7,
1937.

Cast of characters—

Irene Burroughs....................................Vera Allen
Michael O'Hara...............................Douglas Gilmore
Leeds..Bigelow Sayre
Charlotte Marley.............................Eleanor Audley
Hutchins Stubbs....................................Fred Leslie
Leonora Stubbs...............................Edith Atwater
Clyde Rochester.................................David Byrne
Susan Trexel...............................Gertrude Lawrence
Barrie Trexel...................................Paul McGrath
Blossom Trexel...................................Nancy Kelly
Leontine.......................................Katherine Deane
Act I.—Terrace Room in Irene Burroughs' House in the Country.
Act II.—Scene 1—Guest Room in Burroughs House. 2—Terrace
Room. Act III.—Susan's Sitting Room in her House in the Country.
    Staged by Rachel Crothers; settings by Jo Mielziner.

See page 198.

IN CLOVER

(3 performances)

A comedy in three acts by Allan Scott. Produced by John and Jerrold Krimsky at the Vanderbilt Theatre, New York, October 13, 1937.

Cast of characters—

Electa Hornblow	Zamah Cunningham
Harriet Freeman	Claudia Morgan
James Freeman	Myron McCormick
Frederick L. Parsons	Jose Ferrer
Archie Gaunt	Joseph Sweeney
Isabelle Gaunt	Helen Strickland
Mary Jane Walker	Louise Platt
Hank Thornton	Bertram Thorn
Dr. Brewer	Albert Bergh
Polly LaVarre Brewer	Dennie Moore
Eddie, a guest	Don McClure
Guest	Joan Macomber
Guest	Sally Gabler
Guest	Pete Barker
Claire, a guest	Carmen Lewis
Willowy Chap	Robert Crane

Acts I, II and III.—Living Room in Old New England Home.
Staged by Bretaigne Windust; setting by Norris Houghton.

James and Harriet Freeman, tired of the city and intent on finding a quiet little place in the country where they may reasonably raise a family, take a place in Connecticut from a grasping native agent, Electa Hornblow. Their comic and disillusioning adventures include being swindled by the natives and imposed upon by their visiting city friends. In the end they give up and go back to town.

WISE TOMORROW

(3 performances)

A drama in three acts by Stephen Powys. Produced by Bernard Klawans at the Biltmore Theatre, New York, October 15, 1937.

Cast of characters—

Tony Campion	Edith Barrett
Norman Weldon	Naunton Wayne
Peter Marsh	Theodore Newton
Helen Reitz	Rosemary Ames
Bob Ebury	Calvin Thomas
Joan Campion	Gloria Dickson
Diana Ebury	Josephine Victor
Colley	Olive Reeves-Smith
Alice	Florence Edney
Newsman	Joseph Taulane

Act I.—Scene 1—Living Room of Campions' Apartment in the East Sixties, New York. 2—Joan's Dressing Room in Summer Theatre. Acts II and III.—Campions' Living Room.
Staged by Hugh MacMullan; settings by Watson Barratt.

Diana Ebury is an aging actress who resents being forced to give up her career. By obtaining and retaining control over the career of a young and talented actress, Joan Campion, Diana hopes to continue a power in the theatre, perpetuating her hold upon her public through the success of her protégée. Joan's friends, led by her fiancé, Peter Marsh, and her more normal sister, Tony, fight to break the power of Diana over Joan, but are defeated. Even after Diana dies she directs Joan's life through the estate she leaves her protégée as her heir.

WALL STREET SCENE

(3 performances)

A comedy in three acts by John Lawrence. Produced by Mary MacArthur Noble at the Comedy Theatre, New York, October 18, 1937.

Cast of characters—

J. M. Barnes	Ernest Hanes
Miss Cleary	Marie Fleming Zellers
Dan	Rudi Lederer
Sue Barnes	Vola Blakely
Jimmy Standish	Tito Gari
Timothy Fisher	John Moe
David Blade	Cecil Natapoff
Rittenmayer	Frank Elco
P. J. Harland	Charles Locaster
Miss Palter	Barbara Rossiter
Bob Havergal	Peter Brandon
Mrs. Montgomery Kent	Carolyn Whitney
Mrs. Brady	Hope Spingarn
Joan Brady	Betty Jane Tyler
White	Raymond Volpe

Act I.—Scene 1—Private Office of J. M. Barnes. 2—Board Room. Act II.—Scene 1—Fisher's Office. 2—Wire Room. Act III.—Private Office of J. M. Barnes.
Staged by Wallace House; settings by Edward Fitzgerald.

An exposé of the manner in which a gullible buying public was put on the sucker list before the New Deal brought about the Security Exchange Commission and stopped at least a few of the crooked systems. In this play a couple of crooked brokers rent desk room with an honorable firm and carry on from there.

ANGEL ISLAND

(21 performances)

A mystery comedy in three acts by Bernie Angus. Produced by George Abbott at the National Theatre, New York, October 20, 1937.

Cast of characters—

Carma Grainger	Lea Penman
Eunice	Betty Field
Leo Grainger	Carroll Ashburn
Garth	Eric Wollencott
Sylvia Jordan	Arlene Francis
John Kavanaugh	Clyde Fillmore
Sidney Powell	Morgan Conway
Lucy Powell	Edith Van Cleve
Aimee Lattimer	Maidel Turner
Marco Elwood	Nigel Blake
Arlene Richfield	Louise Larabee
Alec Richfield	David Hoffman
Trig	Thomas Graham
Lola	Alma Dickson
Gail Marsh	Joyce Arling
Jeff Kingsley	Clayton Collyer
Bessie	Doro Merande

Act I.—Scenes 1 and 3—Living Room of Old Stone Dwelling, Angel Island off Coast of Carolina. Acts II and III.—Living Room and Kitchen.

Staged by George Abbott; settings by John Root.

The Leo Graingers have bought Angel Island and moved into an ancient homestead. There are reports of pirate treasure hidden in the house or on the grounds. An assortment of week-end guests are not above making search for the treasure, but before they get far one (Lucy Powell), who knows too much, is found stabbed to death with a silver ice pick. Less than an hour later another meany, Alec Richfield, is also put away by the ice pick route. A trap is set for the murderer and he falls into it, being shot to death by the trappers. He turns out to be the master himself.

MANY MANSIONS

(158 performances)

A drama in two acts and fifteen scenes by Jules Eckert Goodman and his son, Eckert Goodman; incidental score by Milton Lusk. Produced by Many Mansions, Inc., at the Biltmore Theatre, New York, October 27, 1937.

Cast of characters—

```
Peter Brent.................................Alexander Kirkland
Roger Crandall..............................Gage Clarke
Edgar Brent.................................George Lessey
Mrs. Edgar Brent............................Suzanne Jackson
Martha Brent................................Gretchen Davidson
Maid........................................Ann Clark
George Graham...............................Walter Coy
Dick Barton.................................Ted Fetter
Joan Hollis.................................Flora Campbell
Jack Worthington............................Peter van Buren
Bob Edmunds.................................Dan Duryea
Harvey Phillips.............................Maurice Hunt
Spencer Winton..............................Charles Sedgwick
Morgan Grange...............................Wendell Phillips
Dean Redmond...............................Lewis Dayton
Bishop Graves...............................Vaughan Glaser
Hank.......................................Franklin Gray
Ella.......................................Nell O'Day
Mrs. Roberts...............................Katherine Squire
Rev. Josiah Ward...........................Seth Arnold
Dr. Charles Hammond........................William Post
Whittaker..................................Roger Fox
Kay........................................Paula Miller
Rita.......................................Hilda Reis
Petrosino..................................Auguste Aramini
Inspector Warren...........................Robert Mulligan
Bishop Jordan..............................Joaquin Souther
Miss Lawrence..............................Ellen Hall
Clerk......................................William Price
```

Act I.—Scene 1—Bedroom of Peter Brent. 2 and 7—Study of Rev. Roger Crandall. 3—Breakfast Room in Peter's House. 4—Alston Country Club. 5—Student's Room in Theological Seminary. 6—Peter's Room in Seminary. 8—A Pulpit. Act II.—Scenes 1 and 6—The Bartons' Home. 2—Rev. Josiah Ward's Study at Irontown. 3—Sacristy of a Metropolitan Church. 4—The Chapel. 5 and 7—Office of Bishop Graves.

Staged by Lee Strasberg; settings by John Koenig.

Peter Brent, hearkening to an inner urge for service in the church, overrides the objections of his family, his fiancée, Joan Hollis, and his local minister, Roger Crandall, and studies for the ministry. His disillusionment begins with his discovery of his fellow divinity students compromising with the flesh and the devil. As a curate he is discouraged when he would interest young people in the church, is disciplined when he tries to save an innocent girl caught in bad company from arrest, and is finally brought before the bishops and unfrocked for his rebellious acts. But not until he has flayed the compromising churchmen for their hypocrisies.

AS YOU LIKE IT

(17 performances)

A comedy in two acts by William Shakespeare. Revived by The Surry Players under the sponsorship of Dwight Deere Wiman at the Ritz Theatre, New York, October 30, 1937.

Cast of characters—

A Banished Duke	Robert K. Adams
Frederick	Alan Handley
Amiens	Alan Handley
Jaques	Frederick Tozere
Le Beau	Jack Lydman
Charles	Hayden Rorke
Oliver	Staats Cotsworth
Jaques	Jack Lydman
Orlando	Shepperd Strudwick
Adam	Norman Budd
Touchstone	Whitner Bissell
Corin	Jabez Gray
Silvius	K. Edwin Shaw
William	Alan Handley
First Page to the Banished Duke	Ramon Blackburn
Second Page to the Banished Duke	Royce Blackburn
Rosalind	Katherine Emery
Celia	Anne Revere
Phebe	Connie Nickerson
Audrey	Helen Wynn

Lords Belonging to the Two Dukes, Foresters and Other Attendants: Barbara Townsend, Janet Marshall, Connie Nickerson, Helen Wynn, Hayden Rorke, David Stevenson, Robert Allen, Jack Lydman, Jabez Gray, Pendleton Harrison.

The Two Acts Lie First Near Oliver's House; Afterwards Partly in the Usurper's Court and Partly in the Forest of Arden.

Staged by Samuel Rosen; settings by Studio Alliance; costumes by Lucinda Ballard and Scott Wilson.

The Surry Players spent one summer in intensive study and a second summer in producing four plays at Surry, Me. Their production of "As you Like It" was seen by Dwight Deere Wiman, who gave them a chance on Broadway. "As You Like It" was last revived in New York by the Shakespeare Theatre Company at the Shakespeare Theatre (formerly Jolson's) the season of 1932-33, when sixteen performances of the comedy were given.

AMPHITRYON 38

(153 performances)

A comedy in a prologue and three acts by Jean Giraudoux; adapted by S. N. Behrman; music by Samuel L. M. Barlow. Produced by The Theatre Guild at the Shubert Theatre, New York, November 1, 1937.

Cast of characters—

Jupiter	Alfred Lunt
Mercury	Richard Whorf
Sosie	George Meader
Trumpeter	Sydney Greenstreet
Warrior	Alan Hewitt
Alkmena	Lynn Fontanne
Amphityron	Barry Thomson
Nenetza	Kathleen Roland
Kleantha	Jacqueline Paige

Echo...Ernestine de Becker
Leda...Edith King
    Acts I, II and III.—In and about Amphitryon's Palace.
    Staged by Bretaigne Windust under supervision of Alfred Lunt
and Lynn Fontanne; settings by Lee Simonson; costumes by Valentina.

See page 262.

* I'D RATHER BE RIGHT

(266 performances)

A musical comedy in two acts by George S. Kaufman and
Moss Hart; music by Richard Rodgers; lyrics by Lorenz Hart.
Produced by Sam H. Harris at the Alvin Theatre, New York,
November 2, 1937.

Cast of characters—

Peggy Jones..Joy Hodges
Phil Barker..Austin Marshall
The President of the United States...............George M. Cohan
His Secretary..Ralph Glover
The Postmaster General...............................Paul Parks
The Secretary of the Treasury.....................Taylor Holmes
The Secretary of State..............................Marion Green
The Secretary of Labor...........................Bijou Fernandez
The Secretary of the Navy...........................David Allman
The Secretary of Commerce.............................Al Atkins
The Secretary of Agriculture........................Robert Bleck
The Secretary of War..................................Jack Mills
The Secretary of the Interior.................Charles McLoughlin
The Attorney-General.................................Robert Less
The Chief Justice....................................John Cherry
James B. Maxwell...................................Florenz Ames
Federal Theatre Director.........................Joseph Macaulay
Social Service Messenger...........................Georgie Tapps
The President's Mother........................Marie Louise Dana
A Butler..Joseph Allen
Sistie..Evelyn Mills
Buzzie..Warren Mills
Tony...Joseph Macaulay
Joe...Joe Verdi
The Acrobats..........................Jack Reynolds, Sol Black

Margaret Sande, Irene McBride, Georgie Tapps, Fred Nay, Jack
    Barnes, Clarise Sitomer, Jack Whitney, Edward Harrington,
    Jeanette Bradley, Lili Mann, Warren Mills, Jack Whitney,
    Martin Fair, Austra Neiman, Don Cater, Tina Rigat, Joe Gran-
    ville, Georgie Tapps and Margaret Sande.
Singing Girls: Virginia Berger, Cecil Carey, Ruth Clayton, Geraldine
    Hamilton, Linda Kellogg, Marie Nash, Erminie Randolph, Jane
    Richardson, Emily Stephenson and Mary Jane Walsh.
Singing Boys: Chas. Bywater, Len Frank, John Fulco, Joe Granville,
    Jack Kearney, Jack Leslie, Wm. Marel, John McQuade, Bob
    Spencer, Norman Van Emburgh and Herbert Wood.
Dancing Girls: Jeanette Bradley, Jeanette Lee, Eleanor Dewitt, Kate
    Fredric, Ruth Gormley, Georgette Lampsi, Velma Lord, Lili
    Mann, Austra Neiman, Tina Rigat, Patsy Schenk, Betty Schlaf-
    fer, Clarise Sitomer and Dorothy Waller.
Dancing Boys: Jack Barnes, Don Cater, Martin Fair, Jay Hunter,
    Beau Tilden, Edward Harrington, Robert Howard and Fred Nay.
Dave Allman's Band.

Acts I and II.—Central Park, New York. July 4.
Book staged by George S. Kaufman; setting by Donald Oenslager; costumes by Irene Sharaff; modern clothes by John Hambleton; choreography by Charles Weidman; dances staged by Ned McGurn.

Peggy Jones and Phil Barker are discouraged because Joe cannot get a promised raise until the President of the United States balances the budget. Falling asleep in Central Park, Phil dreams that he meets President Franklin D. Roosevelt, who promises to see that the budget is balanced so Peggy and he can marry. The President gets into difficulties with the Supreme Court and a variety of fantastic complications arise to delay the consummation of the young people's hopes.

GOLDEN BOY

(250 performances)

A drama in three acts by Clifford Odets. Produced by The Group Theatre at the Belasco Theatre, New York, November 4, 1937.

Cast of characters—

Tom Moody	Roman Bohnen
Lorna Moon	Frances Farmer
Joe Bonaparte	Luther Adler
Tokio	Art Smith
Mr. Carp	Lee J. Cobb
Siggie	Jules Garfield
Mr. Bonaparte	Morris Carnovsky
Anna	Phoebe Brand
Frank Bonaparte	John O'Malley
Roxy Gottleib	Robert Lewis
Eddie Fuselli	Elia Kazan
Pepper White	Harry Bratsburg
Mickey	————
Call Boy	Bert Conway
Sam	Martin Ritt
Lewis	Howard De Silva
Drake	Charles Crisp
Driscoll	Charles Niemayer
Barker	Mladen Sekulevitch

Act I.—Scenes 1 and 3—Office of Tom Moody. 2 and 5—The Bonaparte Home. 4—A Park Bench. Act II.—Scene 1—Gymnasium. 2—Park Bench. 3—The Office. 4—Dressing Room in the Arena. Act III.—Scene 1—Office. 2—Dressing Room. 3—Bonaparte Home.
Staged by Harold Clurman; settings by Mordecai Gorelik.

See page 295.

ANTONY AND CLEOPATRA

(5 performances)

A drama in two parts and fourteen scenes adapted by William Strunk, Jr., from the tragedy by William Shakespeare; music by

Virgil Thomson. Revived by Laurence Rivers, Inc., at the Mansfield Theatre, New York, November 10, 1937.

Cast of characters—

Mark Antony	Conway Tearle
Octavius Caesar	John Emery
M. Aemilius Lepidus	E. Malcolm Dunn
Sextus Pompeius	Averell Harris
Domitius Enobarbus	Thomas Chalmers
Eros	Wilfrid Seagram
Scarus	Frederic Voight
Dercetas	Richard Ross
Demetrius	Charles Bowden
Philo	Henry Adrian
Thyreus	Stephen Fox
Agrippa	Ralph Chambers
Dolabella	Henry Saunders
Proculeius	Wilton Graf
Menas	John Parrish
Canidius	George V. Dill
Alexas	William Barwald
Mardian	Robert Williamson
Diomedes	Fred Hanschi
A Messenger	Lawrence Fletcher
Cleopatra, Queen of Egypt	Tallulah Bankhead
Octavia	Regina Wallace
Charmian	Fania Marinoff
Iras	Georgia Harvey
A Dancer	Kamila Staneska

Musicians: Sidney Halpern, Arnold Sattler and Alfred Ross.
Ladies of the Court: Virginia Spottswood, Derby Dale.
Cup Bearers: Barbara Ellis and Valeska Von Momerty.
Slaves: Mary Shannon and Miriam Cousens.
    Act I.—Scenes 1 and 3—Rome—Caesar's House. 2 and 6—Alexandria—Cleopatra's Palace. 4—Misenum—Between the Camps. 5—Misenum—On Board Pompey's Galley. Part II.—Scene 1—Athens—Antony's House. 2—Rome—Caesar's House. 3, 5, 7 and 8—Alexandria—Cleopatra's Palace. 4—Actium—Antony's Tent. 6—Near Alexandria—the Battlefield.
    Staged by Reginald Bach; settings and costumes by Jo Mielziner.

The last previous revival of "Antony and Cleopatra" was made by the Selwyns and Adolph Klauber with Rollo Peters and Jane Cowl in the name parts in 1924. Previously it was the opening attraction at the New Theatre which a group of millionaires built for New York in 1909, when E. H. Sothern and Julia Marlowe played the parts. It has been revived from time to time by Shakespearean stock companies.

YOUNG MR. DISRAELI

(6 performances)

A comedy in three acts by Elswyth Thane. Produced by Alex Yokel at the Fulton Theatre, New York, November 10, 1937.

Cast of characters—

Isaac Disraeli	Ben Webster
Maria Disraeli	Molly Pearson
Sarah Disraeli	Lora Baxter

Benjamin Disraeli.............................Derrick de Marney
Tita..Donald Arbury
Henrietta..Selena Royle
Mrs. Wyndham Lewis..............................Sophie Stewart
Rook..Alice John
Wyndham Lewis.......................................Edgar Kent
Edward Bulwer.................................Harry Redding
Caroline Norton...............................Lenore Sorsby
Rosina Bulwer..................................Frances Amherst
    Act I.—Bradenham. Act II.—Scene 1—Park Street, London. 2—
Grosvenor Gate. Act III.—Grosvenor Gate.
    Staged by Margaret Webster; settings and costumes by David
Ffolkes; music directed by Henri Berchman.

Benjamin Disraeli as a young man has just seen a first novel
(*Vivian Grey*) published and is hopeful that its sale will help
him get out of debt. Failing this he turns to politics, first as
a radical and later as a Tory. Advancing to leadership among
the Conservatives, he suffers a bit of booing instigated by his
rivals on the occasion of his overaccentuated maiden speech,
but is soon headed toward the cabinet he was later to adorn. His
romance is tied in with that of the widow of his best friend,
Wyndham Lewis, whom his eloquence swept into his arms the
first year of her mourning.

JULIUS CAESAR

(157 performances)

A tragedy by William Shakespeare; incidental music by Marc
Blitzstein. Revived by Orson Welles and John Houseman at
the Mercury Theatre, New York, November 11, 1937.

Cast of characters—

Julius Caesar.....................................Joseph Holland
Octavius Caesar.................................Francis Carpenter
Marcus Antonius...............................George Coulouris
Publius..Joseph Cotten
Marcus Brutus.....................................Orson Welles
Cassius...Martin Gabel
Casca...Hiram Sherman
Trebonius..John A. Willard
Ligarius...Grover Burgess
Decius Brutus....................................John Hoysradt
Metellus Cimber................................Stefan Schnabel
Cinna...Ted Reid
Flavius...William Mowry
Marullus..William Alland
Artemidorus......................................George Duthie
Cinna, the Poet...................................Norman Lloyd
Lucius..Arthur Anderson
Calpurnia..Evelyn Allen
Portia...Muriel Brassler
    Staged by Orson Welles; setting by Samuel Leve; music directed
by L. I. Epstein.

A modern dress version of the Shakespearean tragedy trimmed
to its essential scenes and played without scenery. Resembling

in effect a CIO conspiracy to make way with a dictator of the
Mussolini type.

PLACES PLEASE!

(3 performances)

A comedy in three acts by Aurania Rouverol. Produced by
Jack Curtis at the Golden Theatre, New York, November 12,
1937.

Cast of characters—

Sam	Richard Hunter
Mary Cole Farnum	Ruth Abbott
Lida	Olga Burgoyne
Johnny Gibbons	Don Dillaway
Anthony Farnum	Robert T. Haines
Sylvia O'Connor	Jean Rodney
Floy Farnum	Lillian Emerson
Stanley Lane	Henry Hull, Jr.
Roberta Farnum	Bette Butterworth
Alden Alexander Elliott	Matthew Smith
Mrs. Rhoda Wheeler	Claire Devine
Mrs. Agnes Elliott	Eleanor Malcolm
Mrs. Louisa Wilcox	Marie Falls
Carter	John L. Kearney
Doctor Selby	Richard Stirling
Carolyn Page	Rosalie Norman
Monty	Wilfred Henry

Also Sylvia Stuart, Jane Slater, Tweedy Tinklefaugh and Arthur
Silby.

Act I.—Floy Farnum's Dressing Room. Theatre in Boston. Act
II.—The Elliott Living Room, Boston. Act III.—Scenes 1 and 2—
Boston Theatre Green Room. 3—Floy's Dressing Room.

Floy Farnum, of the acting Farnums, decides to give up the
theatre and marry Alden Elliott, a very superior Bostonian.
Alden's stiff-backed mother refuses to accept Floy as one of
her Back Bay set, which makes Floy pretty mad. She leaves
Alden and Boston, returns to the acting Farnums in time to
score the success of her stage life. After which she decides to
continue on in the old way and marry Johnny Gibbons, the
stage manager.

TOO MANY HEROES

(16 performances)

A drama in two acts by Dore Schary. Produced by Carly
Wharton at the Hudson Theatre, New York, November 15, 1937.

Cast of characters—

Mrs. Halsey	Leslie Bingham
Nora Williams	Elspeth Eric

```
Mr. Halsey.......................................Francis Pierlot
Jeb Williams........................................James Bell
Harry Halsey.....................................Richard Keene
Danny Parker.....................................Jean Barrere
Tommy Potter....................................Thomas Fisher
Wilson............................................Paul Ashley
Cosgrove.........................................James Backus
Hartman.......................................Lawrence Forsythe
Lassiter............................................Jack Lee
Ranger.........................................Randolph Wade
Burton........................................Charles McClelland
Mr. McMillan...................................Clyde Franklin
Andrews.........................................Rex Williams
First Deputy....................................Marion Willis
Sheriff Bailey..................................Joseph Sweeney
Second Deputy..................................John Huntington
Stevenson.......................................Anthony Ross
John Nolan.......................................Lew Eckles
Third Deputy.................................Herschel Cropper
Fourth Deputy..................................Royal C. Stout
Carrie Nolan....................................Shirley Booth
Peters........................................Ernest Woodward
Capt. Miller....................................Robert Reed
Nielson.........................................Bjorn Koefoed
Factory Workers, Townspeople and Children.
```
Act I.—Scene 1—Jeb Williams' Home. 2—Warehouse. 3—County Jail. Act II.—Scenes 1, 4 and 5—Jeb Williams' Home. 2—County Jail. 3—Mr. McMillan's Office.

Staged by Garson Kanin; settings by Jo Mielziner.

Jeb Williams is happily married to Nora and has a job in the mill. The mill superintendent's daughter is kidnaped, abused and murdered by two drunken millhands. A mob is organized to lynch them. Jeb, peace-loving and law-abiding, rebels against joining the mob. Forced in by the sneers of his wife and his friends, it is Jeb who strikes one of the prisoners over the head with an iron bar and kills him. Thereafter Jeb is tortured by his conscience. He tries to give himself up to a Sheriff who is trying to forget the whole business. He tries to help the widow of the man he killed. The town turns against him. His wife leaves him. He is killed by another mob when he tries to defend the woman he would protect.

MADAME BOVARY

(39 performances)

A drama in three acts by Gaston Baty, taken from the novel by Gustave Flaubert, adapted by Benn W. Levy. Produced by The Theatre Guild at the Broadhurst Theatre, New York, November 16, 1937.

Cast of characters—

```
Emma Bovary...............................Constance Cummings
Monsieur Rouault.................................Arthur Griffin
Charles Bovary................................Harold Vermilyea
Homais.........................................Ernest Cossart
```

Mme. Lefrancois	Alice Belmore-Cliffe
Hippolyte	John O'Connor
Binet	Robert Vivian
Leon Dupuis	Carl Harbord
Lheureux	Ernest Thesiger
Felicite	Valerie Cossart
Justin	O. Z. Whitehead
Mme. Homais	Viola Roache
Mme. Caron	Hazel Hanna
Rodolphe Boulanger	Eric Portman
Girard	Maurice Manson
Mme. Bovary, Senior	Eda Heinemann

Companions: Ann Freschmann, Frances Harison, Jacqueline de Wit, Lilyan Miller, Mary McCormack and Gladene Parr.

Act I.—Scene 1—Balcony of Rouault Farm at Les Bertaux. 2—Inn of the Lion d'Or at Yonville L'Abbaye. 3—Living Room of the Homaises. 4 and 5—Sitting Room of the Bovarys. Act II.—Scene 1—Homais' Pharmacy. 2—Emma's Bedroom. 3—Bovary's Sitting Room. 4—La Huchette—Rodolphe's Sitting Room. 5—Emma's Bedroom and Rodolphe's Sitting Room.

Staged by Benn W. Levy; settings by Lee Simonson, adapted from original production of Gaston Baty.

Emma Bovary, radiantly happy the night of her marriage to the dull country doctor, Charles Bovary, suffers a first disillusionment when Charles goes to sleep with his head in her lap. As life grows increasingly disappointing Emma seeks to recover its glow, first by practically forcing an elopement upon Rodolphe Boulanger, who leaves her in the lurch, and later by indulging in a sordid affair with Leon Dupuis. With debts crowding in, Emma finally takes to poison and death to effect her escape.

FATHER MALACHY'S MIRACLE

(125 performances)

A comedy in three acts by Brian Doherty adapted from a novel by Bruce Marshall. Produced by Delos Chappell at the St. James Theatre, New York, November 17, 1937.

Cast of characters—

Mac	John Robb
Peter	Ralph Cullinan
Andrew Gillespie	Donald Beddoe
Father Flaherty	John Call
Annie	Mary Wickes
Canon Geoghegan	Robert S. Harrison
Father Malachy	Al Shean
George Bleater	Victor Beecroft
Winnie Gideon	Audrey Ridgwell
Phyllis Holt	Elisabeth Royce
Bessie Blaine	Maud Burnes
Heather Blue	Marian Miller
Greta Stacey	Jeanne Gilmore
James Shyman Bell	Anthony Blair
Gertie Gill	Wauna Paull
Reverend Humphrey Hamilton	Frank Greene
Peggy McNab	Margaret Curtis
Constable	Thomas P. Dillon
Mrs. McNab	Lillian Brennard Tonge

```
Archie MacDonald...............................Howard Clark
Nora MacDonald.................................Ann Winthrop
Jock Worlock..............................Charles Furcolowe
Bert Cameron.....................................Stanley Grady
A Waiter.....................................William H. Malone
A Second Waiter.............................Clement O'Loghlen
Robert Gillespie, Bishop of Milothian.............St. Clair Bayfield
Timothy Battle.....................................Paul Porter
Cardinal Vassena.........................Benedict MacQuarrie
Sir James Vickers...........................Herbert Standing
Lady Pamela Vickers...........................Virginia Lomas
Bunty Glencannon..............................Connie Crouell
Nessie Macintosh.............................Christie Tiffany
Sam Hicks................................Charles F. O'Connor
Mary Lou Hicks...............................Margot Sterling
Bar Man........................................David Baldwin
```
     Act I.—Scene 1—Street in Edinburgh. 2—Sacristy of the Church
of St. Margaret of Scotland. 3—Bar of the "Garden of Eden." Act
II.—Living Room of the Presbytery of St. Margaret of Scotland.
Act III.—Scene 1—Living Room of Presbytery. 2—Bar of Garden
of Eden Casino on Bass Rock.
     Staged by Worthington Miner; settings by Jo Mielziner.

Father Malachy comes from a monastery to continue his work
in the Church of St. Margaret of Scotland in Edinburgh. A
simple soul of simple faith he accepts a dare from an Anglican
neighbor, the Rev. Hamilton, to prove that miracles are as easy
for God in the twentieth century as they were in the time of
Christ. He prays for the removal of the Garden of Eden dance
hall and God, answering the prayer, takes the dance hall to an
island twenty miles away. In place of restoring the faith of the
world Father Malachy's miracle gets a lot of people into trouble
and in the end he is obliged to ask another miracle that will
return the Garden of Eden to its old stand.

ROBIN LANDING

(12 performances)

A drama in three acts by Stanley Young. Produced by Sidner
Harmon and T. Edward Hambleton at the 46th Street Theatre,
New York, November 18, 1937.

Cast of characters—

```
Laban.........................................Fred  Stewart
Lieutenant  Phelps................................Leslie  Denison
Grant Eaton.........................................Ian Keith
Dr. Titus.....................................S. Thomas Gomez
Tim...........................................Harry  Sothern
Lamont.....................................Morton L. Stevens
Sippi...........................................Kathryn  Grill
Father Duval..................................Robert  Marzano
David Eaton................................Richard Paul Spater
Fink.........................................Whitford  Kane
Kane Eaton.....................................Louis Calhern
Linda Eaton...................................Nan Sunderland
Wilson........................................Percy Helton
```
     Acts I, II and III.—Kentucky Trading Post in 1770.
     Staged by Halsted Welles; setting by Donald Oenslager; costumes
by Jean Sutherland.

Grant Eaton has fled from northern civilization after misunderstandings with his wife Linda and his brother Kane and opened a trading post in the wilderness of Kentucky. Eighteen years later the wife and the brother follow after. Thinking Grant dead Linda and Kane have married. Grant also has married, taking to wife the Indian woman, Sippi, and fathering her half-breed son, David. Grant would be revenged upon Linda and Kane, but the discovery of Linda's continuing love for him and his own loyalty toward his Indian family get in the way of his revenge. He is stabbed and blinded by Kane, who, in turn, is stabbed and killed by one of Grant's followers. Leaving Linda to stay on with Grant in the wilderness to recover as much of their love as possible.

THE BOUGH BREAKS

(3 performances)

A drama in three acts by James Knox Millen. Produced by Peggy Cleary and Paul Berney at the Little Theatre, New York, November 19, 1937.

Cast of characters—

```
The Boy............................................Leon Janney
The Girl...........................................Cyrilla Dorne
The Boy's Mother...................................Eleanor Brent
     Acts I, II and III.—The Living Room.
     Staged by Curtis Cooksey; setting by O. L. Raineri.
```

The Boy is in his last year of college. The Girl is employed in a shop. They meet and want to marry. The Boy's Mother, bitterly disappointed and maternally jealous, is determined to save her son. The Boy and the Girl declare themselves married in the sight of God. In spite of which the Mother pursues her opposition until the Boy's mind is unhinged and he kills himself. Leaving the Girl possessed of all that he left, which is the child she is carrying. This gives Mother pause.

WORK IS FOR HORSES

(9 performances)

A comedy in three acts by Henry Myers. Produced by Anthony Brown at the Windsor Theatre, New York, November 20, 1937.

Cast of characters—

Millie Prentiss....................................Connie Gilchrist
Cornelius Prentiss.................................Robert Keith
Pauline Prentiss...................................Patricia Carroll
Wilbur Tripp......................................Jack Warren
Clara Manning.....................................Eula Guy
T. V. Nash..John Westley
George Shattuck...................................James Todd
    Acts I, II and III.—Living Room of the Prentiss Flat, Amsterdam
Ave., New York.
    Staged by Anthony Brown.

Cornelius Prentiss is a genial but useless loafer. Work, in his philosophy, is for horses and other burden-bearing animals. For twenty-five years he lives on the earnings of his wife, Millie, and then plans virtually to sell his daughter, Pauline, to a big business man and continue his useless existence at her patron's expense. The big business man fights back and the plan fails. Pauline marries the boy who has seduced her. Cornelius is threatened with being forced to work when an aunt dies and leaves him several thousand dollars. Cornelius is back in the old armchair.

THE GHOST OF YANKEE DOODLE

(48 performances)

A drama in two acts by Sidney Howard. Produced by The Theatre Guild, Inc., at the Guild Theatre, New York, November 22, 1937.

Cast of characters—

Sara Garrison....................................Ethel Barrymore
John Garrison....................................Frank Conroy
Patience Garrison................................Marilyn Erskine
Michael Garrison.................................Jack Kelly
The Honorable Edward Callory.....................George Nash
Doris Garrison...................................Kathleen Comegys
Roger Garrison...................................John Drew Devereaux
Joan Garrison....................................Barbara Robbins
Robert Garrison..................................Eliot Cabot
Martin Holme.....................................Richard Carlson
Mary...Ethel Intropidi
James Madison Clevenger..........................Dudley Digges
Ockleford..Don Costello
Steve Andrews....................................Russell Hardie
Buck Anson.......................................Donald Black
A Sergeant.......................................Edward Butler
Burke..Lloyd Gough
Dr. Miller.......................................Howard Roberts
    Acts I and II.—Library of Home of the late John Garrison, now
occupied by his widowed daughter-in-law, Mrs. Paul Garrison, in one
of the older Western American cities. Eighteen months after the
next world war.
    Staged by John Cromwell, Theresa Helburn and Lawrence Langner;
setting by Woodman Thompson.

The Garrisons are an old, established American family. Sara, whose husband, Paul, was an aviator killed in the World War, is maintaining the Garrison home eighteen months after the beginning of the next war. The government is trying to keep out by preserving a strict neutrality. The Garrisons are ardent pacifists, even though the Garrison business is threatened with bankruptcy unless it violates the neutrality act and sells munitions of war to Japan. An old suitor of Sara Garrison's is James Clevenger, powerful publisher of a chain of newspapers. Clevenger is trying to induce Sara to marry him. At the crisis of his wooing he swings the influence of his newspapers in favor of war, bringing prosperity to the Garrisons, but widening the breach between Sara and himself.

OF MICE AND MEN

(207 performances)

A drama in three acts by John Steinbeck. Produced by Sam H. Harris at the Music Box, New York, November 23, 1937.

Cast of characters—

George...Wallace Ford
Lennie.......................................Broderick Crawford
Candy.......................................John F. Hamilton
The Boss......................................Thomas Findlay
Curley..Sam Byrd
Curley's Wife......................................Claire Luce
Slim..Will Geer
Carlson..Charles Slattery
Whit...Walter Baldwin
Crooks...Leigh Whipper
        Act I.—Scene 1—Sandy Bank of Salinas River. 2—Bunk House. Act II.—Scene 1—Bunk House. 2—Crooks' Room. Act III.—Scene 1—Barn, 2—River Bank. Agricultural Valley in Central California.
        Staged by George S. Kaufman; settings by Donald Oenslager.

See page 31.

* PINS AND NEEDLES

(264 performances)

A musical revue by Arthur Arent, Marc Blitzstein, Emanuel Eisenberg, Charles Friedman and David Gregory; music and lyrics by Harold J. Rome. Presented by International Ladies' Garment Workers' Union Players at Labor Stage Theatre, New York, November 27, 1937.

Players engaged—

Lydia Annucci
Sol Babchin
Sadie Bershadsky
Anne Brown
Sam Dratch
Zitta Edinburgh
Al Eben
Anthony Fazio
Tillie Feldman
Irene Fox
Sandra Gelman
Eugene Goldstein
Hyman Goldstein
Enzo Grassi
Nettie Harary
Hattie Hausdorf
Lynne Jaffee
Harry Kadison
Hyman Kaplan
Rose Kaufman

Bella Kinburn
Al Levy
May Martin
Murray Modick
Betty Morrison
Miriam Morrison
Jean Newman
Rose Newmark
Olive Pearman
Joseph Roth
Ruth Rubinstein
Fred Schmidt
Moe Schreier
Paul Seymour
Isaac Sides
Sidney Sklar
Mae Spiegel
Millie Weitz
Beatty Uretsky

Staged by Charles Friedman; settings by S. Syrjala; dance direction by Gluck Sandor; choreography by Benjamin Zemach.

BARCHESTER TOWERS

(40 performances)

A comedy in three acts adapted by Thomas Job from a novel by Anthony Trollope. Produced by Guthrie McClintic at the Martin Beck Theatre, New York, November 30, 1937.

Cast of characters—

Mrs. Proudie	Florence Edney
Bishop Proudie	Frederick Graham
Mr. Slope	John Williams
Miss Trefoil	Pamela Simpson
Dr. Stanhope	Oswald Yorke
Madeline Neroni	Ina Claire
Ethelbert Stanhope	Mackenzie Ward
Butler	Henry Vincent
Eleanor Bold	Ruth Matteson
Mr. Arabin	Damian O'Flynn
Miss Thorne	Effie Shannon
Archbishop	J. M. Kerrigan

Act I.—Scene 1—Bishop's Library in Dean Trefoil's House. 2—Dr. Vesey Stanhope's Drawing Room. Act II.—Lawn in Miss Thorne's Estate at Ullathorne. Act III.—Dr. Stanhope's Drawing Room.

Staged by Guthrie McClintic; settings by Jo Mielziner.

Madeline Neroni, recently returned to the English cathedral town of Barchester, after eleven years in Italy, and following a pretty serious quarrel with her Italian husband, enters merrily into a social crisis arising over the selection of a new dean for the Barchester diocese. Madeline favors a young liberal, Arabin, whose chief opposition is a certain Mr. Slope. To embarrass Mr. Slope before the archbishop Madeline puts champagne in his ginger beer mug. Madeline also forces young Arabin to propose to her when she knows he is in love with Eleanor Bold, and before she is sure that she (Madeline) is a widow. When she hears that her husband has been discovered playing cards at Monte Carlo she is quite satisfied to turn Arabin back to Eleanor and return to Italy.

HOORAY FOR WHAT!

(200 performances)

A musical comedy in two acts conceived by E. Y. Harburg; book by Howard Lindsay and Russel Crouse; lyrics by E. Y. Harburg; music by Harold Arlen; orchestrations by Don Walker. Produced by the Messrs. Shubert at the Winter Garden, New York, December 1, 1937.

Principals engaged—

Ed Wynn	June Clyde
Paul Haakon	Vivian Vance
Jack Whiting	Leo Chalzel
Robert Shafer	Ruthanna Boris
Don Popikoff	Detmar Poppen
Charles Senna	Marcel Rousseau
Franklyn Fox	Will Ferry
Arthur Kay	Al Baron
Five Reillys	The Briants
Al Gordon's Dogs	Sue Hastings Marionettes

Staged by Howard Lindsay; dances directed by Robert Alton; music directed by Robert Emmett Dolan; settings by Vincente Minnelli; costumes by Raoul Pene Du Bois; supervision by Vincente Minnelli.

"Chuckles" Wynn, a horticulturist of indefinite parts, invents a gas intended to destroy the insects that eat his fruit. The gas proves equally devastating to humans as well and is eagerly sought by delegates to the League of Nations at Geneva, who would obtain the formula as soon as possible that they may hurry along the next war. Chuckles manages, after a two-hour pursuit, to elude the delegates and save the world.

BROWN SUGAR

(4 performances)

A melodrama in three acts by Bernie Angus; incidental music by Haven Johnson. Produced by George Abbott at the Biltmore Theatre, New York, December 2, 1937.

Cast of characters—

Bartender	Richard Huey
Tom Warfield	T. Burton Smith
Trot	John T. L. Bunn
Lonny	Martin de C. Slade
Charlie	Ira Johnson
Ruby	Kathryn Lavall
Slim	Alvin Childress
Sam	Juan Hernandez
Rosalinda	Christola Williams
Sylvester	Richard McMyers
Tar	Paul Johnson
Musken	Eric Burroughs
Louella	Beulah E. Edmonds
Sarah	Ruby Elzy
Jeb	Bertram Holmes
Officer Leroy	Julian Miles
Man	Jimmy Waters
Rosco	Haven Johnson
Henry	Canada Lee
Lily May	Georgette Harvey
Lucille	Butterfly McQueen
Walter	William Tinney
George	Allen Tinney
Stella	Beth Dixon
Cleo	Irene Hill
Pete Malley	John Shellie
First Mate	Ernest Rowan
Officer Kent	George W. Smith
O'Hara	George Fitzpatrick
McQuade	Fred Wallace

Act I.—Scenes 1 and 2—In Harlem.   Act II.—Scenes 1 and 3—Lily May's Apartment.   2—Louella's Kitchen.   Act III.—Scene 1—Louella's Kitchen.   2—Dock at Foot of Mester Street.

Staged by George Abbott; settings by Cirker and Robbins; costumes by Helene Pons.

Rosalinda, a night club beauty, has put powders in a white man's liquor and he is dead. Rosalinda turns to big Sam Jackson for love and comfort and Sam seeks to hide her in his wife's (Louella's) flat. Louella is awful jealous, but submits, even going so far as to charm a policeman in order to take his mind off the pursuit. Sam finally escapes aboard a freighter. Rosalinda is taken in by the police and Louella is hopeful of happier days to come.

MERELY MURDER

(3 performances)

A comedy in three acts by A. E. Thomas based on a novel by Georgette Heyer. Produced by Laurence Rivers, Inc., at the Playhouse, December 3, 1937.

Cast of characters—

Kenneth Vereker	Rex O'Malley
Violet Williams	Muriel Hutchison
Rudolph Mesurier	Stiano Braggiotti

```
Murgatroyd...............................Jessamine Newcombe
Leslie Rivers.......................................Betty Jenckes
Tony (Antonia) Vereker..........................Claudia Morgan
Inspector Hannaside..............................Edward Fielding
Giles Carrington................................George Macready
Harry Chippendale.............................Lawrence Fletcher
Sergeant Armstrong..............................Charles Campbell
    Acts I, II and III.—Studio Living Room in the Vereker Flat.
    Staged by Miriam Doyle; setting by Watson Barratt.
```

Kenneth and Tony Vereker, brother and sister, irresponsibles with an artistic urge, are greatly surprised and a little pleased to hear that an absent stepbrother whom both loathed has been mysteriously stabbed to death.   Kenneth expects to come into quite a bit of money.   The Verekers consider it a great joke to let Scotland Yard believe them guilty of the murder.   A second brother, long believed dead, also turns up with plenty of motive for the killing, seeing that he comes into the money before Kenneth.   The second brother is also stabbed to death, and still there is no arrest.   The mysterious murderer is finally discovered to be an outsider who hoped to marry into the family and get her hands on the inheritance that way.

LOVE IN MY FASHION

(2 performances)

A comedy in three acts by Charles George.   Produced by Morris Green and James J. Fero at the Ritz Theatre, New York, December 3, 1937.

Cast of characters—

```
Mrs. Robert Andrews..............................Thais Lawton
Pamela Pennington..................................Luella Gear
Celia Pennington..................................Tookie Hunter
Dwight Langdon....................................Richard Jack
Elsie Andrews...................................Dorothy Bernard
Gardner Dickinson................................William David
Grace Tillman.....................................Claire Carleton
Mrs. Minnie Sterling..........................Ruth Chorpenning
Mrs. Franklin Coleman................................Day Eliot
Elaine Carley...................................Louise Kirtland
Christopher Coffman............................G. Albert Smith
Ryder Pennington..............................Donald Mackenzie
Mrs. Madge Duval....................................Julio Brown
Rev. Stephen Cartwright.........................Sherling Oliver
    Acts I and III.—Living Room of Mrs. Andrews, Baltimore, Mary-
land.   Act II.—Christopher Coffman's Establishment in Virginia.
    Staged by Melville Burke; settings by Cleon Throckmorton.
```

Pamela Pennington, man crazy, no sooner buries her first husband than she begins planning to marry a second, selecting the mortician who buried the first.   The mortician is killed in a railway wreck and Pamela starts after No. 3, who would be the minister officiating at the second's funeral service.

EDNA HIS WIFE

(32 performances)

A monodrama in eleven scenes adapted by Cornelia Otis Skinner from the book by Margaret Ayer Barnes; music by Elliott Jacoby. Produced by Miss Skinner at the Little Theatre, New York, December 7, 1937.

Scene 1—Edna—Blue Island, Illinois—1900. 2—Mrs. Losser, Edna's Mother—1900. 3—Florrie Brophy, a Woman Who Lives Across the Hall—1902. Edna (Before Dinner). Edna (After Dinner). 4—Susan Peebles, Edna's Neighbor and Closest Friend—1913. 5—Dolly McElroy, a Chicago Society Woman—1913. 6—Pearl, Edna's Sister—Chicago, July 6, 1915. 7—Edna—1918. 8—Jessica, Edna's Daughter—1925. 9—Edna—1930. 10—Katharine Boyne, a Sculptress—1930. 11—Edna (Morning)—1937. Edna (Evening).
Settings by Donald Oenslager; costumes by Helene Pons.

Miss Skinner played all eight characters, introducing Edna Losser at the brakeman's picnic at which she met Paul Jones and decided to give up Al Reimer. Thereafter she introduced her mother, sister and intimate friends. The story carries through Edna's unhappy life with her ambitious and ruthless husband, culminating in her discovery of Katharine Boyne, who had been Paul Jones' mistress for sixteen years, and her pathetic acceptance of the situation thus created.

SIEGE

(6 performances)

A drama in three acts by Irwin Shaw. Produced by Norman Bel Geddes at the Longacre Theatre, New York, December 8, 1937.

Cast of characters—

Escobar	Abner Biberman
Bazan	Jackson Halliday
Pierito	Charles Keane
Perez	Harold Moffet
Pacheco	David Leonard
Gomez	Edwin Thatcher
Savin	Leopold Badia
Dr. Castro	J. Hammond Dailey
Guiterra	Sheldon Leonard
Diaz	William Edmunds
Teresa	Rose Hobart
Tormes	Hunter Gardner
Cruz	John Irwin
Marcial	Rollin Bauer
Manero	Maurice Gosfield
Mrs. Perez	Zamah Cunningham
Villista	William Franklin
Captain Bellite	Norman Stuart

Acts I, II and III.—East Tower of Fortress on Mountain Peak in Spain.
Staged by Chester Erskin; setting by Norman Bel Geddes; costumes by Frances Waite.

A few hundred loyalists are beleaguered in an ancient fort on a mountain peak in Spain. During the last days of their defiance both romance and strife break out among them. Guiterra, the bullfighter, takes Teresa, wife of Diaz, a pacifist. Guiterra, in a show of courage, goes for food and loses a leg. Helpless, his courage oozes and he whimpers for surrender. Diaz, the pacifist, turning hero in the emergency, shoots Guiterra to quiet his whimpering and leads the last assault.

SOMETHING FOR NOTHING

(2 performances)

A comedy in three acts by Harry J. Essex and Sid Schwartz. Produced by Stuart Drake, Inc., at the Windsor Theatre, New York, December 9, 1937.

Cast of characters—

Jenny Perkins	Lulu McConnell
Bobby Perkins	Joe Brown, Jr.
"Doc" Piper	Edgar Stehli
Kenneth Scott	Ben Lackland
Una Perkins	Sylvia Field
Will Perkins	Seth Arnold
Mr. Pinkie	Richard Taber
Mr. Boyle	Millard Mitchell
Dr. Kipper	Kent Thurber

Acts I, II and III.—Perkins' Living Room, Paducha, New York.
Staged by Harry Wagstaff Gribble; setting by Nicholas Yellenti.

The Perkins family is contest crazy. At work on the titles of a hundred cartoons for which a gum concern has agreed to pay a prize of a hundred thousand dollars they discover the inventor of the contest, Kenneth Scott, has selected their home as his hideout. He is supposed to have all the correct answers in his bag. Kenneth is stalked by crooks and wheedled by the Perkins crowd. When Una Perkins, who loves him, thinks her family has stolen the answers she goes to New York to expose the fraud. The Perkinses win honestly, but are denied the money.

LOVE OF WOMEN

(8 performances)

A drama in three acts by Aimee and Philip Stuart. Produced by Messrs. Shubert in association with Milton Shubert at the Golden Theatre, New York, December 13, 1937.

Cast of characters—

Jacqueline Vesey	Cathleen Cordell
Mr. Wingate	Sayre Crawley
Mrs. Wingate	Molly Pearson
James Harkiness	Leo G. Carroll
Philip Vesey	Michael Goff
Brigit Wingate	Heather Angel
Vere Malcolm	Valerie Taylor
John Bourdillion	Hugh Sinclair

Acts I and III.—Living Room of Vere's and Brigit's Cottage, Block Beach Cottage, Sussex, England. Act II.—Patio of Cottage. Staged by Leo G. Carroll; settings by Raymond Sovey.

Vere Malcolm and Brigit Wingate, playwrights, have been working and living together for five years. With their first success, which draws newspaper attention to them, certain people begin to question the relationship, broadly intimating that it stems from an abnormal sex attraction. Brigit's family is particularly interested in "saving" their daughter from scandal. John Bourdillion, a young doctor, would get Brigit away because he is in love with her. The girls are inclined to fight the charges and defy the scandal. Bourdillion, convincing both that they should lead normal sex lives through mating and marrying, takes Brigit away with him.

FICKLE WOMEN

(1 performance)

A drama in three acts by Murray Brown. Produced by S. Mario Castagna and Irving E. Bizman at the Nora Bayes Theatre, New York, December 15, 1937.

Cast of characters—

Billie Bronson	Emilie Elden
Alice Bronson	Mildred Rowlette
Marty Bronson	S. Mario Castagna
Edna Walker	Naomi Ravelle
Ralph Walker	Murray Brown
Tony Marillo	Jerry Guardino
John Keenan	William Pharr
Captain Morgan	Edgar Winslow
Betty Stewart	Virginia Elliott
Detective Woods	Garri Rose
Dolores	Caprice Petite

Ann Crane...Alice Craven
District Attorney...................................Paul Long
Matron...Bessie Petts
      Staged by Murray Brown.

Betty Stewart, who had been on call, is moved by sympathy for Billie, the child of Alice Bronson, white slave victim, to reform and take care of the kid. She helps the police and the G-men find Billie Bronson's mother. During a raid on Edna's call house Betty shoots and kills Marty Bronson, Alice's white-slaving husband, which was a good thing.

TELL ME PRETTY MAIDEN

(28 performances)

A comedy by Dorothy Day Wendell. Produced by George Bushar and John Tuerk at the Mansfield Theatre, New York, December 16, 1937.

Cast of characters—

Jane Housman.......................................Ivy Troutman
Myrtle Binner......................................Ellen Love
Glory Dawn...Constance McKay
Waiter...Charles Atkin
Jimmie Manhoff.....................................Otto Hulett
Albert Horning.....................................Harold West
Margo Dare...Doris Nolan
Mrs. Darrell.......................................May Buckley
Mrs. Corey...Susanne Willa
Bobbie Darrell.....................................Charles Powers
Policeman..Arling Alcine
Detective..Glenn Coulter
Hortense...Beatrice Kay
Clementine...Ann Thomas
Stella...Emily Devine
Sadie..Florence Herrick
Hallie...Ruth Conley
The Mick...Nellie Burt
Miss Pillsbury.....................................Lalive Brownell
Gabby..Jean Mann
Tommy Wentworth....................................Alan Bunce
Headwaiter...Walter Armin
Max..Gustave Weinburg
His Girl Friend....................................Nellie Burt
Spectators.................Karl Kohrs, Richard Mercer, Leon Rubin
      Act I.—Scenes 1 and 3—The Oval Room in a Smart Mid-Western Hotel. 2—Margo's Home. Act II.—Scenes 1 and 3—The Oval Room. 2—Margo's Convent. Act III.—Scenes 1 and 3—The Oval Room. 2—The Maison Riche.
      Staged by Arthur Sircom; settings by Watson Barratt.

Margo Dare, who has just scored a great success as an actress, is being interviewed by the press. Asked about her childhood she recalls a jasmine-scented garden in the South. The scene changes and Margo's garden is revealed as Maggie Darrell's backyard of a tenement in New York. Back to the interview, Margo recites her first stage experience at the convent. The changing scene exposes the convent as a house of correction. Again Margo tells of her romantic meeting with the man who is backing her show, which is shown to have been an accidental contact at a night club the time Maggie's brother was being chased by police. The backer's romance, however, is proved to be real.

BETWEEN THE DEVIL

(93 performances)

A musical comedy in two acts by Howard Dietz and Arthur Schwartz. Produced by the Messrs. Shubert at the Imperial Theatre, New York, December 22, 1937.

Cast of characters—

Peter Anthony }
Pierre Antoine }................................Jack Buchanan
Natalie Rives ....Evelyn Laye
Harry Morley......................................William Kendall
Freddie Hill......................................Charles Walters
Claudette Gilbert......................................Adele Dixon
Gaston..Noel Cravat
Maney..Ralph Sumpter
Marie..Natasha Dana
The Savoy Club Boys........Andy Love, Jack Lathrop, Bob Wacker
Waiter...Albert Amato
Bartenders......................Ward Tallman, Vernon Hammer
Annabelle Scott....................................Vilma Ebsen
Raymond Maurois....................................Jules Epailly
English Policeman..................................Maurice Kelly
The Debonaires: Harold Murray, Jack Voeth, Maurice Kelly, Buddy
    Hertelle and Edward Gale.
The Lady Guests: Bunny Waters, Jessica Pepper, Joyce Duskin,
    Tilda Getze, Kay Cameron, Virginia Daly, Ruth Joseph, Helen
    Hudson, Dorothy Compton, Lee Stephenson, Loretto Dennison
    and Linda Lee.
The Gentlemen Guests: Albert Amato, Ward Tallman, Vernon Ham-
    mer, Jack Richards, Frank Gagen, Erick Brotherson.
    Act I.—Scene 1—Roof Terrace off Hotel Ballroom in London. 2
and 6—The Anthony's Drawing Room. 3—Claudette's Apartment in
Paris. 4—Bar off London Restaurant. 5—Entrance to Natalie's Lon-
don House. Act II.—Scene 1—The Drawing Room. 2—Entrance to
Natalie's House. 3—Natalie's Bedroom. 4—Street in Paris. 5—
Claudette's Apartment. 6—Foyer to London Hotel Ballroom. 7—
Roof Terrace.
    Staged by Hassard Short and John Hayden; dances by Robert
Alton; music direction by Don Voorhees; settings by Albert Johnson;
costumes by Kiviette; co-supervision of Edward Duryea Dowling.

Peter Anthony, believing the Claudette Gilbert he, as Pierre Antoine, had loved and married in Paris has been lost in a shipwreck, proceeds to love and marry Natalie Rives in London. Whereupon Claudette walks into the first act very much alive and in excellent voice. Peter finds living bigamously rather pleasant, but it does keep him dodging between London and Paris, and dodging his wives as well, practically every minute.

THREE WALTZES

(122 performances)

A musical romance in three parts adapted by Clare Kummer and Rowland Leigh from the play of Paul Knepler and Armin Robinson; music of first part after Johann Strauss, Sr., of second part after Johann Strauss, Jr., of third part by Oscar Straus. Produced by the Messrs. Shubert at the Majestic Theatre, New York, December 25, 1937.

Cast of characters—

ACT I
VIENNA 1865

Herr Baltramini	Ralph Bunker
Kalliwoda	Ivy Scott
Marie Hiller	Kitty Carlisle
Karl Brenner	Glenn Anders
Sebastian	Len Mence
Countess von Hohenbrunn	Marguerita Sylva
Egon von Hohenbrunn	Harry Mestayer
Herbert von Hohenbrunn	Alfred Kappeler
Felix von Hohenbrunn	Earl McDonald
Leopold von Hohenbrunn	Charlie Arnt
Field Marshal Count Maximilian von Hohenbrunn	George Baxter
Count Rudolph von Hohenbrunn	Michael Bartlett
Herr Difflinger	Wheeler Dryden
Lilli	Ruth MacDonald
Orderly	William Newgord

Ballet Girls—Wanda Cochran, Paula Kaye, Joan Engel, Marion Broske, Jean Sharp, June Sharpe, Ellen Gibb, Dorothy Hardy.
The Ballet Boys—Boris Butleroff, Michael Mann, Milton Barnett, Barry Gunn, Harold Taub, David Preston, Richard D'Arcy, Mischa Pompianov.

ACT II
PARIS 1900

Charlotte Hiller	Kitty Carlisle
Conductor	Trueman Gage
Andre Coroit	Ralph Magelssen
Manager	Alfred Kappeler
Author	Ralph Bunker
Reporter	Earl McDonald
Karl Brenner	Glenn Anders
Lilli Castelli	Ruth MacDonald
Steffi Castelli	Rosie Moran
Baron Delauney	Victor Morley
Viscount Rene Duval	John Barker
Count Otto von Hohenbrunn	Michael Bartlett
Leopold von Hohenbrunn	Charlie Arnt
Barmaid	Adele Rich
Marquise de Campo	Marion Pierce
Willi	Fred Sherman
Baroness de Launey	Ann Andrews
Louis	Wheeler Dryden
Page Boy	William Newgord
Gendarme	Earl McDonald
Dr. Cavaneu	George Baxter

ACT III

ENGLAND 1937

```
Sackville..........................................George  Baxter
W. Wagstaff Wolf...................................Louis  Sorin
Miss Waring........................................Adele  Rich
Cameraman.......................................Alfred  Kappeler
Franzi Coroit Hiller..............................Kitty  Carlisle
Trevor...........................................Earl  McDonald
Freddie..........................................Fred  Sherman
Karl Brenner.....................................Glenn  Anders
Max, Count von Hohenbrunn....................Michael  Bartlett
Musical Director..............................Wheeler  Dryden
Lilli Castelli....................................Ruth  MacDonald
Counterman..........................................Len  Mence
Leo.................................................Truman  Gage
```
Electricians, Stage Hands, Grips, Gaffers and Extras

Act I.—Rehearsal Room, Kartnertor Theatre, Vienna. 2—Coffee Room of Countess von Hohenbrunn. 3—Marie's Living Room. Act II.—Scene 1—Back Stage, Theatre Varieties, Paris. 2—Before the Curtain. 3—The Bar. 4—Maxim's Café. 5—Private Dining Room at Maxim's. 6—Charlotte's Dressing Room. Act III.—Denham-Buckinghamshire Films Ltd. Studio and Studio Cafeteria.

Staged by Hassard Short; dances by Chester Hale; settings by Watson Barratt; costumes by Connie de Pinna.

In Vienna, in 1865, Count Rudolph von Hohenbrunn is in love with Marie Hiller of the ballet. Marie gives him up at the request of his family. In Paris, in 1900, Count Otto, son of Count Rudolph, is in love with Charlotte Hiller, daughter of Marie Hiller. Marie is killed by Otto's jealous mistress. In London, in 1937, Franzi Hiller is making a picture of her grandmother's, Marie Hiller's, great romance in 1865 and accepts Count Max von Hohenbrunn, grandson of Rudolph, as her leading man. This time they are permitted to marry.

A DOLL'S HOUSE

(144 performances)

A drama in three acts by Henrik Ibsen; acting version by Thornton Wilder. Revived by Jed Harris at the Morosco Theatre, New York, December 27, 1937.

Cast of characters—

```
Nora Helmer.......................................Ruth  Gordon
Ellen.............................................Jessica  Rogers
Porter...........................................Harold  Johnsrud
Thorwald Helmer...................................Dennis  King
Christina Linden.................................Margaret  Waller
Doctor Rank.........................................Paul  Lukas
Nils Krogstad.......................................Sam  Jaffe
Anna...............................................Grace  Mills
Emmy........................................Lorna  Lynn  Meyers
Ivar.............................................Howard  Sherman
```
Acts I, II and III.—Home of Thorwald Helmer in Christiana. Staged by Jed Harris; setting by Donald Oenslager.

"A Doll's House" was first introduced to America by Helena Modjeska in Louisville, Ky., in 1883. This version was called "Thora" and included a happy ending following the reconciliation of the Helmers. The Ibsen text, in the William Archer translation, was later played by Minnie Maddern Fiske in 1889 and 1890 and frequently revived by that actress thereafter. American Noras have included Alla Nazimova, Eva Le Gallienne, Ethel Barrymore, Hortense Nielsen and Beatrice Cameron (Mrs. Richard Mansfield). The text used by Ruth Gordon in the revival of 1937 was prepared by Thornton Wilder and introduced originally at the Central City, Colo., drama festival the summer of 1937.

WESTERN WATERS

(7 performances)

A drama in three acts by Richard Carlson. Music arranged by Lehman Engel. Produced by Elsa Moses at the Hudson Theatre, New York, December 28, 1937.

Cast of characters—

```
Abigail..........................................Maxine  Stuart
Abijah  Plummer..................................Robert  Thomsen
Davie............................................Jackie  Grimes
Danny...........................................Jimmie  Lydon
Penelope........................................Joan  Wheeler
Jacques Pitou...................................Robt.  Shrewsbury
Granny..........................................Mabel  Paige
Josiah Cutler...................................Thomas  Chalmers
Gramp...........................................H.  Dudley  Hawley
Rev. Barnabas Harpe...........................S.  Thomas  Gomez
Jabe Knuckles.................................Morton L.  Stevens
Kaintuck......................................Van  Heflin
```
      Acts I, II and III.—Flatboat Floating Down the Ohio River.
      Staged by Elsa Moses and Richard Carlson; setting and costumes by Boris Aronson.

Josiah Cutler, leaving Massachusetts at the close of the seventeenth century in the hope of filing claim to some of the rich farming land in the Ohio valley, is stopped at Pittsburgh. Loading family and livestock on a flat-bottomed boat, the Cutlers start floating down the Ohio River. Their boat is boarded by a wild man called Kaintuck, who proceeds to take charge of the cruise. This uncovers the presence of a fake parson in Rev. Barnabas Harpe, who has been taken along for the ride and who is planning to scuttle the ship and grab land for himself. Kaintuck falls in love with Penelope Cutler, marries her when he has to, and helps Josiah beat back the would-be pirates.

ONE THING AFTER ANOTHER

(15 performances)

A drama in three acts by Sheldon Noble. Produced by Walter Craig at the Fulton Theatre, New York, December 28, 1937.

Cast of characters—

Winkie Butts	Charles Lawrence
Gus	William Foran
A Waiter	Joe Bates Smith
Harry Dill	Stephen Kent
Boss Gilray	Richard S. Bishop
Morgan	Kenneth Daigneau
Bob Barnard	Arthur Pierson
Kay Trevor	Kathryn Givney
Don Weston	Eddie Nugent
Marcia Hancock	Louise Larabee
Judy Canfield	Kathleen Fitz
Jack Thompson	Brandon Peters
Pete	Joseph Vitale
Lefty	Ben Laughlin
Chatterbox	Fred Howard
Eloise Woodward	Ann Mason
Sheriff Casper Blakesley	William Nunn
Myron	John Kane

Act I.—The Mirabar Night Club in Mid-Western City. Acts II and III.—A Deserted Barn.

Staged by Walter Craig; settings by John Root.

Eloise Woodward, who is quite definitely in society, sends a group of her juniors on a treasure hunt to the Mirabar Night Club the very same night that Boss Gilray plants a trio of kidnapers in the same spot to snatch a certain member of the millionaire set who is to be held for ransom. Treasure hunters and kidnapers get their paths frightfully crossed and all end up at a barn with a variety of amusing and vicious intentions. An adjustment of complications brings the curtain down.

STRAW HAT

(4 performances)

A satirical comedy in three acts by Kurt Unkelbach. Produced by Nat Burns at the Bayes Theatre, New York, December 30, 1937.

Cast of characters—

Madame Karnoff	Esther Leeming
Louise	Sylvia Leigh
Mary	Toni Merritt
Betty	Maxine Roscoe
Tillie	Frances Clay
Johnny	Louis Schultz
Denny	Phyllis Goodwin

```
Joe..............................................William A. Terry
Ossie..............................................Frederick A. Bell
Mac Bodeen........................................Nat Burns
Laureen Lee....................................Barbara Combes
Leslie Arnold......................................Frank Gibney
Lu Miller........................................Gordon Peters
Anthony Marks................................Melbourne Ford
Mrs. Marks...............................Ruth Thane-McDevitt
```

Acts I, II and III.—Living Room in Home of Eagle Beach Players, Eagle Beach, N. H.

Staged by Nat Burns; setting by Buell Scenic Studio.

Ossie, who comes from the farm, loves Louise, who is prepared to make any sacrifice to get into the theatre as an actress. Louise, making a try for Hollywood preferment by throwing herself at an executive, is maternally repulsed. Ossie, without guile, is accepted as a great success.

THE SHOEMAKER'S HOLIDAY

(69 performances)

A play by Thomas Dekker. Revived by Orson Welles and John Houseman at the Mercury Theatre, January 1, 1938.

Cast of characters—

```
The King........................................George Coulouris
Sir Hugh Lacy..................................Frederic Tozere
Rowland Lacy......................................Joseph Cotten
Askew..........................................William Mowry
Sir Roger Oteley..................................John Hoysradt
Master Hammon....................................Vincent Price
Master Warner..................................John A. Willard
Master Scott......................................George Duthie
Simon Eyre, the Shoemaker........................Whitford Kane
Roger..............................................Norman Lloyd
Firk..............................................Hiram  Sherman
Ralph..............................................Elliott  Reid
Dodger........................................Francis Carpenter
A Dutch Skipper.................................Stefan Schnabel
A Boy...........................................Arthur Anderson
Serving Man....................................William Alland
Rose, of Sir Roger.................................Alice Frost
Sybil..............................................Edith Barrett
Margery................................Marian  Warring-Manley
Jane..............................................Ruth Ford
```

Attendants: William Howell, Charles Baker.

Soldiers: Charles Baker, Tileston Perry, George Lloyd, Frederick Ross, Frederick Thompson, John Berry.

Shoemakers: Richard Wilson, William Herz, James O'Rear, Frank Westbrook.

Scene—London Streets and Houses.

Staged by Orson Welles; costumes by Millia Davenport.

Simon Eyre, master shoemaker, and his troup of apprentices, become mildly involved in the romantic doings of Rowland Lacy, who sends a substitute to represent him at the wars in France while he stays in London, disguised, to complete his conquest of Rose, daughter of Sir Roger Oteley. Simon is later elected

Lord Mayor of London and declares a shoemakers' holiday. The comedy was first produced in London on New Year's Day, 1600, and first revived professionally in New York on New Year's Day, 1938.

TIME AND THE CONWAYS

(32 performances)

A drama in three acts by J. B. Priestley. Produced by Crosby Gaige, Inc., in association with Jean V. Grombach and George Greening at the Ritz Theatre, New York, January 3, 1938.

Cast of characters—

Hazel...Hazel Terry
Carol...Mary Jones
Alan...Godfrey Kenton
Madge...Joan Henley
Kay...Jessica Tandy
Mrs. Conway..............................Dame Sybil Thorndike
Joan Helford...............................Helena Pickard
Gerald Thornton...............................Norman Wooland
Ernest Beevers...............................Guy Pelham Boulton
Robin...Christopher Quest

Acts I, II and III.—Sitting Room in Mrs. Conway's House, a Detached Villa in a Prosperous Suburb of a Manufacturing Town, Newlingham, England.

Staged by J. B. Priestley and Irene Hentschel; setting by P. Dodd Ackerman.

The Conways, a British family of the upper middle-class, consisting of a widowed mother, four daughters and two sons, are living in fair contentment in one of England's smaller manufacturing centers. On an evening in the autumn of 1919 they are giving a house party. During the charades the most serious-minded of the daughters, Kay, is led to a thoughtful observation of her family. There is Alan, satisfied to be a clerk. Robin, just out of the air service, who hopes for an easy and quick fortune. Hazel, a beauty, with an eye out for a rich husband. Carol, the youngest, with thoughts of the stage. Madge, a bit of a radical, with thought of social reforms, and Kay herself, with an ambition to write. Kay is dreaming of these things and her vision provides a second act in which are shown twenty years later the successive failures scored by the family. Back again to the charades, with Kay pretty depressed by what she knows of the Conways' future.

THE CRADLE WILL ROCK

(108 performances)

A musical drama in ten scenes by Marc Blitzstein. Presented by Sam H. Grisman as a Mercury Theatre production at the Windsor Theatre January 3, 1938.

Cast of characters—

Moll	Olive Stanton
Gent	George Fairchild
Dick	Guido Alexander
Cop	Robert Farnsworth
Reverend Salvation	Charles Niemeyer
Editor Daily	Bert Weston
Yasha	Edward Fuller
Dauber	Jules Schmidt
President Prexy	LeRoy Operti
Professor Trixie	George Smithfield
Professor Scoot	Charles Niemeyer
Doctor Specialist	Frank Marvel
Druggist	John Adair
Mr. Mister	Will Geer
Mrs. Mister	Peggy Coudray
Junior Mister	Maynard Holmes
Sister Mister	Dulce Fox
Steve	Howard Bird
Sadie Polock	Marian Rudley
Gus Polock	George Fairchild
Bugs	Geoffrey Powers
Larry Foreman	Howard da Silva
Ella Hammer	Blanche Collins
Clerk, Reporter, Professor Mamie	Marc Blitzstein

Chorus: Helen Carter, Lucille Schly, Robert Clark, Larry Lauria, E. Sidney, Lilia Hallums, Ralph Ramson, Billy Bodkins, Alma Dixon, Abner Dorsey.

The Scene Is Steeltown, U. S. A., During a Union Drive.

Staged by Marc Blitzstein who also produced the music at a piano.

Mr. Mister is an economic royalist who practically owns and controls Steeltown. He corrupts the press, bulldozes the church, selects his own Liberty Committee and arranges for the assassination of a labor organizer. He is, however, unable to beat the hosts of labor back. They are pretty overwhelming at the final curtain. This is the WPA production that was canceled in Washington and later staged in New York without scenery, costumes or properties, the composer playing the score and serving as announcer at the piano, the actors arising on cue and doing their bits.

LONDON INTIMATE OPERA COMPANY

A repertory of early English Operas revived by Wendell Phillips Dodge at the Little Theatre, New York, January 4, 1938.

THOMAS AND SALLY

A Pastoral Opera by Dr. T. A. Arne (1710-1778)

Sally...Winifred Radford
The Squire.................................Frederick Woodhouse
Thomas...Geoffrey Dunn
Scene—A Village.

THE BRICKDUST MAN

A Musical Entertainment by Charles Dibdin (1745-1814)

John...Geoffrey Dunn
Molly...Winifred Radford
Scene—Bedford Square, London.

TRUE BLUE or THE PRESS GANG

Musical Interlude, The Words and Music by Henry Carey (1685-1743)

Nancy...Winifred Radford
Dreadnought................................Frederick Woodhouse
True-Blue..Geoffrey Dunn
Scene—Arbor in the Commodore's Garden.

DON QUIXOTE

An Opera Devised by Francesca Allinson With Music by Henry Purcell (1658-1695)

Sancho Panza...............................Frederick Woodhouse
Don Quixote....................................Geoffrey Dunn
Maritornes......................................Winifred Radford
Scene—Courtyard of an Inn.

The repertory included rediscovered masterpieces of the 17th and 18th Century English music by Henry Purcell, Charles Dibdin, Samuel Arnold, Henry Carey and Dr. Thomas Augustine Arne, with other works by G. B. Pergolesi, J. S. Bach and W. A. Mozart. The second week beginning January 11, 1938, the program included "Love in a Coffee Cup" by Johann Sebastian Bach; Charles Dibdin's songs, "Peggy Perkins," "The Token" and "Jack at the Opera" sung by Geoffrey Dunn; "Colin and His Wife" by Henry Purcell, "The Grenadier" by Charles Dibdin, "Every Maid Her Own Mistress" by G. B. Pergolesi, English version by Geoffrey Dunn.

Arrangements and adaptations by Frederick Woodhouse, Geoffrey Dunn and Gwenn Knight.

RIGHT THIS WAY

(15 performances)

A musical comedy in two acts by Marianne Brown Waters with additional songs by Sammy Fain and Irving Kahal and additional dialogue by Parke Levy and Allen Lipscott; music by Brad Greene and Fabian Storey. Produced by Alice Alexander at the 46th Street Theatre, New York, January 4, 1938.

Cast of characters—

Bomboski	Leonard Elliott
Lissa	Leona Stephens
Mimi Chester	Tamara
Jeff Doane	Guy Robertson
Josie Huggins	Blanche Ring
Flora Baldwin	Leona Powers
James Withington	Milton Parson
Ship's Captain	Joey Ray
Spaulding	Joe E. Lewis
Rich Traveler	Jack Gilchrist
Leland	Hugh Ellsworth
An American	Jack Williams
Phil Doane	Henry Arthur
Judy March	Thelma White
Butlers	Jack Gilchrist, Joey Ray
Mimi's Assistant	Dorothea Jackson
Comptesse De Marco	Dorothy Maris
Peasant Vendor	Leona Stephens
An American in Paris	Jack Williams
The Girl	Zynaid Spencer

Act I.—Scene 1—Mimi's Studio in Paris. 2—Pier in L'Havre. 3—Sun-Porch of Mimi's and Jeff's Home in Massachusetts. 4—Exterior of Symphony Hall in Boston. 5—Garden of Mimi's and Jeff's Home. Act II.—Scene 1—Mimi's Hat Salon, Paris. 2 and 4—Street in Paris. 3—Market Place at Dawn. 5—Mimi's Studio.

Staged by Bertram Robinson and Alice Alexander; music directed by Max Meth; dances by Marjery Fielding; settings by Nat Karson; costumes by Miles White.

Mimi Chester and Jeff Doane, she a model and he a newspaper correspondent, are living pleasantly in sin in Paris when Jeff is called home and insists on marrying Mimi and taking her with him. In America they fall victim to the humdrum of married life and separate. Back to Paris for the necessary forgive and forget duets.

THE GREATEST SHOW ON EARTH

(29 performances)

A comedy in three acts by Vincent Duffey and Irene Alexander. Produced by Bonfils & Somnes, Inc., at The Playhouse, New York, January 5, 1938.

Cast of characters—

Scheherazade....................................Alice Belmore Cliffe
Rajah...John Alexander
Slimy...Edgar Stehli
Leo...Anthony Ross
Princess...Dorothy Patten
Kitty...Margaret Perry
Narcissus...Jack Davis
Adonis...Alan Handley
Freddie...William Whitehead
Cub...Junior Eric Burtis
Honey...Shirley Poirier
Mr. Bear..Arthur Griffen
Mrs. Polar.......................................Gertrude Barton
"Pee"..John Gerard
Laddie..Frank Lovejoy

Act I.—Scene 1—Quarters of Rajah and Scheherazade, Norton Brothers' Circus. 2—Leo's Apartment. 3—Dormitory. 4—At Mr. Bear's. 5—Laddie's Place. Act II.—Scene 1—Leo's Apartment. 2—The Dormitory. 3—Laddie's Place. Act III.—Scene 1—Leo's Apartment. 2—Laddie's Place. 3—Rajah's Quarters. 4—Mr. Bear's.

Staged by George Somnes; settings by John Root; costumes by Frank Bevan.

In the menagerie of a traveling circus Slimy, the snake, has heard that it is the keeper's plan to mate Kitty, younger sister of Princess, the leading lioness, with Laddie, a handsome cub with whom Kitty is deeply in love. Hating the keeper, Slimy suggests to Leo, mate of Princess, that when the keeper comes for Kitty he (Leo) kill him and escape to the hills with Princess, who is an expectant mother. Laddie and Kitty can follow. Leo, being a noble lion, at first rejects the plan, but agrees at Princess' pleading. When the break is made the keeper is killed, Leo and Princess are shot, Kitty and Laddie get away. Slimy is left to work on the bear cubs, who will soon be big and strong enough to kill another keeper.

YR. OBEDIENT HUSBAND

(8 performances)

A comedy in three acts by Horace Jackson. Produced by Marwell Productions, Inc., at the Broadhurst Theatre, New York, January 10, 1938.

Cast of characters—

Mrs. Scurlock..................................Dame May Whitty
Mistress Binns....................................Brenda Forbes
Prue..Florence Eldridge
Podd...Frieda Altman
Richard Steele.......................................Fredric March
Joseph Addison.......................................J. W. Austin
Partridge...Martin Wolfson
Elizabeth..Marilyn Jolie
Patrick...Harold Thomas

```
Silas Pennyfield.....................................Walter Jones
Lady Envil..........................................Helena Glenn
Lord Envil.........................................Leslie Austen
John Gay...........................................John Pickard
Mrs. Howe........................................Ethel Morrison
Thomas Howe, M.P..............................A. J. Herbert
Lady Warwick Mrs. Addison....................Katherine Stewart
Lord Finch...................................Montgomery Clift
```
        Act I.—Upstairs Sitting Room of Steele's Home in Bury Street,
London. Acts II and III.—Drawing Room of Steele's Home.
        Staged by John Cromwell; settings by Jo Mielziner.

Richard Steele is a great journalist and a great lover, but
an uncertain husband. He does a bit of winebibbing, before
and after quarreling with Prue, his somewhat excitable but always
loving wife. From all sorts of places and all parts of town
Richard writes Prue impeccable little notes explaining that he
will not be able to be with her as soon as expected. When he
does arrive there are more quarrels. The bailiffs are usually
on the trail of Richard, and finally Prue would leave him. She is
held by circumstances long enough for her to change her mind,
and another grand reconciliation is in action at the curtain.

STOP-OVER

(23 performances)

A drama in three acts by Matt Taylor and Sam Taylor. Produced by Chase Productions, Inc., at the Lyceum Theatre, New
York, January 11, 1938.

Cast of characters—

```
Bartley Langthorne..............................Sidney Blackmer
Arthur Darrow.................................Harry M. Cooke
Bessie Latimer..................................Muriel Kirkland
Ed Latimer.......................................Edwin Cooper
Mrs. Scanlon.................................Alice Ann Baker
Father Conley.................................Robert Thomsen
Janet Archer.......................................Jean Rodney
Ben Farnham....................................Calvin Thomas
Marie Farnham................................Norma Chambers
Peter Farnham...................................Billy Redfield
Benjamin Farnham, Jr..........................Ramon Blackburn
Jerry Farnham...................................Eugene Schiel
Dick McKernan...............................Staats Cotsworth
Matt Scanlon....................................Arthur Byron
Lew Foster....................................James Shelburne
Dr. Ralph Greyson..............................Donald Cameron
```
        Acts I, II and III.—Living Room of Langthorne Homestead on
the Post Road Between Albany and New York.
        Staged by Worthington Miner; setting by Norris Houghton.

Bartley Langthorne, romantic actor, is tired and disgusted with
life. Seeking privacy and a rest, he reopens his country place
on the Albany Post Road. Mischievous kids have, it being
Halloween, stuck a "Tourists Accommodated" sign on his lawn,

and before he can settle down various passers-by move in on him. The confusion is added to by the arrival of Matt Scanlon, a crook wanted by the police, who is the husband of Langthorne's housekeeper and has come to stay the night, while a jury is considering the case of his son, being tried for murder. Scanlon, armed, forces a promise from everybody present to stay in the house until he gets a head start toward Canada in the morning. The night is made exciting by various interruptions, romantic and dramatic, the situation being cleared by the escape of Scanlon.

TORTILLA FLAT

(5 performances)

A comedy in three acts by Jack Kirkland based on a novel by John Steinbeck. Produced by Jack Kirkland and Sam H. Grisman at the Henry Miller Theatre, New York, January 12, 1938.

Cast of characters—

Johnny Pom Pom	Eddie Craven
Pablo Sanchez	Harry Bellaver
Mrs. Morales	Mary Servoss
Pilon	Robert Keith
Sweets Ramirez	Erin O'Brien-Moore
Torrelli	Joseph M. de Villard
Big Joe Portagee	Harold Moffet
Danny	Edward Woods
Jesus Maria Corcoran	Mark Schweid
Emilio	Samson Gordon
Caporal	Peter Beauvis

Acts I and III.—Danny's House, Tortilla Flat, Monterey, California. Act II.—Scene 1—Pilon's House. 2—Danny's House.
Staged by Jack Kirkland; settings by Mordecai Gorelik.

Danny, a *paisano* living in a group of *paisanos* near Monterey, Cal., discovers that he has inherited a couple of shacks. Danny dislikes the thought of owning property and the responsibilities certain to follow. He would refuse his inheritance, but his craftier friends, including Sweets Ramirez, a town girl, induce him to keep the shacks and let them live with him. Danny tries a few weeks of reform, living with Sweets Ramirez, but is glad in the end when one shack burns down and he can set fire to the other.

ALL THAT GLITTERS

(69 performances)

A comedy in three acts by John Baragwanath and Kenneth Simpson. Produced by George Abbott at the Biltmore Theatre, New York, January 19, 1938.

Cast of characters—

```
Lord Sutton.........................................David Orrick
Morgan (Muggy) Williams...........................Allyn Joslyn
Dave Hamlin...........................................Royal Beal
Jackie...............................................Jean Casto
Honey...............................................Beverly Phalon
Eléna................................................Arlene Francis
Charlie..............................................Everett Sloane
Mrs. E. Mortimer Townsend.......................Helen Gardner
George Ten Eyck.....................................Judson Laire
Frances Fellowes................................Edith Van Cleve
Kitty Clarke........................................Carmel White
William Fellowes.................................Edward Lester
Saunders...........................................Colin Dawson
Sally..............................................Florence Britton
Atwood Post.......................................Barry Sullivan
Hutchins.........................................George W. Smith
Edwards..............................................Kenneth Bates
```

Act I.—Apartment of Dave Hamlin. Act II.—Living Room of Park Avenue Apartment of Mrs. William Fellowes. Act III.—Veranda of Ten Eyck Country House on Long Island.

Staged by George Abbott; settings by John Root.

Muggy Williams is by instinct a practical joker. When Mrs. E. Mortimer Townsend, society leader, snubs Muggy's prospective fiancée, Kitty Clarke, Muggy determines to be even. Meeting Eléna, an attractive party girl recently arrived from South America, Muggy arranges to introduce her to Mrs. Townsend as a Spanish countess. Mrs. Townsend is charmed with Eléna and introduces her to society. As Muggy is about to enjoy his revenge Eléna hooks herself a society husband in the distinguished person of George Ten Eyck, one of Muggy's best friends. Eléna's triumph is short-lived. She reverts to type and elopes with a playboy, but not before Mrs. Townsend has promised to be good if Muggy will keep his joke out of the papers.

IF I WERE YOU

(8 performances)

A farce in three acts by Paul Hervey Fox and Benn W. Levy, suggested by an idea in Thorne Smith's novel. Produced by Paul Hervey Fox at the Mansfield Theatre, New York, January 24, 1938.

Cast of characters—

```
Arthur Blunt.........................................Bernard Lee
Miss Haller..........................................Mona Moray
Nora.................................................Betty Field
Helena Batty.........................................Janet Hill
Nellie Blunt...................................Constance Cummings
Kenneth Batty..................................Harold Vermilyea
Cook.............................................Marie de Becker
Maxie Maybrick....................................Irving Morrow
A Constable.....................................John M. O'Connor
Dr. Alexander...................................J. Malcom Dunn
```

Act I.—Scene 1—The Blunts' Living Room in a Not Very Pros-
perous Suburb Near London. 2—The Blunts' Bedroom. Acts II and
III.—The Living Room.
Staged by Benn W. Levy; settings by Raymond Sovey.

Arthur Blunt is a bio-chemist who has been experimenting
with the transposition of harmones that will change a male into a
female organism. Nora, an Irish maid in the Blunt house, hearing the conversation, determines to practice one of the witch's
spells her Irish aunt had taught her, which is supposed to
accomplish a like result. The spell works and the Blunts awaken
with their bodies changed. Mrs. Blunt is coarse-voiced and
strident, Mr. Blunt is thin-voiced and effeminate. It takes another act to find the witch, change the brew and get the Blunts'
sex reversed.

* BACHELOR BORN

(171 performances)

A comedy in three acts by Ian Hay. Produced by Milton
Shubert in association with Ruth Selwyn at the Morosco Theatre,
New York, January 25, 1938.

Cast of characters—

Charles Donkin	Frederick Leister
"Bimbo" Faringdon	Lester Lonergan, III
Victor Beamish	Gavin Muir
Frank Hastings	Aubrey Mather
Ellen	Sally Fitzpatrick
Barbara Fane	Phoebe Foster
"Button" Faringdon	Peggy Simpson
Matron	Josephine Brown
Rosemary Faringdon	Helen Trenholme
Chris Faringdon	Jane Sterling
Philip De Pourville	Stephen Ker-Appleby
Flossie Nightingale	Arthur Gould-Porter
Rev. Edmund Ovington	Philip Tonge
Sir Berkeley Nightingale	Francis Compton
Travers	William Packer
"Pop"	Gary McCully
"Old Crump"	Bertram Tanswell

Act I.—Mr. Donkin's Study in the Red House, Marbledown School.
Act II.—Scene 1—Bedroom of Rosemary and Chris. 2—Mr. Don-
kin's Study. Act III.—Mr. Donkin's Study.
Staged by Frederick Leister; settings by Watson Barratt.

Charles Donkin, middle-aged housemaster at Marbledown
School in England, is faced with the problem of giving house
room to the three daughters of the woman he had in his youth
wanted to marry. "Button," Rosemary and Chris Faringdon,
with their Aunt Barbara Fane, settle down at Marbledown, or
try to, and immediately stir up considerable excitement. Hating

the headmaster, the Rev. Ovingdon, who is unjust to Donkin, the young people organize meetings of protest and before they are through indirectly manage the removal of Ovingdon and the promotion of Donkin.

* SHADOW AND SUBSTANCE

(169 performances)

A drama in three acts by Paul Vincent Carroll. Produced by Eddie Dowling at the Golden Theatre, New York, January 26, 1938.

Cast of characters—

```
Brigid.............................................Julie  Haydon
Dermot Francis O'Flingsley.........................Lloyd  Gough
Thomasina Concannon.............................Valerie  Cossart
Father Corr.......................................Henry  Sothern
Father Kirwan........................................Len  Doyle
Very Rev. Thomas Canon Skerritt...............Cedric  Hardwicke
Miss Jemima Cooney................................Sara  Allgood
Francis Ignatius O'Connor.......................Gerald  Buckley
Martin Mullahone,..............................John  L.  Kearney
Rosie Violet.....................................Almira  Sessions
```
      Acts I, II and III.—Living Room of Canon Skerritt's Parochial House in Ardmahone, One of the Small Towns Lying Around the Feet of the Mourne Hills in County Louth, Ireland.
      Staged by Peter Godfrey; setting by David M. Twachtman; art direction by James C. Scully.

See page 87.

JOURNEYMAN

(41 performances)

A drama in three acts dramatized by Alfred Hayes and Leon Alexander from Erskine Caldwell's novel. Produced by Sam Byrd at the Fulton Theatre, New York, January 29, 1938.

Cast of characters—

```
Clay Horey...............................Raymond  Van  Sickle
Dene Horey......................................Eugenia  Rawls
Semon Dye...........................................Will  Geer
Sugar.............................................Helen  Carter
Tom Rhodes...................................Charles  Kennedy
Lorene............................................Ruth  Abbott
Hardy............................................Frank  Wilson
Vearl...........................................Tommie  Baker
Ralph.........................................Geo.  Oliver  Taylor
Pete...........................................John  O'Shaughnessy
Jack.............................................David  Clarke
Fanny's Little Girl.............................Shirley  Poirier
```
      People in the Revival Scene: Herta Ware, Helen Dortch, Lily Winton, Mossette Butler, Agnes Ives, Frank Phillips, Dorothy Brack-

ett, Charles Gordon, Emerin Campbell.
Acts I and II.—Clay Horey's Farm, Rocky Comfort, Georgia. Act
III.—Scene 1—Rocky Comfort Schoolhouse. 2—Clay Horey's Farm.
Staged by Erskine Caldwell and J. Edward Shugrue; settings by
Nat Karson.

Semon Dye, posing as an itinerant preacher, invades the share-
cropper country of the South, cheating the farmers with loaded
dice and the women with promises of salvation. Dye wins Clay
Horey's farm, livestock and wife in a crooked crap game, holds
a religious revival, takes up a small collection and leaves for
fresher fields.

SUNUP TO SUNDOWN

(7 performances)

A play in three acts by Francis Edwards Faragoh. Produced
by D. A. Doran at the Hudson Theatre, New York, February
1, 1938.

Cast of characters—

Brockwell	Carl Benton Reid
Slim	Earl J. Brisgal
Cesare	Frank Mannino
Jakey	Jimmy Lydon
Pogriski	Leslie Barrett
Pearl	Maxine Stuart
Karen	Nonnie Edwards
Rosa	Frances Dworkin
Stanley	Sydney Lumet
Tessie	Sylvia Florant
Ramon	Nat Mintz
Marta	Florence McGee
Andy Turner	Eugene Gericke
Sam Fitch	Percy Kilbride
Alden Turner	Walter N. Greaza
Buddy Turner	Jack Jordan
Feher	Thomas Fisher
Gonzales	Jasper Mangione
Di Marco	Joseph Singer
Mrs. Di Marco	Ludmilla Toretzka
Mrs. Hopkins	Eula Guy
Mrs. Gonzales	Mary Tarcai
Dr. Toliver	James Todd

Other Workers, Parents, Members of the Committee, etc.: Margaret
Moore, Mills Brooke, Nancy Bashein, Henry Bashein, Gordon
Pollock, Harris Berger, Ormand Lydon, Billy Mintz, Charles
Proctor, Anthony Maggi, Stanleu Povitch, Margery Britton, Ruth
Tobin, Lester Florant.
Acts I and III.—Tobacco Barn. Act II.—Another Barn.
Staged by Joseph Losey; settings by Howard Bay.

Andy and Marta are two of the children employed on a
tobacco plantation. Marta is a Mexican girl too young to marry
legally but old enough to bear a child. Andy is a native boy
growing tall in his late teens. Marta and Andy, knowing Marta

is to have a baby, try to marry. When they cannot Andy runs away. The other children try to fix it for Marta to marry Buddy, Andy's younger brother, but the authorities laugh at them. Marta and all her family, hired under one contract, are fired and are forced to move on. Buddy and the others try to stage a strike but don't know how. They go back to working as the plantation owner dictates.

* ON BORROWED TIME

(161 performances)

A comedy in three acts by Paul Osborn, dramatized from a novel by Lawrence Edward Watkin. Produced by Dwight Deere Wiman at the Longacre Theatre, February 3, 1938.

Cast of characters—

Pud	Peter Miner
Julian Northrup (Gramps)	Dudley Digges
Nellie (Granny)	Dorothy Stickney
Mr. Brink	Frank Conroy
Marcia Giles	Margaret O'Donnell
Demetria Riffle	Jean Adair
A Boy	Dick Van Patten
Workmen	Edgar Henning, Andy Anderson, Elwell Cobb, Nick Dennis
Dr. Evans	Clyde Franklin
Mr. Pilbeam	Richard Sterling
Mr. Grimes	Lew Eckels
Sheriff	Al Webster

Act I.—Scenes 1 and 2—The Living Room in an American Town. 3—Granny's Bedroom. 4 and 5—The Tree. Act II.—Scenes 1, 3 and 4—The Tree. 2—The Living Room. Act III.—The Tree.
Staged by Joshua Logan; settings by Jo Mielziner.

See page 122.

* OUR TOWN

(159 performances)

A drama in three acts by Thornton Wilder. Produced by Jed Harris at the Henry Miller Theatre, New York, February 4, 1938.

Cast of characters—

Stage Manager	Frank Craven
Dr. Gibbs	Jay Fassett
Joe Crowell	Raymond Roe
Howie Newsome	Tom Fadden
Mrs. Gibbs	Evelyn Varden
Mrs. Webb	Helen Carew
George Gibbs	John Craven

Rebecca Gibbs....................................Marilyn Erskine
Wally Webb.....................................Charles Wiley, Jr.
Emily Webb.......................................Martha Scott
Professor Pepper....................................Arthur Allen
Mr. Webb.......................................Thomas W. Ross
Woman in the Balcony............................Carrie Weller
Man in the Auditorium............................Walter O. Hill
Lady in the Box...............................Aline McDermott
Simon Stimson...................................Philip Coolidge
Mrs. Soames.....................................Doro Merande
Constable Warren..............................E. Irving Locke
Si Crowell...Billy Redfield
Baseball Players......Alfred Ryder, William Roehrick, Thomas Coley
Sam Craig...................................Francis G. Cleveland
Joe Stoddard................................William Wadsworth
People of the Town: Carrie Weller, Alice Donaldson, Walter O. Hill,
   Arthur Allen, Charles Mellody, Katharine Raht, Mary Elizabeth
   Forbes, Dorothy Nolan, Jean Platt, Barbara Brown, Alda Stan-
   ley, Barbara Burton, Lyn Swann, Dorothy Ryan, Shirley Osborn,
   Emily Boileau, Ann Weston, Leon Rose, John Irving Finn, Van
   Shem, Charles Walters, William Short, Frank Howell, Max Beck,
   James Malaidy.
Acts I, II and III.—Grover's Corners, N. H., 1901 to 1913.

See page 67.

THE BRIDAL CROWN

(1 performance)

A drama by August Strindberg with music by Michael von
Zadora. Produced by Experimental Theatre, Inc., at the Vanderbilt Theatre, New York, February 5, 1938.

Cast of characters—

The Mother of Kersti..............................Anne Gerlette
Kersti...Aurora Bonney
Mats...Dehner Forkum
Midwife..Aletta Stever
The Grandfather................................Richard Kronold
The Grandmother.................................Jane MacDwyer
The Father......................................Wesley Towner
The Mother......................................Sylvia Blumberg
Brita..Marion Rahill
Anna...Elizabeth Edwards
Lit-Karen.......................................Rosalind Carter
Lit-Mats..Mildred Loscht
Stig Matsson..Sey Bockner
The Verger.....................................Willard Duckworth
The Soldier................................Alexander McLaughlin
The Bridesmaids.....................Edith Charles, Lilian Walden,
                                    Jeanne Fagen, Adela Engel
The Servants......................Leafie Wilbur, Anne Martin,
                                Masha Pankevich, Karen Johnston
The Pastor.......................................Nikita Soussanin
Mats' Relatives...........Lee Kresel, Ralph Norton, Harold Reifer,
                              Leah Margulies, May Bolhower
Kersti's Relatives........Ralph Portnow, David Slayton, Anita Haas,
                          Martha Mattey, Henry Shereshefsky
The Wanderer...................................Alexander Basset
The Guard.....................................Arthur H. Menkin
The Headsman.......................................Lee Kresel
The Voice of the Water Spirit....................Raymond Brown
The Voice of the Child in White....................Karen Johnston

The Voice of the Mocker...........................Mildred Loscht
    Scene 1—A Forest Near the Pasture.   2—The Mill.   3—Kersti's
House Before the Wedding.   4—The Mill After the Wedding.   (Intermission.)   5—The Church Courtyard.   6—The Ice on the Lake.
    Staged by Andrius Jilinsky; settings by Eugene Dunkel; costumes
and marionettes by Stasy Uskinsky, Madame Balieff, Mary Towner
and the New York Players Workshop.

Kersti, who has borne Mats an illegitimate child, gives it into
the keeping of a midwife witch in exchange for a crown that
only a virgin can wear at her wedding.   Kersti and Mats are
married, but Kersti throws the crown into the millrace.   In the
search for it the body of the dead infant is found.   Kersti is
banished to an island, where, after a good deal of further persecution, she is released by death.

HOW TO GET TOUGH ABOUT IT

(23 performances)

A comedy in three acts by Robert Ardrey.   Produced by
Guthrie McClintic at the Martin Beck Theatre, New York, February 8, 1938.

Cast of characters—

Joe...Karl Malden
Mannheim..Hans Hamsa
Vergez..Jose Ferrer
Billy Boy......................................Millard Mitchell
Mrs. Clugg.......................................Connie Gilchrist
Peschino...Jack Riggo
Clugg..Ralph Riggs
Dan Grimshaw...............................Myron McCormick
Kitty...Katherine Locke
Dokey...George J. Lewis
Susie...Ruth March
Matt Grogan..Kent Smith
Eldridge..George Nash
Powers...Fred Howard
    Act I.—Scenes 1 and 3—Back Room at Mrs. Clugg's Café.   2—
Kitty's Room.   Acts II and III.—Dan's Houseboat.
    Staged by Guthrie McClintic; settings by Norris Houghton; costumes by Helene Pons.

Kitty is waiting on table in the café of Mrs. Clugg when she
is fascinated by the tall talk and handsome figure of Matt
Grogan.   For three months the two live together and then Grogan
decides to move on.   Take what you want when you want it and
go merrily on your way when you are so moved is the Grogan
philosophy.   To enjoy life a guy has to be tough about a lot
of things.   Kitty, fired from the café, is destitute when she stops
by Dan Grimshaw's houseboat.   Dan, a ne'er-do-well boatbuilder,
is an idealist at heart.   He takes Kitty in and re-establishes her

self-respect. Grogan comes back and takes her away again. In the end Kitty, who is also prey to an idealism she doesn't understand, comes back to Dan for good.

ROOSTY

(8 performances)

A drama in a prologue and two acts by Martin Berkeley. Produced by Albert Lewis at the Lyceum Theatre, New York, February 14, 1938.

Cast of characters—

Dip	Abner Biberman
Alec	Harold Johnsrud
Mary	Tucker McGuire
Stuff Nelson	William Harrigan
Roosty Nelson	James McCallion
Sergeant Pryor	Ernest Woodward
Judge Marlow	William Fay
Mrs. Adams	Zamah Cunningham
Attendant	Salo Douday
Ed Schuster	Russell Hardy
Kate Grant	Katherine Emery
Mrs. Martha Schuster	Mary Morris

State Troopers and Plainclothes Men.
Prologue.—A Hideout in the Adirondacks. Act I.—Scene 1—A Judge's Chamber. 2 and 3—Living-Dining Room of Schuster Farm House. Act II.—Living-Dining Room of Schuster Farm House.
Staged by Lee Strasberg; settings by Nat Karson.

Roosty Nelson, son of the bandit, Stuff Nelson, is hiding out with his father in the Adirondacks, following a holdup in which a policeman has been killed. The pursuing posse closes in, Stuff escapes, but Roosty is taken. In court chambers Roosty is committed to the care of Ed Schuster, an honest and likable farmer, who has nearly completed the regeneration of Roosty when Stuff comes for his son. Roosty is torn between affection for his father and interest in the exciting business of banditry and the honest life Schuster has helped to make attractive. He stays with the farmer.

ONCE IS ENOUGH

(105 performances)

A comedy in three acts by Frederick Lonsdale. Produced by Gilbert Miller at the Henry Miller Theatre, New York, February 15, 1938.

Cast of characters—

```
Eric Lindon........................................John Williams
Morton.............................................Lewis Dayton
Lady Plynne (Dorothy)..........................Margaret Vyner
Lord Rayne (Reggie).............................Archibald Batty
Lord Whitehall (Hugo)...........................Walter Piers
Lady Whitehall (Molly)..........................Nancy Ryan
Lord Plynne (Archie)............................Wilfrid Seagram
Lady Bletchley (Emily).............................Rosalind Ivan
Duchess of Hampshire (Nancy)........................Ina Claire
Paul...............................................Austin Trevor
Charles Pleydell...................................Eric Cowley
Duke of Hampshire (Johnny)......................Hugh Williams
Liz Pleydell......................................Viola Keats
A Footman.........................................Guy Kingsford
```
        Acts I, II and III.—Home of the Duke of Hampshire.
        Staged by Gilbert Miller; setting by Raymond Sovey.

Nancy, Duchess of Hampshire, is threatened with the loss of
Johnny, the Duke of Hampshire, who believes that he has fallen
too hopelessly in love with Liz Pleydell ever to think of falling
out again. Nancy, believing it were better policy to condone an
adultery at home than to force an elopement to South Africa, tries
to reason with Johnny. She makes little headway until Liz discovers that she (Nancy) has no intention of divorcing Johnny.
After that Liz draws away and there is no elopement. Nancy
and Johnny thereupon patch up a reconciliation of sorts.

MURDER IN THE CATHEDRAL

(21 performances)

A drama in two acts by T. S. Eliot. Produced by Gilbert
Miller and Ashley Dukes at the Ritz Theatre, New York, February 16, 1938.

Cast of characters—

```
Thomas Becket....................................Robert Speaight
First Priest........................................Harold Scott
Second Priest.......................................Denis Carey
Third Priest....................................Christopher Casson
Fourth Priest......................................Sidney Warne
Messenger............................................David Gill
First Tempter and Knight..........................Russell Napier
Second Tempter and Knight.........................Denis Green
Third Tempter and Knight.........................Norman Chidgey
Fourth Tempter and Knight.....................E. Martin Browne
```
    Chorus of Women of Canterbury: Phoebe Waterfield, Marjorie An-
        derson, Nina Evans, Valerie Hall, Joy Harington, Pamela Keily,
        Janet Lewis, Lois Miller, Henzie Raeburn.
        Act I.—Scene 1—Archbishop's Hall, Canterbury Cathedral, 1170.
    2—The Cathedral.   Act II.—Altar Steps of Cathedral.
        Staged by E. Martin Browne; settings by Andre Bicat; costumes
    by Stella Mary Pearce.

English version and English setting of the Eliot drama brought over from London following its 600th performance on the other side. The first American production was made by the Popular Price Theatre unit of the Federal WPA Theatre at the Manhattan Theatre, New York, March 20, 1936, and ran for thirty-eight performances. (*Best Plays 1935-36.*)

CASEY JONES

(25 performances)

A drama in three acts by Robert Ardrey. Produced by The Group Theatre at the Fulton Theatre, New York, February 19, 1938.

Cast of characters—

Jed Sherman	Van Heflin
Casey Jones	Charles Bickford
Mac	Joseph Sawyer
Elgy	Curt Conway
Brakeman	Charles Thompson
Old Man	Howard Da Silva
Gassiman	Clancy Cooper
John Collins	Charles J. Dingle
Mrs. Jones	Frances Williams
Jones	Robert Strauss
Portsmouth Jones	Peggy Conklin
Mrs. McGuiness	Eunice Stoddard

Act I.—Scene 1—Locomotive Cab of Chicago-Bound Train. 2—Outside Roundhouse, Chicago. 3—Basement Pool Room. 4—Locomotive Cab St. Louis-Bound Train. Act II.—Scene 1—Basement Pool Room, Mrs. McGuiness' Rooming House. 2—Roundhouse, Chicago. 3—Locomotive Cab, St. Louis-Bound Train. 4—Roof of Mrs. McGuinnes' Rooming House. Act III.—Station at Fort Henry.
Staged by Elia Kazan; settings by Mordecai Gorelik.

Casey Jones, the best engineer on the railroad that employs him, is fifty years old and suffering the first intimations of a physical breaking up. His eyes are going bad, but he will not give up. He takes out No. 4 and pushes her from Chicago to St. Louis in five hours for a record. They take him off the run when he thinks he sees a signal and doesn't, and then fails to see a signal set for him. They make him stationmaster of a whistle stop. Casey can't take the whistle stop, flags No. 4 and goes out into the world hoping to start a new life at 50.

WINE OF CHOICE

(43 performances)

A comedy in three acts by S. N. Behrman. Produced by The Theatre Guild, Inc., at the Guild Theatre, New York, February 21, 1938.

Cast of characters—

```
Charles Dow Hanlon.................................Herbert Yost
Togo.........................................Akihiko Yoshiwara
Binkie Niebuhr.............................Alexander Woollcott
Wilda Doran....................................Claudia Morgan
Dow Christophsen..............................Theodore Newton
Laddy Sears.......................................Donald Cook
Ryder Gerrard.....................................Leslie Banks
Leo Traub.........................................Paul Stewart
Collins..........................................John Maroney
```
    Acts I, II and III.—Living Room of Binkie Niebuhr's Guest Cottage on Estate of Kingdon Sears, Long Island.
    Staged by Herman Shumlin; setting by Lee Simonson.

"Binkie" Niebuhr, an epigrammatic Lithuanian with a penchant for fathering favorite protegées, takes up the problem of Wilda Doran, actress, with whose mother Binkie was once in love. Wilda, having indulged a couple of affairs in her search for love and the more abundant life, is sought in marriage by an old lover, Senator Ryder Gerrard of New Mexico, and also by Laddy Sears, a playboy who is helping her to a screen career. Perversely she falls in love with Dow Christophsen, Communist, who refuses to let love come between him and the onrushing revolution. Wilda surrenders to the Communist; Binkie tries to arrange a marriage; the Communist runs out and Wilda returns to her search for happiness.

CENSORED

(9 performances)

A melodramatic comedy in three acts by Conrad Seiler and Max Marcin. Produced by A. H. Woods, Ltd., at the 46th Street Theatre, New York, February 26, 1938.

Cast of characters—

```
Millicent Redmond..............................Marian Shockley
Arthur Redmond (Red)............................Frank Lovejoy
Charlie Thorpe (Tubbs)...........................Percy Kilbride
Robert Stewart....................................Bram Nossen
Babe Verona...................................Marjorie Peterson
Joe Verona........................................Don Costello
Smoke............................................Hubert Brown
Pike............................................Richard Bengali
Jerry..............................................Dave Mallen
A German Soldier...................................Alvin Zobel
Claudette......................................Phyllis Cornell
Williams............................................Fred Sears
Evette........................................Catherine Lovelace
Annette........................................Phyllis Holden
Toots..............................................Edith Arnold
Beula.............................................Alyce Litwyn
A Soldier........................................Matt Ammann
Mitzi............................................Gloria Pierre
Samuel Blodgett...................................Ralph Holland
Block............................................Arthur Hughes
```

```
Sloan...................................................Leon Stern
Wilbur Sweetwood................................W. A. Burnell
Marguerite.......................................Phyllis Hamilton
Court Clerk..........................................Fred Sears
Prosecutor.........................................Ryder Keane
Court Stenographer...............................Jack Neilan
Judge Cameron....................................Perce Benton
Defense Counsel...............................Hunter Galloway
Miss Clutterbuck................................Carolyne Norton
Miss Billie Folkstone............................Phyllis Dobson
Foreman of the Jury............................Frank Andrews
Orderly..........................................Edward Whitley
```
Act I.—Scene 1—Living Room in Apartment of Arthur Redmond, New York City. 2—Opening Night of "Censored" Showing Trench in France, 1918. 3—Tavern in Small French Town. Behind the Lines. Act II.—Corridor Outside Courtroom and Courtroom, New York City. Act III.—Scenes 1 and 2—Trench in France, 1918.
Staged by Max Marcin; settings by Nicholas Yellenti.

Arthur Redmond is an unsuccessful playwright with a war play. He secures the backing of a gangster, Joe Verona, who wants something against which to charge off his excess profits. The Redmond play, "Censored," is produced, goes sexy back of the lines in France, is raided by the police and the case is taken to court. The Judge agrees to dismiss Redmond and the actors if the playwright will permit a lady reformer named Clutterbuck to rewrite it. She does and the effect is awful.

SAVE ME THE WALTZ

(8 performances)

A comedy in three acts by Katherine Dayton. Produced by Max Gordon in association with Sam H. Harris at the Martin Beck Theatre, New York, February 28, 1938.

Cast of characters—

```
Prince Paul.....................................Lauren Gilbert
Princess Claudine.................................Jane Wyatt
Kirsten.........................................Molly Pearson
King Frederick IV.............................Leo G. Carroll
Queen Elizabeth...............................Mady Christians
A Footman.......................................Derek Fairman
The Countess Zubowska.......................Laura Hope Crews
Von Bethmann...............................Arthur Chatterton
Jon Brasch.........................................John Emery
Count Von Strogonov...........................Reginald Bach
Dmitri.........................................George Macready
Elfrida Von Zedlitz-Wetzel.......................Brenda Forbes
Elmer Wetzel...............................Fred Irving Lewis
Prince George of Holstein-Gastnau.................Leslie Barrie
Chancellor of Holstein-Gastnau...................James Seeley
Chapek.........................................Francis Pierlot
Stroock...........................................Arnold Korff
Duca...........................................Hayden Rorke
Princess Helene of Slogatz.......................Martha Sleeper
Peasant Women.......................Mary Reeves, Mary Howes
```
Acts I and II.—Living Room in Country Residence of Royal Fam-

ily of Jadlovia. Act III.—Office of Jon Brasch, Formerly the Salle des Fêtes in Town Palace.
Staged by Robert B. Sinclair; settings by Jo Mielziner; costumes by John Hambleton.

Jon Brasch, dictator of the mythical kingdom of Jadlovia, can gain much for the political advantage of his country if he can arrange a marriage between Princess Claudine of Jadlovia and the slightly goofy Prince George of Holstein-Gastnau. He visits the castle in which the royal family of Jadlovia is practically exiled to promote the marriage and falls desperately in love with Princess Claudine himself. Thereafter he is much too soft a ruler for the dictatorship and winds up as a mere fiancé.

WHO'S WHO

(23 performances)

A musical revue in two acts assembled by Leonard Sillman; music by Baldwin Bergerson, James Shelton, Irvin Graham and Paul McGrane; sketches by Leonard Sillman and Everett Marcy; lyrics by June Sillman, Irvin Graham and James Shelton. Produced by Elsa Maxwell at the Hudson Theatre, New York, March 1, 1938.

Principals engaged—

Rags Ragland	Imogene Coca
Michael Loring	June Sillman
James Shelton	Mildred Todd
Joseph Beale	Edna Russell
Peter Renwick	Leone Sousa
Johnnie Tunsil	Beatrice Graham
Mara Alexander	Lotte Goslar
Remi Martel	Elizabeth Wilde
Bowen Charleton	Henrietta Boyd

Jack and June Blair
Chet and Mort O'Brien

Staged by Leonard Sillman; technically supervised by Macklin Megley; settings by Mercedes; costumes by Billi Livingston.

THERE'S ALWAYS A BREEZE

(5 performances)

A comedy in three acts by Edward Caulfield. Produced by Joseph M. Hyman and Irving Cooper at the Windsor Theatre, New York, March 2, 1938.

Cast of characters—

Tommy Hammond	Leslie Barrett
Lita Hammond	Anne Baxter
Mrs. Weatherby	Cecilia Loftus

```
Carrie Hammond................................Blanche Sweet
Julia Weatherby..................................Leona Powers
Oscar Jarvis....................................Curtis Cooksey
Ernest Hammond................................William Lynn
Miss Jerome's Maid..............................Sarah Floyd
First Detective.................................George Volk
Second Detective............................Boris de Vadetzky
Harold O'Brien...................................Otto Hulett
Abe Sherman...................................Hume Cronyn
Inspector Martin...............................Herbert Duffy
Asst. Dist. Atty. Roberts.........................Gordon Nelson
Lilly Jerome.....................................Jeanne Hart
Mr. Buckman.............................Alexander Campbell
Marie...........................................Rena Mitchell
```
      Acts I, II and III.—Living Room of Hammond Home in the Sub-
urbs.
      Staged by Harry Wagstaff Gribble; setting by Frederick B. Fox.

Ernest Hammond, for twenty-five years a bank clerk with no
chance to break the bond, is summoned to the love-nest of his
immediate superior. There he meets the superior's mistress and
is witness to a fight in which the boss tries to brain the mistress
with an andiron. Grabbing a gun from the girl's hand Ernest
shoots in her defense. The boss is killed, and Ernest, believing
he is responsible, surrenders to the police and tells all. The
police think him goofy and refuse to hold him. When he finally
does get himself arrested the whole family revels in the publicity.
When the real murderer appears everybody is disappointed, and
Ernest flatly refuses to return to the bank.

I AM MY YOUTH

(8 performances)

A drama in three acts by Ernest Pascal and Edwin Blum.
Produced by Alfred de Liagre, Jr., at The Playhouse, New York,
March 7, 1938.

Cast of characters—

```
Benjamin Place................................Gordon Richards
William Godwin................................Charles Waldron
Mary Jane Godwin..................................Viola Roache
Mary Wollstonecraft Godwin.........................Sylvia Weld
Claire Godwin.......................................Jean Bellows
Fanny Wollstonecraft Godwin.....................Linda Watkins
Percy Bysshe Shelley.............................Frank Lawton
Harriet............................................Arden Young
Boggs............................................Robert Vivian
```
      Acts I, II and III.—Drawing Room of William Godwin's House in
Skinner Street, London, in 1815.
      Staged by Alfred de Liagre, Jr.; setting and costumes by Donald
Oenslager.

William Godwin, liberal socialist, is besieged by young Percy
Bysshe Shelley, poet, to write a book that shall refute Malthus'
defeatist theory about the inevitability of poverty. This, thinks

Shelley, will do much to correct child labor conditions in the Welsh mines. Later Shelley, deserting his wife, elopes with Godwin's daughter, Mary Wollstonecraft Godwin. Another of the Godwin girls becomes the mistress of Lord Byron. Godwin continues his work, assisted by his supposed daughter Fanny. Mrs. Godwin, jealous of Fanny, leaves her home, and when Fanny discovers that she is the illegitimate child of Godwin's second wife by another man she commits suicide.

EMPRESS OF DESTINY

(5 performances)

A drama in three acts by Jessica Lee and Joseph Lee Walsh. Produced by Frederick Ayer in association with Ilya Mottyleff at the St. James Theatre, New York, March 9, 1938.

Cast of characters—

Mme. Tchoglokov	Helen Raymond
Footman	Robert Payson
Tchoglokov	Con MacSunday
Johanna	Frances Woodberry
Elizabeth	Mary Morris
Todorsky	Leo Kennedy
Catherine	Elissa Landi
Peter	Glenn Hunter
Mlle. Shafirov	Harda Normann
Saltycov	Damian O'Flynn
Narychkin	Lionel Ince
Bestushev	A. J. Herbert
Williams	Edward Lester
Mlle. Vorontzov	Jacqueline de Wit
Orlov	Stiano Braggiotti
Shuvalov	William David
Second Footman	Manuel Bernard
Alexis	Leo McCabe
Dashkov	Enid Cooper
Major Domo	George Lambert
Prince George	Pass Le Noir
Yelagin	Leslie Austen
Panin	C. N. Hammond
Segur	Jean Del Val
Stephan	Fred Smith
Monk	William David
Potemkin	Dennis Hoey
Bauer	George Lambert
Zubov	Karl Loewenthal
Paul	Ben Starkie

Act I.—Scene 1—Bridal Chamber of the Grand Duke Peter. Moscow. 1744. 2—Room in the Summer Palace. 1752. Act II.—Scene 1—A Room in the Winter Palace. St. Petersburg. 1760. 2—Room in the Winter Palace. 1762. Act III.—Scene 1—Room in the Winter Palace. 1773. 2—Tent at Sebastopol. 1787. 3—Pavilion in the Royal Gardens. Summer. 1788.

Staged by Ilya Mottyleff; settings and costumes by Robert van Rosen.

Catherine the Great, who was a fairly obscure German girl when she was picked as the bride of an impotent Prince Peter, is dismayed, not to say disgusted, when Peter would have her play at wooden soldiers with him on their wedding night. Succeeding episodes carry Catherine through adventures with various lovers. In the end she deposes Peter and becomes Empress, later taking up a career as a playwright.

THE HILL BETWEEN

(11 performances)

A drama in three acts by Lula Vollmer. Produced by Robert Porterfield at the Little Theatre, New York, March 11, 1938.

Cast of characters—

Anna	Dorothy Patten
Julie	Sara Haden
Brent	Philip Ober
Ellen	Lili Zehner
Paw Robbins	W. O. McWatters
Tobe Carter	Henry Brown
Gil Winters	Richard Ellington
Cale Stubbs	Gilbert Fates
Agnes Riddle	Mildred Dunnock
Bessie Peal	Eugenie Carson
Aunt Frone	Nell Harrison
Martha Litt	Joan Vanderwall
Lucy Wallis	Therese Wittler
Wash Bitters	Jim Robertson
Dolph Collins	Bill Benner
Grandpaw Sanders	William Crimans
Larz	Philip Faversham
Tobias Allen	Robert Dryden

Guests: Roberta Bellinger, Margaret Winkler and Ford Bowman.
Acts I, II and III.—The Robbins Home Somewhere in the Southern Mountains.
Staged by Elizabeth Hull; setting by Tom Adrian Cracraft.

Brent Robbins, born and brought up in the Southern mountains, has gone outside and acquired both an education and a stylish wife, Anna. After building up a good practice as a doctor, Brent takes Anna on a trip to his old home. Here Anna meets Julie, a girl who had sent Brent forth from the mountains at the sacrifice of her love. Also a passel of neighbors and kin. Anna, feeling the old home influences taking a new hold on Brent, tries to get him away. Brent, becoming interested in two or three sick folk, stays on. Anna flirts with Larz, letting him kiss her. Larz, feeling that, according to the code, he has violated his friendship for Brent, tries to kill himself. Brent, resentful and disillusioned, would stay on in the hill country, but again Julie sends him "outside."

SPRING THAW

(8 performances)

A comedy in three acts by Clare Kummer. Produced by Max Gordon at the Martin Beck Theatre, New York, March 21, 1938.

Cast of characters—

Eddie...Mary Philips
Beekman...J. P. Wilson
Willie...Roland Young
Myrtle...Jane Gordon
Dr. Parkinson....................................Robert Wallsten
Bee...Lillian Emerson
Georges Lebard....................................Guido Nadzo
Bernice..Natalia Danesi
Mrs. Garsh.......................................Esther Mitchell
Luke Beebe..Maurice Wells
    Act I.—Living Room in Willie Granger's House, New York City.
Act II.—Scene 1—Bee's Bedroom. 2—Georges' Bedroom. 3—Living Room. Act III.—The Grangers' Camp in the Adirondacks.
    Staged by Arthur Hopkins; settings by Donald Oenslager; costumes by Bianca Stroock.

Willie, a patient husband, puts up with the urge for amorous adventure that attacks his young wife, Bee, in the spring. If Bee wants to run away with Georges, a bad pianist, it is all right with Willie. Let her run and get it over with. But Bee and Georges are forever missing boats and trains. They finally get to Willie's Adirondack camp, but Willie is there before them. It is cold. There is only one bedroom with a fireplace. Willie appropriates the room and the bed. Bee crawls in with him. So does Georges. Willie is in the middle.

SCHOOLHOUSE ON THE LOT

(55 performances)

A comedy in three acts by Joseph A. Fields and Jerome Chodorov. Produced by Philip Dunning by arrangement with George Jessel at the Ritz Theatre, New York, March 22, 1938.

Cast of characters—

Lawrence M. Stone............................Robert H. Harris
Sampson...Buford Armitage
Sam...Charles Wagenheim
Miss Fish...Eda Heinemann
Frank...William Foran
George Lewin.....................................Averell Harris
Herman Godansky...................................Walter Armin
Peter Driscoll....................................Onslow Stevens
Joe Woods.......................................Gerald A. Cornell
Dolly Shepard.......................Betty Philson or Jean Harris
Cynthia Wayne...................................Nancy Sheridan

Carol Birch...Mary Mason
Jeannette Logan.................................Eleanor Flagg
Peggy Walsh......................................Hylah Coley
Susie...Lucille Low
Philip Heming.............................Edward Ryan, Jr.
Bobby...Jack Kelly
Terry...Joe Brown, Jr.
Donnie...Donald Brown
Natalie.......................................Natalynne LaGoff
Benny..James Moore
Charlie Landers.................................Carter Blake
Mickey..Sidney Lumet
Texas..June Curtis
J. Robert Fowler...............................Frederic Clark
Make-Up Man.....................................Paton Price
J. G. Hamilton.................................Houseley Stevens
Jimmy Merritt.................................Gerard Sloane
Janice...Nancy Barnwell
Mr. Zarbel......................................Thomas F. Tracey
Newspaper People, Guests, Studio Employees: Julanne Sack, David
   Pelham, Robert Pelham, Nate Sack, Richard Manning, Virginia
   Dunning, Edward Barry.
   Act I.—Scene 1—L. M. Stone's Office, Mercury Pictures, Holly-
wood. 2—Schoolhouse on the Mercury Lot. Act II.—Scene 1—
Stone's Office. 2—The Schoolhouse. Act III.—Stone's Office.
   Staged by Philip Dunning; settings by Arne Lundborg.

Peter Driscoll, in Hollywood to investigate the request of
Mercury Pictures, Inc., for an additional loan of $2,000,000, is
witness to the rebellion of Dolly Shepard, 7, the spoiled darling
of the studio, when Carol Birch, schoolteacher on the Mercury
lot, refuses to give Dolly a good report card. Dolly gets Miss
Birch fired. Peter gives Dolly a good spanking. The studio,
thinking to blackmail Peter into granting the loan, prefers charges
against him for having made a "sex attack" upon the child.
Compromises are effected and Peter marries Carol.

* WHITEOAKS

(104 performances)

A drama in three acts adapted by Mazo de la Roche from
her novel, *Whiteoaks of Jalna*. Produced by Victor Payne-
Jennings at the Hudson Theatre, New York, March 23, 1938.

Cast of characters—

Adeline (Gran Whiteoak).......................Ethel Barrymore
Aunt Augusta...............................Lenore Chippendale
Uncle Ernest.....................................Wyrley Birch
Uncle Nicholas.............................Reynolds Denniston
Renny..Robert Shayne
Piers...Richard Carlson
Finch..Stephen Haggard
Wakefield.......................................Peter Fernandez
Meg..Olive Reeves-Smith
Pheasant...Ethel Colt
Mr. Patton.......................................Joseph Roeder
Boney...Himself
Merlin...Rex

Acts I, II and III.—The Whiteoaks House, "Jalna," Ontario, Canada.
Staged by Stephen Haggard; setting by Norris Houghton.

Gran Whiteoak, still alive and active at 101, is completely aware of the subtle scheming many of her relatives are doing in the hope of being named in her will. Her interest in the career of the least stable of her grandchildren, young Finch, who would devote his life to a study of music, is stimulated by visits with that young man. The old lady makes Finch her heir, causing considerable consternation when she dies.

ALL THE LIVING

(53 performances)

A drama in three acts by Hardie Albright, adapted from Dr. Victor R. Small's book *I Knew 3000 Lunatics*. Produced by Cheryl Crawford in association with John Stillman, Jr., at the Fulton Theatre, New York, March 24, 1938.

Cast of characters—

Superintendent Henry Burns, M.D.................Charles Dingle
Robert Cole, M.D...............................Irving Morrow
Gilbert Kromer, M.D............................Sanford Meisner
David Grosh, M.D...............................Joaquin Souther
Ann Stalling, R.N..............................Elizabeth Young
Mildred Welch..................................Virginia Stevens
Thomas Jefferson Gardy.........................John Alexander
John Merritt, M.D..............................Leif Erickson
Steward..Edward Downes
Mrs. Kate Selks................................Ruth Yorke
Selks..William Franklin
Mrs. Jenkins...................................Alice John
Alec Jenkins...................................Alfred Ryder
Old Man Adams..................................John McKee
Preacher.......................................Herschel Cropper
Dorty..Marion Willis
Victor Piazza..................................Louis Polan
Newton...Harry D. Southard
Gimmie...Esther Owen
Hazel Webb.....................................Sheila Trent
Governor Davis.................................Ernest Rowan
Mrs. Edisto....................................Sarah Winfree
Miss Jessie Travis.............................Ann Dunnigan
First Monopoly Player..........................Judah Bleich
Second Monopoly Player.........................Michael Snider
Miss Keyes, R.N................................Grace Coppin
Rip..Donald Lawder, Jr.
First Student Nurse............................Jean Rodney
Second Student Nurse...........................Lois Montgomery
Hallboy..Frank Wilson
Ernest M. Vogel, M.D...........................Thomas Coffin Cooke
Patients.......................Katherine Bard, Gretchen Comegys,
                                          Julia Lathrop, Kurt Keller
    Acts I and III.—Staff Conference Room and Corridor Section.
Act II.—Scene 1—Sun Room in Hospital Building. 2—Dr. Merritt's Room.
    Staged by Lee Strasberg; settings by Harry Horner.

Gilbert Kromer, on the staff of a state hospital for the insane, perfects a formula which, from his experiments with rabbits, he feels will heal many mentally defective humans. Because of political and other influences he is denied an opportunity for experimentation with humans. John Merritt, a new associate, carries through such experiments and proves the Kromer formula effective. Both Kromer and Merritt are in love with Ann Stalling, nurse. She prefers Merritt, but is loyal to Kromer until the latter nobly sacrifices his prior claim upon her affections.

THE SEA GULL

(41 performances)

A drama in four acts, translated by Stark Young from Anton Chekhov's Russian play. Revived by The Theatre Guild, Inc., at the Shubert Theatre, New York, March 28, 1938.

Cast of characters—

Irina Arkadina, Madame Trepleff	Lynn Fontanne
Constantine Trepleff	Richard Whorf
Peter Sorin	Sydney Greenstreet
Nina	Uta Hagen
Shamreyeff	Harold Moffet
Pauline	Edith King
Masha	Margaret Webster
Boris Trigorin	Alfred Lunt
Eugene Dorn	John Barclay
Semyon Medvedenko	O. Z. Whitehead
Yacov	Alan Hewitt
Cook	S. Thomas Gomez
Housemaids	Jacqueline Paige, Ernestine De Becker

Acts I and II.—Lawn Outside Sorin's Country Place. Acts III and IV.—Room Inside Gorin's Country House.

Staged by Robert Milton; settings by Robert Edmond Jones.

Anton Chekhov's "The Sea Gull," written in 1896, produced in 1897 in St. Petersburg, was a failure. Revived as the first play of the Moscow Art Theatre a year later its success was pronounced. It was first played in the United States by the Washington Square Players in May, 1916, in Marian Fell's translation, with Mary Morris, Helen Westley, Ralph Roeder and Roland Young playing the leads. Revived in April, 1929, by a co-operative company including Walter Abel, Dorothy Sands and Barbara Bulgakov; again in September, 1929, by Eva Le Gallienne's Civic Repertory Company, with Josephine Hutchinson, Merle Maddern and Jacob Ben-Ami, and again in 1930 by the Bulgakov Associates.

PASQUALE NEVER KNEW

(3 performances)

A comedy in three acts by Clemente Giglio. Produced by the author at the Nora Bayes Theatre, New York, March 30, 1938.

Cast of characters—

Donna Rosa	Augusta Merighi
Maria	Stella Bruno
Pasquale	Clemente Giglio
Mike	Vincenzo Rondinone
Marianna	Lina Maresca
Filomena	Giannina Lizzio
Mr. Charles	Gino Giovanetti
Armando	Sandro Sandrino
Perrelli	Nino Di Salle
Giovanni	Tito Vuolo
Teresa	Adele Giglio

Acts I, II and III.—In the Italian Quarter of New York.
Staged by the author.

Pasquale was the father of four children. It was his dream that each of them, when grown and prosperous, would donate ten dollars to the maintenance of their mother and father. It did not turn out as Pasquale expected it would. One daughter was seduced by an assistant district attorney. Another was charged with the murder of her employer. One son was arrested for speeding and his brother turned out something of a poolroom loafer. Pasquale never knew exactly what was going on.

REUNION

(1 performance)

A drama in prologue and three acts by Ambrose Elwell, Jr. Produced by Kenneth W. Robinson and Norman H. White, Jr., at the Nora Bayes Theatre, New York, April 11, 1938.

Cast of characters—

Landlord	Donald MacDonald
Bill Newton	Arthur Holland
John Edwards	Andrew J. Fox, Jr.
Drake Carlin	Gilbert King
Ebel	Haakon Ogle
Brules	Dearon Darnay
Ahrend	Wilbur Valsch
McEwen	Ted Peckham
Ruth Wilton	Dodee Wick
Von Machen	Robert J. Lance
Mary Carlin	Blanche Haring
Helen Newton	Cleda Hallett
Ambulance Driver	Raymond Nelson
Guard	James Young

Prologue and Act III.—John Edwards' Apartment near Harvard Square, 1927. Act I.—Chemist's Dressing Room, Von Machen Chemical Co., Berlin, Germany, 1937. Act II.—John Edwards' Apartment, Berlin.

Staged by Freeman Hammond.

John Edwards was graduated from Harvard the year his wife died. She had been a loyal supporter, taking a job as waitress to help John through his senior year. John's grief threatened to break him. His friends sent him to Berlin to forget. In Germany he was engaged by the Nazis to perfect a poison gas. Many women admired him, but he was loyal to his memories. He got into trouble with the Germans, came back to Harvard for the tenth reunion of his class, met the widow of one of his best friends, and loved her right off.

* WHAT A LIFE

(81 performances)

A comedy in three acts by Clifford Goldsmith. Produced by George Abbott at the Biltmore Theatre, New York, April 13, 1938.

Cast of characters—

Mr. Nelson	Arthur Pierson
Miss Shea	Ruth Matteson
Miss Pike	Edith Van Cleve
Mr. Patterson	William Mendrek
Bill	Eddie Bracken
Miss Eggleston	Maidel Turner
Mr. Vecchitto	Daniel Ocko
Henry Aldrich	Ezra Stone
Barbara Pearson	Betty Field
Gertie	Elena Salvatore
Mr. Bradley	Vaughan Glaser
Miss Wheeler	Joyce Arling
George Bigelow	James Corner
Mrs. Aldrich	Lea Penman
Mr. Ferguson	Jack Byrne
Mary	Butterfly McQueen

Students: Mitzi Miller, Ralph Bell, Marguerite Lodge, Teresa Keane, Blaine Fillmore, Isla Vaile.

Acts I, II and III.—Principal's Office in Central High School.

Staged by George Abbott; setting by Cirker and Robbins.

See page 332.

THE MERRY WIVES OF WINDSOR

(4 performances)

A comedy by William Shakespeare. Revived by Robert Henderson and Estelle Winwood at the Empire Theatre, New York, April 14, 1938.

Cast of characters—

Shallow...Horace Sinclair
Slender..Albert Carroll
Sir Hugh Evans..................................Edward Harvey
Master George Page...............................J. W. Austin
Sir John Falstaff...................................Louis Lytton
Bardolph..Philip Dakin
Nym..Maury Tuckerman
Pistol..Le Roi Operti
Anne Page...Ann Pendleton
Mistress Alice Ford...................................Joan Storm
Mistress Margaret Page........................Estelle Winwood
Simple...Charles Henry
Mine Host of the Garter.......................Ainsworth Arnold
Robin..Buddy Buehler
Rugby..Cliff Heckinger
Dame Quickly......................................Effie Shannon
Dr. Caius...Peter Brocco
Master Fenton....................................William Post, Jr.
Master Frank Ford.............................Henry Mowbray
A Servant..Frank Parish
Men and Women—Mae Noble, Henry Kline, Jessie Graham, Judith
  Alden, Edith Campbell, Lex Barker, Ruth Belmore, Ludmilla
  Toretzka, Carrie Bridewell, Polly Klock, Marguerite Tebeau,
  Ada Humphries, Clara Cubitt.
A Young Man and Woman.........Solon Harger, Charlotte Maye
Parts I and II.—Windsor and the Neighborhood.
Staged by Robert Henderson; settings by Howard Bay.

The late James K. Hackett staged an important revival of
"The Merry Wives of Windsor" in 1916, with Viola Allen his
co-star. The same year Sir Beerbohm Tree, escaping war-torn
England, revived the comedy in America with Henrietta Crosman
and Constance Collier in the cast. A 1917 revival included
Thomas A. Wise, Constance Collier and Isabel Irving. In 1928
Otis Skinner, Mrs. Fiske and Henrietta Crosman were co-starred
in it in a Players' Club revival. Robert Henderson's first revival
was staged in Los Angeles in 1937, with Louis Lytton the Falstaff.

THE WILD DUCK

(3 performances)

A drama in two acts by Henrik Ibsen. Revived by Henry
Forbes at the 49th Street Theatre, New York, April 16, 1938.

Cast of characters—

Gina Ekdal...Jane Lyon
Hedvig...Arlene Haber
Old Ekdal.......................................Edgar Henning
Hialmar Ekdal.................................Emerson Russell
Gregers Werle..................................William Challee
Relling...Traver Hutchins
Molvik..J. Allen Hamilton
Werle...Eric Franson
Mrs. Sorby.......................................Myrtle Miller
Acts I and II.—Hialmar Ekdal's Studio.
Staged by Henry Forbes; setting by Harry L. Abbott and Edward
Sundquist.

Other revivals of "The Wild Duck," following its original production by Wright Lorimer in 1906, have been that sponsored by Arthur Hopkins in 1918, with Alla Nazimova as Hedvig, and one staged in 1925 by the Actors' Theatre with Blanche Yurka as Gina and Helen Chandler as Hedvig. Miss Yurka again played Gina and Linda Watkins the Hedvig in a 1928 revival by the same organization.

THE CIRCLE

(72 performances)

A comedy in three acts by W. Somerset Maugham. Revived by William A. Brady at The Playhouse, New York, April 18, 1938.

Cast of characters—

Arnold Champion-Cheney, M.P..................Bramwell Fletcher
Spaulding..May Marshall
Mrs. Shenstone................................Audrey Ridgwell
Elizabeth...Tallulah Bankhead
Edward Luton.......................................John Emory
Clive Champion-Cheney.........................Cecil Humphreys
Benson...James E. Corbett
Lady Catherine Champion-Cheney.................Grace George
Lord Porteous...Dennis Hoey
      Acts I, II and III.—Drawing Room at Aston-Adey, Arnold Champion-Cheney's House in Dorset, England.
      Staged by Bretaigne Windust; setting by Donald Oenslager.

For thirty years Lady Catherine Champion-Cheney and Lord Porteous have been living in sin in Italy because Clive Champion-Cheney refused to divorce the lady after she had eloped with his best friend and deserted her five-year-old son. Elizabeth Champion-Cheney, married to the son, hearing the aging elopers have returned to England, invites them to her home. There Lady Catherine not only sees her grown son for the first time, but renews at least a speaking acquaintance with his father. She also discovers that her daughter-in-law is about to elope with a handsome house guest. Both Lady Catherine and Lord Porteous advise against the rash act, citing their own unhappy exile as proof that it doesn't work, but the young people will not be stopped. The circle is completed when they bolt for London in a private car.

ESCAPE THIS NIGHT

(11 performances)

A melodrama in three acts by Robert Steiner and Harry Horner. Produced by Robinson Smith at the 44th Street Theatre, New York, April 22, 1938.

Cast of characters—

Joe Gans	Frank Gould
Alfred Morton	Albert Bergh
Mrs. Underwood	Mrs. Charles Willard
Pete	Jack Tyler
Steve	Hume Cronyn
Mrs. Richter	Ellen Hall
Mr. Richter	Arnold Korff
Policeman Murphy	Bradford Kirkbride
Sally Turner	Francesca Bruning
The Monocled Man	Gage Clarke
Wilson "Alabama" Rice	Walter Coy
Joan	Helen Golden
Eunice	Margaret Ormsby
Two Gossipy Women	Virginia Chauvenet, Irene Cattell
Miss Ellswood	Virginia Tracy
Jimmey	Ronald Brogan
Laurence Harding	John Halloran
Mr. Brock	Calvin Thomas
Higgins	Donald Black
Inspector Brogan	Edward Butler
Ruth	Dorothy Littlejohn
Miss Sanders	Betty Jenckes
Mr. Winters	Robert Allen
Miss Clark	Virginia Chauvenet
Mr. Mathews	Maurice Wells
Ruth's Mother	Irene Cattell
Library Guard	Harry J. Fisher
Mr. Lawson	Donald Cameron
Rogers	Arthur Griffin
First Marine	George Mathews
Second Marine	Giles Kellogg
College Boy	Giles Kellogg
The Reading Boy	Peter Kinnell
The Business Man	Peter Carhartt
Mr. Thompson	John Toll

Passers-by, Nuns, People in Library, Hoboes, etc.: Phyllis Cornell, Gertrude Clemens, Enid Cooper, Frances Kay, Barbara Paige, David Wayne, Richard Freeman, Peter Carhartt, Peter Kinnell, Dearon Darnay.

Act I.—Scene 1—In the Shadow of the Lion. 2—Outer Corridor and Reading Room. Act II.—Scene 1—Braille Room. 2—Balcony. 3—Outer Corridor and Reading Room. 4—Corridor. Act III.—Scene 1—Outer Corridor. 2—Braille Room. 3—Shadow of the Lion. Staged by Robert Steiner; settings by Harry Horner; costumes by Helene Pons.

Mr. and Mrs. Richter have come to America hoping to escape from the persecution of a dictator-run country. Mr. Richter is an author. He has prepared the manuscript of a book that will expose his enemies. A pursuit gang closes in on the Richters. Mrs. Richter is shot and killed in the Braille room of the New York Public Library. Mr. Richter is captured and held prisoner in the same room. Wilson Rice, a college football player taking a casual interest in the case, reaches Richter before the gang can harm him, which apparently frees the old man to go on with his writing.

HEARTBREAK HOUSE

(48 performances)

A drama in three acts by George Bernard Shaw. Revived by Orson Welles and John Houseman at the Mercury Theatre, New York, April 29, 1938.

Cast of characters—

Ellie Dunn	Geraldine Fitzgerald
Nurse Guinness	Brenda Forbes
Captain Shotover	Orson Welles
Lady Utterword	Phyllis Joyce
Hesione Hushabye	Mady Christians
Mazzini Dunn	Erskine Sanford
Hector Hushabye	Vincent Price
Boss Mangan	George Coulouris
Randall Utterword	John Hoysradt

Acts I, II and III.—Captain Shotover's Home in Sussex, England. Staged by Orson Welles; settings by John Koenig; costumes by Millia Davenport.

In the English country home of Captain Shotover, 88-year-old eccentric, are gathered a varied group of humans selected to represent divisions of a disintegrating civilization. The time is the second year of the World War. The argument covers the questions and answers of a sort of Shavian questionnaire. There is a thread of story involving a questioning girl, a big business realist, a small business idealist, and several social parasites. In the end the Heartbreak House that is England is bombed in an air raid. The world première of "Heartbreak House" was staged by the New York Theatre Guild in 1920.

WASHINGTON JITTERS

(24 performances)

A comedy in two acts by John Boruff and Walter Hart, based on a novel by Dalton Trumbo. Produced by The Theatre Guild, Inc., in association with the Actors Repertory Company at the Guild Theatre, New York, May 2, 1938.

Cast of characters—

Radio Announcer	Erik Walz
Harvey Upp	Anthony Ross

Mehafferty..Harry Shannon
Sam Dawson.....................................Robert Porterfield
Senator Marple...................................Francis Pierlot
Hamilton Dill.......................................Forrest Orr
Congressman Fusser............................Bertram Thorn
Secretary..Norma Chambers
Henry Hogg.......................................Fred Stewart
Eula Keefer......................................Helen Shields
Mrs. Nelson.......................................Kathryn Grill
Guide..David Clarke
Tourist...Dorothy Brackett
Senator Briggs..Will Geer
Waiter...Douglass Parkhirst
1st Senator.......................................Edwin Cooper
2nd Senator......................................David Clarke
Jerry...Kendall Clark
Clerk...John O'Shaughnessy
Perigord......................................Robert Thomsen
Manager...Erik Walz
Waiter at Carleton..........................Douglass Parkhirst
Senator Ransom............................John O'Shaughnessy
McGinty...David Clarke
Miss Preston.......................................Rose Keane
Photographer....................................Kendall Clark
Mrs. Dwight....................................Lesley Stafford
Coward....................................George Oliver Taylor
A Sign-Painter....................................Edwin Cooper
Jenny Bronson..................................Dorothy Brackett
Hostess..Norma Chambers
Jed...David Clarke
Footmen.......................John Huntington, Charles Gordon
   Acts I and II.—Washington, D. C.
   Staged by Walter Hart and Worthington Miner; setting by Lawrence L. Goldwasser.

Henry Hogg, a Washington sign painter during the early days of the New Deal, is delivering a "Co-ordinator" job to the office of the ASP project. With the sign on the chief's desk Henry is discovered by a gossip columnist and interviewed on the state of the nation. Henry thinks it terrible. The interview is printed, Henry is accepted as the new co-ordinator of ASP, and proceeds to run the office with a high hand. When the deception is discovered Henry cannot be fired because he never has been hired. Fearing the result of an investigation of a loosely and wastefully run administration Henry's deceived sponsors decide to promote his candidacy for the presidency on a ticket that shall throw the politicians out and reorganize the government.

EYE ON THE SPARROW

(6 performances)

A comedy in three acts by Maxwell Selser. Produced by Girvan Higginson at the Vanderbilt Theatre, New York, May 3, 1938.

Cast of characters—

Philip Thomas	Montgomery Clift
Nancy Thomas	Katherine Deane
Freeman	Edgar Stehli
Roger Sanford	Barry Sullivan
Ted Strong	Philip Ober
Barbara Thomas	Catharine Doucet
Fejac Strode	Leslie King
Jim Wright	Perce Benton
Rostican	Stiano Braggiotti
Florence Augden	Dorothy Francis
O'Mara	Francesca Lenni
Thomas Hosea	Edward Fielding
Rent Collector	Ernest Woodward
First Moving Man	Lester Damon
Rug Man	Sandy Strouse

Act I.—Barbara's Upstairs Sitting Room in the Thomas Residence, New York City.   Acts II and III.—Apartment on 12th Street.
Staged by Antoinette Perry; settings by Emeline C. Roche.

Barbara Thomas, who has always had everything, including a Park Avenue apartment and a wealthy publisher husband, returns from Europe, following the death of her husband, to find that her children, Philip and Nancy, on the advice of the family attorney, have sold everything at auction in an attempt to satisfy the creditors of the estate. Barbara cannot understand. Moving into a 12th Street apartment she continues flightily trying to continue living as she always has lived. Haled to court for debt Barbara finds an old friend in the judge and marries him.

THE MAN FROM CAIRO

(22 performances)

A comedy in three acts adapted by Dan Goldberg from the French of Yvan Noe. Produced by Michael Todd at the Broadhurst Theatre, New York, May 4, 1938.

Cast of characters—

Rudolph	Donald Randolph
Louis	Charles Adler
Kornay	A. J. Herbert
Roszicka	Geraldine Kay
Istvan	Joseph Buloff
Janos	Richard Rauber
Bela	Frank Downing
Leni	Helen Chandler
Henrietta	Viola Roache
Trudi	Ann Thomas
Tailor Boy	Jack Hasler

Act I.—Overflow Lounge of Café Rudolph.   Acts II and III.—33 Lehel Street, Budapest.
Staged by Harry Wagstaff Gribble; settings by Frederick B. Fox.

Istvan is a government clerk living modestly in Budapest who suffers an urge for romance and an escape from the routine of his life. He secretly buys himself a dress suit and once a month dolls up and goes adventuring as a romantic man about town. In the Café Rudolph Istvan meets Leni, who is unhappy in love, convinces her that he is a poet and a dreamer who can bring her great happiness, and disappears. Leni traces him to his flat, meets his dull and buxom wife, is properly disillusioned and returns to her first lover. Istvan (whose name is really Leon) still has his dream—and his dress suit.

*I MARRIED AN ANGEL

(46 performances)

A musical comedy in two acts adapted by Richard Rodgers and Lorenz Hart from a Hungarian play by John Vaszary; music by Rodgers; lyrics by Hart; orchestration by Hans Spialek. Produced by Dwight Deere Wiman at the Shubert Theatre, New York, May 11, 1938.

Cast of characters—

Major Domo	David Jones
Two Guests	The Dunham Brothers
Olga Madayn	Hene Damur
Peter Mueller	Charles Walters
General Lucash	Morton L. Stevens
Willy Palaffi	Dennis King
Countese Peggy Palaffi	Vivienne Segal
Anna Murphy	Audrey Christie
Harry Mischka Szigetti	Walter Slezak
Angel	Vera Zorina
Justice of the Peace	Arthur Kent
Valet de Chambre	David Jones
Femme de Chambre	Marie L. Quevli
Modiste	Ruth Urban
1st Vendeuse	Janis Dremann
2nd Vendeuse	Marcella Howard
The Skater	Apples Apgar
Duchese of Holstein-Kuhhoff	Katherine Stewart
1st Clerk	David Jones
2nd Clerk	Arthur Kent
1st Stenographer	Barbara Towne
2nd Stenographer	Sylvia Stone
Lucinda	Marie L. Quevli
Clarinda	Janis Dremann
Philomena	Marcella Howard
Rosalina	Barbara Towne
Seronella	Sylvia Stone
Arabella	Diana Gaylen
Florabella	Althea Elder
Premier Danseur	Charles Laskey

Ladies of the Ballet: Genevieve Cooke, Ronnie Cunningham, May Block, Marion Davison, Eleanor Fiata, Petra Gray, Ruth Haidt, Isabelle Kimpall, Nancy Knott, Evelyn Lafferty, Sonia Larina, Beatrice Lynn, Maria Monnig, Gedda Petry, Shirley F. Shaffer, Betty Jane Smith, Alma Wertley, Virginia Williams.

Gentlemen of the Ballet: Milton Barnett, Edward Brinkmann, Boris Butleroff, Harold Haskin, Michael Mann, Jack Quinn, Nicolai Popoff, John M. Wray, Harold Taub, Nikolas Vasilieff.

Act I.—Scenes 1 and 6—Willy's Salon. 2 and 5—Willy's Study.
3—Suite in Paris Hotel. 4—Honeymoon Ballet. Act II.—Scene 1—
Palaffi Bros. Bank. 2—Angel's Boudoir. 3 and 6—Harry's Salon.
4—Dream of Roxy's Music Hall. 5—Harry's Study.
    Staged by Joshua Logan; settings by Jo Mielziner; costumes by
John Hambleton; choreography by George Balanchine; music directed
by Gene Salzer.

Willy Palaffi, a good catch as catches go, is ever so particular.
Better bachelorhood than the wrong mate. After an experience
or two Willy swears that he would not think of marrying any
one less than an angel. Whereupon down comes an angel from
heaven and Willy marries her. Angel's wings are rather in the
way at first, but she loses them quickly—on her wedding night
in fact. Thereafter she first tries being an angel and always
telling the truth, but this gets Willy in a good deal of trouble
with his business associates. Then Angel learns to be deceptive
and human and the situation is saved.

* THE TWO BOUQUETS

(23 performances)

An operetta in three acts by Eleanor and Herbert Farjeon.
Produced by Marc Connelly in association with Bela Blau at
the Windsor Theatre, New York, May 31, 1938.

Cast of characters—

Kate Gill...Marcy Wescott
Laura Rivers.....................................Patricia Morison
Mrs. Gill...Viola Roache
Mr. Gill...Leo G. Carroll
Edward Gill.......................................Leslie French
Amelia..Enid Markey
Albert Porter.....................................Alfred Drake
Julian Bromley...................................Winston O'Keefe
Flora Grantley....................................Jane Archer
Bella Manchester.................................Joan Wetmore
Patty Moss.......................................Gabrielle Brune
George...Robert Chisholm
Guests, Thespians, and Regatteers: Jane Archer, Helen Carroll, Elsie
    Eyre, Harriette Henning, Doris Moore, Ronnie Raymond, Mar-
    garet Stewart, Erika Zaranova, Robert Arnold, James Burrell,
    Burr Crandall, Sanders Draper, Tony Kraber, Robert Rounse-
    ville, Tom Scott, John Tyers.
    Act I.—Conservatory at Mr. and Mrs. Gill's in Twickenham. Act
II.—Gardens of the Gills' Home. Act III.—River Bank, Twicken-
ham.
    Staged by Marc Connelly; music directed by Macklin Marrow; set-
tings by Robert Barnhart; costumes designed by Raoul Pene du Bois;
dances staged by Leslie French.

Kate and Laura are quite in love with Albert and Julian, and
Albert and Julian are likewise smitten, though timid. To approach their inamoratas the young men buy two bouquets and
trust them for delivery to the uncertain Edward Gill. Edward

mixes the bouquets and distresses the girls and the boys. So it goes until 11 o'clock. After that explanations and finale.

FEDERAL THEATRE PROJECT FOR NEW YORK

(Important Activities June 15, 1937—June 18, 1938)

SWING IT

(60 performances)

A musical comedy by Cecil Mack and Milton Reddie; music by Eubie Blake. Produced by the Variety Theatre unit of the WPA Federal Theatre Project at the Adelphi Theatre, New York, July 22, 1937.

Cast of characters—

Jake Frye	Edward Frye
Gabby	George Booker
Skadmoose	Ernest Mickens
Miranda	Blanche Young
Nate Smith	Walter Crumbley
Bud	Joe Loomis
Sadie	Frances Everett
Mame	Genora English
Ginger	James Mordecai
Steve	Sonny Thompson
Bob	Sherman Dirkson
Rusty	Henry Jines
Dusty	James Green
Chin Chin	Al Young
Su San	Dorothy Turner
Jamaica Joe	John Fortune
"Mom" Brown	Cora Parks
Smoky	Richard Webb
Sonny	Leo Bailey
Gladys	Olena Williams
Ethel	Marion Brantley
Bill	Norman Barksdale
Swipes	Lawrence Lomax
Flatfut	Frank Jackson
Sheriff	Al Young
Jasper	James Boxwell
Amy	Anita Bush

Staged by Cecil Mack and Jack Mason; settings by Walter Walden and Victor Zanoff; costumes by Maxine and Alexander Jones.

THE TRIAL OF DR. BECK

(24 performances)

A melodrama in three acts by Hughes Allison. Produced by the WPA Federal Theatre Project at the Maxine Elliott Theatre, New York, August 9, 1937.

Cast of characters—

Court Clerk..Frank Ferguson
Judge Archer......................................Clifford Dempsey
District Attorney Madison.........................Frank Harrington
Defense Attorney Collings...........................Earl Sydnor
Assistant District Attorney.......................Kenneth Woodruff
Patrolman James.....................................Jethro Webb
Inspector Timothy O'Malley.....................Thomas McKenna
Dr. John Beck...................................Kenneth Renwick
Ella Gordon...Jane Ferrell
George Doolittle.....................................Elvis Mason
Lulu Doolittle......................................Carrie Adams
Hilda Redd..Lulu King
Oscar Brooks....................................Aurelius Lawrence
Dr. Julius Sims......................................Stewart Ward
Carrie Jones.......................................Virginia Girvin
Elenore Hopkins...............................Dorothy Washington
Ruth Ellen..Harriette Harris
Ralph Judd.......................................Joseph McCallion
Herman Philips.....................................Norman Lewis
Mary Hudson...LaVerne Pine
George B. Shaw..................................William Bendix
Acts I, II and III.—A Court Room.
Staged by Louis M. Simon; setting by Rollo Wayne.

Dr. John Beck is on trial, charged with the murder of his wife,
with whom it is easily proved he was not in love. The trial,
bringing a parade of character and other witnesses to the stand,
reveals the doctor as an idealist with some notion of bringing
about the eventual merging of the black and white races through
selected marriages. The real murderer of Mrs. Beck is finally
disclosed and the doctor freed. The author is a Negro playwright
of promise.

A HERO IS BORN

(50 performances)

An extravaganza by Theresa Helburn based on a fairy tale
by Andrew Lang; music by A. Lehman Engel; lyrics by Agnes
Morgan. Produced by the WPA Federal Theatre at the Adelphi
Theatre, New York, October 1, 1937.

Principals engaged—

Chief Steward....................................Edward Forbes
Chief Cook......................................Raymond Southwick
Queen of Pantouflia............................Margaret Wycherly
The King...Frederic Tozere
Time..Walter Burke
Tony..William Vaughan
Lady Kathleena...................................Marjorie Brown
Lady Molinda......................................Helen Morrow
Prince Prigio.......................................Ben Starkie
Zoroaster..William Phelps
Gaston..John Farman
Lady Rosalind......................................Drue Leyton
Viscount Piffle...................................Harry Redding
Lady Piffledown...................................Janet Rathbun

```
Lord Kelso.........................................George LeSoir
Count Piffledown...................................Robert Bruce
Thomas Benson...................................Harry Sothern
William...........................................Walter Burke
Lord Chief Justice...........................Charles Henderson
```
    Acts I and II.—In and about the Castle of Pantouflia.
    Staged by Agnes Morgan; settings by Tom Adrian Cracraft; costumes by Alexander Saron; production supervised by Edward Goodman.

The day Prince Prigio is christened the Fairies bring him an assortment of many gifts. His mother, the Queen, does not believe in fairies and hides them all. When the Prince, who becomes something of an intellectual prig, is grown to manhood he finds the gifts, including a pair of seven-league boots, a cap of darkness, which makes him invisible, a wishing cap, which grants its wearer any wish and the magic carpet, which carries him to any place he wishes to go. With these aids to happiness the Prince acquires a Princess and a variety of adventures, learning that the smartest thing of all is not to pretend to be too smart.

THE FIREMAN'S FLAME

(204 performances)

A musical melodrama in three acts by John Van Antwerp; lyrics by Ted Fetter; music by Richard Lewine. Produced by John and Jerrold Krimsky at the American Music Hall, New York, October 9, 1937.

Cast of characters—

```
Napoleon Markham..............................Alan Handley
Miss Snodgrass..................................Anna Erskine
Miss Cabot.....................................Julia Hartwell
Harry Howard......................................Ben Cutler
Moze...........................................Harry Meehan
Nozzle...........................................Isham Keith
Mrs. Howard...................................Cynthia Rogers
Jenny.............................................Rose Lieder
Daphne Vanderpool............................Cynthia Rogers
Adolphus Vanderpool..........................Philip Bourneuf
Vesta Violet.....................................Grace Coppin
Bedlington.....................................Sellwyn Myers
Bowery B'hoy...................................Bruce Gordon
Policeman..........................................Lee Burke
Rensselaer...................................George Stinchfeld
Mayor Wickham...............................Howard Fischer
```
    Act I.—Scenes 1 and 3—Outside the Firehouse. 2—Garret Room. 4—Street in Front of Vanderpool Mansion. 5—Room Inside Vanderpool Mansion. 6—Fireman's Ball at Academy of Music. Act II.—Scene 1—Acker, Merrill and Condit's Soda Parlor. 2—Room Inside Vanderpool Mansion. 3—Inside Firehouse. 4—Office of Vanderpool and Izzard, Wall Street. 5—The Battery. Act III.—Office of Vanderpool and Izzard. 2—Outside Vanderpool Mansion. 3—Inside Firehouse. 4—Broadway Panorama. 5—Street in Front of Vanderpool Mansion.
    Staged by John and Jerrold Krimsky; musical numbers staged by Morgan Lewis; settings by Eugene Dunkel; costumes by Kermit Love.

Harry Howard is a hero. Shut out of the Red Heart Hose Boys he joins the more humble Bluebirds and is privileged to rescue Adolphus Vanderpool, the millionaire fox of Wall Street, and his beautiful foster daughter from the flames. This makes the Red Hearts black with envy and they frame Harry, making it appear that he had deliberately dated the wicked Vesta Violet. It is the old Fox himself who makes a happy ending possible.

PRODUCTIONS BY WPA FEDERAL THEATRE PROJECT

PROCESSIONAL

(81 performances)

A play in three acts by John Howard Lawson; revised by author; score by Earl Robinson. Revived by the WPA Federal Theatre at the Maxine Elliott Theatre, New York, October 13, 1937.

Cast of characters—

Boob Elkins	Robert Gehr
Isaac Cohen	S. Boonio
Sadie Cohen	Ruth Gilbert
Smith	Bert Weston
Jake Psinski	Joe Kramm
Felix	Myron Paulson
Joe Green	George Moor
Slop	Paul Sperrin
Gore	Theodore Gros
Angelo	James Rodis
Wayne Whifflehagen	Edward Wright
The Flute Player	Clarence Redd
The Bazooka Player	Maurice Fallet
The Accordion Player	Sam Lazare
The Drummer	Thomas Dumont
Pop Pratt	Bert Norton
McCarthy	Eddie Lester
Bill	Edward Segal
Philpotts	Fred Bael
The Sheriff	Leslie M. Hunt
Man in Silk Hat	Clifford Mack
Old Maggie	Clara Marsh
Mrs. Euphemia Stewart Flimmins	Isabel Bonner
Dynamite Jim	George Mathews
First Soldier	Robert Sherwood
Second Soldier	Sam Kuster
Third Soldier	George Fairchild

The Klansmen and Miners: E. W. Ashworth, John Anderson, Leon Colker, Solomon Goldstein, Julian Garfield, Willie Kaufmann, James Kelly, Edward Hemmer, George Sinclair, Aurelio Tobias, Jack Walters, Robert Worth.

The Miners' Wives: Helen Carter, Agatha Entwistle, Rose Mary, Marion Rudley, Josephine Smith.

Soldiers: Scot Don, Julian Taliaferro, John Gary, John Hamdown, Jack Smith, George Bardi.

Act I.—Scene 1—Street Scene Outskirts of Large Town in West

Virginia Coal Fields During a Strike. 2—The Jail. 3—Labor Temple. Act II.—Scene 1—A Barn. 2—Entrance to Mine. 3—Outskirts of Town. Act III.—Hilltop Above the Town.

Staged by Lem Ward; settings by Manuel Essman; music directed by Dante Carrozzini.

"Processional" was first produced by the Theatre Guild at the Garrick Theatre, New York, January 12, 1925. George Abbott and June Walker headed the cast. It ran for ninety-six performances. A West Virginia coal mine town in the throes of a strike is revealed in a jazz-time review of the American scene, embracing reactionaries backed by state soldiery and the common people hounded by reforms and reformers, including a Ku Klux Klan.

MOON OF THE CARIBBEES

IN THE ZONE

BOUND EAST FOR CARDIFF

THE LONG VOYAGE HOME

(68 performances)

Four one-act plays of the sea by Eugene O'Neill. Revived by the WPA Federal Theatre Project at the Lafayette Theatre, New York, October 29, 1937.

Cast of characters—

MOON OF THE CARIBBEES

Yank	Canada Lee
Jack	Joseph Pope Jones
Lamps	Oliver Foster
Chips	Walter Duke
Old Tom	Service Bell
Bella	Jacqueline Martin
Pearl	Rose Poindexter
First Mate	Edward Fleischer

IN THE ZONE

Smitty	Wardell Saunders
Davis	Joseph Slocum
Ivan	Oliver Foster
Swanson	Walter Duke
Scotty	Paul Johnson
Jack	Joseph Pope Jones
Driscoll	Lionel Monagas
Cocky	William Cumberbatch

Bound East for Cardiff

Yank..Canada Lee
Driscoll...Lionel Monagas
Cocky.......................................William Cumberbatch
Davis..Joseph Slocum
Scotty...Paul Johnson
Smitty...Wardell Saunders
The Captain...................................Thurman Jackson
First Mate....................................Edward Fleischer

The Long Voyage Home

Fat Joe...Arthur Wilson
Nick..Thurman Jackson
Mag..Jacqueline Martin
Driscoll...Lionel Monagas
Cocky.......................................William Cumberbatch
Olson..John B. Johnson
Ivan..Oliver Foster
Kate..Amy Bates
Freda...Hilda Offley
First Rough....................................Kenneth Renwick
Second Rough.....................................Walter Duke
      Staged by William Challee; settings by Perry Watkins.

* ONE-THIRD OF A NATION

(124 performances)

A Living Newspaper about housing by Arthur Arent based on
research by the editorial staff of the Federal Theatre Project.
Produced by Philip Barber at the Adelphi Theatre, New York,
January 17, 1938.

Principals engaged—

Charles Dill	Peter King
Roy Le May	George A. Ryan
Nat Loesberg	Thurlow Bergen
Charles Deigham	Bernard Pate
May Ritchie	Clarence R. Chase
Jennie Wren	Joseph Dixon
John Pote	Virginia Daly
Pat McCullagh	Mira Dark
Edwin Whitner	Ed Brandon
Max Hirsch	Peggy Coudrey
Dick Fitzgerald	James J. Coyle
Wayne Nunn	Lawrence Hawley
Richard Keller	Zack Maccubbin

      Scene—Cross-Section of Tenement House, New York City.
      Staged by Lem Ward; setting by Howard Bay; lighting by Moe
Hack.

A survey of the housing problem focused principally upon the
old-law tenements. The story action goes back to the land
grants from which great American fortunes have sprung, illus-
trating the successive waves of overpopulation followed by waves
of housing problems, epidemics, plagues, rent strikes, etc., bringing the question back to about where it was—"What are we
going to do about it?"

DIFF'RENT

PYGMALION

CAPTAIN JINKS OF THE HORSE MARINES

NO MORE PEACE

CORIOLANUS

A repertory of five plays. Revived by Charles Hopkins for the WPA New York State Federal Theatre Project at the Maxine Elliott Theatre, New York, January 25, 1938, to February 12, 1938.

DIFF'RENT

By Eugene O'Neill

(4 performances)

Cast of characters—

Captain Caleb Williams	Erford Gage
Emma Crosby	Leonore Sorsby
Captain John Crosby	Gene Webber
Mrs. Crosby	Rose Morison
Jack Crosby	Douglas Campbell
Harriet Williams	Irene Taylor
Alfred Rogers	Jay Velie
Benny Rogers	Frank Daly

Acts I and II.—Parlor of Crosby Home, New England Seaport Village.

PYGMALION

By George Bernard Shaw

(2 performances)

Cast of characters—

Miss Eynsford Hill	Irene Taylor
Mrs. Eynsford Hill	Joan Croydon
A Bystander	Harry Clifton
The Bystander	George McSweeney
Freddy	Erford Gage
Liza	Norma Downey
Colonel Pickering	Jay Velie
Henry Higgins	Frank Daly
A Sarcastic Bystander	Harry Jenkins
Taxi Driver	George Shields
Mrs. Pierce	Rose Morison
Alfred Doolittle	Douglas Campbell
Mrs. Higgins	Louise Huntington
The Parlor Maid	Ruth Masters

Pedestrians: Allan Dailey, Gene Webber, W. O. McWatters, John

Giasi, Robert Youmans, Charles Berre, Ruth Masters, Sonia Shand, May Kelly, Willard Foster, Henry Pemberton, Wayland Strong, Edward Hankel, Lee Carney, Victor Casmore, J. Harry Jenkins and Murray Lindsley.

Act I.—Portico of St. Paul's Church, Covent Gardens. London. Acts II and IV.—Higgins' Laboratory in Wimpole Street. Acts III and V.—Mrs. Higgins' Flat on Chelsea Embankment.

CAPTAIN JINKS OF THE HORSE MARINES

By Clyde Fitch

(2 performances)

Cast of characters—

Capt. Robert Jinks	Erford Gage
Charles Le Martine	Frank Daly
Augustus Bleeker Von Vorkenburg	Douglas Campbell
Professor Belliarti	W. O. McWatters
The Herald Reporter	Jay Velie
The Tribune Reporter	Allan Dailey
The Times Reporter	John Randolph
The Sun Reporter	Robert Youmans
The Clipper Representative	Harry Clifton
A Newsboy	Charles Berre
An Official Detective	Wayland Strong
A Sailor	Harry Jenkins
A Policeman	Gene Webber
A Telegraph Boy	John Giasi
Madame Trentoni	Leonore Sorsby
Mrs. Greenborough	May Kelly
Mrs. Jinks	Louise Huntington
Mrs. Stonington	Ruth Masters
Miss Merriam	Rose Morison
First Ballet Lady	Irene Taylor
Second Ballet Lady	Murray Lindsley
Third Ballet Lady	Lee Carney
Fourth Ballet Lady	Sonia Shand
Fifth Ballet Lady	Rose MacDonald
Sixth Ballet Lady	Norma Downey
The Widow's Brat	Joyce Saxelby
Seventh Ballet Lady	Florence Carrette
Mary	Signe Gulbrandsen

Sailors, Domestics and New Yorkers: George Shields, Victor Casmore, Wayland Strong, Edward Hankel, Willard Foster.

Act I.—Landing Dock of Cunard Steamship Company in New York. Acts II and III.—Madame Trentoni's Parlor in Brevoort House.

NO MORE PEACE

Translated by Edward Crankshaw from the original by Ernst Toller; lyrics by W. H. Auden

(4 performances)

Cast of characters—

Napoleon	Douglas Campbell
St. Francis	Jay Velie
The Angel	Norma Downey
Noah	George McSweeney
Samuel	Dann Malloy

Lot..Gene Webber
Laban...W. O. McWatters
David..Erford Gage
Jacob..John Randolph
Rachel...Leonore Sorsby
The Fat Man....................................Gordon Burby
The Little Man.................................John Giasi
The Thin Man...................................Robert Youmans
Cain...Frank Daly
Sarah..May Kelly
Doctor...Wayland Strong
Socrates.......................................Charles Berre
Warder...Harry Clifton

Act I.—Scene 1—Olympus. 2—City Hall in Dunkelstein. Act II.—Scenes 1, 3 and 5—Olympus. 2—Cell in Dunkelstein Prison. 4—Dunkelstein City Hall.

CORIOLANUS

By William Shakespeare

(Acting version by Charles Hopkins)

(6 performances)

Cast of characters—

1st Citizen......................................Willard Foster
2nd Citizen......................................Henry Pemberton
3rd Citizen......................................Harry Jenkins
4th Citizen......................................George McSweeney
5th Citizen......................................Victor Casmore
6th Citizen......................................Edward Hankel
7th Citizen......................................Allan Dailey
Menenius Agrippa.................................Gordon Burby
Coriolanus.......................................Erford Gage
Cominius...W. O. McWatters
Titus Lartius....................................V. L. Granville
Roman Senator....................................George Shields
Sicinius Veluttus................................Frank Daly
Junius Brutus....................................Charles Berre
Tullush Aufidius.................................Jay Velie
1st Volscian Senator.............................Dann Malloy
2nd Volscian Senator.............................Henry Pemberton
Volumnia...Leonore Sorsby
Virgillia..Joan Croydon
Valeria..Norma Downey
Gentlewoman......................................Rose Morison
Roman Herald.....................................John Randolph
Aedile...Robert Youmans
1st Serving Man..................................Wayland Strong
2nd Serving Man..................................Gene Webber
3rd Serving Man..................................Douglas Campbell
Messenger..Edward Hankel
Lieut. to Aufidius...............................Allan Dailey
1st Guard..Wayland Strong
2nd Guard..Allan Dailey
Young Caius Martius..............................Peter Seip
1st Conspirator..................................George McSweeney
2nd Conspirator..................................Allan Dailey
3rd Conspirator..................................Dann Malloy
1st Lord...Willard Foster
2nd Lord...Frank Miller

Act I.—Scenes 1, 6 and 9—Roman Street. 2—Senate House, Corioli. 3—Martius House in Rome. 4—Battlefield Between Roman and Volscian Camps. 5—The Roman Camp. 7—Roman Capitol. 8 and 11—Roman Forum. 10—Room in House of Coriolanus in Rome.

12—Near the City Gate, Rome.   Act II.—Scene 1—Before Aufidius House, Antium.   2—Hall, Aufidius' House.   3 and 7—Street in Rome.   4—A Camp.   5—Advanced Post of Volscian Camp Before Rome.   6—Tent of Coriolanus.   8—A Public Place, Antium.

The five plays of this repertory were staged by Charles Hopkins and the lighting directed by Feder.   The settings and costumes were designed by Ben Edwards with the exception of "No More Peace" whose scene was loaned by Lester Lang from the design by The Experimental Theatre, Vassar College.

"Diff'rent" was first produced in New York by the Province-town Players at the Princess Theatre, February 4, 1921, with James Light as Captain Caleb Williams and Mary Blair as Emma Crosby.   "Pygmalion" had its New York début at the Park Theatre, October 12, 1914, with Mrs. Patrick Campbell and Philip Merivale playing the leads.   "Captain Jinks of the Horse Marines" was first played at the Garrick Theatre, February 4, 1901, with Ethel Barrymore as Madame Trentoni.   Boston appears to have been the only American city favored with previous revivals of Shakespeare's "Coriolanus."   John McCullough played the tragedy there in 1878.   Tomasso Salvini and Viola Allen revived it, also in Boston, in 1885, with Salvini speaking Italian, Allen English.   A production in German was given in New York in 1866 by Hoym and Frau Becker-Grahn.

* HAITI

(82 performances)

A play in three acts by William Du Bois; incidental music by Leonard de Paur.   Produced by James R. Ullman for the WPA Federal Theatre Project at the Lafayette Theatre, New York, March 2, 1938.

Cast of characters—

Toussaint L'Overture	Louis Sharp
Christophe	Rex Ingram
Jacques	Alvin Childress
Bertram	Canada Lee
Andre	Louis Smith
Guy	Frederic Gibson
Haitian soldiers	William Clayton, Arnold Wiley, Lester Palmer, Archie Savage
Daughter	Zola King
Mother	Mary Barnes
First woman	Jacqueline Ghant Martin
Old man	J. Louis Johnson
Second woman	Susie Sutton
Third woman	Lulu King
Josef	Richard McCracken
Boule	Emile Hirsch
Duval	David Enton

Phillipe..Alfred Allegro
Roche..Lou Polan
Boucher...William Sharon
Armand...William Greene
Jean..Byron Lane
LeClerc..Bernard Paté
Odette...Elena Karam
Pauline....................................Catherine Lawrence
Aimee...Lena Halsey
First servant....................................Benny Tattnall
Second servant....................................James Wright
Haitian soldiers: Herbert Glynn, J. Pope Jones.
   Acts I, II and III.—House on Island of St. Domingue, Haiti.
   Staged by Maurice Clark; setting by Perry Watkins; costumes by
James Cochran.

Henry Christophe, one-time emperor of the Haitian domain, moves back into the mountains with his troops when the French take over the island in 1802. Later, with tropical fevers and internal dissensions weakening the invaders' forces, Christophe sweeps down from the hills with his black warriors and all but drives the remaining French into the sea. Between these events there is a good deal of spying, intrigue and domestic tragedy.

* PROLOGUE TO GLORY

(70 performances)

A drama in two acts by E. P. Conkle; incidental music by Hans Bruno Meyer. Produced by the WPA Federal Theatre at the Maxine Elliott Theatre, New York, March 17, 1938.

Cast of characters—

Abe Lincoln..................................Stephen Courtleigh
Denny...Jimmie Lydon
Tom Lincoln......................................John West
Denton Offut.....................................Paul Byron
Sarah Lincoln....................................Lida Snow
Emory Potter...................................Robert Robson
Mentor Graham...................................Robert Lowe
Dr. Allen......................................Henry Buckler
Ann Mayes Rutledge............................Ann Rutledge
Squire Bowlin Green............................Tom Morrison
Jack Armstrong................................Roderick Maybee
Aunt Polly Green...............................Kitty Cosgriff
David Rutledge...................................Robert Miller
Mrs. Rutledge................................Lillian Shrewsbury
Colonel Rutledge..............................Gustave Gordon
Granny Rutledge.................................Clara Marsh
Henry Onstott..................................William Phelps
Carrie..Joan Flicker
Others in the cast: James Houston, Herbert Jelley, George Cowell,
   George Averill, James Bradleigh, Tom Greenway, Charles Leeper,
   John McNulty, Arthur W. Shackett, Seymour Malmude, Frank
   Norton, Robert Toms, Elizabeth Bilencova, Isabel Keightley,
   Charles Henderson, Harlan Knight, Frank McKinney, Jean
   Nelson, Frank Eldred, Josephine Fox, Charles Burrows, Winifred
   Crawford, Sharon Stephens, Elizabeth Widmer, Violette Villiers,
   Blanche Newcomb, Wilbur Cox, Philip C. Jones, Al Durand,
   Gordon Hamilton, Carl Robinson, Sidney Williams, Lawrence

O'Brien, Edwin Platt, Louis Hallett, James Kennedy, Edith Ansley, June Victor, Patricia Ramsey, Harry Mathias, Samuel Van Dyke and Leon Colker.
Act I.—Scene 1—Blackberry Thicket Near Tom Lincoln's Farm. 2—Main Street, Salem. 3—Interior of Denton Offut's Store. 4—Interior of Forum Club's Cabin Meeting Place. Act II.—Scene 1—Lawn Behind Rutledge's Inn. 2—Outside Blacksmith Shop, Petersburg. 3—Room in Rutledge's Inn. 4—Porch at Bowlin Green's.
Staged by Leo Bulgakov; supervised by Morris Ankrum; settings by Walter Walden; costumes by Mary Merrill; lighting by Feder.

See page 233.

TROJAN INCIDENT

(26 performances)

A dance-drama in prologue and one act based on Homer and Euripides and adapted by Professor Philip H. Davis; music by Wallingford Riegger. Produced by Dillard Long for the WPA Federal Theatre Project at the St. James Theatre, New York, April 21, 1938.

Cast of characters—

Odysseus	Marcel Roussenu
Agamemnon	Frank Curran
Menelaus	Joseph Kramm
Thersites	Michael Cisney
Talthybius	Colfax Sanderson
Hecuba	Isabel Bonner
Cassandra	Tamiris
First Soldier	Edward Segal
Andromache	Jane Taylor
Astyanax	Peggy Romano
Attendant	Willie Kaufman
Helen	Evelyn Swenson Eden

Prologue.—Tent of Odysseus. Act I.—Plain Outside Troy.
Staged by Harold Bolton and Tamiris; settings by Howard Bay.

The plight of the Trojan women following the fall of Troy is set forth by Hecuba and illustrated in the dance by Cassandra. Menelaus finally recovers Helen, but doesn't seem very happy about it.

* ON THE ROCKS

(6 performances)

A play in two acts by George Bernard Shaw. Produced by the WPA Federal Theatre Project at Daly's Theatre, New York, June 15, 1938.

Cast of characters—

Sir Arthur Chavender	Philip Bourneuf
Hilda Hanways	Victoria Horne
Sir Broadfoot Basham	Lyster Chambers

Flavia Chavender.................................Charlotte Gloer
Lady Chavender....................................Muriel Starr
David Chavender...............................Joseph Anthony
Tom Humphries...........................C. MacLean Savage
Aloysia Brollikins..................................Ardis Gains
Viscount Barking...........................Houseley Stevens, Jr.
Alderman Blee.......................................John Lynds
Old Hipney..Harry Irvine
The Lady in Grey..............................Estelle Winwood
Sir Dexter Rightside.............................Edward Forbes
Admiral Sir Bemrose Hotspot.......................Doan Borup
Mr. Glenmorrison...............................Donald Arbury
Sir Jafna Pandranath...........................Mervin Williams
The Duke of Domesday...........................George LeSoir
    Acts I and II.—Cabinet Room, No. 10 Downing Street.
    Supervised by James R. Ullman; staged by Robert Ross; setting by
Edwin J. Schruers.

Sir Arthur Chavender, Prime Minister of England, finds his government sorely beset by problems. There are fomenting revolutions on every side. Nor can Sir Arthur hope to bring order out of a threatened chaos. When his wife insists that he take a holiday he takes with him the works of the leading social reformers, including Marx, Lenin and Stalin. Back from his retreat Sir Arthur starts upon a broad program of nationalization. Again he is confronted by the opposition of various selfish interests. Either he goes too far or not far enough. Even the people whom his program is intended to help are dissatisfied. In the end Sir Arthur resigns. Outside No. 10 Downing Street mobs are gathering and singing "England, Arise!"

OTHER FEDERAL THEATRE ACTIVITIES

"Power" produced by the Living Newspaper Unit continued at the Ritz Theatre into the 1937-38 season ending its run of 118 performances on July 10, 1938. After a few minor changes in the news sketches and also in the cast it was brought back to Broadway, this time to the 49th Street Theatre where it remained from February 12th to the 26th and again from March 23 until April 2, 1938, closing with 142 performances to its credit; "Professor Mamlock" continued at Daly's Theatre until July 10, 1938, ending with 76 performances; Paul Green's plays: "Unto Such Glory" and "Hymn to the Rising Sun" played at the Ritz Theatre for 4 performances and then at the Adelphi Theatre for 18 more thereby adding 22 to the 10 of the previous season, making a total of 32 performances; "How Long, Brethren" and "Candide," two dance dramas, continued at the Nora Bayes Theatre until August 4, 1937, closing with 48 performances, and "The Case of Philip Lawrence," George MacEntee's drama produced by the WPA Negro Theatre at the

Lafayette Theatre continued until July 31, 1937, adding 47 performances to the 8 of the previous season making 55 for the total.

The Federal Theatre also presented "Showing Off," a vaudeville revue, for 5 performances the first five days of February, 1938, and John Charles Brownell's "Brain Sweat" with the new name of "Mississippi Rainbow" for 15 performances in early March, both at the 49th Street Theatre. From April 2 to May 7, 1938, "The Tailor Becomes a Store Keeper" was presented at Daly's Theatre for 21 performances. "How Come, Lawd" was revived at the 49th Street Theatre for 2 performances.

"Horse Play," written for children by Dorothy Hailparn, directed by Evelyn Ellis and designed by Perry Watkins was produced at the Lafayette Theatre by the Negro Theatre Unit with Doe Doe Green in the principal role. It was presented 19 times between August 27 and September 24, 1937. "Young Folks Dances" was given 21 afternoon performances at the 49th Street Theatre between December 23, 1937, and January 15, 1938. During this period "How Long, Brethren" was playing at the same theatre in the evenings.

During the Christmas holidays the Federal Theatre presented children's ballets, folk dances, marionette shows, vaudeville, "Advent" and "Nativity" (religious plays), Christmas carols and a festival for children performed ten times through November and December at the Maxine Elliott Theatre. There were also four festivals for children during the Easter Holidays, and in May and early June at the Hippodrome "Treasure Island," Jules Eckert Goodman's dramatization of the Robert Louis Stevenson story was presented for matinée performances. Rhoda Rammelkamp designed the costumes and the cast included William Vaughan and Warren Lyons.

During the summer of 1938 the Federal Theatre produced several Gilbert and Sullivan operas in a tent.

OFF BROADWAY

"The Cradle Will Rock," by Marc Blitzstein, at the close of the 1936-37 season, had been given three performances at the Venice Theatre as an unofficial venture by the heads of Project 891 of the WPA Federal Theatre, after Washington had banned the production as a government enterprise because of labor complications. The producer was announced as Helen Deutsch. Before the closing date, July 1, 1937, nineteen performances had been given. On December 5, 1937, John Houseman and Orson Welles gave the operetta its first official showing in the beginning of a series of Sunday night performances at the Mercury Theatre, which lasted through the Christmas holidays. January 3, 1938, began a regular Broadway engagement at the Windsor Theatre under the sponsorship of Sam H. Grisman, the details of which may be found in the chapter devoted to plays produced in New York in an earlier section of this volume.

"Kingdom of 137," Arthur Smith's play about slum clearance, was another holdover from the previous season, having been presented at the Lavanburg Center June 11, 12, 13 and 19, 1937, and later, sponsored by the East Side Tenants Union, produced at the Auditorium July 21 to 25, 1937.

The Bulgarian National Theatre Company of Sofia, which had arrived in New York June 5, 1937, after an American tour, presented at the Heckscher Theatre, August 14, 15 and 16, 1937, "The Rebels," by Ivan Vazov, a play depicting life in Bulgaria's struggle for freedom; "The Maskers," by Racho Sgoyanov, a play founded on the life of woodcarvers; "The Cricket on the Hearth," a Bulgarian adaptation of the Dickens story.

At the Villa Venice, August 30, 1937, Louise Howard presented "Here's Hoping," a play by Goodman Lipkind, with a cast including Daphne and Marita Sylva, daughters of Marguerite Sylva. At the same theatre, October 17, 1937, Miss Howard presented an intimate and casual entertainment called "Whims of '37," which was written by Miss Howard and William Lord with music by Claude and Howard Latham.

Robert Porterfield made his annual pilgrimage to New York from Abingdon, Virginia, bringing his Barter Theatre to the Heckscher Theatre, October 10, 1937. The tickets were sold

461

as usual for a stated amount of money or its equivalent in potatoes, sugar or what not. "Macbeth" was the play, Margaret Wycherly playing Lady Macbeth, and John Cromwell, Macbeth.

The Willis Productions produced "The House of Cantrell," a comedy by Kermit Vance at the Comedy Theatre, October 11, 1937. "Allergic Summer," a comedy by John Stevens, comparing life in Greenwich Village with that of the Mid-West, was produced by John C. Beresford and Edward Farnham the week beginning May 9, 1938, at the Chanin Auditorium. "Paradise P M," a comedy by Elmer Greensfelder who wrote "Broomsticks, Amen" in 1934, was produced by Edith Becton at the McDowell Theatre, May 10, 1938, with Jane and Patti Pickens in the cast.

Catherine A. Bauman started her sixth season of "Sunday Night Events" in December, continuing through the season at the Barbizon-Plaza Theatre. Elizabeth B. Grimball produced "Blessed Are the Debonair," by Robert Raynolds in January, 1938, at the same theatre.

"The Dynasty," by Arthur Goodman, was produced by the New York Discovery Theatre and staged by Laurence Robinson at the Cultural Federation Auditorium, December 12 and 13, 1937.

Paul and Virginia Gilmore opened their season at the Cherry Lane Theatre with a revival of "As Husbands Go" October 25, 1937. This was followed by "The Drunkard." "As Husbands Go" moved uptown to the Fifth Avenue Theatre, where it played until the end of February. "Three Men on a Horse" followed "The Drunkard" at the Cherry Lane, February 2, 1938, and was still running at the end of the season.

The season of 1937-38 saw an unusually large number of groups staging plays in the metropolitan area. Many of these were old timers but there was also a mushroom growth of new associations.

The Little Theatre Players presented "Peace Interlude," by Dr. Evan Shea at the West 54th Street Theatre, June 24, 1937. The play was staged by Mario Castagna, who, with Frank Francis and Irving Bizman produced "Daylight and Dark," by John S. Brown at the Comedy Theatre, August 2, 1937, with the same Little Theatre Players in the cast.

The Show Shop, founded in London in 1935 by Ruth Putnam Mason, opened July 5, 1937, at the Cherry Lane Theatre. Three plays were presented during a sixteen-week engagement ending October 23, 1937. In December this group, as The American Show Shop, Inc., including H. W. Closson as musical director and

Nicholas Yellenti as art director, leased the President Theatre, renamed it American Show Shop and repeated the Cherry Lane repertory, the first presentation on Broadway being "Murder Sails at Midnight," a three-act mystery play by Kurtz Gordon, staged by Ida Rauh, settings by Elfred Grover. During January it alternated with a poetic drama called "That Rib of Adam," by F. G. Manley, with music by Henry W. Closson. The third production was Lodevick Vroom's "One Every Minute," produced February 28, 1938, staged by George B. Dowell and designed by William Kline.

The Professional Plays and Players produced "His Royal Highness," by Franklyn Aarons, at the Comedy Theatre, August 23, 1937. The Negro Theatre Guild revived "How Come, Lawd?" by Donald Heywood, at the 49th Street Theatre, September 30, 1937. Charles Adler staged the play and the cast included Rex Ingram, Mercedes Gilbert and Leigh Whipper.

The Irish Repertory Players opened their second subscription season October 31, 1937, under the direction of J. Augustus Keogh, assisted by Anita Grannis, with "The White Headed Boy," by Lennox Robinson. Others were "Candida," by George Bernard Shaw, January 16, 1938; a triple bill of one-act plays: "Duty," by Seumas O'Brien (played for the first time in New York); "Riders to the Sea," by John Millington Synge; "The Rising of the Moon," by Lady Gregory, April 1, 1938; and "The Well of the Saints," by Synge, which was still running when the season came to an end in June. Augustin Duncan appeared in "The Well of the Saints." These plays were presented at the Heckscher Theatre with the exception of "Candida," which was produced at the Master Institute Theatre.

The Stagecrafters Association produced "Taking the Count," a comedy by Vivian Mayo, and staged by Deane Taylor, at the Chanin Auditorium, November 12, 1937. The American Actors' Company revived the Euripedes tragedy, "The Trojan Women," in a translation by Edith Hamilton, with Mary Hunter directing the play at the Master Institute Theatre, January 1, 1938.

The Episcopal Actors' Guild gave a matinée performance, February 11, 1938, of "The Pilgrim," a one-acter by Charles Vildrac, translated from the French by Ruth Collins Allen. Augustin Duncan and his daughter Andrea (in her first appearance on the stage), Margherita Sargent and Dulce Fox were in the cast. The Thursday Night Club at the Little Church Around the Corner presented "King John," in a version by James Bell and Robert Buckner.

The Play Room Club, Inc., sponsored by Maxwell Anderson, Gilmore Brown, Barrett H. Clark, Dorothy Gish, Brock Pemberton, Rollo Peters, and Herman Shumlin, started its season in December, 1937, at its West 20th Street Theatre with "The Infernal Machine," adapted by Carl Wildman from Jean Cocteau's play. This was followed February 27, 1938, by "Cheapside," by James Parish, staged by Joan Hathaway. "A Comedy of Good and Evil," by Richard Hughes, which had had its American première May 3, 1935, in a production by the Harvard Dramatic Club, was presented April 7, 1938. The fourth and last production was "No Laughter in Heaven," by Martha Pittinger, May 15, 1938. It was staged by Mervin Williams and Al Ward with settings by Neil Ferguson.

"The Moon-Peddler," a satire on astrologists by Henry Allen Vaux, staged by Freeman Hammond, was produced by the Metropolitan Players at the Heckscher Theatre, January 4, 1938. May 17, 1938, this group produced "Thanks for Tomorrow," a melodrama by Le Roy Bailey.

The New Theatre League presented a program at the Mercury Theatre, January 30, 1938, in which Fred Keating was Master of Ceremonies and Morris Carnovsky acted in a monologue called "The Bishop of Munster," by H. Kraft. Robert K. Adams staged Ben Bengal's "Plant in the Sun" and a one-act play by Theodore Kaghan, "Hello, Franco." June 10, 1938, the League sponsored two Negro groups presenting a one-act play program at the Nora Bayes Theatre. The plays were "Don't You Want to be Free," by Langston Hughes, with music by Carroll Tate, performed by the Harlem Suitcase Theatre, and Alice Holdship Ware's "Mighty Wind a Blowin'," done by the New Haven Progressive Players.

The Try-out Guild began its career February 17, 1938, at the Roosevelt Theatre with a performance of "He Was Like a Continent," a satire in blank verse in two acts by Philippa Burrell, staged by Nicholas Grey with an Equity cast. The play continued until February 20, 1938.

Michael Blankfort's play dealing with the siege of Alcazar, "The Brave and the Blind," was presented by the Current Theatre at the Artef Theatre, June 17, 1937. It had previously been offered by the Rebel Arts Players at Labor Stage. The Current Theatre produced "Fingers," a long one-act play by Jackson Segil, staged by Wendell K. Phillips for seven performances ending March 7, 1938.

Social Stage produced "Tornado," by Lajos Egri, at the Nora

Bayes Theatre with Kalman Marki as director March 10, 1938, and The Stagers produced "No Answer," by Day Tuttle, at the Bayes Theatre. This play had been tried out at Yale in 1936. It was staged by Donald Wetmore.

The Snarks produced Helen Martin's adaptation of Pierre Chine's "L'Heure H" which was presented in Paris at the Theatre de Humour in December of 1935. The Snarks called the adaptation "The Hour." The production was at the Heckscher Theatre, April 5, 1938. The Vagabond Players at the Fifth Avenue Theatre, April 18, 1938, produced "The Prince of Liars," announced as the work of Sydney Grundy. It was staged by Robert Currier and the sets designed by Albert Allen.

The Tower Club at the Beekman Tower Theatre, April 24, 1938, presented "Worse Things Happen at Sea," by Keith Winter, a play which had opened in London in the spring of 1935 and in America August 31, 1937, in Suffern, New York.

A group of young performers which started out as American Theatre Council Unit No. 570, largely graduates of the Workers' Laboratory Theatre, produced two one-act plays, "Plant in the Sun," by Ben Bengal, which won the New Theatre League contest this season, and "Transit," an adaptation by Philip Stevenson from Albert Maltz's "Season of Celebration." They were staged by Art Smith and Lewis Leverett at the Nora Bayes Theatre April 24, 1938, and continued with Sunday night performances and a few matinées until late in May. At this time they called themselves the "Plant in the Sun Company." Studio Group No. 559 of the Committee of the Apprentice Theatre of the American Theatre Council were the actors in John Rodell's "Play it for Comedy," which had one performance at the Lyceum Theatre, April 11, 1938. Studio Group 545 of the same association gave one performance of "Three Sisters," staged by Philip Loeb and under the direction of Antoinette Perry at the Ambassador Theatre. The Apprentice Group also produced a one-act play by Thornton Wilder, staged by Hope Lawder at the Plymouth Theatre, May 16, 1938.

The Actor-Worker Project presented an anti-war drama by Joseph Moore called "Peace and Plenty" at the Chanin Auditorium, May 2, 1938, and the Playwrights Theatre, another new group, produced "Dark Clouds," a play by Alexander Greendale at the Nora Bayes Theatre, May 6, 1938. Six and Company gave four one-act plays by Philip Bloom at Yorke Center May 8, 1938. The plays were "The Actress," "Jeffrey Does a Book," "No Edged Thing" and "The Jungle." In June this group produced "Death of Spring," by Alfred D. Geto, staged by J. J. Robbins. The East Side Dramatic Group at the Grand Street Playhouse gave "End of a Cycle," by Arthur Smith, staged by Leonard Schwartz.

MONODRAMA

Cornelia Otis Skinner, whose monologues have reached the stage of regular play production, may be found in an earlier part of this book. Cecilia Loftus was presented by Bernard Hart and Bill Doll in a revival of her impersonations, sketches and impressions in a series of Sunday night performances starting March 27, 1938, at the Little Theatre and ending May 8, 1938, at the Lyceum Theatre. Her impersonations included mimicry of Ethel Barrymore, Sophie Tucker, May Irwin, Florence Reed (in "Shanghai Gesture"), Pauline Lord (in "The Late Christopher Bean"), Mrs. Patrick Campbell in Hollywood, Nora Bayes singing "Shine on, Harvest Moon," Ada Rehan in "Twelfth Night," Mrs. Fiske in "Mary, Mary, Quite Contrary," Jeanne Eagels in "Rain," and a variety of others.

Helen Howe appeared at the Little Theatre, April 4, 1938, with "These People," a title chosen for her sketches and caricatures. The solo-dramas included "Fountain Service," "In a New York Department Store," "In a West Side Hotel Bedroom," "Case History," "Mary Cum Laude" and "This Present."

PUPPETS

Columbia University opened its eighth marionette season October 23, 1937, at the McMillin Academic Theatre with Sue Hastings' Marionettes in "Alice in Wonderland." The final performance, December 18, 1937, was "Snow White and the Seven Dwarfs" and "The Marionette Carnival" by the Rufus Rose Marionettes.

The WPA Federal Theatre during the Christmas holidays presented "The Dragon Snee Zee," a Chinese fable, and "Nicola," a Punch and Judy Show at the Maxine Elliott Theatre.

The Tatterman Marionettes of Cleveland presented "Taming of the Shrew" under the auspices of the New York Chapter of the Puppeteers of America at Carnegie Hall, March 14, 1938. Hunter College Make-Up Box, a dramatic organization of the college, presented "One Summer's Day" and "They Refuse to be Resurrected," March 25, 1938. The Children's Theatre of Columbia University gave a spring festival from March 26 to April 16, 1938, at the McMillin Academic Theatre, including "Cinderella," "Little Black Sambo," "Micky Mouse Circus," "Winnie-the-Pooh" and "Peter Rabbit."

Jan Gay presented Agrippino Manteo's Marionettes at the Nora Bayes Theatre, April 27, 1938, in a scene from Ariosto's "Orlando Furioso" in Italian and an abridged version of "Macbeth" in English, and Gilbert Josephson presented for one week starting April 18, 1938, at the Windsor Theatre, Sue Hastings' Marionettes, Reno and Calvert's Punch and Judy Show and Uncle Don's Easter Circus.

CHILDREN

The Juvenile Art Theatre revived "Quality Street," by J. M. Barrie, with a cast of professional children August 29, 1937, at the Comedy Theatre. Their second production was Molnar's "The Swan" at the same theatre. In December at the Chanin Auditorium "Rebecca of Sunnybrook Farm," by Kate Douglas Wiggin and Charlotte Thompson, was revived by the child actors and in April, 1938, at the Little Theatre "Tom Sawyer" and "Growing Pains." "Tom Sawyer" was repeated at the Nora Bayes Theatre in June.

The WPA Federal Theatre Project began a nine-day autumn festival for children at the Maxine Elliott Theatre beginning October 30, 1937, including a presentation of Charlotte Chorpenning's "The Emperor's New Clothes," "Horseplay," produced by an all-Negro cast; "Pierre Patelin," translated by Mauritz Jagendorf from a farce reputed to have been written by Lope de Vega; "Jack and the Beanstalk," by Charlotte Chorpenning, and a Tom Thumb revue. In January and February at the 49th Street Theatre the Federal Theatre produced "Hansel and Gretel" and Children's Dance Ballets featuring "Mother Goose" and folk dances.

The Children's Art Theatre at the Nora Bayes Theatre presented three one-act plays early in December: "The Purse of Fortunatus," "Mother Holle" and "Little Red Riding Hood." From December 27, 1937, through New Year's Day the repertoire included "Hansel and Gretel," "The Jealous Sister," "Hiding a Prince," "Out of a Cave," "Fourth Kingdom" and "The King's Arrowmaker." A Children's Christmas Carnival produced at the Windsor Theatre by Gilbert Josephson lasted through the holidays, showing Tony Sarg's Marionettes in "Robinson Crusoe,"

"Toto the Clown," Albert Theis and his midgets, Dorothy Gordon and Uncle Don. The Children's Repertory Theatre presented "The Bumble Bee Prince," Rimsky-Korsakoff's opera, during the holidays at the St. James Theatre.

During the Easter holidays the Lilliput Theatre gave two play-lets: "A Kiss in Xandu" and "Knave of Hearts" with dance, mime and puppet shows. During the month of April the King-Coit Children's Theatre produced "The Golden Cage," arranged by Catharine Cook Smith from poems by William Blake, with music by Arthur Whiting at 135 East 40th Street. "Pinocchio," a narrative ballet described as a dance-play, dramatized by Dorothy Coit with music by M. Wood Hill and under the direc-tion of Edwin Strawbridge, was presented by Junior Programs, Inc., April 9, at Mecca Auditorium.

College Plays in New York

The Washington Square Players of New York University opened their annual repertory season with Shaw's "Androcles and the Lion" in late October and closed in May with "Julius Caesar." About seventeen plays by Shakespeare, Sheridan and Shaw were presented during November and December. In February "The Victors," by Stanley Kauffman, was produced.

The Mask and Wig Club of the University of Pennsylvania produced a musical comedy called "Fifty-Fifty" at the Center Theatre, December 4, 1937. Louis C. Madeira IV and George Elliott Hess wrote the book, Clay A. Boland and M. Jaffe com-posed the music and the direction was in the hands of Paul B. Hartenstein, Robert Brown and Walter F. Keenan.

Fordham University Mimes and Mummers presented Sidney Howard's "Yellow Jack" with a cast of twenty-nine students directed by Harry C. Schnibbe, as its annual varsity production, December 9 and 10, 1937.

Princeton's Triangle Club produced for its forty-ninth annual presentation a romantic farce in musical comedy style by Alex-ander H. Lehmann, Jr., called "Fol-de-rol," December 17 and 18, 1937. Jose Ferrer directed the thirty-eight actors. Music and lyrics were written by Richard Uhl, Sanders Maxwell, Dixon Morgan and Charles Davis.

"You've Got Something There," the forty-fifth annual show of Columbia University was presented at the Astor, March 31, 1938. The musical comedy was written by Isadore Diamond with music by Lee Wainer and lyrics by Lupin Fein. Paul Winkopp directed the performance, the dances were staged by Frank Gagen and John Morrissey directed the music. During the season The Morningside Players presented "I Made Iron," by Richard Allan Arm, with a cast of twenty faculty members, students and alumni directed by Milton M. Smith, February 4, 1938, and four dramatic groups comprising the Columbia Theatre Associates presented a revival of "A Comedy of Errors" at Earl Hall, April 26, 1938.

The ninety-second annual musical production of the Hasty Pudding Club of Harvard, "So Proudly We Hail," was presented at the Waldorf-Astoria April 8, 1938. The book was by Nathaniel G. Benchley, Benjamin Welles and John McD. Graham, music by B. Welles, Allan J. Lerner, Stanley Miller and J. David Lannon.

The New York City College's oldest undergraduate club, The City College Dramatic Society, celebrated its golden jubilee April 21 and 22, 1938, at the Pauline Edwards Theatre with the production of "In the Groove," a satirical musical revue. The revue plot was written by Mortimer Cohen, Lew Zuckerman, Jerry Albert, David Dawson, Newton Meltzer, Nathan Hentel and Arthur Jacobs; music and lyrics by George Lenchner, Don Wynick, Jack Gould and others. A cast of more than fifty was directed by Leroy Zehren and the dances were directed by J. William Cody.

FOREIGN LANGUAGE PLAYS

The French Theatre of New York, Inc., with a French company, Theatre des Saisons, started their 1937-38 season in late October with Pierre Barbier's adaptation of Carlo Gozzi's old Venetian comedy, "Le Roi Cerf," at the Barbizon-Plaza, directed by André Barsacq. Moussi Abadi played the leading role. "Le Voyage de Monsieur Perrichon," by Eugene Labiche, with Jean Daste playing the lead, was presented November 1, 1937; "Knock," by Jules Romains, November 15, 1937; "Jean de la Lune," by Marcel Achard, December 13, 1937; Molière's "La Jalousie du Barbouille," directed by Maurice Jacquemont and "Le Médecin Malgré Lui," directed by Jean Daste, December 27, 1937; "Nationale 6," by Jean Jacques Bernard, directed by André Barsacq, January 10, 1938; "Y'Avait Un Prisonnier," by Jean Anouilh, January 24, 1938; "Un Caprice" and "Fantasio," by Alfred Musset, February 7, 1938.

Teatro d'Arte under the direction of Giuseppi Sterni produced

"Il Medico Delle Pazze," by Sterni, in September of 1937, and "La Signora Dalle Camelie," by Dumas, with Sterni as Armando and Yolanda Deste as Marguerita Gautier, in early October. Clementi Giglio produced "The Ugly Daughter," an Italian play written by the producer, at the Nora Bayes Theatre, August 28, 1937. "La Surena Varada," a Spanish drama by Alejandro Casona, was produced and staged by Enrique de Rosas at the Nora Bayes Theatre in October, 1937, with Enrique de Rosas, the Argentine actor, and Blanca Tapia in the principal roles.

The Artef Players revived "200,000" and "The Outlaw" in December of 1937. "The Good Soldier Sweik," dramatized by the actor Mark Schwerd from the novel by Yaroslav Hasek, continued until January 31, 1938, with seventy-six performances. February 8, 1938, Ossip Dymow's "The East Side Professor" was presented and seventy performances were given.

The Yiddish Art Theatre celebrated its eighteenth anniversary in November, 1937. The 1937-38 season was started September 20, 1937, at the Venice Theatre, with "The Brothers Ashkenazi," which Maurice Schwartz and I. J. Singer dramatized from the Singer novel. Kurt Katsch was one of the leading actors in the play. At the Public Theatre "My Malkele" ended a five months' run January 2, 1938, with Mollie Picon and Aaron Lebedeff playing the principal characters. "Bublitchki," a musical comedy by William Siegel with music by A. Ellstein, had its première January 15, 1937, with Mollie Picon and Jacob Zanger in the leading roles. "The Jesters," a comedy by Joseph Tunkel with music by Pola Kadison and dances by Pauline Kanor, was produced by Workmen's Circle and directed by James Shigorin at the Nora Bayes Theatre, March 13, 1938.

STATISTICAL SUMMARY

(LAST SEASON PLAYS WHICH ENDED RUNS AFTER JUNE 18, 1937)

Plays	Number Performances	Plays	Number Performances
Abie's Irish Rose	46	Excursion	116
Babes in Arms	289	Having Wonderful Time	372
Boy Meets Girl	669	Show Is On, The	237
Brother Rat	577	Tovarich	356
Cat and the Canary, The	9	Yes, My Darling Daughter	405

LONG RUNS ON BROADWAY

To June 18, 1938

(Plays marked with asterisk were still playing June 18, 1938)

Plays	Number Performances	Plays	Number Performances
Abie's Irish Rose.....	2,532	Broadway	603
*Tobacco Road	1,940	Adonis	603
Lightnin'	1,291	Street Scene	601
The Bat	867	Kiki	600
Three Men on a Horse	835	Blossom Time	592
The Ladder	789	Brother Rat	577
The First Year.......	760	Show Boat	572
Seventh Heaven	704	The Show-Off	571
Peg o' My Heart.....	692	Sally	570
The Children's Hour..	691	Strictly Dishonorable..	557
Dead End	687	Good News	551
East Is West	680	The Music Master....	540
Irene	670	The Boomerang	522
Boy Meets Girl......	669	Blackbirds	518
A Trip to Chinatown..	657	Sunny	517
Rain	648	Victoria Regina	517
*You Can't Take It with You	645	The Vagabond King...	511
The Green Pastures...	640	The New Moon......	509
*The Women	632	Shuffle Along	504
Is Zat So............	618	Personal Appearance ..	501
Student Prince.......	608	Bird in Hand........	500
		Sailor, Beware!	500

DRAMA CRITICS' CIRCLE AWARD

Meeting April 18, 1938, the New York Drama Critics' Circle took four ballots before a three-fourths majority vote was given to John Steinbeck's "Of Mice and Men" as the best play of American authorship produced during the season of 1937-38. Thornton Wilder's "Our Town" received the second highest number of votes on all four ballots. Other plays included in the voting were Mark Blitzstein's "The Cradle Will Rock," E. P. Conkle's "Prologue to Glory" and Clifford Odets' "Golden Boy."

The citation accompanying the award of the circle's silver plaque to Mr. Steinbeck's drama reads: "For its direct force and perception in handling a theme genuinely rooted in American life; for its bite into the strict quality of its material; for its refusal to make the study of tragical loneliness and frustration either cheap or sensational, and finally for its simple, intense and steadily rising effect on the stage."

At the same meeting Paul Vincent Carroll's drama, "Shadow and Substance," was awarded a scroll as representing the best theatrical importation of the year.

The Drama Critics' Circle awards to date have been:

1935-36—Winterset, by Maxwell Anderson
1936-37—High Tor, by Maxwell Anderson
1937-38—Of Mice and Men, by John Steinbeck

PULITZER PRIZE WINNERS

"For the original American play performed in New York which shall best represent the educational value and power of the stage in raising the standard of good morals, good taste and good manners."—The Will of Joseph Pulitzer, dated April 16, 1904.

In 1929 the advisory board, which, according to the terms of the will, "shall have the power in its discretion to suspend or to change any subject or subjects . . . if in the judgment of the board such suspension, changes or substitutions shall be conducive to the public good," decided to eliminate from the above paragraph relating to the prize-winning play the words "in raising the standard of good morals, good taste and good manners."

The committee awards to date have been:

1917-18—Why Marry? by Jesse Lynch Williams
1918-19—None
1919-20—Miss Lulu Bett, by Zona Gale
1920-21—Beyond the Horizon, by Eugene O'Neill
1921-22—Anna Christie, by Eugene O'Neill
1922-23—Icebound, by Owen Davis
1923-24—Hell-bent fer Heaven, by Hatcher Hughes
1924-25—They Knew What They Wanted, by Sidney Howard
1925-26—Craig's Wife, by George Kelly
1926-27—In Abraham's Bosom, by Paul Green
1927-28—Strange Interlude, by Eugene O'Neill
1928-29—Street Scene, by Elmer Rice
1929-30—The Green Pastures, by Marc Connelly
1930-31—Alison's House, by Susan Glaspell
1931-32—Of Thee I Sing, by George S. Kaufman, Morrie
           Ryskind, Ira and George Gershwin
1932-33—Both Your Houses, by Maxwell Anderson
1933-34—Men in White, by Sidney Kingsley
1934-35—The Old Maid, by Zoe Akins
1935-36—Idiot's Delight, by Robert E. Sherwood
1936-37—You Can't Take It with You, by Moss Hart and
           George S. Kaufman
1937-38—Our Town, by Thornton Wilder

PREVIOUS VOLUMES OF BEST PLAYS

Plays chosen to represent the theatre seasons from 1909 to 1937 are as follows:

1909-1919

"The Easiest Way," by Eugene Walter. Published by G. W. Dillingham, New York; Houghton Mifflin Co., Boston.

"Mrs. Bumpstead-Leigh," by Harry James Smith. Published by Samuel French, New York.

"Disraeli," by Louis N. Parker. Published by Dodd, Mead and Co., New York.

"Romance," by Edward Sheldon. Published by the Macmillan Co., New York.

"Seven Keys to Baldpate," by George M. Cohan. Published by Bobbs-Merrill Co., Indianapolis, as a novel by Earl Derr Biggers; as a play by Samuel French, New York.

"On Trial," by Elmer Reizenstein. Published by Samuel French, New York.

"The Unchastened Woman," by Louis Kaufman Anspacher. Published by Harcourt, Brace and Howe, Inc., New York.

"Good Gracious Annabelle," by Clare Kummer. Published by Samuel French, New York.

"Why Marry?" by Jesse Lynch Williams. Published by Charles Scribner's Sons, New York.

"John Ferguson," by St. John Ervine. Published by the Macmillan Co., New York.

1919-1920

"Abraham Lincoln," by John Drinkwater. Published by Houghton Mifflin Co., Boston.

"Clarence," by Booth Tarkington. Published by Samuel French, New York.

"Beyond the Horizon," by Eugene G. O'Neill. Published by Boni & Liveright, Inc., New York.

"Déclassée," by Zoe Akins. Published by Liveright, Inc., New York.

"The Famous Mrs. Fair," by James Forbes. Published by Samuel French, New York.

"The Jest," by Sem Benelli. (American adaptation by Edward Sheldon.)

"Jane Clegg," by St. John Ervine. Published by Henry Holt & Co., New York.

"Mamma's Affair," by Rachel Barton Butler. Published by Samuel French, New York.

"Wedding Bells," by Salisbury Field. Published by Samuel French, New York.

"Adam and Eva," by George Middleton and Guy Bolton. Published by Samuel French, New York.

1920-1921

"Deburau," adapted from the French of Sacha Guitry by H. Granville Barker. Published by G. P. Putnam's Sons, New York.

"The First Year," by Frank Craven. Published by Samuel French, New York.

"Enter Madame," by Gilda Varesi and Dolly Byrne. Published by G. P. Putnam's Sons, New York.

"The Green Goddess," by William Archer. Published by Alfred A. Knopf, New York.

"Liliom," by Ferenc Molnar. Published by Boni & Liveright, New York.

"Mary Rose," by James M. Barrie. Published by Charles Scribner's Sons, New York.

"Nice People," by Rachel Crothers. Published by Charles Scribner's Sons, New York.

"The Bad Man," by Porter Emerson Browne. Published by G. P. Putnam's Sons, New York.

"The Emperor Jones," by Eugene G. O'Neill. Published by Boni & Liveright, New York.

"The Skin Game," by John Galsworthy. Published by Charles Scribner's Sons, New York.

1921-1922

"Anna Christie," by Eugene G. O'Neill. Published by Boni & Liveright, New York.

"A Bill of Divorcement," by Clemence Dane. Published by the Macmillan Company, New York.

"Dulcy," by George S. Kaufman and Marc Connelly. Published by G. P. Putnam's Sons, New York.

"He Who Gets Slapped," adapted from the Russian of Leonid Andreyev by Gregory Zilboorg. Published by Brentano's, New York.

"Six Cylinder Love," by William Anthony McGuire.

"The Hero," by Gilbert Emery.

"The Dover Road," by Alan Alexander Milne. Published by Samuel French, New York.

"Ambush," by Arthur Richman.

"The Circle," by William Somerset Maugham.

"The Nest," by Paul Geraldy and Grace George.

1922-1923

"Rain," by John Colton and Clemence Randolph. Published by Liveright, Inc., New York.

"Loyalties," by John Galsworthy. Published by Charles Scribner's Sons, New York.

"Icebound," by Owen Davis. Published by Little, Brown & Company, Boston.

"You and I," by Philip Barry. Published by Brentano's, New York.

"The Fool," by Channing Pollock. Published by Brentano's, New York.

"Merton of the Movies," by George Kaufman and Marc Connelly, based on the novel of the same name by Harry Leon Wilson.

"Why Not?" by Jesse Lynch Williams. Published by Walter H. Baker Co., Boston.

"The Old Soak," by Don Marquis. Published by Doubleday, Page & Company, New York.

"R.U.R.," by Karel Capek. Translated by Paul Selver. Published by Doubleday, Page & Company.

"Mary the 3d," by Rachel Crothers. Published by Brentano's, New York.

1923-1924

"The Swan," translated from the Hungarian of Ferenc Molnar by Melville Baker. Published by Boni & Liveright, New York.

"Outward Bound," by Sutton Vane. Published by Boni & Liveright, New York.

"The Show-off," by George Kelly. Published by Little, Brown & Company, Boston.

"The Changelings," by Lee Wilson Dodd. Published by E. P. Dutton & Company, New York.

"Chicken Feed," by Guy Bolton. Published by Samuel French,

New York and London.

"Sun-Up," by Lula Vollmer. Published by Brentano's, New York.

"Beggar on Horseback," by George Kaufman and Marc Connelly. Published by Boni & Liveright, New York.

"Tarnish," by Gilbert Emery. Published by Brentano's, New York.

"The Goose Hangs High," by Lewis Beach. Published by Little, Brown & Company, Boston.

"Hell-bent fer Heaven," by Hatcher Hughes. Published by Harper Bros., New York.

1924-1925

"What Price Glory?" by Laurence Stallings and Maxwell Anderson. Published by Harcourt, Brace & Co., New York.

"They Knew What They Wanted," by Sidney Howard. Published by Doubleday, Page & Company, New York.

"Desire Under the Elms," by Eugene G. O'Neill. Published by Boni & Liveright, New York.

"The Firebrand," by Edwin Justus Mayer. Published by Boni & Liveright, New York.

"Dancing Mothers," by Edgar Selwyn and Edmund Goulding.

"Mrs. Partridge Presents," by Mary Kennedy and Ruth Warren. Published by Samuel French, New York.

"The Fall Guy," by James Gleason and George Abbott. Published by Samuel French, New York.

"The Youngest," by Philip Barry. Published by Samuel French, New York.

"Minick," by Edna Ferber and George S. Kaufman. Published by Doubleday, Page & Company, New York.

"Wild Birds," by Dan Totheroh. Published by Doubleday, Page & Company, New York.

1925-1926

"Craig's Wife," by George Kelly. Published by Little, Brown & Company, Boston.

"The Great God Brown," by Eugene G. O'Neill. Published by Boni & Liveright, New York.

"The Green Hat," by Michael Arlen.

"The Dybbuk," by S. Ansky, Henry G. Alsberg-Winifred Katzin translation. Published by Boni & Liveright, New York.

"The Enemy," by Channing Pollock. Published by Brentano's,

New York.

"The Last of Mrs. Cheyney," by Frederick Lonsdale. Published by Samuel French, New York.

"Bride of the Lamb," by William Hurlbut. Published by Boni & Liveright, New York.

"The Wisdom Tooth," by Marc Connelly. Published by George H. Doran & Company, New York.

"The Butter and Egg Man," by George Kaufman. Published by Boni & Liveright, New York.

"Young Woodley," by John Van Druten. Published by Simon and Schuster, New York.

1926-1927

"Broadway," by Philip Dunning and George Abbott. Published by George H. Doran Company, New York.

"Saturday's Children," by Maxwell Anderson. Published by Longmans, Green & Company, New York.

"Chicago," by Maurine Watkins. Published by Alfred A. Knopf, Inc., New York.

"The Constant Wife," by William Somerset Maugham. Published by George H. Doran Company, New York.

"The Play's the Thing," by Ferenc Molnar and P. G. Wodehouse. Published by Brentano's, New York.

"The Road to Rome," by Robert Emmet Sherwood. Published by Charles Scribner's Sons, New York.

"The Silver Cord," by Sidney Howard. Published by Charles Scribner's Sons, New York.

"The Cradle Song," translated from the Spanish of G. Martinez Sierra by John Garrett Underhill. Published by E. P. Dutton & Company, New York.

"Daisy Mayme," by George Kelly. Published by Little, Brown & Company, Boston.

"In Abraham's Bosom," by Paul Green. Published by Robert M. McBride & Company, New York.

1927-1928

"Strange Interlude," by Eugene G. O'Neill. Published by Boni & Liveright, New York.

"The Royal Family," by Edna Ferber and George Kaufman. Published by Doubleday, Doran & Company, New York.

"Burlesque," by George Manker Watters. Published by Doubleday, Doran & Company, New York.

"Coquette," by George Abbott and Ann Bridgers. Published by Longmans, Green & Company, New York, London, Toronto.

"Behold the Bridegroom," by George Kelly. Published by Little, Brown & Company, Boston.

"Porgy," by DuBose Heyward. Published by Doubleday, Doran & Company, New York.

"Paris Bound," by Philip Barry. Published by Samuel French, New York.

"Escape," by John Galsworthy. Published by Charles Scribner's Sons, New York.

"The Racket," by Bartlett Cormack. Published by Samuel French, New York.

"The Plough and the Stars," by Sean O'Casey. Published by the Macmillan Company, New York.

1928-1929

"Street Scene," by Elmer Rice. Published by Samuel French, New York.

"Journey's End," by R. C. Sherriff. Published by Brentano's, New York.

"Wings Over Europe," by Robert Nichols and Maurice Browne. Published by Covici-Friede, New York.

"Holiday," by Philip Barry. Published by Samuel French, New York.

"The Front Page," by Ben Hecht and Charles MacArthur. Published by Covici-Friede, New York.

"Let Us Be Gay," by Rachel Crothers. Published by Samuel French, New York.

"Machinal," by Sophie Treadwell.

"Little Accident," by Floyd Dell and Thomas Mitchell.

"Gypsy," by Maxwell Anderson.

"The Kingdom of God," by G. Martinez Sierra; English version by Helen and Harley Granville-Barker. Published by E. P. Dutton & Company, New York.

1929-1930

"The Green Pastures," by Marc Connelly (adapted from "Ol' Man Adam and His Chillun," by Roark Bradford). Published by Farrar & Rinehart, Inc., New York.

"The Criminal Code," by Martin Flavin. Published by Horace Liveright, New York.

"Berkeley Square," by John Balderston. Published by the Macmillan Company, New York.

"Strictly Dishonorable," by Preston Sturges. Published by Horace Liveright, New York.

"The First Mrs. Fraser," by St. John Ervine. Published by the Macmillan Company, New York.

"The Last Mile," by John Wexley. Published by Samuel French, New York.

"June Moon," by Ring W. Lardner and George S. Kaufman. Published by Charles Scribner's Sons, New York.

"Michael and Mary," by A. A. Milne. Published by Chatto & Windus, London.

"Death Takes a Holiday," by Walter Ferris (adapted from the Italian of Alberto Casella). Published by Samuel French, New York.

"Rebound," by Donald Ogden Stewart. Published by Samuel French, New York.

1930-1931

"Elizabeth the Queen," by Maxwell Anderson. Published by Longmans, Green & Co., New York.

"Tomorrow and Tomorrow," by Philip Barry. Published by Samuel French, New York.

"Once in a Lifetime," by George S. Kaufman and Moss Hart. Published by Farrar and Rinehart, New York.

"Green Grow the Lilacs," by Lynn Riggs. Published by Samuel French, New York and London.

"As Husbands Go," by Rachel Crothers. Published by Samuel French, New York.

"Alison's House," by Susan Glasgow. Published by Samuel French, New York.

"Five-Star Final," by Louis Weitzenkorn. Published by Samuel French, New York.

"Overture," by William Bolitho. Published by Simon & Schuster, New York.

"The Barretts of Wimpole Street," by Rudolf Besier. Published by Little, Brown & Company, Boston.

"Grand Hotel," adapted from the German of Vicki Baum by W. A. Drake.

1931-1932

"Of Thee I Sing," by George S. Kaufman and Morrie Ryskind; music and lyrics by George and Ira Gershwin. Published by Alfred Knopf, New York.

"Mourning Becomes Electra," by Eugene G. O'Neill. Published by Horace Liveright, Inc., New York.

"Reunion in Vienna," by Robert Emmet Sherwood. Published

by Charles Scribner's Sons, New York.

"The House of Connelly," by Paul Green. Published by Samuel French, New York.

"The Animal Kingdom," by Philip Barry. Published by Samuel French, New York.

"The Left Bank," by Elmer Rice. Published by Samuel French, New York.

"Another Language," by Rose Franken. Published by Samuel French, New York.

"Brief Moment," by S. N. Behrman. Published by Farrar & Rinehart, New York.

"The Devil Passes," by Benn W. Levy. Published by Martin Secker, London.

"Cynara," by H. M. Harwood and R. F. Gore-Browne. Published by Samuel French, New York.

1932-1933

"Both Your Houses," by Maxwell Anderson. Published by Samuel French, New York.

"Dinner at Eight," by George S. Kaufman and Edna Ferber. Published by Doubleday, Doran & Co., Inc., Garden City, New York.

"When Ladies Meet," by Rachel Crothers. Published by Samuel French, New York.

"Design for Living," by Noel Coward. Published by Doubleday, Doran & Co., Inc., Garden City, New York.

"Biography," by S. N. Behrman. Published by Farrar & Rinehart, Inc., New York.

"Alien Corn," by Sidney Howard. Published by Charles Scribner's Sons, New York.

"The Late Christopher Bean," adapted from the French of René Fauchois by Sidney Howard. Published by Samuel French, New York.

"We, the People," by Elmer Rice. Published by Coward-McCann, Inc., New York.

"Pigeons and People," by George M. Cohan.

"One Sunday Afternoon," by James Hagan. Published by Samuel French, New York.

1933-1934

"Mary of Scotland," by Maxwell Anderson. Published by Doubleday, Doran & Co., Inc., Garden City, N. Y.

"Men in White," by Sidney Kingsley. Published by Covici, Friede, Inc., New York.

"Dodsworth," by Sinclair Lewis and Sidney Howard. Published by Harcourt, Brace & Co., New York.

"Ah, Wilderness," by Eugene O'Neill. Published by Random House, New York.

"They Shall Not Die," by John Wexley. Published by Alfred A. Knopf, New York.

"Her Master's Voice," by Clare Kummer. Published by Samuel French, New York.

"No More Ladies," by A. E. Thomas.

"Wednesday's Child," by Leopold Atlas. Published by Samuel French, New York.

"The Shining Hour," by Keith Winter. Published by Doubleday, Doran & Co., Inc., Garden City, New York.

"The Green Bay Tree," by Mordaunt Shairp. Published by Baker International Play Bureau, Boston, Mass.

1934-1935

"The Children's Hour," by Lillian Hellman. Published by Alfred Knopf, New York.

"Valley Forge," by Maxwell Anderson. Published by Anderson House, Washington, D. C. Distributed by Dodd, Mead & Co., New York.

"The Petrified Forest," by Robert Sherwood. Published by Charles Scribner's Sons, New York.

"The Old Maid," by Zoe Akins. Published by D. Appleton-Century Co., New York.

"Accent on Youth," by Samson Raphaelson. Published by Samuel French, New York.

"Merrily We Roll Along," by George S. Kaufman and Moss Hart. Published by Random House, New York.

"Awake and Sing," by Clifford Odets. Published by Random House, New York.

"The Farmer Takes a Wife," by Frank B. Elser and Marc Connelly.

"Lost Horizons," by John Hayden.

"The Distaff Side," by John Van Druten. Published by Alfred Knopf, New York.

1935-1936

"Winterset," by Maxwell Anderson. Published by Anderson House, Washington, D. C.

"Idiot's Delight," by Robert Emmet Sherwood. Published by Charles Scribner's Sons, New York.

"End of Summer," by S. N. Behrman. Published by Random House, New York.

"First Lady," by Katharine Dayton and George S. Kaufman. Published by Random House, New York.

"Victoria Regina," by Laurence Housman. Published by Samuel French, Inc., New York and London.

"Boy Meets Girl," by Bella and Samuel Spewack. Published by Random House, New York.

"Dead End," by Sidney Kingsley. Published by Random House, New York.

"Call It a Day," by Dodie Smith. Published by Samuel French, Inc., New York and London.

"Ethan Frome," by Owen Davis and Donald Davis. Published by Charles Scribner's Sons, New York.

"Pride and Prejudice," by Helen Jerome. Published by Double-day, Doran & Co., Garden City, New York.

1936-1937

"High Tor," by Maxwell Anderson. Published by Anderson House, Washington, D. C.

"You Can't Take It with You," by Moss Hart and George S. Kaufman. Published by Farrar & Rinehart, Inc., New York.

"Johnny Johnson," by Paul Green. Published by Samuel French, Inc., New York.

"Daughters of Atreus," by Robert Turney. Published by Alfred A. Knopf, New York.

"Stage Door," by Edna Ferber and George S. Kaufman. Published by Doubleday, Doran & Co., Garden City, New York.

"The Women," by Clare Boothe. Published by Random House, Inc., New York.

"St. Helena," by R. C. Sherriff and Jeanne de Casalis. Published by Samuel French, Inc., New York and London.

"Yes, My Darling Daughter," by Mark Reed. Published by Samuel French, Inc., New York.

"Excursion," by Victor Wolfson. Published by Random House, New York.

"Tovarich," by Jacques Deval and Robert E. Sherwood. Published by Random House, New York.

WHERE AND WHEN THEY WERE BORN

Abba, Marta .... Milan, Italy 1907
Abbott, George .... Hamburg, N. Y. 1895
Abel, Walter .... St. Paul, Minn. 1898
Aborn, Milton .... Marysville, Cal. 1864
Adams, Maude .... Salt Lake City, Utah ... 1872
Adler, Luther .... New York City 1903
Adler, Stella .... New York City 1904
Aherne, Brian .... King's Norton, England ...1902
Akins, Zoe .... Humansville, Mo. 1886
Alexander, Katherine .... Arkansas 1901
Alexander, Ross .... Brooklyn, N. Y......... 1904
Allenby, Peggy .... New York 1905
Allen, Adrianne .... Manchester, England 1907
Allen, Viola .... Huntsville, Ala. 1869
Allgood, Sara .... Dublin, Ireland 1883
Ames, Robert .... Hartford, Conn. 1893
Ames, Winthrop .... North Easton, Mass. 1871
Anders, Glenn .... Los Angeles, Cal. 1890
Anderson, Judith .... Australia 1898
Anderson, Maxwell .... Atlantic City, Pa. 1888
Andrews, A. G. .... Buffalo, N. Y........... 1861
Andrews, Ann .... Los Angeles, Cal. 1895
Anglin, Margaret .... Ottawa, Canada 1876
Anson, A. E. .... London, England 1879
Anspacher, Louis K. .... Cincinnati, Ohio 1878
Arling, Joyce .... Memphis, Tenn. 1911
Arliss, George .... London, England 1868
Arthur, Julia .... Hamilton, Ont. 1869
Ashcroft, Peggy .... Croydon, England 1907
Astaire, Fred .... Omaha, Neb. 1899
Atwell, Roy .... Syracuse, N. Y.......... 1880
Atwill, Lionel .... London, England 1885

Bainter, Fay .... Los Angeles, Cal. 1892
Baker, Lee .... Michigan 1880
Bankhead, Tallulah .... Huntsville, Ala. 1902
Banks, Leslie J. .... West Derby, England 1890

Barbee, Richard .... Lafayette, Ind. 1887
Barrett, Edith .... Roxbury, Mass. 1904
Barrie, James Matthew .... Kirriemuir, Scotland 1860
Barry, Philip .... Rochester, N. Y. 1896
Barrymore, Ethel .... Philadelphia, Pa. 1879
Barrymore, John .... Philadelphia, Pa. 1882
Barrymore, Lionel .... London, England 1878
Barton, James .... Gloucester, N. J. 1890
Bates, Blanche .... Portland, Ore. 1873
Baxter, Lora .... New York 1907
Beatty, Roberta .... Rochester, N. Y. 1900
Beecher, Janet .... Chicago, Ill. 1884
Behrman, S. N. .... Worcester, Mass. 1893
Bell, James .... Suffolk, Va. 1891
Ben-Ami, Jacob .... Minsk, Russia 1890
Bennett, Richard .... Cass County, Ind. 1873
Bennett, Wilda .... Asbury Park, N. J. 1894
Bergner, Elisabeth .... Vienna 1901
Berlin, Irving .... Russia 1888
Best, Edna .... Sussex, England 1900
Binney, Constance .... Philadelphia, Pa. 1900
Blackmer, Sidney .... Salisbury, N. C. 1896
Boland, Mary .... Detroit, Mich. 1880
Bolger, Ray .... Dorchester, Mass. 1906
Bondi, Beulah .... Chicago, Ill. 1892
Bordoni, Irene .... Paris, France 1895
Bowman, Patricia .... Washington, D. C. 1912
Brady, Alice .... New York 1892
Brady, William A. .... San Francisco, Cal. 1863
Brady, William A., Jr. ...... New York 1900
Braham, Horace .... London, England 1896
Brent, Romney .... Saltillo, Mex. 1902
Brian, Donald .... St. Johns, N. F. 1877
Brice, Fannie .... Brooklyn, N. Y. 1891
Broadhurst, George H. ...... England 1866
Broderick, Helen .... New York 1891
Bromberg, J. Edward .... Hungary 1903
Bruce, Nigel .... San Diego, Cal. 1895
Bryant, Charles .... England 1879
Buchanan, Jack .... England 1892
Buchanan, Thompson .... Louisville, Ky. 1877
Buckler, Hugh .... Southampton, England ... 1886
Burke, Billie .... Washington, D. C. 1885

Digges, Dudley .... Dublin, Ireland 1880
Dillingham, Charles B. .... Hartford, Conn. 1868
Dinehart, Allan .... Missoula, Mont. 1889
Dixey, Henry E. .... Boston, Mass. 1859
Dixon, Jean .... Waterbury, Conn. 1905
Dodson, John E. .... London, England 1857
Doro, Marie .... Duncannon, Pa. 1882
D'Orsay, Lawrence .... England 1860
Dressler, Eric .... Brooklyn, N. Y. 1900
Dressler, Marie .... Cobourg, Canada 1869
Drew, Louise .... New York 1884
Duncan, Augustin .... San Francisco 1873
Dunn, Emma .... England 1875
Dunning, Philip .... Meriden, Conn. 1890
Dupree, Minnie .... San Francisco, Cal. 1875
Durante, Jimmy .... New York City 1893

Edeson, Robert .... Baltimore, Md. 1868
Edney, Florence .... London, England 1879
Eldridge, Florence .... Brooklyn, N. Y. 1901
Ellerbe, Harry .... Georgia 1905
Ellis, Mary .... New York 1900
Elliston, Grace .... Wheeling, W. Va. 1881
Ellinger, Desirée .... Manchester, Vt. 1895
Elliott, Gertrude .... Rockland, Me. 1874
Elliott, Maxine .... Rockland, Me. 1871
Eltinge, Julian .... Boston, Mass. 1883
Emery, Gilbert .... Naples, New York 1875
Emery, Katherine .... Birmingham, Ala. 1908
Emerson, John .... Sandusky, Ohio 1874
Errol, Leon .... Sydney, Australia 1881
Ervine, St. John Greer ...... Belfast, Ireland 1883
Evans, Edith .... London, England 1888
Evans, Maurice .... Dorchester, England 1901

Fairbanks, Douglas .... Denver, Colo. 1883
Farmer, Frances .... Seattle, Wash. 1914
Farnum, William .... Boston, Mass. 1876
Farrar, Geraldine .... Melrose, Mass. 1883
Fassett, Jay .... Elmira, N. Y. 1889
Faversham, William .... Warwickshire, England ... 1868
Fenwick, Irene .... Chicago, Ill. 1887
Ferber, Edna .... Kalamazoo, Mich. 1887

Ferguson, Elsie .... New York 1883
Field, Sylvia .... Allston, Mass. 1902
Fields, Lew .... New York 1867
Fields, W. C. .... Philadelphia, Pa. 1883
Fischer, Alice .... Indiana 1869
Fiske, Minnie Maddern .... New Orleans, La. 1867
Fontanne, Lynn .... London, England 1887
Forbes-Robertson, Sir J. ...... London, England 1853
Foster, Claiborne .... Shreveport, La. 1899
Foster, Norman .... Richmond, Ind. 1907
Foster, Phœbe .... New Hampshire 1897
Foy, Eddie, Jr. .... New Rochelle, N. Y. 1906
Franklin, Irene .... St. Louis, Mo. 1878
Frederick, Pauline .... Boston, Mass. 1884
Friganza, Trixie .... Cincinnati, Ohio 1870
Frohman, Daniel .... Sandusky, Ohio 1850

Gahagan, Helen .... Boonton, N. J. 1902
Garden, Mary .... Scotland 1876
Gaxton, William .... San Francisco, Cal. 1893
Gaythorne, Pamela .... England 1882
Geddes, Norman Bel .... Adrian, Mich. 1893
George, Grace .... New York 1879
Gerald, Ara .... New South Wales 1902
Gershwin, George .... Brooklyn, N. Y. 1898
Gershwin, Ira .... New York 1896
Gielgud, John .... London, England 1904
Gillette, William .... Hartford, Conn. 1856
Gillmore, Frank .... New York 1884
Gillmore, Margalo .... England 1901
Gish, Dorothy .... Massillon, Ohio 1898
Gish, Lillian .... Springfield, Ohio 1896
Glaser, Vaughan .... Cleveland, Ohio 1873
Gleason, James .... New York 1885
Glendinning, Ernest .... Ulverston, England 1884
Golden, John .... New York 1874
Gordon, Ruth .... Wollaston, Mass. 1896
Gottschalk, Ferdinand .... London, England 1869
Granville, Charlotte .... London 1863
Granville, Sydney .... Bolton, England 1885
Greaza, Walter .... St. Paul, Minn. 1900
Green, Martyn .... London, England 1899
Green, Mitzi .... New York City 1920

Greenstreet, Sydney .... England 1880
Grey, Katherine .... San Francisco, Cal. 1873
Groody, Louise .... Waco, Texas 1897
Gwenn, Edmund .... Glamorgan, Wales 1875

Haines, Robert T. .... Muncie, Ind. 1870
Hale, Louise Closser .... Chicago, Ill. 1872
Hall, Bettina .... North Easton, Mass. 1906
Hall, Laura Nelson .... Philadelphia, Pa. 1876
Hall, Natalie .... North Easton, Mass. 1904
Hall, Thurston .... Boston, Mass. 1882
Halliday, John .... Brooklyn, N. Y. 1880
Halliday, Robert .... Loch Lomond, Scotland ...1893
Hamilton, Hale .... Topeka, Kansas 1880
Hampden, Walter .... Brooklyn, N. Y. 1879
Hannen, Nicholas .... London, England 1881
Hanson, Gladys .... Atlanta, Ga. 1887
Harding, Lyn .... Newport, England 1867
Hardwicke, Sir Cedric .... Lye, Stourbridge, England..1893
Harrigan, William .... New York 1893
Harris, Sam H. .... New York 1872
Harrison, Richard B. .... London, Ontario 1864
Hart, Vivian .... Texas 1905
Haydon, Julie .... Oak Park, Ill. 1910
Hayes, Helen .... Washington, D. C. 1900
Hazzard, John E. .... New York 1881
Hedman, Martha .... Sweden 1888
Heggie, O. P. .... Australia 1879
Heineman, Eda .... Japan 1891
Heming, Violet .... Leeds, England 1893
Hepburn, Katharine .... Hartford, Conn. 1907
Herbert, Evelyn .... Brooklyn, N. Y. 1900
Herne, Chrystal .... Dorchester, Mass. 1883
Hobert, Rose .... New York 1906
Hodge, William .... Albion, N. Y. 1874
Hopkins, Arthur .... Cleveland, Ohio 1878
Hopkins, Miriam .... Bainbridge, Ga. 1904
Hopper, de Wolf .... New York 1858
Hopper, Edna Wallace .... San Francisco, Cal. 1874
Holmes, Taylor .... Newark, N. J. 1872
Howard, Leslie .... London, England 1890
Howard, Sydney .... Oakland, Cal. 1891
Hull, Henry .... Louisville, Ky. 1893

Hunter, Glenn .... Highland Mills, N. Y. 1896
Huston, Walter .... Toronto 1884
Hutchinson, Josephine ...... Seattle, Wash. 1898

Inescort, Frieda .... Hitchin, Scotland 1905
Ingram, Rex .... Dublin, Ireland 1892
Irving, Isabel .... Bridgeport, Conn. 1871
Irwin, May .... Whitby, Ont. 1862

Janis, Elsie .... Delaware, Ohio 1889
Joel, Clara .... Jersey City, N. J. 1890
Johann, Zita .... Hungary 1904
Jolson, Al .... Washington, D. C. 1883
Johnston, Moffat .... Edinburgh, Scotland 1886
Joy, Nicholas .... Paris, France 1892

Kane, Whitford .... Larne, Ireland 1882
Kaufman, George S. .... Pittsburgh, Pa. 1889
Kaye, A. P. .... Ringwood, Hampshire,
                             England 1885
Keane, Doris .... Michigan 1885
Keith, Ian .... Boston, Mass. 1899
Keith, Robert .... Scotland 1899
Kelly, Walter C. .... Mineville, N. Y. 1875
Kennedy, Madge .... Chicago, Ill. 1890
Kerrigan, J. M. .... Dublin, Ireland 1885
Kerr, Geoffrey .... London, England 1895
Kershaw, Willette .... Clifton Heights, Mo. 1890
Kilbride, Percy .... San Francisco, Cal. 1880
King, Dennis .... Coventry, England 1897
Kingsford, Walter .... England 1876
Kingsley, Sydney .... New York 1906
Kirkland, Alexander .... Mexico City 1904
Kosta, Tessa .... Chicago, Ill. 1893
Kruger, Alma .... Pittsburgh, Pa. 1880
Kruger, Otto .... Toledo, Ohio 1895

Lackaye, Wilton .... Virginia 1862
Landi, Elissa .... Venice, Italy 1904
Larimore, Earl .... Portland, Oregon 1899
Larrimore, Francine .... Russia 1898
La Rue, Grace .... Kansas City, Mo. 1882
Lauder, Harry .... Portobello, Scotland 1870

Laughton, Charles .... Scarborough, England 1899
Lawrence, Gertrude .... London 1898
Lawson, Wilfred .... London, England 1894
Lawton, Frank .... London, England 1904
Lawton, Thais .... Louisville, Ky. 1881
Lean, Cecil .... Illinois 1878
Lederer, Francis .... Karlin, Prague 1906
Le Gallienne, Eva .... London, England 1900
Leiber, Fritz .... Chicago, Ill. 1884
Lenihan, Winifred .... New York 1898
Leontovich, Eugenie .... Moscow, Russia 1894
Levey, Ethel .... San Francisco, Cal. 1881
Levy, Benn .... London, England 1900
Lewis, Mabel Terry .... London, England 1872
Lillie, Beatrice .... Toronto, Canada 1898
Locke, Katherine .... New York 1914
Logan, Stanley .... Earlsfield, England 1885
Loraine, Robert .... New Brighton, England...1876
Lord, Pauline .... Hanford, Cal. 1890
Lorraine, Lillian .... San Francisco, Cal. 1892
Lou-Tellegen .... Holland 1881
Love, Montagu .... Portsmouth, Hants 1877
Lowell, Helen .... New York 1866
Lunt, Alfred .... Milwaukee, Wis. 1893

Mack, Andrew .... Boston, Mass. 1863
Mack, Willard .... Ontario, Canada 1873
Macdonald, Donald .... Denison, Texas 1898
Mackay, Elsie .... London, England 1894
MacKellar, Helen .... Canada 1896
March, Fredric .... Racine, Wis. 1897
Margo .... Mexico 1918
Marlowe, Julia .... Caldbeck, England 1870
Marshall, Herbert .... London, England 1890
Massey, Raymond .... Toronto, Canada 1896
Matthews, A. E. .... Bridlington, England 1869
Matthison, Edith Wynne ..... England 1875
Maude, Cyril .... London, England 1862
McClintic, Guthrie .... Seattle, Wash. 1893
McCormick, Myron .... Albany, Indiana 1906
McIntyre, Frank .... Ann Arbor, Mich. 1879
Meek, Donald .... Glasgow, Scotland 1880
Meighan, Thomas .... Pittsburgh, Pa. 1879

Melba, Nellie .... Melbourne, Australia 1866
Menken, Helen .... New York 1901
Mercer, Beryl .... Seville, Spain 1882
Meredith, Burgess .... Cleveland, Ohio 1909
Merivale, Philip .... Rehutia, India 1886
Merman, Ethel .... Astoria, L. I. 1909
Miller, Gilbert .... New York 1884
Miller, Marilyn .... Findlay, Ohio 1898
Mitchell, Grant .... Columbus, Ohio 1874
Mitchell, Thomas .... Elizabeth, N. J. 1892
Mitzi (Hajos) .... Budapest 1891
Moore, Grace .... Del Rio, Tenn. 1901
Moore, Victor .... Hammonton, N. J. 1876
Moran, Lois .... Pittsburgh, Pa. 1909
Morgan, Claudia .... New York 1912
Morgan, Helen .... Danville, Ill. 1900
Morgan, Ralph .... New York City 1889
Morris, Mary .... Boston 1894
Morris, McKay .... San Antonio, Texas 1890
Muni, Paul .... Lemberg, Austria 1895

Nagel, Conrad .... Keokuk, Iowa 1897
Nash, Florence .... Troy, N. Y. 1888
Nash, Mary .... Troy, N. Y. 1885
Natwick, Mildred .... Baltimore, Md. 1908
Nazimova, Alla .... Crimea, Russia 1879
Nielsen, Alice .... Nashville, Tenn. 1876
Nolan, Lloyd .... San Francisco, Cal. 1903
Nugent, J. C. .... Miles, Ohio 1875
Nugent, Elliott .... Dover, Ohio 1900

O'Brien-Moore, Erin .... Los Angeles, Cal. 1908
O'Connell, Hugh .... New York 1891
Odets, Clifford .... Philadelphia 1906
Olcott, Chauncey .... Buffalo, N. Y. 1862
Oldham, Derek .... Accrington, England 1892
O'Malley, Rex .... London, England 1906
O'Neill, Eugene Gladstone ..... New York 1888
O'Neill, Nance .... Oakland, Cal. 1875
Ouspenkaya, Maria .... Tula, Russia 1876
Overman, Lynne .... Maryville, Mo. 1887

Painter, Eleanor .... Iowa 1890
Pawle, Lenox .... London, England 1872
Pemberton, Brock .... Leavenworth, Kansas 1885
Pennington, Ann .... Philadelphia, Pa. 1898
Perkins, Osgood .... Boston, Mass. 1892
Perry, Margaret .... Denver, Colo. 1913
Philips, Mary .... New London, Conn. 1901
Pickford, Mary .... Toronto 1893
Pollock, Channing .... Washington, D. C. 1880
Post, Guy Bates .... Seattle, Wash. 1875
Power, Tyrone .... London, England 1869
Powers, James T. .... New York 1862
Powers, Leona .... Salida, Colo. 1900
Powers, Tom .... Owensburg, Ky. 1890
Pryor, Roger .... New York City 1901

Quartermaine, Leon .... Richmond, England 1876

Rains, Claude .... London, England 1889
Rambeau, Marjorie .... San Francisco, Cal. 1889
Rathbone, Basil .... Johannesburg 1892
Reed, Florence .... Philadelphia, Pa. 1883
Rennie, James .... Toronto, Canada 1890
Revelle, Hamilton .... Gibraltar 1872
Richman, Charles .... Chicago, Ill. 1870
Ridges, Stanley .... Southampton, England 1891
Ring, Blanche .... Boston, Mass. 1876
Ring, Frances .... New York 1882
Robinson, Edward G. .... Bucharest, Roumania 1893
Robson, May .... Australia 1868
Rogers, Mary .... Rogers, Ark. 1916
Roos, Joanna .... Brooklyn, N. Y. 1901
Ross, Thomas W. .... Boston, Mass. 1875
Royle, Selena .... New York 1905
Ruben, José .... Belgium 1886
Rumann, Siegfried .... Hamburg, Germany 1879
Russell, Annie .... Liverpool, England 1864

Sanderson, Julia .... Springfield, Mass. 1887
Sands, Dorothy .... Cambridge, Mass. 1900
Santley, Joseph .... Salt Lake City 1889
Sawyer, Ivy .... London, England 1897

Wiman, Dwight Deere .... Moline, Ill. 1895
Winwood, Estelle .... England 1883
Witherspoon, Cora .... New Orleans, La. 1891
Wood, Peggy .... Brooklyn, N. Y. 1894
Worlock, Frederick .... London, England 1885
Wright, Haidee .... London, England 1868
Wycherly, Margaret .... England 1883
Wyndham, Olive .... Chicago, Ill. 1886
Wynyard, Diana .... London, England 1906
Wynn, Ed. .... Philadelphia, Pa. 1886

Yorke, Oswald .... London, England 1868
Young, Roland .... London, England 1887
Yurka, Blanche .... Bohemia 1893

Zabelle, Flora .... Constantinople 1885
Ziegfeld, Florenz, Jr.......... Chicago, Ill. 1868

NECROLOGY

June 15, 1937—June 18, 1938

Ames, Winthrop, producer, 66. After Harvard, edited art and architectural magazine; staged modern and classical plays, Castle Square Theatre, Boston; director New Theatre, New York; built Little and Booth Theatres, New York; produced "The Pigeon," "Old English," "Escape," "Beggar on Horseback," etc.; retired from Broadway in 1932. Born North Easton, Mass.; died Boston, Mass., November 3, 1937.

Atteridge, Harold, librettist, 51. Wrote book and lyrics for more than forty Shubert productions (many in collaboration) beginning with "Vera Violette" (1911); wrote "Dream Girl" which contained the last complete score by the late Victor Herbert. Born Lake Forest, Ill.; died Lynbrook, L. I., New York, January 15, 1938.

Barrie, Sir James Matthew, playwright and novelist, 77. One of England's most popular dramatists whom America adopted wholeheartedly; wrote "Peter Pan," "The Little Minister," "The Admirable Crichton," "What Every Woman Knows," etc.; *Sentimental Tommy* and many other novels. Born Kirriemuir, Scotland; died London, England, June 19, 1937.

Belasco, Edward, theatrical producer, 63. Formerly associated with Homer Curran and Henry Duffy in San Francisco; produced "Cat and the Fiddle," "Grand Hotel," "Front Page," "Devil's Plum Tree," etc.; brother of the late David Belasco. Born San Francisco, Calif.; died San Francisco, October 9, 1937.

Buchanan, Thompson, playwright, 60. Drama critic *Louisville Herald;* editor Goldwyn pictures in Hollywood; dramas included "A Woman's Way," "Civilian Clothes" and "Pride"; married Joan Lowell, author of "The Cradle of the Deep." Born New York City; died Louisville, Ky., October 15, 1937.

Burnham, Charles, producer, 80. Brought "The Mikado" from England for its first production in New York, Union Square Theatre, 1885; several years president of Managers Association; retired after sixty years in theatre. Born New York City; died Winter Park, Fla., January 19, 1938.

Cabot, Eliot, actor, 39.   Studied for stage in London; first appearance in New York in "Six Characters in Search of an Author"; was Helen Hayes' leading man in "Coquette"; joined Theatre Guild company in 1922.   Born Boston, Mass.; died New York City, June 17, 1938.

Carew, James, actor, 62.   Veteran actor prominent in England and America; married Ellen Terry, with whom he appeared in many stage successes; retired in 1936.   Born Goshen, Ind.; died London, England, April 4, 1938.

Carter, Mrs. Leslie, actress, 75.   First New York appearance, "The Ugly Duckling" (1890); first London appearance, "The Heart of Maryland" (1898); others "Zaza," "Du Barry," "Andrea," etc.; under management of David Belasco until her marriage to W. L. Payne in 1906.   Born Lexington, Ky.; died Brentwood Heights, Santa Monica, Calif., November 13, 1937.

Chaliapin, Feodor, singer, 65.   Celebrated Russian basso; famous for portrayal of Boris Goudonoff, Ivan the Terrible, Mephistopheles, etc.; wrote *Pages from My Life.*   Born Kazan, Russia; died Paris, France, April 12, 1938.

Cliff, Laddie (Clifton Albyn Perry), actor, 46.   Famous English comedian; first seen in New York at Colonial Music Hall, 1907; member Folies Bergere Company, New York (1911).   Born Bristol, England; died Montana, Switzerland, December 8, 1937.

Clive, Colin (Clive-Greig), actor, 37.   Career started in 1919 in England; played Captain Stanhope in "Journey's End"; starred in many films; married Jeanne de Casalis, French actress and playwright.   Born St. Malo, France; died Hollywood, Calif., June 25, 1937.

Dazey, Charles Turner, playwright, 85.   First play "Rusticana." "In Old Kentucky" brought him fame and fortune.   Born Lima, Ill.; died Quincy, Ill., February 9, 1938.

Donaghey, Frederick, music and drama critic, 64.   Critic for *Chicago Tribune, Philadelphia Enquirer* and *Public Ledger, New York Herald*; general manager for William A. Brady; Chicago manager for Klaw & Erlanger, George C. Tyler, Liebler Company; adapted Bisson's "The Marriage of a Star"; wrote "The Girl at the Gate" and other plays.   Born Philadelphia, Pa.; died Chicago, Ill., November 8, 1937.

Earle, Virginia, actress and singer, 62.   Musical comedy star of the nineties; début at age of 12 in juvenile opera company playing "Mikado"; toured with Pike Opera Company; traveled two years in Australia; married Frank Lawton, comedian. Born Cincinnati, Ohio; died New Jersey, September 21, 1937.

Emery, Edward, actor, 77. Member of old English theatrical family; with Wilson Barrett, Charles Hawtrey and Sir Charles Wyndham; in America supported Mrs. Fiske, Ethel Barrymore and Margaret Anglin; married Georgia Waldron; father of Edward Emery, Jr. Born London, England; died New York, May 7, 1938.

Fellows, Dexter William, press agent, 66. Internationally known as circus press representative for Barnum, Bailey, Ringling, etc., for more than forty years. Born Boston, Mass.; died Hattiesburg, Miss., November 28, 1937.

Ferguson, Frank, actor, playwright, 74. Began stage career in Boston in light opera; was dramatic critic *Boston Home Journal;* wrote forty-one one-act plays; played with Mary Shaw; headed his own company in vaudeville. Born Boston, Mass.; died New York City, September 8, 1937.

Forbes, James, playwright, 66. Associated with American stage for fifty years; started as actor; dramatic critic *Pittsburgh Dispatch* and *New York World;* wrote "The Chorus Lady," "The Traveling Salesman," "The Famous Mrs. Fair," etc. Born Salem, Ontario; died Frankfort-on-the-Main, Germany, May 26, 1938.

Forbes-Robertson, Sir Johnston, actor, 84. Prepared at Royal Academy to be an artist; début on stage 1874; toured with Ellen Terry in "The Wandering Heir"; played leads with Modjeska, Henry Irving, Mary Anderson; first appearance in New York, 1885, as Orlando in "As You Like It"; co-starred with Mrs. Patrick Campbell; popular in "The Passing of the Third Floor Back"; final appearance London, 1913, "Hamlet"; final appearance New York, 1914, with his wife, Gertrude Elliott; final appearance on any stage at Sanders Theatre, Harvard University, in "Hamlet." Born London; died St. Margaret's Bay, Dover, England, November 6, 1937.

Furniss, Grace Livingston, playwright, 74. Wrote "A Colonial Girl," "The Pride of Jennico" (with Abby Sage Richardson), "Mrs. Jack," "Gretna Green," etc. Born New York City; died New York City, April 20, 1938.

Gershwin, George, composer, 38. First score for musical comedy, "La La Lucille" (1919); others included "Lady Be Good," "George White Scandals," "Strike Up the Band," "Girl

Crazy," "Rosalie" (with Sigmund Romberg), "Of Thee I Sing" and "Porgy and Bess." Born Brooklyn, New York; died Hollywood, Calif., July 12, 1937.

Gould, Howard, actor, 74. Started as call boy in 1882 at Boston Museum; four years with Daniel Frohman, playing "Prisoner of Zenda," "The Witching Hour," "Madame X," etc. Born St. Anthony, Minn.; died Winthrop, Mass., February 3, 1938.

Greenwald, Joseph, actor, 60. Gained prominence as Jewish comedian; toured in "Abie's Irish Rose"; was taking part of Mr. Bonaparte in "Golden Boy" on the road when he collapsed on stage. Born New York City; died Santa Barbara, Calif., April 1, 1938.

Hards, Ira, actor, director, 65. Acting début (1893) under Charles Frohman; staged many Broadway productions including "Dracula," "Jarnegan," "The Bishop Misbehaves," etc. Born Geneva, Ill.; died West Norwalk, Conn., May 2, 1938.

Henderson, John Raymond, press representative, 48. Became Sir Johnston Forbes-Robertson's press agent; subsequently represented E. H. Sothern and Julia Marlowe, George Arliss, Ethel Barrymore and Katharine Cornell. Born Colorado Springs, Colo.; died in seaplane accident Athens, Greece, October 1, 1937.

Horniman, Annie Elizabeth Fredericka, producer, 76. Private secretary to W. B. Yeats; first connected with play production in 1894; opened Abbey Theatre, Dublin, Ireland, 1904, producing Irish plays; Midland Theatre, Manchester, 1907; Gaiety Theatre, Manchester, 1908; produced over 200 plays including "Hindle Wakes," "The Mob," "The Younger Generation," etc. Born Forest Hill, London, England; died London, August 6, 1937.

Kennark, Jane (Lothian), actress, 75. Début in "Pearl of Savoy" (1880); member touring company Madison Square Theatre; was original Estrella in "Arizona"; played stock in many cities. Born Cincinnati, Ohio; died New York City, February 11, 1938.

Kingston, Gertrude (Silver), actress, 68. Associated with stage for fifty years; with Henry Irving and Beerbohm Tree; American début "Captain Brassbound's Conversion" (1915); planned and built Little Theatre in John Street, London. Born London, England; died London, November 8, 1937.

Losee, Frank, actor, 81. Fifty years on stage; trained with Amaranth Society of Brooklyn; member Hooley's Stock Company and Union Square Stock Company under A. M. Palmer; played leads in many companies; appeared in pictures with Mary Pickford, Marguerite Clark and Pauline Frederick. Born Brooklyn, New York; died Yonkers, New York, November 14, 1937.

Lowell, Helen (Robb), actress, 71. Began career of fifty years with children's company singing "Pinafore"; first adult appearance title role in "Iolanthe"; created Dearest in "Little Lord Fauntleroy" and Miss Hazy in "Mrs. Wiggs of the Cabbage Patch"; remembered as Ma Fisher in "The Show Off" and in many pictures; impersonated Mary Roberts Rinehart's "Tish" for the radio. Born New York City; died Hollywood, Calif., June 29, 1937.

Marquis, Donald Robert Perry, playwright and novelist, 59. On staff of *New York American, New York Sun, New York Tribune* and many other newspapers; famous as humorist; plays were "The Old Soak," "Out of the Sea," "Everything's Jake" and "The Dark Hours." Born Walnut, Ill.; died Forest Hills, New York, December 29, 1937.

McWade, Robert, actor, 56. Represented third generation of American stage family; first appearance with Murray Hill Stock Company, 1902; toured as Simonides in "Ben Hur"; played in support of many stars both stage and screen. Born Buffalo, New York; died Culver City, Calif., January 20, 1938.

Mitchell, Theodore, press representative, 63. Drama critic of *Cincinnati Enquirer;* press agent for Lillian Russell, John Drew, Klaw and Erlanger and others; with the late J. J. McCarthy publicized "Birth of a Nation," "The Covered Wagon," "Broken Blossoms," etc; founder and president of Theatrical Managers, Agents and Treasurers Union. Born Lexington, Ky.; died Beechurst, L. I., New York, February 23, 1938.

Monroe, Frank, actor, 73. First stage appearance in "East Lynn" (1884) in Baltimore; played in "The Virginian," "Checkers," "Cheating Cheaters," etc.; with James Herne in "Sag Harbor"; detective in original production of "Alias Jimmy Valentine." Born Jersey City, New Jersey; died Bay Shore, L. I., New York, June 19, 1937.

Morrison, Howard Priestly, actor, director, 66. First appearance 1894 in "Fate"; first production, 1910, "New York"; other productions: "The Fascinating Widow," "Smilin' Through," "Mama's Affair," "Easy Come, Easy Go," "The Challenge of Youth," "The Barker," "Best Years," etc.; last engagement playing Grandpa Vanderhof in road show of "You Can't Take It with You." Born Baltimore, Md.; died Kew Gardens, L. I., New York, January 26, 1938.

Morton, James J., vaudeville actor, 76. Began theatrical career singing topical songs for Healey and Bigelow's Hibernian Minstrels; said to be originator of "rag time words"; long in vaudeville; organizer and two years president of Vaudeville Comedy Club. Born Boston, Mass.; died Islip, L. I., New York, April 10, 1938.

Moses, Harry, producer, 64. Chicago merchant who left trade for theatrical production; produced Zoe Akins' dramatization of Edith Wharton's "The Old Maid," which won Pulitzer award; Vicki Baum's "Grand Hotel" (with Herman Shumlin) and others. Born Chicago, Ill.; died New York City, August 31, 1937.

Muldener, Louise, actress, 84. Supported many stars; played Juliet to Edwin Booth's Romeo; was with Joseph Jefferson, Mary Anderson, Marie Wainwright, Walker Whiteside, Henry E. Dixey and the elder Salvini. Born Brooklyn, New York; died New York City, May 10, 1938.

Paulding, Frederick (Dodge), actor and author, 78. First child born in military reservation at West Point; son of Col. Richard Irving Dodge; first stage appearance at 15 in London with Sir Henry Irving in "The Lyon's Mail"; played "Hamlet" 400 times before he was 20; member of Jefferson-Florence Comedy Company; wrote "Two Men and a Girl," "The Woman's Hour," "Trooper Billy," etc. Born West Point, New York; died Rutherford, New Jersey, September 6, 1937.

Perkins, Osgood, actor, 45. First stage appearance as Homer Cady in "Beggar on Horseback" (1924); prominently cast in "The Front Page," "Tomorrow and Tomorrow," "Good-Bye Again," "The School for Husbands" and "Ceiling Zero"; played in the opening of "Susan and God" in Washington, D. C. the night he died. Born West Newton, Mass.; died Washington, D. C., September 21, 1937.

Pinchot, Rosamond, actress, 33. Selected by Max Reinhart to play the nun in "The Miracle"; also played in "Henry IV," "Danton Tod," "St. Helena" and "The Eternal Road"; appeared in screen play "The Three Musketeers." Born New

York City; died Old Brookfield, L. I., New York, January 24, 1938.

Romano, Charles, actor, 38. Came to United States from England in 1921 with Henry Esmond; played here in: "Romance," "Will Shakespeare," "Gentlemen Prefer Blondes," "Seventh Heaven," "Berkeley Square," etc.; served with British army in Gallipoli campaign. Born London, England; died New York, August 9, 1937.

Seagram, Wilfrid, actor, 54. First appearance on stage, London, 1910; début New York same year in "The Scarlet Pimpernel" with Fred Terry; toured in "Disraeli" with George Arliss; late appearances were in "Accent on Youth," "Antony and Cleopatra" and "Once is Enough." Born Finchley, England; died New York City, May 28, 1938.

Smith, Edgar McPhail, librettist, 80. Began stage career as actor; wrote or adapted more than 150 plays and musical comedies including "The Spider and the Fly," "The Grand Vizier," "The Merry World," etc. Born Brooklyn, New York; died Bayside, Queens, New York, March 8, 1938.

Strickland, Helen, actress, 75. Prominent on stage for sixty years; played in "The Bachelor Baby" (with Francis Wilson), "Dark Victory" (with Tallulah Bankhead); "Macbeth" (with James K. Hackett) etc.; wife of Robert Conness, actor. Born Boston, Mass.; died New York City, January 11, 1938.

Tell, Alma, actress, 45. First appearance as Ethel in "Peg o' My Heart," 1914; subsequently stock in Philadelphia, Rochester and Portland, Me.; toured in "Eyes of Youth"; several years in Hollywood. Born New York City; died San Fernando, Calif., December 30, 1937.

Tree, Lady (Helen Maud Holt), actress, 73. Widow of the late Sir Herbert Beerbohm Tree; London stage début 1883; appeared in New York in 1908 as Clytemnestra in "Electra" with Mrs. Patrick Campbell. Born London, England; died London, August 7, 1937.

Van Dresser, Marcia, soprano, 60. Joined Bostonians in 1898; toured country four years; with Metropolitan Opera Company; sang in grand opera in Europe; member Chicago Opera Company. Born Memphis, Tenn.; died London, England, July 11, 1937.

Weaver, John Van Alstyn, playwright, 45. Book editor *Chicago Daily News* and literary editor *Brooklyn Daily Eagle;* wrote novels and poetry; most successful play, "Love 'Em and Leave 'Em," written with George Abbott; adapted "Tom

Sawyer" for screen; married Peggy Wood, actress. Born Charlotte, N. C.; died Colorado Springs, Colo., June 15, 1938.

Wharton, Edith (Newbold Jones), author, 75. Famous novelist, many of whose books have been adapted to the stage: "Age of Innocence," adapted by Margaret Ayer Barnes, "Old Maid" by Zoe Akins, "Ethan Frome" by Lowell Barrington and revised by Owen and Donald Davis. Born New York City; died Pavilion Colombes, France, August 11, 1937.

THE DECADES' TOLL

(Persons of Outstanding Prominence in the Theatre
Who Have Died in Recent Years)

	Born	Died
Aborn, Milton	1864	1933
Ames, Winthrop	1871	1937
Bacon, Frank	1864	1922
Baker, George Pierce	1866	1935
Belasco, David	1856	1931
Bernhardt, Sarah	1845	1923
Coghlan, Rose	1851	1932
Crabtree, Charlotte (Lotta)	1847	1924
Crane, William H.	1845	1928
De Koven, Reginald	1861	1920
De Reszke, Jean	1850	1925
Dillingham, Charles Bancroft	1868	1934
Ditrichstein, Leo	1865	1928
Dressler, Marie	1869	1934
Drew, John	1853	1927
Drinkwater, John	1883	1937
Du Maurier, Sir Gerald	1873	1934
Duse, Eleanora	1859	1924
Fiske, Minnie Maddern	1865	1932
Galsworthy, John	1867	1933
Gershwin, George	1898	1937
Goodwin, Nathaniel	1857	1920
Gorky, Maxim	1868	1936
Greet, Sir Philip (Ben)	1858	1936
Hawtrey, Sir Charles	1858	1923
Herbert, Victor	1859	1924
Hopper, De Wolf	1858	1935
Lackaye, Wilton	1862	1932
Mantell, Robert Bruce	1854	1928
Miller, Henry	1858	1926
Morris, Clara	1848	1925
O'Neill, James	1850	1920
Patti, Adelina	1843	1919

	Born	*Died*
Pinero, Sir Arthur Wing	1855	1934
Pirandello, Luigi	1867	1936
Rejane, Gabrielle	1857	1920
Rogers, Will	1879	1935
Russell, Annie	1864	1936
Russell, Lillian	1861	1922
Schumann-Heink, Ernestine	1861	1936
Sembrich, Marcella	1859	1935
Shaw, Mary	1860	1929
Smith, Winchell	1862	1933
Sothern, Edwin Hugh	1859	1933
Terry, Ellen	1848	1928
Thomas, Augustus	1857	1934
Warde, Frederick	1851	1935
Whiffen, Mrs. Thomas	1845	1936
Wilson, Francis	1854	1935
Ziegfeld, Florenz	1869	1932

INDEX OF AUTHORS

INDEX OF PLAYS AND CASTS

515

INDEX OF PRODUCERS, DIRECTORS AND DESIGNERS